AGING

THE SOCIAL CONTEXT

Second Edition

TITLES OF RELATED INTEREST FROM PINE FORGE PRESS

Aging: Concepts and Controversies, Third Edition by Harry R. Moody

This Book Is Not Required, Revised Edition, by Inge Bell and Bernard McGrane

Community Resources for Older Adults: Programs and Services in an Era of Change by Robbyn Wacker and Karen Roberto

Dimensions of Human Behavior: The Changing Life Course by Elizabeth Hutchison

Dimensions of Human Behavior: Person and Environment by Elizabeth Hutchison

Media/Society: Industries, Images, and Audiences, 2nd Edition by David Croteau and William Hoynes

Multiculturalism in the United States: Current Issues, Contemporary Voices by Peter Kivisto and Georganne Rundblad

The Social Worlds of Higher Education: Handbook for Teaching in a New Century by Bernice Pescosolido and Ronald Aminzade

Sociology for a New Century, by York Bradshaw, Joseph Healey, and Rebecca Smith

Worlds Apart: Social Inequalities in a New Century by Scott Sernau

Worlds of Difference; Inequality in the Aging Experience, Third Edition by Eleanor Palo Stoller and Rose Campbell Gibson

The Pine Forge Press Series in Research Methods and Statistics

Social Statistics for a Diverse Society, Second Edition by Chava Frankfort-Nachmias and Anna Leon-Guerrero

Investigating the Social World: The Process and Practice of Research, Third Edition by Russell K. Schutt

Aging, Social Inequality, and Public Policy by Fred C. Pampel

AGING
THE SOCIAL CONTEXT

Second Edition

Leslie Morgan
University of Maryland Baltimore County

Suzanne Kunkel
Miami University

Pine Forge Press

Thousand Oaks, California ■ Boston ■ London ■ New Delhi

For information:

 Pine Forge Press
A Sage Publications Company
2455 Teller Road
Thousand Oaks, California 91320
sales@pfp.sagepub.com

SAGE Publications Ltd.
6 Bonhill Street
London EC2A 4PU
United Kingdom

SAGE Publications India Pvt. Ltd.
M-32 Market
Greater Kailash I
New Delhi 110 048 India

Publisher: Stephen D. Rutter
Assistant to the Publisher: Ann Makarias

Library of Congress Cataloging-in-Publication Data

Morgan, Leslie A.
    Aging: The social context / Leslie Morgan, Suzanne Kunkel.-- 2nd ed. p. cm.
    Includes bibliographical references and index.
    ISBN 0-7619-8731-2 (Cloth: acid-free paper)
    1. Aged--United States. 2. Aging--United States. 3. Gerontology--United States.
I. Kunkel, Suzanne. II. Title.
HQ1064.U5 M6818 2000
305.26--dc21

                                                                    00-012864

Printed in the United States of America
            05   06   07   7   6   5   4   3   2

This book is printed on acid-free paper that meets Environmental Protection Agency standards for recycled paper.

About the Authors

Leslie Morgan is Professor of Sociology in the Department of Sociology and Anthropology at the University of Maryland Baltimore County (UMBC). She has authored or co-authored three previous books and has published over 30 articles and book chapters. Her research has focused on a variety of issues related to aging, including widowhood, economic well-being, family relationships, and housing alternatives.

Suzanne Kunkel is Director of the Scripps Gerontology Center and Associate Professor in the Department of Sociology, Miami University. She has published more than 25 articles, research monographs, and book chapters, primarily in the areas of the measurement of health and projections of health care needs for the older population. She is currently Past President of the Association for Gerontology in Higher Education.

About the Publisher

Pine Forge Press is a new educational publisher, dedicated to publishing innovative books and software throughout the social sciences. On this and any other of our publications, we welcome your comments and suggestions.

Please call or write us at

Pine Forge Press
A Sage Publications Company
2455 Teller Road
Thousand Oaks, CA 91320
(805) 499-4224
E-mail: sales@pfp.sagepub.com

Visit our World Wide Web site, your direct link to a multitude of online resources:
http://www.pineforge.com

CONTENTS

5 Psychological Perspectives on Aging / 143
by Michael Marsiske, Melissa M. Franks, and Benjamin T. Mast

6 Sociological Perspectives on Aging / 183

III Social Institutions and Aging

IV The Future

In this second edition of *Aging: The Social Context*, we have worked to sharpen and strengthen our original focus, to expand some of the topics included within that focus, and to provide updated information. We were assisted in this task by feedback from users of the book. Our intent with the first edition was to provide an alternative to existing texts, which generally focus on summaries of current and classic research on aging. These existing texts give limited attention to the value and uses of the social construction/social context approach to the study of age and aging. Our second edition continues to emphasize the depth, richness and breadth of the social construction perspective. Through examining aging individuals' opportunities, choices and experiences as the product of their individuality interacting with the surrounding social structure, we hope to highlight how aging is much more than an individual journey through time. Our emphasis on encouraging students to step back from the typical individual-based point of view to examine social structure is designed to help students see the play of these social forces in all of our lives and their implications specifically for aging. As in the first edition, we make explicit reference to the social construction of age throughout the text as we review and synthesize the literature on various topics. The emphasis on factors related to social location– especially gender, race, ethnicity, and social class– and the impact of these contextual variables in creating diverse realities of aging, continues to be an important thread throughout this edition.

In our teaching experience, most students can relate easily to aging through their personal or family experiences. Seldom do they come to the course understanding the implications of the aging of societies or the critical ways that the dynamics of aging work to reshape the major institutions of society. It is this macro-level, structural perspective on aging that we wish to add to our readers' intuitive understanding of individual aging—and to correct some misunderstandings that they may bring from their personal experience about what it means to grow older. Since human aging does not occur in isolation, but rather is fundamentally social, it is critical to examine interactions with the surrounding society, which show how we shape and are shaped by the social contexts in which we grow older.

We have used two major vehicles–discipline-based chapters and special "applying theory" inserts within chapters–to present major theoretical and analytical frameworks from social gerontology and the core disciplines which inform the field. Theoretical perspectives throughout the text are connected to age-related issues and problems, such as retirement, health care, and economic inequality. These analyses explicitly look at varying questions, assumptions, and conclusions that derive from these theoretical viewpoints. We take a broad look at societal institutions (such as the family, the economy, employment and retirement, politics and public policy, and social services and health care) that affect older adults and are affected by the aging of our society. Students will acquire tools for analyzing social issues and societal institutions from different theoretical points of view and different ideological frameworks from reading these chapters.

In addition to emphasizing theoretical perspectives and social construction, a third guiding focus is on the cross-cutting of age with gender, race, ethnicity, and social class. One manifestation of this focus is the consistent discussion of heterogeneity and diversity among older adults. These discussions of diversity in later life allow a reformulation of the basic questions in the field—away from the question "What changes does aging bring about for the typical older person?" to questions such as "What are the variables on which older people differ from one another? What are the patterns of difference on those variables, and why do those differences exist?" Consistent discussion of diversity among older people, and of how it is patterned, helps to further illustrate the fact that the experiences and meanings of age and aging are socially constructed, and are not predictable results of a set of fixed biological processes.

Teaching with This Book

We have directed this text to undergraduate or beginning graduate students in social gerontology or sociology of aging courses. Because we have included chapters on physical and psychological aging in Part II, the book is appropriate for multidisciplinary survey courses, especially those taught from a sociological point of view. These chapters broaden the usefulness of the text and allow a discussion of how the important influences of both psychology and physiology interact with social forces to shape the meanings and experiences of aging. These chapters were written by experts from those discipline. In the second edition these chapters have been revised with editorial support from the authors to present a "seamless voice" speaking to the reader.

We have also included some special pedagogical features that we think help students to absorb critical theories and concepts. First, we have interspersed among the chapters six "speculative essays" on timely and sometimes unusual topics to encourage lively discussion and application of ideas presented in various chapters. A second teaching feature is a series of within-chapter inserts focusing on applying theories. Each of these inserts augments the more basic theoretical issues presented in the discipline-based chapters in Part II of the book. In each case, the theory is applied either to an individual's own aging or to policy or practice. The "insert" format gives instructors greater flexibility as to how, when, and how fully to utilize these theories in their teaching.

Third, we have highlighted key terms in each chapter with bold type when they are introduced and defined. These key terms are listed for study purposes at the end of each chapter and are included in a glossary at the end of the book for easy reference. In the second edition we have added "Questions for Thought and Reflection" at the end of each chapter and essay to prompt consideration of key issues presented in the chapter and serve as a focal point for classroom discussion.

Other New Features of the Second Edition

In addition to the augmented features mentioned above, the second edition includes new and updated web sites at the end of every chapter in our "Web Wise" sections. Instructors may wish to investigate these sites and may build student assignments or exercises around them. We have also endeavored to make the visual presentation more engaging by including photos and cartoons in the text, in addition to the graphs and charts found in the first edition. The majority of graphs and charts have been updated with more recent data, and the text in all chapters has been refreshed with new information that has appeared since completion of the last edition.

Beyond editorial revision, the chapters on Physiology and Psychology include considerable new information. In the case of the physiology of aging, new findings and further information have been presented. In the psychology chapter a new section, focusing on memory and memory change, is included in this edition. Other chapters have been reorganized so that material appears in only one chapter, removing redundancy. Finally, at the suggestion of some reviewers, we have enhanced information on death and dying, family caregiving, memory and other topics that were viewed as receiving insufficient attention in the first edition.

Our original and continued purpose in writing has been to provide a new type of textbook on social gerontology/sociology of aging, one that is neither encyclopedic in its coverage of research findings nor overly weighted down with jargon. We hope that we have brought added strength in this second edition to the message about the dynamics of aging within a changing social world.

ACKNOWLEDGMENTS

With any project of this size, there are a large number of people who make important contributions to its completion. We would like to acknowledge the technical support provided by the staff at Pine Forge Press. Second, we must acknowledge our co-authors, who contributed to several chapters. Robert C. Atchley, at Naropa University, contributed to the material in Chapter 1. Helxine Alessio, from Miami University's Department of Physical Education, Health and Sports Studies, took on the difficult task of describing the sometimes-challenging research conducted on the physiology of aging. Melissa M. Franks and Benjamin T. Mast, from the Institute of Gerontology and the Department of Psychology at Wayne State University, along with their colleague Michael Marsiske, from the Institute on Aging and the Departments of Health Policy and Epidemiology and Clinical and Health Psychology at the University of Florida, tackled the chapter outlining the "state of the art" in the psychology of aging. We appreciate the contributions of these collaborators and their willingness to work within our focus on aging in social context.

We also need to thank our support systems on our individual campuses. For Leslie Morgan this includes the staff at the Department of Sociology and Anthropology at UMBC and especially Research Assistant Erika Schukraft. For Suzanne Kunkel appreciation is extended to a long list of colleagues and friends at Miami University's Scripps Gerontology Center. Special thanks go to Cheryl Johnson, Betty Williamson, Thelma Carmack, and Jerrolyn Butterfield for their careful and cheerful support. Christine Bellomo provided vigilant, thorough, and energetic help with the final stages of this edition.

We would also like to acknowledge our mentors and colleagues (both proximate and remote) who have shaped our professional lives and perspectives. These include Robert Atchley, Vern Bengtson, Kevin Eckert, William Feinberg, Joe Hendricks, Norris Johnson, David T. Lewis, Matilda White Riley, Neal Ritchey, Pauline Robinson, Mildred Seltzer, and Judith Treas, among others we have inadvertently overlooked.

A set of reviewers for the first edition, and reviews drawn from the users of the first edition, have provided us with helpful feedback during the development of this second edition. They include:

Gloria D. Gibson	Towson University
Joe Hendricks	Oregon State University
Charlie Stelle	University of Connecticut
Shirley Varmette	Southern Connecticut State University
Jane Straker	Miami University, Ohio
Merril Silverstein	University of Southern California
Elisabeth Burgess	Georgia State University
Nancy Gilliland	Moorhead State University
Sue Humphers-Ginther	Moorhead State University
Ed Rosenberg	Appalachian State University

Finally, we would like to acknowledge our friends and families, especially our parents, Dick and Gerry Morgan and Ted and Lois Kunkel, and, for Suzanne, daughters Emma and Hannah. These are the people who give us our roots and our wings, help us keep perspective, and remind us of the importance of balance in our lives.

Understanding Aging: Frames of Reference

We are all aging. Most of us have at least a common-sense understanding of aging on an individual level, having viewed the maturation and aging process of ourselves and those around us. Each of us has passed through major "turning points,"—becoming an adolescent or entering college—and we have expectations regarding the way that our futures will unfold as we move through the remaining stages of the life course. We have seen changes in our physical selves, in our mental capabilities, in the way we think about ourselves, and in the way people treat us because of changes in our ages.

A deeper understanding of aging requires, however, that we move beyond our individual experience and broaden our view to understand how processes from the level of the individual cell to the overall society influence us and, in turn, are influenced by us as we progress through life. Human aging occurs in a social context that defines aging and the stages of life, giving them a meaning that we, as members of a common culture, share. Each of us responds to these meanings, sometimes to reinforce them and sometimes to alter them; that dynamic is what we mean by aging in social context. Our social understanding of aging and the stages of life shapes our decisions and choices, and how we live our lives in turn influences our understanding of what it means to be 20 or 80.

The first part of this book explores central ways of discovering the implications of aging as a process occurring in this dynamic social context. Chapter 1 describes the social construction perspective in greater detail, identifying aging as a socially constructed concept that we, by using and accepting, make an important part of our shared social reality. Its taken-for-granted nature renders it nearly invisible to us, as we constantly use an individual's age for a variety of social purposes in everyday life. By making the age structure of society and social roles visible, we identify the ways in which your life is organized by society through a system of socially constructed and culturally transmitted ideas about aging and the life course.

Chapter 2 examines in some detail the techniques that researchers use to study aging. Because the study of aging is fairly "young," some of the research techniques are borrowed from other, "older" disciplines; there are also some exciting new approaches to address aging issues more directly. Of central importance in this chapter is the discussion of the key concepts of aging, period, and cohort effects. These three interacting forces are central to understanding the fit of individual aging with the larger-scale processes of societal aging that will help to shape our collective futures. Even if other sections of this chapter are skipped or saved for a later portion of your course, we suggest that you read this pivotal section early in order to better understand these issues, which will reappear in subsequent chapters.

The demography of aging—the population dynamics that shape the growth and aging of any population—is discussed in Chapter 3. Understanding that not only individuals but also societies are aging is critical for living and working in the decades to come. The dynamics of aging in developing countries and postindustrial countries vary considerably, although the forces that shape these dynamics are the same. Demography presents a very different frame of reference for examining aging, which again points out the critical role of the social context in which individuals grow, mature, and eventually age.

Each of these ways of understanding aging adds an important lens through which to view the world around us. Later sections of the book will present the ways diverse disciplines examine the aging process. We will also look at the sometimes complex interactions between the aging of individuals and social groups and institutions.

CHAPTER 1

Aging and Society

with Robert Atchley

"The individual does not act alone, although conscious beings will do and act as if they had control over their lives and could do what best pleased them.... No person really acts independent of the influences of our fellow human beings. Everywhere there is a social life setting limitations and influencing individual action. People cooperate, compete, combine, and organize for specific purposes, so that no one lives to him/herself." (Blackmar, 1908, p. 3–4).

Aging is something that happens to all of us. It is a natural and virtually inevitable process. Yet older people are often the subject of bad jokes and negative stereotypes, and many people in our society dread growing old. A quick visit to the birthday card section of your local card shop will confirm our preoccupation with aging. Despite this preoccupation, our ideas about what aging really means are notably diverse. Consider:

- At age 40, people in the labor force are legally defined as "older workers" by the Age Discrimination in Employment Act.
- Cliff's mother died when she was 73. At age 47, Cliff had become the oldest generation in his family.
- In 1989, United Airlines Captain Al Haynes was credited with saving the lives of over a hundred people in a plane crash in Iowa. His years of experience were cited as the major factor in his ability to respond so effectively to the emergency. A few months after this dramatic event, Captain Haynes turned 60 and was forced to retire.
- "Until the mid-sixteenth century.... few people knew exactly how old they were (Cole, 1992, p. 5)."
- Most people who are age 75 do not think they belong in the "old" age category.
- At age 16, people are "old enough" to be licensed drivers, at age 18 they are "old enough" to vote, and at age 21 they are "old enough" to drink alcohol. Why do we say "old enough"?
- Men can join the senior professional golf tour at age 50. The senior tour in men's tennis is for those age 35 and older.
- There is no age at which a man is too old to legally marry or to father children.
- Members of the armed forces can retire as early as age 37.

- At age 90, Ludwig Magener won the national swimming championship in six masters' swimming event.
- The human genome project could potentially extend life expectancy significantly. What will it mean to be 75, if life expectancy is 200? What will happen to our ideas about education, careers, and grandparenthood?

These examples illustrate two very important points. First, our society has many different formal and informal social definitions of age and aging. Second, the meanings, definitions, and experiences of aging vary across cultures and across time. So, questions about when aging begins, or what it is, can only be answered by paying attention to the social contexts in which aging takes place.

Dimensions of Aging

If you ask the person behind you in line at the grocery store checkout to define "aging," she might reasonably respond that it means growing older. But, what does growing older mean? Is it simply the passage of time, having another birthday? Increasingly, scholars argue that chronological age is a relatively meaningless variable (Ferraro, 1990; Maddox, 1988). Age is only a way of marking human events and experiences; these events and experiences are what matters, not time itself (Botwinick, 1978). Time's passing is of concern only because it is connected, however loosely, with other changes: physical, psychological, and social.

Physical Aging

The passage of time for human organisms is related to a large number of specific physical changes such as gray hair, wrinkling of skin and decrements in reproductive capacity, immune system response, and cardiovascular functioning. An interesting question about these physical changes is whether they are inevitable, natural consequences of growing older. In fact, research shows that some of the changes we think of as normal are modifiable, preventable, and related to socially influenced lifestyle choices and cultural practices. For example, while some wrinkling of the skin and some loss of arterial elasticity appear to be related to physical aging processes, it is clear that the magnitude of change and speed of deterioration are affected by lifestyle choices and culture. We know that wrinkling of the skin is accelerated and accentuated by sun exposure and by smoking, and some of the changes over time in cardiovascular functioning are related to diet, exercise, and smoking. Similarly, most of us know 70 year olds who are as active, healthy, and vigorous as an average 40 year old. Increasing evidence shows enormous variability in physical aging among individuals; this growing evidence of variability has resulted in new ways of describing aging.

In the past, researchers searched for the "normal" changes that accompanied aging; a most important part of this search was to distinguish normal age changes from pathological or disease processes that became more prevalent

Exhibit 1.1   *Variability of Physical Aging*

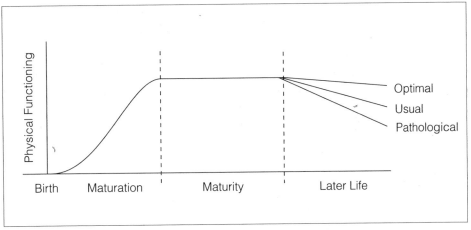

Adapted from: Machemer, 1992.

with age but were not caused by aging. With the growing knowledge about the modifiability and variability of physical aging processes, the distinctions among usual, optimal, and pathological aging emerged (Rowe and Kahn, 1988). "Optimal" aging is characterized by minimal loss of physical function and a healthy, vigorous body; "pathological" aging is aging accompanied by multiple chronic diseases and negative environmental influences. "Usual" aging refers to the typical or average experience– somewhere in between pathological and optimal. Exhibit 1.1 illustrates this view of the variability of physical aging (Machemer, 1992). These distinctions reflect new ways of thinking about physical aging as a variable, contingent, and sometimes modifiable set of processes that often have important social components.

As we continue to find that the changes we call physical aging are merely age-linked and not age-caused, that they are in fact modifiable, we are forced to reconsider the question of what aging means as a physical process. The ever-increasing evidence that individuals vary greatly in their experience of physical aging suggests that few if any of the significant aspects of aging are purely or even primarily physical. These issues are discussed further in Chapter 4.

Psychological Aging

Psychological aging processes include changes in personality, mental functioning, and sense of self during our adult years. Some changes are considered a normal part of adult development, some are the result of physiological changes in the way the brain functions, and some psychological dimensions show little change at all in later year. As in the case of physical aging, a wealth of research has explored the complexities of these processes.

For our purposes, several generalizations are important. First, personality does not undergo profound changes in later life; most personality traits, self-concept and self-esteem remain fairly stable from mid-life on. For example, people do not become wise, grumpy, or rigid in their thinking as a result of growing older; the grumpy old man was very likely a grumpy young man. Although the developmental challenges and opportunities we encounter do vary through our lives, the strategies we use to adapt to change, to refine and reinforce our sense of self, to work toward realizing our full human potential are practiced throughout our adult lives. The simple passage of time seldom requires or causes fundamental changes to these basic personality structures and strategies.

Similarly, loss of cognitive functioning is not an inevitable result of aging. Just as significant loss of physical function is not inevitable or universal, so too memory and other cognitive skills may remain stable or even improve with age. However, it is important to be accurate here. Research on the physiology and psychology of aging shows that, in the absence of disabling disease, aging causes only minimal declines in functioning until around age 85, at which point about 25% of elders begin to show frailty even in the absence of disease. Chapter 5 provides more detail on the psychological aspects of aging.

Social Aging

If aging brings only relatively small universal and inevitable changes in physical or cognitive functioning, in the basic structure of personality, and in the trajectory of adult development, why does it matter in people's lives? In this book, we argue that, at least before age 85, age is significant primarily because of the social meanings, structures, and processes attached to it. Gray hair, wrinkles, longer reaction time, and even some short-term memory loss matter only because the social world in which we live has defined those characteristics as meaningful. Much of the social meaning of aging is tied to erroneous beliefs about the effects of aging on physical and mental capabilities. Aging does not inevitability cause us to become rigid in our thinking, forgetful, or unable to carry out our favorite physical or intellectual activities. For most people aging is a process of change that is so gradual that we compensate for most of it so that it has little impact on our lives.

The importance, meanings, and implications of the changes people experience as they age are heavily influenced by, or we might even say constructed by, the social reality in which those changes take place. Society uses age to assign people to roles, to channel people into and out of positions within the social structure, as a basis for allocation of resources, and as a way to categorize individuals. In its most benevolent form, using age to allocate opportunities is a reasonable mechanism. For example, our society has rules about minimum ages for employment; these laws were designed to protect young people from being exploited, and, according to some, they are good for the labor force because they control the flow of new workers into the labor market. In a more constraining way, however, age artificially and inequitably limits the opportunities of people. Gray hair and wrinkles, perhaps the most visible signs of aging, and the chronological age of 65— the most often-used criterion of old age— have no effect on physical functioning or cognitive capability. They do, however, have profound effects on social interactions and role opportunities for individuals in the social world. Whether we would seriously consider someone as a possible candidate for a job, or as an interesting partner in social interaction is, in fact, influenced by our assessment of the age of that person and what that person's age symbolizes to us. Again, it is not because age 65 or gray hair are symptomatic of competence or incompetence or of a boring or dazzling personality, or even that visible signs of aging are inherently unattractive or attractive. We make these assessments because we live in a society that has constructed the meaning of aging in particular (primarily negative) ways.

It is important to think about the extent to which the very same processes work at other ages and stages of life. In our culture, it is possible to be "too young" just as it is possible to be "too old" for certain roles and opportunities. We have very clear social prescriptions, often in the form of federal and state laws, about when a person is old enough to drive a car, get married, and be president of the United States. In these examples, "old enough" seems to imply the window of opportunity between legally too young and socially too old.

Social aging is a *multidimensional* and dynamic force. It includes the transitions into and out of roles, expectations about behavior, societal allocation of resources and opportunities, negotiations about the meaning and implications of chronological age, and the experience of individuals travelling the life course and negotiating life stages. Chapter 6 explores these issues in detail, and the chapters in Part Three apply the concepts of social aging to the major dimensions of our social lives.

The ways in which the experiences of aging are largely constructed by society is an example of an important sociological idea: the "social construction" of reality. This concept suggests that reality does not exist "out there," waiting to be measured and known. Rather, reality is created out of interactions among humans and by the social institutions in which people live their lives. For an illustration of the gap between physical reality and people's lived experience aspect of aging, think about witnesses to an unusual event, such as an auto accident. While we know that there are "facts" in such a situation— for example, the color of the cars, the direction and speed they were traveling—eyewitness accounts often vary greatly on even these details. Human beings pay attention to different things, remember different things, and report different things. If one of the people in the accident is a friend of a witness, the witness might be motivated (consciously or unconsciously) to notice and report details that will be favorable to the friend. In our everyday lives, we see differences in how people interpret a word, phrase, or gesture. And we can observe the ways in which people communicate in order to make sense out of the social world, reconstructing events, providing meaning, creating accounts of what is happening.

So, we construct reality out of interaction. Social institutions also play a major role in creating the experiences of individuals living in society. We will explore this idea throughout this book.

Population Aging

Beyond the "social construction" of aging, social forces influence the experience of aging in another important way. Societies themselves experience aging. As the proportion of population in the "older" age categories increases, profound changes in the social structure take place. **Societal aging**— these demographic, structural, and cultural transformations— affects every aspect of social life, from social institutions to the experiences of aging individuals. Health care, education, and the economy are good examples of social organizations and institutions that are affected greatly by the growth of the older population. Our health care system faces special challenges as we plan for the long-term care needs of increasing numbers of older people. The impact of population changes on the educational system in the United States can be seen in the growing number of attempts to address the needs of older learners and in the growing number of college and university programs targeting the older population. Some of you may have summer Elderhostel programs at your institutions or free tuition available for students over age 65. The University of Massachusetts at Boston has a certificate program in gerontology; over half of the hundreds of people who have earned that certificate are over the age of 60. The impact of population aging on our society is discussed in greater detail in the chapters of Part 3.

Societal aging, and its consequent increase in the proportion of older adults, requires societies to make adjustments in many areas of social life.

Another impact of the growth of the older population is the increased visibility of aging. Because there are more older people in the general population, more people are aware of the diversity among older individuals. As older people become more numerous and visible, stereotypical attitudes and discriminatory practices that disadvantage older people are more likely to be challenged. For example, in comparing magazine advertisements in the year 2000 to those from 1980, we see a definite increase in both the number of ads that feature older people and in the average age of many models (other than the "supermodels" who still are very young). While most people in ads are still young, the increased visibility of older people begins to change our images of aging.

The aging of a population influences how aging itself is a social construction. As cohorts of different size and with unique characteristics move through the age structure, they are affected by, but also have an impact on, the experience of being older. The baby boomers will experience aging in a very different way than the current generation of older people. There are growing challenges to pervasive negative stereotyping of older people, including age discrimination legislation, increasing visibility of and diversity among older people, and increased targeting of products and services to an aging market. When these social changes combine with the political activism that has historically characterized the baby boomers, and with their potential power in the marketplace and in the polling booths, their experiences and definitions of aging will be altered. We are already seeing more middle-aged and older people in advertisements and as lead characters in TV shows. In addition, products and services designed for middle-aged and older generations are appearing with increasing frequency.

The aging of groups of older people also has an impact on social institutions such as the economy and health care. For example, the current generation of older people grew up during the Great Depression. Their investment, purchasing, and savings habits have been shaped by that experience; they tend to save at higher rates than other groups of adults, especially the baby boomers, and they are less likely to make risky investments or purchases. The baby boomers grew up during relatively comfortable economic times, are not good savers, and are more likely to make non-essential purchases. During the past decade we have seen tremendous growth in the "games for adults" industry; a walk down the games aisle at your neighborhood toy store will reveal a very large number of board games designed for adults, far beyond the number available just ten years ago. This trend is related to the purchasing power, leisure preferences, and buying habits of baby boomers. You can use your imagination to think about new leisure, health care, or convenience products for aging baby boomers. Thus the aging of cohorts (groups of people born at the same time), as a dimension of population aging, has an impact on the economy: on product and service development, on savings, and on consumer demand patterns.

With these examples we do not mean to oversimplify societal aging, or social change in institutions such as the economy. Rather these examples are intended to illustrate how the experiences of aging, and the social contexts in which they take place, change over time as a result of the aging of unique cohorts. As new groups of people go through stages of growing older, they bring with them a unique historical profile, and they alter meanings, values, and norms associated with growing older. The movement of new groups into old age also places new demands on the social system. Changes to the social structure emerge in response to the size, characteristics, and demands of each new group of older people. The intricacies of this dynamic recreation of the meanings, opportunities, and values associated with the later stages of life will be discussed in further detail in later chapters. For our purposes at this point it is important to acknowledge that societal aging is a significant dimension of the social processes of aging. We can define societal aging as the demographic, structural, and cultural transformations a society undergoes as the proportion of its population that is aging increases.

Ways of Categorizing People by Age

As we consider the many dimensions of social aging, we need a way to mark or measure the age of individuals. Most often people are categorized using chronological age, functional status, or life stage. Each type of measure has advantages and disadvantages, and the decision to use any measure should be based on the conceptual assumptions and frames of reference underlying them.

Keep in mind that whether we use chronological age, functional need, or life stages, we are applying socially constructed labels and definitions, which allow us to treat people as members of meaningful social categories. We use these definitions in many ways: to determine the proportion of people in various age groups, to predict significant attributes of specific individuals, to select a specific target for social action or policy, to define a subject of study, and in many other ways. Remember, all these definitions, including chronological age, are human creations designed to serve a purpose. In selecting definitions of aging or age categories, we need to be conscious of our underlying purpose and select our definitions accordingly.

Chronological Age

This is one of the simplest assessments of age and thus it reduces administrative complexity. Chronological age is used in our society as the basis for determining many social roles (voting, driving, marrying, holding public office), for eligibility in social programs (such as Social Security, AARP membership, or Older Americans Act services), and inclusion in research projects.

The use of chronological age to mark major life transitions is taken for granted in modern urban societies. However, it is a relatively recent development coinciding with the rise of bureaucratic industrialism (Moody, 1993). The industrial economy required that human lives be ordered efficiently so that work years coincided with the years assumed to be associated with peak productivity. Chronological age was adopted as a simple way to define a worker's life stage.

The meaningfulness of chronological age is questioned in many ways today, however. The number of birthdays an individual has had tells us little in and of itself. The fluidity and multiplicity of today's life styles defy the use of bound-

Marking the passage of years is celebrated in many cultures.

aries so rigid as numerical age (Moody, 1993). When it is possible to have two career peaks—one at age 40 in your first career, and a second at age 60 in your second career; when it is increasingly common to find people having children when they are forty— about the age at which others are becoming grandparents— the usefulness of chronological age as a life stage marker is indeed questionable.

In the world of social policy and programs, the validity of age-based policies and programs is being questioned at another level (Torres-Gil, 1992). The age for eligibility for full benefits under Social Security is gradually being raised, so that by the year 2027 you will need to be 67 to retire with your full benefit. Older Americans Act services, for which people are eligible at age 60, are increasingly being targeted to groups within the older population with the greatest need: frail, low-income, and minority groups. In general, policies seem to be moving away from such a central focus on chronological age. We will discuss these policy issues in greater detail in Part III, but these policy shifts are further examples of the challenges to the meaningfulness of chronological age.

Functional Age

What measures or markers of age will we use if chronological age continues to lose its meaning, significance, and utility? In the case of policies, programs, and services, increasingly common is the "targeting" of services to specific groups of people in need of certain kinds of assistance. For example, if we are interested in identifying people who have physical limitations that require assistance by another person, we can use measures of functional need such as Activities of Daily Living, a generic term for several scales that measure an individual's ability to accomplish, without assistance, routine personal care activities such as bathing, eating, dressing, and getting in and out of bed. Such measures are useful if we are interested in targeting home care programs to those who need them because of physical frailty. To the extent that we continue to use age as a convenient way to determine eligibility for services, we are assuming that age is a proxy for the need for those services. Functional status is a way to move beyond that negative assumption about age, but it is obviously a much more complicated way to grant access to programs and services.

Life Stage

As lives progress, people tend to reach certain plateaus of stability (life stages) punctuated by period of change. Thus people can be categorized as being in roughly comparable circumstances, such as adolescence, young adulthood, middle age, and later maturity. We can assume that people going through the "empty nest" transition have living adult children and are in the process of launching them into lives as independent adults. We can assume that people in very old age (sometimes call "old-old" age, referring to people 85 and above) are probably physically frail and live quite simple lives. **Life stages** are thus broad social categories that encompass changes in social roles, physical changes, and societal and self-definitions of transition.

Life stages roughly correspond to chronological age ranges, but are much more fluid, dynamic, and socially negotiated than chronological definitions of age. For example, when is someone an adult? When they move out of their parents' home, reach age 18 or age 21, have a child, have a full-time job, act mature? Life stages rely on some information about physical changes, but are much more attentive to social attributes such as the roles people play. For example, the "empty nest" described above implies something about chronological age, but derives its meaning from the new family roles and relationships emerging during that stage. The concept of life stage will be discussed further in Chapter 6, when we explore the sequences of roles people move into and out of as we go through our lives. We will specifically discuss life stages within the family and within the economy, emphasizing the shared expectations about what roles we should be playing at what ages.

Ageism

With all of the possible ways to assess and define age, and the limitations of any single approach, it is fair to ask why we continue to use age in so many aspects of social life. In part, we use social categories to help organize our world. As children, we learn to generalize across sensory stimuli so that every situation is not completely new and confusing. Unfortunately, our use of social characteristics such as age, gender, and race to categorize people often leads to stereotypes, prejudice, and discrimination. **Ageism** is "a systematic stereotyping of and discrimination against people because they are old, just as racism and sexism accomplish this with skin color and gender" (Butler, 1989). At the heart of any kind of "ism" (ageism, racism, sexism, classism) is the creation of an "other." Creating an "other" means seeing people as different from ourselves because of some characteristic they do or do not possess. We then feel comfortable in making sweeping generalizations about members of that "other" category, seeing them as not full human beings. Although these categorizations make the world simpler, they deny members of the "other" category an opportunity for full engagement in social life. Damaging stereotypes of older people can take many forms. We are all familiar with the views of older people as lonely, frail, needy, and deserving of our help. This "compassionate ageism" (Binstock, 1991a) now exists side-by-side with other stereotypical views: older people are cute and interesting; older people are wise and funny; older people are greedy and selfish and economically more advantaged than any other group. While the content of these ageist views does vary considerably, the impact is the same. Older people are seen as "other"— in either positive or negative light– different from us, but all like each other.

We often use visual, informal assessments to decide if a person is "old" or not. Be aware, however, that such categorizations limit the opportunities available, both for formal social participation and for informal interaction, to the person assigned to the "older" category. For example, think about your reactions to someone who seems "old" and strikes up a conversation with you as you wait to cross the street. If you have any kind of automatic negative reaction to that person, you may unconsciously limit the possibilities for interaction. As further illustration of the power of these visual assessments, we can think about why it is considered such a compliment to say to someone, "You don't look 50 (or 30 or 80)!" Why is it so desirable to look younger than your age? And what "should" 50 look like??

The Rise of Old Age as a Social Category

We tend to take for granted the idea of categorizing people by age. We aren't often conscious of the many ways in which this categorization takes place, or of its impacts. It is often difficult to take a step back from our everyday lives in order to reflect on why we organize our social lives the way we do. Social science, especially sociology, helps us to gain this more reflective attitude. The notion of systematically studying any aspect of society developed in conjunction with the industrialization of Western Europe in mid- to late- nineteenth century. The era's grand masters of social theory, Comte, Spencer, Durkheim, Weber, and Marx, focused on the ideological and cultural shift that transformed the West from agrarian, small-scale societies to urban mass societies. They also observed the shift from the family as the basic economic unit to individual achievement and performance in a complex division of labor. They either said nothing at all about age, aging, or generations, or referred to these topics only in passing, perhaps because they were more interested in society as a whole than in the details of individual life structure.

However, in the 1950s social theorists began thinking and writing about age, aging, generations, and the life course. Their work remains relevant today.

Generational Consciousness

The first serious attempt to look at the social important of age groups was made by the German sociologist Karl Mannheim in an essay titled "The Problem of Generations," which was first published in German in 1927 but was not published in English until 1952. Mannheim defined **generation** as a category of people born within a specific historical era or time period, much the same way that we define **cohort** today—a group of people born at the same time. For Mannheim, a generation was also characterized by common world views that distinguished them from other generations. Mannheim was keenly aware that accident of birth did not automatically create these common understandings and world-views; he observed that social and social-psychological processes led some members of a generation to develop an identity and consciousness with their age peers. Mannheim believed that generational consciousness arose not from merely being born at the same time but from being exposed to the same kinds of experiences in a common intellectual, social and political environment. Thus, belonging to a generation is a combination of a *state of mind* and an age grouping.

Each generation reacts to their social and historical time. Today's "Gen Xers" are categorized as technologically savvy, cynical about the materialistic values of preceding generations, and jaded by growing up in a world of violence, but there are different subgroups within "Gen X." Mannheim suggested that each generation may comprise a number of specific units, each with a unique consciousness. For example, the 1980s saw the young adult cohort split between the *Yuppies* (young, upwardly mobile professionals) with a self-centered life philosophy that influenced social change in the economy particularly, and the *environmentalists,* with their concerns about creating an economically and physically sustainable future for life on the planet Earth. These generational units, although the same ages, were often in conflict.

Mannheim believed that much of the potential for conflict between generations stemmed from the tendency of older generations to hold on too long to their generational philosophy. "Any two generations following one another always fight different opponents... While the older people may be still combating something in themselves or in the external world in such a fashion that all their feelings and efforts and even their concepts and categories of thought are determined by that adversary, for the younger people this adversary may simply be nonexistent" (Mannheim, 1952, pp. 298-299). For example, the defining theme of needing to be free from want that drove the "Great Depression" generation was not the defining theme of the generations that followed them, such as the "World War II" generation or the "1960s" generation.

Mannheim also suggested that different generations would cooperate under certain conditions. For example, during times of slow social change, the younger generations tend to model themselves after those immediately ahead of them in the generational structure. But in times of rapid social change, the older generations, in order to adapt, are more likely to be influenced by younger generations, who often have a less cluttered history and therefore a clearer picture of social trends. Mannheim also thought that intergenerational conflict is minimized by the fact that each generation spends much of its time interacting with people of the generations nearest them and little time interacting with distant generations. The adjacent generations serve as mediators and interpreters of the much older or much younger generations. Much of Mannheim's commentary about intergenerational dynamics seems relevant to today's debates about "generational equity" and "intergenerational warfare" which are discussed in Chapters 9 and 11.

Mannheim's ideas about generations, generational consciousness, and the succession of generations, remain useful and have served as major building blocks for sociological theories of aging, which are discussed in Chapter 6. However, Mannheim sidestepped the central question of *aging*. He acknowledged that aging is part of the dynamics of generations, but he does not explicitly consider what that part might be.

The Aging Population as a Social Force

Warren Thompson, like Mannheim, drew attention to issues related to aging in the late 1920s and early 1930s. However, Thompson used a demographic perspective to ponder the effects of population aging on society. As a student, Thompson had become interested in the interplay between population and social structure. In 1930, the President's Research Committee on Social Trends gave Thompson and his colleague, P.K. Whelpton, the assignment of projecting

Exhibit 1.2   *Distribution of the Population by Five-Year Age Periods: 1880–1930 and 1930–1980*

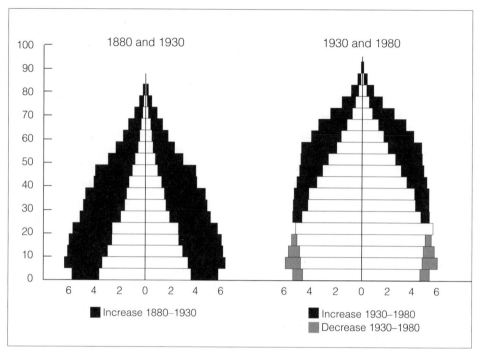

Source: Thompson and Whelpton, 1933.

the population of the United States from 1930 to 1980 and identifying significant population trends that should be taken into account in national planning.

The rapid growth of the older population and the aging of the population as a whole were identified by Thompson and Whelpton (1933) as perhaps the most fundamental expected change in the population of the United States. Exhibit 1.2 shows how dramatically Thompson and Whelpton expected the population age structure to change in what, for a large population, was a very short period of time. Even though Thompson and Whelpton had no way to anticipate the post–World War II baby boom, their projections concerning growth in the proportion the older population represented of the total were very much on target. The actual proportion of people age 65 and over in the United States in 1980 was 11.9 percent compared to their projection of 12.1 percent.

Thompson and Whelpton assumed that retirement would continue to occur at age 65 and speculated that funding retirement pensions would be a major social challenge for the future. "...(T)he problem of old-age pensions is one thing in 1930 with 5.4 percent of the population over 65 years of age but will be a different thing in 1980 when the proportion over 65 years of age will probably be more than twice this large (over 12 percent)" (Thompson and Whelpton,1933, p.165). Writing before Social Security was enacted, they were understandably concerned about the potential social disruption that might come when a large proportion of the population would be retired but with no widespread institutions in place to provide continued retirement income. They were also concerned that poverty at older ages could be even greater than they anticipated "if, as is quite commonly believed, industry and commerce are scrapping men at earlier ages than formerly and if they hire older men only at very low wages" (Thompson and Whelpton,1933, p. 170). (The use of "men" in this quote reflects the reality that, in the 1930s, the vast majority of paid workers were, indeed, men.)

Assuming that elders are more politically and socially conservative than the average American, Thompson and Whelpton suggested that an increase in the proportion of older people in the population might lead to stronger defense of the status quo in politics and less innovation and risk-taking in business. Older people would presumably be less ready to abandon out-dated social policies and business practices. To their credit, however, Thompson and Whelpton pointed out that social innovation could still be fostered through intentional planned effort by middle-aged and older members of society to search for creative and more efficient business methods.

In their discussions of employment and income problems for an aging population, Thompson and Whelpton tended to portray older Americans as a social problem. However, social problems refer to difficulties that categories of people encounter not because of their own qualities but because of the way they fare in the operation of the social system. C. Wright Mills (1959) spoke of the distinction between private troubles that arise from accidents of personal history and social problems that arise from inequities built into the concepts, laws, rules and procedures we live by. Thompson and Whelpton were writing specifically about the social problem of poverty arising from the practice of compulsory retirement at age 65 in the absence of retirement pensions. But in an entirely different vein, they noted that the processes of adult development could have a beneficial influence on social cultural trends. They wrote:

> Youth is more concerned with doing things, forging ahead, and making a place in the world. Age is apt to be more reflective, perhaps because the spur of poverty is less sharp, the inner drive is weaker, or time and thought have brought about a change of ideas as to the goal of life. The mere shift in age distribution, therefore, may lead to more interest in cultural activities and increased support for the arts. Such developments in turn will influence the outlook and taste of the whole population(1933, p.168).

Here they acknowledged that elders were not simply a social problem or a category toward which policy might be directed, but also people who were continuously evolving and could become social resources and agents for change. This potential role for the older population was not characteristic of traditional agricultural societies but of modern, mass society.

The Life Course and the Transition to Old Age

A further key step in the development of old age as a social category came through the comparative, cross-cultural work of an anthropologist, Ralph Linton (1942). Social anthropology is concerned with identifying cultural universals, patterns that appear in all human cultures, as well as links between culture and personality. Linton advanced the thesis that all known societies have been stratified by at least two human characteristics, age and sex. The definitions of age and age categories, the number of age categories, and the rules governing transitions from one age to another have varied considerably across societies, but in all societies old men and old women have been differentiated from one another and from adult men, adult women, boys, girls, and infants. Linton's very simple and basic statement of fact still appears to be true over 50 years later.

Linton suggested that the modernization of society has affected the status of the old by transforming age from a key status location in the social structure to just one of many individual attributes. Thus *old* shifted from a meaningful adult category with rights and duties to simply a qualifying adjective used to make other role expectations more precise—for example, older worker.

Another important concept that permeated Linton's work was the idea of a **life course,** formed by a succession of age-sex categories. In all societies, males who survived infancy would go on to experience boyhood, ascend to adult manhood, and then are either elevated to or relegated to the position of old man, depending on whether the society was accepting or rejecting in its treatment of old men. A parallel sequence existed for females.

Linton believed that these life course age-sex categories are arranged in a hierarchy of social influence. In most societies, the adult males have been the most influential, although occasionally Linton discovered cases where elder men have had the most influence. He found another kind of variability. In many cases, elder women experienced increased freedom when they went through the transition from adult to older woman. Women sometimes experienced

> …the removal of many of the social and especially the ceremonial disabilities to which adult women are subject. Thus old women are almost universally exempted from seclusion and chaperonage. They also tend to be allowed much more power than young women. Even in societies which are strongly patriarchal in theory it will be found that a surprisingly large number of families are ruled by strong willed mothers and grandmothers. Lastly, a very large proportion of the societies which exclude adult women from participating in religious ceremonies and contact with sacred objects remove such restrictions after the menopause. To cite a single example, the Comanche excluded adult women from contact with 'medicine' objects and from the practice of supernaturalistic healing, and thought that it was impossible for them to acquire 'power.' Old women, on the other hand, could acquire and use 'power' on exactly the same terms as men and were treated as equals by male 'power' holders. It was even a common practice in this tribe for medicine men to train their wives in the techniques of healing when they had

reached middle age, transferring their own powers to them immediately after the menopause so that, if they were widowed, they could still carry out the husband's practice (Linton, 1942, p.594).

Despite these interesting exceptions for women, Linton argued that adult categories have typically been the high point of life course existence, and the roles of elders have been referenced back to adult status or derived from it. In most societies, elders who have lost their physical or mental powers have almost always immediately lost the influence appropriate to the individual's status as old man or old woman. In a few cases, however, the influence of elders increased steadily with age.

In addition to looking at life stages and age-sex categories, Linton discussed transitions from one age-sex category to the next. He was impressed with the capacity of humans to make sometimes quite abrupt and substantial changes without showing signs of mental distress. Linton believed that the transition from adulthood to old age was a particularly difficult one, because the loss of power is not satisfactorily offset by a decline in obligations and because formal values about respect and authority granted to older people may not be carried out in actual practice (1942).

Linton's work has been an extremely important resource for the social perspective on aging. It drew attention to the process that connects age to social position and influence. It used the sociological concepts of status and role to explicate a complex social structure made up of interconnected role obligations and opportunities. It presented the life course as a progression of age grades, thus linking the issue of aging with life stages. Finally, it drew our attention to the importance of life course transitions and hinted at a human adaptive capacity to deal with life changes.

Social Perspectives on Aging

In their work, the social scientists described above provide excellent illustrations of understanding age as a social category. Throughout our discussion of old age and aging, we have referred to the way society creates and perpetuates our ideas about who is old, how they should act, and how we treat them. We will continually return to the ideas of social construction as we discuss the many aspects of aging. While many fields of study discuss society, social changes, and peoples' lives, two perspectives in particular are helpful frameworks from which to understand the social context of aging: *social gerontology* and the *sociology of aging*.

Social gerontology

Many social gerontology courses are taught in departments of sociology by sociologists and much of the material included in social gerontology courses consists of research on aging by sociologists. However, social gerontology has a

Exhibit 1.3   *In social gerontology, the sociology of aging is but one of many contributing disciplines.*

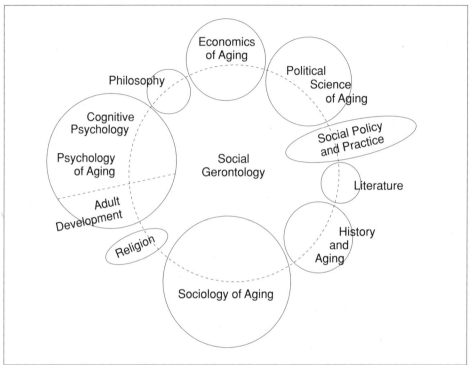

broader range of interests than the sociology of aging. **Social gerontology** is a multidisciplinary field that includes research, policy, and practice information from all of the social sciences (including sociology) and the humanities (see Exhibit 1.3). A specific example may help you understand its scope.

Long-term care — the ongoing provision of health care and assistance with activities of daily living to chronically disabled people — is a major area of interest within the field of aging. Nursing homes provide long-term care, but increasingly the focus within the field of aging is on the development of less restrictive alternatives such as home-delivered care. When care is given in the elder's home, most of the time family members provide the care, but formal service providers are increasingly being employed in conjunction with family. Whether care is provided in institutions or at home, making sure that the quality of care is adequate is a major issue. This area of concern is called quality assurance.

Social gerontology approaches quality assurance from a broad multidisciplinary perspective (Applebaum and Austin, 1990). Social workers and nurses might specialize in developing standards of care and in assessing the care needs of the long-term care client. Ethicists might look at the moral basis for decision-making about care. Psychologists might be concerned with the impact of care on the emotional well-being of clients. Policy researchers could focus on the development of regulations addressing quality of care. Political scientists might look at the various interest groups trying to influence funding and regulation of quality assurance efforts. Economists might look at the cost of quality assurance as a part of the overall cost of long-term care. Anthropologists could study how professionals and paraprofessionals develop language to discuss care quality. Sociologists might study how different stakeholders define the standards of quality. To understand the many facets of quality assurance in health care for older adults, social gerontologists draw on the insights of many disciplines.

Disciplinary Perspectives on Aging

In comparison to the interdisciplinary approach of social gerontology, there are many disciplines that contribute to the understanding from their distinct perspectives. In this text, you will be exposed to psychological perspectives, biological and physiological frameworks, and, predominantly, sociological perspectives on aging. Like social gerontologists, sociologists interested in aging may also address different aspects of quality assurance. However, to a sociologist, the sociological concept of social control is the essence of quality assurance. **Social control** refers to the formal and informal ways that society constrains the behavior of its members (individuals, groups, and organizations). Laws, rules, and regulations are obvious tools of social control. Conforming to the norms of a group such as our family or our friends is a less obvious but equally constraining mechanism of social control. Sociologists thus have a fairly well-developed concept of quality assurance as a social territory consisting mainly of socialization, rules, and sanctions.

Sociological theory takes us a further step toward understanding by offering explanations for social control. For example, is the purpose of social control (quality assurance in this case) to promote order and achieve social values, rather than exploitation and selfish gain? Or is the purpose of social control to preserve a power system which dominates thought and action for the benefit of a powerful few? Although sociologists might agree on a basic definition of what social control is, they might disagree strongly about the purposes of social control and the processes by which it operates.

Both social gerontology and the sociology of aging share an interest in sociological work applied to aging. The main difference is the context within which this work is placed. The **sociology of aging** is concerned with understanding aging from sociological perspectives and applying that understanding to sociology in general. **Social gerontology** is concerned with understanding aging from a variety of perspectives and integrating information from various social science and humanities disciplines to achieve an understanding of aging in general, and to apply that understanding to resolving problems and creating policy.

Although the sociology of aging and other disciplinary perspectives can be differentiated from social gerontology, in the actual study of aging the boundaries among them are often blurry. Often studies focus on a topic that falls both within the domain of social gerontology and within the traditional domain of sociology and economics or psychology. However, as a field, sociology has not been particularly interested in the sociology of aging. Aging has generally been seen as a fringe topic rather than a serious area of scholarship dealing with one of the most important social trends societies will confront over the next 50 years. By contrast, the field of aging (gerontology) has been very interested in the sociology of aging. Thus we can profitably explore some of the key issues in sociology.

The Sociological Imagination.

The promise of the sociological perspective has nowhere more powerfully, passionately, and eloquently expressed than in C. Wright Mills' classic presentation of the sociological imagination. He suggested that the promise, and the responsibility, of sociology lies in giving individuals the tools to make the distinction between "personal troubles" and "public issues." We can make this distinction if we have a social context and a sense of history from which to understand their personal experiences. The ability to shift perspectives, to analyze an experience or an issue from many levels of analysis, and to see the intersection of these many levels of mutual influence, is the fruit of the sociological imagination. If you develop a new understanding of your own attitudes about older people because of what you learn about how societies construct meanings of age, you will have experienced the sociological imagination. If you understand how an older individual's situation of economic disadvantage is a product of social forces rather than simply personal choice or chance, you are applying the sociological imagination.

"No social study that does not come back to the problems of biography, of history, and of their intersections within a society has completed its intellectual journey"(Mills, 1959, p. 5). Mills suggests that there are three basic questions we must continually ask in exercising our sociological imagination. First, what is the structure of this particular society as a whole? How does it differ from other varieties of social order? Second, where does this society stand in human history? What are the essential features of this period? Third, what "varieties" of people prevail in this society and in this period? How are these types "selected and formed, liberated and repressed, made sensitive and blunted?" With these questions, Mills focused our attention on the broad structures and forces that shape our personal stories.

Note particularly Mills' third question which suggests that social order and historical period actually select in favor of certain kinds of people. This is a profoundly different view of human nature than most of us are familiar with. Yet understanding your personal biography as a product of social structure and history is the heart of sociology. Armed with this understanding, we can go on to understand how, "by the fact of our living, we contribute, however minutely, to the shaping of our society and to the course of its history, even as we are made by society and its historical push" (Mills, 1959, p.4). Also, seeing public issues creates new ways to seek answers, rather than every person for him/herself. Age-based policies developed as a consequence of seeing aging as a public issue. Social Security developed as a consequence of the Great Depression, when poverty became seen as a public matter, not an individual problem.

Micro and Macro Perspectives.

Mills' discussion of history, society, and biography draws our attention to the intersection of individual experience and broad social forces. Probably most of us agree that our behaviors, attitudes, and even our feelings are shaped partly by our personalities and partly by the social situation in which we live. Sociologists vary a great deal on the relative importance given to individual responses to social influences (**micro** concerns) and to the social structures— organizations and institutions— that create the conditions requiring a response from individuals (**macro** concerns) varies a great deal. The camera lens is in many ways an apt metaphor. A standard lens depicts a modest visual field and a modest amount of close-up detail. The wide-angle lens captures a much wider visual field, but the images of specific objects within the field usually show less visible detail compared to images produced by the standard lens. The telephoto lens allows the camera to focus on distant objects in greater close-up detail, but the width of the visual field is very narrow. If we look at three photographs of the same general visual field taken with different lenses, we can see that none of the photographs captures everything that the human eye is capable of seeing. Which photograph is the most useful depends on the purpose to which the photograph is to be put. Similarly, different questions about the social context, meanings and experiences of aging require different perspectives along the micro-macro continuum.

The same difference can also be seen in the sociology of aging. Several major streams of research are concerned with understanding micro-level issues such as the adaptation of individuals to the changes that accompany aging. This body of work considers the individual's adjustment to changes in his/her social situation, such as retirement. A more macro perspective seeks to understand, explain, and predict the social construction of those conditions to which the individual must respond. In the example of retirement, a more macro perspective would ask why there is anything to adjust to; where did retirement come from, and what purposes does it serve? How does retirement affect companies? How does retirement related to employment and unemployment? How does retirement reflect and affect the overall economy of a society?

Another example of the distinction between micro and macro approaches within the sociology of aging can be drawn from the vast area of health care. Some sociological work focuses on the health behaviors of individuals: how older patients adjust to life in a nursing home, who goes to the doctor most often, how doctors and patients interact, and how stress and health problems are linked. These are the kinds of questions that mark a micro-level perspective.

A macro-level framework would focus on organizational and system-level issues, such as the impact of population aging on the structure of our health care system, the equality of access to health care among different groups in our society, and the differential distribution of health hazards across different groups in our society.

This micro-macro distinction is one of the energizing tensions within the field of sociology; each perspective enriches the other and can push the other to greater clarity, heuristic value, and applicability. There is no single superior way to perceive and interpret "reality." There are many ways of identifying, classifying, and organizing our experiences of the social world. The micro-macro distinction is one way of categorizing ideas and information.

Summary

As you can see, aging is a broad and diverse field of study. In recent decades, as the population has aged, aging has steadily become a very important topic addressed by many different disciplines and perspectives.

Social perspectives on aging help us to understand the historically unique role of the elderly in our society today. In Part I of this book, the frames of reference used throughout the book are introduced, discussed, and illustrated. In this chapter we present the basic dimensions of aging and ways of categorizing people by age, as well as an overview of social perspectives on aging. Chapter 2 is an overview comparing different techniques and tools for studying aging; it also discusses some pragmatic considerations in the design and implementation of research in the field. This chapter seeks to provide you with some of the necessary skills to evaluate existing research on aging. Chapter 3 rounds out our overview of social perspective on aging by discussing the aging of society and the impact of "distant" demographic forces such as cohort size on the lives of aging individuals.

Part II takes us into the disciplinary views of aging: physical aging (Chapter 4), psychological aging (Chapter 5), and social aging (Chapter 6). Part III covers major social structures and institutions: the family, work and retirement, the economy, health care, and politics. Finally, in Chapter 12, we offer a view of the future of aging.

Our goal in this book is to illustrate the kinds of work leading us to a new understanding of the social context and social constructions of aging. An understanding of how social theorists and researchers think about, analyze, critique, and investigate questions related to aging is our major focus, although we also draw on the latest scholarship on physical and psychological aging. In the process we will note areas that have not received adequate attention, and offer some suggestions about why certain questions and issues have remained unasked and unexamined. This latter course requires some speculation on our part, but we decided it would be more challenging and interesting, and might inspire some of you to fill in the gaps in our understanding of aging.

Web Wise

At the end of each chapter we present a number of web sites that may be relevant to further investigation of select topics presented in that chapter. Some are oriented toward research, while others focus on policy or practice. For each site we provide the address and a brief description of what is included or tips on links you may wish to pursue. To get you started, we have included a few "how to" web sites, describing how to access, use, and cite information from the web. Another included site encompasses a directory to many other web sites that you may find useful if you are interested in a topic for which we did not list a particular site.

Beginners Central

http://www.northernwebs.com/bc/

This site, copyrighted and maintained by Northern Webs, has won awards from web groups for its help to those new to the web. It has a multi-chapter tutorial that you can read, download, or print that ranges from simple to complex topics. Like most good sites, it is updated regularly and has a lot of links to helpful resources.

Internal Tutorials

http://www.albany.edu/library/internet/index.html

This site, maintained by Laura Cohen, Webmaster and Network Services Librarian at the State University of New York at Albany, covers many of the same topics as Beginners Central, including numerous "how to" sections with clear, printable directions. There is some correspondence in the information, but not a complete overlap.

Using Web Resources in Writing a Paper

MLA-Style Citations of Electronic Sources

http://www.cas.usf.edu/english/walker/mla.html

One problem that new (and sometimes experienced) users of the internet have is how to cite and give credit to electronic sources, including web sites, gopher sites, and other electronic media. This site, created by Janice Walker, an expert in this field from the Department of English at the University of South Florida, gives specific and concrete examples of how to cite materials in bibliographies and links to a page giving information on how to do in-text citations. If you will be writing a paper where you may use web-based information, this will be useful to you. It also includes a bibliography and has won several awards.

Sites to Help Locate Other Sites on Aging

AOA Internet and E-mail Resources on Aging: An Online Directory
http://aoa.dhhs.gov/aoa/pages/jpostlst.html

Joyce Post, a librarian at the Philadelphia Geriatric Center, has made a name for herself by compiling and categorizing resources related to aging. This site, done in cooperation with the Administration on Aging, includes over two thousand sites and listservs related to aging and can be searched to find more specific information. I suggest going to "General Resources" or checking items marked as "Best Bets."

Andrus Gerontology Center Library

http://www.usc.edu/Library/Gero/

The library at the University of Southern California's Andrus Center has a useful on line list leading to most of the main aging resources available via the web. I found the "Web Resources" page especially useful. The resource links are organized topically under major categories, such as "Organizations and Associations" and "Psychology and Sociology" to help guide you to relevant websites. It also includes links to electronic journals (E-journals) and newsletters that may be of use to you.

Key Terms

ageism	micro approach
cohort	social aging
generation	societal control
life course	social gerontology
life stage	societal aging
macro approach	sociology of aging

Questions for Thought and Reflection

1. Take a look at a few magazine ads that feature older people. What are your reactions to those advertisements? What are they selling? What images of older people are being portrayed?

2. John Glenn recently completed his much publicized return to space. His age (he is in his 70s) was a major topic of conversation. Why is the American public so fascinated, amazed, and possibly wary of a 75-year old astronaut?

3. Respond to the statement that "You're only as old as you feel." Do you agree or disagree? What are some of the things that influence how old we "feel"?

4. What does the phrase, "social construction of aging" mean to you?

5. What are some of the causes, consequences, and solutions to ageism?

TOPICAL ESSAY

Will They Play the Rolling Stones at the Nursing Home?

What kinds of music do you listen to now? Whether it's classical or hip-hop, politically informed or "head banging," your taste in music may not be as simple as you think. First, recall what music you listened to five or ten years ago. Next compare your tastes with those of your parents or grandparents. Can you imagine what the music favored by people of your children's or grandchildren's generation is going to sound like? One thing is for certain: it probably will be very different from what you listen to today; and your musical tastes and preferences today may be far from accidental.

Analyzing the social aspects of music is in some ways like analyzing the social aspects of age; both are aspects of daily life that most of us approach with a "taken-for-granted" attitude (Martin, 1995). Music, like growing older, just seems to "happen" and to be part of everyday existence, rather than some puzzle to be solved. Although age has not been dealt with in a very systematic fashion in connection with music (Martin, 1995), there are some interesting questions that we can pose about music and aging. Although most attention in the sociology of music has focused on classical music (perhaps because it has been the music of powerful elites in many Western societies), some contemporary analysts also examine class, race, and age as elements of musical preferences (Epstein, 1994; Martin, 1995). Such issues as how and when musical preferences are formed and change and how the trends in popular music evolve over time have also been addressed in a preliminary fashion by social and cultural researchers. Here we examine some possible connections of music with the concepts of age, period, and cohort. (See chapter 2 for more detail on these concepts.)

Do Popular Music Styles Have a Life Cycle?

Music, like many aspects of each culture, evolves from its particular roots and traditions over time. Every era in each culture has its own "sound" as well as its sights, smells, and tastes. The 1995 fiftieth anniversary celebration of the end of World War II recalled not only the political events of the day, but the music and performers memorable to the cohorts who shared in that era. In a sense, the music is connected with the events (period effects) that shaped the lives of everyone, but especially of youth most affected by the war. Members from cohorts born later might think of this music as being "old fashioned," both by virtue of being out of date compared to contemporary styles and by its connection to a bygone era.

Perhaps musical styles and songs, as well as their performers, could be described as going through "life stages." Many musical styles make their entries as brash youth, breaking the rules and raising the ire of older generations. Parents in the 1920s were concerned with the moral decay implicit in the fast-paced music behind the dances in vogue, such as the Charleston. The same issues arose with the birth of rock-and-roll. Chagrin among elders toward adolescents' musical tastes is certainly not new!

With the passage of time, these new musical forms become institutionalized and accepted as part of the musical marketplace. As the musical style matures, we may hear versions of these songs converted into "muzak" for elevators or shopping mall background. By this point in their life cycles the songs, their performers, and the styles have become an accepted part of the culture, perhaps as their advocates move into more mature and responsible social roles. Emphasizing the importance among youth of separating their music from that of older cohorts, Epstein claims that,

> As generations of rock fans grow up, and have families of their own, they bring their music with them into adulthood. This makes it necessary for rock music to change, to mutate . . . Once a music is co-opted into the mass culture, it can no longer be considered confrontational, as is demonstrated by the Beatles song 'Revolution.' Revolution was once considered a controversial song about radical political change; now it is used in television commercials to sell shoes. (Epstein, 1994, p. xvii).

The once-shocking Rolling Stones passed this milestone when one of their hits became the anthem for a major software advertising campaign in 1995.

Artists age along with their audiences. New performers rocket to stardom, often to fade from the scene after a few years (Martin, 1995). Just remember that the most innovative, cutting edge musical artists of today will, if you wait long enough and their music endures, become "oldies," both musically and chronologically!

Do Cohorts Have Fixed Musical Preferences?

Especially compelling for each cohort seems to be the music associated with the events of young adulthood and "coming of age." Couples may have "their" song to mark their romance and marriage; young adults recall their passage to maturity with the songs they heard as they surmounted major milestones toward adulthood. Perhaps Mannheim was right in suggesting that the strongest influences upon us are those we encounter in late adolescence and young adulthood, since they form the standards against which we evaluate whatever comes later (1952). In music, at least, this would suggest that each cohort's tastes become set in young adulthood. If this hypothesis is true, then no music would compare to the music of our youth in its impact on us.

Setting of musical tastes in late adolescence and demographic trends go a long way to explain why many major cities now have at least one "oldies" station, playing the hits of the 1960s and 1970s. Radio station managers have come to believe that each cohort's tastes are fixed in young adulthood, so that baby boomers will continue to listen to the music of that era throughout their lives. The large size of the cohorts of the baby boom, and their current location in their high-earning middle-years, makes them a very valuable market for advertisers. In past years, radio advertisers pushed fast cars and the newest fashions to the Boomer market; but now products marketed to this group include insurance, minivans, and "relaxed fit" jeans. So what if Mick Jagger is past 50 and the surviving Beatles are becoming grandfathers? The logical outcome of this

"fixing" of musical tastes, of course, is that eventually they will need to play the Rolling Stones in nursing homes.

In contemporary nursing homes one may hear at least two kinds of music. For afternoon sing-alongs or performances the most favored music is comprised of the "old songs," reflecting the youthful period of the residents To estimate when these songs were most popular, take the current year and subtract about 60-70 years to when the residents were in their teens and twenties. Even those residents with cognitive impairment seem to recall the words of the songs of their youth, and seem to be cheered by hearing them. The other music to be heard in nursing homes, however, is that played by the staff, reflecting a younger generation and their tastes in music. Although it may satisfy the workers, we would guess that the musical tastes of most workers would not win many converts among the residents.

But do we all become fixed in our musical tastes in young adulthood? Is musical preference really a cohort-related trait? Probably not completely. There are those who cultivate a taste for other types of music as they mature. A fan of hip-hop may eventually cultivate a taste for jazz or the classics. There once was a "maturation hypothesis" regarding music, the absolute opposite of the cohort hypothesis derived from Mannheim. The maturation hypothesis argued that musical tastes routinely changed as we matured. Musical preferences, like our bodies, were thought to change in a predictable way. "Easy listening" radio stations once hoped for a major boost, expecting that the baby boomers, once they achieved middle age, would convert from the music of their youth to the style and performers of music that had been favored by their parents in mid-life. Instead of a high decibel level and a heavy beat, they hoped that mature Boomers would be more interested in a milder and more settled sound. That change failed to materialize in large enough numbers to maintain the "easy listening" format in many radio markets; and some of these stations converted to talk radio or oldies formats.

Just to throw our neat musical cohort scheme into chaos, there are occasional aberrations. An example is the mid-1990s embrace of singer Tony Bennett by young adults. Bennett is a star closer to their grandparents' than their parents' generation; he has not altered his pop style to accommodate his youthful fans. Unlike stars of most generations, Bennett, having already become "chronologically advantaged" relative to this new audience, will not have the luxury of growing older with them for too many years in the future.

Questions for Thought and Reflection

1. Since music plays such a role in our memories of events in our lives, what songs, artists, musical events so far in your life do you think will mark significant events or turning points for your birth cohort?

2. Is music likely to always serve as something that separates groups at different stages of the life course? Are there any forces that encourage people of different ages to share musical tastes and preferences?

CHAPTER 2

Studying Aging:
Analytical Frames of Reference

"...(N)ever begin a sentence with 'The elderly are...' or 'The elderly do...' No matter what you are discussing, some are, and some are not; some do, and some do not. The most important characteristic of the aged is their diversity. The average can be very deceptive, because it ignores the tremendous dispersion around it. Beware of the mean." (Quinn, 1987, p. 64)

Despite the perennial desire to understand how and why people age in a physical sense, the study of the social aspects of aging is a relatively recent phenomenon; the vast bulk of research has been done in the past thirty years. The research techniques that were initially applied to the study of aging in a social context were borrowed from the disciplinary research traditions of sociology, economics, history, and other fields, and then applied to the study of processes and products of aging in social life. The traditions and assumptions of these transplanted analytical frames of reference have shaped both the types of questions that are asked and the manner in which we seek answers to them. More recently, however, the study of aging has matured and developed its own, unique approaches to answering the key questions. Both the traditional and the newer, more innovative methodological frames of reference are the subject of this chapter.

Mainstream social science research has dealt with "age" for years as a variable in research. Many social phenomena are expected to vary by age, but often age is included as a **control variable**: a factor whose influence is statistically removed in order to examine, without interference from its effects, the real relationship under consideration (Ryder, 1965). For example, a study of the effect of parental social class on educational attainment of children might control for age, since it is well known that each successive group born into American society (to date) has achieved a higher collective level of education than its predecessors (see Exhibit 2.1). Removing the effect of age in this case would enable the researcher to draw conclusions regarding the effects of social class on schooling, without clouding the issue with differences in education that are simply due to age. This control-variable approach to examining age is still typical of studies where topics other than aging are the main focus.

The study of aging, however, redirects our attention to age as the central variable of interest, with the correlates and consequences of aging the focus of attention. The earliest research on social aspects of aging focused on the aged as a group, considering their circumstances (such as poverty and ill health) as social problems and examining ways to intervene on both the individual and

Exhibit 2.1   *Educational Attainment by Various Cohorts*

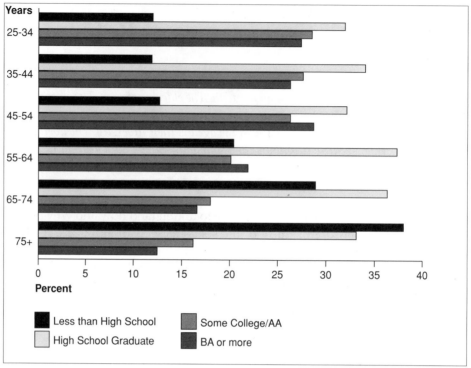

Source: Day and Curry, 1998.

the societal levels. More recently, however, the focus has shifted from study-ing "the aged" as a population category to studying *aging* as a social process (Campbell and O'Rand, 1985). This shift has prompted a move away from research methods that focused on analysis of a static group (those over 65 or some other arbitrary age) to studies of dynamic processes in society as groups of individuals move through the life course's various stages to later life. The addition of this dynamic view and application of the life course perspective have raised a whole range of new questions and prompted the development of new methodological approaches to answer them. So, although the roots of research in aging reach into the most enduring traditions of several social sci-ence disciplines, researchers are constantly struggling to find new and better ways to examine the dynamics of aging within an ever-changing society.

Why Do We Conduct Research?

There are a number of important reasons to conduct research on aspects of the social world. The most central motive is a deep curiosity: How do the various facets of this social world interact to shape the lives of individuals, groups, and

Exhibit 2.2   *Reasons to Conduct Research*

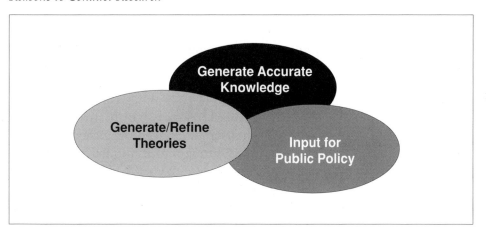

major social institutions such as the economy, contributing to the stream of social change that we all encounter as we move through our lives (Schutt ,1996)? Thus, the first impulse of research is to generate accurate knowledge about the social world in which we live (see Exhibit 2.2).

The interest in research goes deeper than this curiosity and desire for knowledge. Social scientists, like all scientists, are committed to a fuller understanding of how and why things (in our case, the social world) work the way they do. This understanding requires building theories that both explain and predict social behavior on the micro level of the individual, on the macro level of the social institution or society, or on any intermediate level between these two extremes. The second major purpose of doing research, then, is to generate, test, and refine theories. Ironically, the purpose of any specific piece of research is not to validate a theory, but to refute it. Since most theories are created and promoted because they seem logical and plausible, it is often easy for us to accept their propositions as intuitively appealing. As with many other scientific fields, the study of aging has had theories that seemed intuitively appealing when first proposed, but which were subsequently proved to be inadequate or false. Some examples of both successful and unsuccessful theories will be described in subsequent chapters. Scientific method requires that we do as much as we can to test a theory by trying to prove it to be wrong, thereby invalidating it and prompting us to move on to develop new or alternative theories to explain what we see. In this way, progress is made toward understanding social phenomena, including the processes of aging.

A third and increasingly compelling reason for conducting research on aging is to provide input for public policy and intervention. This type of research, referred to as **applied research** or evaluation research, uses scientific methods to provide answers to important questions of policy and practice (McAuley,

1987). Studying whether a particular service-delivery technique to support family caregivers of older adults with physical or cognitive health problems, for example, would be an applied evaluation study with direct implications for policies and programs. In an aging society and an aging world, the fate of individuals and groups as they grow older becomes inextricably linked to the well-being of the overall society. For example, older, widowed women make up one of the most consistently poor components of the older population, with many of them relying on modest Social Security survivor benefits as their sole source of income (Burkhauser and Smeeding, 1994). As society changes and more women are employed throughout adulthood, however, the plight of this group may improve as more aging women have their own pensions, savings, and Social Security benefits (Morgan, 1991). Making plans and policies based on current situations, without research insights on elders of the future, might lead to serious mistakes. More and more, health care practitioners and public policy makers are applying the findings of research on aging to strategies for intervention in the lives of individual older persons or on the local, state, or federal level.

Issues in the Collection of Scientific Evidence

Rules of the Scientific Method

The social sciences have built their reputations as being "scientific" through adherence to the rules of **scientific method**. These rules, subject to continuing debate, both provide basic guidelines for gathering information correctly (with oversight by peers) and maximize the likelihood of challenging incorrect theories. In this sense, the scientific method represents the agreed-upon rules of acquiring knowledge from the social world surrounding us; it is the approved process for generating scientific knowledge. Included in these rules are the concepts of **empiricism, objectivity, and control** (Singleton, Straits, and Straits, 1993).

"**Empiricism** is a way of knowing or understanding the world that relies directly or indirectly on what we experience through our senses" (Singleton et al., 1993, p. 30). Empiricism means that science rejects revelations from psychics or oracles, unsupported opinions by experts or authority figures, and personal intuition. Instead, scientists use their senses to generate observations and limit their questioning to those issues for which empirical information can be gathered. Beyond the empirical realm are philosophical questions regarding the meaning of life; within its realm, however, are more concrete concerns regarding how human groups operate on a daily basis to construct the social world.

The second concept, **objectivity**, means lack of bias. Objectivity is a goal of science even though it is difficult for scientists to separate themselves from what they study. Scientists determine objectivity by whether two independent observers agree on the results of a given scientific measurement or test. This requirement prompts scientists to outline in detail the logic involved in their methods of observing the world so that others can evaluate them for objectivity (Singleton et al., 1993). This review by peers is critical to quality control in the scientific method.

The third component, **control**, refers to scientists' efforts to remove from their methods any bias or error that may distort results (Singleton et al., 1993). Researchers must always consider alternative explanations for their observations and try to rule them out of consideration by their methods. This task is especially difficult in studying social life, because human beings cannot be reared (or, for our purposes, grow old) within a controlled environment, such as an experimental laboratory. Much of the work in developing complex research designs involves efforts to control these alternative explanations for phenomena under investigation.

While debates on the scientific method continue, researchers involved in the study of aging are working to develop techniques that will enable them to identify the effects of aging on individuals and on the larger society. A variety of approaches, as we shall see, are being employed to try to better understand aging and related phenomena.

The Role of Theory in Selecting Question/Method

Theories are often described as the driving force behind research, dictating both the specific questions that need to be asked and the choice of the most appropriate analytical techniques to answer them. For example, during the 1960s and 1970s, the theoretical contention between disengagement and activity theories led to considerable research on the concept of life satisfaction among the elderly. (These theories will be discussed in greater detail in Chapter 8.) Today, these theories are seldom discussed, and contemporary research gives only minimal attention to life satisfaction (Markides, Liang, and Jackson, 1990).

Research methods are sometimes viewed simply as tools to enable the testing of theoretical propositions, allowing them to be supported or refuted. In truth, the relationship between theory and methods is more dynamic (Campbell and O'Rand, 1985). By constraining what the researcher is able to do, the methodologies available often stimulate the development of theory in certain areas while blocking it in others. A theory that cannot be tested through research, although it may be intriguing, is not scientifically viable (Achenbaum and Bengtson, 1994). Again, a good example is disengagement theory (discussed in detail in Chapter 8). The theory was intriguing, but it could not be tested effectively in research. For this and other reasons, interest in the theory soon waned, and researchers looked to other theories that provided more viable avenues for advancing knowledge. Although theory shapes methodology, the relationship is actually a reciprocal one, with feedback from methodology to theory development, as shown in Exhibit 2.3. Theory can be "research-driven" (Campbell and O'Rand, 1985), just as research is often "theory-driven."

Exhibit 2.3   *Synergy between Theory and Research Methods*

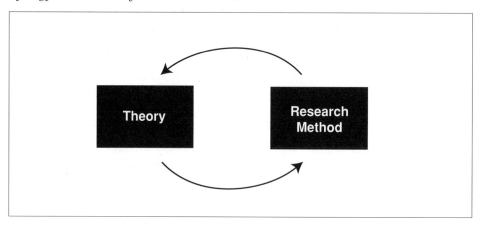

Qualitative versus Quantitative Approaches

Most of the techniques drawn from other social science traditions that have been applied to the study of aging are **quantitative approaches** — that is, they tend to examine numerical data using statistical techniques. The numerical data may derive from medical records, the census, an experiment, or from a survey of individuals, states, or companies; the data are then analyzed in such a way as to suggest that the numbers are meaningful reflections of reality. For example, a person reporting limitations in five Activities of Daily Living (ADLs)—a common measure of functional health status—is assumed in a quantitative approach to be more disabled than a person reporting only two such limitations. Although widely used, quantitative approaches have also been widely criticized for ignoring subjective interpretations by respondents and cultural differences in meaning, and for inhibiting theorizing by turning complex social life into a set of numbers (Cole, 1995). In contrast to these quantitative approaches are numerous **qualitative analysis** techniques.

"Qualitative research starts from the assumption that one can obtain a profound understanding about persons and their worlds from ordinary conversations and observations" (Sankar and Gubrium, 1994, p. vii). Qualitative research is thus based not on numbers, but on words, meanings, and conceptualizations. Key to the qualitative approach are the acknowledgment of (1) people's inherent ability to know and communicate things about their own lives, one another, and their respective worlds; (2) the researcher's role in obtaining the facts of experience; and (3) the importance of seeking to understand the multifaceted and complex nature of human experience from the perspective of subjects (Sankar and Gubrium, 1994). Thus, instead of using questions with multiple-choice answers, which construct the meaning of the social situation for the respondent in advance, qualitative researchers tend to focus their research efforts on in-depth interviewing, life-history collection, and observation, sometimes as a participant, in a social setting. The goal is to represent the participants' reality as faithfully as possible from their points of view (Sankar and Gubrium, 1994). The researcher, rather than being only minimally present for the administration of a questionnaire asking yes/no questions or for numerical ratings of the subject's health, is an active participant in eliciting meanings from the informants, whose reality is often recorded on audio- or videotape for later analysis.

For example, Gay Becker (1993) analyzed the aftermath of stroke in a sample of 100 victims. Her analysis was based on repeated interviews with the sample, participant observation in a stroke rehabilitation ward of a hospital, and observation of patient-practitioner interactions over a five-year period. The interviews, once transcribed, were used to identify central themes that appeared throughout the data. Those themes became the basis of theoretical explanations and hypotheses for further consideration. Among her key conclusions was that victims viewed stroke as a major life-course disruption, requiring victims to reconstruct their lives with new expectations and patterns of behavior.

In this case, Becker examined the event (stroke) from the perspective of those living through it to learn how they, not physicians or researchers, socially constructed the major issues. As an observant outsider, the qualitative researcher may see aspects of the situation that are missed or taken for granted by those in the situation. The hallmark of qualitative research is looking at the meanings central to social actors, not those that may be imposed by the perspective and goals of the researcher. However, it is important to point out that these two approaches-qualitative and quantitative-represent two different, not necessarily opposing, frames of reference for examining the social world and are sometimes combined in research studies.

Units of Analysis

One critical issue in any research study is understanding the appropriate **unit of analysis**, which reflects the particular elements under study (blood cells, families, health care delivery systems) and relates to the micro/macro continuum discussed in Chapter 1. If you are a biologist, at the micro level the smallest units of analysis include chemical compounds and components of the cell, whereas the macro level may include entire complex organisms, such as mice or human beings. In the social sciences the continuum differs by discipline: Psychologists move from intra-individual phenomena (micro) to the complex behavior of the person in social interaction (macro); sociologists take the individual as the micro end of their disciplinary continuum and entire societies as the macro end. In each case, the units of analysis along these continua vary in complexity and size, ranging from the smallest and often simplest units (at the micro end) through a variety of intermediate-level units to the largest and most complex units of analysis at the macro end of the continuum. The unit that is chosen for any given study derives from the question at hand and dictates the techniques most appropriate for seeking answers.

Scientists can address different aspects of the same topic using many different units of analysis. For example, the social phenomenon of early retirement can be examined with the individual as the unit of analysis (addressing questions such as the effects of early retirement on economic well-being or marital satisfaction), on the company level (How does early retirement affect the quality of the pool of workers?), or on the societal level (How do the economies of Western societies fare when there is large-scale early retirement?). Selecting the appropriate unit of analysis for a research project is a challenge generic to research studies of aging. This selection is often problematic. For example, researchers will discuss matters such as "relationships in later-life families" having interviewed only one person from the family. In such cases they are misstating the unit of analysis for their research (it is the individual, not the family). In the chapters that follow, you will find reports of research using a variety of units of analysis from small to large. Keep in mind that what happens at these various levels is very much interconnected.

Critiques of the Scientific Methods: The Sociology of Knowledge and Research Activism

Most of us take the information we get, especially from authoritative sources, for granted. We assume that the information is factual and unbiased. But there are many questions that we can, and perhaps should, ask about it. How do certain ideas come to the forefront in a society? Why do particular theories become popular and taken for granted by researchers or the public? Why do certain discoveries get coverage in popular media, whereas others disappear from view? We assume that experts know what they are talking about, use appropriate means to determine and present facts without the influence of political or ideological slants. But these assumptions are not necessarily true. One subfield of sociology, the **sociology of knowledge**, has made knowledge its subject matter. Sociologists of knowledge assume that we need to question how we know what we know and to examine the social influences on sources of information that most of us take for granted. Science is a social enterprise and a human activity that is shaped by the setting and the historical context in which it is performed. Researchers bring their personal frames of reference, including ideologies, expectations, interests, and experiences, to the research setting, sometimes unwittingly confounding what they find in their studies with what they wish to see.

These problems of potential bias are much more pertinent in the social sciences than they are in biology or physics, for example, where the topics the scientist is studying are more removed from personal interests and goals. When scientists study people and society and how they operate, however, they touch upon topics in which all social scientists have a strong vested interest. It becomes quite difficult to maintain the "objectivity" that scientists are supposed to have regarding their subject matter when the processes under study affect them and all of the people important to them. Because we are all aging and have family and friends who are aging, these issues become very personal.

The way scientists ask questions is influenced by their own backgrounds and biases, and also by external forces. Research, like fashion, has trends that are shaped by a variety of external forces, including political trends, the availability of funding to support research on various topics, and the popularity of particular research methodologies. Social scientists' decisions about what to study and how to study it are also shaped by the society around them. As interest groups gain political power, they influence public debate about, and funding for research. A good example of these external forces is the dramatic increase in funding from the mid-1980s to the 1990s for research on both the physical and social aspects of Alzheimer's disease (Adelman, 1995). Although scientists identified the disease in 1906, they "rediscovered" it during the 1980s with the assistance of advocacy groups who predicted that large numbers of the oldest old would face this disease in the future. Funding for research grew tremendously, resulting in increasing knowledge about Alzheimer's disease, its impact on the health care delivery system, and its effects on family members who provide care and support to its victims (Adelman, 1995). Although most diseases receive research funding that reflects their burden on the population, Alzheimer's disease is not alone, since both AIDS and breast cancer, receive greater funding than would seem warranted by the number of people affected and their lethality (Gross, Anderson and Powe, 1999). Legislators and those who fund research are engaged in actively socially constructing the relative seriousness of diseases. In another social/political context, funding might have been allocated in an entirely different fashion.

Knowledge is not neutral; it is socially constructed. Economics, politics and the personal interest of scientists and their sponsors influence scientific knowledge. The sociology-of-knowledge perspective emphasizes the importance of looking at research on aging with a critical eye for implicit assumptions, potential biases, and alternative conclusions.

A second major critique has to do with the issue of *activism* among researchers versus the objectivity mandated by the scientific method. It is as difficult for researchers studying aging as it is for other researchers of human behavior or society to separate themselves completely from the topic they study and remain objective. We are all aging! Social scientists continue to dispute whether science should even attempt to be objective, value-free, or value neutral. Some researchers argue that they should be activists, taking a stand on critical social issues of importance and providing applied research findings oriented toward solving these problems. There are compelling arguments on both sides of the debate. Those espousing an objective approach to science suggest that it is critical for researchers to acknowledge and work to overcome any biases or preconceptions they may have. In this way, the research may be more valid, reflecting viewpoints other than those of the researcher, and may have more credibility with any audience. A study finding beneficial effects of nursing home placement, for example, would be more credible if conducted by an independent researcher with no vested interest than if conducted by a group funded by the nursing home industry. Those on the other side argue that it is fundamentally impossible for us to put aside our personal frames of reference in conducting research. Rather, we ought to acknowledge the assumptions and biases that have directed us to select particular topics for study and approaches to studying them. Instead of pretending value neutrality, researchers should acknowledge and work with their biases to achieve applied research that is oriented toward improving the circumstances of some group or solving some problem. They may carry their activism to testifying before legislative bodies or lobbying on behalf of the causes they choose, combining research with individual political activism.

Special Concerns In Studying Aging

Most research on the social world is complex, because it involves the relationships of individuals, groups, and the larger society. These mutually influential components of the social world are in constant flux. Studies of aging not only share in these complexities but add other concerns unique to research into social aging. We address several of these special concerns here.

The Dilemma of Age, Period, and Cohort

When a researcher studying political participation finds that the percentage of the population that votes is higher in upper age groups (see Exhibit 2.4), what exactly does that tell us? Does it mean that advancing years or changes resulting from aging make us more politically active or involved? Not necessarily. There are, in fact, three related influences that shape changes across age groups and over time: aging, period, and cohort effects. Understanding these three forces is central to understanding the complexity of aging in a social context.

Many researchers are interested in learning about the effects of **human aging**, that is, the changes that occur as individuals accumulate years and move through the life cycle. When most people think of the effects of aging, they think first of the physical effects, such as wrinkling of skin or graying of hair. Yet there is clearly a social side to aging as well. For example, we may want to know whether and how aging influences individuals' productivity at work, happiness in marriage, choices in saving or spending money, or religious participation. But answering these questions is not as simple as it first appears. Our initial inclination would be to observe, for example, workers of various ages to learn how productive they are at a specific task and then draw comparisons by age. But would any differences that appear be *only* the result of aging?

It is very difficult to isolate the effects of aging in research, because human

Exhibit 2.4   *Percentage Voting in Congressional Elections by Age: 1966–1994*

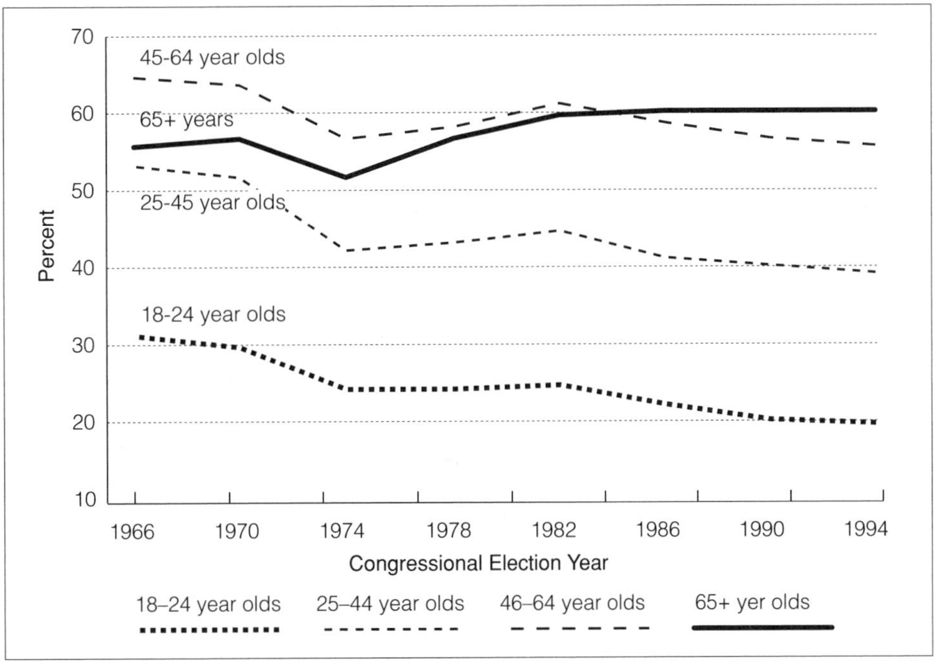

Source: U.S. Bureau of the Census, 1996b, U.S. Bureau of the Census, 1977.

aging or maturation does not occur in a vacuum. Instead, the process of aging is surrounded by social, economic, and historical events that influence the lives of individuals and groups as they age. Beyond aging, a second force that is sometimes responsible for differences between age groups derives from the historical period. **Period effects** emerge from the major events that occur while we are trying to study aging. For example, if we studied a cross-section of adults twenty-five years ago and again today and saw that the same people knew much more about AIDS now than they did before, should we conclude that their increased knowledge is a result of aging? Of course not. The period effect of growing public awareness of AIDS has influenced individuals of all ages over that same time period—at the same time that the adults were aging 25 years. Because individual aging and period effects are tied together by time, it is important to attempt to separate period effects from those of aging. The time at which we measure knowledge of AIDS, not the fact that the respondents are older, is the real issue with period effects. Often we think of major wars, economic booms or busts, and dramatic modifications in the norms and values of society as altering people's experiences as they age (Schuman and Scott, 1989). It is important to recognize, however, that more "everyday" period effects—for example, the introduction of new technologies such as personal computers and cellular phones—can also have profound effects.

Finally, **birth cohorts**—groups of individuals born at approximately the same time in history and sharing a collection of historical life experiences—often differ from each other in important ways. Cohort effects are differences between groups sharing major life events such as birth, marriage, college entry at different points in historical time. Some behaviors common among older people today are not necessarily caused by age. For example, if a research study found that appreciation of the music of bandleader Lawrence Welk was higher among older birth cohorts, would it mean that you would come to like this music as you aged? No; the older cohorts today, who came of age during the era when Lawrence Welk's music was popular, have continued to like it as they have aged. Their preference is a cohort effect: It has moved with them as they aged; the preference was not "caused" by aging.

A breakthrough article by Ryder (1965) identified the critical nature of the cohort in understanding processes of aging in society. Paralleling some of Mannheim's ideas about "generation" discussed in Chapter 1, Ryder identified the flow of birth cohorts through society as both creating and institutionalizing change in society over time. "Each cohort has a distinctive composition and character reflecting the circumstances of its unique origination and history" (p. 845). Members of a cohort share a slice of history and the social and cultural influences of their time, differentiating them from cohorts who preceded them or those that follow. Thus, each cohort has a life of its own. Cohort traits, such as its size or its race or gender composition, influence outcomes for the larger society and shape the life chances of individuals within the cohort (Easterlin, 1987).

The diagram in Exhibit 2.5 is a graphical representation by Riley and her colleagues (1987; 1994) of the triple forces of aging, period, and cohort. In this diagram, time is represented by the movement from left to right on the horizontal axis, and age is represented on the vertical axis. The diagram shows three birth cohorts, A, B, and C, each born at a different point in history. For each cohort, we can move from the year of birth on the horizontal axis diagonally upward as time passes and each group ages. Thus, the diagonal black bars represent the aging component. The white vertical bars represent period effects, the first clearly being World War II, the second perhaps the Vietnam War, and the third (potentially) the widespread integration of computers into everyday life. (The fourth is a hypothetical event yet to happen.)

You can see that most of the cohorts intersect each of these period events, but they do so at different ages and stages of their lives. For members of the oldest cohort, World War II occurred when they were in their 50s, the age to be parents of soldiers. Members of the next cohort, born in 1920, were young adults, likely to be heavily involved in actual fighting or war work on the home front. The 1950 cohort did not experience that war directly, but was undoubtedly influenced by its aftermath. For them the second event, the Vietnam War, fell at about the same time in their life spans (their early 20s), as World War II did for the 1920 cohort. In contrast, the Vietnam War was too late to have much effect on

Exhibit 2.5　*Changing Lives and Sociocultural Change*

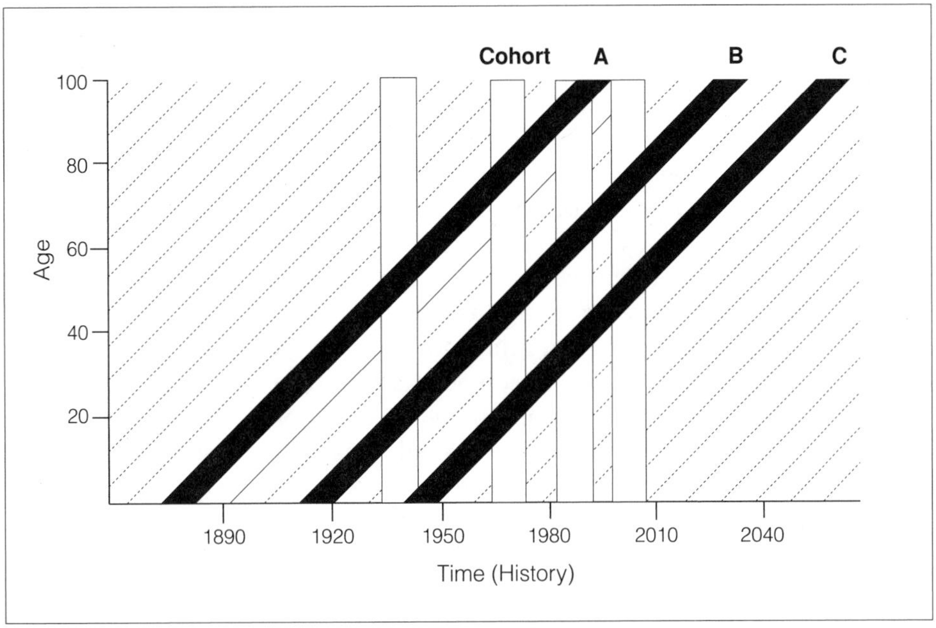

Source: Riley, 1987.

the surviving members of the cohort born in 1890, who were by then about 80. Thus, different cohorts face the same historical events (period effects) at different stages of the life course, and therefore relate to them differently. Such period effects may influence these cohorts as a collectivity in ways that will persist throughout their lifetimes (Riley, 1987).

Any large-scale event, such as a lengthy war or a significant economic downturn, is likely to have an impact on everyone in the society, but the effects are differential based on membership in different birth cohorts. Young adult cohorts, those most likely to be called upon to fight in the event of war, are likely to experience a life-changing effect from the war. At the same time, the birth cohorts who are parents or grandparents of these fighting-age adults, while doubtless affected by the war (worry over the outcome, shortages of goods and services) are unlikely to feel the same magnitude of effect on their lives from the same historical event (Pavalko and Elder, 1990). More mundane examples also apply. Certainly being a teenager in the 1990s was different from being one in the 1930s, even though many of the issues of aging/maturation faced by teenagers were the same. These sorts of accumulated differences throughout life may make the two cohorts very different when they reach their third or eighth decade of life.

Because they are so closely interrelated, these three factors (aging, period, and cohort effects) are extremely difficult to disentangle in research (Firebaugh and Chen, 1995). More complicated research designs, such as some described later in this chapter, can often assist in separating one type of effect (for example, a cohort effect) from the other two, but no currently available statistical technique enables us to routinely distinguish the relative inputs from each of these three factors (Schaie and Hertzog, 1982). Unfortunately, little research has systematically addressed the ways to sort out this vexing puzzle (George, 1995).

To return to our initial example in Exhibit 2.4, when we see variations by age in voting behavior, it is not apparent from a comparison across age group whether aging, period, or cohort effects, or some combination of them, is at work. If we make the assumption that it is all from aging, we commit what is called a **life course fallacy**—interpreting age differences in data collected at one time across birth cohorts as if the differences were *caused by* the process of aging, without ruling out other possibilities (Riley, 1987). Although it may be the case that adults do become more politically aware with the accumulation of experience (aging), and therefore act upon that awareness in the voting booth, this interpretation is not the only possibility. A second explanation for this difference by age may relate to cohorts and their experience. Older cohorts, raised at a time when most people were more patriotic, may feel a greater duty to vote, and may have voted at higher rates all of their lives when compared with younger cohorts. The age difference in voting, therefore, could be a **cohort effect**. A third possibility is a **period effect**, where a political event, issue or candidate could increase or decrease the voter turnout or voter registration rates (Firebaugh and Chen, 1995). Finally, it is quite possible that the pattern of voting behavior is a result of some combination of aging, cohort, and period effects. Despite the research difficulties in disentangling these three forces in the complexities of social life, some research has succeeded in doing so. By way of illustration, we will describe three specific research studies in which one of the three factors was successfully separated from the other two.

Aging Effects: Criminal Behavior by Age

Research has clearly established that not all citizens are equally likely to commit crimes. As Exhibit 2.6 shows, many of the crimes of greatest concern to society are committed by adolescents and young adults (gambling is an exception). Further, peak ages for commission of these crimes have remained consistent or declined since 1940 (Steffensmeier, Allan, Harer, and Streifel, 1989). Teenagers and young adults commit (and are arrested for) substantially more crime than are children or more mature adults. Why do we think this is an aging effect? In large measure the answer rests on the fact that similar age-related patterns of criminal behavior have been reported in many different societies and in different historical periods, diminishing the potency of explanations based on period or cohort. Although the amount of age difference in criminal behavior and the size of the decline with advancing age vary, many crimes show similar patterns of variation by age (Steffensmeier et al., 1989). When a pattern as apparently consistent as this appears, then we cautiously conclude that there is an aging effect.

Exhibit 2.6   *Peak Ages for Commission of Various Crimes in 1940, 1960, and 1980.*

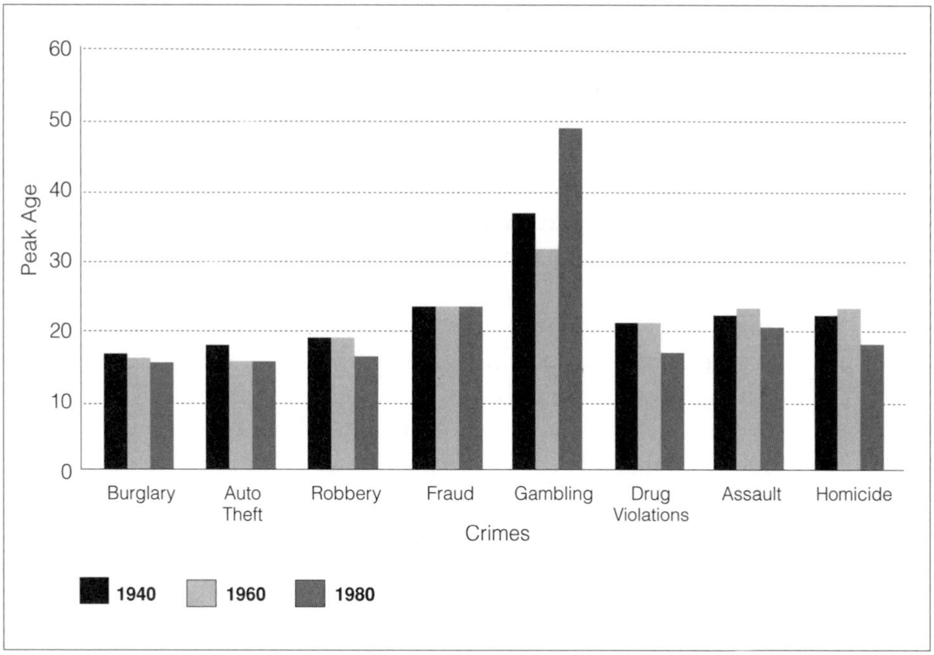

Adapted from: Steffensmeier et al., 1989.

But how is aging implicated in crime? Certainly criminal activity may be somewhat related to physical aging, in that some crimes require strength, speed, or agility to execute. More plausible, however, are the social explanations for crime: "Society at large is faced perennially with an invasion of barbarians . . . [and] every adult generation is faced with the task of civilizing those barbarians" (Ryder, 1965, p. 845). The barbarians to whom Ryder refers are, of course, the youthful cohorts being socialized to the ways of society and their roles as adults. Teenagers and young adults have fewer links or responsibilities toward work and family, and so are not well integrated into the social world. Since they are incompletely socialized and have not fully matured, teenagers and young adults face fewer constraints against committing crimes than do their older counterparts. The explanation suggests that as individuals mature and gather more responsibilities and linkages to the social order (that is, increase their **social integration**), the costs of crime rapidly grow to outweigh its benefits, discouraging participation in illegal activities (Laub, Nagin and Sampson, 1998; Steffensmeier et al., 1989).

A number of research studies have verified that the age structure of a society is indeed one of the key predictors of the rates of crime (Cohen and Land, 1987), but the picture has recently become a little cloudy. One analysis of homicide found cohort differences to be responsible for a dramatic increase since the mid-1980s in homicides committed by youth ages 15-24 (O'Brien, Stockard and Issacson, 1999). For nearly all other crimes, however, the effect of age continues to predominate, such that, all else being equal, a larger youth population will translate into higher rates for many types of crime.

Cohort Effects: The Case of Voting among the Nineteenth Amendment Women

Although it is typically very difficult to sort out age, period, and cohort effects, sometimes social life provides a "natural experiment" enabling researchers to clearly identify the consequences of cohort membership. In one such study, Firebaugh and Chen (1995) examined the changes in voting behavior of women in conjunction with passage of the Nineteenth Amendment to the Constitution, giving women the right to vote. The researchers noted that the voting rates of women just after passage of the amendment were much lower than those for men, but that this gap gradually narrowed over the years and then disappeared. Why?

To examine the issue, the researchers compared the voting behavior of three ten-year birth cohorts of white women: those born before 1896, who were denied the vote in young adulthood; those born between 1896 and 1905, who spent their childhoods before women could vote, but could themselves vote when they came of age; and those born between 1906 and 1915, who were raised after the enactment of the amendment. Firebaugh and Chen hypothesized that the experience of lacking the franchise (the right to vote) would have a lasting cohort effect on the first group, and that each of the later two cohorts would be more likely to vote than the first cohort, because this oldest group had been socialized to think that women should not vote and had themselves been prohibited from voting in their youth.

To make the test even more stringent, the voting behavior examined was from much later: national elections between 1952 and 1988. The analysis revealed a true and enduring cohort effect from the passage of the Nineteenth Amendment. Women from the earliest cohort, who had been kept from voting as young women, were less likely than either of the subsequent cohorts to vote throughout their lives. Even though they did get to vote as soon as they reached adulthood, the women in the second cohort, who were socialized during the era when women could not vote, were still less likely to do so thirty years later than their younger counterparts, who were raised when women had the vote. Thus, the critical experience of youth lasted throughout life and differentiated these three cohorts of women in their voting behavior.

Finally, the authors offered an explanation as to why the gender gap in voting rates shrank over time. This reduction was the result of changes in the composition of the voting population. As the older cohorts of women, who were less likely to vote, died and were replaced by women of later cohorts more likely to vote, the gap systematically disappeared. Thus, this change probably did not reflect changes in the voting behavior of individuals or even of cohorts.

Exhibit 2.7   *Changes over Time in Divorce Rates: 1930–1993*

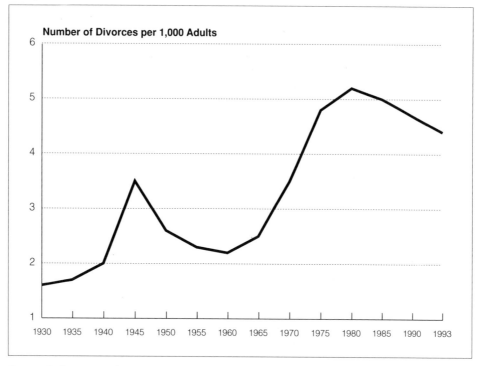

Sources: U.S. Bureau of the Census, 1975, U.S. Bureau of the Census, 1998b.

Rather, the explanation derives from the so-called **cohort composition effect**. As cohorts age and their members die, they are replaced in the population (here, the voting-age population) by younger cohorts whose behaviors and attitudes may differ. This gradual shift in the composition of the voting population, then, accounts for the disappearance of the voting gap between women and men.

Period Effects: The Case of World War II and Divorce

Although the annual rate of divorce has shown a long-term increase that leveled off in the 1980s (Cherlin, 1992), dramatic variations in divorce rates have occurred at particular points in historical time. One such point was World War II, with a notable increase in divorce rates in the years just after the war's end (see Exhibit 2.7). This short-term phenomenon was a **period effect**, sometimes explained as the result of marriages hastily made before men went off to fight, sometimes explained by the stress of long separation from spouses. Pavalko and Elder (1990) examined this period effect in closer detail using a cohort of males, about half of whom entered military service. Their analysis suggested a period effect for divorce throughout society (the divorce rate for all social groups increased at the end of the war) and that the effect was greatest for those closest to the war. Men who served in the military had more divorces than those who did not, and those who experienced combat had the highest divorce rates of all.

Surprisingly, however, it was not the marriages established between 1942 and 1945 (the war years) that were the most likely to be terminated. Some soldiers reported that their experiences in the war enabled them to meet partners who otherwise would have been outside their social range, perhaps forming better matches rather than poorer ones. It was not a case of "hasty" marriages failing; the marriages that had been established well before the war, and therefore were most disrupted by the changes that wartime life brought, were the most vulnerable to divorce.

Separating "Normal" from "Pathological" Aging

In Chapter 1 we mentioned the difficulty in separating out the "normal" aging of the body from diseases that are age-related but not age-caused. Similar problems arise in studying the social phenomena associated with aging. If people typically experience a decline in response time at the wheel of a car or in purchasing power in the marketplace as they age, can we say that these factors are part of the normal process of aging? Often we cannot. Some social phenomena are clearly age-related; for example, the probability of widowhood for women is clearly related to the ages of their husbands. But any times the chain of causation is indirect at best. The decline in response time may result from illness, rather than age per se. The decline in income, though common, is a consequence of the manner in which society constructs the systems for income-maintenance for older people who have retired and the fact that women, with fewer economic resources in current older cohorts, outlive men. Because we have institutionalized retirement and developed income-replacement strategies that derive from employment and do not always keep up with inflation, many people see their purchasing power erode. A majority of these survivors are older women. So just as physical pathology is hard to separate from the biological components of aging, social effects are intertwined with the social processes of growing older.

There is nothing natural or inevitable about doing things this way in the social world; age systems are socially constructed. In agricultural economies, where the ownership of land often remains in the hands of the oldest generation, their power and economic security may endure until death. We must remain vigilant to avoid assumptions that because something is common or typical, it is somehow socially "normal." This critical eye enables us to identify and address, through policies and programs, problems of older persons that are not inevitable parts of the aging process but that could in some instances be thought of as social pathologies in need of "treatment" through policy intervention.

Increasing Variability with Aging

Dale Dannefer (1988b) points out another difficulty related to the study of aging. He argues that there is now an ample body of both psychological and sociological research demonstrating that individuals in a cohort become more differentiated (or, in sociological terms, **heterogeneous**) as age increases.

> Older people have been thought to be more dissimilar from one another than are younger people in terms of physical health status, intellectual capacity, and psychological functioning, material resource availability and life-style. Although such comparisons are often used to contrast different age groups or strata at one point in time, they also implicitly connote a life-course pattern toward greater heterogeneity among age peers. (p. 360)

The processes involved in creating this increased variability are complex and the growing differentiation with advancing age creates challenges for research. Dannefer argues that neither our theories nor our research methods are well equipped to deal with this pattern. Adequate study of variability with aging would require both very large samples and longitudinal data (data collected on the same individuals over long periods of time.) This kind of research on many subjects over a long period of time is expensive.

Many of our current approaches to describing age-related changes focus on **measures of central tendency**, such as averages (means) that define how a typical person is doing. We then compare across ages to find any differences

Both social structural differences and unique life histories result in variation among older adults.

associated with age. If we find a difference, we think we may have identified an effect arising from aging, period or cohort. In fact, on some items older people differ more from one another than they do from younger age groups! Measures of central tendency ignore the variability within each cohort, making such measures less adequate to describe older than of younger groups. It is this "mean" that Quinn warns us about in the quote that began this chapter. Alternative measures are available, and Dannefer urges their use in the study of aging populations.

Adequate Samples for the Question under Study

What are samples, and how do researchers use them? As Nesselroade so simply put it, "A **sample** is a small part of anything (or a few of a larger number of somethings) that is (are) used to show the nature of the whole" (1988, p. 13). In most social science research, a sample is a few units of analysis (people, families, businesses, city governments, or countries) out of all of the possible pertinent units of analysis (the population) that you wish to study (see Exhibit 2.8). The units in the sample reflect the location along the macro/micro continuum that has been selected as appropriate for the question at hand, with the number of units in any given sample being highly variable and the number of samples potentially to be drawn from any large population infinite.

The goal is to have a sample that represents the entire population (sometimes also called the universe), because it is too costly in time and money to reach every member of that population, and good estimates can be developed from a sample of what would have been found had the entire population been included. This is especially challenging given the diversity among older adults. A study of the entire population of the United States is conducted every decade when the census is taken. The census, by not using a sample, is more the exception than the rule. Since it is impossible to interview every person who is widowed, for example, researchers select a sample believed to represent in most critical ways the larger population from which it was selected (all widowed persons).

A wide variety of sampling techniques can be applied to various types of quantitative and qualitative research (McAuley, 1987). Many of these techniques are directly applicable to studies of aging, where attention is often focused on constructing samples based on age (for example, a survey studying how attitudes toward Social Security vary by age). Sampling by age is a difficult task, because there is no simple way to identify or reach large and representative groups of people across the full range of ages. For example, there is no roster of retirees or persons over age 65 from which we can easily draw samples (McAuley, 1987). Although the Social Security system has information about most older adults, the information is confidential, and not available to researchers.

The study of aging encompasses more than just age in selecting participants

Exhibit 2.8   *The Relationship among Population, Sample, and Unit*

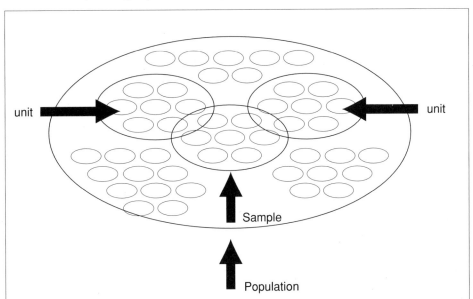

for research. Sometimes researchers are interested in locating individuals from more specific groups or "rare populations": daughters providing at-home care for a frail parent; older adults who have maintained high levels of creative productivity in the arts; or African Americans anticipating retirement in the next few years. Efforts to examine specific groups require additional attention to sampling and sometimes the use of special sampling techniques (Kalton and Anderson, 1989). Not only may these groups be statistically rare, but they may also be resistant to participating in research for a variety of reasons (McAuley, 1987). To develop a high-quality sample in these cases requires considerable resourcefulness.

Studies that focus attention on the oldest individuals in society, who are often frail or cognitively impaired, raise additional concerns. Researchers are ethically bound to use extreme caution in conducting interviews or observations with such samples, given the relatively higher risks of stress, fatigue, and health impacts of upsetting a normal routine. Gatekeepers, such as relatives or health care providers, are often reluctant to give permission for frail persons in their care to participate in research studies. Special protections, including detailed reviews of research methods for risk factors when older subjects are involved, work to minimize problems for such vulnerable samples.

Early research on aging was plagued by samples that were small, local, and unrepresentative of the larger population (Cutler, 1995). Researchers could draw conclusions only in very limited fashion because there was no certainty that their results pertained to the population as a whole. Until fairly recently, most studies underrepresented some groups, making it difficult, for example, to study aging in minority populations (LaViest, 1995; Markides et al., 1990). In fact, many studies were conducted using "convenience" samples that tended to over-represent white, middle-class individuals. The development in large, nationally representative samples that enable researchers to examine many issues of concern in aging has marked a major advancement in the field (Cutler, 1995; Kasl, 1995).

Cohort-Centrism, Dynamism, and the Limitations of Current Knowledge about Aging

As we have already noted, the scientific study of aging is a relatively recent development. For example, early research on retirement began in the 1950s and grew dramatically in the decades that followed. Most of what we know about how retirement affects individuals, families, the labor market, and the overall economy is drawn from the 1970s through today. The same could be said about a wide range of topics associated with aging.

Our knowledge of retirement is, therefore, limited to cohorts of workers who were entering or already in retirement at those particular time periods, with all of their related cohort experiences of economic upturns and depressions, education, war, and employment. They represent a truly narrow slice of history upon which to build a knowledge base. Riley (1987) warns against the **fallacy of cohort-centrism**, whereby an erroneous assumption is made that future (or past) cohorts will age (have aged) in the same fashion as current cohorts under study. We should expect research findings to change as new cohorts, with vastly different experiences in health care, the labor market, the family, and in other domains of their lives, approach and enter retirement. These newer groups will retire from a global economy that has changed dramatically in the past twenty to thirty years. Similarly, processes that are influenced by period effects in other areas of aging, even biological aging, should be expected to change as conditions experienced by the individual alter through historical time.

In studying aging, part of the problem is that we attempt to study a moving target. Matilda White Riley describes this dynamic aspect of the study of aging from her perspective of examining cohort flow through the age structure of society over time (1987). She describes two, interrelated dynamisms as underlying this interplay of individual aging and social change. The first process is the *aging of people* in successive cohorts who grow up, grow old, die, and are replaced by people in subsequent cohorts. Because the members of these successive cohorts age in different ways, they contribute to social change. "When many individuals in the same cohort are affected by social change in similar ways, the change in their collective lives can produce changes in social structure" (p. 9).

For example, Riley explains the rising economic well-being of older adults using the "cohort composition" explanation described earlier. The reduction in the poverty level of the older population has been brought about by deaths among the oldest cohorts, who were the least financially secure, and the movement into older ages of their replacement cohorts, more of whom retired with pensions and assets to combine with Social Security benefits. Thus, according to Riley, the fates of particular elderly persons have not improved over the past decades. Instead, the movement of cohorts into and (through death) out of the older population has changed the composition of, and thus society's view of, the economic security of the older population (1987).

Studying contemporary older adults captures experiences unique to their cohort.

Second, there is constant *change in society* as people of different ages pass through the social institutions organized by age. As society changes, people in different cohorts age in different ways. The economic boom following World War II and the increased availability of pensions has enabled more older persons today to retire at earlier ages. Early retirement, in turn, has created a boom in housing, travel, and leisure pursuits for this economically advantaged group, to which the economy has had to react by providing products and services. "The key to this understanding lies in the *interdependence* of aging and social change, as each transforms the other" (Riley, 1987, p. 2).

The problem, according to Riley, is that we are attempting to study the process of aging within the context of constant change in the social world. Social changes, in turn, modify the process of and the adaptations to aging among successive cohorts, making it more difficult to determine what, if anything, is caused by aging on the macro or micro level. One such dynamic, described below, is change in the size and composition of birth cohorts, which, according to economist Richard Easterlin, may have important influences on the lives of various cohorts.

■ ■ ■ ■ ■ ■ ■ ■

APPLYING THEORY
Cohort Size and Life Chances: The Easterlin Hypothesis

Do you believe that your personal fate and your opportunities are entirely in your own hands? Is it only your individual abilities and choices that determine how your life will turn out? Economist Richard Easterlin has formulated a very interesting and controversial theoretical argument about the opportunities individuals get in society (what sociologists call **life chances**). His premise is a simple one: The life chances of individuals are influenced to a significant degree by the size of the cohort into which they were born. "For those fortunate enough to be members of a small generation, life is—as a general matter—disproportionately good; the opposite is true for those who are members of a large generation" (1987, p. 3). Prompted by the obvious impact of the "baby boom" cohorts (which he refers to as a generation), and recognizing an apparently cyclical movement from large to small "generations," Easterlin argues that cohort size affects the well-being and outcomes experienced by a cohort's individual members. Members of large cohorts compete for attention and positions in families, schools, and the labor market; members of smaller cohorts see their fortunes advance relatively easily by comparison. When the members of larger cohorts are unable to achieve their high aspirations, Easterlin argues, they take actions such as having fewer children, and they experience higher rates of unemployment, divorce, suicide, crime, and political alienation (1987).

Although Easterlin has presented a compelling case in his book *Birth and Fortune*, other researchers have demonstrated its limitations as an explanatory scheme. To test one of Easterlin's predicted negative outcomes for large cohorts, Kahn and Mason (1987) analyzed survey data on political alienation from 1952 through 1980. They found that period effects (such as, the Vietnam War or Watergate) had more to do with political alienation than did cohort size. Political alienation fluctuated over time in similar patterns for all cohorts, rather than differentially for cohorts of different sizes.

In other studies examining cohort size and crime, findings are mixed. One analysis showed that larger cohort size was related to the commission of homicide (O'Brien et al., 1999) but others showed, contrary to Easterlin's prediction, that larger cohorts were not especially prone to crime (Steffensmeier, Streifel, and Harer, 1987). These authors argued that looking only at cohort size is too simplistic and that prediction of criminal behavior needs to take into account the larger social and economic climate as well. Nonetheless, the age structure of society does influence crime in important ways.

As the debate on the validity of Easterlin's hypothesis on cohort size continues, it may be important for you to consider the size of your cohort (either your birth cohort or the cohort with which you entered school, job, or marriage) and to contemplate whether the size of that group is likely to shape your opportunities and, as a result, your life chances as you move through your life course.

■ ■ ■

Designs Targeted to Studies of Aging

In this section we outline some of the analytical frames of reference that have emerged more recently to address the special concerns in the study of aging. Although many of them are also applied to other types of questions, these innovative approaches have signaled great strides forward in the study of aging.

Longitudinal/Panel Studies

Longitudinal studies, sometimes also called panel studies, attempt to provide us with the means of isolating aging from cohort or period effects by following a sample of units of analysis (cells, individuals, states, corporations, or societies) over time to observe how they change (or remain unchanged). The most often used type of longitudinal study is one in which individuals in a sample are repeatedly surveyed about their lives over a period of years or even decades. Longitudinal designs are contrasted with **cross-sectional studies**, in which data are collected at one point in time, generating a snapshot of differences between age cohorts. Although it is not a panacea for all of the analytical problems we have been discussing (Campbell, 1988), the use of longitudinal data drawn from the study of a sample over time is generally touted as a necessity in the study of social processes of aging, because the commitment in time, financial resources, and effort involved in collecting significant longitudinal data can be staggering, with the benefits sometimes not seen for years (Campbell and O'Rand, 1985). In addition, researchers face challenges in conducting longitudinal studies that are not characteristic of cross-sectional work.

> Despite the researcher's efforts, some respondents will be lost, requiring extensive tracking, and may possibly never be found. The investigator must deal with thorny measurement issues. Should questions be repeated, even if the early data from the study show them to be flawed? And even if questions are repeated in exactly the same form, the structure and meaning of concepts they indicate may have changed over time. What if new concepts emerge that seem germane to the original research objectives? (Lawton and Herzog, 1989, p. vi)

Yet longitudinal data are critical to disentangling the effects of age, cohort, and period on processes of individual aging and social change over time. Especially useful are longitudinal studies that include a **cohort sequential design**. Exhibit 2.9 shows a hypothetical sequential design, following three cohorts over four time periods. Each group is re-interviewed at five-year intervals. Note that this design makes it possible to compare across cohorts and time periods; for example, comparing cohort 2 at age 29-30 at time 1 with cohort 3 at the same age at time 3. In a cohort sequential design, more than one cohort is followed longitudinally, enabling further separation of the effects of aging, period, and cohort. A recent study, for example, included fifteen birth cohorts (every 3 years between 1916 and 1958) and collected data annually for eleven years, provid-

Exhibit 2.9   *Cohort Sequential Design*

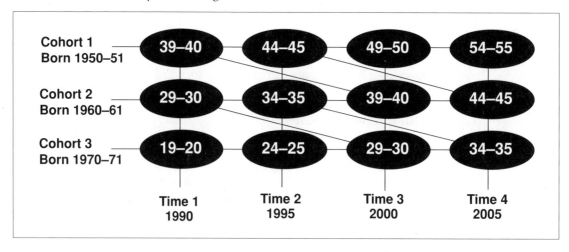

ing a substantial amount of information to sort out age, and cohort effects for disease and disability (Reynolds, Crimmins and Saito, 1998). In the earlier example of women's voting patterns following ratification of the Nineteenth Amendment, by focusing on a span of behavior (voting patterns from 1952 to 1988) with three distinct cohorts, the researchers used a sequential design to clearly isolate cohort effects.

Secondary Analysis

"**Secondary analysis** refers to the study of existing data initially collected for another purpose" (Liang and Lawrence, 1989, p. 31, emphasis added). Although secondary analyses need not use longitudinal data or even survey data (for example, secondary analysis of medical records) (Palmore, 1989), many of the most valuable contributions to our knowledge of aging have involved longitudinal surveys of aging samples.

A growing number of large, national longitudinal secondary analyses of studies originally designed to examine very specific issues (such as economic status, employment, utilization of health services, and family relationships) have been employed by other researchers in secondary analyses to answer questions about aging beyond those envisioned by their original designers. Many such data sets are available from computerized archives, making them readily accessible to researchers for secondary analyses (Inter-University Consortium for Political and Social Research, 1985; Liang and Lawrence, 1989). You can locate examples through web sites listed at the end of this and some other chapters. These studies have been used to dramatically expand knowledge in a number of areas about aging, despite having been designed with other goals in mind. Newer longitudinal studies, including the Health and Retirement Survey initiated in 1992 with large samples of women and men, will update the knowledge provided by panels initiated in the 1960s and 1970s (Juster and Suzman, 1995). Without a doubt, these longitudinal studies used in secondary analysis have added considerably to our store of knowledge about aging.

The growth in these large, national data sources available to researchers for secondary analysis is a mixed blessing. As Kasl (1995) points out, although these studies provide both a longitudinal design and a large, national sample, which would probably otherwise be unavailable to most researchers on aging, they offer information on a limited number of variables. Researchers may not be able to measure concepts of interest (such as health status, family cohesiveness, or political involvement) in ways that are ideal; essentially they must work within constraints of what the data provide. If a key variable is missing, then the researcher must choose between not using the data at all or attempting to work around this limitation.

Event History Analysis

One of the newer tools in the study of aging is called **event history analysis**. In aging research we are often interested in when a particular life event happens or in the social forces that shape its occurrence. Event history analysis attempts to address these issues. This frame of reference draws our attention to a particular event of interest, such as retirement, enactment of a new social policy, entry into a nursing home, or divorce.

As its name suggests, event history analysis focuses on when and how particular events happen to the person or group of interest. Based on longitudinal data, this technique explores how much time passes before the event of interest occurs, the rates of occurrence of particular events (for example, widowhood within a population), and how these rates change with the passage of time (Does the rate of widowhood increase as women age?) (Campbell and O'Rand, 1985). This type of analysis allows us to answer questions related not only to when something occurs, but also to the relationships, if any, between events—for example, marriage and childbirth, or passage of a new retirement policy and changes in the behavior of retirees.

Although event history analysis is most frequently used on the individual level, examining the impact of specific life events, it can also be applied to large-scale (macro) events. It would be equally valid, however, to look cross-nationally at how changes in eligibility age for retirement influence when workers retire in various countries, using the country as the unit of analysis. Regardless of the unit of analysis, it is essential that the unit under study have the potential to undergo a particular change that may have identifiable consequences of interest.

A key to analyses of this type is being able to pinpoint the timing of the event of interest (Campbell and O'Rand, 1985). Current studies often enable us to know only that retirement or marriage or death took place between the third and fourth round of interviews in a longitudinal panel, but not the specific month or year of the event in question. A second complication in this type of analysis is known as censoring. If we are following a large sample to examine the timing and rate of a particular event—say the onset of dementia, which occurs at widely different ages in a population above age 70—this event would already have occurred for some people, not yet have occurred for others, and never occur for still others. In the cases where the event doesn't occur and we don't know its timing, the event is considered "censored," and not available for analysis. Therefore, unless we can wait thirty or forty years to ensure that everyone in the sample has either shown signs of dementia or died without doing so, event history analyses are always dealing with censoring. Censoring simply means that we lack knowledge of when those remaining people will experience the event of interest, if ever. Fortunately, techniques are available to assist in dealing with the problems of censoring.

As a specific example of event history analysis, Moen, Dempster-McClain, and Williams (1989) conducted a study of women's role involvement and longevity. They used a sample of married mothers (originally ages 25-50) who had been interviewed in both 1956 and 1986. The event of interest was mortality. Most women in the sample (76 percent) had survived the thirty-year period and were therefore censored as to the timing of their eventual demise. Another 5 percent could not be located and were also considered censored as to time of mortality. Only 19 percent of the sample had died during the interval between interviews. Knowing the dates of death for the women who died, however, enabled the researchers to utilize complex statistical techniques to evaluate the relationship between longevity and the number of social roles held earlier in life.

The researchers were interested in whether the number of social roles (aside from being a wife and mother) was related to longevity. They found, after controlling for social class and age in 1956, that the number of social roles did help to predict longevity. Women who were more involved earlier in their lives, especially those who belonged to clubs or organizations, had greater longevity than those who did not. The authors concluded that social integration of midlife women has beneficial effects that translate into greater life expectancy. The event history approach enables researchers to examine a variety of life course events that are of considerable interest. Rather than focus on "the aged," this technique emphasizes the dynamic nature of aging over time.

Life History and Reminiscence

Some researchers choose to address questions of time, aging, and social change at a more individual level, asking older persons to look back over their lives, emphasizing the transitions and events that served as turning points. This **life history or reminiscence** approach is not only used for research purposes, but is also considered by many to be therapeutic for older persons themselves (Parker, 1995). Review of past life events may occur spontaneously by an older person alone or in conversation, through a structured interview process or in a group workshop. It is these latter two settings that have been involved in research and therapeutic activities. As a research tool, life history interviewing is somewhat controversial. Many methodologists argue that retrospection (looking back) involves a mental reconstruction of the past that is subject to bias (Hagburg, 1995). This reconstruction, however, may be what is of interest, rather than a factual accounting of the events as they happened. For example, what is of interest to a researcher today may not be the exact realities of the Great Depression of the 1930s or World War II but how those events and times are recalled over the course of many years, and how they influence today those who experienced them.

Bo Hagburg, in a life history study focusing on close personal relationships throughout the life cycle, examined satisfaction with events surrounding retirement. Hagburg (1995) found that positive recollections of relationships in childhood and adolescence were associated with a positive reaction to the experience of retirement. Retirees remembering earlier life stages and the significant people in them most positively were most likely to be satisfied in retirement. Neither the current mental status nor the cognitive ability of the retiree explained this relationship. Instead, satisfaction with retirement was linked to a positive report of relationships to significant others during childhood and adolescence.

Much of the life history or reminiscence work is qualitative in nature, focusing on descriptions of past events and how they are interpreted through the passing years. This qualitative approach is not necessarily the case, however. The Hagburg study, for example, used statistical means to correlate aspects of life history with current events and characteristics.

In addition to these research techniques that focus specifically on issues surrounding aging, a range of mainstream techniques from other scientific disciplines can also be productively applied to the study of aging issues. We now turn our attention to some of those techniques.

Mainstream Methodologies Applied to Aging Issues

In this section we describe some examples of how traditional approaches to research, used in a range of disciplines, have been applied to the study of aging. These examples identify ways in which researchers have adapted these techniques to questions on aging. You should expect to see numerous examples of these methodologies in the chapters that follow.

Macro Approaches

Most of us think about aging as an individual-level phenomenon. If we think about health care, family, or retirement, most of us initially think about the implications for the individual. Yet other levels along the micro/macro continuum can be highly instructive in understanding issues of aging in a social context. Instead of addressing retirement from the point of view of the individual's decision or outcomes, we can look at how retirement affects the economy and labor force. Rather than considering the utilization of health services by individuals, we might examine how social policies shape the health care delivery system. This approach to research, utilizing the wide-angle macro lens instead of the close-up lens described in Chapter 1, reflects the **macro approach** to the study of aging.

A good example is the set of related studies by Estes and her colleagues (Estes, Swan, and Associates, 1993). Through several related research projects, this team attempted to explain how a major modification in social policy, the Prospective Payment System (or PPS) under Medicare, modified the health care delivery system in the United States. The PPS was Medicare's attempt to control increasing costs by limiting the amounts Medicare was willing to pay health care providers. Estes and her colleagues used a multi-method approach to address this complex problem, including telephone interviews with hospital discharge planners and service provider organizations, interviews with state and local policymakers and representatives of major provider organizations, detailed case studies in three communities, and secondary analysis of data from a variety of governmental and private sources. From all of these pieces of the puzzle, this team put together a picture of the complex changes to the health care delivery system brought about by the advent of the PPS.

Although the findings from such a large-scale and data-rich study cannot be summarized briefly, one aspect of the macro analysis conducted by the Estes team related to community-based care. They found that the PPS reduced the length of hospital stays for Medicare recipients. Although that reduction was anticipated, what was not expected was a slowing in overall hospital admissions under Medicare, lowering hospital occupancy rates significantly. Physicians reported pressures to discharge patients and to conduct tests on an outpatient basis, changing their existing approaches toward delivering care to patients. Evidence on the quality of care is mixed. There are indications of poorer outcomes such as higher mortality and more readmissions to the hospital. Other analyses show no reduction in quality of care. The other major result of the PPS has been the relocation of many types of care to settings outside of the hospital, including home and outpatient care providers. Under PPS, hospitals more often discharged patients to nursing homes, rehabilitation facilities, or home health care programs because their medical needs continued to be greater than could be met at home (Estes et al., 1993). Home health care has increased dramatically since the advent of PPS, including the use of very high-tech equipment at home. Interestingly, hospitals, in an effort to recover some of the income lost from inpatient days, have branched out into subacute care and home health programs.

In studies such as this one, the macro approach takes a giant step back from the individual level of analysis and focuses its analytical attention on the manner in which major institutions, such as the health care delivery system, react to political, economic, or value changes in society. Paired with individual-level studies, these macro approaches often provide compelling answers to why certain social changes have the consequences they do.

Experimental and Quasi-Experimental Research

Studies with true experimental designs are perhaps the classic form of research under the scientific method. An **experimental design** involves taking a sample and subjecting it to some sort of intervention, treatment, or stimulus to determine whether that intervention has some specific outcome. Experiments enable us to control many other differences in an attempt to guarantee that only the experimental factor is the cause of the observed outcome (Schutt, 1996). Essential to true experiments is having both an experimental group, whose members are subject to the intervention, and a control group for comparison. A second requirement is that the units of analysis (cells, people, businesses) are assigned randomly to either the experimental or the control group (Schutt 1996). An experiment on the effects of exercise on aging bones, for example, might randomly assign individuals to either a control group, which continues its prior level of activity, or an experimental group, which begins an intensive period of exercise to determine whether bone structure is altered after a year. Tests both before and after the exercise intervention could also help to identify any changes due to aging over that time period. An experiment for family caregivers might randomly select some families for a program of respite care for six months and compare them with controls to determine if they show lower levels of stress. Even macro-level experiments are possible, when a policy is altered in some states and not in others, but researchers are less often able to randomly assign macro-level units of analysis to an experimental and control group.

For obvious reasons it is impossible to conduct the purest form of experiments on human aging, because we cannot control all aspects of the environment and experience of an experimental subject to guarantee that nothing other than our experimental factor (whether aging itself, a drug, or a social policy) causes of any change we see. In addition to the technical problem of establishing the causes of change, there are ethical problems with experimenting on humans. For example, randomly assigning people to experimental and control groups may involve delaying or denying a necessary intervention to someone. In addition, it is likely that most of the issues of concern in aging, as in most research on human endeavors, involve multiple causes generating multiple outcomes (Davitz and Davitz, 1996). Many types of experiments can be conducted that are relevant to human aging, but some experimental designs cannot be implemented.

To examine many social phenomena, we often must turn to **quasi-experimental designs**—research designs that are not true experiments, but that contain at least one key element of an experiment (Schutt, 1996). Quasi-experiments do not permit us to control all of the other factors influencing the sample, yet move the research toward the goal of eliminating alternative explanations for what we observe (Campbell and Stanley, 1963). Major types of quasi-experimental designs include studies that have both an experimental and a comparison group, but where assignment is not random. An example might be a study of a sample of cities, only some of which have received funding for a new case management program to assist frail elders. We could follow the outcomes of frail elders in cities with and without the new program to see whether it improved living conditions, but we would be unable to rule out many alternative causes because the cities were not randomly assigned to the experimental and control groups.

The other major type of quasi-experimental design is a study that evaluates results before and after intervention, but involves no control group. We might plan a study providing training to older adults in money management. We could evaluate their sense of competence both before and after the training, but would be unable to rule out alternative explanations (such as the effect of having additional social contact with their peers during the training) as having contributed to the results. Clearly researchers need to think carefully about the nature of any experimental or quasi-experimental design they propose and the alternative explanations for the results they find.

Surveys

Surveys are probably the most widely used methodology in social science research, including studies of aging. Survey methodology is highly diverse, from telephone marketing surveys about your favorite soap to surveys of cities, states, or nations on their social policies or laws. The essential nature of a **survey** is asking structured questions (in person, by telephone, or in a pencil-and-paper format) to a sample of units of analysis (whether persons or organizations) in order to answer research questions (Fowler, 1988). Survey methodology is used in both cross-sectional and longitudinal research, surveys are frequently used for applied and evaluation research, and the data from surveys often become the raw material for secondary analysis.

Many surveys on aging are large-scale, nationally representative, longitudinal studies that have served as the basis for considerable amounts of published research in recent years. A good example is a set of studies begun in the late 1960s called the National Longitudinal Surveys (NLS) (Center for Human Resource Research, 1995; Shaw, 1983). These longitudinal surveys focused initially on four cohorts: young men (14 to 24 years), young women (14 to 24 years), mature women (30 to 44 years), and mature men (45 to 59 years). Each sample was repeatedly interviewed over a number of years at one- to two-year intervals, with the interviews for the two women's cohorts continuing into the mid-1990s. The intent of the studies was to follow sufficiently large groups (each sample started with more than 5,000 individuals) over time to examine major life-cycle changes in behavior, employment, family, and residency. The NLS project has added other cohorts, and its detailed data on a variety of variables have now been used by thousands of researchers internationally. A bibliography lists more than 2,500 research reports generated from these major longitudinal surveys (Fahy, 1995).

Usually, however, survey efforts are much more modest in scope. Individual researchers, lacking the massive resources required to mount the type of effort required for the NLS, may select a local sample of a few hundred individuals to address a variety of questions, such as the health consequences of providing care to an older spouse. It is this type of survey research that predominates in the literature on aging. Although more limiting in terms of the conclusions one can draw (Is a sample from Pennsylvania also representative of people living in the Southwest?), smaller-scale studies have constituted the bulk of survey research.

Comparative Studies

Comparative studies examine the similarities and differences of a social phenomenon (in our case, aging) in different cultures or societies. In some instances, the comparison is an explicit one; in others, a description of one culture's ways of handling the process of aging and their older population is written by and for members of another culture, allowing them to draw their own comparative conclusions. It is entirely possible to have comparative work within a country, for example a comparison of the status of Amish or Hispanic American elders with that of middle-class American seniors of European descent.

A classic example is Palmore's comparative study of aging in Japan and the United States. Palmore (1975) compared two highly industrialized and technically advanced cultures that differed substantially on the older person's integration into and status in society. Palmore identifies the roots of this difference in two areas. First, the *vertical focus of relationships* in Japan means that most interactions are not among equals but among those with more or less status, including age-conferred status; older Japanese adults would be interacting more often from a position of age-based status, giving them an advantage not found in the United States. Second, *piety toward older kin*, an outgrowth of the worship of ancestors in Japanese culture, means that older people receive favorable treatment and a place of honor within the family. Unconditional duty of children toward their parents meant that more than three-fourths of Japanese over 65 were living with their children when Palmore did his research. This was a pattern of choice, not necessity. Older relatives contributed to the good of the household through work and advice, and many were in good health and able to support themselves financially. At the time Palmore was writing, more than half of Japanese men over 65 remained in the labor force, contradicting notions that modern industrialized economies necessarily discard older workers through retirement (Palmore, 1975). Despite an accepted retirement age in most large companies of around 55 years of age, many workers who were self-employed or worked in a family business could easily continue their employment to age 70 and beyond.

Exhibit 2.10   *Picking an Aproach: Critical Questions*

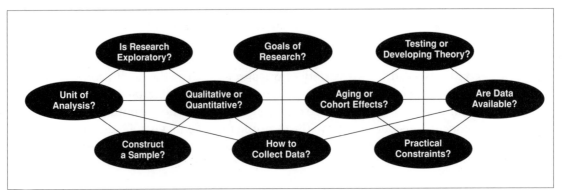

1. **How much do we already know about the topic to be studied?** The less that is known, the more exploratory the study, and the less we can rely on research precedents of others. In exploratory research we need to think more broadly about the question and its potential connections to theory and related social phenomena.

2. **What are the goals of the research?** Are we conducting research in order to inform policy or advocate a social issue or is the research purely oriented toward the development of knowledge? Applied research (where policy and/or intervention are goals) less often derives explicitly from and tests aspects of a theory (although it sometimes does so). It may also be more constrained in terms of time available, since policy formation sometimes cannot wait for lengthy research to be completed.

3. **Are we interested in testing or developing theory?** If a relevant theory is available that fits our topic, then we may wish to use the research not only to gain practical knowledge but also to test the tenets of the theory. In other areas, there may appear to be no theory that is relevant (although some might argue that we simply haven't looked hard enough). In that case, research may serve to generate theoretical propositions or a full-fledged theory. The connection to theory is relevant in most research, including much of applied research, with either theory building or theory testing as a central goal.

4. **What is the appropriate unit of analysis?** As with the previous question, a researcher can address a single issue on a variety of levels. Very different information is needed if we study the impact of caregiving on family relationships or the impact of family caregiving on the health care delivery system.

Throughout Palmore's book, explicit contrasts with trends and behaviors of the elderly in the United States paint a picture of the role that culture plays in shaping the lives of people as they age. It is sometimes only through such comparisons that our culturally based assumptions are illuminated and our understanding of aging in our own culture enhanced.

Historical Analyses

Researchers from many disciplines have benefited from historical analyses of aging. In a sense, **historical studies** are a different type of comparative analy-

5. **Are there compelling reasons to select a qualitative or quantitative approach to the topic under study?** For many questions either approach is useful. In some cases (such as a study of health care costs in various age groups), the meanings attached by those participating might be a less critical concern. In many other instances, however, research topics may be fruitfully addressed by qualitative studies, focusing on the meanings of social experiences to the participants. Clearly we can study the passage into retirement, for example, by examining the social and economic factors predictive of a choice to retire at a particular point in the life cycle, as quantitative analysts have done. It is also at least as valuable, however, to interview individuals moving through this process to understand how they think about it and define the importance of this rite of passage in their lives.

6. **Are we attempting to identify aging effects or cohort differences?** If we are seeking aging effects, we need to consider the use of longitudinal data and techniques such as event history analysis that focus on process and change. Simple cross-sectional comparisons of age groups will not enable us to identify aging effects adequately.

7. **Are data relevant to the topic already available, or do they need to be collected?** For some topics, the expense and time required to mount a longitudinal study is prohibitive. Secondary analysis of existing longitudinal studies can be a fruitful choice when those studies ask the right questions.

8. **Do we need to construct a sample?** Whether we need to use sampling depends in part on the source of data and the unit of analysis. If we are studying states or major labor unions, there may be few enough to collect information from the entire population. For many studies on the individual level, however, drawing a sample is the only practical solution.

9. **How best should data be collected?** Should we observe people in naturally occurring setting, perform experiments on them, interview them, or give them a problem-solving task? More than one possibility may provide useful information, and combining techniques is often beneficial.

10. **What practical constraints do we face in conducting research?** Both time and resources may significantly limit the scope of a research project. If the study must be completed within six months, for example, this time constraint would preclude certain types of data collection (such as a multi-year longitudinal study). Similarly, practical considerations may limit the size or location of a sample and the techniques used to collect information (for example, a telephone survey instead of in-person interviews).

---

sis, usually implicitly comparing the current situation with that of the same culture or society in the past. According to historian Peter Laslett, this type of comparison is necessary because the extreme rapidity of societal aging means that societies "have to be brought up against the facts of aging as they always used to be and compare them with the very different facts as they now are" (1995, p. 4). Historical analyses have focused on a variety of issues, including the sociopolitical context resulting in the establishment of Social Security (Quadagno, 1988), varied conceptualizations of aging and the life cycle in different historical periods (Cole, 1992), and a better understanding of the operations of daily family life in the early United States (Hareven, 1994, 1995). Using archival materials ranging from early censuses, cultural archives, and political records to newspapers, family Bibles, and personal diaries, historians often construct the past in a more realistic fashion than our cultural memories portray it.

Historical analysis reveals the past and helps us to understand the origin of social norms and social policies that shape the experiences of aging for individuals in the contemporary social world. One example would be the effects of industrialization on the lives of older persons. During the transition from a predominantly agricultural to an industrial economy in England, there was a brief period when the cottage industry flourished. Rather than having centralized places where manufacturing took place, individuals and families worked at home and returned the finished product for modest pay (Quadagno, 1982). An example of this pattern is the ribbon-weaving town of Chilvers Coton in England, where women and children worked at home at their looms while adult men worked in the mines or the nearby factory for higher wages. Older women continued to work at home weaving silk ribbon, as did surviving older men (Quadagno, 1982). When this home-based system became less profitable, the cottage industry disappeared and much of the population migrated out of the area. Especially hard hit among those who remained were older men and women, who were unable to find employment in the new industries that grew to replace ribbon weaving.

"Although cottage industry existed to a significant degree for only a brief moment in history, many of the stereotypes of the golden age of aging are based on a romanticized view of cottage industry and the wrenching effects of industrialization and urbanization upon it" (Quadagno, 1982, p. 61). In fact, this research suggests that in England the rise of industrialization initially increased the likelihood that older persons would share a household with their children in comparison to what was happening in rural areas. During this time older people were taken in if they could contribute to the family economy by working as a ribbon weaver; by caring for small children, enabling the mother to work in a factory; or by bringing some other source of income with them that would augment family resources (Quadagno, 1982).

Thus, historical analyses provide a deeper understanding of how the status of older people was changed by period effects such as the Industrial Revolution, and how the policies to address their needs have evolved. In an era of rapid social change, understanding the historical context through which current conditions were created is critical to preparing ourselves for future aging of the population.

Picking The Right Approach To Answer An Aging Research Question

A researcher with a question about aging has a complex task in constructing a strategy to derive an answer. One way to approach the task is to ask and answer a series of interrelated questions regarding both conceptual and practical concerns that shape the research process. Although we pose the questions in a particular order here, they are all connected, and the researcher may start from any number of locations, perhaps asking most or all of these questions before completing a research design.

Exhibit 2.10 includes the key questions and shows some, but not all, of the possible interconnections among them.

This not an exhaustive list of the questions that a researcher might consider in developing a research design, nor does Exhibit 2.10 outline all of the possible interactions among these issues. Going through these questions, however, does point out how connected many aspects of the research process are and how decisions in one area often direct the answers in others.

Summary

Researchers studying aging in a social context have a growing number of options. Not only can they draw from traditional techniques from several disciplines, but the field has added some specific methodologies, such as longitudinal and event history analyses, to the methodological arsenal. Increasingly, data are available on selected topics following multiple cohorts over twenty to twenty-five years, allowing us to disentangle some of the changing nature of cohorts as they age. The growing number of nationally representative studies, including lengthy panels on a wide range of topics, has increased researchers' abilities to address important issues without trying to collect their own data in an era of restricted research funding. The recent rise in popularity of qualitative techniques has enriched the information on many subjects in which statistical analyses, though useful, can cause the flavor and meaning of the results to be lost.

The quality of research on aging has improved substantially in recent decades, but numerous challenges remain (Cutler, 1995). Researchers continue to compete for financial support to perform research on aging, and the knowledge builds selectively as research funding for biomedical concerns outstrips that for the social sciences. The need for high-quality applied research on aging escalates as the population ages and we seek solutions to many related social issues. The main challenge for researchers is to clearly identify their research problem, its appropriate unit of analysis, the population from which a sample is to be drawn, the best way in which to collect information (surveys, observations, review of historical records), and specific techniques for analyzing that information in order to answer the original question. Only then can we be confident that our base of knowledge about aging in a social context is sound. Many studies on aging show failings in one or more of these steps, in part because of the "youth" of the field, and in part because of the practical constraints on research. It is the skill to match methodology to the problem that is the hallmark of important research to advance our knowledge of aging.

Web Wise

Fedstats Site

http://www.fedstats.gov

The Fedstats web site is intended to provide users with easy access to government statistics on a wide range of topics. The site organizes and provides access to information that is collected and made available on-line or through publications from numerous federal agencies. It is a "one stop shopping" site and allows you to search by topic for information that may be relevant to you across a range of governmental agencies.

AgeLine

http://research.aarp.org/ageline/home.html

AgeLine is a resource that has been around for a while and is very useful to researchers, including students with paper assignments. It is a searchable database of thousands of articles from journals and magazines on topics related to aging. AgeLine, supported by AARP, has a thesaurus of aging terms that can be used as keywords in a search on a particular topic. Helpful on line "how to" descriptions make this an easy way to identify and review the abstracts of materials you might find useful to your own research or project. It even includes a "How to" chapter on researching a term paper!

HRS/AHEAD Studies

http://www.umich.edu/~hrswww/

This site provides information on two of the largest research projects to collect information about the economic, social, and health status of older adults. The two studies, the Health and Retirement Study (HRS) and the Asset and Health Dynamics among the Oldest Old Study (AHEAD) are still collecting data. Information on design of these studies, their goals, funding, and initial publications are provided on this very active site. Anyone interested in seeing the "nuts and bolts" of large-scale data collection would do well to visit this site. Both are large, national, longitudinal studies funded by the National Institute on Aging, with a variety of rich data that will be useful to researchers and policy makers.

National Archive of Computerized Data on Aging (NACDA)

http://www.icpsr.umich.edu/NACDA/

The National Archive of Computerized Data on Aging, located at the University of Michigan's Inter-university Consortium for Political and Social Research (ICPSR), has been a substantial resource for researchers interested in secondary analysis of existing databases. NACDA archives and maintains a large number of datasets that can be retrieved by members of ICPSR for research purposes. The site lists research studies by topic, providing an abstract for each, and gives information on downloading information or datasets, if you are eligible. NACDA enables researchers to benefit from the data collection efforts of many of their colleagues to answer questions relevant to the field. This is not the "friendliest" site we found, but a perusal of the NACDA holdings section will give you a flavor of what this organization is all about and perhaps some ideas for your own research.

Key Terms

applied research	life course fallacy
birth cohorts	life history
cohort composition effect	longitudinal studies
cohort effects	macro approach
cohort sequential design	measures of central tendency
comparative studies	objectivity
control	period effects
control variable	qualitative analysis
cross-sectional studies	quantitative approaches
empiricism	quasi-experimental designs
event history analysis	sample
experimental design	scientific method
fallacy of cohort-centrism	secondary analysis
heterogeneous	social integration
historical studies	sociology of knowledge
human aging	survey
life chances	unit of analysis

Questions for Thought and Reflection

1. Researchers on aging continue to debate whether research on humans can be objective and whether social scientists should be activists. Pick a topic or question you think should be the focus of research and critically examine why you selected this topic. Do you have a personal or family interest? Could you really be objective about that question.

2. Conducting research is always complicated. Taking a question or topic that interests you, go through the ten questions posed in the final section of this chapter to consider how you might begin to shape a strategy to answer your question.

3. Examining your own life, identify some events or historical transitions that you think might influence your aging to make it different from that of your parents or grandparents.

4. Think about your life and the life of one of your grandparents. What are the commonalities that you expect to find in the childhood and adolescence of these two lives? What differences do you expect in those and later stages? What causes the differences between you and your grandparent?

CHAPTER 3

Aging People in an Aging World: Demographic Perspectives

"Demographic forces have not been stilled... They will continue to cause social change and to shape social programs for the balance of our lives and beyond" (McFalls, 1998, p.3)

Many people are concerned about he future of Social Security, and are discussing it in many different settings, from newsmagazine cover stories to debates on the floor of Congress to everyday conversations with family and friends. You are no doubt familiar with the issues; you may be worried about whether Social Security will be there for your generation and about how much you will have to pay in taxes to keep it going. The "crisis" in Social Security, which will be discussed in greater detail in Chapter 8, is defined by and will be resolved as a matter of public policy and public sentiment. The battle lines are drawn by political processes and societal values. However, another influence is at work in framing the Social Security debate: the demography of our aging society. The number of beneficiaries receiving Social Security and the number of workers contributing to the system have a direct impact on the amount of money workers will have to pay in taxes to keep Social Security viable. The size of the older population ahead of you in line for Social Security helps to determine how much you will have to pay in taxes during your prime working years. The "crisis" of Social Security is founded in and driven by demography. As we shall see, politics and economics have as much to do with the debate as demography, but the numbers are the starting point.

The demographics of an aging society and an aging world are a very important part of the social context of aging. As you will see, many aspects of culture and social life, including those that help shape the experiences of aging, are affected by the size, structure, and composition of a society's population. So, as we begin this discussion of the demography of aging, put aside any preconceived ideas you may have about demography as thinly disguised math, "dry social accounting" (McFalls 1998), and ultimately irrelevant to you. As you see in the case of Social Security, demography is shaping public policy and your future. Even the number and kinds of jobs available to you when you enter (or re-enter) the job market will be determined in part by demography, especially the size of the generations just ahead of you.

The Aging Of Societies

Not only does demography deal with trends and information that are personally relevant to you, demographic forces have a great impact on society as a whole. One of the most important worldwide trends is **societal aging**. Societal aging refers to the social and demographic processes that result in the aging of a population—the transition to an age structure with increasing numbers and proportions of older people and decreasing proportions at the youngest ages. The specific forces involved in, and measures of, societal aging are discussed later in this chapter. For now, our focus is on the general impact of population aging on a society.

The size and composition of the older population influences the most basic features of social life, from television commercials to ethical debates about end-of-life medical treatment. Families, the health care system, education, government, media, and the economy are all affected by the "age" of a population. Two brief examples will help to illustrate this point.

First, consider the number of advertisements and commercials that deal in some way with age and aging. Some of these ads present negative messages about aging and try to sell products that slow down or alter the visible signs of aging. Others use a positive message, such as the Nike Air ad featuring Nolan Ryan; this ad talks about "94-year-old swimmers, 89-year-old weightlifters. . . . People who forgot to retire . . . and never got old." Analyzing the effectiveness and purposes of negative versus positive age-based advertising is interesting. But for our purposes the main point of these ads is their mere existence. Advertisements featuring aging in some way, the appearance of middle-aged and older characters on television, and the design of new products for midlife people are all recent developments, and they are related to the increasing average age of our population. As a large proportion of our population (the baby boom generation) enters midlife, marketers and advertisers are responding to this shift by including a new range of images, messages, and products. The "relaxed fit" jeans are clearly targeted to the middle-aged baby boomers. As a result of the aging of the U.S. population, "in one way or another, every social institution in American society has had to accommodate to older people's needs, court their favor, or mobilize their resources and contributions" (Treas, 1995, p. 2).

For another example of the impact of population aging on social life, think about the differences between India and the United States. India is a relatively "young" society: only 5 percent of its population is age 65 or over, and average life expectancy is about 60. The United States is considered to be an "aging" society, with nearly 13 percent of its population in the 65+ category and an average life expectancy of about 76. As we will see in our discussion of population pyramids, "young" societies have high birthrates (fertility) and high death rates (mortality), whereas "aging" societies have low fertility and low mortality. Many aspects of social life , including the availability of health care, the level of economic development, and the status of women, are related to these birth and death patterns that produce population aging. For example, health care in India is focused almost exclusively on maternal and child health, family planning, and immunization. The United States spends its health care dollars very differently; Medicare, government-sponsored health insurance for older people, is the largest and most expensive publicly funded program in the country (Lassey et al., 1997). The availability of public education, access to safe water and sufficient food, and the demands that compete for limited government resources are very different in the two countries. In the United States, we take clean water for granted (though there is increasing evidence that perhaps we shouldn't); education through age 18 is guaranteed as a basic right of all citizens; virtually all people over the age of 65 receive government-sponsored health care; and nearly 90 percent of the older population is eligible for a public pension (Social Security). In India, all of the major causes of death in children are directly linked to the lack of clean water and food; two-thirds of older men and more than 90 percent of older women are illiterate; there is no national policy of health care for older people, and virtually no public pension system. Although the different "age" of the two populations does not fully explain these basic and profound differences, the age of a population is a contributing factor. One Indian scholar summarizes the significance of population aging this way: "The aging of society reflects the triumph of civilization over illness, poverty, and misery, and the decline in human fertility" (Goyal, 1989, p. 10).

In this chapter, we will present the aging of societies as an important process that affects our everyday lives, even though it may seem, at a macro level, distant from us. We will discuss how societies age, how we can tell they are "aging," and why it matters. We will also present an overview of the demographic characteristics of the older population in the United States, focusing on some of the uses of such information for policy and planning.

How Do Populations Age?

The simple answer is that populations grow older when fertility and mortality are low. We will see this pattern in comparing the population pyramids of aging and young societies. Population aging occurs when large numbers of people survive into old age and relatively few children are born. Life expectancies are high, and the proportion of the population age 65 and above is high. But how does mortality decline? How does a whole society of people decide to have fewer children? An important framework for understanding these changes is the demographic transition theory.

■ ■ ■ ■ ■ ■ ■ ■
APPLYING THEORY
Demographic Transition Theory

The demographic transition is a pattern of interrelated social, economic, and demographic changes that result in rapid population growth and aging. The prototypical transition pattern occurred throughout Western Europe in the nineteenth and early twentieth centuries. The first aspect of the transition is related to mortality (the rate of death in a society). During the transition, the

Societies with aging populations face different concerns than those with a higher proportion of children.

economies of these countries went through enormous shifts, changing from an agricultural base to an industrial mode of production. At the same time, these countries experienced mortality decline as a by-product of economic development. They gained control over infectious diseases, improved the availability of clean water, and saw the emergence of more advanced medical technology. This shift from high and somewhat variable mortality (variable because of epidemics) to lower mortality is shown in Exhibit 3.1. As you can also see in Exhibit 3.1, fertility remained high longer than did mortality, but then began to decline. In this transition phase, the lag between mortality decline and fertility decline set the stage for rapid population growth; mortality was not "removing" nearly as many people from the population as before, and continued high fertility was adding lots of new people. Finally, with sustained low mortality and low fertility, population aging occurs. Exhibit 3.1 shows the curves for population growth and for growth in the aged population that result from the demographic transition.

Thus far we have been discussing the demographic transition as a pattern of change in mortality and fertility that accompanied industrialization. Yet we have referred to the demographic transition *theory*. As you know, a theory goes beyond description to search for explanations and ultimately to make predictions. *Why* did mortality and fertility decline accompany economic development in Western Europe? Is the pattern of decline consistent? What will happen in nations that are just beginning to enter the transition phase? Data on the consistency of the prototypical pattern suggest that

Exhibit 3.1   *A Simplified Diagram of the Demographic Transition*

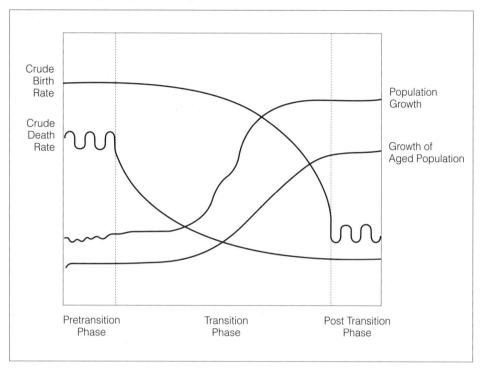

Adapted from: Yaukey, 1985 and Myers, 1990.

even in Western Europe there were variations in the timing of fertility and mortality declines. More important, causal connections between the demographic trends and industrialization are not well established. In Western Europe, the stages of the demographic transition are related to, "and in part caused by, industrialization, urbanization, and the spread of literacy and education" (Matras ,1990, p. 27). An industrial economy created, for the first time, an economic surplus; all members of a society could be supported by a smaller number of workers. For this reason, it was not necessary for families to have large numbers of children. It may seem unusual to imagine that people decide how many children to have based on such a rational calculation. However, there is an extensive literature in demography about the many factors, including the "cost and benefits" of having children, that go into such a personal and emotional decision.

We can understand more about the strengths and weaknesses of the demographic transition theory when we consider how well the pattern and predictions are holding for the developing regions of the world that are still "young." The declining mortality rates in these countries are characteristic of the beginning of the second stage of the demographic transition. Whether, when, and how quickly declining birthrates will follow mortality declines is questionable. Matras (1990) points out that Mexico, Nicaragua, and Jordan have all experienced dramatic mortality declines, but show little evidence of downward trends in birthrates. Such a decline is necessary for these and other developing nations to move into the third (post-transition) stage, characterized by an older population, a low rate of population growth, a stable low mortality, and a fluctuating but low fertility. When and how any given country reaches the post-transition stage depends on an array of cultural, ideological, and social factors that are not thoroughly understood. In developing nations there is some evidence to suggest that mortality is having a greater impact on population aging than it did in developed nations. This departure from the classic model (Coale, 1959), in which fertility has the primary impact on population aging, points to the caution we must exercise in applying existing models of change to developing nations. Furthermore, in the United States, Western Europe, and Japan, population aging proceeded along with economic development. In developing nations, partly because of the importing of technology to control fertility and mortality, population aging can occur ahead of economic development. These forces will very likely have an impact on the timing and nature of population aging in the developing regions of the world.

■ ■ ■

In agricultural economies there were typically few older adults and they usually worked to support themselves.

Exhibit 3.2   *Population Pyramid Summary for United States, 2000*

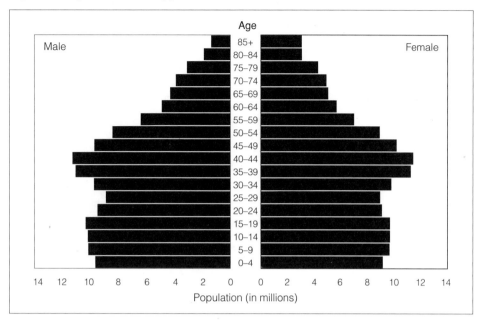

Source: U.S. Census Bureau, International Data Base web site.

Measures of Population Aging

How can we tell if a population is aging? What distinguishes a "young" population from an "aging" population? The five commonly used measures of population aging are *population pyramids, proportion aged, mean and median ages, dependency ratios,* and *life expectancy.* Each of these measures tells part of the story of a society's "age."

Population Pyramids

A **population pyramid** is a graphic illustration of the age and sex structure of a population. It shows the relative proportion of a population that is a given age and sex. These proportions are sometimes shown as a percentage of the total population, and sometimes as the actual number of people in that age/sex category. Population pyramids truly are pictures worth a thousand words. They capture and illustrate at a glance many past, present, and future demographic trends. Only three things directly determine the shape of a pyramid: fertility, mortality, and migration. The numbers of people being born, dying, and moving into or out of a location will affect the relative size of all of the age and sex groupings for that location. You can see the impact of fertility, mortality, and migration in shaping a population structure in the examples of population pyramids discussed throughout this section.

Exhibit 3.3   *Population Pyramid Summary for United Arab Emirates, 2000*

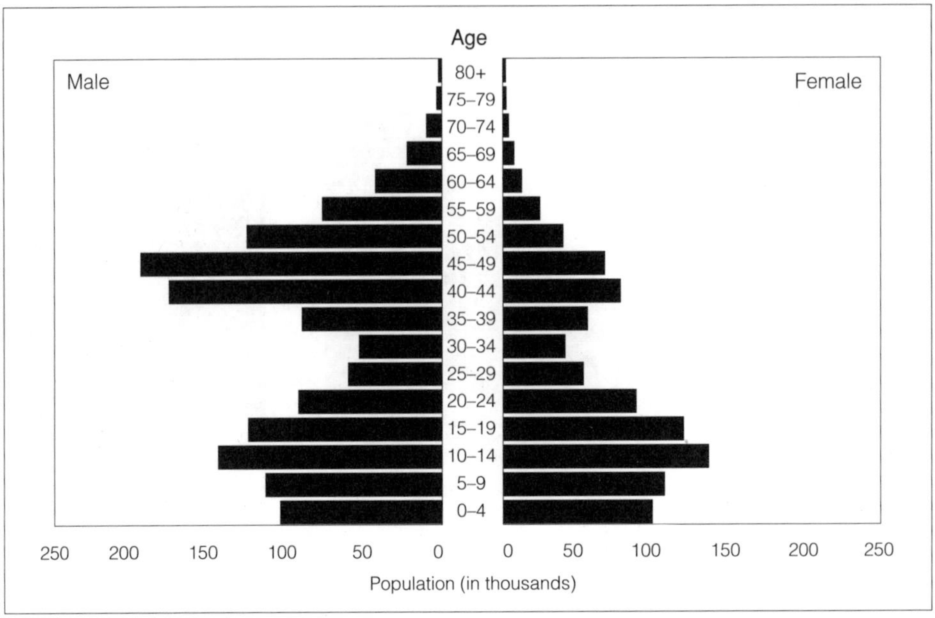

Source: U.S. Census Bureau, International Data Base web site.

Exhibit 3.2 shows the population pyramid for the United States in 2000. The "bulge" of people in the 35- to 49-year-old range is the infamous and fateful "baby boom," the large number of children born after World War II, between 1946 and 1964. Thus we see the powerful impact of a past fertility trend reflected in the shape of our pyramid today. We can also see the slightly lopsided top of the pyramid, which shows the greater number of older women than men. This imbalance is a manifestation of past and current trends in mortality: Women live longer than men do. (We will discuss this phenomenon in greater detail later in this chapter.)

Based on the age/sex structure illustrated in the 2000 pyramid, we can make some predictions about the shape of our population pyramid in the future. The most significant feature of that shape will be the movement upward of the baby boom generation. Demographers sometimes refer to this as the "pig-in-the-python," conjuring up the earthy image of watching a whole pig move slowly through the digestive tract of a large snake. So, too, the baby boom bulge moves through the population pyramid of the United States. The midlife baby boomers of today are the older generations of tomorrow; and young adults today are the middle-aged of the near future!

The population pyramid for the United Arab Emirates (Exhibit 3.3) has a very unusual shape. Working-age men far outnumber women of the same age. Why would this be so? We know that there are only three possible influences on the shape of a pyramid: fertility, mortality, and migration. In this case, the

Exhibit 3.4   *Population Pyramids of Different Shapes*

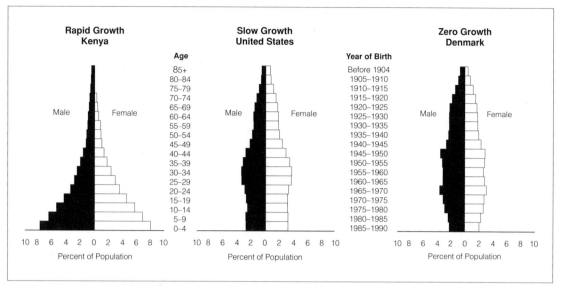

Source: McFalls, 1991.

imbalance in the numbers of working-age men and women is due to the immigration of thousands of people from Asia and other parts of the Middle East to work in the oil fields. These workers are nearly always men who migrate into the UAE without their families (McFalls, 1998; U.S. Bureau of the Census, 2000).

For most countries, migration does not currently play such a big role in the age and sex structure; fertility and mortality are by far the more powerful influences. However, for smaller geographic units, such as states and counties within the United States, migration can be an important factor. Think about what the population pyramid would look like for a small county that builds a 500-unit, state-of-the-art, low-cost retirement community that can accommodate 1,000 older people. This desirable location would attract people from all around the area, including neighboring counties; the relative size of the older population for the "receiving" county would be affected immediately and significantly. If the receiving county had a small, rural population, a large number of new, older residents could create a T-shaped population pyramid.

The shape of a population pyramid thus tells us something about the past, present, and future of a society—not only the fertility, mortality, and migration trends, but also something about life in that society. Population pyramids often take on one of three basic shapes; each stylized shape distinguishes, in a general way, demographic patterns and other aspects of social life, such as a stage in the demographic transition and level of economic development. Exhibit 3.4 shows the three basic shapes. The "true" pyramid, or fast-growth shape, is characteristic of young countries with high fertility and high mortality, such

Exhibit 3.5a   *Population Pyramid for Sub-Saharan Africa: 1990*

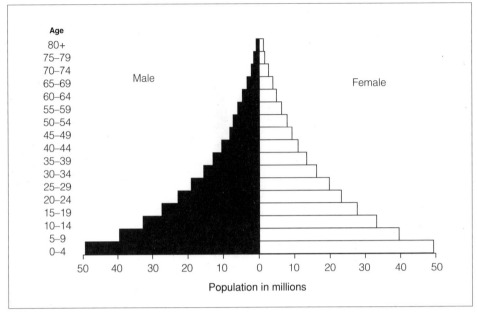

Source: Lutz, 1994.

Exhibit 3.5b   *Population Pyramid for Western Europe: 1990*

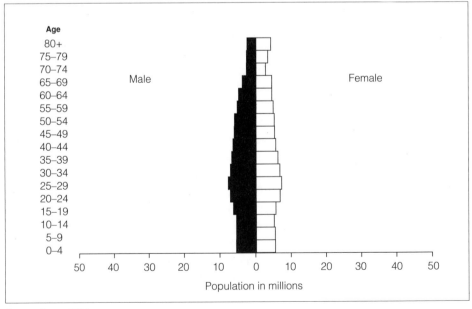

Source: Lutz, 1994.

as Kenya. The slow-growth, beehive-shaped pyramid reflects low mortality and fertility, as in the United States. The rectangular, or no-growth, pyramid shows the effects of sustained very low fertility and very low mortality, as in Denmark. In Exhibit 3.5 we see more dramatic illustrations of the "true" and rectangular pyramids. Some demographers have suggested a fourth pattern: the collapsing or inverted pyramid, which is narrowest at the base. The bottom half of the pyramid for Denmark (in Exhibit 3.4) has this shape and it is possible that Denmark will eventually have an inverted pyramid, if current levels of extremely low fertility are maintained.

Students are often curious about which pyramid is most "desirable" for a society. That question has no simple answer; each of these pyramid shapes represents a different set of challenges. For example, a pyramid with a wide base and narrow apex describes a society with lots of children, large families, and high rates of mortality; in such a society, the major focus of public policy and of the health care system will probably be on maternal and child health, and on family planning. In a society with a rectangular pyramid, it is fairly certain that some public policy and tax resources will be devoted to caring for older people. So, there is no "best" shape for a population pyramid; our views on which kind of challenge we find most acceptable is determined by economic development, and by political, cultural, and social values.

Population pyramids are elegant, informative, intuitively useful representations of the age and sex structure of a society. They give information about how old or young a society is and provide an indication of the level of economic development, the state of advancement in medical technology, and the nature of the resource allocation dilemmas faced by a society.

Proportion Aged

A very straightforward measure of population aging is to consider the proportion of a society that is older. Older than what? you might ask. Good question, we would say. Most reports of *proportion aged* use 65 as the marker, but some, especially those comparing countries around the world, use 60, so it is wise to be careful about the precise definition of "proportion aged." Exhibit 3.6 shows the proportion of population that is age 65 and over for a broad selection of countries. These proportions range from a low of 2 percent to a high of 17 percent (United Nations, 1994). The average proportion of the population 65 and over for the more developed world is 13 percent; for less developed nations, it is 5 percent.

The proportion aged is most often used in conjunction with other demographic information about a society to round out the picture of aging in that society, and to make comparisons among nations or across historical time periods. Proportions aged are less complicated and also less informative than population pyramids. Trends in the proportion aged in a society can provide us with an important indicator of population aging.

Exhibit 3.6   *Measures of Population Age for Selected Countries: 1994*

	Percent 65+ *	Mean Age **	Median Age **	Life Expectancy at Birth*
Kuwait	2	23.8	21.2	75
Kenya	3	19.6	14.2	56
Nepal	3	23.5	18.8	54
Brazil	5	26.2	22.7	66
India	5	25.9	21.8	60
China	7	29.3	25.8	68
New Zealand	11	34.0	31.1	76
United States	13	35.3	33.1	76
Japan	14	37.3	37.2	79
Denmark	15	38.6	37.2	75
Sweden	17	40.1	39.3	78

*Data Source: World Population 1994, U.N. Department of Economics and Social Information and
          Policy Analysis.
**Data Source: Keyfitz and Flieger, 1990.

Mean and Median Ages

Like the proportion aged, mean and median ages are single numbers that are often used in conjunction with other measures of population aging. You are no doubt familiar with the differences between a mean and a median: the **mean** is the arithmetic average of a range of numbers; as such, it is very sensitive to, and affected by, extreme values. The **median** is the midpoint of a range of numbers, the point at which half the cases fall above and half below. The second and third columns of Exhibit 3.6 show quite a range of mean and median ages. Sweden, by many measures the "oldest" country in the world, has an average age of 40; the median age is very close (39). Kenya, one of the "youngest" countries in the world, has an amazingly low median age of 14; half of the people in Kenya are under the age of 14! The mean age for Kenya is nearly 20; the difference between mean and median age is greater than for any other country in the table. Curiosity about these patterns would lead us to investigate the recent history, fertility patterns, political turmoil, natural disasters, and food shortages that might have befallen a country with an unusual demographic pattern.

Dependency Ratios

Dependency ratios are, as the term suggests, measures of the proportion of a population that falls within age categories traditionally thought to be economically dependent: those under age 15 (the youth dependency ratio) and over age 64 (the aged dependency ratio). We can take issue with the definition of any-

Exhibit 3.7   *Dependency Ratios for Selected Countries: 1994*

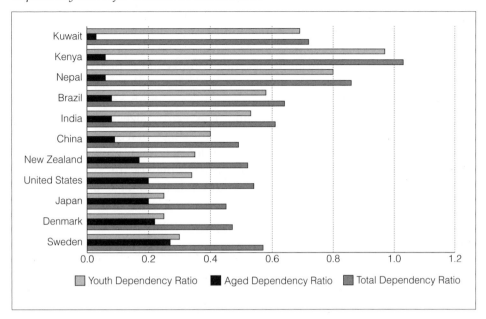

Source: Data calculated from information in World Population 1994, U.N. Department of Economics and Social Information and Policy Analysis.

one under 15 or over 64 as automatically being economically dependent, especially in countries where people work long before age 15 and sometimes long after age 65. In fact, a recent discussion of dependency ratios in the United States uses age 18 instead of age 15 (Treas, 1995). Despite this limitation, however, dependency ratios are useful as general comparative indicators of the relative proportions of working-age versus non-working-age people. As such, they point to different patterns across states or nations of demand on economic and social resources, such as health care, tax dollars, and the educational system.

The aged dependency ratio is similar to proportion aged, but is calculated in a slightly different way and interpreted in a very different way. The proportion aged in a society is simply the number of older people divided by the total population. The aged dependency ratio is the number of older people divided by the number of people ages 15 to 64. It is interpreted as the number of older people for every working-age person (sometimes stated as the number of older people per 100 working-age people).

Exhibit 3.7 shows the youth, aged and total dependency ratios for the same selection of countries as Exhibit 3.6. Of these, the country with the highest total dependency ratio in the list is Kenya, which has 103 non-working-age citizens for every 100 working-age citizens. Countries such as the United States, Japan, and Sweden have roughly two working-age people for every non-working-age person. If you look at the two components (aged and youth) of the total dependency ratio for countries with very high total dependency ratios and those with relatively low ones, you see that most often the youth dependency ratio contributes disproportionately to a high overall ratio. This pattern would be predicted by the demographic transition theory. As you will recall, high fertility and high mortality are typical of a country in the pre-transition or early transition phase. Lots of children are being born, and lots of people are dying, producing a low proportion of older people and a high proportion of children relative to the working-age population. The relative sizes of the youth and aged dependency ratios are also reflected in the shape of a country's population pyramid.

One final point about dependency ratios is important for us to keep in mind. Although the numbers and patterns may be (to some of us) interesting in and of themselves, they are most often used to make an argument, defend a position, or change a public policy. In the United States, the increasing proportion of older persons and the accompanying increase in the aged dependency ratio has "prompted concern and even alarm about society's capacity to pay for pensions, to finance health care, and to provide the personal assistance that disabled older adults need in their daily lives" (Treas, 1995, p. 6). Although it is certainly reasonable to debate the nation's ability, obligation, and strategies to provide these important programs and services, these issues have been used to fuel a political agenda built on the rhetoric of burden. Using "voodoo demographics" (Schulz 1986), proponents of the burden perspective present data such as the aged dependency ratio to conclude that the number of workers will be insufficient to support age-based entitlement programs for the huge baby boom generation lurking just around the bend. They argue that the economic burden of an aging population will become unfair and unbearable in the near future. Their proposed solution is to cut programs and alter eligibility criteria for those programs. Although we may decide to take such action, the demographics of our aging society are not the driving force behind either the problem or the solution. Interestingly, while the aged dependency ratio in the United States is increasing steadily, the youth dependency ratio has been declining, so that our current total dependency ratio is lower than it was in the 1960s and 1970s (Treas, 1995). Our ability to meet the needs of our aging population depends not simply on numbers of old people in relation to working-age people, but on the economic health of our nation and on conscious decision making on the part of politicians and voters.

Life Expectancy

The final measure of population aging we will discuss is life expectancy. **Life expectancy** refers to the average length of time the members of a population can expect to live. It is not the same as **life span**, which refers to a theoretical biological maximum length of life that could be achieved under ideal conditions. We have calculations of the life span of species that can be raised in those optimal conditions, but for humans it is not ethically viable or possible to control the environment. For humans, we gauge the maximum possible life span by using the most recent reliable data on how long a single individual has actually lived. Currently, the life span for humans is estimated to be about 120 years, based on the experience of a French woman who died in 1997 at the age of 122 (Los Angeles Times, 1997; Russell and McWhirter, 1987).

Life expectancy, then, is the *average* experience of a population. It is calculated from actual mortality data from a single year and looks at what would happen to a hypothetical group of people if they moved through their lives experiencing the mortality rates observed for the country as a whole during the year in question. The last column in Exhibit 3.6 shows the different life expectancies for the sample of countries we have been discussing. As you probably expected, countries with the lowest percentages of aged persons, lowest median and mean ages, and age/sex structures most resembling pyramids are also those countries with the lowest life expectancies. These measures of societal aging are correlated.

For a better understanding of life expectancy, Exhibit 3.8 gives a great deal more detail about average length of life in the United States; it shows the average number of years of life remaining for people of different age, sex, and race categories in the United States in 1990. To use the table, look at the left-hand column to find a target age, then read across to the race and gender category that is of interest to you. Find the number of years in the appropriate cell of the table, and add those years to the age in the left-hand column to obtain the life expectancy for someone of that age, gender, and race. For example, the life expectancy for a 40-year-old black female in 1990 was 76.8 (40 plus 36.8).

As you spend some time calculating life expectancies from this table, you will notice some interesting sources of variation. Average length of life varies depending on age, race, and sex. Life expectancy at birth (all races, both sexes) in 1990 was 75.4; but life expectancy at age 75 is an additional 11 years (to about 86). For every year of life a person survives, his/her life expectancy goes up. So, the longer you live, the longer you can expect to live , and you can quote us on that!

The race differential in life expectancy is evident in Exhibit 3.8. African American men of all ages have the lowest life expectancies. African American women have life expectancies lower than European American women do but higher than European American men do. Notice, however, that the differences between African Americans and European Americans (within gender categories) become smaller and smaller as age goes up. The difference in life expectancy at birth for African American and European American baby boys is 8.2 years. African American males who make it to age 85, though, have life expectancies almost equal to those of European American males (5.0 and 5.2 years, respectively), and African American females at age 85 have life expectancies almost equivalent to those of European American females of the same age. This decrease and of the African American/European American difference in life expectancy is called **convergence**; the eventual reversal (at the oldest ages) of the difference is called the *crossover effect*.

Exhibit 3.8   *Abridged Life Expectancy Table by Race and Sex: U.S., 1990*

Age	All Races, Both Sexes	European American Males	European American Females	African American Males	African American Females
0	75.4	72.7	79.4	64.5	73.6
5	71.2	68.5	75.0	61.0	70.0
10	66.3	63.5	70.1	56.1	65.1
15	61.3	58.6	65.2	51.3	60.2
20	56.6	54.0	60.3	46.7	55.3
25	51.9	49.3	55.4	42.4	50.6
30	47.2	44.7	50.6	38.2	45.9
35	42.6	40.1	45.8	34.1	41.3
40	38.0	35.6	41.0	30.1	36.8
45	33.4	31.1	36.2	26.2	32.4
50	29.0	26.7	31.6	22.5	28.2
55	24.8	22.5	27.2	19.0	24.2
60	20.8	18.7	23.0	15.9	20.5
65	17.2	15.2	19.1	13.2	17.2
70	13.9	12.1	15.4	10.7	14.1
75	10.9	9.4	12.0	8.6	11.2
80	8.3	7.1	9.0	6.7	8.6
85+	6.1	5.2	6.4	5.0	6.3

Source: Vital and Health Statistics

These observations suggest two questions: Why is there a race differential in life expectancy at all, and why does it diminish and even reverse itself at the oldest ages? In answer to the first question, most of the race differential in mortality is explained by differences in socioeconomic status (Rogers, 1992; Queen et al., 1994). African Americans in the United States have historically been economically disadvantaged and continue to have unequal access to educational, occupational, and economic opportunity; the numerous health disadvantages that accompany this lack of access show up in higher mortality. We will discuss these racial differences in health status, prevalence of diseases, and causes of death in greater detail in Chapter 10.

The second question, regarding the convergence in the race differential in life expectancy, has received some attention, but no definitive answer. One suggested explanation is that the data are unreliable. Among the current generation of older African Americans, the lack of "official" date-of-birth information may be responsible for some misreporting of age (Preston, Elo, and Rosenvaike,

1996). Another hypothesis for the convergence effect is that because African Americans who make it to the oldest ages do so in spite of many disadvantages and long odds, they may be "survivors;" that is, they may have some complex set of physiological and social psychological survival advantages.

A final variation in life expectancy that is readily apparent in Exhibit 3.8 is the gender difference. At every age, for both races, females have higher life expectancies than do males. How can we explain this "excess male mortality"? You probably have some ideas on the subject; whenever we present this question in classes, in speeches, or in casual conversation, we never wait long for responses. Many are thoughtful and scientific; some are creative. A colleague offered the hypothesis that the stuff that men cough up and spit out has life-sustaining properties; because women in most cultures don't spit, they live longer (McGrew, 1989).

More plausible and thoroughly researched explanations for the sex differential fall into two major categories: biological explanations and social/behavioral explanations. Biological explanations are based on the premise that females have a physiological advantage that results in greater longevity, whereas sociobehavioral explanations focus on lifestyle choices, socialization, risk taking, stress, and occupational hazards. There is evidence supporting both kinds of explanations.

One example of empirical support for the biological basis for the sex differential in mortality comes from the sex ratio. About 120 males are conceived for every 100 females conceived, but by the time of birth that ratio is down to about 105 males for every 100 females. Assuming that social and behavioral factors do not play a role in utero, we conclude that male fetuses are less viable than female fetuses. Another bit of evidence for the physiological basis is heart disease: Prior to menopause, women have significantly lower rates of heart disease than men do, but after menopause women's rates increase to approximate those of men. Apparently estrogen (which is high during the childbearing years but low after menopause) provides some protection against at least this one major cause of death.

The "superior biological viability" argument does not tell the whole story, though. Waldron (1993) found that as much as risk-taking and other unhealthy behaviors such as smoking could explain as much as 50 percent of the sex differential in mortality. Men in U.S. culture are socialized to drive fast, drink alcohol, and smoke; they are also less likely to see a physician on a regular basis, and less likely to use social support networks to deal with stress. All of these factors help to explain men's shorter life expectancies.

No doubt the life expectancy difference between men and women is explained by some combination of biological, social, and behavioral influences. Sorting out the explanations is interesting in and of itself, but also has important implications for health promotion and enhancement. The longevity differential had been consistently widening from 1900 until 1972 in the United States, but has been narrowing since the late 1970s (National Center for Health Statistics, 1994), primarily as a result of slower gains in life expectancy for women. For many decades, everyone's life expectancy has been improving, but the rate of improvement does vary. AIDS is having a very significant effect on the rate of improvement in longevity, but life expectancies are still increasing slightly. The recent narrowing of the gender differential in mortality is partly explained by the fact that improvements in life expectancy for women have slowed due in part to increases in women's rates of smoking.

The same pattern of "excess male mortality" holds true for most other countries around the world, though the difference between men's and women's life expectancies is often not as great in the developing nations. For the United States in 1990, the difference in life expectancy at birth was seven years; in the European Community, females on average lived about six years longer; in less developed regions, the difference was less than three years (Keyfitz and Flieger, 1990). In very few countries, the difference is in the opposite direction. For example, in Nepal, life expectancy at birth is 51.5 for men and 50.3 for women; in India, life expectancy for men and women is nearly equal. The smaller or reversed gender difference in longevity in the developing nations is due primarily to maternal mortality: deaths among women during pregnancy and childbearing. We saw this same pattern in the United States in the late nineteenth century, when knowledge, services, and technology surrounding childbirth were less well developed and less available.

Thus far, we have seen that life expectancy varies by age, by race, by gender, and by your country and the social and economic development of your nation and your group. Many other factors help to determine how long any individual is likely to live. To get a sense of these other influences and how they can affect an average expectation of life, spend a few minutes taking the "life expectancy test" in Exhibit 3.9. After you have answered all of the questions, sum up your added and subtracted years of life. Take your total number, find yourself on the life expectancy table (Exhibit 3.8), and calculate how long you are likely to live. Obviously, this is not a scientific prediction of your life expectancy, but it should be interesting for you to consider how long your life might be, and how you feel about it. Does it seem too long or too short?

The life expectancy test shows the importance of heredity, lifestyle, social forces, and other social characteristics such as marital status. For many of these influences on longevity, their impact is intuitively obvious, but perhaps the relationship between marriage and life expectancy was a surprise to you. This relationship is quite well established; it has been observed consistently in our country and in other nations as well (Hu and Goldman, 1990). Married people live longer than unmarried people do. There are two major explanations for this phenomenon (Weeks, 1994). First is the "selectivity" hypothesis (that healthy people are more likely to get married). The second is that marriage is good for your health: Having a stable intimate relationship is conducive to good health, and the availability of caregiving support is an important health advantage. The highest death rates are for divorced males.

Exhibit 3.9   *The Abridged Life Expectancy Test*

Have any of your grandparents lived to age 80 or beyond? If so, add one year for each grandparent living beyond that age. Add one-half year for each grandparent surviving beyond the age of 70. _____

If any parent, grandparent, sister, or brother died of a heart attack, stroke, or arteriosclerosis before the age of 50, subtract four years for each incidence. If any of those close relatives died of the above before the age of 60, subtract two years for each incidence _____

Do you prefer vegetables, fruits, and simple foods to foods high in fat and sugar, and do you always stop eating before you feel really full? If your honest answer to both questions is yes, add one year. _____

How much do you smoke! If you smoke two or more packs of cigarettes a day, subtract twelve years. If you smoke less than a pack a day, subtract two years. If you have quit smoking, congratulations, you subtract no years at all! _____

How much do you exercise? If you exercise at least three times a week at one of the following: jogging, bike riding, swimming, taking long, brisk walks, dancing, or skating, add three years. Just exercising on weekends does not count. _____

If you enjoy regular sexual activity, having intimate sexual relations once or twice a week, add two years. _____

If you are married and living with your spouse, add one year. _____

If you are a separated or divorced man living alone, subtract nine years, and if you are a widowed man living alone, subtract seven years. If as a separated, divorced, or widowed man you live with other people, such as family members, subtract only half the years given above. Living with others is beneficial for formerly married men. _____

Women who are separated or divorced should subtract four years, and widowed women should subtract three and a half years. The loss of a spouse through divorce or death is not as life-shortening to a woman, and she lives about as long whether she lives alone or with family, unless she is the head of the household. Divorced or widowed women who live with family as the head of their household should subtract only two years for the formerly married status. _____

If you are a woman who has never married, subtract one year for each unmarried decade past the age of 25. If you live with a family or friends as a male single person, you should also subtract one year for each unmarried decade past the age of 25. However, if you are a man who has never married and are living alone, subtract two years for each unmarried decade past the age of 25. _____

Do you generally like people and have at least two dose friends in whom you can confide almost all the details of your life? If so, add one year. _____

The numerous influences on life expectancy are relevant to all of us as individuals. They are also part of the complex picture of how, why, and when a population "ages."

Global Aging

Why does the aging of a population matter to individuals or to societies as a whole? In many ways, this entire book is about the effects of population aging on social institutions such as work, the family, the economy, and the health care system. In Chapter 6 we will see that the naming of life stages is partly a result of how long people in a society live. For example, *adolescence* is a fairly recent idea; in earlier eras, when people married and had children in their early teens and only lived to their thirties, there was no "preparatory" stage of life.

Beyond the impact of societal aging on our lives as individuals and as members of a society, one of the most far-reaching consequences of population aging is that the entire world is aging. The world's elderly population is increasing by about 800,000 persons *per month*! (Kinsella and Taueber, 1993). The aging of a society is accompanied by, and is a catalyst for, enormous social change. Some of the greatest impacts of population aging are in the areas of health care and social policy. Developed nations such as the United States are still struggling to adapt health care and social service systems to the challenges presented by the aging of their populations. In developing nations, the aging of a population presents even greater challenges for two primary reasons. First, the infrastructure for planning and providing health care and social services is often not well developed. And, as we noted in the case of India, such services are most often aimed at family planning and maternal and child health; it is extremely rare to find a developing nation with a health care system that addresses the long-term care necessitated by the chronic conditions of later life. Second, the crucial policy debates that take place in the developed nations regarding the distribution of responsibility for care of the elderly among family, government, and individuals have not taken place in most of the less developed nations. In those countries, the number of people surviving to old age has been so small as to obviate the necessity for such discussion.

The issues arising from the aging of the world population, and the growing numbers of older people in developing nations, are receiving increasing attention, for good reason. In 1990, 57 percent of all older people (60+) lived in developing countries, and this proportion is expected to increase to 69 percent by the year 2020 (U.S. Bureau of the Census, 1991b). These figures seem surprising, given the relatively low proportion aged, life expectancy, and median age in these countries. But consider that, in 1994, about 80 percent of the world's total population lived in the developing nations. Take India as an example. Even though only 5 percent of India's population is aged 65 or above, with a population of almost a billion people, that 5 percent adds up to a lot of older people. Because so much of the world's population is concentrated in these regions, and because these regions are beginning to experience population aging, a very high proportion of the world's older people will be living in these areas.

In recognition of the many complex and momentous issues opportunities and challenges raised by the aging of the globe, the United Nations designated 1999 as the International Year of Older Persons. A sweeping, ambitious, and inspirational "International Plan of Action on Ageing" was created by representatives from countries around the world. This plan, and some accompanying principles to guide policy development, call for attention to demographic realities, to the humanitarian issues related to the situation of older people, to the problem of global inequality that will make it difficult for developing nations to meet the basic needs of their populations, and to our assumptions that old age is inevitably a time of decline, diminished capacity, and alteration of basic human needs. On a philo-

Many nations around the world face issues related to the aging of their populations.

sophical note, the World Assembly offered that "A longer life provides humans with an opportunity to examine their lives in retrospect, to correct some of their mistakes, to get closer to the truth, and to achieve a different understanding of the sense and value of actions. This may well be the most important contribution of older people to the human community" (United Nations, 1998). The demographic facts of global aging indeed have far-reaching consequences.

The trends in population aging have produced a range of responses. At one end of the spectrum is the alarmist call to action and deep concern over the lack of attention given to aging-related policy and planning issues. Driven by the rapidly increasing numbers and by the less than stellar example of the United States in planning for our aging population, this position suggests that time is growing short for making decisions about how to care for the older population. At the other end of the continuum are critics who dismiss the alarmist position as ethnocentric: Westerners are defining the problem and calling for a solution that mirrors their own. In some research conducted in Nepal, a number of senior health and planning officials said that aging was not a problem in Nepal, and that they were not ready to believe it will be a problem just because Americans said so (Kunkel and Subedi, 1997). They were convinced that older people would be well taken care of by their families and would impose no significant new burden on the health care system. Certainly the enormous pressures of maternal and child health in Nepal take precedence over a longer-range issue that may be adequately handled, at least for a time, by family caregiving.

What will happen to older people in the developing nations? An overview of modernization theory will help provide a context for the problems, solutions, and biases involved in the issue of global aging.

■ ■ ■ ■ ■ ■ ■ ■

APPLYING THEORY
Modernization Theory

As we saw in our earlier discussion of demographic transition theory, economic development and other sociocultural forces are very important in determining the timing, nature, and magnitude of the declines in fertility and mortality that cause a population to age. The importance of explicitly examining ideological and cultural change is borne out by modernization theory as well.

The basic premise of modernization theory is that the status of older people declines as a society modernizes. Changes such as urbanization, industrialization, the changing nature of work, health advances, and population growth combine to erode the position of honor, prestige, and respect accorded to older people in simpler societies. Thus, "with increasing modernization the status of older people declines" (Cowgill, 1974, p. 124). In nonmodernized societies, older people supposedly enjoy high status, and family members meet their physical and emotional needs; they require external assistance only when modernization disrupts the traditional (mostly agrarian) family's economic and social support measures. Based on modernization theory, we would expect that in most rural, agrarian developing countries the elderly enjoy high status and their long-term needs are readily met by families.

Modernization theory enjoys a great deal of intuitive appeal and some empirical support. However, it has also been challenged by some research studies and has been criticized for using unclear and inconsistent definitions of social status, oversimplifying the processes of modernization, and ignoring intervening variables such as ideology and value systems.

Perhaps the most significant assumption made by modernization theory is that the extended family in developing societies typically cares for its older members. According to Tout (1989), "in some instances, reliance on the traditional extended family may not be the normally acceptable panacea, but may for the old person be a gruesome and cruel experience of dependence, deprivation, and degradation" (p. 300). The situation of widows in India is one clear example of this less than idyllic circumstance of family care. In today's Indian society, most widows do not throw themselves on their husband's funeral pyre as tradition once mandated; instead, the widow is taken care of by her husband's family. However, she has very low status in the family, is often viewed as a burden, and is sometimes the victim of verbal and physical abuse.

In a review of family demography in developing nations, Martin and Kinsella (1994) provide further grounds on which to question the stereotypical model of multigenerational households providing care for elders. They found that intergenerational co-residence is declining in many developing countries, and that the likelihood of sharing a residence is inversely related to age of the elder. This latter fact suggests that multigenerational households are more likely to be based on the needs of sons and daughters than on the needs of older family members. If the needs of elders were the primary motivation, we would expect the prevalence of co-residence to increase with advancing age.

Some though not all, of the developing nations studied by Martin and Kinsella are still characterized by an extended family structure. Nepal is one example. Based on this criterion, we might expect the status of the elderly in Nepal to be high. However, research conducted by Goldstein and his associates (1983) in both rural and urban Nepal found that the equation of membership in an extended family with status, security, and satisfaction for the elderly person is misleading. They found that economic factors (unemployment, low wages, inflation) and social factors (less property as a result of the division of inheritance, migration of eldest sons to urban areas) had affected relationships within the family, often leaving the elderly at the mercy of younger family members. Findings from the study indicated that the status of and care for older people depended on the elders' ability to control property and income. These researchers conclude that, given the socioeconomic conditions of most developing societies and the inability of governments to provide substantial social service programs, there are likely to be increasing numbers of elderly parents with neither property, pensions, nor savings in their old age. This image—older people exchanging promises of economic reward for receipt of care in later years—forces Western scholars to rethink our idealized vision of life in developing nations.

■ ■ ■

Demographic Characteristics of Our Aging Population

The causes, consequences, and measurement of population aging are large-scale issues. Powerful forces, such as fertility and mortality, alarmist warnings about the consequences of global aging and assumption-laden measures of dependency ratios may seem far distant from your life. However, we hope that you have begun to see that population aging affects us as individuals and as families. It affects our government, public policy, health care system, and our economy. A description of our older population will help bring this picture into sharper focus.

In this section, you will find some illustrations of demographic description of the older population in the United States. The purpose of this section is not to provide extensive detail about every conceivable demographic characteristic, but to provide a general description of the older population, to give you

Exhibit 3.10   *Percentage Living in Nursing Homes by Age and Sex: U.S., 1990*

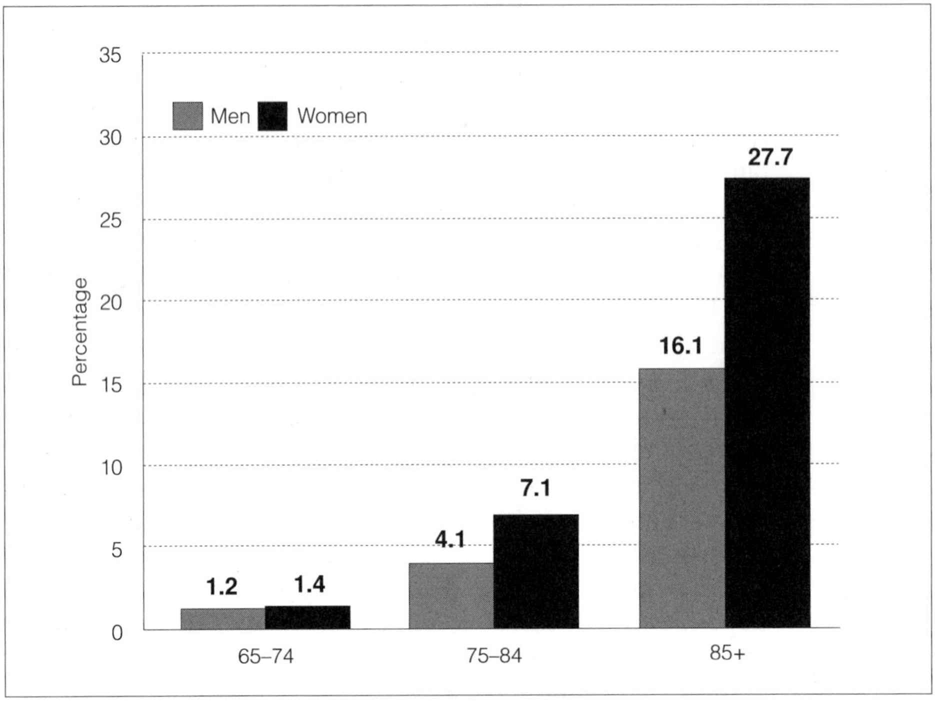

Source: Bureau of the Census Press Release CB93-117, June 28, 1993.

an idea of the kinds of information available, and to encourage you to think about how and why such information is useful. We will also direct your attention to the fact that most of these characteristics vary a great deal within the older population. Among the many population characteristics that we could describe are labor force participation, living arrangements, ethnic diversity, geographic distribution, education, and sex ratios. Some of the most important demographic characteristics, such as health, income, and marital status, will be discussed in greater detail in later chapters and will not be presented here. The major disadvantage of not including them here is that these characteristics provide some of the best illustrations of the great variation in the older population, a point that is important to keep in mind. The major advantage to leaving certain demographic characteristics until later in the book is that we don't want to press our luck in convincing you that demography provides a fascinating, lively, and useful perspective on the issues of aging. Therefore, we will focus on three demographic variables and their interpretations.

Information about the *living arrangements* of older people is important for community planners, housing designers, researchers interested in social support networks, and those of us curious about the validity of prevailing societal images. Contrary to a common stereotype, most older people do not live in nurs-

Exhibit 3.11 *Living arrangements of the population age 65 and older, by sex and race and Hispanic origin, 1998.*

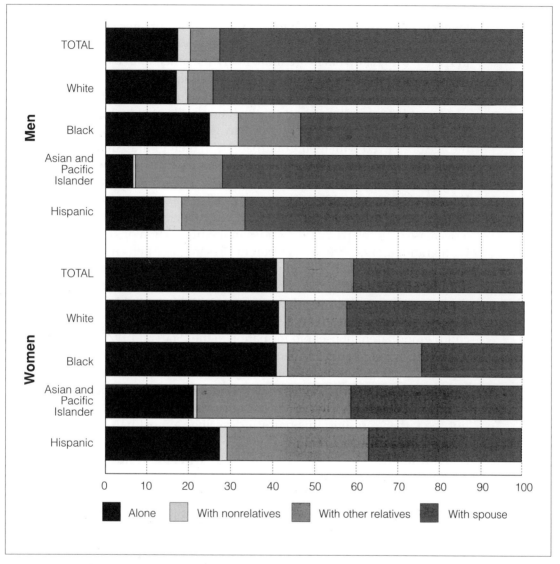

Note: Hispanics may be of any race.
Source: Federal Interagency Forum on Aging Statistics, 2000.

ing homes. As you can see from the graph in Exhibit 3.10, only a very small proportion lives in nursing homes: about 5 percent of all people 65 and over. This percentage does increase considerably by age; almost 25 percent of the 85+ population live in nursing homes, but it is still not anywhere near a majority.

As we see from the charts in Exhibit 3.11, living arrangements for non-institutionalized older people vary by age and sex. When we compare men and women in the same age category, we see that women are much more likely to live alone than men are; men are more likely to live with a spouse throughout their lives. This pattern reflects differences in marital status. Because women live longer than men, and tend to marry men who are about three years older, women are much more likely than men to become widowed in later life. You can also see in Exhibit 3.10 that women are more likely than men to live in nursing homes. That pattern is partly explained by the availability of spouse caregivers. This gender difference in marital status is discussed further in Chapter 7.

One of the interesting trends in the households of older people is the presence of grandchildren in their homes. In 1993, 5 percent of all children under the age of 18 lived with their grandparents in their grandparents' home, not in the parents' home with grandparents present. This pattern is more common than it was in 1970, when 3.2 percent of children lived with grandparents (U.S. Bureau of the Census, 1994). There is a growing literature on grandparents who "parent" their grandchildren (see Chapter 7). However, there has actually been a decrease over the past two decades in the proportion of kids who are living with grandparents with neither parent present (30.2 percent of the grandparent/grandchild households fitted this pattern in 1993, compared with 43.3 percent in 1970). This change is probably a manifestation of the very different social conditions that produce grandparent/grandchild households. Whereas absence of parents (through death or divorce) was a more likely impetus for the grandchild/grandparent household formation in the 1960s and 1970s, in recent years economic problems, employment difficulties, and drug and alcohol abuse have rendered more parents unable to care for their children. Thus, the likelihood that neither parent would be present has declined. In fact, the most common structure for a grandchild/grandparent household is to have the mother (but not the father) present; this pattern describes almost half of the grandparent/grandchild households.

How are the households in which older people reside distributed geographically? This question may appear to be of interest to a limited number of people, but the **geographic distribution** of the older population (across states, among cities and suburbs, across counties) actually has far-reaching consequences for a location's tax base, educational system, demand on health and social services, and voting patterns. The numbers of older people, the proportion they represent in a given location, and how they got there (by aging in place or by migration) are all related to the consequences of the distribution of the older population.

Many of the states that have large numbers of older people happen to be states with large populations. Ohio, Pennsylvania and New York are examples of states with large populations and large numbers of older people. The *proportion* of older people in a given location is affected more by the age structure of the state than the size of its population; these population pyramids, as you know, are shaped by fertility, mortality, and selective migration. California has a proportion aged that is lower than for the United States as a whole, partly because of the migration of younger people into the state. Florida has the highest proportion of older people in the nation (18.6 percent), partly because of immigration of older people. Although it is true that a large proportion of the older people who relocate do move to Florida, it is not true that most older people move to Florida. Less than 5 percent of the older people migrate across state lines; those who do are likely to end up in states such as Florida, Arizona, and Texas. These states, and other locations that receive large numbers of older people, have to factor in increased (and sometimes seasonal) demands for services and amenities.

A number of other interesting trends and issues relate to the distribution and redistribution of the older population. Longino, Jackson and Zimmerman (1991) have described a model for understanding the causes and consequences of multiple moves by older people, ranging from a move motivated by the attractiveness of a particular location to moves motivated by the need for long-term care. Like research on these multiple moves, investigations into seasonal migration are increasing in number. Because the presence of "snowbirds" in a given location has important consequences for the economy and service delivery system in those locations, such research has policy and planning implications.

In addition to where people live geographically and with whom they live, information about where they are "housed" is also important for policy, quality of life, and service design. Housing availability, accessibility, and quality are of major concern to all of us. For older people with fixed incomes and increased likelihood of health problems, appropriate and acceptable housing options are more challenging. Over 60% of older homeowners have lived in their current homes for 20 years or more, speaking to an emotional as well as financial investment. Deciding how and when to make a change, and finding desirable and feasible options, are complex and difficult processes. Even though three-quarters of older people own their own homes (a higher proportion than any other age group), "reduced income and frailty can place at risk their many years of financial, physical, and emotional investment in home and neighborhood" (U.S. Dept of Housing and Urban Development, 1999). Affordable, appropriate housing represents a public policy and planning challenge; it is also a matter of personal and family concern encompassing a vast array of issues such as independence, autonomy, security, and the meaning of home.

The **sex ratio** is a measure used by demographers to summarize the gender composition of a population. Traditionally, the sex ratio is presented as the number of men for every 100 women; calculated by dividing the number of men by the number of women, it has been called the "masculinity ratio" (Yaukey, 1985). In the United States, among people of all ages, the ratio of men to women is about 95 to 100. Among the older population, however, the sex ratio is very unbalanced, and it makes more sense to talk about a "femininity ratio": the number of older women for every 100 older men. For the population 65+, the ratio is 147 women for every 100 men; among those 85 and above, it is 256 women for every 100 men. These ratios capture the differential impact of mortality on men and women. The imbalance has implications for remarriage possibilities following widowhood, for the economic well-being of the oldest old, for living arrangements, and for service needs.

Centenarians are people aged 100 and over. They are an interesting part of the demographic picture of our older population. In 1980, there were only about 15,000 centenarians around; that number had almost doubled by 1990, and is projected to grow to around 834,000 by the year 2050 (Velkoff, 2000). These long-lived people have experienced incredible social change and major historical events. There is growing interest in studying centenarians for the many contributions they can make to our understanding of aging. Obviously we can learn from their perspectives on the social world. In addition, scientists speculate that the demographics of centenarians may provide clues to factors that influence longevity (Velkoff, 2000).

Summary

Interpreting and Using Demographic Data about the Older Population

In describing a few demographic characteristics of the older population, we have suggested some possible uses for demographic data. Such information is the foundation for a wide range of professional endeavors, including product design and development, community planning, market research, education about aging, and public policy development. You can use demographic information to support a position you are taking in a term paper or presentation. We all use such data to help us understand the realities of aging.

As we use such data about the older population, it is extremely important not to overgeneralize, not to make blanket statements about all older people or about the "typical" older person. So, while we encourage you to use demographic data as a valuable tool, we caution you to see it as a way to uncover the complexities and varieties of aging.

The Fallacy of the Demographic Imperative

Throughout this chapter we have been encouraging you to see the importance and usefulness of demographic information. We make those same points in the final section of this chapter. However, it is essential to keep in mind that "demography is not destiny." Friedland and Summer (1999) illustrate various interpretations of even commonly accepted demographic wisdom. You have heard and read a lot about the baby boomers, and what their aging will mean to you and to society. Friedland and Summer point out that we can get a different sense of the magnitude of the "baby boom problem" if we consider not just the total number of people in that birth cohort, but also the additional people born solely because of the higher birth rate. The higher birth rate during the baby boom added about 12.3 additional children beyond the number that would have been born if the pre World War II birth rates had been in place. If we think about it this way, the baby boom does not seem as large. These authors also clearly demonstrate how economic s and policy play roles at least equal to demography in shaping our destiny.

Although the numbers may seem compelling, we have illustrated several times throughout this chapter that numbers are only part of the picture. In the case of Nepal discussed earlier, it is quite clear that the "demographic imperative"—the aging of Nepali society—is, at this point, anything but an imperative for planning and policy. What any society decides to do about the aging of its population depends not simply on how many older people there are, but on the political, social, and moral values of the society.

The same warning can summarize our discussion of the "uses" of the dependency ratio to foretell impending economic disaster for American society. The numbers themselves are open to interpretation, and choices about which numbers to present are often very strategic decisions, because some "facts" better support an agenda than others. So, while we encourage you to consider demographic information as a useful resource, we also urge you to be aware of the social and political context that generates the numbers and directs their uses. Keep this warning in mind as you use demographic "facts," and as you critically analyze anything you read that uses such information.

While demographic information provides an essential framework from which to understand the aging of societies, it is equally important to remain aware of the overarching impact of economics, politics, power interests, and societal values as we decide how to deal with the challenges of aging. "We need not believe ourselves to be at the mercy of blind forces such as demographic and economic imperatives, as if these existed outside the realm of public discussion and debate" (Robertson, 1991, p. 147)

Our Demographic Future

As we have discussed throughout this chapter, the increase in the size and proportion of our older population has an impact on every aspect of social life. In the United States, the number of older people is projected to exceed 70 million by the year 2030, at which time all of the baby boomers will have reached age 65. Older people will represent about 20 percent of our population by then: one in every five people you see on the sidewalks and in the grocery store will be 65 or older!

Around the world, the increase in the size of the older population is equally dramatic and consequential. As we saw earlier in this chapter, a high proportion of older people will live in developing nations by the year 2020. Those nations will see their older populations grow by an average of 160 percent between 1991 and 2020. Exhibit 3.12 shows the percentage increase in older population projected for a sampling of countries around the world. The challenges

Exhibit 3.12   *Projected Percentage Increase in Population Aged 60 and over: 1991–2020, Selected Nations*

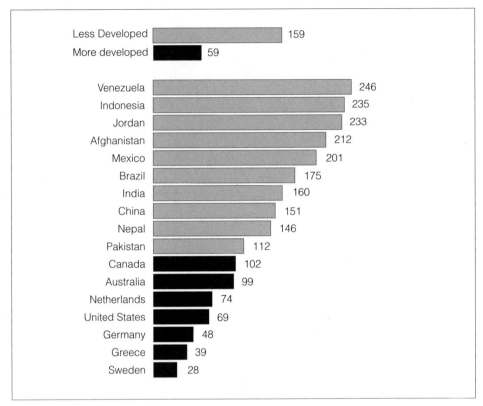

Adapted from: U.S. Bureau of the Census, *Global Aging*, 1991.

facing the nations in which rapid population aging will compete with maternal and child health concerns are enormous. Of equal magnitude are the challenges for the global community to define and understand problems and to propose and implement solutions.

When populations age, health care systems are profoundly affected. As large numbers of people survive to old age, the special health care needs of that group, for ongoing long-term care due to chronic illnesses, pose a major challenge. An interesting question about future generations of older people is whether they will be healthier and need less care than current generations. There are a range of predictions concerning this aspect of our future (see, for example, Kunkel and Applebaum, 1992; Manton and Liu, 1984, 1993). One way of thinking suggests that our advanced medical technology is highly successful at keeping people alive, but not at preventing or managing chronic conditions and the resulting disabilities. Thus, people who might have died of an illness in the past are now being kept alive longer, but in poor health. Others suggest that improvements in

Exhibit 3.13 *Resident Population by Race and Age Group: U.S., 1990 and Projection for 2020*

April 1, 1990

	All Races	European American	African American	Asian	Hispanic American
All Ages	**240,710**	**204,764**	**30,483**	**7,454**	**22,054**
Under 25	90,342	73,120	13,648	3,101	11,035
25-44	80,755	67,481	9,739	2,719	7,300
45-64	46,371	40,082	4,604	1,189	2,659
65-84	28,162	25,260	2,269	421	1,055
85+	3,960	2,761	223	29	91

July 1, 2020

	All Races	European American	African American	Asian	Hispanic American
All Ages	**325,942**	**254,791**	**45,409**	**22,653**	**51,217**
Under 25	108,233	79,475	18,748	8,663	22,325
25-44	83,214	63,819	11,877	6,663	13,904
45-64	81,147	65,748	9,920	4,899	10,241
65-84	46,390	39,642	4,373	2,115	4,152
85+	6,959	6,106	490	312	595

Percent Changes 1990-2020

	All Races	European American	African American	Asian	Hispanic American
All Ages	**31.1**	**22.1**	**49.0**	**203.7**	**129.1**
Under 25	19.8	8.7	37.4	179.4	102.8
25-44	3.0	5.4	22.0	145.1	90.5
45-64	75.0	64.0	115.5	312.0	257.0
65-84	64.7	56.9	92.7	402.4	293.6
85+	125.9	121.2	119.7	975.9	553.8

Source: Metropolitan Life Statistical Bulletin, 1994.

preventative health measures, growing knowledge about treatment of chronic diseases, and new levels of awareness about health-enhancing behaviors bode well for future generations of older people to live longer and be healthier.

Along with the numbers of older people, their health status, and their long-term care needs, another important aspect of our demographic future is the increasing racial and ethnic diversity of the United States as a whole, and the older population in particular. Most projections suggest "that there is likely to be a substantive shift in the racial composition of the U.S. resident population" (Kranczer, 1994, p. 21). Exhibit 3.13 shows the numerical and percentage increases in different age and race/ethnicity groups projected to occur in the United States between 1990 and 2020. The highest rates of increase will occur among people 65 and above who are of Asian or Hispanic origin. For example, the number of Asian American elders aged 85 and above will increase by nearly 1000 percent between 1990 and 2020! Obviously, since the number of Asian Americans 85 and older in 1990 is small, it takes relatively few additional people to produce a very high percentage increase. Nevertheless, this trend of increasing diversity in the older population is of great importance for service providers and planners, and for students and scholars who are trying to understand and describe the experiences of aging in the United States. Because ethnic and racial identities often play a central role in shaping those experiences, we need to be aware of this important aspect of diversity among the older population.

As we proceed with our look at the experiences of aging, demography will provide a lens to see the diversity of characteristics, situations, and needs of the older population. Demography shows us the aging of our society and how it compares to other aging societies around the world. The demographic big picture of patterns of fertility, mortality, and migration, and the demographic composition of the older population may at first seem remote. But these demographic descriptions of our aging society can help you understand your future: your life, your family, the country you will be running, and the planet of which you are a citizen.

Web Wise

Below is a list of sites that can provide you with information on demography of the aging population in the United States and in various countries around the world. Note that not all of the information is free and that some of it refers you to published (hard copy) materials.

Age Data

http://www.census.gov/population/www/socdemo/age.html

This is a linked web site maintained by the U.S. Census Bureau. It provides access to national, state, or local sources of information on demography from the Census Bureau. International data are also available. There is a search process available for a $40 fee for any census from 1900 to 1990 to request specific sets of information. In general, the census provides both statistics on current populations and projections for population change/growth through these sites and their printed publications.

National Institute on Aging

http://www.nih.gov/nia

The National Institute on Aging (NIA), part of the federally-funded National Institutes of Health, is involved with both basic and applied research on physical, social and psychological aspects of health as people age. Their web site provides information on their research agenda including extramural research (funding to outside groups, such as university-based researchers) on biology of aging, behavioral and social research, neurosciences and neuropsychology, and geriatrics. In addition, NIA funds its own research labs (internal programs) and provides a number of free publications that are available via E-mail requests. To find out what is "hot" in aging research, one good place to look is the NIA web site.

International Data Base (IDB) from U.S. Census Bureau

http://www.census.gov/ipc/www/idbnew.html

Ever want to know what population pyramids will look like for Albania, Guatemala, or Sierra Leone in 2025? Visiting the IDB site provided by the U.S. Census Bureau will enable you to look at projections for population and detailed characteristics of various countries or regions of the world. Choose from a large number of countries and look at the aging rates of the populations (via population pyramids) or at statistics in tables. It is also possible to download IDB data, but review the requirements in advance and be prepared for a large data set!

Key Terms

centenarians	mean
convergence	median
dependency ratios	population pyramid
geographic distribution	sex ratio
life expectancy	societal aging
life span	

Questions for Thought and Reflection

1. How does the age structure of a society affect social institutions such as health care, education, and politics?

2. Find some examples, in newspapers or magazines, of the ways in which demographic information about the older population is used to present a particular agenda or message. How might the same information be presented differently to convey a different message?

3. We know that aging is a phenomenon affecting all countries around the world. Think about some of the ways in which societal aging presents unique challenges in some of the countries you are familiar with.

4. How does the life expectancy in a county affect the way in which social life is organized– for example, number of years spent in school, age at marriage, age for entry into the labor force?

Dimensions of Aging

Having been introduced to some initial frameworks through which we can view aging in social context, we turn in this section to a closer examination of the perspectives of three specific disciplines pivotal to understanding aging in social context. As Chapter 1 discussed, the study of aging involves a wide range of traditional academic disciplines (such as biology, history, economics), some with a much higher level of involvement and longer tradition of studying aging than others. The field of social gerontology represents an interdisciplinary combination of a number of these disciplines directed toward the study of aging, including the interactions among biological, psychological, social, and economic aspects of the process.

This section presents the perspectives of three disciplines often considered to be "core disciplines" in social gerontology: health/physiology, psychology, and sociology. Many interdisciplinary programs require courses in these three disciplines on the assumption that they are central to understanding human aging in social context. Each of these disciplines carves out its own particular niche to examine the dynamics of aging. Each discipline traditionally asks a different set of questions, and each identifies particular units of analysis and research methodologies as relevant to their questions.

Physiologists, for example, might be interested in the effects of enzymes or hormones on individual cells and how they age. Their largest unit of analysis is one human body and the interactions between aging organ systems within it. Some psychologists also begin their research at a very minute unit of analysis; within a single person they can study psycho-physiological and cognitive processes and reactions. The largest scale of psychological research is the level of social psychological process involving multiple individuals. Psychologists and physiologists often rely on experimental and quasi-experimental techniques to address the kinds of questions they pursue. Sociologists focus on the human individual as the smallest unit of analysis, and can broaden their scope to examine the complexities of entire societies. Taking a macro-sociological approach, sociologists look at societies using historical and survey research techniques. Because the disciplines identify different units of analysis as important, they undertake different , but sometimes overlapping, styles of collecting data.

Similarly, the disciplines tend to focus on different aspects of and issues in the aging process as the sources of their questions. Not surprisingly, psychologists tend to focus their attention on age-related changes in cognition or age-based differences in learning, memory, or attitudes—a range of topics we would easily identify as psychological. Similarly, sociologists often focus on how class, ethnicity, gender, and other variables shape the processes and outcomes of aging.

The questions are also driven by the fundamental issues and theories in each of the disciplines. One question, such as how individual functioning changes with advancing age, would be addressed quite differently by each of these three disciplines. First, each of the disciplines would define "functioning" differently. Sociologists might look at ability to get along in the community, family interactions, or economic well-being; psychologists might focus on cognitive performance or measures of psychological well-being; physiologists might look at pulmonary output, coronary function, bone density, or hormonal/enzyme balance in the blood. Because each discipline constructs the concept of "functioning" differently, these scientists' attempts to answer this question could be complementary, not competitive, but might also disagree. For example, an individual might cope quite well in the social world, despite having some degree of cognitive impairment, depression, or serious health limitations. Each discipline, then, offers a unique viewpoint on the processes of aging that augments our overall understanding.

Each of these disciplines is the product of a sociohistorical process of development, which has identified boundaries and methodologies that are appropriate to the field. Examining this from a sociology of knowledge perspective, we can note that each of these disciplines carves out aspects of the aging process as its particular domain. This, too, is a social construction that adherents of these disciplines often recognize as artificial and sometimes limiting.

In the study of aging, it quickly becomes obvious that the disciplines have much to teach each other, and cross-disciplinary questions and research are common. Although the chapters that follow tend to highlight the distinctions among these three core disciplines, it is important to point out that understanding aging more fully often requires crossing the boundaries we have constructed between them.

CHAPTER 4

Physiology of Human Aging

by Helaine Alessio

"Aging defies easy definition, at least in biological terms. It is not merely the passage of time. It is the manifestation of biological events that occur over a span of time. The biology of aging has come a long way from being the domain of quacks and merchandisers bent on exploiting people's vanity to sell cosmetic repairs. Today it is one of the last major biological frontiers" (Hayflick, 1994).

One of the most fascinating areas of research and personal interest in aging is the physiology of aging. Practical questions, such as, "How will my body look and function over time?" or basic research questions, such as, "What controls the body's rate of aging?" are key questions asked by individuals interested in living long, healthy lives and researchers interested in understanding the physiological dimensions of aging. In this chapter you will be introduced to the basic concepts relating to the physiology of aging We will describe how scientists separate universal age-related changes from both the usual changes we see and from disease. We will cover some key ways we evaluate physiological aging, and some contemporary theories among those studying the physiology of aging to explain how aging occurs in the body and its systems.

What Is Physiological Aging?

Physiological aging refers to changes with the passage of time in the structure and processes of tissues, major organs and systems of the body that can ultimately affect our health, behavior, functional capacity, and survival. But not all of the changes that we see in older persons are due to physiological aging. While many persons experience similar physiological changes over time, some changes are not inevitable. Results from longitudinal studies, following large numbers of people over many years, reveal new information about physiological aging that helps us to understand two key distinctions: the first is between "usual" aging and "inevitable" aging, and the second distinction is between "normal" aging and "disease."

Usual and Inevitable Aging

We have all observed changes in the health and physical bodies of individuals as they age. But which of these changes are inescapable? Do our actions or inactions in terms of our own health bring about some of the changes? The distinction between usual and inevitable aging is one dimension of the answer.

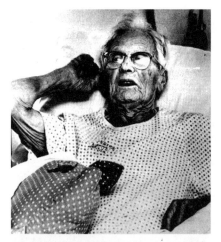

There is broad variation in the health status of older adults; understanding the difference between inevitable and usual aging is key.

Usual aging changes refer to the complex of changes that we typically see in individuals as they move into and through later life. Included among usual aging changes are increases in blood pressure and weight and loss of hearing and visual acuity. The *inevitable* changes are those that seem to be universal, perhaps through being somehow genetically or biologically programmed or the unavoidable result of living through time (Lee and Paffenbarger, 2000; Snowden, Kemper, Mortimer, Greiner, Wekstein, and Markesbery, 1996).

Examples of inevitable physiological changes include graying of the hair, baldness, and facial wrinkles. With rare exceptions, less pigment is produced in the hair follicles over time, hair becomes thinner, and skin loses its smoothness. These changes vary among individuals, but they do appear to be inevitable, albeit unpopular. On the other hand, no disease has been connected with natural graying of hair, baldness, or facial wrinkles (Schnor, Nyboe, Lange, and Jensen, 1998).

Usual changes associated with aging are numerous and familiar. By labeling them *usual* we mean that, although they typically occur, they are not the result of a fundamental process of aging. Often, instead they result from lifestyle choices, such as smoking, poor diet, exposure to risk factors in the environment like pollution, sun, and noise, that can affect physiological systems in most people. For example, in all men and women, walls of the arteries *usually* thicken and blood pressure increase with age. But the extent to which these usual changes occur varies across groups in the population. Extent of blood pressure increase is much greater among African Americans compared to African, Euro-Caucasian, or Asian populations. The fact that there is variation in whether and the degree to which changes such as this occur indicate that it reflects a usual, not an inevitable, physiological change with aging.

There is a range of inevitable physiological aging changes that may become labeled as diseases if they are severe. For example, age-related loss of bone den-

Exhibit 4.1   *Reaction Time and Age*

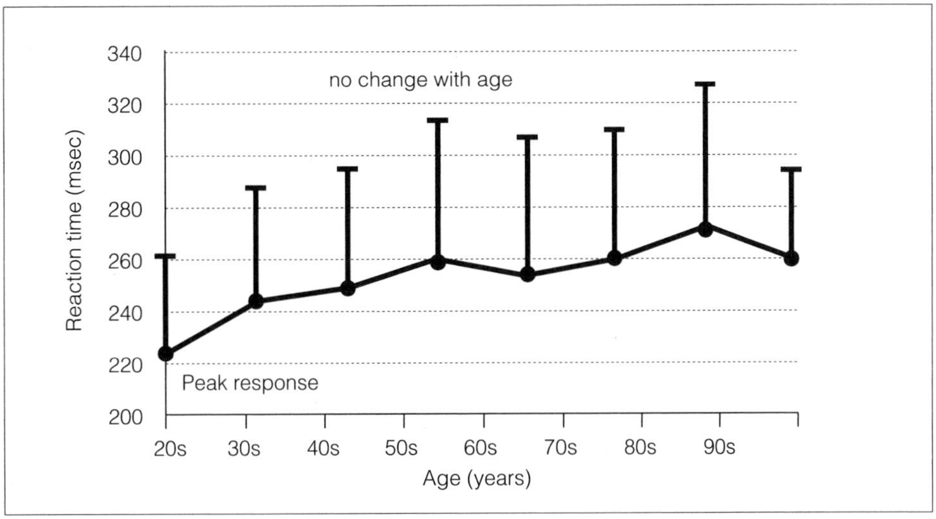

Source: Fozard et al., 1994.

sity via loss of calcium becomes osteoporosis in its advanced form; enlargement of the prostate gland (benign prostatic hyperplasia), or a severe loss of brain cells (dementia) can both come to be labeled as diseases in their extreme forms. It is not the type of change (usual or inevitable) that determines whether something is *disease*, but rather its severity.

Normal Aging and Disease

The other important dimension of physiological aging has to do with differentiating *normal* aging from *disease*. By a disease, we typically mean a condition that is considered problematic or risky to the individual's functioning or long-range well-being. Typically, diseases meet medical criteria as being a problem and may require treatment or intervention of some sort. For example, sensory losses, arthritis, and other usual aging changes may be considered *normal* aging if symptoms are limited, but may be labeled *disease* if they are likely to interfere with functioning or longevity. Normal aging, then, constitutes the complex of physiological changes that occur in acceptable ranges, whether they are *inevitable* or *usual* changes of aging.

Normal aging may be best characterized by stability over time. Exhibit 4.1 shows age-associated changes in simple reaction time from the Baltimore Longitudinal Study of Aging (Fozard, Vercruyssen, Reynolds, Hancock, and Quilter, 1994). Reaction time depends on neuromuscular function in which the brain, upon being stimulated (in this case, upon hearing a sound), signals the appropriate skeletal muscle group (in this case, the arm) to move and hit a target as quickly as possible. The twenty-year-old group clearly had the fastest and the seventy-year-old group had the slowest reaction times. But the most striking results are the reaction times of all age groups between the youngest (20-year-old) and oldest (70-year-old) groups. No clear age-associated changes occurred between 30 and 60 years! This implies that although peak performance is likely to occur in young adulthood, over time, neuromuscular function is well maintained and does not usually deteriorate with age.

Some physiological changes that were considered to be *normal* consequences of aging have been re-labeled as *disease*. For example, hearing loss is no longer considered to be an inevitable consequence of aging (Mader, 1984). Comparative studies of hearing ability in native populations around the world indicate that exposure to noise is a major factor in determining the extent of hearing loss (Goycoolea, Goycoolea, Rodriguez, Farfan, Martinez, and Vidal, 1986). In this case, a condition that was considered both *inevitable* and *normal* has been re-labeled as *usual* and *disease*.

Other examples of usual age-related physiological changes include increased blood cholesterol, increased body fat, decreased lean body mass, and loss of bone density; all of these show a great deal of variability across groups and individuals as they age. In fact, variability in most physiological measures tends to increase with age, suggesting that as we age we become more physiologically diverse from our peers than we were in childhood and youth (Spirduso, 1995). This increased variability is a product of the interaction between genetics and environment, revealing the complexity of human physiological aging. Individuals in later life are physiologically quite diverse, but share some common aging characteristics. The fact that they experience different times of onset, rates of change, and magnitude of physiological changes, even the inevitable ones, makes it difficult to predict physiological items on the basis of age in many cases (Cavalieri, 1992).

Diseases Associated with Aging

As one ages, the chances of dying from a disease increase dramatically (Exhibit 4.2). These are only a few of the diseases and chronic conditions that affect mortality as one ages, but they are some of the most dramatic in terms of their consequences for the individuals, their families/friends, and the larger society. Continued, intensive tracking of diseases in contemporary cohorts may reveal that death from all diseases is decreasing across the life span, which would explain the increase in life expectancy. Both genetics and environment influence many of the diseases reported to occur among older adults. Most studies that track disease in adulthood agree on two points: 1) there is a direct connection between age and disease, and 2) with increased age, the chances of suffering from more than one disease (termed comorbidity) increases. **Comorbidity** makes diagnosis and treatment of diseases in older persons more complicated, since the treatment for one disease (e.g. anti-inflammation for arthritis) may

Exhibit 4.2   *Age and Risk of Diseases*

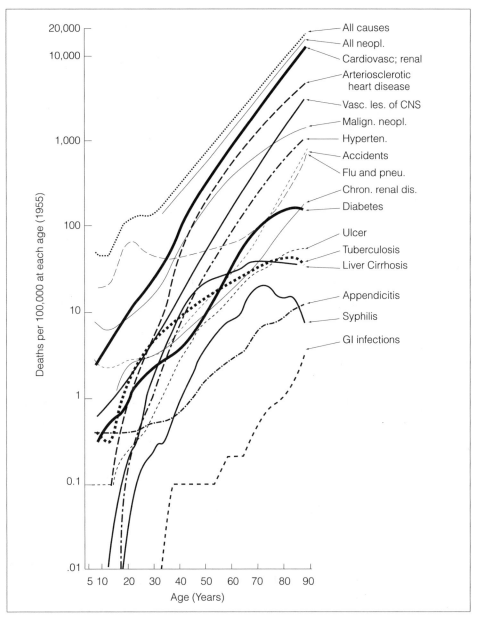

Source: Timiras, 1994

interfere with treatment for another disease (medication for stomach ulcers or acid reflux). It is important to point out, however, that having a disease does not mean that older people are permanently disabled or institutionalized. Many of the age-related diseases can be treated or managed with medication, diet, exercise, and/or therapy (See Chapter 10).

An example of an age-related disease is **atherosclerosis,** a progressive accumulation of fat on the inside of arteries carrying blood throughout the body. It is difficult to treat, because it develops slowly during youth, with little to no symptoms. By age 65, however, nearly half of all Americans are treated for some form of atherosclerosis. Over time, fat accumulation impedes blood flow, raises blood pressure, and increases blood clotting. The result can be disability or sudden death from hemorrhage or blood clots, but both prevention and treatment have changed the outcomes from this age-related disease. Control of atherosclerosis is the reason that physicians encourage individuals to pay attention to their diet and cholesterol intake, since its development is slow and progressive over decades. Medical treatment with daily aspirin, blood pressure medications, cholesterol lowering medications, or estrogen replacement therapy, work with diet and exercise as interventions.

Few diseases associated with aging ignite such intense fear as **Alzheimer's disease** and **Parkinson's disease**, both neurological-based disorders found most frequently, but not exclusively, among older adults. We turn first to Alzheimer's disease, which results in loss of mental and eventually, physical function. The general term dementia is defined as a global deterioration of intellectual and cognitive functions characterized by defects in all five major mental functions: 1) orientation, 2) memory, 3) intellect, 4) judgment, and 5) affect (Timiras, 1994). Both Alzheimer's and Parkinson's disease can result in dementia for their sufferers, most of whom are beyond age 70. In the U.S., approximately 5% of persons aged 65 and older suffer from Alzheimer's disease (Evans, 1996), representing about 4 million persons. That number is predicted to increase in the near future, but the increase is likely to occur in the oldest–old (older than 80 years) age group, in part due to more people living longer.

Although the causes of these diseases are not well understood, their effects are well known. In Alzheimer's disease, for example, the brain develops an accumulation of **neurofibrillary tangles** and **plaques** in the cerebral cortex (where high-level thinking occurs) and in the hippocampus (involved in memory). These tangles and plaques apparently interfere with the brain's normal functioning. The resulting memory loss, confusion, and eventual loss of physical functioning occur as the plaques and tangles take over more of the brain.

A well-known longitudinal study on Alzheimer's Disease has used as its sample an order of nuns from Michigan who participated in a battery of physical and mental tests every few years up until death. After death, they all agreed to donate their brains to science. Reports from this study (Snowden, 1997) find an association between depression, poor language skills, and the onset of Alzheimer's symptoms. The study provides only limited support for a genetic link in Alzheimer's disease, so we know little more about the causes of this disease now than when its discoverer (Alois Alzheimer) named it in the early 1900's.

In Parkinson's disease, rigidity of the limbs, tremor, and loss of motor function are core symptoms. The disease, named after its first describer (James

Parkinson) in 1917, is caused by a biochemical imbalance in the brain between two **neurotransmitters** (dopamine and acetylcholine). This imbalance was not discovered until a half-century after the complex of symptoms was identified, because several alternative explanations were suspected first. Approximately 1% of adults in the U.S. suffer from Parkinson's disease, and most of them are over age 65 (Hampton, 1991).

Features that give the appearance of reduced mental functioning often accompany the physical disabling characteristics of Parkinson's Disease. But it is mainly the nerve cells involved in locomotion that are damaged. This results in four cardinal symptoms: 1) rigidity, 2) tremor, 3) bradykinesia (slow movements), and 4) postural instability (Canter, Torre, and Mier, 1961). A key brain chemical in this process is dopamine, and a drug (L-dopa), which is a building block of dopamine, is often used to treat this disease. Dopamine levels normally decrease with aging, but when a critically low level is reached, and the ratio of dopamine to acetylcholine changes too dramatically, then the signs and symptoms of Parkinson's occur. Besides L-dopa, other treatments include administering monoamine oxidase (MAO) inhibitors, which prevent the breakdown of dopamine, antioxidant supplements to reduce free radical attack on dopamine cells, cell transplants, and exercise to build up dopamine naturally. Parkinson's disease, like Alzheimer's is a progressive and debilitating disease, most frequently found among older adults.

Environment versus Genetics

During the 20th Century, life expectancy increased from approximately 50 years to 75 years in the United States (Metropolitan Life Insurance Company, 1991). Long life expectancy, the average number of years an individual is expected to live, is a key indicator of healthy aging of an individual or of a population group. In the 21st Century, more people than ever before will live to advanced ages, as we learned in Chapter 3. In trying to understand why life expectancy has grown and will continue to increase, researchers have studied both environmental and genetic factors.

It has been estimated that **environment** accounts for about 65% of the variance in life expectancy (Herskind, McGue, Holm, Sroensen, Harvald, and Vaupel, 1996). The environment includes the range of factors to which the body is exposed, including food, water, heat/cold, noise, toxins, etc. The importance of environment to life expectancy was evident in the United States during the early 1900s when improved sanitation (e.g. water and sewage systems, antibacterial techniques) became widespread and many infectious diseases (e.g. diphtheria, tuberculosis, gastritis, pneumonia), came under control.

The importance of the environment to life expectancy and quality of life in the next 100 years will mainly derive from improvements in lifestyle, rather than sanitation. What people eat, where they live, how they use cars or firearms and whether they smoke or exercise: the cornerstones of environmental forces that influence life expectancy in the future will be behavioral.

Further changes in life expectancy over the next century are likely to come from advances in **genetics**. Genetics describes how genes, the coded segments of DNA in every cell that control cell development and function, work. Genes influence life expectancy and physiological aging, and account for approximately 35% of the variance in humans (Herskind, McGue, Holm, Sroensen, Harvald, and Vaupel, 1996). The number of potential years that the human species could live, if negative factors such as disease or accidents, did not occur, is referred to as the life span. Interest in how genes regulate life span has peaked in part due to the impact of genetic experiments where manipulations of single genes (or parts of single genes) have increased life span in other species rather dramatically. Most of this work has been performed in simple animal models, such as flies, worms, and rodents. For example, Orr and Sohal (1994) reported a 40% increase in life span in fruit flies after they inserted an extra copy of a gene for a protein that defends against harmful cell reactions. If extra copies of select proteins can be inserted successfully in more complex animal models with similar results, the human life span could be stretched to 150 years or more!

Other recent genetic experiments have attempted to identify and modify "age" genes, which, when turned on, appear to cause cell death. By disabling these "age" genes in adult worms, researchers have enabled these altered worms to live twice to four times as long as typical worms (Johnson, Sinclair, and Guarente, 1999). Schachter and associates (1994) placed special genes that may relate to aging into three categories: 1) genes that influence longevity, 2) genes responsible for cell function and repair, and 3) genes associated with age-related diseases. Recent study of the human genome has identified many genes responsible for diseases and death. Currently, there is mixed evidence on whether or not there are one or more genes that relate specifically to aging or longevity in humans (Miller, 1999).

At the pace we are currently discovering genes relating to aging either directly or indirectly, nearly 1000 more age genes will be identified by the end of the 21st Century (Miller, 1999). Other animals, including humans, may benefit from "extra" or altered genes, but the expectations regarding changes in human aging are for modest increases, due to the complex interactions of our relatively long lives (compared to worms or fruit flies) with environmental factors. Any major genetic manipulations to expand life span are likely to take place some years in the future.

Markers Of Physiological Aging

Although most of us utilize physiological cues to approximate the age of people we meet and know, as we have seen, such markers are not very reliable ways to gauge aging, since they vary significantly among individuals. Physiologists, desiring a more precise view on changes in the body and its organs and systems, utilize a range of markers to reflect aging and changes in the body.

According to Richard Sprott (1999), **biomarkers of aging** should be able to be obtained in a short segment of an animal's life span, and yet accurately reflect the aging rate and predict longevity. He describes four desirable properties of useful biomarkers of aging:

1. Be relatively easy to evaluate without harming subject;
2. Be reproducible and reflect physiological age;
3. Show significant changes over relatively short periods of time;
4. Represent functions that are important to health and daily activities.

Aging and Rate of Aging

Two criteria define aging on a physiological level: 1) the probability of death at any point in time increases with age, and 2) representative changes in physical traits occur in all cases. While we've already discussed the increasing rate of mortality in Chapter 3, the second issue will be discussed here. For a biomarker to be aging, it must have properties as described by Sprott and must occur in all cases. We are beginning to see regularities in the changes that occur with aging, in cross sectional longitudinal studies. The Baltimore Longitudinal Study, the Framingham Study, the Harvard Alumni Study, and the Nun Study previously mentioned have all been following individuals for many years. Some of the changes in aging people that researchers had thought were normal aging can be defined as disease based on this data. Longitudinal research shows real differences in the health and survivorship of varying groups and cohorts over time.

Based upon comparisons of survival data during the past 10,000 years, a similar rate of aging seems to apply to humans and some other primates. Finch and his colleagues (1990) described an eight-year **mortality-doubling time** for humans and a three-month mortality-doubling time for mice. The mortality doubling time is the span of years it takes from an initial age for the rate of mortality in a species to double. For example, a 40 year old is twice as likely to die at age 48, four times as likely to die at age 56, and eight times as likely to die at age 64. Of course, the 40-year-old started with a fairly low rate. These species-specific mortality-doubling times suggest that the aging rate for any given species is genetically programmed or fixed.

Yet, within the same individual, not all of the organs or tissues in the body age or change at the same rate. Your vision or lung function may change earlier or later than that of your best friend. And, if we look at different individuals, age changes in particular organs, such as the skin or the kidney occur at different rates. Therefore, the aging rate is unique to every individual. In the large aggregates, however, regularities appear in terms of mortality rates.

Ever since Benjamin Gompertz described human death in terms of mathematical probability, there has been a lot of interest about why, how, and when we die. Instead of being just an individual and family transition, looking at large numbers of individuals' longevity gives us different pictures and raises new questions. The Gompertz function that is plotted in Exhibit 4.3 shows that the

Exhibit 4.3   *Gonpertz Plot of Age-Specific Mortality*

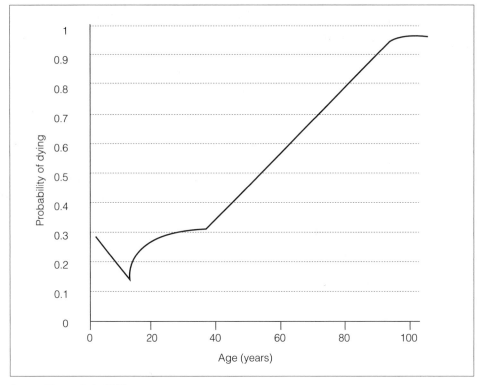

Source: Carey et al., 1992

older one becomes the greater the chance of dying, much as Finch and his colleagues had confirmed with mortality-doubling. The curve is exponential, so that the rate of change in death is not the same for all groups. The increased risk of dying is greater for a 60-year-old than for a 20-year-old (where the curve is still fairly flat). In the oldest age range, however, there is a marked deceleration in the curve among the oldest survivors, suggesting that those who reach advanced ages can expect to live even longer (Carey, Liedo, Orozco, and Vaupel, 1992). It is likely the interaction of genes and environment will continue to affect longevity.

Persistent Capacities

An important, but often overlooked fact about physiological aging is that most physiological systems endure over time. The old heart continues to beat, although it can never beat as fast as a young heart when under stress. Old lungs continue to transfer oxygen to the blood, although they may need to work harder compared to younger lung tissue to maintain sufficient oxygen content in the blood.

Exhibit 4.4   *Mean body composition for different ages in a typical man and master's athletes*

	Typical Men			Masters Men		
Age (years)	Body Weight (pounds)	Body Fat (percentage)	Lean Body Mass (pounds)	Body Weight (pounds)	Body Fat (percentage)	Lean Body Mass (pounds)
20	152	15	136	176	18	143
40	160	20	123	170	20	136
60	171	24	116	171	20	137

Exhibit 4.5   *Mean body composition for different ages in a typical woman and master's athletes.*

	Typical Women			Masters Women		
Age (years)	Body Weight (pounds)	Body Fat (percentage)	Lean Body Mass (pounds)	Body Weight (pounds)	Body Fat (percentage)	Lean Body Mass (pounds)
20	132	27	107	128	27	92
40	150	30	82	136	27	100
60	152	34	60	135	28	99

Source: Kavanagh et al., 1989; Fine et al., 1999

Homeostasis is the ability of a physiological system to function properly both at rest and when under stress. Virtually all older adults without advanced or complicated diseases can function sufficiently in a rested or non-stressed state. If homeostasis is compromised, then **functional reserve** is called upon to restore proper functioning. Functional reserve refers to the body's ability to respond to changes in the internal environment by recruiting more cells into action in order to restore homeostasis. If the functional reserve is inadequate, the physiological system under stress, as well as co-dependent systems, will fail to function properly.

Aging is associated with a reduced functional reserve capacity. So the body of an older person responds differently to the stress of acute illness, increased anxiety, or increased physical activity. It may simply be more challenging to the organs and systems of the older body to respond to an unusual physical demand. Compared with the older adult, a younger person will show less deviation from homeostasis and a faster recovery to baseline levels of functioning after a physiological stress of any type. Again, the degree of functional capacity decline is slow with aging and varies among individuals.

Common images of older adults have led us to expect an increased incidence of disease with age and some loss of function. While change is apparent on many levels, what is not obvious from these images is that aging usually occurs with little loss of function. Exhibits 4.4 and 4.5 show body composition changes in a *typical* man and a *typical* woman, and in men and women who compete in masters level sports competition. These represent usual and ideal body composition from youth to advanced age. **Master's athletes** of all ages have lower fat and higher lean body mass compared to typical men and women of similar ages. In contrast to the stereotypes of old people as being frail, sickly, and dull-witted, most aging changes in healthy men and women are reflected in slight changes in skin texture, body fat, joint movement, and memory. Recent research indicates that many of these mild age-associated changes can be prevented, attenuated, or delayed by improved lifestyles, as discussed at the end of this chapter.

Cell Death

Cell death is a definitive marker of aging, representing the endpoint of life. Cells die throughout the bodies of individuals at all ages. Concerns arise, however, when cells are not replaced at all or not replaced at rate to maintain functioning within the tissue or organ. For example, the plaques and tangles of Alzheimer's disease are in part responsible for the death of regular brain cells, resulting in some of the changes we see in that disease. Cell death and aging are related, but research has not demonstrated that aging causes the death of cells or an increase in its rate. Cell death can be a passive outcome of cell damage (necrosis) or from an active, programmed process (**apoptosis**). In **necrosis**, cells will burst, and gradually break apart in what appears as a messy death (Timaris, 1994). Apoptosis, in contrast, is a more controlled and less messy death. Programmed death of certain cells and their components may not be necessarily bad, since animal studies suggest it helps clear out old and precancerous cells (Wang, Nishigori, Yagi, and Takebe 1991; Grasl-Kraputt, 1994). Since cells are programmed only to survive for so long, aging research looks to alter the programming as a means to extend the function of tissues, and perhaps extend longevity. It is likely to be some time before scientists have keys to unlock the programming of cell death in ways that will have medical applications to extend or improve life.

Theories Of Aging

Descriptive aging studies provide information on what usually happens to our bodies over time and the diseases that are associated with advanced age. In order to modify the rate or extent of these changes in our bodies, research is also designed to explain why aging occurs and what controls aging processes in the body. Often, studies are set up to test whether the major tenets of one of the theories are supported. Theories of physiological aging can provide clues to understanding the process as well as to developing interventions for slowing down deleterious aging effects and facilitating healthy cell and tissue functioning.

Over 300 physiological aging theories have been investigated over the centuries. Although each one has a distinctive angle on the cause of aging, there is a lot of overlap and many shared concepts or mechanisms. General aging theories include external or internal causes. External causes include environmental elements such as food, bacteria, radiation, and pollutants as major life-threatening causes. Internal causes are believed to be programmed events leading to cellular changes or death. External and internal causes of aging are not mutually exclusive—many aging theories refer to both.

There are two major categories in which the major theories of investigation today fall: 1) **Error theories of aging** and 2) **Programmed theories of aging**. Error Theories of Aging argue that aging is external to the workings of the species. To be part of the Error theory group, some mechanism must exist whereby the cells or tissues of the body are attacked by an environmental assault. Damage incurred from this assault accumulates over time, and then causes the cell to malfunction or die. Programmed aging theories, on the other hand, hold that aging is internal to the species and is the natural and expected result of a purposeful sequence of events written into the genetic code. Although most studies are categorized under one heading or the other, they frequently include elements from both types of theories. Below are brief descriptions of the current set of error and programmed theories of aging under active investigation by researchers in biology and physiology. You will see these overlaps as you read through their specific descriptions.

Error Theories of Aging

Free Radical Theory

The **free radical theory** of aging as originally described by Harman in 1956, has been time-tested, and has emerged as a viable model for aging research and intervention. The term, free radical, refers to atoms or molecules having an unpaired electron in their outer electron shell, thus making them seek an electron to form a stable pair. As long as an electron in their outer shell remains unpaired, free radicals indiscriminately pluck hydrogens and their accompanying electrons from cellular proteins, lipids, sugars, and nucleic acids. This action will bring stability to the original radical while at the same time, bringing instability and damage to the molecule giving up a hydrogen and electron (Exhibit 4.6). It falls in the Error Theories category because cell damage accumulates over time and destroys the cell.

Mitochondrial Theory of Aging

Mitochondria are key organelles in the cell responsible for energy production necessary for cell function, repair of cell damage, and restoring homeostasis. The mitochondria facilitate the movement of hydrogens and electrons down an energy gradient within the cell to a point where they are picked up by oxygen to form water. If some electrons exit this process, oxygen may not receive pairs

Exhibit 4.6   *Oxygen Radical Attack on a Lipid or Fat*

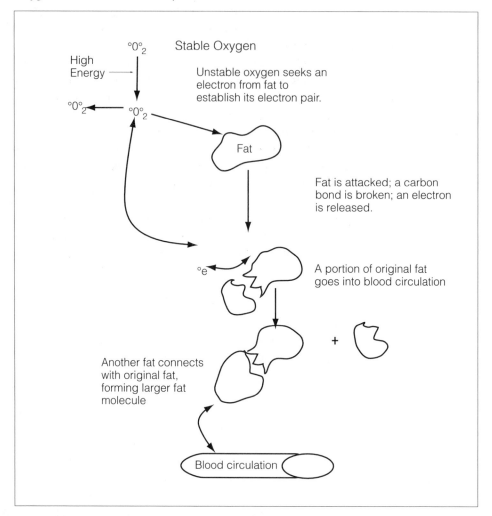

of electrons, and free oxygen radicals may form. Old mitochondria often lose the ability to transfer hydrogens and the electrons to oxygen in this process, and therefore, form more free radicals within the cells, which create damage in the fashion described above. Again, this is primarily an error theory since cell damage results from the failure of a necessary cell process resulting in damage.

Wear and Tear

Wear and tear portrays the human body as a machine in which overworked parts wear out sooner than desired. The main concept of the Wear and Tear theory is that the deleterious changes often observed in physical functioning with aging

Exhibit 4.7   *Metabolic Rate and Maximum Life Span Potential in Various Primates*

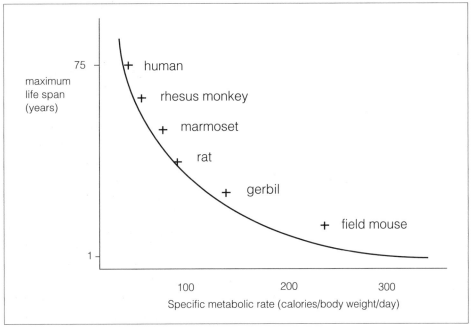

Source: Cutler, 1982

are the result of time-dependent use or abuse. In the late 1800's, Weismann presented his thoughts that the gradual wearing down of somatic cells (virtually all bodily cells except those involved in sexual reproduction), was a major cause of aging. His published work (1891) has stimulated much discussion over the past century and led to variations of the original idea. The theory has been directly related to metabolic rate, placing it in the Error Theory category, whereby animals with the lowest metabolism rates (such as tortoises and humans), as indicated by oxygen consumption, live proportionally longer than animals with faster rates of metabolism (such as mice) (Exhibit 4.7). Colder environmental temperature has been reported to slow down metabolism and aging rate while warmer temperature hastens metabolism and aging rates (Everitt, Porter, and Steele, 1981; Fanestil and Barrows, 1965; Strehler, 1962). Lower metabolism slows the wear and tear resulting in slower or delayed aging of the organism.

The ideas behind the Wear and Tear theory have been dismissed by most biogerontologists because the theory does not describe the mechanisms responsible for the loss of function. Nor does the theory recognize that tissues such as muscle show significant improvement and growth following bouts of work, like physical labor or exercise in which controlled cellular damage is inflicted. But an essential concept of the Wear and Tear Theory is that there is a failure or reduced capacity to repair cell damage over time. It is this concept that has led to developments of other aging theories, and those theories are proving to be more amenable to rigorous scientific investigation.

Cross-Linking

Connective tissue, collagen, is found in the skin, blood vessels, bone, cartilage, tendons and organs all over the body. Collagen is elastic and provides flexibility and selective permeability to many tissues, permitting the body to move and nutrients, wastes, and other materials to move through organs and systems. If collagen loses its elasticity, cell transport, waste removal, and pressure changes will occur and the cell will experience damage. Over time, collagen and other connective tissues undergo what is called **cross-linking**, a process by which proteins that normally exist separately, bind to each other and form a bond or cross link.

One of the best known cross linking processes occur when protein and glucose molecules react to form **advanced glycosylated end products** (AGEs) (Cerami, 1985). This reaction between glucose and proteins in the eye lens causes AGE's, results in a residue buildup that impairs vision, referred to as cataracts. Cross-linkages have been shown to increase with age and to be associated with disease (e.g. cataracts). Nevertheless, research has not shown that damage to specific cells that experience cross-linking generalizes to cause damage and death of the entire organism.

Error Catastrophe

The fifth and final example of the Error Theory category is what is called the **Error Catastrophe Theory**. According to this theory, accumulated effects from errors in synthesis of proteins in the body results in catastrophic outcomes over time. This theory focuses on the production of proteins and enzymes within the body. Production of new proteins and enzymes is vital because they supply the fundamental support for cell structure and control cellular function. Errors in forming new proteins and enzymes may occur in the genetic information stored in DNA, or in the process of transcribing the information to RNA or in translation, when new proteins are actually formed from the code. Although errors that occur in any or all of these steps may be slight, any error that results in even one alteration in a new protein will cause that new protein to be less functional compared to the earlier, correct version.

According to this theory, these small errors build and accumulate over time. Proteins produced from the altered protein will continue down the same path, so that the initial error, albeit small in relation to other proteins that are properly created, will increase exponentially with age. Ultimately, according to this theory, these errors build to a level sufficient to cause some sort of catastrophic outcome, from significantly diminished function in some tissue or organ of the body to even death (Sharma, 1994).

Programmed Theories of Aging

Hayflick Phenomenon

In the early 1960's, researchers (Hayflick and Moorehead, 1961) observed that young skin cells cultured in a petri dish continued to divide up to fifty times. As the number of divisions approached fifty, the rate of cell replication slowed and eventually halted. This set number of replications met the criteria of a Programmed Theories of Aging in that aging appears to be a phenomenon programmed into the cell. The **Hayflick Phenomenon**, then, is the pre-programming of cells for a set number of replication, after which the cells die.

There are two notable exceptions to the Hayflick Phenomenon that are well known to most people: cancer and germ cells. Both of these types of cells divide many more than fifty times, and, in the case of cancer, uncontrolled cell replication is characteristic of the disease process. What controls the rate of division for normal versus abnormal cancer cells? Recent research by has determined that the regulation of the Hayflick phenomena, whether it be fifty divisions in a normal cell or fifty thousand in a cancer cell, is directed by the expression of telomerase (Bodnar, Ouellete, Frolkis, Holt, Chiu, Morin, Harley, Shay, Lichteiner, and Wright, 1998), the focus of our next Programmed Theory of Aging.

Telomerase Theory

One of the newer entrants in the set of theories explaining physiological aging focuses on telomerase. **Telomerase** is an enzyme that repairs and replaces part of the telomere lost during cell replication. You can think of the telomere as a "tail" on the DNA strand that works like a clock controlling the rate of replication and the ultimate number of cell divisions that are possible. Telomeres usually shorten with each replication and therefore, with aging, they are likely to reach a shortened length at which point, replication no longer occurs. This theory is considered to be a Programmed Theory because it occurs in all members of a species and indicates an internal, programmed process, determining change with the passage of time and cell replications. Exhibit 4.8 provides a graphic representation of a telomere.

The action of telomerase can restore and re-lengthen the telomere, which has the effect of increasing cell replication beyond the normal test tube limits. Ironically, every cell has the capability to produce telomerase, but telomerase genes are actively suppressed in normal cells, permitting the telomere to shorten in the programmed fashion, while they are activated in cancer cells, permitting uncontrolled cell replication. Thus, the process of lengthening the telomere also appears to risk the development of cancer. A telomerase inhibitor may shorten the telomere, reducing replication in cancer cells, while a telomerase activator lengthens the telomere and increases cell divisions. Recent studies in which a telomerase gene was inserted to re-extend telomeres to their youthful length resulted in cells that demonstrated characteristics of "young" cells (Fossel, 1998).

Exhibit 4.8   *Telomere Theory of Aging*

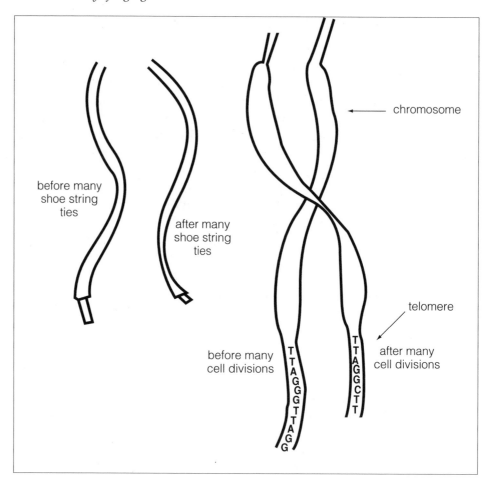

Telomerase research, while still in its infancy, has much potential for better understanding aging and disease intervention.

Neuroendocrine Theory

The **Neuroendocrine theory** suggests that changes/diseases in the neurological system of the body, which affect the endocrine system, are implicated in physiological aging. To understand this theory we need to have some understanding of these two systems, which fulfill critical functions for the human body. First, the nervous system of the body is discussed.

There are three major types of cells within the nervous system of the body: neurons, glial cells and endothelial cells. **Neurons** are cells that transmit nerv-

Exhibit 4.9   *Aging Changes in a Neuron*

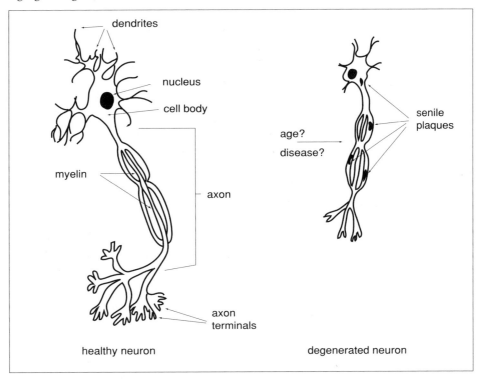

ous signals. **Glial** cells are brain tissue which provide physical support to neurons but do not transmit nervous impulses, **Endothelial** cells are those inside the cerebral capillaries supplying blood that provide a barrier to protect the brain tissues from harmful metabolites and toxins. Proper nervous system function requires a nerve signal emitted from a specific area of the brain be sent along an intact neuron "glued" in the proper place by glial cells and protected from biochemical waste products and toxins by the blood/brain barrier of healthy endothelial cells. To complete the functional circuitry of the nervous system, the signal encounters a synapse or gap between the branching tips of neurons known as dendrites, where neurotransmitters such as acetylcholine, dopamine, and epinephrine gather to assist the signal across a cell membrane to the next neuron down the line. The signal continues down the chain of neurons until it reaches the target tissue or organ, where it activates cells. A healthy neuron will carry a nervous signal quickly and effectively to the target tissue, but a degenerated neuron will fail to properly stimulate the target cell (exhibit 4.9). If the target cell or tissue is frail or not functioning properly, the end response may not be adequate, but that would not be the fault of the nervous system. It could, for example, be the result of a frail, atrophied muscle that, upon neural stimulation, produces very low force.

For a long time, it was accepted that death of neurons was a direct and inevitable result of aging. Researchers found an approximate 10% loss of brain mass among healthy 70-80 year old human brains (Dura, London, and Rappoport, 1985). But, emerging data cautions that the loss of neurons, leading to the reduction of brain mass, may be a sign of disease, rather than inevitable aging processes (Morrison and Hoff, 1997). Age related changes in neurons and increases in senile plaque formation, neurofibrillary tangles, associated with Alzheimer's disease, build up of lipofuscin, another substance found in older brains, all contribute to various degrees of decline in nervous system function. In contrast, Green and associates (1983) found that when old rats were placed in a novel, stimulating, "Disney-like" environment, neuron connections increased as well as performance on cognitive tasks (1995). It is currently accepted that neurons, when stimulated regularly, survive well into old age and continue to sprout new connections with other nerves.

The second system involved in this theory is the body's endocrine system, which consists of **glands, hormones and target cells.** Glands are organs that produce and secrete hormones into the blood. The **hormones** are molecules secreted by the glands to act on distant, target cells. The receptors on **target cells** allow select hormones to activate their receptors and initiate a subsequent series of reactions inside the cell. Among the glands included are the thyroid, parathyroid, pituitary, adrenal, pancreas, gonads, and ovaries. Aging changes may occur as a result of shrinkage of certain glands (e.g. thyroid, thymus), lower production of certain hormones (e.g. growth hormone, testosterone, estrogen), or reduced sensitivity of target tissues to certain hormones (e.g. glut 4 cell receptors require more insulin to transport glucose inside the cell). One target of the nervous system is sending signals to the glands of the endocrine system when they need to produce hormones to get various tasks accomplished within the body. Because the nervous system relies on a target cell for a response to the original nerve signal, the nervous system and endocrine system work together to accomplish an ultimate goal. Since aging can influence functioning of the nervous system in negative ways, the endocrine system may also fail to complete the necessary tasks to maintain tissues and organs of the body, resulting in a predictable loss of functioning, disease, and death. The complexity of the nervous and endocrine systems have not discouraged investigations, using a wide range of interventions that include hormone replacement therapy for men and women, cell receptor enhancers and blockers, exposure to novel stimuli, and cognitive therapies to control nervous functioning.

Somatic Mutation Theory

According to the **Somatic Mutation Theory**, defects in somatic cell DNA occurs either by mutations (e.g. standard base pairs or added, deleted, or rearranged) or damage (e.g. the DNA's double helix structure is broken). Regardless of whether DNA experiences mutations or damage, the effects are similar: gene

Exhibit 4.10   *Ways in which regular exercise affects aging processes and morbidity.*

Cardiovascular System

Health Component	Usual Aging Change	Effects of Exercise	Effects on morbidity
Blood Pressure	Increase	Maintains or decreases	Lower risk for hypertension
Cardiac Output (Heart's ability to pump)	Decrease	Increase	Lower risk for all cardiovascular diseases
High density lipoproteins	Decrease	Increase	Lower risk for atherosclerosis
Triglycerides (blood fat	Increase	Decrease	Lower risk for atherosclerosis

Musculoskeletal System

Muscle strength	Decrease	Increase	Lower risk for sarcopenia
Muscle endurance	Decrease	Increase	Lower risk for sarcopenia
Muscle flexibility	Decrease	Increase	Lower risk for lower back pain
Bone mineral content	Decrease	Increase	Lower risk for osteoporosis

Regulatory System

Blood sugar	Increase	Decrease or Maintain	Lower risk for diabetes melitus
Metabolic rate	Decrease	Increase	Lower risk for obesity
Body fat	Increase	Decrease	Lower risk for some types of cancer
Cognitive Function	Decrease	Increase	Lower risk for dementia

expression will be modified. That means there will be a greater risk for some diseases. When Szilard first introduced this theory in 1959, he proposed that aging was the result of abnormal chromosomes. Several studies from the 1960s–80s supported the Somatic Mutation Theory, with reports that unstable chromosomes were related to a shortened life span (Curtis, 1964; Salk, An, Hoehn, and Martin, 1981). The Somatic Mutation theory does not fully explain age-related changes, because for instance, there are many examples of chromosomal aberrations that have little to no affect on aging rate or life span. It lost favor to other theories during the 1980s and early 1990s. Recently, however, there has been a renewed interest in the Somatic Mutation Theory led by Woodruff and Nitikin (1995) and Thompson, Woodruff, and Huai (1998) with new and convincing evidence linking somatic gene damage and shortened life span. As in many instances, results from aging research investigating this theory has assisted in advancing our understanding of both aging and disease processes.

Dysdifferentiation Theory

Cells in the body are differentiated in order to accomplish various goals. So, cells in the blood are unlike those in the liver or bone, since they perform specialized functions for the body. Cutler (1982) proposed that with aging there is a time-dependent loss of proper **differentiation** or distinction between cells and dysdifferentiation. In this process, distinct cells begin over time to look less different from each other and more alike. These cell changes appear to be internal to different species and so it is considered a programmed aging theory. When cells begin to move away from their unique, differentiated forms, this is called cell drift. The causes of cell drift and the rate of drifting are as yet, unknown.

The major predictions of the Dysdifferentiation hypothesis are that: 1) older cells will look different than younger cells of the same type and 2) older cells from various types of tissues will lose their uniqueness and look more like other older cells from different tissues. For example, blood cells and bone cells will become more like each other with age. Presumably, this dysdifferentiation would result in a diminished capacity of these cells to perform their unique and differentiated functions within the body.

Immunological Theory

The body's **immune system** is responsible for protecting it against infections and substances that should not be within particular tissues. It has long been believed that age-related breakdown of the immune system is responsible for high rates of cancer, autoimmune disease, and infection, found in elderly compared to young adults (Woods, Evans, Wolters, Ceddia, and McAuley, 1998). Blood levels of antibodies (necessary to defend against antigens) begin to decline shortly after sexual maturation is reached (Nordin and Makinodan, 1974), and the incidence of tumors, which are fought by the immune system, increases in old age (Ershler, 1993). In doing its work, the immune system must distinguish the body's own healthy cells from unhealthy cells, such as tumors, and from invaders, called antigens, in order to activate proper defenses.

With advancing age, the immune system's response time and effective against antigens decreases. It also confuses the body's own healthy cells with antigens, and sometimes initiates attacks on itself—a condition referred to as autoimmune response. Autoimmune antibodies tend to increase with age. Current research is investigating whether or not these changes are programmed, perhaps linked to the shrinking of the thymus gland over time, since it is the thymus's job to prepare immune cells for attack against a specific aggressor. When the thymus decreases in size, so too does its ability to adequately prepare immune cells to attack the appropriate aggressor cells, setting up a situation for mistaken attacks against oneself. Autoimmune diseases include many age-related conditions such as rheumatoid arthritis, Addison's disease, Lupus, and Multiple sclerosis.

Anti-Aging Interventions

Humans have always sought ways to stop or reverse the aging process. The use of animal tissue replacement, cell injections, special plant extracts, and other elixirs have attempted, but always failed, to stop the aging process and delay death. The following are examples of interventions that have recently gained favor in slowing down the aging process, and in some cases, diseases that are associated with aging.

Estrogen Replacement Therapy

Estrogen replacement therapy (ERT) in post-menopausal women has been shown to have a range of positive effects. It results in greater retention of calcium and phosphorus in bones, improved blood flow to the brain, and reduced risk of atherosclerosis (Peterson, Courtois, Peterson, Peterson, Davila-Roman, Spina, and Barzilai, 2000; Grady, Rubin, Petitti, Fox, Black, Ernster, and Cummings, 1992; Williams, Adams, and Klopfenstein, 1990; Pak, 1983). Most studies also agree that ERT reduces the risk of coronary heart disease (Bush, 1990). Possibly ERT has a positive effect on the "good" cholesterol (HDL or high density lipoproteins), which gather "bad" cholesterol (LDL or low density lipoproteins) and fat from arterial walls and transport them to the liver for disposal. However, it appears that HDL levels are more influenced by testosterone levels in the blood than by estrogen. ERT may indirectly influence this process by increasing the ratio of estrogen to testosterone. Estrogen can also benefit skin through the estrogen receptors on the skin, which result in increased water content and skin thickness.

But use of ERT is not without risks. ERT has been associated in research with greater risks of uterine cancer and gallstones. Most physicians that prescribe ERT use the lowest doses possible to achieve benefits to minimize these risks. It is accepted by most health professionals that the benefits associated with ERT are not limited to women. However, few men consider ERT to improve their bone mineral content or HDL levels.

DHEA

Dehydroepiandrosterone (DHEA) is the most abundant steroid hormone found in the blood. Produced by the adrenal gland, DHEA is designated as a biomarker of aging because it satisfies two criteria: 1) DHEA levels decrease with age, and 2) DHEA is higher in longer-lived species (Cutler, 1982). Unlike the well understood functions of other steroids such as estrogen, testosterone, progesterone, and cortisol, the specific functions of DHEA are not clear. DHEA can be converted into testosterone and estrogen, possibly enhancing reserve supplies when needed. DHEA is also believed to act as an antioxidant (see earlier theories for discussion of antioxidants) and a regulator of immune function.

Although not entirely understood, studies on animals have shown remarkable correlations between DHEA and tumor reduction, immune function, decreased body fat, increased lean body mass, and reduced risks for diabetes and atherosclerosis (Ho, Hansen, Chen, and Holloszy, 1998). But compared to humans, animals have meager amounts of DHEA. So, increasing the levels in animals would not be expected to produce similar results as supplementation of DHEA in humans. Early tests on DHEA's potential as an anti-aging hormonal supplement do show some encouraging results. A study of 60 adults, (ages 66-84 years), found higher levels of DHEA associated with greater physical activity and with greater aerobic fitness, in particular (Bonnefoy, Kostka, Patricot, Berthouze, Mathian, and LaCour, 1998). These initial results suggest promise for the beneficial effects of DHEA on health and function, but not necessarily on life expectancy. Further research on DHEA will shed greater light on its potential and on its safety as a supplement for humans.

Growth Hormone Replacement

The role of **growth hormone** in aging has generated much interest and prospect for the way it imparts benefits for men in a similar way that estrogen replacement imparts benefits for women. As its name suggests, growth hormone is associated with growth and development of the body during childhood and youth. Growth hormone deficiency is associated with reduced lean body mass, increased fat, reduced protein synthesis, reduced skin thickness, and reduced energy levels (Nelson, 1995). By age 65, growth hormone levels decrease by 50% compared to peak levels between age 20-30 years.

Use of growth hormone supplements for frail older adults was originally believed to enhance Neuroendocrine function and energy expenditure to a level in which the adults could raise their own level of activity for every day tasks and further increase their natural production of growth hormone. Research where frail older adults received six months of growth hormone supplementation showed promise, with increases in lean body mass, reduced fat, and increased energy levels (Rudman, Feller, Nagraj, Gergans, Lalitha, Goldberg, Sclenker, Cohn, Rudman, and Mattson, 1990). But twelve months of growth hormone supplementation resulted in serious side effects that outweighed the benefits (Cohn, Feller, Draper, Rudman, and Rudman, 1993), suggesting that more is not always better. Safer ways to supplement growth hormone are under development (Silverman and Mazzeo, 1996).

Caloric Restriction

Of all the interventions that may influence aging and mortality, only **caloric restriction** has been shown in different laboratories to consistently influence both the rate of aging and mortality. The major drawback is that these positive changes have only been observed in lower-level animal such as rodents and fruit flies, and to more limited extent, in rhesus monkeys (Verdery, Ingram, Roth, and Lane, 1997; Weindruch, 1996). In caloric restriction, animals are fed a nutritionally dense diet that contains the recommended dietary allowances for protein, vitamins, and minerals, but in a fewer number of calories. Caloric reduction is dramatic; generally the caloric intake for these animals is approximately 60-70% of the normal amount, a significant reduction. For an average weight human who usually consumes 2000 calories per day while meeting dietary requirements, this would mean getting the same nutrients but reducing the calories to 1400 per day.

The side effects of dramatic caloric restriction over a life span include a slower maturation rate and an adult body size that only reaches 85% of the average. The main benefit is that animals on a caloric restricted diet live longer and have a longer mortality rate doubling time compared to animals with unlimited access to food (Weindruch, Walford, Fligiel, and Guthrie, 1986; Yu, Masoro, and McMahon, 1995). In addition, the number of tumors and types of cancers are lowered by caloric restriction, so not only do they live longer, but also healthier (Sonntag, Lynch, Cefalu, Ingram, Bennet, Thornton, and Khan, 1999).

Since studies have proceeded in rodents, experimental data on humans is needed to verify whether caloric restriction operates in the same way in a much larger mammal. In the Biosphere 2 experiment, a dozen scientists were sealed into a domed ecosystem and forced to eat a caloric restricted diet for nearly two years. They reported reduced body weight, blood pressure, cholesterol, blood glucose, and white blood cell count in all participants (Walford, Harris, and Gunion, 1992). These physiological biomarkers are the opposite of changes that occur typically with aging. It is no surprise that only one of the original Biosphere 2 project's scientists, continues on a caloric restricted diet to this day as an ongoing experiment on long-range outcomes in a single human.

Exercise

The importance of **exercise** to life span was clear to our ancestors, who relied on speed and strength to outrun predators, forage for food, and build their own shelters. In the 21st Century, the importance of exercise to life span persists.

Exhibit 4.11   *Association Between All-cause Mortality and Physical Fitness in Men and Women*

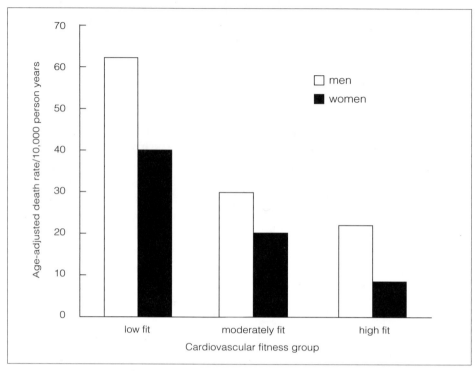

Source: Blair et al., 1989

Many large scale research studies have shown that regular exercise reduced one's risk of disease and death (Morris, Kagan, Garner, and Raffle, 1966; Paffenbarger, Laughlin, Gima, and Black, 1970, Paffenbarger, Wing, and Hyde, 1978; Blair, Kohl, Paffenbarger, Clark, Cooper, and Gibbons, 1989). Regular exercise tends to promote changes in the body that are directly opposed to age-related changes. Exhibit 4.11 lists ways in which age and exercise affect mortality, cardiovascular disease, cancer, diabetes, and other conditions.

What are the mechanisms behind the anti-aging effects of exercise? There are several possibilities. Single bouts of exercise increase metabolism during exercise, increase steady blood flow through the arteries, which removes some fatty deposits from the blood vessel walls, facilitates sugar and fat clearance from the blood, and raises growth hormone levels. Regular exercise is associated with lower resting metabolic rate, higher protein synthesis (necessary for muscle and bone growth), lower build-up of fat, higher HDL ("good" cholesterol), lower levels of total cholesterol and triglycerides, lower body weight, enhanced cell receptor sensitivity to some hormones, and improved cell repair. Essentially, exercise addresses all the processes that are supposed to cause aging according to the aging theories discussed earlier in this chapter (Rogberg and

Roberts, 1999). Regular exercise has also been associated with elevated levels of antioxidants (Alessio and Goldfarb, 1988; Alessio and Blasi, 1997; Alessio, Cao, and Goldfarb, 1996; Ji, 1995), reduced lipid peroxidation (Alessio, Goldfarb, and Cutler, 1988), and other biomarkers of oxidative stress (Sen, 1995).

Several longitudinal studies have found a link between regular exercise and longevity. The Harvard Alumni study by Paffenbarger and associates (1976) reported a 2-7 year increase in life expectancy depending on other risk factors in men who were physically active, expending an average of 2000 calories a week in physical activities, over the years following graduation. Consider that a 30 minute jog requires approximately 300 calories in an average sized adult and that all forms of physical activity (e.g. steps, walking to and from a car, etc.) were used in this study to reach a sum of 2000 calories per week. The striking results from the Harvard Alumni studies, which continue today to report results of physical activity on risk of death, were that low levels of physical activity (less than 500 calories per week) were significantly related to increased death rates from all causes. So, being inactive is not simply neutral, it has negative effects! By increasing physical activity to moderate levels (500-1900 calories per week), risk of death decreased significantly. While raising physical activity to a high level (2000+ calories) did not reduce the chances of dying over moderate activity levels, other benefits to health were visible. Clearly, inactivity is the greatest risk factor.

Blair and associates (1989) expanded on this line of research by including 3000 women as well as men as subjects and provided direct evidence of physical activity via tests for oxygen consumption. When the subjects were divided into categories of low, moderate, and high levels of cardiovascular fitness, the results reinforced those from the Harvard sample (Exhibit 4.11). Physical activity, if performed on a regular basis that reaches an intensity level adequate to "turn on" the mechanisms associated with these positive outcomes, link exercise to reduced morbidity (disease/health problems) and mortality. Studies of world-class athletes suggest that, while their life expectancies are longer than those of typical humans, they do not exceed or stretch the upper limit of life span (Sarma, Sahi, Koskenvuo, and Kaprio, 1993).

A reduction of muscle strength does appear to be a major component of normal aging (Evans, 1995). But, sometimes, frail elderly experience muscle wasting to a point where the disease sarcopenia is indicated. Sarcopenia is severe loss of muscle mass that may be brought about by prolonged physical inactivity, inadequate protein intake, and/or disease. In contrast, **masters athletes** participate and compete in regular, intense physical activity and sports. Age of masters athletes ranges from 30 to 100+ years. Researchers are slowly gathering information about physiological function, health, and longevity in master's athletes to learn more about aging versus disease processes. Unlike their age-matched peers, master's athletes suffer few if any, chronic health conditions (Spirduso, 1995; Kavanagh, Mertens, Matosevic, Shephard, and Evans, 1989). Benefits associated with regular exercise training can occur up to and even beyond age

Research demonstrates benefits to exercise, even at advanced ages.

99 (Rubenstein, Josephson, Trueblood, Loy, Harker, Pietruszka, and Robbins, 2000; Fiatronne, O'Neill, Doyle, Clements, Roberts, Kehayias, Lipsitz, and Evans, 1993). An important benefit of regular exercise is that it improves functional performance of older adults, which can lead to maintaining or regaining independence (Cress, Buchner, Questad, Esselman, deLateur, and Schwartz, 1999). Exercise strategies have traditionally focused on aerobic or endurance activities, however, recent evidence suggests that exercises that increase muscle strength and power (e.g. using free weights) should also be included in regular exercise activities for older adults. The maintenance and development of muscle power in advanced age has been shown to reduce the risk of falling (Rubenstein, Josephson, Trueblood, Loy, Harker, Pietruszka, and Robbins, 2000).

Tannins

Tannins are substances commonly found in red wines and many teas. In recent years they have gained popularity as being both healthy beverages and anti-aging drinks. The "French paradox" describes the situation of the French who eat large amounts of high fat food (e.g. cheese, red meat), yet have relatively low levels of cardiovascular disease and cancer, illnesses associated with fat consumption in other parts of the world. One explanation for this paradox is that the French drink wine every day, which is high in tannins. Tannins act as **antioxidants** in the gastrointestinal tract and remove free radicals and related active oxygen species before they enter into the circulation to attack cells and tissues (Maxwell, Cruickshank, and Thorpe, 1994). By acting in the digestive system, tannins spare other antioxidants; therefore more antioxidants (e.g. Vitamin C, E, and glutathione) can enter the general blood circulation and defend against damage from oxidation. Green tea, a common drink among Asians, is also high in tannins. It has been associated with reduced risk for cardiovascular disease and cancer in populations that consume it (Zeyuan, Bingying, Jinming, and Yifeng, 1998). Further research is needed to understand the potential anti-aging effects of drinking tea and wine.

Summary

The puzzle of physiological aging is a complex one. Although we have many clues and theories, as yet we have not identified the mechanisms that are responsible for the changes that occur in the body, its systems, tissues, and cells, with the passage of time. It may be that multiple mechanisms are responsible for normal aging and yet others account for many of the age-related conditions and diseases that we see as part of usual aging. It is likely that both genetics and environment play roles in the multitude of changes, small and large that occur as the body ages. Unlike cross sectional studies that compare different age groups at one point in time, longitudinal studies that follow the same persons for many years have distinguished between inevitable and usual aging changes as well as normal aging and disease. A 70-year-old who participated in a research study in the 1960s has many different life experiences compared to a 70-year-old participant in a study today. Different opportunities and barriers over the course of one's lifetime will affect health and function in different ways. Some aging changes that we thought were inevitable are now believed to be a bit more under our control and may usually occur in some but not all persons. We no longer accept that disease is a natural part of aging. The diversity among older adults is much greater than previously thought and one can find large numbers of healthy, disease-free older adults as well as adults requiring assistance due to ill health and low functional ability. As scientists try to learn more about healthy aging, many biomarkers of aging have come in and out of favor. Recent long term studies have reported how some conventional biomarkers of aging are remarkably stable over time. Death, the ultimate biomarker of aging, is now being separated into death by necrosis and death by apoptosis. Scientists are learning how cell death caused by damage suffered by the cell differs from death that is programmed by the cell itself. This distinction relates to the two general categories of aging theories: error and programmed, and the continued investigations of theories falling and in many cases, overlapping, in these categories, will shed light on aging versus disease processes and future interventions. But until then,

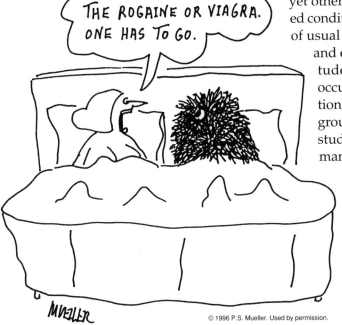

THE ROGAINE OR VIAGRA. ONE HAS TO GO.

MUELLER

© 1996 P.S. Mueller. Used by permission.

Pharmaceutical products to address age-related concerns are expanding rapidly.

some people will turn to their own anti-aging solutions, and will supplement hormones, restrict daily food intake, become more active, drink green tea, or look for other anti-aging potion. It is interesting that in the high-technology world we live in today, many centurions, when asked how they have managed to live past 100 years old, often answer: "I eat right, I keep busy, I get enough sleep, and I don't worry."

Web Wise

National Institute on Aging

http://www.nih.gov/nia/

This web site is the home of the National Institute on Aging. It has links that are useful for researchers and laypersons—especially the health links. They include research, educational, and popular media links on aging and health. Informative, timely and useful information on physiological aging can be obtained from the NIA web page.

http://cpmcnet.columbia.edu/dept/dental/Dental_Educational_Software/ Gerontology_and_Geriatric_Dentistry/normal_aging/ physiologic_changes.html

This web site contains a timely overview of physiological aging. It reads like a tutorial from which the serious student and layperson can each benefit. Tables, graphs, and pictures elucidate many of the statements and findings. It has helpful links to other educational sites.

Go60.com

http://www.go60.com/

This is a straight forward web site designed to help seniors age with grace and good health. Timely news articles are included in its easy to access links. Not all address physiological aging, but many do, and they report from news wires on recent advances in health science and medicine.

Key Terms

advanced glycosylated end products (ages)

antioxidants

apoptosis

atherosclerosis

Alzheimer's disease

biomarkers of aging

caloric restriction

comorbidity

cross-linking

Dehydroepiandrosterone (DHEA)

disdifferentiation

endothelial cells

environment

error catastrophe theory

error theories of aging

estrogen replacement therapy

exercise

free radical theory

functional reserve

genetics

glands

glial cells

growth hormone

Hayflick phenomenon

homeostasis

hormones

immune system

master's athletes

mortality doubling time

necrosis

neuroendocrine theory

neurofibrillary tangles and plaques

neuron

neurotransmitters

Parkinson's disease

physiological aging

programmed theories of aging

somatic mutation theory

tannins

target cells

telomerase

wear and tear theory

Questions for Thought and Reflection

1. What are the physiological changes that accompany normal aging? Do these normal physiological changes explain the vulnerability of older adults to the diseases associated with aging? Take into account theories about the process of physiological aging in your answer.

2. Which anti-aging interventions require the most involvement of doctors and other health care providers? Which can be done by people without professional help? Are there any policies that could encourage people to practice the interventions they can do without medical help, like exercise?

3. Estrogen replacement therapy (ERT) is one of the most widely prescribed anti-aging treatments for women past the age of menopause, even though it has acknowledged side effects. How would you formulate a public health policy to determine who should and should not take ERT?

4. Construct a sample exercise program for a non-athletic person trying to avoid the negative effects of aging. Think about forms of exercise that build cardiovascular fitness and maintain or build muscle mass that would be fun and could fit into family and work life. What is the minimum you would advise?

TOPICAL ESSAY

Face Lifts and Frozen Heads

A recent episode of CBS's 48 Hours depicted the lengths people will go to in order to stay young, appear young, or feel young. Titled "Forever Young," the show focused on a wide range of techniques, treatments, and products designed to deal with some visible, physical, psychological, or social aspect of aging. This range included cosmetic surgery, knee replacement, nutrition and exercise programs, and retirement community living. The documentary also depicted some obviously questionable techniques, including "live cell therapy," in which allegedly live cells are injected to rejuvenate all of the major organ systems of the body. There was also a segment on cryogenics—freezing bodies or just heads (for a reduced price) until such time as a cure for the condition that caused the demise of the cryonically suspended person could be found. At that time the person would be "thawed out" and cured of their previously fatal condition. If only the head was frozen, it would be attached to a body created by cloning, using DNA from the frozen head. Based on information from one company that "looks after" the cryonically suspended, the cost of freezing an entire body was about $100,000; for a head only, the cost was about $35,000. It is easy to be skeptical about cryogenics and to question the motivations of people who choose it. To some viewers this technique seems a desperate, ill-fated, and costly attempt at immortality. But what about face lifts, exercise programs, and knee replacements? We can probably draw lines between frozen heads, face lifts, and knee replacement, and we probably pass judgement on people who choose these various options. But we won't all draw the same lines or make the same judgements. Trying to make a distinction between which efforts are reasonable and which are scams assumes that some efforts to fight aging are morally or socially acceptable and some are not. With procedures that seem like scams to us, we ask why anyone would undergo the cost, false hopes, and pain for something so silly. However, some people have the same reaction to face lifts-why go to the expense and pain to maintain a false illusion? We could argue that knee replacement, exercise programs, and retirement communities are reasonable attempts to improve the quality of one's life; cosmetic surgery is often seen as less acceptable because it is based on appearances and vanity; having your head frozen is probably the least acceptable or reasonable "anti-aging" technique because it is based on fear of death and on untested technology. Obviously, there are others who would argue that cosmetic surgery is really no different from exercise and proper nutrition-all are aimed at helping individuals maximize their later years, feel as good as possible both physically and psychologically.

The wide range of techniques available to "fight aging," and the apparent differences among them, can generate interesting discussions. We can talk about which procedures we find reasonable and acceptable in general, and which we find irrational or silly; we can also reflect on which actions we might take personally, and which we would never consider. We can learn a lot from such discussions; you might be surprised at which of your colleagues would have a face lift, who might dye their hair, who exercises to outrun the spectre of aging, and who might even consider cryonic suspension. The more challenging intellectual task is to explore what all of these treatments and techniques have in common. Consider the possibility that the differences among them are merely a matter of degree. In such an exploration, the differences between medically sound and fraudulent procedures, between those chosen for vanity and those chosen for health, are not as significant as the similarities. Face lifts, frozen heads, exercise, and knee replacement are all attempts to "fight" aging. Some attempts seem more graceful, natural, and reasonable. Some are aimed at combating the appearance of age, some are aimed at maximizing health in old age, and some are attempts to live forever. But all are fundamentally "anti-aging" efforts.

Now the interesting question is not why someone chooses a particular procedure—be it hair coloring, face lift, or cryonic suspension. The more basic question is why someone chooses any of these techniques? While there are lots of possible ways to answer this question, we can compare and contrast two different sociological explanations—a symbolic interactionist perspective, and a critical perspective. Both frameworks consider the way in which societal pressures influences individual choices, but they have very different starting points, units of analysis, and focus. In general, a critical perspective questions the ideology and the political and economic agendas underlying a given social arrangement, while a symbolic interactionist framework looks at how people negotiate their social world, including sense of self.

You will recall that symbolic interactionism describes the process whereby social interactions help individuals develop and maintain a sense of who they are; in turn, these interactions reinforce society's values and norms as the members of society reflect back to each other messages about appropriate behavior, roles, and appearances. In our youth-oriented culture, looking "old" can potentially be a disadvantage. Older people are often treated as invisible, or are actively shunned. We discriminate against older people in many ways, so some people may choose to mask the visible signs of aging by staying active and healthy, or through face lifts or hair coloring. In a segment of the 48-Hours "Forever Young" episode, one physician who specializes in face lifts refers to looking old as a "cosmetic disability," and one of his clients said that she was having the surgery done so that she would "fit in." If, as symbolic interactionism suggests, we rely on messages from the larger society to maintain or reinforce our sense of self, taking measures to fight aging may seem a reasonable attempt to avoid being victimized by ageist attitudes and discrimination. Indeed, many of us might argue that people have a right to take any anti-aging action that helps them compete in a youth-oriented job market, keeps them from being stereotyped, or just helps them feel better.

However, a more critical perspective on the measures available to combat aging would suggest that succumbing to such societal pressures only help to reinforce ageist attitudes. Refusing to buy into those attitudes may be one way to change them. For example, " . . . a woman who allows her hair to gray naturally . . . is, in effect, challenging the ageism of a society that tells her she should be ashamed of her age and should make every effort to disguise it" (Gerike 1996, p. 162). In addition, a critical analysis of our attempts to stay forever young would point out that the expense associated with most of these techniques precludes their availability to many groups in society. Only people who have money can have face lifts, freeze their heads, or move to a retirement community. Unequal access to these options means that "staying young" is an opportunity only for middle and upper class people and helps to reinforce social inequalities. Finally, a critical analysis of the '"forever young" phenomenon suggests that there are powerful economic forces at work in creating and sustaining the market for anti-aging products and services. The multi-billion dollar cosmetics industry, and the rapid growth in use of cosmetic surgery (Wolfe 1991) are evidence of a large market for these efforts to fight aging. We know that our ageist society helps to create the demand for such services, but the industries themselves have a stake in perpetuating that demand and may, in fact, be the dominant force creating that market. A critical perspective, therefore, would ask us to more deeply analyze an individual's actions as a product of powerful social and economic institutions, and not simply a matter of personal choice to feel better. So, before we judge people who choose to have their heads frozen or their faces lifted, we need to thoughtfully reflect on the social, economic, and psychological origins of their choices. Social forces have created the problem of ageism, and have created one set of solutions (anti-aging techniques) that are economically beneficial to a number of industries. The economic success of these industries relies on perpetuating the problem so that people will buy the solutions.

Societal norms and attitudes, manifested as individual attitudes and behaviors, have given rise to a very ageist, discriminatory world. Aging individuals sometimes respond to the threat of stereotypes and discrimination by trying to "pass" for middle-aged or younger. A rapidly expanding anti-aging industry serves to create, sustain, and fill the need for techniques and treatments to remain "forever young" in a society where the alternative—growing old gracefully—invites invisibility, stereotyping, and disdain.

Questions for Thought and Reflection

The range of techniques that people employ to "stay young" raises lots of questions. These techniques range from those that we might consider to be reasonable attempts to improve the quality of our lives (e.g., knee replacement) to those considered to be scams (e.g., freezing heads).

1. What do you think is "reasonable"? If your position is that it is OK for people to do whatever they need to feel better, think about why they need to feel better.

2. Who really benefits from the many industries surrounding the preservation of youth (e.g., cosmetic surgery, cosmetics, spas, anti-aging drugs)?

CHAPTER 5

Psychological Perspectives on Aging

by Melissa M. Franks, Institute of Gerontology and Department of Psychology, Wayne State University; Michael Marsiske, Institute on Aging, Departments of Health Policy & Epidemiology and Clinical and Health Psychology, University of Florida; and Benjamin T. Mast, Institute of Gerontology and Department of Psychology, Wayne State University

The elderly person...has a specifically difficult task: At a time of increasing biological vulnerability, demands due to developmental tasks of old age...require strengths and adaptation. Moreover, the occurrence of most of these events is not under human control... On the one hand, autonomy and agency are asked for to deal with these tasks.... On the other hand.... the elderly person must be able to transform agency... into behavioral dependency, delegating control in order to adapt successfully. For the elderly person staying in control and mastering aging is like walking a tightrope.
(M. Baltes, 1996, p. 158)

In this chapter, our goal is to provide non-psychologists with an overview of current concepts, theories, and research in the psychology of aging. Psychological research is one of the most active areas of social and behavioral inquiry into aging; psychologists compose a large segment of the membership of the Gerontological Society of America, the premier aging research organization. Although psychologists, like sociologists or anthropologists or economists, consider themselves social and behavioral scientists, they have some fairly unique ways of both approaching research questions and of conceptualizing the important areas of study in aging. Our goal in this chapter is to provide you with a flavor of both of these issues from the psychologist's point of view. We will begin with a brief discussion of how we define psychology and then turn to the broad theoretical approach within which most psychological gerontologists work.

Defining a Psychological Approach to Aging

What is psychology? **Psychology** is commonly defined as a science of mind and behavior. This definition highlights the interest of many psychologists in studying internal mental processes (such as thinking and feeling) along with their behavioral manifestations. Popular depictions of psychology frequently emphasize clinical psychology, or psychotherapy, which is an applied sub-discipline of psychology. Clinical psychologists use the science of psychology to intervene in the problem behaviors and difficulties of thinking and feeling that some individuals experience. Later in this chapter, we will consider a major area of focus for clinical psychologists: namely, mental health and aging.

The psychology of aging has focused primarily on four major areas: (1) Research on **cognition** seeks to describe and explain the changes in memory, problem solving, and other mental abilities that occur with aging. (2) Research on **self and personality** focuses on understanding how elders' perceptions of themselves and their abilities change with age, and how these changes influence their behaviors in the everyday world. (3) Research on **social relations** seeks to understand the changes in later life in our social relationships, as well as in perceptions of others in our social environment. Finally, (4) the study of **mental health and aging** is an emerging area of applied psychology. Research and practice in this domain focus on losses of cognitive function, the sense of self, and social networks that can lead to pathological psychological functioning, and on helping individuals adapt to these losses.

Psychology, more than microsociological approaches, is concerned with individual behavior. Even when they study the behavior of individuals in groups, psychologists are typically interested in how the group influences individual behavior, when sociologists focus on the inter-personal aspects. With regard to aging, then, psychology is concerned with understanding the factors that lead to, or result from, individual aging. Psychologists ask questions such as, "Who changes in later life, and who doesn't?" or "What are the consequences for the aging individual of having higher levels of internal resources, such as better memory or more self-confidence?"

Before considering how psychologists actually try to answer some of these questions, we will first consider a major theoretical perspective that has emerged in the psychology of aging which structures much of the way we present the field. Specifically, we consider psychological views of successful aging.

Psychological Perspectives on Successful Aging

One way or another, everyone studying processes of aging is implicitly interested in understanding successful aging. Biologists and physicians are interested in understanding why some cells, tissues, and organs decline with age, and why others do not. Economists are interested in understanding why some traits or experiences give rise to better economic outcomes for older adults than others do. Psychologists are interested in understanding why some individuals adapt more easily to the challenges of aging than others. Psychologists give a special meaning to the term successful aging. To psychologists of aging "successful" aging does not mean "optimal" or "problem-free" or "better than average." Instead, **successful aging** implies that individuals are satisfied or contented with their lives; that is, that they have found ways of maximizing the positive in their lives while minimizing the impact of inevitable age-related losses.

One danger that arises when we talk about "successful aging" is that it seems to set up the expectation that there are "norms of success," or that we expect all

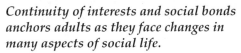

Continuity of interests and social bonds anchors adults as they face changes in many aspects of social life.

individuals to have a positive old age. For some, a concept like "successful aging" seems to set up the expectation that we can have an old age that is without loss or decline (Cole, 1983; Rosenmayr, 1989; Rowe and Kahn, 1998).

Psychologists interested in successful aging have tried to argue that it does not necessarily mean a universally positive, unburdened old age. Baltes and Carstensen (1996) note "A single individual may be physically ill but psychologically strong, feel despair about family but contentment about work, and experience great dissatisfaction but a profound sense of meaning in life" (p. 399). Indeed they argue, *"We cannot predict what any given individual's successful aging will look like until we know what are the domains of functioning and goals that that individual considers important, personally meaningful and in which he or she feels competent"* (p. 399, emphasis original).

In studying successful aging, psychologists generally focus on whether elders experience life satisfaction and well-being. This approach has a long tradition in aging research (Erikson, Erikson, and Kivnich, 1986; Jung 1960) and certainly characterizes much of the contemporary scholarship on the topic (for example, Baltes and Baltes, 1990; Brandtstädter, Wentura, and Greve, 1993; Heckhausen and Schultz, 1995; Marsiske, Lang, Baltes and Baltes, 1996; Ryff 1991; Staudinger, Marsiske, and Baltes, 1995; Whitbourne, 1985). In popular terms, successful aging research can be likened to the cliche, "It's not how old you are, it's how old you feel." Psychologists, thus, focus on the meaning and well-being that individuals maintain in the face of losses to interpersonal ties and physical and cognitive functioning.

Beyond well-being, many successful aging models have focused on trying to understand how individuals maintain adaptive functioning in the face of declining resources (see Marsiske et al. 1996, for a review). How do individu-

Berman   By Jennifer Berman

How we view and evaluate changes that are inevitable with aging is a major influence on psychological adaptation.

als with cognitive or physical loss, for example, go on achieving their critical daily tasks? Baltes and Baltes (1990) have proposed one influential model, which they call **selective optimization with compensation**. That model posits two major processes through which elders can maintain high levels of functioning in critical life domain (See also Freund and Baltes, 1998).

The first process, *selection*, suggests that, across the life span, we cannot do all things. Rather, we must all select from an array of choices the one or two options we will follow; for example, we cannot develop multiple professional careers, and so must pick a particular career path. With age, resources available to the individual (cognitive, physical, social, and economic) may begin to shrink; as a result, the selection pressure on individuals may become even greater. Individuals may need to reduce demands on their time and energy, both physical and cognitive. If we focus our resources on the domains that are most important to us, Baltes and Baltes argue we may be able to maintain adequate functioning longer.

The second process, *compensation*, refers to our ability to find alternative ways of achieving important tasks. If we usually walk to the store, for example, but develop a physical impairment that hinders our doing so, then compensation would involve finding an alternative way of getting to the store: for example, using a walker, using a wheelchair, or having a family member provide transportation assistance. To the extent that older individuals are successful in compensating for losses, they may be able to prolong their period of active life involvement. We will see a good example of compensation later in the section on cognitive functioning.

Throughout the chapter, we focus on the ways that individuals can maintain optimal psychological functioning, despite the variety of losses they may experience with aging. For us, this focus is the unifying theme of psychological research on aging.

In the remainder of this chapter, we will examine the four major areas studied in the psychological aging literature. We will begin with cognitive aging, followed by aging of the self and personality, and then consider how psychologists look at social relations in later life. Finally, we will look at how these three domains (cognition, self, and social relations) may be affected when individuals experience psychological and brain-related changes that would be classified not as "normal aging," but rather as "pathological aging." Specifically, we consider mental health and aging.

Cognitive Aging

Modern experimental psychology is largely based on **cognition,** which is the study of mental functioning, including memory, problem solving, intelligence, attention, speed and perception. In the psychology of aging, no single topic receives more attention than the study of cognition. Our review of psychological aging will pay considerable attention to various aspects of cognitive aging.

Why is cognition so important to the study of aging? First, cognition is an area of psychological functioning that shows some of the most dramatic effects of aging. As we will see, there is substantial evidence that increased age carries both significant risks and benefits in terms of our ability to perform a variety of mental tasks as we age. Second, cognition is assumed to be important to quality of life. Specifically, psychologists believe that declines in the ability to perform cognitive tasks may lead to other problems, such as lessened ability to perform critical tasks of daily living, such as cooking and managing money. Psychologists believe that our mental capabilities—abilities like remembering, solving complex problems, paying attention, or performing other mental tasks—are a key component of our ability to take care of our everyday environment and ourselves. Therefore, studying how such mental capabilities change and what might cause such changes is an important area of investigation (Willis, 1996).

When we use the term cognition, what do we mean? That question has no simple answer; research on cognitive aging has turned out to be a very broad and multidimensional area. Psychologists have used many different research techniques to study cognition. Many of us think about cognition as "what we know," or "how we solve problems," or "mental capacity." In this chapter, we focus on the most important investigations of cognitive and intellectual aging.

What do we know about cognitive aging? Think about what you know and what you believe about mental functioning in later life. Do most people decline or improve their memory and intelligence as they get older? Would older adults perform as well as younger adults on most standard intelligence tests? When older adults do show decline in an area of cognitive functioning, is this decline irreversible? Are age differences in cognitive functioning due solely to changes in the aging brain, or are they due to changes in the social context of aging (for example, changes in mental demands associated with retirement)?

Paul Baltes and his colleagues (Baltes, 1987; Staudinger, Marsiske and Baltes, 1995) have offered one useful summary of what we know about these questions. Based on the research results, they formulate a series of summary "propositions" about life-span developmental psychology, which relate in part to cognitive changes with aging. We summarize each of these five major ideas below with a review of the evidence that supports them. Because of the general interest in memory aging, we also focus specifically on memory as an example of cognitive aging.

The Complexity of Cognition

Cognition is not a single thing. It has many different components (for example, memory, speed, attention, verbal ability), and adult development and aging do not necessarily have the same effect on each component. We might describe the complexity of cognition as being multidimensional and multidirectional.

As already noted, there are many different ways of studying cognition. Researchers taking the **information processing approach** study a wide array of tasks, including individuals' abilities to remember word lists, autobiographical life events, and details of text passages. They also study attention, especially the ability to perform one task while simultaneously doing another. Tests of attention range from how quickly a person pushes buttons on a computer keyboard when a particular image appears on the screen to how quickly a person decides if a given word spoken or shown is a real "word." For a good set of reviews of this literature on information processing and speed see Creak and Salthouse (1992).

Psychologists have also developed a diverse group of experiments using the **psychometric approach**. Experiments developed with this approach include tasks that measure verbal ability, usually the ability to recognize or define words. Other psychometric tasks measure spatial ability, such as the ability to recognize objects when they are rotated, flipped or moved. Test yourself in this kind of spatial ability: compare these symbols: ↗ ↘ ↖ ↑ In order to test reasoning, psychometric researchers ask subjects to look at a series of alphabetic or numeric characters and identify what pattern unifies them. Try this sample reasoning task: In the series c m d c n d c ___ , what would come next? If you guessed o, you did well on this reasoning task, because you realized that there was an alphabetic series m-n-____ embedded between the repeated c's and d's. For a review of these kinds of tasks, see Schaie (1996) or Horn and Hofer (1992).

Several theorists, looking at this wide array of tasks, have argued that they can really be summarized in two broad categories. One category, which has been called "fluid intelligence" (Horn and Hofer, 1992) or the "mechanics of intelligence" (P. B. Baltes, 1993), refers to basic information processes such as attention, memory, reasoning, and speed of responding. A second category, which has been called "crystallized intelligence" (Horn and Hofer, 1992) or "pragmatics of intelligence" (P. B. Baltes, 1993), refers to the kinds of knowledge we accumulate through formal and informal schooling and life experience. This category might include our knowledge of languages; it might also include the professional and personal knowledge and expertise we have accumulated.

The evidence is now fairly clear that when we compare adults of different ages on the two dimensions of **fluid mechanics** and of **crystallized pragmatics**, we get very different aging patterns. Exhibit 5.1 displays a summary figure of these two dimensions of intelligence by age offered by Baltes (1993). The figure suggests that the fluid mechanics of intelligence begin to decline fairly early in adulthood, although the actual age when this change begins remains subject

Exhibit 5.1   *Baltes's Summary of the Two Major Categories of Intellectual and Cognitive Functioning. The fluid mechanics show relatively early loss. The crystallized pragmatics, on the other hand, appoear to increase or remain stable until very late life.*

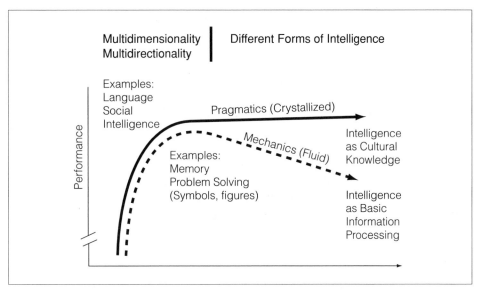

Source: Smith and Marsiske, 1997.

for discussion and debate (Schaie, 1994; 1996).

However, crystallized pragmatics appear to increase or remain stable until individuals are at least in their 60s, on average. When individuals' knowledge levels are tested on vocabulary, basic facts in recent history, and specific job-related knowledge, knowledge does not show a clear decline as subjects age. In fact, the curves suggest there may be "benefits of experience" that lead to enhanced performance into very old age. Baltes and Staudinger (1993), for example, have argued that their measure of wisdom, the kinds of knowledge people have for answering advice questions, shows stable performance into old age. In fact, they found that those performing at the highest levels of wisdom included disproportionately more older adults than younger adults.

The multidimensional nature of cognition makes it difficult to answer questions about change with aging in a simple fashion. Taken together, the research literature suggests the importance of a multidirectional and multidimensional conception of adult cognition and intelligence. No single ability and no single direction (gain, loss, or stability) can summarize all of adult cognition and intelligence.

It should be mentioned, however, that relatively few studies have looked at what happens to the cognitive performance of the "oldest old"—individuals in their 80s, 90s, and older. Because the survival of large numbers of people to these ages is a fairly recent demographic phenomenon, it has been difficult to collect data on such very old individuals. However, two major recent data collections— the Georgia Centenarian Study (Poon, Martin, Clayton, Messner, Noble, and Johnson, 1992) and the Berlin Aging Study (Lindenberger, Mayr, and Kliegl, 1993)—have examined cross-sectional trajectories of cognitive and intellectual functioning in these very old adults. As you might expect, these very old individuals have a relatively high level of physical and sensory impairments. Correspondingly, there appears to be a fairly strong negative, linear age trajectory in their cognitive functioning. At these ages, both fluid and crystallized intelligence show negative effects of aging for all educational and socio-economic groups, but diversity in performance persists even among the oldest old.

Development as Gain/Loss

At all points of the life span, development always consists of both gain and loss. In early life, for example, as we gain more and more ability to engage in logical thinking, we lose the ability to believe in magic. In later life, even as we might lose some ability to do some kinds of mental tasks (for example, some kinds of memory get worse), we might gain others (for example, wisdom or knowledge about the world).

Cognitive gains and losses occur throughout the adult life span. Some theorists have argued that what changes with age is that the relative proportion of losses to gains increases, so that in old age we experience proportionately more losses than gains (Baltes and Baltes, 1990).

Perhaps more interesting, from a cognitive perspective, is how the gains and losses can *interact* with one another in producing everyday cognitive performance. An interesting example comes from the work of Salthouse (1991), who tried to demonstrate a process he called "cognitive compensation" in his work with younger and older expert typists. Salthouse showed that younger and older typists differed significantly in what might be called typing "mechanics;" specifically, on simple measures of typing (motor tapping) speed, older adults were much slower than younger typists were. However, on a measure of overall typing speed, there was no difference between younger and older typists. How did older typists perform at the same level as younger typists, despite age differences in basic tapping speed? It appeared that older adults were looking much farther ahead in their to-be-typed material than younger adults. In other words, older typists may reduce the amount of time spent looking at the to-be-typed material to compensate for their slower tapping speed. This example, which has since been replicated (Bosman, 1993), is a fascinating example of compensation, because it suggests that a gain in one kind of competence (looking farther ahead when you type) can be used to offset a loss in another (typing speed). Expressed more generally, by relying on those systems in which older adults experience gains or stability of performance, they may be able to minimize the everyday effects of losses.

Exhibit 5.2   *Pattern of Older Adults' Training Gains in Intellectual Measures.*
Trained older adults are compared with untrained control subjects. Measures on the left represent measures of what was trained (figural relations). Measures on the right represent untrained abilities. Scores represent performance of older adults following training. Clearly, on measures of the trained ability, older adults show substantial benefits of cognitive training.

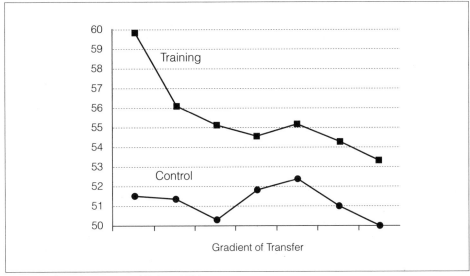

Source: Willis, Blieszner, and Baltes, 1981.

Cognitive Performance is Modifiable

When we measure older adults' cognitive performance, we get a snapshot of how well they are functioning at a moment in time, but it tells us very little of what they are capable. This concept is familiar to all of us if we think about "good days" and "bad days" for taking any type of examination. We do better on a good day, a day on which we feel well, we have minimal anxiety, we feel rested and refreshed, and we believe in our own ability. But if we are tested on a bad day, our performance may not be as good. Moreover, even if our current performance is quite low, it doesn't mean that with a little training and practice we couldn't do much better.

Researchers have demonstrated in several studies that training and practice can substantially enhance the cognitive performance of older adults. Even when individuals show losses or declines in cognitive ability, these losses can be reversed. A large body of research now suggests that cognitive performance can be substantially improved, even in very old adults.

Older adults show improvement in cognitive ability in studies using fluid intelligence measures. In the typical study, adults between 60 and 90 years of age have received tutor- or self-guided instruction in strategies needed to successfully solve fluid intelligence problems. Remarkable consistency across studies has been demonstrated. First, older adults demonstrate significant performance gains on the fluid intelligence tests selected for training and practice. Exhibit 5.2 shows a typical pattern of training gains. These results are particularly impressive because, you may recall, it is the fluid mechanics aspect of intelligence that show the most precipitous age-related losses in cross-sectional research (Baltes and Lindenberger, 1988; Baltes, Sowarka, and Kliegl, 1989; Blackburn, Papalia-Finley, Foye, and Serlin, 1988; Denney, 1984; Schaie and Willis, 1986; Willis 1987; Willis and Schaie, 1986). Second, training gains are maintained for older adults for very long periods, often up to a year or more. Some longitudinal studies now suggest that long-term effects of training may be observed up to seven years after training (Willis and Nesselroade, 1990; Willis and Schaie, 1994). The only major group of older adults who appear to have absolutely no gains from this type of training in fluid intelligence tasks are adults with Alzheimer's type dementia (Baltes, Kühl, and Sowarka, 1992). These results suggest that the potential to modify cognitive performance is very much present in older adults and that age-related declines, when found, are not necessarily irremediable.

Cohort Variations in Cognition

The historical and cultural environments profoundly affect age-trends in cognition where they occur. Think about measuring computer skills among older adults. Today's cohorts of older adults might not be expected to perform well, on average, on many computer tasks because computers were not a part of their lives. Personal computers weren't even available throughout much of their adulthood. In contrast, consider today's younger adults, for whom computers are a part of both work and school. Some younger adults have been exposed to computers practically from birth. When these individuals are older, we will probably no longer be able to say, "Older adults might not be expected to perform well, on average, on many computer tasks." In other words, even if older adults today don't perform well on computer tasks, this finding probably has less to do with aging than it does with cohort-related historical opportunities to use computers.

Perhaps the preeminent ongoing data collection in cognitive and intellectual aging is the Seattle Longitudinal Study, which has been collecting data on some individuals since 1956 (Schaie, 1996). One key feature of the Seattle Longitudinal Study is that it includes many different birth cohorts. This feature lets us ask cohort-related questions such as, "How does the intelligence of people born in the 1920s differ from that of people born in the 1930s?" To answer this question, we could look at people born in the 1920s when they are in their 50s (in the 1970s) and compare their performance with the 1930s birth cohort when those cohort members are in their 50s (1980s).

Using this kind of analysis, a cohort-sequential design (see discussion in Chapter 2), Schaie has reported data like those shown in Exhibit 5.3. What this figure shows is that, for at least three abilities (inductive reasoning, verbal mean-

Exhibit 5.3 *Cohort Trends in Intellectual Functioning. Throughout the twentieth century later-born cohorts show substantial advantages on many measures of intellectual ability, although two abilities (number of artihmetic ability and word fluency) actually show some decline throughout the same periodl*

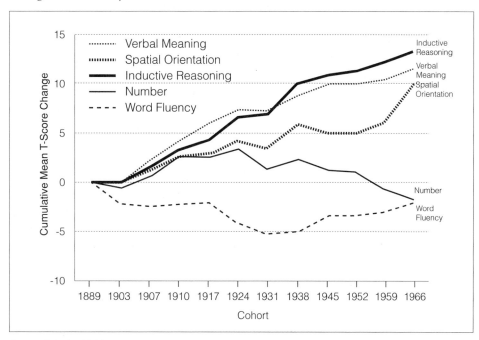

Source: Schaie, 1994

ing, and spatial orientation), there have been sizable positive cohort trends in most aspects of intellectual performance. That is, cohorts born more recently perform better on most of these dimensions of intelligence. For number skills and word fluency, on the other hand, the cohort trends are downward. These findings are of substantial interest to sociologists. They suggest that broad sociocultural changes associated with the progression of the twentieth century have resulted in substantial intellectual performance gains in many cognitive abilities. Reasoning and spatial abilities, as well as verbal abilities, appear to have shown dramatic improvements. It is interesting to speculate on the role of increased participation in formal education, exposure to television and print media, health, or educational quality in producing these trends. In contrast, the ability to perform arithmetic problems and the ability to generate speech (which is what the verbal fluency test measures) appear to have declined. Again, we can only speculate on what kinds of influences, such as increased reliance on calculators, may be responsible. These data underscore the fact that aging itself is a "moving target." Differences between younger and older adults that exist today may have a lot to do with differences in life opportunities that the two age cohorts have encountered, and little to do with actual aging.

Everyday Cognition: The Role of Context

The cognitive abilities we use vary from person to person, depending on the contexts we inhabit. Think about an air traffic controller. A person in this profession will need to develop and enhance such abilities as quick visual searches, speedy decision making, and focused attention. Now, contrast the abilities used by a professional writer. For this person, strong verbal abilities and vocabulary, and the ability to develop logical arguments, are much more important. In other words, our profile of cognitive strengths and weaknesses probably adapts to the kind of life we lead. If we are looking to understand why older adults might perform better than younger adults on some cognitive tasks but not on others, we should probably look at differences in the kinds of cognitive tasks they confront in their daily lives. We need to think about which skills they use and which skills they don't.

How do older adults deal with the everyday consequences of age-related cognitive changes? One way of interpreting the mechanics/pragmatics theory of intelligence is that, on those daily living tasks in which individuals had high levels of experience and knowledge, they may have developed high levels of pragmatically relevant knowledge, supporting continued high-level functioning.

To investigate this topic, several researchers have developed measures of "everyday cognition" or "practical problem solving," which attempt to assess the cognitive components of everyday task performance. Cornelius and Caspi (1987), for example, asked adults how they would deal with a wide variety of everyday interpersonal dilemmas, such as resolving conflicts within the family or with coworkers. Denney and her colleagues (Denney and Pearce, 1989) asked how individuals might solve a variety of instrumental (for example, getting one's lawn mowed when one has a heart condition and no money) and social (such as adjusting to widowhood) problems. Willis, Marsiske and their colleagues (Allaire and Marsiske, 1999; Diehl, Willis, and Schaie, 1995; Marsiske and Willis, 1995; Willis, 1996) presented older adults with everyday printed materials, such as medication labels or nutrition charts. In another test, they asked individuals to solve common everyday problems, such as finding the right medication dosage for a child or cutting a recipe in half.

Evidence for the effects of aging on everyday cognition has been quite varied. In studies that measure everyday information use and social strategy use (Corneluis and Caspi, 1987; Demming and Pressey, 1957; Denney, 1984; Gardner and Monge, 1977; Heidrich and Denney, 1994), research has tended to support the prediction of mechanics/pragmatics theory. On everyday information and social strategy, older adults typically performing as well as, or better than, younger adults do.

A second stream of research on everyday cognition has tried to look more specifically at "basic cognitive competence" with critical tasks of daily living (such as food preparation, medication use, and housekeeping; for example, Morrell, Park, and Poon, 1990; Willis, 1991). These studies emphasize adults' abilities to adapt to unexpected but potentially relevant life situations that require adaptation to new challenges (such as dealing with widowhood or poor weather; see Denney and Pearce, 1989). In research on these kinds of tasks, where individuals have relatively little prior knowledge and experience on which to draw, there has been much less evidence of preserved functioning in later life, with declines resembling those seen for fluid intelligence. However, Willis, Jay, Diehl, and Marsiske (1992) found that even when an average decline is present, a high proportion of older adults show stable performance on everyday cognitive tasks into very old age. Changes in cognition vary from individual to individual.

A Focus on Memory

Aspects of memory have been included in the above discussion. However, memory as a topic holds particular interest for individuals and practitioners, due to anxieties about loss of functioning in this area. Both loss of memory associated with diseases, such as Alzheimer's disease, and what could be considered "normal" changes in memory with aging have been the subject of considerable research interest (Smith, 1996). Anyone over 50 who can't locate their keys may start to wonder whether they are experiencing age-related changes in memory.

Memory is itself a complex area of study. Scientists have broken memory up into different abilities. **Primary memory** is the ability to remember things in the immediate term; for example, being able to recall a list of words or numbers just read to you. **Secondary memory** is the ability to remember events or knowledge acquired at somewhat prior time. **Prospective memory** is the ability to remember to do certain things in the future, such as taking medications at specified times. To be able to remember, the individual must be able to perceive the stimulus, bring it to conscious attention, be able to effectively encode it into long-term storage and retrieve it when called upon to do so (Craik, 1977). Psychologists have long conducted studies of these various aspects of memory in order to discover whether there are aging-related changes to memory processes or performance. Research debunks some "common sense" ideas regarding memory, such as easy recollection by older adults of events many years earlier while forgetting what happened yesterday as "normal" patterns of aging memory changes (Craik, 1977).

Early studies of primary memory, recalling something that was still "in mind," showed minimal age differences in performance (Craik, 1977). Practice improved the performance of younger subjects more than that of older subjects in recalling items in memory span tests, where subjects are asked to recall a list of words, numbers or objects presented to them. Older persons did less well if the items had to be repeated in another order (e.g., backward) or if there was a longer list of items, beyond the capacity of primary memory (Craik, 1977). The concept of **working memory**, the aspect of memory involved in temporary storage and organizing of material being processed, has been identified as a limited resource among older adults, contributing to age-related decrements in some types of memory performance (Hultsch and Dixon, 1990; Smith, 1997). Like a computer, if the aging individual's ability to take in and process new information is limited, this will effectively limit the complexity of cognitive operations that can be performed.

Specific training in memory skills can enhance performance of older adults on cognitive tests like these. (See Baltes and Kliegl, 1992; Kliegl, Smith, and Baltes, 1990; see Verhaeghen, Marcoen, and Goosens, 1992 for a review.) Older adults show dramatic improvements in memory performance as a function of training, although long-term effects of memory training seem to be less durable than those seen with fluid intelligence (Anschutz, Camp, Markley, and Kramer, 1987; Scogin and Bienias, 1988). Individuals who practice particular types of memory skills (e.g., playing chess, remembering names with faces) tend to maintain their capacity for this type of memory as they age (Hultsch and Dixon, 1990), but the improvement does not generalize to remembering other types of information.

Older adults in most classic studies of secondary memory perform less well than do younger adults in recalling either verbal information or visual images (Craik, 1977). The amount of age decline in performance is sometimes modest. Performance of older individuals was better in most studies if lists of verbal items were all from one conceptual domain (e.g., all types of animals or fruits) and if material was familiar to them. Recalling items without cues was more difficult than simply being able to recognize items that had been presented some time before. With secondary memory lessened, ability to organize information prior to storing it is responsible for lower performance on average with advanced age (Craik, 1977). Building skills with verbal or visual "mediators" to assist in organizing the material in some way improves performance of older adults significantly. Better learning and recollection can be prompted with appropriate stimuli to encourage active acquisition of the information being presented (Craik, 1977).

In the past two decades research has focused on refining an understanding of memory identifying individual differences and using memory tests that are more varied and "realistic." It was expected that older adults would perform better on reality-based memory tasks, but this has been disproved by most research (Hultsch and Dixon, 1990). Moving beyond tests that focused on recall of words or digits, memory studies are developing increasingly refined approaches to examining recall and recognition of actions, spatial relationships and faces as well as lists of words or numbers. Attention to individual differences in factors such as verbal ability and to other factors, such as health or education, that may explain age differences in some memory tasks clarifies the understanding of memory processes (Hultsch and Dixon, 1990; Smith, 1997).

Some recent research supports the notion that prospective memory is actually better in older adults than in young adults (Rendell and Thomson, 1999) utilizing a set of "real life" tasks. But experts in memory caution against drawing conclusions prematurely, since researchers continue to refine both their research methods and their understanding of the complex processes that constitute human memory (Smith, 1997).

Cognition: Summary

By way of summary, let us return to the questions we asked you to think about in the beginning of this section. Do most people decline, or improve, their memory and intelligence as they get older? The answer seems to be "both." It is impossible to make a single summary statement about the nature of cognitive aging. Some functions do seem to get worse, but others seem to remain stable or improve.

Would older adults perform as well as younger adults on most standard intelligence tests? On some tests the answer is yes; on other tests, younger adults performed better. Tests of knowledge and experience show much greater advantages for older adults than tests of basic information processing.

When older adults do show decline in an area of cognitive functioning, is this decline irreversible? As the work on modification of cognitive performance shows, we can substantially enhance the performance of older adults through a wide variety of training and practice interventions.

Are age differences in cognitive functioning due solely to changes in the aging brain, or are they due to changes in the social context of aging (for example, changes in mental demands associated with retirement)? Cohort-related studies and studies on "everyday cognition" suggest that the historical era in which we are born and the contexts in which we live powerfully shape the kinds of cognitive tasks we become specialized to do.

Aging of the Self and Personality

Let's do another thought exercise to get at your initial ideas about self and personality. Think about how you would answer the following questions: What is the "self," and how does it relate to personality? Does our personality change as we age, or does it remain stable? Do we, for example, become more "set in our ways," or do we become more mature, content, or wise? What kinds of factors contribute to change and stability in personality?

Let's begin with some definitions. What is **personality**? In general, we tend to think of it as enduring, or stable, ways of behaving and interpreting or responding to situations. We express it in language like "Bob is always so neurotic" or "Martha is a real optimist!" Personality is one manifestation of the broader self-system each of us constructs.

The **self**—a lofty term—encompasses all the beliefs, thoughts, and emotions that come to organize our identities and behaviors. In its simplest form, the self is what we think of when we answer the question "Who am I?" Current views of selfhood portray the self as a multidimensional and dynamic entity, actively involved in psychological and social processes (see review by Markus and Wurf, 1987). The self is most often conceptualized as a system of knowledge structures in which one's experiences are organized. These knowledge structures have been variously labeled as self-schemas (Markus, 1977), as salient identities (Stryker, 1986), or core conceptions (Gergen, 1977). Contained in these knowledge structures are mental representations of what we think about, care about, and spend time and energy on (see review by Markus and Herzog, 1991; Herzog and Markus, 1999) in domains that are important to us, such as health, family, work, or independence. In other words, our various schemas form the core of our self-concept, or what we have come to hold as essential about ourselves.

Personality, then, is one component of the broader self system. The self encompasses all that individuals hold to be true about themselves. It includes sociodemographic descriptors ("I am a woman" or "I am African American"), social role attributes ("I am a mother" or "I am a teacher"), interpersonal attributes ("I am charitable" or "I am generous"), interests and activities ("I like to bowl" or "I like to play basketball"), and personality characteristics ("I am extroverted" or "I am flexible").

Although personality is only one component of the self system, it is the component that has been most widely measured and studied by psychologists throughout this century. Consequently, we begin our consideration of this research with a review of work on personality. We then turn our attention to other ways of measuring self-related functioning. Finally, we revisit the concept of "successful aging" and ask how individuals may defend and modify their beliefs about themselves and their lives in order to maintain high levels of personal satisfaction and well-being.

Personality

Classic psychoanalytic conceptions of adult personality remain a strong anchor for contemporary research on self and personality aging. It is this area of psychology, along with research on mental health and aging, that most conforms to public conceptions of what the study of psychology is all about. Indeed, much of the early work on adult personality development stems from the work of Sigmund Freud. More recently, another psychoanalytic conception of adult personality development has received wide attention, that of Erik Erikson. We highlight Erikson here because he is most widely studied and cited in contemporary psychology, though many other important theorists have done work in this area, including Jung, Loevinger, and Levinson.

Erikson highlighted a series of developmental issues that individuals needed to deal with as they moved through the life course. The resolution of each issue contributes to the reorganization and further development of self and personality. Erikson viewed the first major developmental issue confronted in adulthood as having to do with our roles in the lives of others—especially our children and succeeding generations. He termed the next major developmen-

Exhibit 5.4 *Major Personality Dimensions Identified by the NEO-PI Personality Inventory. "Facets" describe various components of each personality trait.*

Trait	Facets
Neuroticism	Anxiety, hostility, self-consciousness, depression, impulsiveness, vulnerability
Extraversion	Warmth, gregariousness, assertiveness, activity, excitement seeking, positive emotions
Openness to experience	Fantasy, aesthetics, openness to action openness to ideas, open to feelings, open to values
Agreeableness	Trust, straightforwardness, altruism, compliance, modesty, tender-mindedness
Conscientiousness	Competence, dutifulness, order, achievement, striving, self-discipline, deliberation

Source: Costa and McCrae, 1988.

tal crisis of midlife "generativity versus stagnation," in which individuals resolve for themselves what the roles of things like caring, generosity, or teaching are in their lives. The last major issue individuals confront in their lives, according to Erikson, is "integrity versus despair." Erikson postulated that as individuals approach the end of their lives, they engage in a process of life review. In this process, they reexamine the story of their lives and determine how well all the pieces fit together (integrity) and how much of their lives seems meaningless or without purpose (despair).

The core question in the ego approach to personality in Erikson's work is how individuals, by having more and more life experiences, might profit from these experiences. Erikson asserts that by resolving major "crises," people move their personality development in the positive direction of increased maturity, wisdom, acceptance, and contentment.

Although much of the work from the psychoanalytic perspective has been concerned with the conditions under which positive personality development might occur in later life, research in recent decades has focused much more on measuring personality and tracing its normal developmental pattern in adults. This approach attempts to assign each person a "score" on various personality dimensions. The question then becomes how much individuals differ on each personality dimension being studied.

Psychoanalytically based theories of personality emphasize personality change, but empirical studies using personality tests have overwhelmingly found support for stability of personality. There is very little empirical evidence for systematic change or "growth" of personality with advanced age.

Exhibit 5.5   *Seven-year Longitudinal Change in the "Big Five" Personality Dimensions. Adult personality shows considerable stability.*

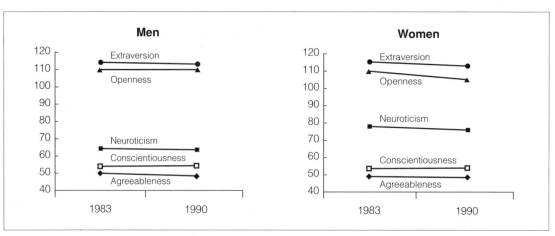

Data Source: Costa and McCrae, 1988.

Throughout much of the twentieth century, many different personality inventories, or paper-and-pencil tests, have been developed (Schaie and Willis, 1996). Across these many inventories, there seems to be substantial evidence that five major dimensions of personality, "the Big Five," can be identified in many different tests. Exhibit 5.4 presents a summary of this "Big Five," as described by Costa and McCrae, (1988).

Despite many different approaches to testing and measuring personality, the consistent conclusion emerges that substantial continuity and relatively little change characterize adult personality development. Exhibit 5.5 summarizes the results of one seven-year longitudinal study conducted on a sample of adults aged 19 to 87 (Costa and McCrae, 1988). Not only has personality stability been reported over intervals of three to six years (Costa and McCrae, 1988); even studies that looked at self-reported personality data from 20- and 45-year intervals have found significant stability (Conley, 1985; Finn 1986; Hann, Millsap, and Hartka, 1986). In addition, over several decades and using many different personality measures, cross-sectional studies comparing younger and older adults have found very little personality difference between age groups. This is a very consistent result (for example, Culligan, Osborne, Swenson, and Offord, 1983; Schaie and Parham, 1976; Siegler, George, and Okun, 1979; Swenson, Pearson, and Osborne, 1973).

The Self

If personality is one component of the self, what kinds of changes might be expected for self-related functioning with advancing age? Do studies of self-con-

Exhibit 5.6   *Schematic Representation of the Self. The self has many inputs and outputs, and includes current, past, and future components.*

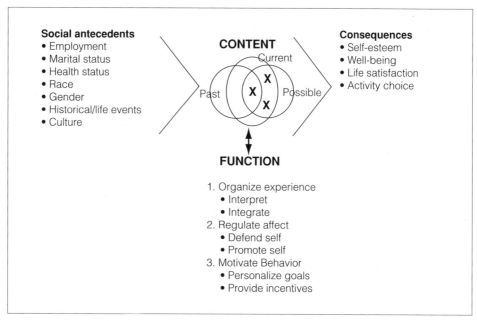

Source: Markus and Herzog, 1991.

cept (which is one common way in which "self" has been measured and studied) show the same stability as personality? Or are measures of the self, which are more complex and qualitative than personality measures, more sensitive to the kinds of "maturity" and "integrity" proposed by the ego theorists?

Efforts to capture the essence of the self have varied in nature and in scope. Some research has relied on individuals to generate self-descriptions in response to such questions as "Tell me about yourself" or "Who am I?" Other research has narrowed the range of options in describing the self by providing respondents a series of potential self-characteristics and having them indicate those that ring true about themselves. Still other work has used some combination and/or variation of these two approaches. For this reason, it is often difficult to summarize or compare research on the self, because how the question is constructed greatly influences how the self is defined and described.

Based on the research, it is clear that the self is made up not only of who we are today, but also of who we once were and who we may become (Markus and Herzog, 1991). Exhibit 5.6 shows a schematic illustration of how we might depict the self. As Exhibit 5.6 shows, the self has both content (past, present, future), and functions (which we will discuss in more detail). Viewing the self across the life course makes it apparent that the self is both stable and changing (Markus and Herzog, 1991). This concept may at first seem contradictory or meaningless. How can the self be stable, but change? As a generalization, the aspects of self we hold most dear can remain constant while at the same time the way we think about them is evolving. Research on the future of the self can illustrate this stable yet changing nature.

Age Trends in Possible Selves

The vision of the self-to-be in the future is most commonly referred to as the **possible self** (Markus and Nurius, 1986). The possible self includes both those aspects of self one hopes to achieve and to incorporate into the self-system and aspects of self one fears attaining. As an example, in a study of older adults' possible selves, the state of one's health was often reported as both a hoped-for and a feared aspect of the self to come (Hooker and Kaus, 1992).

In a cross-sectional study of adults' possible selves, Cross and Markus (1991) found that older adults (aged 60 years and older) generated significantly fewer possible future selves, both those hoped for and those feared, than did younger adults (three groups aged 18-24 years, 25-39 years, and 40-59 years). In fact, the average number of possible selves offered by these four age groups was found to decrease progressively as age increased. The average 18- to 24-year-old hoped for 7.6 important selves in the future, compared with 5.7 hoped-for selves of the average 60-plus adult.

Besides differences in the number of hoped-for selves, the content of the selves also differed across age groups. In regard to the hoped-for selves of the youngest two groups, their responses reflected their expectations of moving into new roles such as marriage and career. For the older two groups, responses focused on hopes for the present self in the future, and less on acquiring new roles or new selves. For example, an 18-year-old may respond by hoping to marry a wealthy executive, whereas a 70-year-old may respond by hoping to be a loving grandparent.

The feared selves of individuals across all age groups contained a common theme of feared physical alterations. This type of response was proportionally highest for the oldest respondents. Generally speaking, the feared selves of the younger groups focused on personal failures or fears that their own lives might be full of disappointment. In the older groups, the fears turned away from the personal to reflect fear of changes thought to accompany the later years of life, such as widowhood and financial insecurity.

Possible selves may be important in the selection and revision of goals, which are central to theories of successful aging (Markus and Herzog, 1991). What we hope to become in the future, as well as what we fear becoming, may influence our current goals and related behaviors in two ways. First, the future component of the self-system is believed to operate as a motivating force guiding and directing the current self toward hoped-for selves and away from feared selves. As an example, in the study by Hooker and Kaus (1992), those older adults for whom health was an important hoped-for or feared self reported engaging in more health-related behaviors and provided more detailed and specific examples of these behaviors than did those older adults for whom health was not such an important or central feature of the future self. Thus, individuals who hold a healthy possible self are more attentive to health-related information and are more likely to take good care of themselves through diet and exercise now in order to achieve the healthy self in the future (or to avoid the unhealthy self).

A second way in which possible selves can contribute to successful aging is that the hoped-for or feared possible selves may serve as guideposts for actions and priorities selected by the current self. That is to say, the consequences of any current experience will be evaluated based on how that experience affects the outcomes hoped for in the future. For example, not contributing to an employer's retirement benefit plan would be more inconsistent with the self of a person hoping for financial security in older age than for someone who is unconcerned with life following their paid work career.

Successful Aging: The Resilient Self and Personality

We have already suggested that a key outcome studied by psychological investigators of successful aging is "well-being" or "life satisfaction" or "sense of meaning." What most contemporary psychologists have come to realize, however, is that the self and personality are themselves adaptive, flexible mechanisms that continuously work to ensure and enhance these levels of well-being.

In this section, we will attempt to tie together several themes from our review of self and personality aging. On the one hand, older adults, both when compared with younger adults and when compared with their own earlier personality ratings (even several decades earlier), demonstrate substantial personality stability. On the other hand, as people reconstruct their views of the future and what it holds, fairly dramatic age-related changes emerge, including a reduction in possible selves and an increase in feared selves, especially in the health domain. How can personality, one component of the self, remain stable when the whole self-system is dynamic?

The answer seems to be that individuals actually reconstruct and change their self-concepts in order to ensure stability of well-being, personality and other related constructs, such as how "in control" of their lives they feel (see Lachman, Ziff and Spiro, 1994 for a review). In other cases, they seem to use new ways of ensuring that they can protect and maintain their existing self-concepts. Let's consider each of these ideas.

Flexible Goal Adjustment: Continuity and Change in the Self

Several theorists (for example, Brandtstädter et al. 1993; Heckhausen and Schulz, 1995; Whitbourne, 1985) have proposed that as individuals are confronted with challenges to their self-concept they find ways of modifying their goals. The age-related reduction in possible selves is one example (Markus and Herzog, 1991). These theorists argue that as we get older we have reduced resources to support our efforts. It becomes harder and harder to balance multiple roles (our hobbies, jobs, family relationships, physical activities, and so on). To avoid exhaustion and overload, one logical solution is to reduce the number of domains in which we are active (e.g., retire or give up a club membership). You may recall that such selection of activity is a core component of the Baltes and Baltes model of successful aging.

Unfortunately, simply giving up areas of activity can be depressing. If we have to give up activities, we may become depressed by the losses we are confronting. One way of protecting against the negative consequences of such giving up is to reconceptualize what is important to us, to say to ourselves, in effect, "Oh well, this goal wasn't so important to me after all."

It is this process of reevaluating our goals—maintaining some and relegating others to our "less important pile"—that researchers of aging discuss under various labels, such as **flexible goal adjustment** (Brandtstädter, Wentura, and Greve, 1993) or **secondary control** (Heckhausen and Schulz, 1995; Schulz and Heckhausen, 1996). The work of Brandstadter, and that of Heckhausen and Schulz, suggests that as we age we become increasingly likely to let go of some goals and increasingly willing to modify and reduce our expectations. Consider an aging marathon runner whose self-concept has always included something like "I am a winning marathon runner." Although the runner may have won many marathons, as he or she ages it is unlikely that marathon wins will always continue. At this point, if the runner engages in secondary control strategies (strategies to reprioritize and reevaluate the importance of goals), the runner's goal might change from "I want to win marathons" to "I want to compete in marathons," or "I want to do well for my age group in a marathon," or "I want to win seniors' marathons." In all three cases, the goal has been transformed to minimize threats to well-being and self-esteem.

The reduction in the number of possible selves may be another manifestation of this kind of goal selection. When we are young, having many different possible selves may be positive and adaptive, because it helps us chart future courses of action and protects well-being if some pathways become blocked. Consider the student who flunks out of medical school. If the student has no other possible selves, this could be a devastating—even irrecoverable—loss. The more selves that might be potentially available, the more likely the student can quickly figure out an alternative pathway to pursue. In contrast, too many possible selves may be exhausting and demoralizing to an older adult confronting an accumulation of age-related physical, cognitive, and social losses. In this case, reducing the number of possible selves, by reducing the number of demands and expectations the elder places on himself or herself, may be more adaptive.

At the same time, it is important not to overstate how much older adults might adjust and modify their goals and possible selves. In fact, the perspective that older adults strive to preserve important aspects of the self guides much of the research on the aging self. In terms of selective optimization with compensation, if we have opted to select or retain a life domain as important—say, a personally important hobby, such as woodworking—we need to find ways to remain satisfied and content with our performance in that domain, even if our objective performance declines. The person for whom work is a very important part of the self-concept will need to find outlets (such as volunteer activities) for their productive energies after retirement. The person for whom parenthood is an important part of the self-concept will need to find outlets (pets, nieces and nephews, grandchildren) in the empty-nest phase.

The current self plays a selective role in choosing to adopt and elaborate past and possible selves that are consistent with or support desired self-concepts, and to discard or modify those that are inconsistent. In this way, the entire self-system is instrumental in engineering a sense of continuity and change across the life course. For this reason, Markus and Herzog (1991) have suggested that the self is the manager of the adaptive processes by which we maintain high levels of well-being and personal meaning into very old age.

Finding the "Right" Basis for Evaluating Ourselves

Another major mechanism that has been proposed is the use of shifting standards of comparison in self-evaluation. At the core of this idea is classical social psychological research by Festinger (1954), Wood (1989), and Taylor and Lobel (1989), which suggests that we evaluate ourselves based on comparisons with others in our environment. The choice of whom we evaluate ourselves against thus becomes important. If we want to motivate ourselves to do better, Taylor and Lobel have argued we will look for those who are better off and set them as the standard **(upward social comparisons)**. On the other hand, if we are feeling threatened or vulnerable, we will tend to compare ourselves with those who are less well off, making ourselves look better by comparison. These **downward social comparisons**, it has been argued, should increase in frequency with age—especially when individuals are evaluating their physical, cognitive, or social status.

Several studies have supported the idea that older adults increasingly use these downward social comparisons. Heidrich and Ryff (1991), for example, asked two samples of older women to describe the comparison processes they used when thinking about their health. Poorer physical health status was linked to more frequent social comparisons. Women in the worst health who used more downward (self-enhancing) social comparisons had low levels of depression, high perceptions of personal growth, and positive relations with other. Their mental health levels were comparable to women in good health! In other words, even for very unhealthy women, downward social comparisons appeared to be quite protective of their mental health.

Taken together, the evidence suggests that the apparent stability of personality and the self-system that has been reported in many studies may not be a passive outcome. Instead the evidence shows that people achieve stable personalities through an active and continuous reconstruction of self-perceptions based on a dynamic underlying system of adaptive mechanisms designed to maintain the sense of well-being and personal integrity.

Self and Personality: Summary

What is the "self," and how does it relate to personality? As we have suggested, the self is a multifaceted description of a person, including past, present, and future components. Personality is one component of the self and reflects our stable and enduring presentations of ourselves to the world.

Does our personality change as we age, or does it remain stable? Do we, for example, become more "set in our ways," or do we become more mature, content, or wise? Psychoanalytically based theories have argued for the movement of adult personality, if we successfully resolve developmental crises, in the direction of wisdom and maturity. Research on personality using paper-and-pencil tests, however, provides substantial evidence for stability.

What kinds of factors contribute to change and stability in personality? In this section, we have reviewed a variety of mechanisms by which individuals achieve both continuity and change in the self, including flexible goal adjustments and changes in the social comparison referents by which people evaluate themselves.

Psychological Perspectives on Social Relations

Because we are social beings, it is not surprising that social scientists would be keenly interested in human social interaction. Understanding adult social interaction is especially compelling given that, unlike the necessity of social contact for survival in the early years of life, social interaction in adulthood and late life is to a large extent voluntary. In light of the frequency with which adults engage one another socially and the demonstrated benefits of social integration to health and well-being (for example, Berkman and Syme, 1979), the study of **social relations** represents an intersection of social science theory and research. This area is the region of greatest overlap with sociology, but psychology focuses its attention much more on individual perceptions of network partners and the quality of social relationships.

In this section, we explore psychological theory and research on the processes whereby social relations can foster older adults' successful adaptation to and compensation for the challenges of the aging mind and body. We first review psychological research pertaining to the social network composition of older adults. We then describe work investigating one way in which social relations benefit other domains of successful aging: physical and cognitive well-being. We finish this section with a discussion of social psychological research concerning the consequences for well-being of negative aspects of social relations.

Let us begin once again with a few guiding questions. What is unique to psychology about the study of social relations? Do the social networks of older adults differ from those of younger adults? How do our social relationships facilitate successful aging? How can social relations interfere with successful aging?

Social Networks of Older Adults

Psychologists, as well as other social scientists, have paid a great deal of attention to individuals' social networks. This interest in social ties and interactions focuses on determining who the important people in our lives are and what makes them so important to us. Much of the work examining social networks has explored the ways in which individuals help one another in times of need and what such help means to the physical and psychological functioning of individuals experiencing stress in their lives (see review by Cohen and Willis, 1985).

Sometimes the structure of a person's social relations is measured by simply tallying the number of close ties, such as whether or not the person is married, the number of children (if any) the person has, and the number of other close family and friends. Structural ties can also include attendance at or membership in civic or religious organizations. In addition to determining the number of close ties, psychologists are often interested in assessing the **psychological closeness** of network members to individuals. In other words, who are the important people in your life, and how close do you feel to them?

One frequently used instrument for measuring closeness of network members is the **social convoy model** (Antonucci and Akiyama, 1987; Kahn and Antonucci, 1980). The term convoy reflects the notion that our networks comprise people we are close to and who travel with us through part or all of our lives. The convoy model is illustrated in Exhibit 5.7.

In this model, the innermost circle represents the person or persons deemed so important that you could not imagine life without them. The middle circle includes other close network members who are important to you. The outer circle is for others who are less close but still important in your network. Together they provide an estimate of the number of ties in your network as well as their relative closeness.

When the number of important network members is compared for younger and older adults, most research indicates that older adults report fewer important others overall than do younger adults. A recent review of the literature on social relations in late life (Lang and Carstensen, 1994) summarizes the findings on the size of individuals' social networks across several studies. This compilation indicates that older adults generally report a total of 5 to 15 important others, whereas younger adults generally report between 15 and 35. This comparison is particularly striking in that the high end of the range for older adults is equal to the low end for younger adults.

Research on social networks of older adults further suggests that their net-

Exhibit 5.7   *Social Network Measurement with the Convoy Circle Diagram.*
Psychologists are interested not only in whom older adults include in their networks, but also in how close they feel to these individuals.

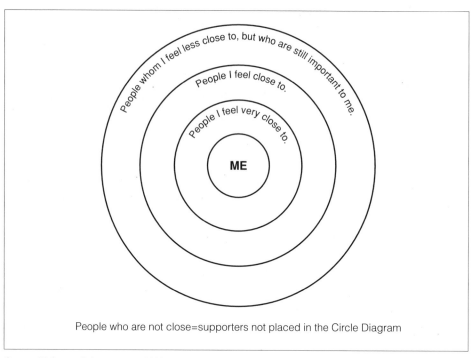

People who are not close=supporters not placed in the Circle Diagram

Source: Kahn and Antonucci, 1980.

works show a high concentration of very important others. Antonucci and Akiyama (1987) examined social network characteristics and psychological closeness in a national sample of adults aged 50 and older. For these older adults, the average size of the network was 8.9, consisting of 3.5 very close intimates, another 3.5 close ties, and an additional 1.9 less close members. A high proportion of the social contacts reported to be important across all age groups consists of family ties, and most of the individuals deemed close or very close are family members (see review by Antonucci and Akiyama, 1995).

One line of psychological research has put forth a potential explanation for the tendency of network structure to reflect a higher proportion of very close ties as we age. Known as **socioemotional selectivity theory** (Carstensen, 1992; 1993), this approach suggests that the move toward smaller networks consisting primarily of the closest ties does not simply reflect the loss of important others through normative transitions such as bereavement or retirement, but is driven by the specific needs of older adults.

According to this theory, our needs for social contact change as we grow older. In earlier periods of life, we desire and seek social contact to meet information-seeking goals. To this end, a broad and more diverse social network affords the greatest opportunity for access to novel information and experiences. In late life, however, we desire and seek social contacts to meet emotional regulatory goals. As we grow older, we become less interested in seeking novel experiences, preferring to engage in established relationships known to provide enjoyment and satisfaction. This selection of social contacts is closely aligned with the theory of selective optimization with compensation, in that it is guided by a desire to maximize time spent in self-affirming and emotionally rewarding interactions.

Social Relations as a Basis for Successful Aging

How can social partners help us select the domains in which we will remain active, and how can they help us compensate for personal losses so that we can continue critical everyday tasks? Many older adults face limitations as a result of declining health and most are assisted by family and friends to maintain their independence. The contributions of others can also have an important influence on our performance on everyday cognitive problems, because individuals confront most of life's difficulties not by acting, or reacting, alone, but by seeking out information, advice, and support from trusted others. One important aspect of social relations, that involving informal caregiving, will be dealt with in a later chapter on families, since it is an area where the work of many disciplines intersects. Other positive and negative aspects of social relations frequently addressed in psychological research on aging are described below.

Social Cognitive Interactions

A new area of research demonstrating the beneficial effects of social interactions for successful aging is referred to in the psychological aging literature as interactive minds (Baltes and Staudinger, 1996; Staudinger and Baltes, 1996) or **collaborative cognition** (Dixon and Gould, 1996). This work is based on the recognition that many cognitive tasks are not completed by a single individual in isolation. Rather, in the real world, individuals process information, recall past events, and make decisions in the company of and with the assistance of others. Think about a husband who loses his keys. In many families, he and his wife will work together, each calling out where they last remembered seeing the keys, trying to help one another find them.

One study of social interaction and cognition has examined the facilitative effects of interacting with others on wisdom and wisdom-related tasks (Staudinger and Baltes, 1996). Wisdom and wisdom-related performance, you may recall, refer to the kinds of knowledge individuals use when they give important life advice to others. The study basically asked the question, "Can others help us to be wiser than we are on our own?" To answer this question, they compared how people performed on standard, solitary versions of the wis-

Convoys of social support, including enduring bonds, contribute to well-being among older adults.

dom task with how they performed under a variety of social conditions. Every person tested was asked to come to the testing session with a close member of his or her social network (a friend or family member).

When individuals had a chance to discuss life dilemmas with others and to think about them, they performed at the highest levels on the wisdom tasks. Interestingly, even when individuals were told to work alone, but to *imagine having a conversation about life dilemmas with their partner*, simply having this imagined dialogue also produced the highest levels of performance on the wisdom task. These two kinds of social dialogues, real and imagined, resulted in the best wisdom scores. Other conditions (discussing the problem with others, but having no time to reflect on it; thinking through the problem on your own; simply performing the task without reflection) did not yield such high performance benefits.

These findings support the perspectives underlying this area of work. First, individuals' levels of achievement on wisdom-related tasks are higher when individuals incorporate the views of others into their own performance, when they collaborate. Second, people learn from others and are able to utilize their insights and abilities even when they are not physically interacting with them. In sum, it can be argued that determining the wisdom-related potential of individuals will be underestimated when the value of the input of important others is neglected.

In a related line of work, Dixon and colleagues (Dixon and Gould, 1996; Gould, Kurzman, and Dixon, 1994) have also investigated cognitive performance of individuals in social settings. As in the studies on interactive minds, they found enhanced cognitive performance when individuals collaborated with others to solve problems such as retelling a story. In addition, they found that older adults collaborated with a partner (in this study, a spouse) through overt discussion of how to successfully complete the task, whereas they collaborated with a stranger through joint efforts to make each other feel comfortable with the task. In contrast to the older adults, younger adults made fewer attempts to complete the task jointly or to support one another. These findings suggest that older adults may be more willing to compensate for low individual performance by interacting with others for assistance with the task at hand and/or support for persevering in the task. As we saw in the interactive minds research, older adults' cognitive performance is heightened by collaboration with others. This research extends the interactive minds findings by suggesting that older adults, more than younger adults, are cognizant of the advantages of collaboration and are more likely to engage in such cooperative activity.

Negative Aspects of Social Relations

To this point, we have highlighted the positive and beneficial effects of being integrated into a network of close others. However, research on social relations also has documented the potential for detriments to well-being from negative interactions with members of one's social network (Antonucci, 1990; Rook, 1990). Here we will focus on two important areas of research concerning the negative aspects of social relations. First, research has demonstrated that negative experiences with social network members can have greater effects on psychological well-being than positive ones. Second, negative consequences to well-being can result from exchanges that network members intended to be supportive.

Family and friends offer opportunities and outlets for relatedness, caring, and concern, as well as help in times of need. At the same time, relationships with family and friends can be sources of tension and conflict. Research suggests that for most people, the close others they nominate as social network members are reported as being supportive more often than problematic (Rook, 1990). Moreover, the ratio of positive to negative social interactions is greater for older adults than for younger adults. For example, older adults are much less likely than younger adults to report that close others "get on their nerves" (see Antonucci and Akiyama, 1995 for a review).

Although most social interactions are positive, when negative interactions do occur, they have been shown to have a greater impact on well-being than do positive interactions (for example, Rook, 1984; Stephens, Kinney, Norris and Ritchie, 1987). In other words, though researchers found that older adults were less annoyed than younger people by everyday interactions with their relatives and friends, negative social interactions upset older people much more.

Rook (1990) offers three potential explanations for this relatively stronger impact on well-being of negative than of positive interactions. First, negative interactions occur less frequently and, therefore, are more noticeable in contrast to expected positive interactions. The relevance of the negative behavior then increases its association with well-being. Second, based on attribution theory, non-normative behaviors may elicit more concern about intent than do normative behaviors. Thus, negative interactions, more than positive ones, may call into question the value of the relationship, and thereby more strongly influence well-being. Third, individual adaptation may be facilitated by a stronger reaction (aversion) to potential threat or harm than to potential benefit. Thus, negative interactions would elicit more arousal than would positive ones and thereby would be more closely linked to affective responses.

Research examining the negative aspects of social relations has identified several ways in which interactions with others can have negative consequences for well-being (see review by Antonucci, 1990). Interactions that are unwanted or unpleasant, such as network members being overly demanding or critical, is one way in which social relations can be detrimental. A second way that social relations can detract from well-being is through well-intended support attempts that are ineffective or excessive. Because many older adults rely on their social networks for some assistance when their daily activities are limited by problems with their health, negative consequences for physical and psychological functioning associated with well-intended support have been the focus of recent gerontological research attention.

In one study from the MacArthur Network on Successful Aging (Seeman, Bruce, and McAvay ,1996), high-functioning older adults reporting greater assistance were compared with those receiving less assistance. Those who received more assistance were found to be at increased risk for impairment in activities of daily living two years later. It was suggested that this association between a high level of support and reduced functioning might stem from the erosion of older adults' beliefs that they can accomplish basic activities on their own. In other words, the assistance they receive from others may undermine their confidence in their ability to care for themselves. This decrease in confidence may then lead to greater reported disability; either actual impairment from reduced physical performance or perceived impairment from reluctance to attempt self-care tasks.

Take, for example, the instrumental task of going to the market to shop for groceries. An older adult who can no longer drive may need to rely on others for help with transportation. If well-intentioned family and friends begin delivering the groceries instead, the older person may come to believe that she is unable to shop for groceries, when initially the disability was only in getting to the market. In this case, support in the form of transportation would be more beneficial for independent functioning than going the extra step to select, purchase, and deliver the needed items.

Other related work has shown that assistance to older adults is beneficial to psychological well-being up to a point, beyond which the effects of additional assistance are as negative as too little aid (Silverstein, Chen, and Heller, 1996;

Exhibit 5.8   *Nonlinear Effects of Support on Well-being. Beyond a threshold, greater support begins to detract from rather than continue enhancing well-being.*

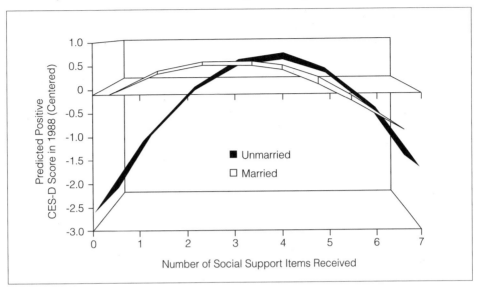

Source: Silverstein et al., 1996.

see also Krause, 1995). This pattern has been referred to as curvilinear or **nonlinear effects of support** on well-being (see Exhibit 5.8). Research evidence suggests that moderate amounts of support are related to enhanced positive feelings but that excessive amounts of support are associated with lowered psychological well-being. Reductions in well-being associated with high levels of assistance represent the unintended negative consequences of oversupport. If too much assistance prevents older adults from overcoming challenges on their own, it denies them the opportunity to bolster their feelings of personal mastery or of independence (Seeman et al. 1996). Erosion of these important personal resources, in turn, leads to the detected reductions in well-being.

Another way in which behaviors intended to be supportive can have negative consequences for well-being is illustrated in the work of Margret Baltes and her colleagues (for example, M. Baltes, 1995; Horgas, Wahl, and M. Baltes, 1996) on a model of **learned dependency**. This model posits that dependent behaviors exhibited by older adults, such as requesting that someone push you in a wheelchair rather than attempting to walk some distance, are, at least in part, a response to pressures from their social environment. Attention to dependence and neglect of independence creates an environment in which social others are "overresponsive" to the limitations of older adults and thus less attuned to their strengths and adaptive capacity. In such an environment, older adults learn to control interactions and contact with others through reducing attempts to act independently, thus increasing their dependence.

Evidence to support this model has been found in both institutional (nursing home) and community settings. As predicted, this research has demonstrated that dependent behaviors are attended to and reinforced more often than independent behaviors. As a result, older adults learn that reduction in self-care activities generates social interaction (e.g., an aide speaking with the person while helping her to the dining room) and positive feedback. This heightened social control is achieved at the cost of functional independence.

In sum, social interactions between older adults and close others are, by and large, positive. Negative interactions do occur, however, and these experiences greatly impact psychological well-being. Moreover, the negative effects of social conflict, interactions that are intended to be supportive, can also affect psychological well-being negatively. Research examining negative consequences of well-intended support indicates that help from others is most beneficial when supportive interactions balance older adults' needs for assistance with their desire for independence. In other words, providing assistance that does not jeopardize the physical or psychological well-being of another involves helping in a way that promotes independence rather than responding only to dependence.

Social Relations: Summary

What is unique to psychology about the study of social relations? Psychologists often bring to the study of social relations an interest in the individual's perceptions of the degree of psychological closeness of network members.

Do the social networks of older adults differ from those of younger adults? Yes, older adults' networks are generally smaller than those of younger adults. This difference is believed to result from the different social needs of older adults.

How do our social relationships facilitate successful aging? Network members often provide a variety of resources for older adults to draw on to assist them in compensating for losses encountered with advancing age.

How can social relationships interfere with successful aging? Network members can impede successful adaptation by neglecting to promote independence in their response to impaired older adults' limitations in health and functioning.

Mental Health and Aging

Thus far we have discussed psychological aspects of successful aging. Although successful aging is important to mental health, considerable psychological interest and research has focused on the differentiation between normal and pathological (or abnormal) aging. The study of mental health and aging, and particularly research into effective assessment and treatment approaches, is commonly referred to as **geropsychology** or clinical gerontology (Lichtenberg, 1999). In discussing mental health, it is important to keep in mind that some older adults experience problems of mental health that continue from earlier life stages. Among psychologists studying aging, most of the interest centers on mental health problems that are especially prevalent among older adults or where onset of the disease/problem is commonly found in later life. Here we will focus specifically on two of the most common pathologies in late life: depression and dementia.

As in previous sections, this discussion is guided by questions for you to consider. What is the overall prevalence of depression and dementia among older adults? Are these disorders more common among older adults than they are among young adults? Are there aspects of depression that are unique in older adulthood? What types of treatments are available for older adults experiencing these disorders, and how effective are these treatments?

Depression

Depression is one of the most common disorders among older adults. The fourth edition of the *Diagnostic and Statistical Manual of Mental Disorders*, or **DSM-IV** (American Psychiatric Association, 1994) characterizes depression as a set of symptoms, including negative mood, loss of interest in formerly pleasurable activities, disruptions or changes in sleep patterns, loss of energy, marked weight loss, feelings of worthlessness, and, sometimes, cognitive difficulties such as trouble concentrating. Depression is a commonly used term, and most people have a general idea of what depression is. However, several distinctions are commonly made regarding the diagnosis of depression.

First, it is important to consider whether the current symptoms represent a single episode of depression (experiencing these symptoms for only one period greater than two weeks) or a recurrent disorder (more than two episodes of these symptoms, each lasting longer than two weeks). If the episode is the first for an adult over the age of 60, he or she is experiencing what has been termed **late-onset depression** (Koenig and Blazer, 1992).

In their review of mood disorders in late life, Koenig and Blazer (1992) provide a brief discussion of late-onset depression. They argue that although late-onset depression has not been formally recognized as a distinct diagnosis, there is support for distinguishing it from depression that first occurs in earlier stages of life. They cite evidence suggesting that late-onset depression is more strongly linked to biological influences and is less likely to be related to a family history of depression than is early-onset depression. Other features found in late-onset depression are more frequent complaints related to physical health and cognitive problems such as difficulty with concentration and memory. Other research, however, questions these apparent differences. Clearly more research needs to be done to address any potential differences between early- and late-onset depression. (Koenig and Blazer, 1992).

Second, it is important to consider whether these symptoms can be better accounted for by factors other than depression, such as bereavement or medical conditions (DSM-IV 1994). If these symptoms can be accounted for by other factors, a diagnosis of depression is not usually given. This distinction is especially important in late life because of the increase in age-related physical and social losses.

Some argue that a significant portion of geriatric depression is reactive or situational depression (Koenig and Blazer ,1992; Staudinger, Marsiske, and Baltes, 1995). Bereavement, for example, is a social loss that, on average, will be experienced more frequently in later life. A reactive depression resulting from the death of a family member or friend is thus more probable because older adults will experience more deaths in their social networks than will younger adults. Similarly, since depressive symptoms may arise as a secondary consequence of medical problems as they age, the diagnosis of secondary depression is especially common among older adults (Cohen, 1990). In the case of secondary depression, treatment would probably focus on the underlying cause (e.g., a medical condition), rather than the psychological symptoms themselves. With these distinctions in mind, we can begin to discuss the prevalence of depression.

Epidemiologists have frequently studied the overall prevalence of depression among older adults. Because of different diagnostic criteria and other classification problems, however, the reported numbers have varied (Staudinger et al. 1995). For example, some studies consider the prevalence of depressive symptoms, whereas others focus on only clinical diagnoses of depression. A **clinical diagnosis** is made when a specified number of symptoms are observed or reported and cannot be better explained by other disorders or medical conditions (DSM-IV, 1994). **Depressive symptomatology,** on the other hand, means experiencing symptoms of depression but not necessarily meeting all the criteria for clinical diagnosis. As we have noted, many older adults experience depressive symptoms related to losses in life or health problems without meeting the strict requirements for a diagnosis of depression.

There is general agreement among researchers that clinically diagnosed primary depression does not increase in late adulthood; in fact, there is some evidence that primary depression is diagnosed less frequently among older adults (Cohen, 1990; Gatz, Kasl-Godley, and Karel, 1996). However, there is some evidence that depressive symptomatology and secondary depression are more common in older adulthood (Cohen 1990). Other researchers have suggested that the rate of depressive symptomatology over the life span may be curvilinear, with the highest rates in young adulthood and very late adulthood or over the age of 85 (Gatz, Kasl-Godley, and Karel, 1996).

Depending on the criteria used, estimates of the prevalence of depression among older adults range from 5 to 44 percent (Staudinger et al. 1995). The rate of diagnoses of primary depression among community-dwelling older adults is at the lower end; assessments of symptomatology are much higher. The prevalence of either diagnosed depression or symptomatology is even higher among older adults who have been institutionalized. Some researchers have estimated that as many as 70 to 80 percent of older adults in long-term care facilities experience some type of depression (see Cohen, 1990).

Treatment of Depression

After a complete medical evaluation has been conducted and a diagnosis made, an appropriate treatment plan can be formulated. The treatment of depression among older adults encompasses a variety of approaches, including pharmacological treatments (medication) and, in more extreme cases, electroconvulsive therapy; however, this chapter will focus on psychotherapeutic interventions. (The interested reader may wish to consult Koenig and Blazer, 1992 for a brief overview of treatment options not covered in this chapter.)

Two common psychotherapeutic approaches to the treatment of depression among older adults are the behavioral and cognitive-behavioral approaches. The behavioral approach to depression focuses on reinforcing positive, self-enhancing behaviors—remaining active and participating in social activities—and extinguishing negative behaviors that maintain depression, such as withdrawal from social activities (Koenig and Blazer, 1992).

It has been argued that **learned helplessness** is common among older adults who are depressed (Seligman and Elder, 1986). These individuals have concluded from their experience that they are helpless and have little control over what happens in their lives. They are more likely to attribute failure to internal causes, such as lack of ability, and attribute success to external causes such as luck (Staudinger et al. 1995). Behavioral therapy seeks to counter learned helplessness by providing experiences that demonstrate to these older adults that they do have control over what happens in their lives.

The cognitive-behavioral approach seeks to augment behavioral schedules by focusing on altering the negative thoughts of older adults from self-blaming attributions to a more adaptive way of viewing themselves and the world (Staudinger et al. 1995). While the behavioral side of the treatment focuses on positive behaviors and their reinforcement, the cognitive aspect focuses on changing the thought processes and content related to these activities.

A third type of treatment for depression is worth noting here. As mentioned earlier, depressive symptomatology that is reactive to age-related losses and stressors like health problems is quite common among older adults. Although these symptoms are significant enough to require attention, they may not be severe enough to warrant official diagnosis and formal treatment. These symptoms may be treated by general emotional support from family members, clergy, or other members of the social network (Koenig and Blazer,1992). The general goal for those involved is to aid the older adult in adapting to the losses that have been experienced.

In general, various forms of psychotherapy for the treatment of depression have proven quite effective among older adults. This observation runs contrary to the historically embedded belief that psychological treatment is less effective in late life than it is for younger members of the population (Staudinger et al. 1995). Many older adults respond quite well to behavioral and especially to cognitive-behavioral approaches (Koenig and Blazer,1992).

Dementia

Depression is not a distinctly age-related disorder. **Dementia**, on the other hand, is experienced almost exclusively in the latter portion of the life span. Although its origins are primarily biological, it is still considered a mental health problem because of its behavioral manifestation of symptoms. The DSM-IV (1994) characterizes dementia as a set of disorders involving multiple cognitive deficits. The most common type of dementia is the **Alzheimer's type** (AD), which occurs in 2 to 4 percent of adults over the age of 65 (DSM-IV, 1994). Beyond age 65, the prevalence of AD increases dramatically, with some estimating that the prevalence doubles with every five-year increase in age (Gatz, Kasl-Godley, and Karel, 1996).

Alzheimer's disease is primarily characterized by memory impairment, along with aphasia (language impairment), apraxia (difficulty with motor function), agnosia (failure to recognize familiar objects), or difficulty with what has been termed "executive functioning" (the ability to plan and organize stimuli). Besides these difficulties, older adults with AD often experience depression, rapid and extreme shifts in emotions, personality changes, and irritability. In the later stages of the disease, they may lose the ability to perform activities of daily living (such as bathing and eating), and some may lose the ability to communicate altogether (DSM-IV, 1994). The course of the disease is often that of progressive decline over a span of three to twenty years (Raskind and Peskind, 1992).

One problem encountered in the diagnosis and treatment of depression and dementia is that many older adults experience both disorders. Dementia is often accompanied by symptoms of depression, and depression is sometimes characterized by apparent memory loss as well as other cognitive difficulties. Diagnoses of depression and dementia are complicated not only by their frequent co-occurrence, but also by the overlaps in their symptoms among older adults. Raskind and Peskind (1992) note that these diagnostic problems can often be solved by completing a thorough medical history and clinical examination. One common way to differentiate dementia from the dementia-like symptoms that can accompany depression is to examine the general time period when the symptoms first appeared. Dementia usually involves a more gradual onset of symptoms, whereas the cognitive symptoms associated with depression commonly have a more sudden onset (DSM-IV,1994).

Treatment of Dementia

The treatment of dementia has proven much less effective than the treatment of depression among older adults. Depression is often attributed to a combination of biological and psychological factors, whereas dementia is primarily based in biological pathology. The treatment of dementia therefore differs from the treatment of depression in its general approach. With depression, the underlying disorder itself is treated; in cases of dementia, the behavioral manifestations and losses associated with the disorder are treated and managed, rather than the disorder itself. Some pharmacological treatments are currently being used to slow the declines associated with dementia. Medications aimed at reducing difficult behaviors have shown modest results at best (Raskind and Peskind, 1992; see Raskind, Risse, and Lampe, 1987 for a review of the use of antipsychotic medication with demented individuals). This chapter will focus solely on cognitive and behavioral approaches to treating dementia.

The cognitive therapy used in the treatment of depression is often considered inappropriate for individuals with dementia because of the cognitive deficits resulting from the disorder. However, other types of cognitive interventions, similar to those discussed earlier in the chapter, have been attempted with demented individuals. This line of work has generally focused on improving memory through an information-processing approach. In general, the evidence supporting memory gains among older adults with dementia are much less impressive than among older adults without cognitive impairments. Mildly demented individuals have shown very slight memory improvements when given more time to study objects to be remembered and more time to respond (Staudinger et al. 1995).

Another cognitive intervention has sought to optimize the strengths that the demented individual has retained. For example, although dementia has profound impacts on many areas of cognitive function, memories from earlier stages of the person's life may remain intact well into the course of the disease. This approach has sought to use those memories to compensate for losses in more recent memories (Staudinger et al. 1995). These interventions have proven somewhat effective, but overall treatment gains have still been minimal.

Behavioral treatments, on the other hand, have shown some promise in terms of maintaining some level of behavioral functioning. These treatments are similar to the behavioral approaches we discussed for depression, although in the case of dementia they have a more operant focus. The operant focus in this case is basically an individually tailored behavior modification program that reinforces certain behaviors while seeking to extinguish others. When combined with certain types of cognitive interventions already mentioned, this approach has yielded some positive results, such as retrieving the ability to remember a family member's name for a short period of time. However, more research is needed to determine the usefulness of this approach (Staudinger et al. 1995).

As with depression, the family and other members of the social network play an important role in the behavior management of the individual with dementia. Raskind and Peskind (1992) note that a significant aspect of any treatment is a "safe, secure, and consistent environment" for the older adult. For some individuals and their families this environment can be achieved at home, but for others the difficult decision must be made to place their loved one in some type of long-term care facility.

Treatment of any type of mental health problem among older adults is complicated by the fact that symptoms are often not recognized. The distinction between what is a normal age-related change and what is pathological is not easily made. Some research has suggested that misconceptions about the mental health of older adults are quite widespread (Palmore, 1988). Cohen (1990) points out that disruption in sleep patterns, memory problems, intellectual difficulties, changes in sexual interests, and severe fear of death are warning signs of mental health problems among older adults. He notes that these symptoms are often overlooked because they are attributed to normal aging processes (Cohen, 1990).

Mental Health: Summary

What is the overall prevalence of depression among older adults, and is it more common in late life than in early life? The answer varies depending on whether one is considering the clinical diagnosis of depression or depressive symptomatology. As a general range, it has been suggested that the rate of depression lies between 5 and 44 percent of older adults. There is little evidence to support the notion that the clinical diagnosis of depression is more common among older adults, but depressive symptomatology is more common than it is among younger adults.

Are there aspects of depression that are unique in older adulthood? Some have argued that late-onset depression should be a distinct diagnosis. There is some evidence to support this claim; however, more work is needed before any conclusive decision can be made.

What is the overall prevalence of dementia among older adults? At age 65 the prevalence of Alzheimer's type dementia is about 2 to 4 percent. The prevalence doubles with every five-year increase in age.

What types of treatments are available for older adults experiencing these disorders? Behavioral and cognitive approaches are frequently used in the treatment of both depression and dementia. The treatment of depression has been much more successful than any treatment of dementia.

Summary

We conclude this chapter by acknowledging that more psychological aging research has been omitted from this "tour of the highlights" than was included. An ever-increasing number of psychologists are interested in understanding individuals' experiences in late life. Other areas of psychological aging research include treatment of other psychopathologies in the elderly, gender and other demographic differences, late-life marriage, the older worker, older adults as caregivers, productive activity, the interface of physical and psychological functioning, detailed analysis of neuropsychological aging, and, information-processing analyses of attention, vision, memory, and speed.

We have chosen to focus on psychological aging research addressing the level and maintenance of functioning in a variety of life domains. The overarching conclusion from this body of work is that, for most older adults, the challenge of psychological aging involves maximizing stability and gains in the face of inevitable age-related changes and losses. We have tried to suggest that a key task for many older adults is coming to terms with, and incorporating age-related changes into, how they view themselves and their roles in the world. A related conclusion and direction for future research, one that will require increased collaboration among the social sciences, is that the adjustments necessary to achieve stability can best be made with a little help from our friends.

Web Wise

Geropsychology Central

http://www.premier.net/~gero/geropsyc.html

This site, organized by Michelle Planche from the Psychology Department at Louisiana State University, is a clearinghouse for information related to the psychology of aging. It focuses on links to sites useful to geropsychology professionals (such as professional organizations and upcoming conferences) and on providing information and services to older adults. The "Senior's Corner" section provides a listing of a variety of services. Other than the rather eerie pictures of cross-sections of brains from dementia patients, this is a very useful site for locating more specific information on psychological issues.

American Psychological Assn. Division 20: Adult Development and Aging
http://www.iog.wayne.edu/apadiv20/apadiv20.htm

The American Psychological Association's Division 20 includes researchers, teachers, and practitioners focusing on adult development and aging. This site is run by that association and includes information relevant to students (information on student organizations and graduate study), teachers (syllabi, film, and text information), as well as a clinician's guide for information on psychopathology and mental health and on-line publications (a newsletter and "vital aging," having to do with psychology's concept of successful aging). It also carries links to many other useful sites.

Alzheimer's Association

http://www.alz.org/

The Alzheimer's Association is the national organization that provides information and resources to families of Alzheimer's disease and advocates on behalf of research and support for victims of this illness. Their site describes caregiver resources, the latest in research and medical treatments, and issues of public policy, among other contents. Links to other sites are included. As an activist organization on an issue related to the mental health of older adults, this site provides a different view of mental health and aging issues.

Key Terms

Alzheimer's type dementia
clinical diagnosis
cognition
collaborative cognition
crystallized pragmatics
dementia
depressive symptomatology
downward social comparisons
DSM-IV
flexible goal adjustment
fluid mechanics
geropsychology
information processing approach
late-onset depression
learned dependency
learned helplessness
nonlinear effects of support

personality
possible self
primary memory
prospective memory
psychological closeness
psychology
psychometric approach
secondary control
secondary memory
selective optimization with compensation
self
social convoy model
social relations
socioemotional selectivity theory
successful aging
upward social comparisons
working memory

Questions for Thought and Reflection

1. The research on the psychology of aging provides numerous clues regarding how individuals may, in the psychologist's sense, age successfully. If you were going to start today to maximize your psychological well-being as you age, what steps would you outline to enhance cognition, maintenance of a positive self, strong social relations and to avoid (inasmuch as it is possible) problems with mental health?

2. Utilizing the Convoy Circle Diagram in Exhibit 5.7, graph your current social network and consider the types of relationships that constitute your personal network. How do you expect this network to expand, contract or change members as you move through your life course?

3. The self is an evolving constant through life. Describe the key processes relating to change in the self as individuals move through the life course. Given what you have learned, do you expect your sense of self to differ from your self today when you reach advanced old age?

4. Psychologists often employ the concepts of gain, loss and adaptation in thinking about cognition. From what you have learned, what common stereotypes about the cognitive abilities of older adults would you now challenge as incorrect?

CHAPTER 6

Sociological Perspectives on Aging

"Like gender or height or the presence/absence of ear lobes, age itself is not a cause of anything. Rather, it is.... a socially significant title that covers complex sociocultural formulations, including some which are directly implicated in personal and collective identities" (Hazelrigg, 1999, p. 96).

In the preceding chapters on the biology and psychology of aging, we focused on the changes, growth, development, and declines that happen *within* individuals as they age. These chapters made it clear that such changes do not happen in a vacuum; people respond to, and are affected by, the social context in which they live. For example, you saw that the prevalence of certain health conditions varies systematically by gender and race. The patterning of health status points to the fact that these conditions are not simply the results of individual behaviors, good fortune, or genetics ; social characteristics play an essential role. In the psychology chapter you read about the link between cognitive abilities of older people and the jobs people held, as well as the richness of their intellectual environment. These findings reinforce the idea that social context can have significant impact on what happens within the individual as he or she ages.

For sociologists who study aging, social context is not just an acknowledged influence on individual change and response—it is the focus of their work. This is the unique contribution sociology makes to the study of aging. Sociology examines the ways in which social life is organized, and the ways in which it affects individual actions and behaviors at all ages. You will recall from the first chapter that the sociology of aging covers a micro-macro continuum, a breadth of interests, theories, and research questions. Sociological research topics range from a focus on how individuals adapt to the changes that accompany aging to a focus on the social structures that strongly influence the situations to which older people must respond. In the example of retirement, a micro focus might look at how an individual's satisfaction with life is affected one year after leaving the job. A micro-level sociological analysis actually overlaps with social psychology as described in the preceding chapter. A macro analysis of retirement would look at the economic, social, and historical conditions that gave rise to retirement as a life stage in the larger society. What purposes does retirement serve for society? What groups in society benefit from retirement?

The sociologists' emphasis on the social context for, and the social construction of, the experiences of aging can be more clearly illustrated if we look at three related but distinct kinds of analysis that are part of the sociology of aging. These three areas do not encompass all of the topics that sociologists interested in aging have examined, but they give a good overview of the field. These three areas are: the life course, the patterning of experience by social characteristics, and social institutions and social change.

In the study of the **life course**, we are interested specifically in the ways in which society sets up a "road map" that influences the timing of the individual choices we make about moving into and out of important social roles such as marriage, parenthood, and employment. When sociologists look at the second area, **the patterning of experiences,** we look beyond the common ways in which society influences all of us to a more careful study of the ways in which society differentially structures the experiences of different groups of people. Race, ethnicity, gender, and social class are the fundamental characteristics by which experiences are patterned. Is aging the same for a poor Native American woman as it is for an economically secure black male? Probably not. This aspect of the sociology of aging, which is often also referred to as the study of **diversity** in aging, looks at patterns of difference and questions the sources of those differences. Finally, sociologists who are interested in the macro end of the continuum often focus on **social institutions and social change.** Social institutions are large-scale, organized systems of activities that fulfill some function for society; the economy, government, education, and the family are all examples of social institutions. The ways that social institutions are affected by aging is an example of this level of analysis. For example, the average age of population in our society has significant impacts on many aspects of our economy, including the aging of the workforce, demand for services, consumption patterns, and savings patterns. The increasing size of our older population has resulted in an increased demand for health care services and a parallel growth in jobs in the field of health care.

We introduce each of these three topics in this chapter, and develop the latter two (diversity and social institutions and social change) throughout the remainder of this book. This chapter builds on the ideas of social construction presented in Chapter 1. We include a brief section on sociological theories of aging to give an overview of the range of frameworks in the field. Finally, at the end of this chapter you should have a stronger sense of the ways in which society creates the meanings and experiences of aging, and of the ways in which social forces shape the choices we make as individuals.

Before we begin our review of the three areas described above, two ideas that have been discussed earlier in this book warrant a brief mention here— the contributions of demography to the sociology of aging, and the value of a sociological imagination. As Chapter 3 discussed, demographic forces (fertility, mortality, and migration) underlie the aging of a population, help to shape social institutions, and at least indirectly have an influence on individual lives. You will recall our discussion of the role of population aging in the challenges facing Social Security, and the current high level of competition for jobs that is partially related to the large number of baby boomers in the work force. The demographic perspective takes the essentially individual events of birth, death, and relocation and sums them up, describes patterns and trends, and considers the causes and consequences of these events from society's point of view. In looking at this interplay between individual behaviors and societal influences and impacts, demography is a fundamentally sociological science. The field of demography enriches, and provides some of the foundation for, other macro-level areas of study within sociology. You will find many references to and uses of demographic information and the demographic perspective throughout this book.

One of the great values of sociology is to lend a broader perspective, what Mills called the sociological imagination. As we discussed in Chapter 1, this perspective places personal circumstances in a social and historical context, and gives us a bigger frame of reference for understanding individual experiences. This chapter, and all subsequent chapters in this text, draw upon the sociological imagination to help us analyze the experiences of aging. Understanding how historical context shapes our own lives and the lives of others is a challenge. "History is an integral part of the lived experience, but it is that very point that causes us discomfort. We want to believe that we can learn the lessons of history...yet at the same time stand outside its reaches" (Hardy, 1999, p. 2).

It is often our tendency in American society to focus on the individual. We are enamored of the concept of free will. We value independence, and our nation is built on ideas about individual choice and individual responsibility. We are curious about the various circumstances people find themselves in, and often take some comfort in attributing success or failure to a person's choices and actions. Such thinking allows us to believe that good fortune will come to us if we work hard and position ourselves correctly, and that ill fortune won't happen to use because we have done the right thing. The sociological imagination allows us to a richer understanding of the contexts and social forces that influence individual lives.

Social Theories Of Aging

As you know, theories are frameworks that help us to organize information and understand our world. Many of the major social theories about aging are presented in detail in various chapters in this book. Here we want to provide an overview of theories in this field, of what specifically they attempt to explain, and of the ideological foundations and assumptions on which they are built. This overview should help you to critique, compare, and contrast the theories that are discussed later in the text.

Before we consider this brief overview, let us consider some prior questions about theory construction. Where do theories come from and how are they developed? In the case of social theories about aging, there is a very wide range of phenomena that are trying to be explained, from individual adaptation to societal changes. How can we understand this wide range of questions to get some sense of coherence in sociological theorizing about aging? Theories reflect historically situated views of what the appropriate questions are and what subject matter should be focused on (Ferraro, 1997). For example, questions about how people adapt to retirement received a lot of attention in the 1970s and 1980s. At that time the attention of researchers, policy makers, and the general public was turned to the experiences of aging people, partly because we were beginning to recognize the tremendous growth of the older population. More people were retired than ever before. Today the research on retirement tends to focus more on political and economic questions, including how to finance retirement and regulate employer pensions. Theories "furnish the boundaries for what we know... A theoretical orientation becomes a habit of the mind... and does not easily recognize contradictory evidence"(Hendricks, 1992, p. 32-33). Theories create competing explanations and new kinds of questions that might be asked.

To understand how a given theory reflects the historical period during which it evolved, Hendricks provides the concept of generations of theory. He suggests that there are three generations of theory in the sociology of aging. The first generation of theory focused on individual adaptation and adjustment. In the next phase, theories began to focus on structural processes and social organization. In the third generation, theories of aging synthesized the individual and structural emphases of the earlier generations. In this phase, theories became "more dynamic and political... recognizing the important of structure...but also seeing people as intentional actors involved in creating social situation and their lives" (Hendricks, 1992 p. 37). As we describe the major theories in social gerontology below, you can identify the "generation" to which they belong. In turning our attention to the ways in which theory development is a product of a particular historical and social context, Hendricks (1992) and Ferraro (1997) are pointing out that knowledge itself is a social construction—a product of dominant ideas and assumptions.

Another way to review the range of social theories about aging is to use the micro/macro continuum. You will recall that the micro end of the spectrum focuses on aging individuals and how they adapt or respond to their social environments. Activity theory is an example of a micro level perspective. Activity theory attempts to explain how individuals adapt to, and compensate for, the changes in their social lives that happen to them as they age. Exchange theory is another micro level theory that is applied to aging. This theory focuses on the interactions between individuals, and the attempts people make to maintain some sort of balance in their exchanges with others. This theory has been successfully applied to a number of aging experiences: caregiving, support networks, and changing family relationships. The macro level focuses on society as a whole, and on how social institutions and social structures influence the experience of aging. Modernization theory proposes that the social status of older people (as a group, not as individuals) declines when societies modernize. Social changes that accompany the economic development of a society, such as child-centered education and industrialization make older people's skills obsolete and make older people themselves less necessary to the functioning of society. With its focus on large scale social institutions, social change, and social status of a group, modernization is a good example of a macro level theory.

Some theories bridge the micro/macro ends of the continuum by discussing both individual actions and societal forces. Disengagement theory, the first formal explicit social theory specifically about aging proposes that aging individuals and society mutually withdraw from each other, and that this process is mutually beneficial. In considering the actions of individuals as they age and the action of society in responding to aging people, disengagement theory is an example of a theory that covers both micro and macro level phenomena.

Social theories of aging thus differ in their micro v. macro focus; they attempt to explain different levels of phenomena because of that focus. Another very important difference among these theories is the assumptions and ideologies that underlie them. There are many ways to draw distinctions among the various perspectives in the sociology of aging (Bengston, Burgess, and Parrott, 1997; Passuth and Bengston, 1988). Most introductory sociology textbooks discuss symbolic interactionism, structural functionalism, and conflict perspectives. These perspectives do indeed cover the rich tradition of sociological theorizing and are a useful method for categorizing theories about aging. We will give examples of aging theories that draw on each of these perspectives and highlight the major assumptions of the perspective.

Disengagement theory posits that mutual withdrawal of society and aging individuals from each other is beneficial for everyone— for the older person who needs to turn his or her energies inward, and for society which needs individuals to make predictable, smooth transitions out of the mainstream so that the flow of life is not interrupted. According to this theory, retirement, a highly organized form of disengagement, helps work organizations to plan for turnover in their labor force, and gives individuals a graceful exit from the pressures of employment and entry into well-deserved leisure. With its focus on maintaining the equilibrium of society, and its assumption that social structures and institutions each perform functions necessary to the status quo, disengagement is a structural functional perspective. Theories derived from this foundation ask what function a given social arrangement fulfills for society.

In contrast, conflict-based theories ask who benefits from a given social arrangement, or whose rules count in the structuring of social life. The political economy of aging is an example of a theory that takes this approach. This theory analyzes the ways in which major social institutions (especially the economy and politics) create a situation of structured dependency for older people (Estes et al., 1984). Instead of discussing the benefits of retirement for society, the political economy of aging asks why retirement exists at all and who really reaps the rewards of this arrangement. This perspective is often the most difficult to grasp at first, because it takes a very critical look at situations we take for granted. Many of us would argue that all of us benefit from retirement; we want to retire, we deserve it, and it is a good way to ensure that there will be jobs for younger people. A political economist would ask us to consider why we want to retire and why jobs have to be taken away from some people so that others can enter the labor force.

Both structural functionalism and conflict and primarily macro-level in emphasis; they focus on social arrangements. Symbolic interactionism is a micro level perspective centering on the interdependence between individuals and society. Individuals develop a sense of self from the feedback they receive from others. They "attempt to understand how others see their behavior by taking on the role of the other" (Passuth and Bengston, 1988: 341). This process generates and reinforces a shared understanding among individuals that is the basis of social order. Activity theory is based on symbolic interactionist principles. In trying to explain positive adjustment to aging, activity theory suggests that people need to replace lost roles and maintain involvement in society. This involvement reinforces one's sense of self, and also helps to bolster the social order we create out of interaction with each other.

Activity theory is markedly different from political economy of aging. The former is a micro level theory that explores how individuals adapt to aging. More importantly, they make different assumptions about the realities of aging. Political economy would ask why there is anything to adapt to; why does aging put people in a situation that requires them to "do the right thing" in order to adjust?

As you encounter more detailed presentations of many sociological theories of aging in this text, you can deepen your understanding of those theories by comparing and contrasting them. Is the theory micro, macro, or mixed? To what "generation" does the theory belong? What assumptions about the appropriate the subject matter are implicit in the theory? What exactly does the theory try to explain and where does it look for answers? Does it presume the functionality of a given arrangement, or does it question why that arrangement exists? Does it presume that individuals need to adapt to aging, or does it question why the situation requiring adaptation came to be? These questions can help you analyze and categorize the variety of sociological theories of aging.

The Life Course

All societies use age in some way to organize social life— to assign people to roles, to regulate interaction, as a basis for division of labor. In our society, we have laws about minimum ages for drinking, driving, voting, and holding some public offices. We also have some expectations about what ages are appropriate for people to marry, enter the job market, and retire. Many people thought that the 63-year old woman who had a baby in 1995 with the aid of in vitro fertilization was definitely too old to have a child. Most of us plan to retire sometime in our 60s. In addition to ideas about appropriate ages for entry into and exit from important social roles, we also share some general expectations about age-appropriate behavior. The dictum to "Act your age" is a clear illustration that we do have some underlying ideas about what we should be doing at

SAY, FELLAS, I JUST RETIRED A COUPLE OF WEEKS AGO. WHERE CAN I GET A GOOD DEAL ON SOME BAGGY SHORTS, A FLOPPY HAT AND A METAL DETECTOR?

Used with permission.

We expect interests and behaviors to differ in various stages of the life course.

various stages in our lives. "Expectations regarding age-appropriate behavior form an elaborated and pervasive system of norms governing behavior and interaction, a network of expectations that is imbedded throughout the cultural fabric of adult life" (Neugarten, Moore, and Lowe, 1965, p. 22-23). These expectations are part of our culture; they are taught to us as we grow up, and continually reinforced throughout adulthood.

These expectations are part of our laws, policies, and organization rules; they are also part of a general timetable we use for major life events. Neugarten and her colleagues observed that people "are aware not only of the social clocks that operate in various areas of their lives, but they are aware also of their own timing and readily describe themselves as 'early', 'late', or 'on-time' with regard to family and occupational events" (1965, p. 23). This social clock is the life course.

The **life course** is a sequence of stages people move through as they age; movement out of one stage and into another is typically marked by a significant event. For example, people enter the stage of widowhood when their partner dies; we enter the childrearing stage following childbirth. The life course is delineated by the roles we are expected to play and the activities in which we are expected to be involved at various ages. Atchley defines the life course as "a cultural ideal consisting of an age-related progression or sequence of roles and group memberships that individuals are expected to follow as they mature and move through life" (1994, p.154). The life course can be applied to many domains of social life, including the family, education, and work. We can, for example, talk about the timing of events in the occupational domain and whether they fit well or poorly with the expectations at the same ages for the family domain. For example, career building comes at an age when many are actively involved in parenting small children, and retirement occurs when society demands few other contributions from us.

Indeed, most of us feel some pressure to achieve milestones at fairly specific ages. Deciding on a major and finding a job after college are two milestones that many college students feel pressured to accomplish within a certain time frame. Think about the following questions, as further evidence of the existence of a life course. Why don't more people work past the age of 65? Why don't people wait until they are in their late thirties to get married? Would you feel comfortable announcing to your family, friends, and professors that you have decid-

Exhibit 6.1 *Christ-centered Wheel of Life: from a Psalter (1339) belonging to Robert de Lisie of Yorkshire*

Source: British Library, London.

Exhibit 6.2 *The Life Cycle of Man and Woman: an anonymous print (London, ca. 1773)*

Photograph: Warburg Institute, University of London.

ed to delay your entry into the job market until you are in your mid-40s and in the meantime you will enjoy your leisure and pick up some odd jobs here and there? The life course carries fairly influential ideas about what we are supposed to do and how we are supposed to behave at various stages of life. It is one of the ways in which society shapes our opportunities, decisions, and behaviors at various ages throughout life.

The idea that human life is organized into a series of stages related to age is not a new idea. There is extensive sociological and anthropological literature about how societies organize themselves, and age and gender are two of the most consistent and powerful dimensions used to fit people into various positions and roles in society. Historian Tom Cole summarizes the evolving images of the life course found in art, religion, and science throughout American history (Cole, 1992). Two examples of these images are reproduced in Exhibits 6.1 and 6.2. These illustrations show different images relevant to different times in history, different cultural values. Exhibit 6.1 has a strongly religious theme, with Christ at the center and all stages of life radiating from that center. The circles used to depict the eternal cycle of life in Exhibit 6.1 portray quite a different image from the more linear stair-step design in Exhibit 6.2. The latter illustration suggests that life is a career, which peaks at midlife. This image "reveals a great deal about changing attitudes toward death, the decline of eternal time, and the growing hope for longevity in secular time" (Cole, 1992, p.111).

Cole's work draws our attention to **historical time**, one of only three kinds of time important in understanding the life course. Historical time refers to a particular point in history, marked by unique values, attitudes, and cultural symbols. Exhibits 6.1 and 6.2 represent very different points in history, each having a different emphasis on the religious and "fateful" view of life, and different attitudes about aging. Historical time thus helps determine the nature and meaning of life stages. Neugarten and Datan explain that the life course encompasses "life time" and "social time" in addition to historical time (1973). **Life time** is a dimension of time that corresponds roughly to a biological timetable; the physiological components of growth, maturation, and growing old are the basis for life time. Infancy, childhood, adolescence, maturity are examples of life time stages. The concept of **social time** refers to the meanings, expectations, and definitions that society gives to life stages. These stages, and their timing, are not "natural" or immutable. They are sometimes linked to "natural" processes such as physiological development, but the roles accessible to us and their link to age expectations are malleable, and are primarily determined by society. This important idea will be further developed when we discuss the age norms that form the basis for our expectations about timing of life events and stages. Historical time intersects with social time to produce a life course unique to a particular point in history along which life time is mapped. In other words, life time is an individual's movement through stages and role changes; society defines those stages and roles, and those social definitions are influenced by location in history. For example, childhood did not exist as a distinct stage of life until industrialization made child labor unnecessary (and illegal), and formal education became a social institution in the seventeenth and eighteenth centuries (Aries, 1962). Similarly, retirement is a fairly recent life stage; life expectancy had to increase sufficiently for enough people to grow old enough to retire.

In summary, the life course is a socially constructed, culturally and historically specific sequence of roles and stages that people are expected to move through as they mature and grow older. The life course is comprised of social roles, and the entry and exit from those roles are influenced by age norms. These two building blocks of the life course require further examination.

Social roles

The concept of "social role" is one of the fundamental building blocks of the life course (and of sociology). It is the mechanism through which real live human beings are linked to the more nebulous structures of social organizations and institutions. There are actually two ways that people are linked to each other in social structures. They fill positions in social networks, and they behave in certain ways when they are in those positions. These two related but distinct ideas were discussed in a classic work by Ralph Linton (1942). Linton refers to the position in social structures as social status, and the expected behaviors and activities that people undertake while in those positions is a social role. **Social status** is a defined position in the social structure of a group or society that is distinguished from and at the same time related to other positions through its designated rights and obligations (Theodorsen, 1969). Many of us use the term status to describe a hierarchy of prestige. In fact, that is one way the term is commonly used. However, the basic sociological definition of status refers to position, but not to the prestige or value of that position.

So a social status is a niche in social structures filled by people. A **social role** is a set of expected activities and responsibilities that go along with that niche. Conveniently, this important concept has an everyday referent; the term "role" conjures up theatrical images of parts to be played. In fact, a social role is essentially that, a part to be played in social life (Goffman, 1969). A role is a set of expectations about how people who occupy a particular position will behave: what they will do,.what they should do, and what they should not do. Roles exist in relationship to other roles; that is, each role has a counterpart. Some examples of reciprocal roles are mother/child, teacher/student, friend/friend. Because roles exist in relation to each other, having shared expectations about what each person will do (or not do) in a given role is essential for social interaction and social order. If we had no idea at all about what to expect when we enter a classroom, that is, no idea what the teacher will do or what the students will do, it would be very difficult to accomplish anything.

A central figure in American social psychology, George Herbert Mead, used the idea of a baseball game to explain the reciprocity of social roles and their importance for social interaction. He points out that every player in a baseball game has to learn how to play her own position, but also has to learn what the responsibilities of the other positions are as well. A good player has to understand the function of every position on the team in order to effectively play her own position. Similarly, role players in society have to understand how their position relates to other roles in the social structure in order to fully participate in society. (Mead)

A social role is the script for the position; it describes the activities and behaviors necessary to the structural position of the status. Role is the dynamic aspect of a status, what the occupant of the position is expected to do and not do. Role behaviors are structured, but not completely. There is room for variation in how we enact a particular role, such as student, worker, daughter. Linton suggested that the distinction between status and role may only be of academic interest, because they are actually opposite sides of the same coin; he stated unequivocally that they are inseparable; there are no statuses without roles, and no roles without statuses.

Sociologist Irving Rosow (1985) disagreed with Linton's statement about the inseparability of role and status, and discussed the possibilities for status and role to be interconnected or not . He proposed that the presence, formality and clarity of both status and role are variable, so that different combinations are possible. Often we have clearly defined roles (a well-written script; clear expectations about behavior) attached to a definite status (a well-defined position in a social structure, including clear interrelationships with other statuses). "Grandmother" is an example of this situation; we have fairly clear expectations about how someone should and should not behave in that role, and it is a well-defined position in relation to other social positions (grandchild). However, Rosow suggests that there are situations where either the role is not clearly defined, or the status is not very specific. "Retired worker" is an example of ill-defined expectations about essential activities. The past connections to the workplace help define the position, but what is one expected to do or not do as a retired worker? Rosow questions whether old age itself, because of the multiple role losses associated with growing older, is a position without substantial role expectations—a "roleless role." This argument has generated some discussion, primarily designed to refute the negative message thought to be implied by the term. But the question draws necessary attention to whether our society provides opportunities for older people to be meaningfully involved in all aspects of social life such as family, work, education, government.

Age Norms

Have you ever seen a small boy dressed in a suit and acting very adult, or someone in their seventies playing hopscotch? Do these images strike you as inappropriate? If so, it is probably because of age norms. The ideas and expectations share by members of a culture about how a person of a certain age should behavior, or how a role should be played, are **norms**. These shared rules guide the behavior of members of a society by specifying what behavior and activities are expected, appropriate, and inappropriate. **Age norms** are those guidelines and expectations for behavior that are in some way specifically related to age. Age norms are "socially governed expectations and sanctions concerning the appropriateness of role acquisitions and behaviors as a function of chronological age" (Burton, 1996, p.199). For example, we have age norms about entry into roles (driving, voting, marrying, working) and exit from roles (retirement, childbearing). We also share age-related expectations about behavior, dress, and speech. To explore your own age norms about behavior and dress, think about how you would react to an 80-year old woman wearing a very short skirt, to a 70-year old couple kissing passionately, a 50-year old man who has not held a full-time job, and 80-year old woman going to college, or a 17-year old male who drives very slowly.

Norms, Age Norms and Roles.

The definitions we have provided for roles and norms sound quite similar. Both of these concepts are related to expected behaviors. Norms, however, are the shared *ideas* and expectations about behavior. Roles are the behaviors associated with a particular social position. The nuances of difference between norms and roles is a topic of ongoing discussion among sociologists. For our purposes, it is sufficient to understand that "role" implies a more or less organized set of interrelated about functions, activities, and behavior associated with a given status or position. Remember the theater reference—a role is a script. Norms are broader and more intangible; they are the ideas we have in our heads, collectively, that allow us know what to expect, that guide a person's behavior while they are playing a role. Role obligations for a particular position are defined by norms, the group's ideas and expectations. Norms are shared expectations; roles are behaviors. They are obviously tightly interrelated.

Age norms are a specific kind of norm; they are shared expectations that are directly linked to age. Age norms govern entry into and exit from roles, and they also dictate more general aspects of social interaction such as attire, demeanor, public behavior, language. Our

The very proper lady was conforming to age norms of her time, while the man with the hula hoop is engaged in an unexpected behavior for his age.

expectation that people should marry in their twenties or early thirties is an example of a role-related age norm; it is a shared idea about when to enter into a particular social role. Earlier in this discussion we asked you to think about your reactions to how people were dressed and how they acted (playing hopscotch, for example). These are examples of general age norms; they are not specifically related to a role. They are related, however, to being a certain age. General age norms influence how individuals act, and how we react to each other.

Ageism.

Our expectations about how people should behave and what kinds of roles they should be engaged in because of their age provide some level of social order and organization. However, an "overapplication" of these expectations can lead to ageism. **Ageism** is "a systematic stereotyping of and discrimination against people because they are old, just as racism and sexism accomplish this with skin color and gender" (Butler, 1989). While ageism may be related to society's use of age to organize social life, it is not a necessary by product of age norms. In other cultures and at other times in history, older people were valued differently. Ageism is a product of complicated demographic, political, ideological, and economic forces (see Scrutton, 1996, for a discussion of the foundations of ageism).

Ageism is alive and well in American society. In an intriguing expose of our discrimination against older people, Patricia Moore used makeup and dress to "disguise" herself as an older woman. Her book, *Disguised* (1985), documents the experiences she had traveling as an old woman and presenting herself in various situations. She encountered both negative and positive forms of ageism; she was ignored, patronized, deferred to, ridiculed, and offered assistance. These were not the reactions she received when she presented herself as a young woman. Even participants at conferences on aging treated Ms. Moore differently, often excluding her from conversation or treating her as if she were invisible (Ferraro, 1997).

Observing age norms and the life course

Age norms operate both formally (through laws, policies, and institutionalized practices), and informally (as a set of expectations that operate in everyday interaction). There are three important components of age norms: (1) they prescribe and proscribe behavior (i.e., tell us what to do and what not to do); (2) they are shared by some social group (such as society, a work organization, or a subculture); (3) they carry with them some element of social control or sanction (there are consequences of failing to behave according to the social expectations). Some sociologists would add a fourth key feature: they must actually constrain peoples' behavior. Settersten and Hagestaad (1996a) and Lawrence (1996) discuss these features of age norms in more detail.

Exhibit 6.3   *Family Life Cycle, U.S. 1880s–1950s: Demographic Description*

	Birth of Wife	1880s	1890s	1910s	1920s	1930s	1940s	1950s
Family Life Cycle Stage	Approximate Period of First Marriage	1900s	1910s	1930s	1940s	1950s	1960s	1970s
Median Age at								
First marriage		21.4	21.2	21.4	20.7	20.0	20.5	21.2
Birth of first child		23.0	22.9	23.5	22.7	21.4	21.8	22.7
Birth of last child		32.9	32.0	32.0	31.5	31.2	30.1	29.6
Marriage of last child		55.4	54.8	53.2	53.2	53.6	52.7	52.3
Death of one spouse		57.0	59.6	63.7	64.4	65.1	65.1	65.2
Difference between								
Ages at birth of first and last children		9.9	9.1	8.5	8.8	9.8	8.3	6.9
Ages at birth of first and marriage of last child		22.5	22.6	21.2	21.7	22.4	22.6	22.7
Ages at marriage of last child and death of spouse (="Empty Nest")		1.6	4.8	10.5	11.2	11.5	12.4	12.9

Adapted from: Glick, 1977; Matras, 1990.

These four component of age norms raise conceptually challenging questions. If age norms must, by definition, be pre- and proscriptive, more or less universal within a group, be associated with some sanction, and actually constrain behavior, how do we know if these criteria are met? Who do we ask, and what do we ask them, to find out if a particular age norm exists, and if it constrains behavior? Are you aware of any pressures to complete certain tasks or take on new roles at a particular time in your life? Is that sufficient evidence that age norms are operating and that you have a life course map, sketched according to age norms, in your head? These questions have fueled a great deal of debate within sociology and are related to the question of the usefulness of the distinctions among role, status, and norms.

The basic dilemma in the measurement of age norms and the life course is the question of what should be measured: what people typically do, or what people say they think they (and others) should do. Both approaches have been used by researchers to document the existence of age norms and a life course. The former strategy— looking at what people typically do— is well-illustrated by the work of Paul Glick (1977), who calculated the median age at major life

Exhibit 6.4   *Consensus in a Middle-Class Middle-Aged Sample Regarding Various Age-Related characteristics*

	Age Range Designated as Appropriate or Expected	Percent who Concur	
		Men (N=50)	Women (N=43)
Best age for a man to marry	20–25	80	90
Best age for a woman to marry	19–24	85	90
When most people should become grandparents	45–50	84	79
Best age for most people to finish school and go to work	20–22	86	82
When most men should be settled on a career	24–26	74	64
When most men should hold their top jobs	45–50	71	58
When most people should be ready to retire	60–65	83	86
A young man	18–22	84	83
A middle aged man	40–50	86	75
An old man	65–75	75	57
A young woman	18–24	89	88
A middle aged woman	50–50	87	77
An old woman	60–75	83	87
When a man has the most responsibilities	35–50	86	80
When a man accomplishes most	40–50	82	71
The prime of life for a man	35–50	86	80
When a woman has the most responsibilities	25–40	93	91
When a woman accomplishes most	30–45	94	92
A good-looking woman	20–35	92	92

Source: Neugarten, Moore, and Lowe, 1965.

events for women (such as marriage, birth of first child, marriage of last child, and death of spouse), from the 1900s to the 1970s. His findings, summarized in Exhibit 6.3, showed very little change in women's median age at marriage, but dramatic increases in the number of years spent in marriage until the death of a spouse, and a substantial decline in the length of time spent in the child-bearing stage. Similarly, Matras has documented the "compression of employment" (1990) into a smaller proportion of the life span, and Uhlenberg (1996) analyzed the impact of increased life expectancy on opportunity for intergenerational relationships throughout the life course. These demographic patterns speak to "typical" behaviors, relatively predictable timetables, and to the evolution of new or altered life stages.

Exhibit 6.5   *Perceived Age Deadlines for Major Family Transitions*

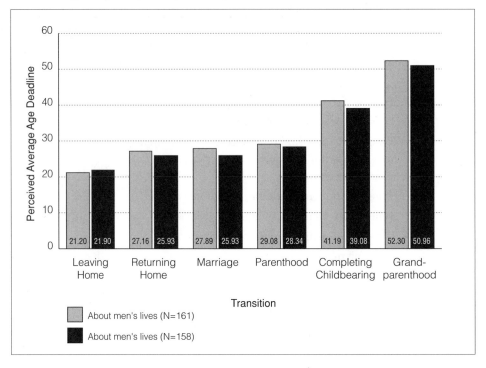

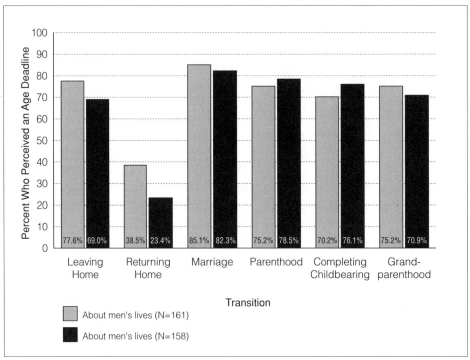

Source: Settersten and Hagestad, 1996.

The second approach to measuring age norms and the life course—asking people what they think about appropriate ages—has been adopted in number of studies. Exhibit 6.4 presents results from one of the classic studies on this topic (Neugarten, Moore, and Lowe, 1965). These findings show a high degree of consensus on appropriate ages for various life stages and behaviors; some of the interesting variations by gender will be discussed in our section on modifiers of the life course. In this same study, researchers asked respondents about their own opinions about appropriate behaviors, and about their perceptions of other peoples' opinions about these issues. There was a difference between personal attitudes and attitudes attributed to others. Age norms were consistently acknowledged to exist in other peoples' minds, but were not always accepted as personally valid or constraining (Neugarten, Moore, and Lowe, 1965).

In a study of perceived age norms among New Zealanders, Byrd and Breuss (1992) concluded that age norms had remained fairly consistent since the Neugarten study. Their study compared findings across age and gender groups, and confirmed the degree of consensus and overall pattern of age norms found in the earlier study. Settersten and Hagestad (1996a) recently found that age norms are still perceived to be relevant for most major life events for both men and women. Exhibit 6.5 shows the percentages of people who perceived deadlines for major family transitions, and the average ages deadlines for those transitions. A strong majority perceive deadlines for all family transitions except returning home. The average ages for these deadlines shows some differences between what is expected for women and what is expected for men. Women are expected to marry and complete childbearing earlier than men. Perhaps more important than the average age deadlines is the standard deviation for these averages— the amount of variation there was in the responses people gave. There was a lot of variation in the ages given for completion of childbearing for men (over seven years), and for grandparenthood (more than seven years), but little range given for the acceptable age for leaving home. This important study suggests that there is a perceived timetable, but that there is some flexibility in the timing of some family events.

Interestingly, these researchers found that, although the majority of respondents perceive age norms, they did not perceive any sanctions associated with violating them. "Being late" did not carry with it significant consequences. Lashbrook (1996) found fairly consistent age norms for promotions in work organizations, but little relationship between being "off time" and job well-being for middle-aged men. The lack of sanction for being off time, and the flexibility in timing led Settersten and Hagestad to conclude that cultural timetables and age norms "may be an important force shaping the life course, but their influence may instead be secondary ... and may be much more flexible in individuals' minds than researchers have assumed" (1996a, p.187).

In summary, there is a fair amount of evidence that people carry around ideas in their heads about when it is appropriate to be at certain stages in one's life, and there are demographic "norms" for when people move into and out of various social roles. There is less evidence that people feel pressured to conform to those expectations and whether they worry about being "off schedule." These two facts seem inconsistent. This apparent inconsistency can be explained in several ways. Foner (1996) suggests that perhaps age norms are only part of the age structuring of society, and age norms are flexible across social contexts. Settersten and Hagestad (1996a) offer that cultural timetables—age norms that we perceive for everyone—can be different from personal timetables that individuals use to construct their life courses (1996a, p.186). This latter explanation reminds us that age structures and other social forces are not totally deterministic. Human beings do take some active role in the creation of their own lives, even when there are contextual factors at work as well. In fact, people have an impact on social structures and social forces. Individuals are not merely reactive; they are, to some extent, "proactive architects" of their own life course trajectories (George, 1996, p.254). Moreover, many individuals collectively can change the nature, impact, and meaning of social structures (Riley, 1996). The role that individuals play in influencing their own lives and even in changing society is always in dynamic reciprocity with the impact of social forces on individuals. Attending to these reciprocal influences is one of the challenges of sociology.

Patterning Of Experience: Diversity In Aging

Looking more deeply and critically at the ways in which society influences the meanings and experiences of aging, some sociologists have focused on how, why, and to what extent the experiences of aging are different for different groups of people. For example, poverty is profoundly more prevalent among black women who live alone than among any other group of older people. Why does this pattern exist? What social forces have produced this structured disadvantage for older black women?

Many scholars have warned against using averages to describe the older population, because there is often more variation among older people than among younger people on some variables. This heterogeneity is very often acknowledged, but not thoroughly examined. Arguing for the need to really analyze heterogeneity, Dannefer (1988a) suggested that research should begin to look for the extent, nature, and patterns of heterogeneity on a wide range of variables. Is the older population as heterogeneous on life satisfaction as they are on income? Are the political attitudes of older people as varied as health status in later life? Does the amount of heterogeneity on health status change as people grow older? What is the pattern of that change? Does heterogeneity increase, decrease, or fluctuate over time? Finding out more about how much heterogeneity exists among the older population, on which variables, and in what pattern, is an important first step in understanding the different experiences people have as they age.

Later life is a product of history, individual experiences and social forces.

But, we need to go even farther than that to really understand the many different realities of aging. Dannefer (1988a) suggests that the next step is to analyze the sources of heterogeneity. How is heterogeneity produced, and what should be done about it? Calasanti (1996a) further refines this position by distinguishing between heterogeneity as variation among individuals, and diversity. Heterogeneity, the extent to which older individuals are different from each other, is what we have discussed in the preceding paragraph. Diversity refers to patterns of difference among groups of people in different social locations. The most common indicators of these social locations are gender, race, ethnicity, and social class. Scholarship on diversity searches for the nature, extent, and causes of differences among groups of older people. In doing so, we acknowledge that the realities of aging are not the same across all groups.

Studying diversity can take one of two directions. We can compare groups to try to understand their difference experiences of aging. There is a fair amount of research that takes this approach, and some of it will be referred to in later chapters. This is a useful but limited approach. The disadvantage of the "comparison" model for studying diversity is that there is always a reference group to whom everyone else is compared. For example, we can say that women have higher rates of diabetes than men, or that older black women have the highest rates of poverty among adults. While this information is instructive, the implicit use of a dominant group as a point of comparison reinforces the reference group's experience as "normal" and minimizes the different social reality inhabited by the "other" groups (Calasanti, 1996a).

The limits of the comparison approach are well-illustrated by the fact that such analyses often categorize people as white/non-white, or male/not-male. This approach assumes that the complexities of life in a particular social category (African American, female, working class) are somehow captured by not being a member of the reference group. But it is very clear that being female is not the same as not being male (Kunkel and Atchley, 1996).

By focusing on groups of people in particular social locations, we can better understand the different worlds of aging. We would ask different questions that delve more deeply into the lives of the members of the group we are interested in. Instead of comparing men's and women's rates of diabetes, we might ask how the rates of diabetes vary among women, by social class and race; or we might attempt to specify exactly how social forces affect the lives of members of a particular group. Listening to the "voices" of those groups better illuminates their situation than focusing on how they are different from the dominant group. The questions we ask, the concerns we attend to, and even the items we include on a survey will be more insightful if we begin with a conviction that reality itself is different for groups in different social positions. For example, Gibson (1996) writes about the retirement experience of older blacks. She introduces the "unretired-retired" status to describe individuals who are 55 or older and not working, but who do not consider themselves retired. This status is most common among poor blacks. They do not meet traditional criteria for retirement, and therefore are never included in studies of retirement. This example clearly illustrates how using the experiences and meanings that are relevant for one dominant group completely undermines our ability to understand the experiences of other groups.

As social research on diversity in aging matures, there is more attention given to diversity as an approach to reality rather than a kind of comparative content. Calasanti argues for an acknowledgement of the constructed and contextual nature of social reality in all theorizing and research. "Being inclusive.. requires acknowledging the unique configuration of a group within the matrix of power relations, being sensitive to the importance of these cross-cutting relations, and not making undue generalizations" (1996a, p.15).

Social Institutions And Social Change

A final area encompassed by the sociology of aging is the study of how society and its social institutions (such as the family, health care, the economy) are affected by, and have an effect on, the aging population. Matilda Riley eloquently argues for the importance of this area of study. She warns against "life-course reductionism," which treats social structures as merely the context for individual lives. She urges an examination of social structures and social change in their own right. "As lives change, new norms develop and become widely accepted and institutionalized in structural transformations" (Riley, 1996, p. 258). All of the chapters in Part III address both the impact of social structures on individual experiences of aging, and transformation of those structures as society ages. For example, the chapter on health care looks at the impact of access to health care on health status of aging individuals; it also presents policy issues, financing debates, and long-term care challenges that have accompanied the aging of our society.

While social change is addressed either implicitly or explicitly in each of these chapters, here we will look at how the life course changes and gets redefined as populations age. Two ideas that have emerged in the gerontological literature recently provide excellent illustrations of the ideas we have been discussing in this chapter. The idea of *structural lag* is based on Matilda White Riley's age stratification theory, which pulls together some of the most important concepts (such as cohort flow, age graded opportunity structures, and the aging of society) in the sociology of aging. A related line of research, on *pro-*

ductive aging, looks at the current and potential opportunities available to older adults for continued contribution to society. Because these two ideas stem from role changes and the life course, and because they capture so well the power, fluidity, and evolution of the life course, we present them in further detail.

Structural lag

In their discussion of structural lag, Riley, Kahn, and Foner (1994) clarify the link between real live human beings and the more formal, less tangible structure of social roles. They define **structural lag** as the tendency for the social structure of roles, norms, and social institutions to change more slowly and thus lag behind changes in peoples' lives. For example, the majority of people retire at around age 65 (and often before). Because of increases in life expectancy, most people will live an average of 15 to 20 years in retirement. But what roles or opportunities exist for people after retirement? What exactly do we expect a retired person to do? What links do they have to the life of the larger society? Society has not kept up with the increase in life expectancy by building opportunities and responsibilities for the new stage of life. Society has lagged behind the changes in peoples' lives; this is what we mean by structural lag.

Another example of the mismatch between society and peoples' lives is the persistence of age norms about completion of education at a relatively young age. The notion that education and career training should be complete by age 25 or 30 "lags behind individual need for continual retraining in the workplace over the person's whole life; and these norms are not in accord with the capabilities of older people and their motivations' (Foner, 1996, p.222). These education and work examples illustrate the gaps that have emerged between peoples' longer lives and the timing of opportunities, roles, and rewards in the life course.

Structural lag occurs, according to Riley and her colleagues, because human lives, including the timing of life course events, change more rapidly than social structures and institutions. One of the questions that grows out of a thoughtful consideration of structural lag is how the degree and nature of lag can and should change. Riley and Riley (1994) suggest a possible direction for change. The Rileys argue that we currently organize social life in a very age-segregated way. Young people are involved in education, middle aged people in work, and older people are immersed in the world of leisure. A more flexible, age-integrated arrangement would open up these three areas of social life for people of all ages. Exhibit 6.6 illustrates these two different arrangements. The Rileys suggest that we should be moving to an age-integrated structure to accommodate the needs, interests, abilities, and contributions of people of all ages. These scholars are optimistic that "age will lose its current power to determine when people should enter or leave these basic social structures (work, education, retirement); nor will age any longer constrain expectations as to how people should perform" (1994, p.110). Whether or not we reach such a state where age is truly

Exhibit 6.6   *Two Idealized Age Structures*

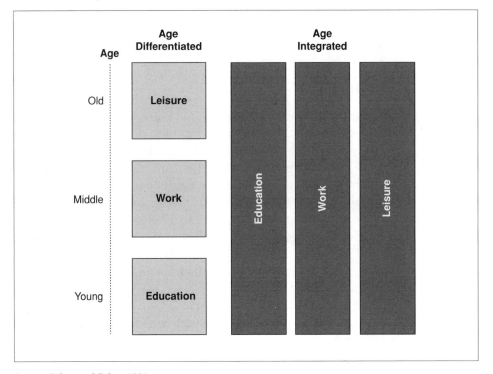

Source: Riley and Riley, 1994.

irrelevant in the near future, there are some changes in age structures that reflect the Rileys' position. Elderhostel programs and over-60 audit policies at many institutions of higher education have opened up the opportunity for continued learning for many older people. The integration of "service learning" or community service into the curriculum at many colleges acknowledges the importance of crossing the artificial work/education barrier that is implied by classroom-only curricula. More flexible career trajectories, including protected time off for child or elder care, suggest a loosening of the boundary between work and leisure.

The concept of structural lag, and the possibility of an age-integrated society, asks us to question our restrictive views of later life, and our constraining age norms that force people into a rigid, age segregated structure of roles and opportunities. This idea can be used to support a position of advocacy for older adults. One of the clear messages in the discussion of structural lag is the unfulfilled potential of a large proportion of the older population, due to lack of formal outlets and recognized positions in which they can make their contributions. This attention to the costly lack of opportunities for contribution is a very helpful backdrop for analyzing the growing body of work on *productive aging*.

Productive aging

Our culture highly values productivity, which is largely defined in terms of paid employment. By this measure, most older adults are "unproductive." Or are they? A perspective which focuses on the ways in which older are, could be, and desire to be productive has been receiving considerable attention from researchers and advocates. One of the hallmarks of the productive aging perspective is a view of older people as an untapped, valuable resource (Caro, Bass and Chen, 1993). The productive aging movement questions the rigid age norms and role structures that preclude the involvement of older people in the economic life of our society. In doing so, both the structural lag concept, and research on productive aging are suggesting some new stages for the life course, and are challenging powerful age norms and stereotypes about older people. **Productive aging** is defined as "any activity by an older individual that produces goods or services, or develops the capacity to produce them, whether they are to be paid for or not" (Caro et. al. 1993:6).

While scholarship in the area of productive aging has grown considerably over the past decade, it is interesting to note that the philosophy underlying the perspective was voiced in a report on the first national conference on aging. The 1951 conference report, "Man and His Years" was titled in the gendered language common during that era, but nonetheless inappropriate on demographic grounds, given the larger number of older women than men. The report states:

> Inevitably, the question has arisen: what shall we do about our old people? Shall we ignore them and dissipate the most mature years of their lives so that they become meaningless as people and as part of our national community? Or shall we look upon their experience, skills, wisdom, and judgement as great national assets which, if properly utilized, could serve the country well while giving meaning to their added years? (Ewing, 1951, p. 1).

Even though the idea of valuing the experience and wisdom of older people seems a noble enough goal, the productive aging movement receives a fair amount of criticism. What counts as "productive" and who decides? Does productive aging include caregiving, informal volunteer work such as helping out a neighbor with babysitting, or does it just include "recognized," formal activities such as paid employment and formal volunteer work? Why is an employment-based strategy offered as the best way to find new meaning and significance in later life? Work-oriented views of "productivity" are criticized as reflecting white, middle class, male experiences (see Holstein, 1993).

The debates about what constitutes "productive" aging and what does not is a very intriguing manifestation of different political and ideological perspectives on aging, work and its link to the economy. However, the most significant thing about the productive aging perspective, for our purposes, is the attention it draws to the ways in which society constructs the experiences of aging by expanding or contracting the opportunities available for older people.

In earlier decades, a lot of aging research focused on how individuals adjust to retirement. Now that people are living longer and will spend an average of 15 or 20 years in "retirement," researchers and advocates are looking for meaningful roles and opportunities for older people. The research on, and discussions about, productive aging, are indeed pushing us to reconsider age norms, role expectations, and the very structure of the life course in later years.

The numbers of people who are living long enough have helped to engender this reconsideration of the life course. Structural lag and productive aging are new ideas that grew out of an aging population; how these ideas play out in terms of policy, practices in the work force, and personal behavior will have an impact on the life course and on social institutions such as the economy, government, and the family.

Summary

We have spent this chapter exploring the mechanisms through which society shapes our choices, our life stages, our experiences of aging. Americans place high value on a sense of individual achievement and responsibility, and so it is often difficult for us to embrace the notion that our destinies are not completely the product of our individual actions. Using a sociological imagination helps us to better understand our own and others' experiences. We can see that our personal circumstances arise, at least in part, from a particular social and historical context. The ways in which experiences in later life are patterned by gender, race, and social class provide examples of the impact and constraints of social location.

Some sociologists take a purely deterministic view and argue that there is no such thing as personal "choice"; they suggest that all action and experience are the result of social location and social influences. Others argue that social influences do indeed have an impact, but that human beings retain free will are never truly completely "socialized." While this debate is ongoing, many scholars are more interested in the interplay between social constraints and individual actions. We have presented this idea of reciprocal influence a few times in this chapter; people are influenced by social forces such as age norms, but they also, collectively, can have an impact on age norms and social structures. "People's lives can only be fully understood as they influence, and are influenced by, the surrounding social structure of roles, groups, nation states, and other social and cultural institutions" (Riley, 1996, p.256).

In our society is it very popular to focus on individual attitudes, the power of positive thinking, and individual responsibility. Comments such as, "Aging is all in your mind," or, "You're only as old as you feel" reflect those values. Now that you have been thinking about the ways in which society shapes our lives, we ask you to reconsider such statements. Is it really so simple? Is personal attitude all that matters? Or are there age-related social forces that do have an impact on what we can do, how we can behave, whether we can find a job, and how "young" we can possibly feel?

Web Wise

A Sociological Tour Through Cyberspace

http://www.trinity.edu/~mkearl/

Sociologist Mike Kearl of Trinity University has obviously invested considerable time in developing a web site with numerous interesting links and great visuals. Aside from general information about the discipline of sociology and links relevant to that discipline, he includes a section entitled "Exercising the Imagination: Subject-Based Inquiries." Two of these subject-based inquiries (Sociology of Death and Dying and Social Gerontology) are especially pertinent to this book. Visit the "Death Clock" and see your probable date of death, or learn how the aging of the population is going to have repercussions in every aspect of social life.

American Sociological Association, Section on Aging and the Life Course

http://www.soc.duke.edu/~aging/index.htm

Just as the psychologists have a specialized division focusing on aging and the life course, the American Sociological Association also has a membership section addressing issues related to aging. This home page gives you access to recent newsletters, membership information, data resources, and a description of sociology's role in the study of aging and the life course. Included are links to other aging organizations and groups.

Key Terms

ageism	patterning of experiences
age norms	productive aging
diversity	social institutions and social change
historical time	social role
life course	social status
life time	social time
norms	structural lag

Questions for Thought and Reflection

1. Speculate about what life would be like if life expectancy was 200 years. How would our social roles and social institutions be affected? What would our family lives and work lives look like?

2. To what extent do you feel constrained by age norms and life course expectations? How aware are your friends of these expectations? Informally "interview" a handful of people and ask them some specific age norm questions (e.g., at what age should a person be settled into a career?). What do the findings from these interviews tell you about the existence and power of age norms?

3. How do societies "use" age? Why does chronological age make any difference whatsoever in our lives? Give some examples of the ways in which social definitions of age have affected your life (or the life of someone you know well).

4. What do you think are the most compelling questions addressed by sociological theories of aging?

Social Institutions and Aging

Social scientists often focus attention on major social institutions, such as the family, the political system, or the economy, as systems by which we organize and carry out our social lives. Whether one views these social institutions as consensual structures with functions to perform for the maintenance and well-being of individuals or whether they strike you as oppressive systems of control and constraint over individual lives, they provide us an organized way of looking more substantively at how aging occurs in a social context. In the chapters that follow we dissect what we know (and often what we don't know) about aging in the areas of the family, employment and retirement, the economy, health and health care, and politics. Specialists in the study of aging have researched many of these topics.

The issues and results we present here must be understood as provisional. This is what we know about how aging has occurred in a particular social context, usually the United States, within a particular historical time, the mid-to-late-20th century. In order to answer questions about social institutions and how they are reacting to the aging of their members, we have crossed disciplinary boundaries to consult the work of sociologists, physiologists, historians, economists and psychologists. We have organized the chapters by level of analysis; the chapter on families focuses more on the individual, for example, while the chapter on politics addresses macro-social issues.

Although we draw separations among them, these domains are clearly interrelated. Who we are, and how we age, derives from our family life, our work, and the economic and health care institutions we encounter as we mature and age. Our individual decisions about family and work are clearly interrelated. Similarly, societies structure their expectations of how peoples' lives will unfold based on their understandings of issues such as the ages at which it is appropriate for someone to be employed and when it might be appropriate for them to retire. As you read, keep in mind that our experiences of middle and later life stages may or may not be the same as what has happened in the past as people aged. Just as we change with aging, so does the social context surrounding us.

Chapter 12, which concludes the book, looks to the future of society both as we grow older and the society itself ages. Exploring the future raises more questions than it answers. We cannot predict how the numerous social, technological, and environmental changes we are encountering today and in the next few decades may reshape our trajectories as aging individuals. Planning for the future means planning for change both in ourselves and in the social world surrounding us.

CHAPTER 7

Aging in Families

"The myth that old people are alienated from their families and children has guided much of social gerontological research about the elderly for the last 30 years. ..[E]ach time evidence has been presented that old people are not alienated from their families, new adherents of the myth rise up" (Shanas, 1979a, p. 3).

Families In The Study Of Aging

Families are a cornerstone of all human societies; they have existed in every human culture in history. Family is the social institution that is perhaps closest to us; we immediately see and feel its influence on our everyday lives. Everyone has a "commonsense" understanding from personal experience of what is meant when we say the word **family**, yet there is some difficulty in coming to a consensus on its definition. Most attention focuses on the concept of the family as the group socially responsible for rearing children, rather than on the family relationships that continue as an important organizing force throughout our lives.

Contemporary Western societies have a wide variety of family forms, contributing to ambiguity regarding the definition of the family. Our own culture had different structures and expectations for family members in past epochs (Hareven, 1995), and other contemporary cultures structure the institution of the family much differently than we do. Nonetheless, the centrality of the family as an organizing social institution cannot be overemphasized. Many of our closest, most enduring social linkages in life are located in the family, in our social roles as child, sibling, spouse, and parent.

Early gerontological theorists hypothesized that the family's importance *increases* as individuals age and other social roles and statuses (such as employment) fall away (Cumming and Henry, 1961). These theorists thought that whatever life space remained to the individual was reallocated to ongoing roles, including important familial roles (Neugarten, Moore, and Lowe, 1968).

Because of gendered views of family roles, early gerontologists also believed that women experienced aging with more ease than did men, a position now contested by research. Women were thought to have two advantages. First, a primary identity with the family, as opposed to employment, primarily guaranteed strong continuity throughout their lives in the kinship system. Second, because family roles involve continual changes with the addition, maturation, and departure of family members, social scientists thought women were more accustomed to changes than were men. They thought men's continuity of identity was in employment, rather than in the family and that men's identities were suddenly interrupted at retirement (Maddox, 1968). We now recognize that these ideas are overly simplistic and stereotypical; both women and men hold core role identities in families and in employment.

Of the social institutions researchers on aging have studied, perhaps the largest body of research is associated with family relationships and their impact on the individual. Most of the research is micro-level in its unit of analysis, focusing on small group or dyadic relationships, or on individuals' reactions to the family. Few researchers have examined macro-level questions, although there are many of interest. We have selected a few interesting studies on aging and the family, mostly on the micro-level.

Research on **later-life families,** those families beyond the childrearing years (Brubaker, 1990a) began as a reaction to the ascendancy of so-called "nuclear family theory" (Sussman and Burchinal, 1968). In the 1950s some family researchers who believed in nuclear family theory focused their study on the isolated and autonomous nuclear family unit, suggesting that extended kin relations were largely irrelevant (Parsons, 1959; Parsons and Bales, 1955). Researchers with this perspective focused on family formation and kinship relations in the first half of family life (Cohler and Altergott, 1995). Under this view of the family, social scientists did not view other kin like grandparents or adult siblings as important to the lives of individuals whom, researchers thought, were focused entirely on their nuclear units.

Family researchers, however, quickly remedied this limiting view of kinship by demonstrating the active interchanges of support and the meaningful bonds of affection that exist among extended kin, albeit in different, and sometimes distant, households (Hill, 1965; Litwak, 1965; Shanas, 1967; Sussman and Burchinal, 1968). Families are, in fact, some of the most important age-integrating organizations in society (Riley et al., 1994). While many other social contexts segregate us by age, families necessarily bring together individuals of various ages and generations in social groups sharing mutual interests, experiences, cultures, and values. It is through family membership that many of us develop both interest in and knowledge of other stages of the life course. As part of this changing view, the typical American family form has been described as the **modified extended family** (Litwak, 1960). Theorists of a modified extended family acknowledge that, although kin may reside in separate households, often at great distance, there remain strong bonds of affection, identity, and support between them. In fact, because the term family often connotes the nuclear group, some authors advocate use of the term kinship, referring to the wider web of relatives both within and beyond the household, to emphasize these intergenerational and interhousehold bonds (Maddox and Lawton, 1993).

The Meanings of Generation

Linking various ages in the family are the biological **generations** that are key to the family's structure. Although the term generation has a wide variety of meanings, including the very distinct one by Mannheim discussed earlier, its meaning within the family is clear and familiar to most of us. In this context generations are "lineage descent positions within families" (Bengtson, Cutler, Mangen, and Marshall, 1985, p. 305). Grandparents, parents, and children in family systems form clearly recognizable social linkages connecting individuals of various ages and cohorts into one of the most influential social institutions, the family. These generations link the history of the family system through time and provide individual members with connections to both the past and the future. The craze for genealogical research and the development of "family trees" reflects our interest in better understanding these linkages with our own ancestors. Similarly, grandparents may feel a stake in the future through the younger generations of children and grandchildren in their families (Bengtson and Kuypers, 1971).

Another meaning of the term generation is as a proxy for cohort. In studying family relationships, as in other areas, we encounter a great deal of difficulty in distinguishing the effects of cohort membership from those of aging, especially since most of the research on aging and families has been conducted only in the past thirty years. This **cohort-centrism** means, for example, that our knowledge of later-life marriage is currently limited to the experiences of couples from cohorts born between approximately 1880 and 1932. Those are the only couples who have reached later life during the research era, showing the limitations of our knowledge. How will future cohorts of older married couples differ? Given the dramatic changes in the overall society, including gender roles within marriage and the increasing experience of divorce and remarriage, it is difficult to project future trends with confidence. It is unlikely; however, that future cohorts will be the same as those we have studied to date.

Aspects of Family Variation

Certainly not all families are alike, and researchers have identified several socially constructed dimensions of diversity on which families vary. One is the family's stage of development, reflecting its size, the ages of family members, and the types of issues being addressed as central concerns. (See the section on Family Life Cycle Theory later in this chapter.). Among other key differences are family form, race/ethnicity, and social class.

In terms of *family form*, a variety of kinship groupings are called family. Family form remains a highly controversial area, because society lacks consensus on whether some of these groups constitute "true" family. For example, there seems to be substantial agreement that a married couple or a single parent living together in a household with children constitutes a family. But if the couple is childless or a grandparent is raising the children, some would withhold the term family. Any society's definition of family, as a socially constructed component of its culture, is subject to change. Individuals in most of the groups just described, and those in other less traditional family forms such as blended families or same-sex couples, with or without children, consider themselves to be families and act accordingly even if law and public policy are not always on their side.

A considerable body of research has examined the potential differences by race or ethnicity in how families operate as members age. Much of the research has focused on African Americans, but recently more attention has been paid to Hispanic, Asian, and European American families. The bulk of research on African Americans suggests that relationships in their families are more interdependent, with members more likely to rely on extended kin and close community (such as church members) for support (Sussman, 1985). For example, African American elders are more often cared for at home by relatives, rather than by formal service providers or nursing homes, when their health fails (Miller, McFall, and Campbell, 1994). Such differences may reflect both cultural variations in family norms of mutual assistance and experiences of discrimination in access to health care.

Differences between middle-class European Americans and Americans from other social classes or racial/ethnic groups are sometimes attributed to stronger norms of familism in the latter groups, a cultural emphasis on communal sharing of resources directed toward those most in need, and a greater emphasis on family bonds and responsibilities. Some researchers have emphasized the apparently greater flexibility in kinship roles among African Americans in particular. African-American families are more likely to establish **fictive kinship**, granting someone who is unrelated the title and rights of a family member, such as "She is like a sister to me." Researchers also found African-American families forming **surrogate family relationships**, wherein family members or others take active role responsibility replacing a parent, child, or caregiver (Burton and DeVries, 1995; Johnson, 1995b).

Most research has shown a higher level of intergenerational exchange and support in African American families than in European American families (Mitchell and Register, 1984; Mutran, 1985). But efforts to identify the distinct influences of race or ethnicity in aging families are often obscured by their associations with social class. When researchers compare families across race or ethnicity, they necessarily include the effects of class differences as well (Mitchell and Register, 1984; Mutran, 1985). Separating these factors can be difficult, but it is not impossible. In one study, Mitchell and Register (1984) examine both simultaneously by carefully sampling both middle-class and poor individuals from the African-Americans and European-Americans populations. For family interaction they found high levels of interaction for both races; about three-fourths of older adults had seen both a child and a grandchild within the prior two weeks. Slightly more African American elders shared a residence with a child or a grandchild, but the major finding of the research was that race makes only a very small difference in family relationships, and that in some instances social class is more important.

Within races, *social class* differences in family relationships have been the

Exhibit 7.1   *Dynamics of Family Norms*

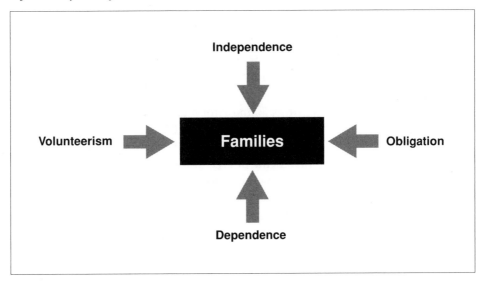

subject of some investigation. The great majority of research has focused attention on middle-class families, with only occasional work focusing on class diversity. Working-class families tend to live in closer proximity, enabling households
in the modified extended family to have more frequent face-to-face contact and
exchange of support (Townsend, 1968). Because working-class spouses maintain more separation in their daily routines and friendship patterns than do middle-class couples (Lopata, 1979), marital relationships less often shape
well-being, and widowhood may be less disruptive (Bengtson, Rosenthal, and
Burton, 1990).

Core Norms and Expectations of Family Relationships

Family relationships are often thought of simply as bonds based on affection.
These critical social linkages are, however, more complex, consisting of many
aspects and dimensions (Silverstein and Bengtson, 1997). What keeps family
members together when relationships are stressed? Why do adult siblings often
assist each other in many ways but seldom help out financially? Why is it often
stressful if an adult child moves back in with her parents following a divorce?
What structures the separations between kin and households in such a way as
to promote privacy and autonomy? Why do we care about privacy and autonomy in family relationships?

Clearly family relationships are governed by culturally based and socially
constructed rules, **social norms**, regarding how members should act toward one
another. These cultural norms for families are specialized in three ways. First,

they are specific to particular role relationships. For example, the issue of privacy may be very different between an adolescent and a parent than between a husband and a wife. Second, these variations in familial norms may be systematically related to membership in social class, racial, ethnic, religious, or regional groupings. One example, noted previously, is the stronger emphasis on mutual help in African American families reported by many researchers. Third, the norms may vary across individual families, so that particular families, besides sharing a joint history and membership in other social groups, may have their own unique family norms to augment or alter the basic cultural rules.

The social norms governing family life include two major dynamics, portrayed in Exhibit 7.1: the degree of independence/dependence of relationships, and the degree to which relationships are ruled by voluntarism or obligation. Families operate at the focal point of these sometimes contradictory dynamics. These two underlying themes, though certainly not capturing all important aspects of family relationships, are central to an understanding of the social issues often faced in families as they and their members age.

Independence and Dependence

Central to the relationships within the U.S. family are issues of **independence and dependence**. Young children are physically and emotionally dependent on their parents, and we expect spouses to have dependencies on each other throughout marriage. Yet we do not expect children to remain dependent on their parents throughout life, nor is a high level of economic, social, or emotional interdependence expected between adult siblings (Suitor, Pillemer, Keeton, and Robison, 1994). These norms may be violated, as when unmarried adult children remain in the home of their parents or return there following a divorce or employment disruption, so-called "boomerang" children (White and Peterson, 1995). Fears of non-normative dependency in later life also influence the relationships between older adults and their offspring. The vigor of such norms is indicated by the fact that dependency of an elderly parent, often termed "being a burden" to the children, is a concern commonly voiced by middle-class Americans (Sussman, 1985).

Living arrangements provide evidence of the norm of independence among adult generations in the United States. As Exhibit 7.2 shows, the oldest cohort are more likely to live with relatives other than a spouse (usually adult children or siblings) than are their younger counterparts. However, neither men nor women, except those in cultural groups which normatively support this behavior, expect to or strive to live with relatives. Instead, most older Americans prefer to live alone (U.S. Bureau of the Census, 1991a). With adequate financial resources and health, older adults choose to live independently of their adult children, although often in relatively close proximity. This pattern has been called **intimacy at a distance** (Rosenmayr and Kockeis, 1963), whereby emotional and social bonds between parents and children are maintained across house-

Exhibit 7.2   *Living Arrangement of Older Americans by Sex and Age: 1995*

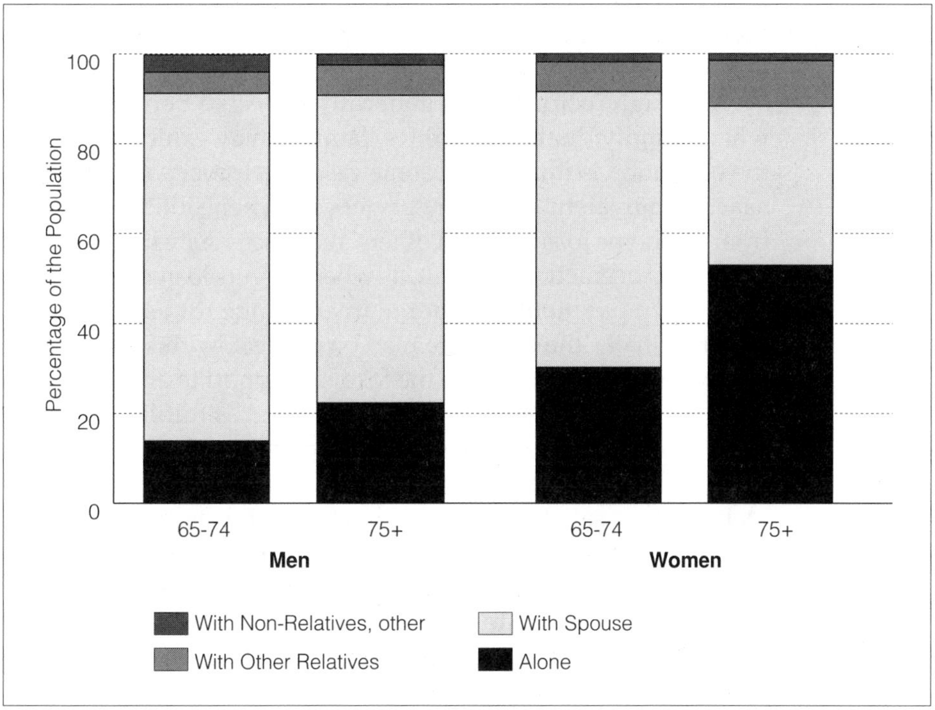

Source: Lugaila, 1998.

holds. This household separation underpins the independence of each of the generations, because neither is subject to the rule of the other as household head.

Norms about dependence of family members have changed over time. The relationships of older relatives to their kin have altered as families, especially those of the middle class, have moved from shared economic function (such as a family farm to provide for the economic survival of the group) toward relationships based on greater voluntarism among kin (Hareven, 1995). Cohler (1983) suggests that self-reliance and autonomy are core values of industrial capitalism; these values inhibit the expression of mutual dependency among two or more generations of adults enjoying family ties of long duration. Instead, there is pressure to maintain at least the guise of independence among adults linked by bonds other than marriage. Because self-reliance and autonomy reflect our particular social, cultural and economic context, these values are not dominant in other societies' family life.

The norm of generational independence is also reflected in the **norm of reciprocity**, as applied within the family. This norm, which directs repayment of social and material debts between individuals or groups, provides an acceptable way of managing dependency within families to maximize the perception of independence. In the family, as in the larger society, the norm of reciprocity dictates that individuals who are recipients of benefits from others have an unpaid debt or obligation until a comparable favor can be returned to the original helper. The common statement "I owe you a favor" is an expression of this social norm in everyday life.

Although reciprocity is generally expected between exchange partners, whether individuals or societies, families may exhibit some flexibility in how the obligation is fulfilled. In some cases, reciprocity may be direct and involve exactly equivalent goods or services, as when siblings help each other move from one home to another. In others, reciprocity may involve exchanges of goods or services deemed equivalent, as when parents loan their adult children money for a down payment on a home in exchange for assistance with household repairs. Finally, the exchange may be indirect, with support received from one family member paid back in the form of support to another family member. For example, reciprocity norms may be deemed as fulfilled when parents provide for their children, who, when grown, pay the debt back by caring well for the grandchildren of the original givers (Antonucci, 1990). In this case, the norm of reciprocity is satisfied quite indirectly, on the assumption that ultimately all members of the group will benefit through the ongoing assistance down through the generations. Even in the absence of direct reciprocity, older kin may define their assistance to younger kin as equivalent (given limited resources) to any help they receive, enabling them to maintain the sense of balanced reciprocity in these relationships (Antonucci, 1990).

The particular form of family reciprocity is based in culture. Akiyama, Antonucci, and Campbell (1990) suggest that European Americans have a linear model of exchange, such that older people always give more to younger people within the family. By comparison, the Japanese culture projects a curvilinear model, in which the middle generation gives more to older and younger. African Americans hold more of a communal model, whereby those with resources share them with kin on an as-needed basis. Other research, however, suggests that the actual patterns of assistance may vary within a culture, as we will see later in the chapter.

Voluntarism and Obligation

Family relationships differ from those of friends in so far as kinship carries with it a higher degree of obligation. "Family are supposed to perform in times of need, friends are not so obligated" (Antonucci, 1990, p. 215). Expectations of mutual responsibility and support have been at the heart of most family systems across cultures and throughout history, but the core of obligation and responsibility is thought by some to be diminishing in recent times (Antonucci, 1990; Jarrett, 1985). The degree of **voluntarism** in these relationships (the extent to which individuals have choices regarding whether and when to meet individual versus family needs) has varied widely. Johnson (1995b) describes the **opportune family,** a form available to the contemporary American middle class, as a system in which individuals can choose the degree to which they invest in themselves (versus the family collectivity), their level of obligation to relatives, and the nature of their significant relationships.

The extent to which **obligation** or duty rules family relationships has changed over time. Since the nineteenth century, families in the United States and many other Western cultures have changed toward a more voluntaristic basis, held together more by sentiment, compared with past linkages based on obligation and duty (Hareven, 1994; Hess and Waring, 1978). The extent to which obligation or voluntarism exists varies among social and cultural categories. As part of their family roles, individuals clearly have both rights and obligations toward one another, including mutual (although not always equal) responsibility of spouses and sometimes asymmetrical obligations between parent and child (Jarrett, 1985). The specific case most studied is that of the adult child's obligation toward the aging parent.

Filial obligation or duty refers to the responsibility that children have toward their parents, as mandated by their culture or as felt by individuals, especially in terms of meeting their needs in later life (Lee, Peek, and Coward, 1998). As with other social norms, filial obligation varies across cultures and historical periods. In some societies and locations, including many U.S. states, laws mandate filial obligation.

Until World War II, norms for American families dictated that one child, most typically a younger daughter, would forgo or delay marriage to remain at home and provide care for her aged parents until their deaths (Hareven, 1995). Although this practice of having a daughter as caregiver has waned, contemporary American society still has strong expectations that adult children will provide support and assistance for an older parent or parents should they require it. These expectations vary among individuals by age, gender, social class and ethnicity, (Stein, Wemmerus, Ward, Gaines, Freeberg and Jewell, 1998). Despite a movement toward a more voluntaristic, opportune family, especially among the middle class, filial obligation has continued relevance in contemporary families (Finley, Roberts, and Banahan, 1988; Hareven, 1995). Social policies, such as those to provide health care and housing, often rely on a considerable volume of care provided by kin, expecting this sense of obligation to provide considerable support to dependent elders.

Not all adult children feel these emotions equally (or equally with their parents), creating potential strain in the parent/child relationship (Jarrett, 1985). Research by Finley and her associates (1988) found that both daughters and sons claimed a high sense of responsibility toward aged parents. Factors such as the degree of affection the child felt toward the parent and the proximity of their residences influenced the degree of filial obligation reported toward a mother. For fathers, however, absence of conflict predicted a sense of obligation among daughters but not among sons. Agreement or disagreement with questions such as "Adult children should give their parents financial help when it is necessary" and "Every child should be willing to share his/her home with aging parents" is used to evaluate the degree to which these obligations are felt. Actual behavior may vary from normative statements made in a survey, however, because it is not socially acceptable to admit conflict, distance, or a lack of felt obligation in these relationships (Jarrett, 1985).

The Cultural Basis of Family Norms: The Chinese Case

Social norms, including those regarding family relationships, are a socially constructed part of culture, varying across cultural groups and even across time within cultures. To illustrate this point, let us examine the cultural norms regarding intergenerational family relationships in China.

According to Charlotte Ikels (1993), the traditional culture of the early twentieth century (pre-Communism) was based on Confucianism "an ethic of familism that not only served as the standard to guide proper family organization for many centuries but was also codified into law" (p. 124). This system emphasized vertical family ties—those between the generations—as more important than horizontal ties, such as those between spouses, which were viewed primarily as a means by which to continue the lineage through offspring.

In earlier times parents arranged the marriages of their children, because they held a strong stake in the selection of an appropriate mate to continue the family line. Because the system was strongly patrilineal, and only members of the male line were considered truly related, the term grandchildren was reserved for the offspring of a son. Sons remained in residence with their parents following marriage, whereas daughters left to be with their new husbands and parents-in-law, who considered them full members of that family only if they bore children. Thus, sons and their wives provided the support system to aged parents within the same household. Each household was under the control of the senior male until his death, at which time the property was divided among the sons. This continued subdivision of property for each new generation sometimes meant that sons needed to leave home to seek economic support elsewhere, including overseas. Sons who emigrated, however, retained their obligation to provide financial support for aging parents back home.

Daughters-in-law were responsible for the physical care of aged parents-in-law and continued this care with offerings to the ancestors after their deaths. If widowed, a daughter-in-law would be discouraged from remarriage because of her responsibility toward the ancestors and her links, through her children, with her husband's kinship group.

Although the advent of the communist regime changed numerous aspects of the traditional family system, many components remain. For example, 73 percent of urban elders and 89 percent of rural elders lived in multigenerational households in the late 1980s, a legacy of the traditional Chinese family norms. Contemporary China is grappling with social changes threatening family traditions and has now formalized family obligations in law and policy to ensure that kin meet the needs of elders in this rapidly aging society (Leung, 1997).

Continuities in Later-Life Families

Brubaker (1990a) defines a later-life family as one that is moving through the child-launching phase and into the postparental phase, in which most couples eventually experience retirement, health limitations, and widowhood. Spousal, parental and sibling relationships are well established by the time families reach this stage. Typically these relationships exhibit considerable continuity in how they operate over time. One approach to understanding family relationships in later life is to examine these continuities.

Not all family relationships are close and affectionate, and some may actually be distant or acrimonious as a result of early-life events or changes that occur with maturation. For example, if a father and adolescent son have had a conflicted relationship, it is unlikely that this conflicted heritage will evaporate without a trace in later life and that they will develop warm and affectionate bonds. Although they may become closer, especially if the son moves through expected normative changes into marriage, parenthood, and employment (Suitor et al., 1994), such a father and son may never become really close. Similarly, a son who has been close to his parents may find himself pulled away from interaction with them by the responsibilities of distant job or his family, but will likely maintain regular contact and an emotional relationship with them throughout their lives.

Family members are typically involved to some degree with one another's lives, providing advice and emotional support, making demands on time and loyalty, and sometimes giving or seeking assistance both across and within generations. This mutual exchange is often so routine as to be hardly noticed as anything special by members of the family. It is these regular, ongoing activities that constitute the bulk of family relationships over the years. On occasion, however, a crisis intervenes to upset the routine operation of established kin relationships. A crisis can be a non-normative event, such as the divorce of an adult child, or the more expected, but no less stressful, illness of an elderly parent. In these circumstances, family relationships may change with shifts in residency, assistance, and interaction patterns that have been long established. Despite the threats posed by crises within the family, continuity is the norm in the quality and nature of most family relationships in later life.

■ ■ ■ ■ ■ ■ ■ ■
APPLYING THEORY
Family Life Cycle Theory and Individual Dependency in the Family

Family life cycle theory is one theoretical "lens" that has been especially pertinent to the study of families as they age. It originated in the 1950s, when the focus in family research was on the nuclear unit. Family life cycle theory focuses attention on the systematic changes that occur in family life over time in conjunction with the maturation of its members. "Families, like individual persons, progress from birth to death in the steps and patterns inherent in the human condition" (Duvall and Miller, 1985, p. 20). According to this developmental approach, family relationships, goals, and routines are differentiated by the stage of development. Families with preschool-age children, for example, are quite different in their focus than are families with teenagers moving toward adulthood or postparental families, whose children have left the household. Thus, it makes sense to recognize these differences and to focus attention on the changes to be expected as members of the nuclear family unit mature.

Because the original theory was developed after World War II in a time of high fertility and low divorce rates, it emerged with a set of stages that were driven by the maturation of the oldest child. For example, when the oldest child became an adolescent, according to this formulation, the family moved into a new stage. This emphasis on stages has been criticized for focusing attention on a traditional, idealized, nuclear family in which family events occur on time and without disruption (Cohler and Altergott, 1995). It fails to recognize the variations in family life (for example, families may have both teenagers and preschoolers at the same time) or account for alternative patterns, such as childlessness, divorce and remarriage, or single parenthood.

More recently attention in this theory domain has turned to understanding the transitions experienced by the family or its members, rather than defining stages. This emphasis on family dynamics opens the theory to greater flexibility in examining family careers (Cohler and Altergott, 1995). Regardless of the usefulness of stages, however, the family life cycle theory accomplished one vital goal. It focused attention on the fact that family life is dynamic, involving predictable changes in relationships, closeness, and problems of central concern to the family based on the changing composition of the household and maturation of its members over time.

Think about family life cycle theory in terms of your own experience. How does the passage of time, paired with the maturation of family members, change the roles, responsibilities, and relationships between you and your kin? One key area of change, mirrored in stages of family development, has to do with the development of children and their dependence on the family. Your own experience was probably of moving from a high degree of dependence as a baby to greater independence as you matured. Later, others may be reliant on you, if you become a partner or parent, and even later you may have a second phase of dependency, should you experience failing health in advanced old age. Those changes in dependency also shaped your relationships with others in myriad ways. Family life cycle theory separates out one link in the chain of generations—a single nuclear family—to point out that our relationships are not static. Just as we as individuals grow and change with the passage of time, so too does the family

▪ ▪ ▪

Key Familial Roles And Relationships

Despite being a small group on the micro/macro continuum, the family has largely been examined from the perspective of the individual member. Research studies tend to focus on individuals as units of analysis, not dyads or the larger family network, often describing relationships only through the eyes of one of the participants. The research described in this section focuses on the dyad, the two-person group, within the family.

Spouses/Aging Couples

The majority of older men (79.1% of those 65-74 and 66.7% of those over age 76) were married in 1997 (Lugaila, 1998). For women the picture is more complex. Women are much more likely than men beyond mid-life to be widowed or divorced. (See Exhibit 7.3.) Marital status also varies by race/ethnicity, such that African-American and Hispanic women are even less likely to be married in later life than women from European backgrounds. These figures on marriage overlook older individuals who are coupled without marriage in either heterosexual or homosexual relationships (Huyck, 1995). These uncounted individuals are often erroneously presumed to be without an intimate relationship because they are not legally married.

Marital relationships for persons born in the United States at the turn of the last century were much shorter than today. M any persons were widowed before their children were grown. This was a matter of life expectancy and age of marriage. Median ages at marriage were then of 21.2 for women and 24.6 for men, and the average life expectancy for European American women was about 51 years and for European American males 48 years. African-American women and men had even lower life expectancies, 35 and 32.5 years, respectively (National Center for Health Statistics, 1989; U.S. Bureau of the Census, 1991a). Today, couples marrying at higher median ages (26 for males, 24 for females) can, because of increased life expectancy, expect to be married fifty or more years. Of course, the majority of marriages don't make it to that landmark, but the reason is primarily divorce rather than death of a spouse (U.S. Bureau of the Census, 1991a). This increasing potential duration of marriage has led to suggestions, only half humorous, that growing divorce rates may be one of the outcomes. Couples who might be able to tolerate a problematic marital relationship for fifteen or twenty years choose not to endure it for fifty or sixty years, opting instead for divorce. The great bulk of divorce still occurs among younger rather than older adults, but this pattern may shift in future cohorts.

Marriage does not remain static in maturity, because the roles and responsibilities of the partners change over time with the launching of children, the deaths of family members, and the addition of grandparental roles (Huyck, 1995). Differences may also exist between marital cohorts (groups married at different times in history) in the manner in which household labor is divided

Exhibit 7.3   *Marital Status by Sex and Age: 1995*

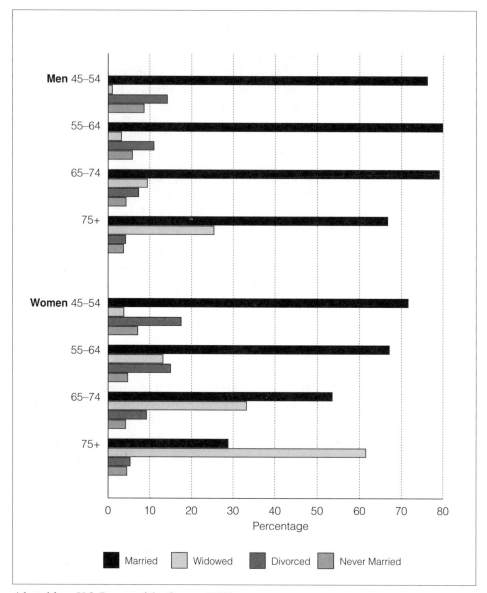

Adapted from: U.S. Bureau of the Census, 1998b.

and gender relations are structured over the course of the couple's life togeth-er. Even in this very personal area, then, it is possible to confuse the effects of aging with cohort or period effects.

Decades ago, deriving her approach from conflict theory, Jesse Bernard (1972) suggested that within each marital relationship were actually two marriages—"her" marriage and "his" marriage—with differing expectations, responsibilities, and pressures. This view, among the pioneering feminist critiques of marital roles, has been supported by years of studies revealing that men benefit than women do from being married. Married men have a greater life expectancy, higher life satisfaction, and better health than single men; married women have no such advantage. Perhaps men get more out of marriage because women do more of the work involved in running the household and in maintaining family relationships, called **kin-keeping** (Bengtson et al., 1990; Rogers, 1995; Schone and Weinick, 1998). Marriage thus benefits men more than women.

Marital Satisfaction over the Life Course

Among the earliest and most persistent themes in the study of marital relations in later life is that of **marital satisfaction** —the degree to which couples are satisfied with their partners and relationships. An early study on marital satisfaction involved a longitudinal comparison of 400 couples married in the early 1930s (Pineo, 1961). In this analysis, in which couples were evaluated soon after marriage and again twenty years later, results showed diminished marital satisfaction, a change that Pineo dubbed "marital disenchantment." Other studies have also confirmed this decline over the first twenty years of marriage (Lee, 1988).

Subsequent cross-sectional analyses of marital satisfaction among couples of different marital durations and ages have suggested that marital satisfaction follows a curvilinear path. Married happiness goes from a peak during the honeymoon to a valley during the rearing of children, bottoming out during the years of raising teenagers, followed by a mid-life improvement as couples move through child launching and into later life. This research has been criticized for concluding that individual couples go through this curvilinear pattern, because the researchers (1) compared across cohorts with very different marital experiences; (2) relied on the average marital satisfaction score to describe a highly variable trait;

Most older couples express high levels of satisfaction wth their relationships.

and (3) ignored the survivorship effect. As time passes, many of the unhappiest couples get divorced, leaving behind a pool of marital survivors who were probably happiest all along (see Glenn, 1998; Weishaus and Field, 1988).

Recent research has not revealed a uniform pattern of change in marital satisfaction or quality with aging. One analysis found no "typical" pattern of change in marital satisfaction in conjunction with aging (Weishaus and Field, 1988). Gary Lee's (1988) cross-sectional research suggests that reduction of parental role overload (as children become adults) is associated with improvements in marital satisfaction. In another study, golden-wedding-anniversary couples, marital survivors, were asked to describe retrospectively (i.e., looking backward over their lives) their levels of marital satisfaction at various times during the family life cycle. The results mirrored the curvilinear pattern of satisfaction for both men and women, but with wives reporting a deeper decline in marital happiness during the middle-age and early old-age periods (mirroring Bernard's concept of "his" and "hers" marital experiences) (Condie, 1989). Other studies have confirmed that the "empty nest," created by the launching of children into adulthood, results in improved marital happiness of partners (White and Edwards, 1990). Recent work by Glenn, which follows five ten-year marriage cohorts over a 21-year period in a cohort-sequential design, found the expected U-shaped pattern when data were examined in a cross-sectional design (1998). Following the experience of individual cohorts, however, did not demonstrate the improvement in the quality of marriage beyond midlife (Glenn, 1998), suggesting that variations in marital satisfaction may be based in differences among cohorts.

Termination of Marriage: Widows and Widowers

The differential in average life expectancy dictates that more women than men will survive their spouses (Kinsella and Taeuber, 1993). Past the age of 65, widows outnumbered widowers 4 to 1 in the United States in 1997 (Lugaila, 1998). As Exhibit 7.4 shows, the incidence of widowhood increases with age, but the gender gap remains throughout. Added to the life-expectancy differential are the facts that women tend to marry men older than themselves and that widowers have ample opportunity to remarry, should they wish to do so (Bengtson et al., 1990). Because of both larger numbers and more pressing problems (such as higher rates of poverty), most of the research has been conducted on widowed women rather than men.

The transition to widowhood is one of the most stressful in life. It takes away a central relationship and a role identity, wife. It changes social relationships with friends. At home widowhood eliminates the division of labor in the household, changes the individual's relationships with kin, and diminishes her economic well-being. Regardless of age, marital roles are highly salient to most individuals, structuring much of their identity and social activities. Even an unhappy marriage influences self-concept and activities. The loss of this rela-

Exhibit 7.4   *Percentage of Males and Females Widowed by Age*

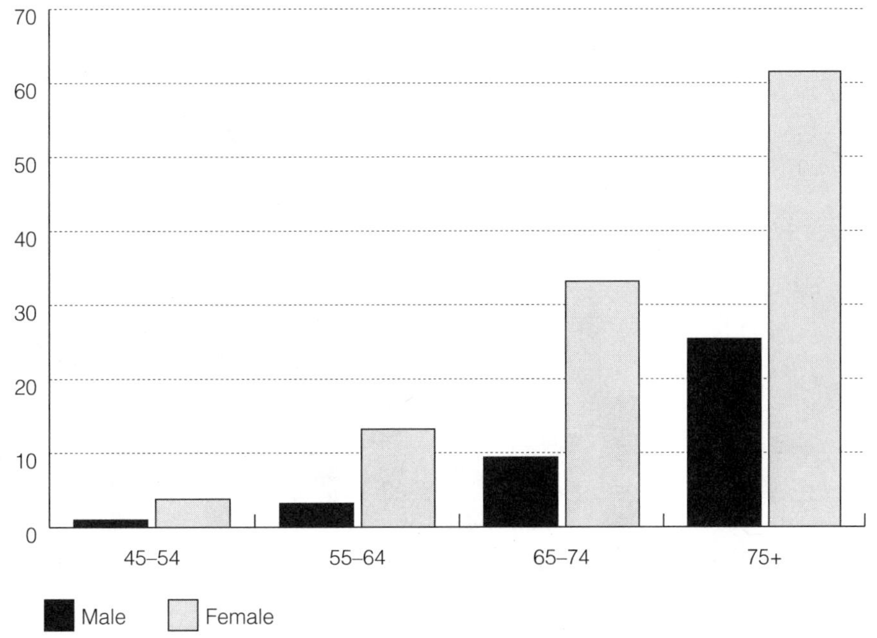

Adapted from: U.S. Bureau of the Census, 1998b.

tionship has both expected and unexpected consequences. Widowed women, for example, experience a disruption in their friendship networks, which are (at least for the middle class) based on couples that interact socially with other couples. Upon being widowed, a woman becomes a "fifth wheel," creating social discomfort if she continues to socialize with her former (married) friendship group (Lopata, 1979). Gradually, most widows change social patterns to spend less time with married friends and more time with other widows.

Cohort effects appear when examining the division of household labor, which was more strictly maintained among cohorts born earlier. A strict division of labor by gender often meant that those who were widowed were unfamiliar with and thus unable to perform certain tasks. Among the oldest cohorts of women, these unfamiliar tasks often included driving an automobile, managing finances, or overseeing household repairs (Lund, Caserta, Dimond, and Shaffer, 1989). Many males went from the home of their parents to that with their wives and never learned how to cook or clean house. In both cases, the strict division of labor meant that the surviving spouse was vulnerable; for example, widowers might not eat properly and widows might manage their money poorly. As we move down the age structure, however, this strict divi-

Exhibit 7.5   *Risks of Being Poor/Near Poor by Household Status and Sex: 1994*

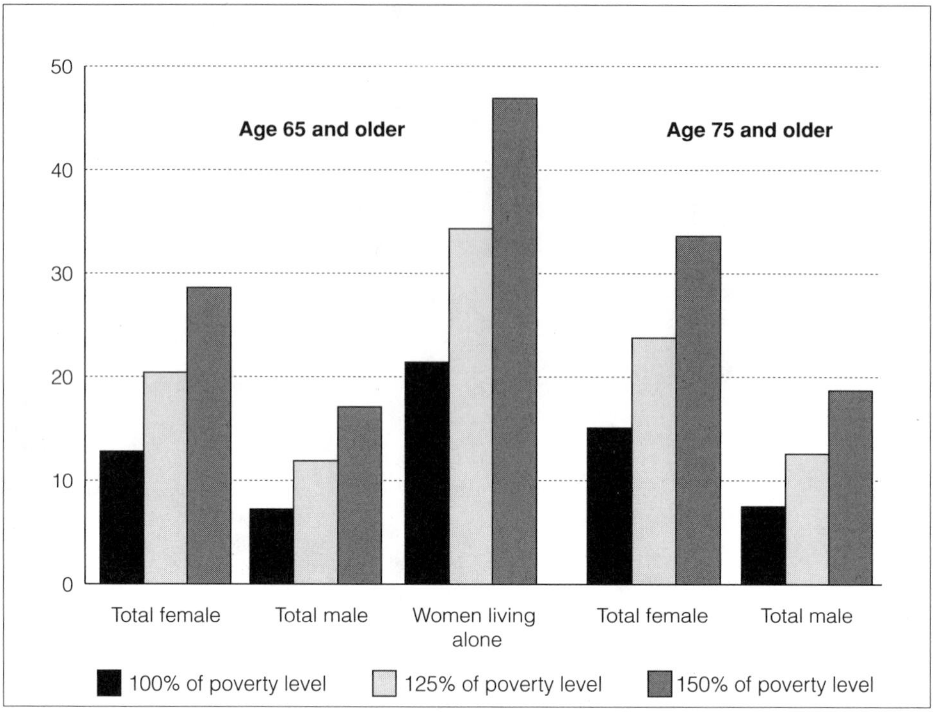

Adapted from: U.S. Bureau of the Census, 1999a.

sion of labor abates, until we reach young cohorts of today, who typically spend some time living on their own and learn most of the basic survival skills once divided into male or female tasks. Although they may fall into "traditional" patterns of gendered tasks if they marry, they will at least have some experience of doing most of those tasks necessary to living independently.

The most important changes in family relationships following widowhood are those relating to children. Relationships with adult children are intensified, as sons and daughters assist in the crisis associated with the death of their parent (Lopata, 1979). Long-term modifications in these relationships, however, tend to be specific by gender. The amount of interaction with adult children increases and persists at the higher level for widows, whereas widowers' levels of contact with adult children continue at levels that existed during their married lives (Morgan, 1984). Why this difference? One possible explanation is the emotionally closer relationships felt toward mothers (Finley et al., 1988). Another is the gendered views of widows as being more vulnerable and in need of emotional and instrumental support following the loss of their spouses (Morgan, 1984). In either case, widowed persons, conforming to norms of independence and "intimacy at a distance," seldom move in with adult children if they themselves are healthy and have adequate income.

Economic security is especially tenuous for widows, in part because of the rules for Social Security and private pensions (see Chapters 8 and 9). As Exhibit 7.5 shows, rates of poverty are significantly higher for widowed women living alone than for other women or for men over age 65. Both Social Security and private pension policies have viewed wives as economic dependents of their husbands, presuming him to be the primary breadwinner. Both systems were established primarily to protect workers (male) and secondarily to protect their dependents (wives and growing children). Social Security, upon the death of the worker, reduces the benefits to a widowed woman who was a traditional homemaker to 66 percent of the couple benefit. Research suggests that the survivor needs 80 percent of the couple's previous income to maintain her standard of living (Burkhauser and Smeeding, 1994). In addition, until 1985 many retiring employees received pensions with no survivor benefits. Thus, many widows moved from having a Social Security benefit plus private pension to having only two-thirds of the prior Social Security benefit. Widowers, in contrast, saw their benefits from Social Security reduced but maintained their private pensions. Under these conditions, is it any wonder that poverty among older, widowed women has been a persistent problem (Burkhauser and Smeeding, 1994)?

Parents and Children

We have already discussed a number of issues that are central to understanding the nature of parent/child relationships. As both the parents and the children mature, the dependencies between them shift, reciprocity becomes a long-term expectation, and there is generally continuity in the contact between generations and its quality (either positive or negative). For most of the adult years, these relationships are governed by the norm of independence. Parenting varies across cohorts, simply because the numbers of children born to cohorts differ, sometimes substantially. As Exhibit 7.6 shows, cohorts of women born between 1906 and 1910 had significantly lower fertility than did their successors born between 1931 and 1935. Thinking about the time frames during which these cohorts of women were having their families, how might you use historical events (period effects) to partially explain these differences? Today, U.S. rates of fertility are much lower, hovering around 1.9 births per woman but varying across class, race, and educational groupings (see Chapter 3).

Beyond these central characteristics, two contrasting themes have characterized discussions of relationships between older parents and adult children over the years. The first, and perhaps most persistent, mythical theme is that adult children neglect and abandon their older parents, indicative of the poor relationships between them (Shanas, 1979a, b). This theme of abandonment was described in the quotation opening the chapter. The second theme is that of family solidarity, support, and affection as descriptive of parent/child bonds in later life. Although these themes have traded places in terms of prominence over time, both probably reflect unrealistic stereotyping of parent/child relation-

Exhibit 7.6   *Variations in Completed Fertility for Cohorts of Women*

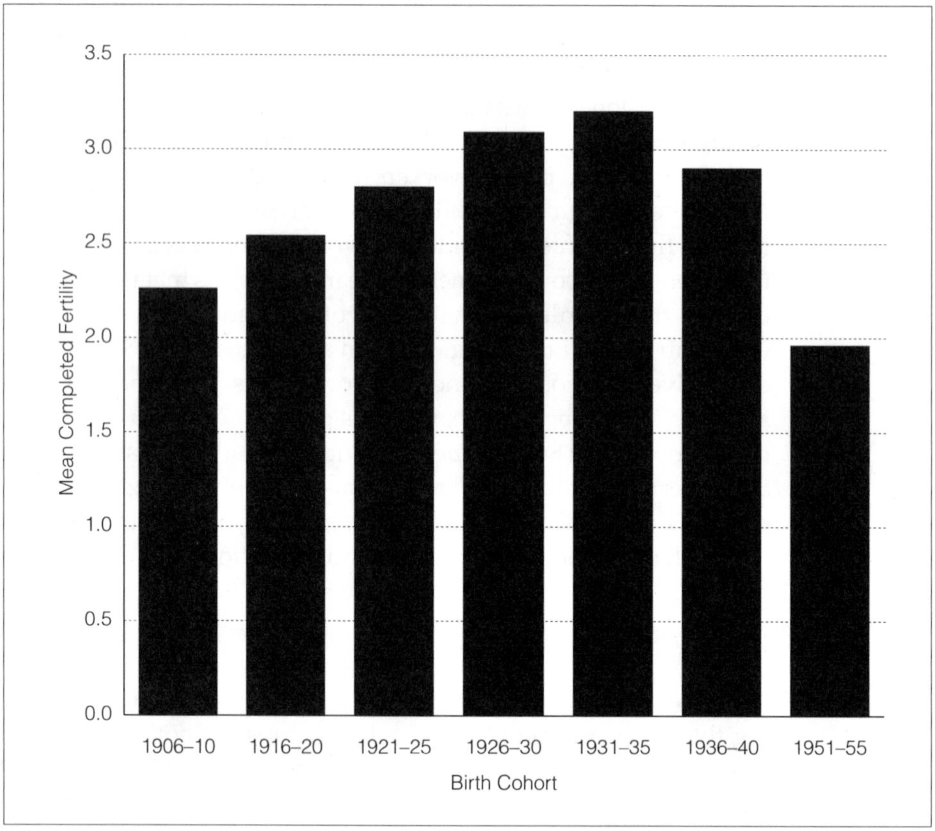

Source: Bachu, 1997.

ships. As is often the case, the truth lies somewhere in between.

There has been a good deal of research on the levels and types of interactions between adult generations in a family. According to research in this area, most older persons are *not* isolated from their families; a majority of interactions are deemed to be positive (Bengtson et al., 1985). Interestingly, it is generally assumed that *more* interaction is *better* for the elderly family members. This oversimplifies relationships between parents and children, where majorities recognize some conflicts in their relationship along with more positive aspects (Antonucci, 1990; Clarke, Preston, Raksin and Bengtson, 1999; Luescher and Pillemer, 1998).

In an effort to overcome the myth of family abandonment of the elderly, researchers may have gone too far in emphasizing support and consensus within the family, overlooking conflict and ambivalence (Luescher and Pillemer, 1998). It would clearly be a mistake to assume that family relationships are untroubled, and that more is always better in terms of family interaction. There is an ample body of evidence demonstrating **neglect and abuse** of older persons by family members, often those providing care for them (Steinmetz, 1988). There is more than one potential explanation for elder abuse. First, abuse and neglect may be a product of violations of the norm of independence. When an older person becomes dependent on a child, for example, it violates this norm and places an unexpected stress on the relationship with a caregiver, especially a child (Steinmetz, 1988). A second hypothesis, not yet thoroughly tested with regard to elder abuse, is that violence is a product of reciprocity; that is, adult children who are violent toward a frail parent are returning violence that they received as children. Indirect support for this argument comes from studies showing that children from violent families are themselves more likely to be violent toward kin (Wallace, 1996). Finally, recent research has examined the fact that many of those committing abuse and neglect are spouses, not adult children. What remains unclear is whether this abuse began after the person reached old age, or whether this pattern of violence is a long-standing characteristic of the marital relationship (Vinton, 1991). Since not all couples experiencing violence divorce, some component of elder abuse may be "spousal violence grown old" (Harris, 1995).

Parent/child relationships are influenced by a variety of factors, including characteristics of the parent and child on the micro level and changes in the age structure of society on the macro level. Increasing life expectancy means that often the "child" caring for an aging parent is herself old, for example, a 65-year-old "child" caring for a 90-year-old parent. Second, smaller family size means a smaller ratio of younger to older family members, lessening the availability of kin for support and kin-keeping functions. Third, mobility has meant that adult children are less residentially proximate to their parents, modifying the numbers and types of interactions possible between them. Not all researchers are convinced that the changes in intergenerational relations will be dramatic or occur quickly. Demographer Peter Uhlenberg (1993) contends that the changes over the next several decades will be slow and gradual, enabling ample time for societal and individual adaptations to changes in the family structure.

Research has consistently suggested that gender of parent and child influences the relationship between them. Mother/daughter dyads are typically closer than any other combination, with more daughters acting as confidantes and fewer likely to disappoint their mothers (see Suitor, Pillemer, Keeton, and Robison, 1994). The relationship most likely to experience conflict is that between a father and son, with cross-gender dyads (mother/son, father/daughter) falling somewhere in between.

Siblings

Most older persons, and indeed most adults, have one or more siblings with whom they continue to interact in later life (Brubaker, 1990b). Sibling relationships have some unique characteristics that differentiate them from other familial ties. First, sibling relationships are likely to be the longest-enduring kinship bonds most of us experience in our lives (Brubaker, 1990a). Whereas a marriage typically starts after twenty or more years of life have elapsed, siblings are often born only a few years apart. Because they live their early lives in temporal as well as physical proximity, siblings essentially share a childhood in the family culture (Cicirelli, 1991). In addition, siblings often share a cohort and its experiences, encountering the same major innovations, historical events, and societal value shifts. Since sisters and brothers, unlike friends, are not chosen, there are no guarantees of closeness or affection in these relationships. Indeed, the aftermath of sibling rivalry or violence can exact a toll on these relationships throughout adulthood (Scott, 1990).

Changes in Contact/Intimacy through Life

Until recently, most of the research on bonds between siblings presumed that, after adolescence, siblings were unimportant in the lives of adults (Bedford, 1995). More recently, limited studies of siblings have suggested a continuing salience of these relationships throughout adulthood (Bedford, 1995; Cicirelli, 1991; Scott, 1990). Although their energies may be absorbed by their jobs, spouses and children in early to middle adulthood, siblings maintain emotional bonds and tend to reactivate their bonds if they have become dormant as they mature and their children depart (Bedford, 1995).

Siblings can and do provide friendship and support to one another as adults (Wellman and Wortley, 1989), often maintaining relationships even when they are geographically distant. Exchanges among siblings seldom include financial aid or substantial assistance with health care, probably because of norms of independence (Suitor and Pillemer, 1993; Wellman and Wortley, 1989). There is some evidence that the amount of intersibling support and assistance declines in old age (Bedford, 1989), but this research is rather limited by small, unrepresentative samples.

Variations in Sibling Linkages

Not all sibling relationships are created equal. A range of social factors helps to construct the outlines of how a sibling relationship will unfold through adulthood and later life. Along with other family relationships, sibling bonds are shown by research to vary across racial/ethnic groups. Two major studies have confirmed that older African Americans rely more on siblings for assistance than do their European American or Hispanic counterparts; these results are especially compelling because socio-economic differences between groups were very small, ruling out that alternative explanation (Bedford, 1995). The norm of independence from siblings may be weaker and expectations of reciprocity and support stronger in the culture of African American families.

The number of siblings is also important, because the amount of support given by any single brother or sister may be limited. The more siblings one has, the more likely as an adult one relies on a sibling as a confidante or provider of support (Connidis and Davies, 1992). But older adults who have other family relationships, such as adult children, may turn to them rather than to a sibling for some types of support. Marital status also influences the interdependence of siblings. Individuals who have never married or those whose marriages have ended appear to turn more to siblings for assistance (see Bedford, 1995). Being married and having one's own children are thought to provide more compelling role involvements, pushing sibling relationships to a somewhat lower priority.

Finally, what is the role of gender in shaping the closeness of sibling bonds? Some early research suggested that relationships with a sister are closer; other studies suggest that same-sex dyads are closer than those consisting of a brother and sister (Bedford 1995; Scott, 1990). Same-sex pairs, especially sisters, are noted for the stronger emotional bonds throughout their lives (Cicirelli, 1991).

Grandparents

What pictures come to mind in thinking about grandparents? Typically we rely on those cultural images fostered by advertisers, including advanced age, gray hair, leisure, kindness, and celebration of family rituals and holiday traditions. Do grandparents really fit this image? What exactly do grandparents do?

Most persons now over age 65 are parents, and most have also become grandparents, often well before reaching old age. Although being a grandparent is a familial role associated in our thinking with later life, most individuals enter grandparenthood earlier (Bengtson et al., 1990). In a recent study the average age at birth of the first grandchild was 47 years, and 62% of grandparents still had a child under age 18 at home when this transition occurred; 45% of those with a grandchild under age 6 were employed 30+ hours a week (Szinovacz, 1998). For women this means spending nearly one-half of life as a grandparent. The timing of becoming a grandparent is highly variable, from well before age 40 to beyond age 60 (Szinovacz, 1998).

Although entry into grandparenthood is variable, once entered it is an enduring role, lasting until the grandparent's death, by which time the grandchildren are often grown and themselves parents (Szinovacz, 1998). The span of this relationship encompasses the aging of the grandparent, so that neither partner in the relationship remains static (Silverstein and Long, 1998). As expected, with the maturation of both parties, the relationship changes over time, with grandparents enjoying their roles best when grandchildren are young (Cherlin and Furstenberg, 1986).

The Waltons Myth: Coresidence of Grandparents

The once-popular 1970s television show "The Waltons," now syndicated, presented a nostalgic view of family life during the Depression. The strong family of three generations included paternal grandparents, their son and his wife, and a large number of their children, ranging in age from late adolescence into childhood. Did the Waltons present a realistic image of family life in the past, with grandparents happily coresiding with their children and grandchildren?

Although a myth persists regarding the high number of **intergenerational households** (with three or more generations) in the past, the number of households including an aging parent has declined from its already low level in the early decades of the twentieth century to even lower figures today (see Chapter 3). Demography offers ample reasons that this type of household was not common. First, the life expectancy of that era was short. It is probable that either Grandma or Grandpa Walton would have died before all of their children had reached maturity. Even if they had both lived, it is even less likely that they would both survive the nearly twenty additional years that would be required to produce grandchildren of the ages shown in the program. Finally, if the grandparents had a large number of children, as their own son subsequently did, a lot of other Walton sons and daughters, married and perhaps with their own children, would not be sharing a household with aged grandparents. Assuming four siblings, for example, only 25 percent of those households could have grandparents for some period of time.

Demography aside, grandparents in that era were less likely to be warm and compassionate than is true in more recent cohorts (Cherlin and Furstenberg, 1986). Grandparents were more often distant authority figures, rather than nurturers of younger children. In short, the idyllic picture of happy multigenerational living portrayed in "The Waltons," though not impossible, was certainly not the commonly lived experience of most families of that era.

Voluntary Nature of Grandparenting in Middle-Class Families

Just what are the duties and rights of a grandparent? As a social role, being a grandparent is not well structured. Early research, mostly on European American, middle-class grandparents, has attempted to identify the roles played by grandparents within the family system and toward the grandchildren (Roberto, 1990). Relatively few clear-cut responsibilities are mandated for grandparents, because their roles, unlike those of parents, typically are not critical to the survival and well-being of dependent children. Given that only recently have large numbers of people lived long enough to spend much time as grandparents, the fact that social norms have not yet been constructed is understandable. This cultural void gives grandparents the opportunity to structure the role in any way they see fit, but it also provides them with few guidelines on how they should act as grandparents (Kennedy, 1990). Probably as a result, much of the early work on grandparenting has focused on how adults view and structure their relationships with grandchildren. Several studies have identified "styles" of grandparental behavior, indicating a wide variation in how the relationships are structured and perceived (Roberto, 1990).

Somewhat less research has examined the relationship from the perspective

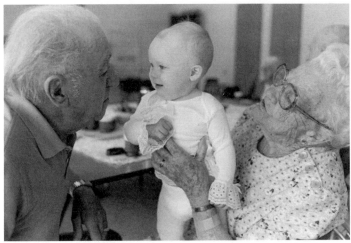

Grandparent roles can vary from formal and distant to warm and nurturing surrogate parents.

of the grandchild. One study (Kennedy, 1990) asked more than 700 college students about their grandparents' roles. "Students tended to agree most strongly with items that described grandparents as being loving, helping and comforting, as providing role models, and sharing family history, as being persons who are important in the lives of young people and persons with whom they have fun." The responsibilities of grandchildren were to "express love and provide help to their grandparents, that they are a part of their grandparents' sense of the future" (Kennedy, 1990, pp. 45-46). Within the sample, female students tended more than males to emphasize the closeness of the relationships, and African American students described grandparenting as a more active role than did their European American peers. Even with these expectations, however, there is a wide range of ways in which grandparents could enact their role obligations (Szinovacz, 1998).

Relationships between grandparents and grandchildren are built within a larger context of family relationships. The middle generation plays a critical role, linking the older and younger generations in the kinship system. This role has been described as the **lineage bridge**, the span connecting the other two generations (Thompson and Walker, 1987). The quality of the relationships between the grandparents and parents, acting as lineage bridges, will inevitably shape the closeness, residential proximity, and frequency and types of interaction between grandparents and grandchildren. This linkage becomes especially important in the case of divorce, where paternal grandparents may lose contact with grandchildren unless they maintain ties to their former daughter-in-law or exercise their legal rights to visitation (Roberto, 1990).

Variations in Grandparenting Roles

Beyond differences based on the respective ages of grandparent and grandchild, other factors that influence the bonds between grandparents and grandchildren include race/ethnicity and gender. Cherlin and Furstenberg (1986) found that African American grandparents take a more active role, correcting the behavior of grandchildren and acting as protectors of the family. These behaviors are sometimes undertaken out of necessity, when the adult child is divorced, un/underemployed, or otherwise less capable of providing for the grandchild (Cherlin and Furstenberg, 1986; Hogan, Eggebeen, and Clogg, 1993). This greater activism is enabled by higher rates of multigenerational households. Studies of household structure have shown that African American families are more likely to have three-generation households, providing grandparents with opportunities to take a more active role toward their grandchildren (Cherlin and Furstenberg, 1986; U.S. Bureau of the Census, 1991a). There has been an increase in grandchildren living with one or more grandparents during the 1990s from 3.2% in 1970 to 5.5% in 1997 (Bryson and Casper, 1999). Exhibit 7.7 shows significant differences by race in the percentages of grandchildren who reside with their grandparents. Within each group, most children live with their mother and one or more grandparents, but a substantial number live with grandparents only, without either parent in the household (Saluter, 1996).

In these and other instances, grandparents take on active roles in lieu of parents, acting as **surrogate parents**. An estimated 3.9 million American grandchildren lived in the same household with their grandparents in 1997 (Bryson and Casper, 1999). The percentages are higher for African American than for European American children. More than 12 percent of African American children live with grandparents, and nearly 40 percent of those have neither of their parents living with them in the household, creating a skipped-generation household. Grandparents acting as surrogate parents take on short- or long-term responsibility for care of grandchildren because of economic or social problems of their adult children (including death, substance abuse, physical or mental illness, and incarceration) (Pruchno, 1999). Research suggests that the establishment of skipped generation or multi-generational households involving grandparents are more often brought about by the needs of *younger* generations for assistance than by the needs of elderly kin for care (Ward et al., 1992). This unexpected undertaking of parenting responsibilities can be stressful for the grand-

Exhibit 7.7   *Children Under Age 18 Living in Grandparents' Households by Race/Ethnicity*

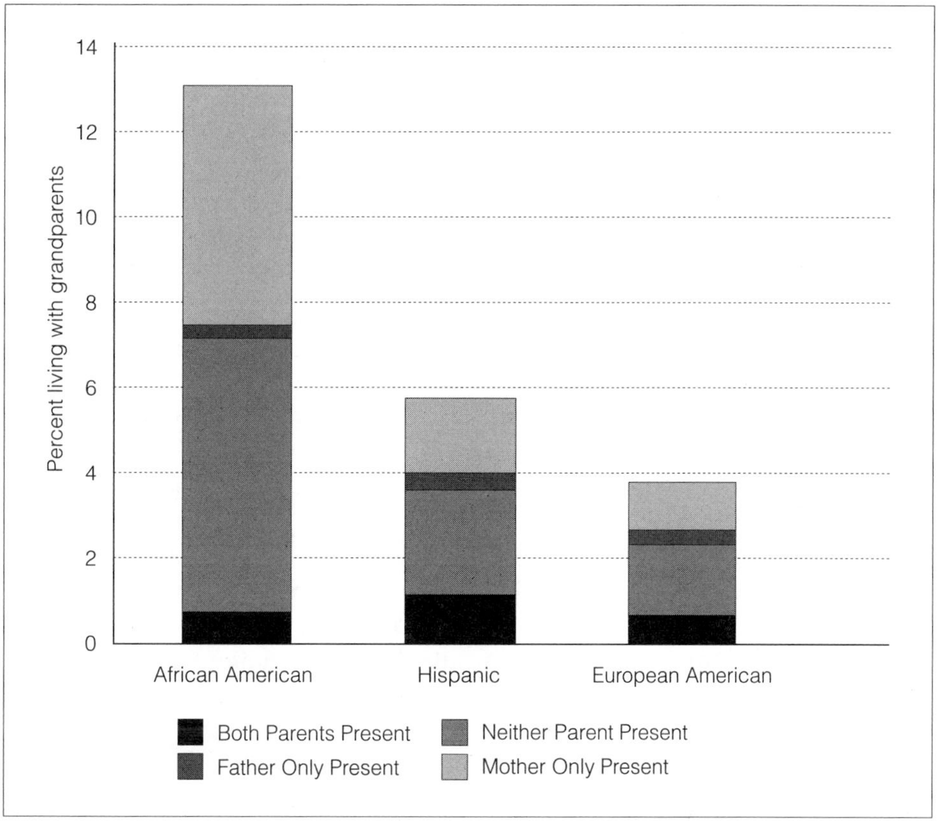

Adapted from: Saluter, 1996.

parents, who may themselves be facing challenges associated with aging (Burton and DeVries, 1995; Pruchno, 1999). On the other hand, some recent research suggests that both adolescent grandchildren and their grandparents may derive some benefits from this multi-generational situation (Kirby and Uhlenberg, 1998).

■ ■ ■ ■ ■ ■ ■ ■
APPLYING THEORY:
Exchange Theory and Family Caregiving

What is really happening when individuals, groups, or societies interact with one another? What is the essence of the social interactions that take place every day on any level from person to person or major corporation to major corporation or nation to nation? One framework for answering these questions derives from **social exchange theory**. This particular theory emphasizes social life as constructed by exchanges among social actors of a variety of valued resources, including material goods, financial resources, and intangible social goods (humor, respect, information) (Dowd, 1975). Exchange theory bridges the micro-macro continuum, because individuals, groups, or even entire nations may form exchange relationships; each exchange partner seeks to maximize their returns in the exchange by getting as much or more back than they give. If one party to the exchange is not receiving an equitable return, that party will withdraw and seek other exchanges. Inequalities of power between exchange partners can be critical. We can easily think of examples such as a friendship, where friends of equal social power provide each other (via exchange) with emotional support, respect, and help in an ongoing fashion. But social exchange may happen on a much larger scale, when labor unions negotiate a new contract with management or when nations in conflict must settle disputes by each giving up desired land, military power, or other resources. Exchanges also occur across levels of the micro-macro continuum, as when individuals exchange with a large organization (such as exchanging work effort for a paycheck).

In exchange theory it is essential to consider whether those making exchanges hold equal power (equal resources), because power influences how the exchange will occur. More powerful exchange partners, whether individuals, corporations, community groups, or nations, have a larger reserve of valued resources to give. Being thus endowed, they have a wide range of potential partners eagerly awaiting an exchange opportunity. Because they can pick and choose among exchange partners, they can control the terms of the exchange to their own benefit.

In applying the concepts of exchange theory to aging, Dowd (1975) has proposed that individuals in Western industrialized societies systematically lose power and resources as they age, putting them at a disadvantage in exchanges. Old age itself is a deficit in social exchange. This may lead to unequal exchange relationships and force older people to behave in ways that are not of their choosing. Dowd defines the process of retirement as one of exchanging the prestige and higher wages of employment for the security of a fixed income and health benefits (pension, Social Security, and Medicare). In an unequal power situation with an employer, employees may be prompted to "choose" to retire either by improvements in the exchange rate if they comply (a "golden parachute" benefits package) or by the prospect of a much less profitable exchange should they stay. Because older persons may lack high incomes and powerful social positions and are, as a group, socially devalued, they must give more to maintain their exchanges, further depleting their limited resources.

Applying exchange theory to the family, we could examine the relative power of participants in the exchange, which may be conditioned by age, gender, family roles (child, parent), or other social factors. We can also examine various types of exchanges that are ongoing in family life and those undertaken under special, crisis conditions. Principles of exchange and reciprocity are sometimes visible in the support of various types that occurs in later-life families, including caregiving for elderly kin. How does exchange play a role? Some people argue that caregiving by adult children is essentially delayed reciprocity, a repayment on a deferred debt for care received while they were children. In this sense, the norm of reciprocity is a special case of exchange theory operating between the generations. Some research suggests that keeping the exchange at least somewhat "even" is important to the well-being of participants. Older relatives who are recipients of support often value the opportunity to help their children or grandchildren in return, even if that support involves simply being a good listener or giving advice. People with physical impairments requiring a lot of assistance can, by broadly defining support that is exchanged, understand that they are still making a contribution (Walker, Martin, and Jones, 1992). Those receiving care who do not feel they are giving anything back experience lower well-being because of their unbalanced exchanges.

■ ■ ■

Families As Providers Of Support

Some theorists think about social institutions, such as the family, in terms of the functions they perform for the larger society and for the individual members. Families have always served both their members and the larger society by providing various types of support and assistance to their members. Researchers have devoted considerable attention to the ways families support their members, especially frail elderly persons. These supports vary across the life course; across class, culture, and ethnic groups; and historically within a given culture. Within families, support flows both within and across generational boundaries.

Intergenerational Support

A thirty-year research tradition has sought to analyze and understand the ongoing patterns of exchange both within and among households of the modified extended family. Among the pioneering work was that of Reuben Hill (1970), who examined the exchanges among three generations of families in the 1950s. That study showed that family members in all generations were typically involved in giving and receiving assistance of various types, including assistance during illness, child care, financial support, emotional support, and household management. The middle generation tends to be net givers of support—that is, they provided more types of help to other generations (their elderly parents and their adult children) than they themselves received. As Exhibit 7.8 shows, the young adult generation more commonly received assistance and gave less. The grandparent generation gave the least and received the most help with household tasks, illness, and emotional support,

Amato and his colleagues (1995) more recently collected data on four types

Exhibit 7.8   *Percentage of Young Adult Children Receiving or Providing Intergenerational Support*

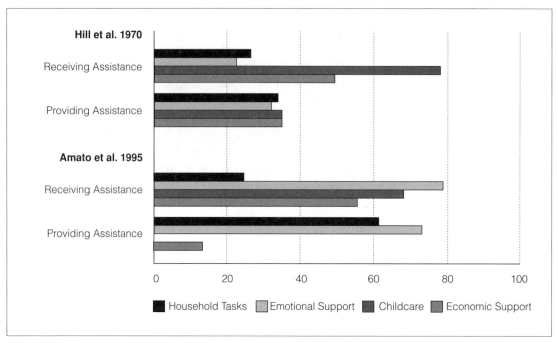

Adapted from: Hill and Associates, 1970; and Amato et al., 1995.

of assistance studied by Hill and his colleagues, sampling exchanges of assistance between just two generations, young adults (19+ years of age, still living at home) and their parents (see Exhibit 7.8). In this newer study, adult children were much more likely to provide assistance with household tasks (understandable because they shared a residence with parents), and many more said they both gave and received advice. The fact that fewer received childcare help than in the Hill study may have to do with the fact that fewer were themselves parents. Finally, fewer reported providing financial gifts or loans to parents than had reported doing so in the earlier study. Either differences in sampling or cohort and period effects might explain the differences in the results.

Another recent study (Hogan, Eggebeen, and Clogg, 1993) examined intergenerational support in a large national sample of more than 5,000 adults who had (1) surviving parents and (2) one or more children under 18 at home. Four specific types of support were examined: financial, caregiving (to a child or parent), assistance with household tasks, and emotional support or advice. Analyses of exchanges between the older two generations indicated that more than half (53 percent) of middle-generation adults were low exchangers, giving or receiving very little and 11 percent were high exchangers, typically both giving and receiving a variety of support with their aging parents. Women were more active as exchangers than were men and coresident parents both received and gave high levels of support. African Americans were, contrary to the findings of previous research, *less* likely to be involved in intergenerational exchanges, a result explained by a shortage of resources within their families.

Finally, the study by Hogan and his associates (1993) revealed that family size influenced the exchange of support. When there were several siblings, each was less likely to receive support from older parents, who had to divide limited resources among several offspring. Older parents, on the other hand, improved the odds of being recipients of support with each additional adult child. This analysis was, of course, a snapshot cross-sectional view of support and did not convey the lifetime experience of giving or receiving support. In fact, Riley suggests that low levels of assistance at any given time may mask a **latent kin matrix**, "a web of continually shifting linkages that provide the potential for activating and intensifying close kin relationships" when and if they are needed (1983, p. 441). Thus, current exchange and support may be much more limited than the potential exchange and support should greater need arise.

More recently research has tended to focus on families as providers of routine support to elders, rather than on the reciprocity of exchanges (Hogan, Eggebeen, and Clogg, 1993). Although this research continues to show that older adults receive considerable assistance from adult children, especially in crises, it would be erroneous to conclude that they are only the recipients of support. Numerous studies also reveal the ongoing support of many types that older adults provide to their grown children and grandchildren (Walker et al., 1992). In fact, most multigenerational households are created in response to the needs (economic, housing, child care) of adult children, rather than the needs of older adults, as was once believed (Ward, Logan and Spitze, 1992).

Family Members as Caregivers to Frail Elders

In times of illness or disability, most older adults receive both emotional and instrumental assistance from kin. Turning to close others for this support can be thought of as a means of compensating for functional losses. Older adults who lack supportive ties on whom they can rely for assistance are at greatest risk for institutionalization when they can no longer care for themselves (see review by Antonucci and Akiyama, 1995). It is estimated that 80 percent of informal care for frail and disabled elders is provided by kin acting as **family caregivers** (Dwyer, 1995).

Families provide a wide array of assistance to kin with health limitations, most of it routine aid in tasks of everyday living that may be so normalized as not to be thought of as assistance by family members (Chappell, 1990; National Alliance for Caregiving, 1997). Although kin are sometimes limited in their health care skills, there are pressures toward placing more responsibility for sophisticated procedures in the hands of relatives to minimize health care costs to insurers and Medicare (Glazer, 1993) (See Chapter 10 for further discussion of health care delivery.)

Caregiver Burden and Rewards

Despite the obvious benefits to older adults' functioning and independence, the stress experienced in providing such care often decreases the physical and psychological health of the caregiver (see review by Schulz, Visintainer, and Williamson, 1990). Family members undertaking these responsibilities often experience stress and **caregiver burden**. The experience of burden—a degree of strain reflecting lower life satisfaction, depression, and a decline in health—is highly variable, depending on the level and type of impairment of the care recipient and a number of aspects of the relationship between the care provider and recipient (Chappell, 1990). For example, adult children seem to be more prone to stress than spouses acting as caregivers, perhaps because the intense responsibility for an aged parent violates the norms of generational independence, as well as presenting the potential for role conflicts with midlife marriage and parenting responsibilities. Caregivers to patients with cognitive impairments leading to behavioral problems (night wandering, agitation, or dangerous and embarrassing behaviors) also report greater caregiver burden (Chappell, 1990; National Alliance for Caregiving, 1997).

One important consequence of assuming the role of primary caregiver, of particular relevance to social relations research, is the limitation imposed on the caregiver's own social relationships. The time and energy required to provide care to an impaired family member drains the resources available to the caregiver for engaging in other role responsibilities or social interactions. Such interference of the caregiving role with other important social roles has been shown to detract from the psychological well-being of the primary caregiver (Stephens and Franks, 1995; Stephens and Townsend, 1997). However, family caregiver research has also found that the increased social involvement with the impaired older family member can be also rewarding to caregivers (Stephens, Franks, and Townsend, 1994) and can bring family members closer together (Stoller and Pugliesi, 1989).

Who Are Family Caregivers?

Nearly two decades of research on informal caregiving have established that most adults receive much of the help they need from a single network member. The person most responsible for the care of an impaired person is referred to as the **primary caregiver**. Other network members who provide assistance both to the primary caregiver and to the impaired older adult are referred to as secondary caregivers (see review by Gatz, Bengtson, and Blum, 1990). Although adult children constitute approximately one-third of family caregivers, their participation is actually surpassed by that of spouses (Stone, Cafferata, and Sangl, 1987). Other relatives (siblings, grandchildren) or friends and neighbors may also be included in informal caregiving groups (National Alliance for Caregiving, 1997).

The provision of care to older adults has been shown to follow a hierarchical pattern (Cantor, 1983; Horowitz, 1985a). Caregivers are selected from available kin, with the role often, but not always, falling first to a physically able spouse (Allen, Goldscheider and Ciambrone, 1999). Because male partners are generally older, more wives than husbands face the duties of caregiving (Chappell, 1990). If a spouse is unavailable or unable to provide the needed assistance, they turn next to adult children.

Among adult children, gender, proximity, marital status, and the prior quality of the relationship can all contribute to the selection of an adult child as primary caregiver (Allen et al., 1999). Daughters are three times as likely as sons to assume the role of primary caregiver. Among the most impaired parents, the disparity between daughters and sons increases such that daughters are four times as likely to assume the primary caregiver role (Stone and Kemper, 1989).

Horowitz (1985b) found notable differences in how sons and daughters performed the caregiver role. Although both groups were highly involved in providing care (27 percent shared a household with their older parent), they differed in the types of care they provided. Aside from the emotional support commonly provided by both sons and daughters, more of the "hands-on" care of transportation, household chores, meal preparation, and personal care fell to

Caregivers, most often daughters, provide both emotional and practical supports.

daughters. Sons involved themselves in male gender-specific tasks (financial management, dealing with bureaucracies) or gender-neutral tasks, spending less time and doing a smaller number of tasks overall than their female counterparts. Most married sons involved their spouses in the caregiving, whereas fewer than half of daughters did so. Perhaps not surprisingly, daughters experienced more stress in association with their caregiving duties, largely because of their greater commitment in time and task responsibility. Sons appear to be more motivated by norms of obligation and familism, whereas daughters are more often motivated by the affection of the relationship, confirming the kin-keeping role of women in the family system (Silverstein, Parrott, and Bengtson, 1995).

Another study by Spitze and Logan (1990) looked at the family's structure, including the number of sons and daughters, in explaining patterns of support to an older parent. Elders with large numbers of children were more likely to coreside with a daughter or son. Receipt of support from kin outside the household was less likely for parents with only sons, showing the importance of having at least one daughter for receipt of interhousehold assistance with daily activities. A second daughter, however, did not substantially improve the likelihood of receiving assistance.

Daily contact for care requires residential proximity, ruling out adult children living at great distances. In some cases an unmarried child, or one without children, will be tapped as caregiver on the assumption that this child will have fewer role conflicts (Brody, 1985). Finally, it is unlikely that an adult child with a conflicted past relationship with the parent will undertake caregiving unless there is no other alternative.

Women in the Middle

It is well-established that female kin provide the bulk of caregiving in both routine and crisis family situations (National Alliance for Caregiving, 1997). Research by Brody (1981) has identified the potential problem of being a **woman in the middle** (also known as being in the **sandwich generation**). These women appear to be caught between the responsibilities of providing care to their own dependent children at home and assisting frail parents or parents-in-law. Both increased longevity and decreased fertility (providing fewer adult children as potential caregivers) are thought to accentuate the problem (Rosenthal, Matthews, and Marshall, 1991). Although this structural problem of being in the middle may be a serious one for those upon whose shoulders it falls, recent research argues that the problem is not as common as once believed. First, the peak demand on adult-child caregivers occurs between the ages of 45 and 54 (17 percent of this age group has a disabled older parent) (Cantor, 1995). By this age most women have raised their children beyond early childhood and into adolescence or young adulthood, times when parental demands may be waning. Second, as longevity increases and disability is delayed, the onset of caregiving responsibilities should occur at later ages for adult children, further reducing the potential for simultaneous, competing demands by older and younger generations (Cantor, 1995). One study, for example, has demonstrated that only 50 percent of women are at risk of this dual responsibility, with fewer actually facing demands from both generations. The potential for being "in the middle" is greatest for younger women, because their parents are surviving and their children are still in the household. But their parents are also still fairly young and healthy, generally not in need of assistance. By the time older parents reach ages where disability becomes prevalent, their grandchildren are typically launched, leaving most women with caregiving responsibility toward only one generation (Rosenthal et al., 1991).

What these studies overlook is that there are other role conflicts, such as being caught between the conflicting responsibilities of employment and caring for an aged parent. This increasingly common role conflict (Matthews and Rosenthal, 1993) may detract from effectiveness at work, and sometimes results in cessation of employment in order to provide care. Although family leave (without pay) is now available, the ongoing demands of care for a parent with chronic health problems often forces choices between reducing/stopping work (with the attendant loss of income and reduction in pension benefits) and purchasing care from the formal sector. In addition, the prospect of delayed onset of disability for aged parents means that the "children" serving as caregivers themselves may be even older than caregivers are today. Although the retirement of adult children may enable them to have more time to attend to caregiving duties, such duties may magnify the children's own issues of aging, such as economic or health problems. Still debated hotly in policy circles is the degree to which family members should be responsible for the later-life income, housing, or health care needs of their members

Social Change And The Family's Future

Neither the family as a social institution nor individual families are static. They respond to changes in the larger society, and they contribute to or accelerate societal changes through the decisions and actions of individuals or family units. As Maddox and Lawton (1993) point out, "Current interest is not on whether groups bonded by kinship persist but how and why they adapt as effectively as they do in response to social change" (p. 2). As we move into the twenty-first century, what predictions can we make about how families may age differently?

Changes in Size/Structure of Families

Increased longevity has created the growing potential for four- and even five-generation families. The advent of the four-generation family was first heralded back in the 1960s (Townsend, 1968). In a **five- or six-generation family**, an individual can simultaneously be a grandparent and a grandchild, provid-

Exhibit 7.9   *Comparison of Family Structure and Size with High versus Low Fertility*

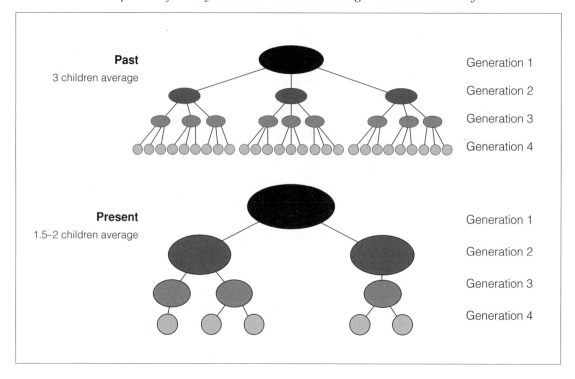

ing an even richer possible set of intergenerational family experiences. The possibilities for exchanges of support across so many generations raise many questions, such as whether all generations will have some responsibility toward the oldest. Will elderly sons and daughters be able to adequately assist their even older parents? What rights and duties does a great-grandparent have toward her offspring three generations removed?

Changes in fertility also have long-term implications for family structure. As fertility rates have stabilized in recent years near replacement rate (just under 2 children per married couple), the "family tree" has changed its shape, a process sometimes called family verticalization. From a narrow base of one couple, fewer children and grandchildren will eventually emerge, leading to a description of this structure not as a tree but as a **beanpole family** (Bengtson et al., 1990). As Exhibit 7.9 shows, the change from a fertility rate of 3 to a fertility rate of 1.5 alters the numbers of siblings, cousins, grandchildren, and great-grandchildren any individual is likely to experience. The beanpole family, resulting from lower fertility, contains fewer siblings, in-laws, nieces, and nephews, and relatively more kin located in other generations. It is unclear whether this change in structure will be accompanied by a systematic change in filial expectations when fewer adult children are available as supporters and caregivers.

Greater Complexity of Family Relations

Although comparatively few of the current older adult population have experienced divorce, the percentage of divorcees will increase dramatically among future cohorts (Crown, Mutschler, Schulz, and Loew, 1993; Uhlenberg, Cooney, and Boyd, 1990). Since the probability of remarriage diminishes rapidly for women as they age, more women will enter later life in divorced status (Uhlenberg et al., 1990). Even among current cohorts of older adults, many have experienced the stress, familial dislocation, and relationship complexity resulting from the divorces of their children or grandchildren. Grandparents may lose touch with grandchildren or find themselves providing housing and childcare assistance to a newly divorced child in conjunction with a transition out of marriage (Johnson, 1995a). These responsibilities may tax the resources of aging couples or individuals.

Increasing numbers of older adults in future cohorts will themselves have been through divorce, often (more so for men) followed by remarriage. Many will have spent a considerable number of years in families with stepchildren (or with stepsiblings). There are probably important but as yet unresearched differences between older persons who are "newly divorced" and those who are "career divorced," having spent numerous years in divorced status as they aged (Brubaker, 1990b). Given the association between divorced status and poorer economic security in later life (Crown et al., 1993; Weaver, 1997), the coming cohorts of elders with their increased experience of divorce give society cause for concern (Uhlenberg et al., 1990).

There are many unanswered questions about family relationships derived from the more complex families that emerge in a society with divorce and remarriage. Will adult children feel strong filial obligation toward a biological parent, stepparent, or both (Ganong, Coleman, McDaniel and Killian, 1998)? How enduring will relationships become between half- or stepsiblings, as they grow older? How are decisions made about the priority of family obligations toward younger and older kin when there is a web of relatives (or former relatives) to whom one may feel some degree of duty? Who will have legal rights in terms of life-and-death health care decisions?

These complex changes in family relationships associated with the increase in divorce and remarriage have only begun to receive attention. Some research has confirmed a decrease in support exchanged or expected between fathers and adult children following divorce and shown less felt obligation toward stepparents (Amato et al., 1995; Cooney and Uhlenberg, 1990; Ganong et al., 1998). In a national sample of adults, relationships for full siblings and step- or half-siblings were compared as to quality and closeness (White and Reidmann, 1992). Full siblings had more contact and higher-quality relationships than stepsiblings, but having spent more time living together as siblings while growing up also increased the amount of contact. Thus, divorce seems to disrupt or diminish the strength of relationships that may be critical to well-being in adulthood and later life.

Exhibit 7.10   *Life-Event Timetables of Selected Female Cohorts*

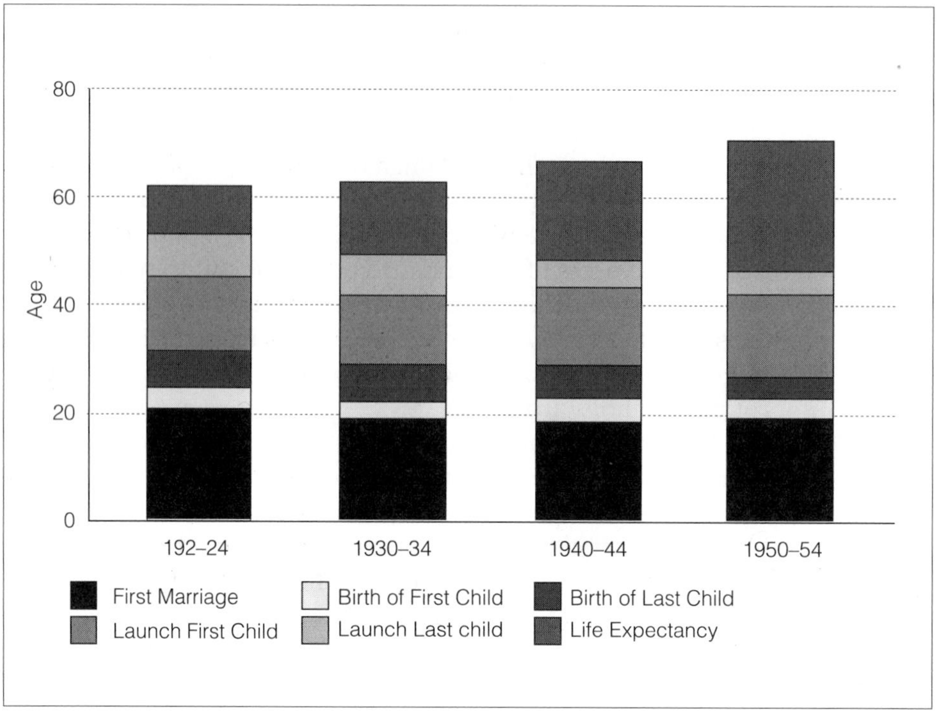

Adapted from: Schmittroth, 1991. Statistical Record of Women Worldwide.

Changes in the Timing of Family Life Events

Major events of family life, such as marriage, birth of children, or child launching, occur at times that are dictated by social norms, cultural traditions, individual decisions, and (sometimes) fate. Ethnic/cultural variations in the timing of family events such as marriage and childbirth were recently discovered in a sample of adolescent girls (East, 1998). Research on are norms described in Chapter 6 shows that, despite considerable variation in when people achieve particular family milestones, cultures often share a degree of consensus (i.e., age norms) regarding the best ages for many of these events. When asked by what age certain major family events (such as marriage or completion of childbearing) should occur for men and women, the majority of people suggest ages within a six-year range, with only slight differences in the timetables for men and women (Settersten and Hagestad, 1996a). There is less consensus on the best age for becoming grandparents, which ranges more widely.

An unanticipated early or late pregnancy or being "left at the altar" (events that throw you "off time") can shape the timing of events throughout an individual's life in ways that influence later outcomes. Expansion of educational attainment, for example, means that select members of the population often

Exhibit 7.11   *Timing of Age-Gapped/Age-Condensed Lives*

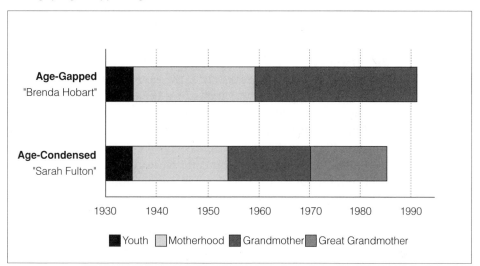

delay the establishment of families, so that these events will occur at later ages than was true for their parents. Others, through teenage childbearing, are accelerating the ages at which family milestones can be reached. Exhibit 7.10 shows the differences in timing of selected family events for members of female cohorts born between the 1920s and the 1950s. Although time of first marriage was surprisingly consistent for these cohorts, differences are visible in both life expectancy and the time spent parenting. Over time, because of reduced fertility and increased life expectancy, the top period, reflecting the postparental stage of life, has expanded. We are spending a smaller percentage of our time as parents and more time before and after parenting.

Despite these overall trends, considerable variation is possible within any cohort. Consider the female generations in two hypothetical families: the Hobarts and the Fultons (see Exhibit 7.11). Brenda Hobart was born in the 1930s, married at age 22, and started her family two years later with a daughter, Beth, followed by three other children. Beth grew to adulthood and continued her education through a master's degree. Having delayed marriage, Beth had her first child, Brenda's first grandchild, when she was 32. This granddaughter plans to be a physician and also to have children late. Brenda became a mother at 24 and a grandmother at 56; her daughter Beth became a mother at 32 and expects to become a grandmother only at age 65. Generations of this family are clearly farther apart in age than dictated by age norms, a pattern referred to as **age-gapped** (Bengtson et al., 1990).

Sarah Fulton married early, bearing her first child, Susan, at 19. Susan became pregnant at age 16 and gave birth to a daughter who followed her mother's example and had a first child at age 15. In this family Sarah became a parent at 19, a grandparent at 35, and a great-grandparent at 50! Susan, the daughter, became a mother at 16 and a grandmother at age 31. In this case, the generations are closer in age (**age-condensed)** in comparison to societal age norms (Bengtson et al., 1990). The potential for an increase in four- or even five-generation families rests on two forces. While individuals are living longer, the choices of family members regarding the age at which to procreate shape the timing of these events. While the Hobarts were experiencing an expansion of the time between generations, the Fultons were seeing increasingly rapid-fire addition of generations. Since early childbearing is associated with several negative outcomes (poorer income, education, and health) for both mothers and children, the relationships between generations for the Fultons, especially the dependence or independence of generations, may differ significantly from the experience of the Hobarts.

Although a set of age norms establishes when events in the family life cycle are expected to take place, these socially constructed norms are subject to change. Events happening on time are not problematic, but family events that happen off time, especially early, are more challenging transitions (Cohler and Altergott, 1995). Grandmothers in age-condensed families are often uncomfortable with the early onset of this role, because it is viewed as occurring "off time" compared with their expectations (see Brubaker, 1990b). Both early childbearing and early widowhood are more stressful than comparable events that are off time by being late.

Summary

What conclusions can we draw about aging families? First, family relationships are maintained throughout life, holding deep personal and social significance for most individuals. Second, a set of social norms directs relationships within families, with variation in those norms by class, race, ethnicity, and gender. Not all persons are expected to act the same toward all other persons; structured relationships have their own norms in addition to general norms regarding obligation and reciprocity. Third, families provide considerable assistance and support to their members, with most of that assistance being viewed as routine or normal. Families take mutual assistance as a given in many of the relationships among individuals. Finally, families are not static, either through their own life cycle or historically. Structural changes with the maturation of members and social changes both modify the tasks faced by kinship groups and their expectations of how to meet these challenges. While families are a durable social institution, we can expect them to continue to change as the society does.

The family as a social institution is a dynamic force within the larger society, both contributing to and responding to social changes in politics, the economy, and other social institutions. But families are also internally dynamic, experiencing ongoing change as new generational units are formed, add members, mature, and eventually pass from the scene as they age and die. Throughout this dynamism, however, are threads of continuity connecting the generations and patterns of family norms that are often passed down as part of familial heritage. Family relationships are a force for continuity in the lives of individuals, bridging decades of societal change.

It is difficult to talk about "family" as though it is a singular phenomenon. Families differ in structure; individual families change in composition and closeness over time; and forces such as class, race, and ethnicity shape the manner in which family life unfolds. We have seen throughout this chapter, for example, that the families of African Americans differ in some important ways from those of European Americans, including more mutual assistance, closer sibling relationships, and a more active role for grandparents in rearing their grandchildren. Such differences are the products both of culture and of generations of socioeconomic disadvantage and discrimination, encouraging greater reliance on kin networks.

Nor should we overgeneralize the positive nature of family relationships. For many of us family ties are close, and many of those ties are positive. Assuming that reliance on family caregivers is better than using formal health care services in all instances, however, ignores the realities of conflict, abuse and neglect that characterize some relationships. For many individuals as they age, however, the continuity and support of familial roles, both as responsibilities and as resources, forge the key linkages that connect them to the social world.

The age-integrating family system is undoubtedly going to continue its pattern of change in the coming decades. Four- and five-generation families will be paired with serial monogamy to create intricate and complex family systems that may be more or less responsive to the needs of older adults of future cohorts. As we all age, the families we build and the manner in which we enact family roles will help to shape the norms for this future and the place of the family within it.

Web Wise

Sites related to the family tend to be "problem oriented." Below are references to three sites that focus on specific problem areas relating to aging families that are "hot" today. Others can be located through the AOA site described in Chapter 1's Web Wise segment.

Caregiver Survival Resources
http://www.caregiver911.com/
Caregiving is a major issue for elderly people, children, and disabled people of all ages. This web site is oriented to provide information and support to caregivers in various situations, including but not limited to caring for older relatives. A variety of resources are offered, including books, an "ask Dr. Caregiv-

er" option, and links to a variety of other resources and more specialized organizations. This could be a good first stop for assistance for someone seeking information or assistance with caregiving problems. This is a very friendly site for caregivers or professionals interested in support or information.

Grandparenting: The Essential Sites

http://www.thirdage.com/grand/

This web site, more a metasite operated by Third Age Media, lists sites and reviews regarding grandparenting. It links the user to a range of these sites related to contemporary grandparenting issues, including topics such as legal issues surrounding grandparents and divorce, how grandparents can maintain family legacies, and grandparents who care for their grandchildren. This is a very friendly site and can take you many places connected with the topic of grandparenting.

National Center on Elder Abuse

http://www.gwjapan.com/NCEA/

This site focuses on the issue of elder abuse. It provides links to a number of sites addressing the issue of abuse, its definition, and prevention. Users can connect to information and advocacy groups that provide statistics, strategies, and interventions.

Key Terms

age-condensed	later-life families
age-gapped	lineage bridge
beanpole family	marital satisfaction
caregiver burden	modified extended family
cohort-centrism	neglect and abuse
family	norm of reciprocity
family caregivers	obligation
family life cycle theory	opportune family
fictive kinship	primary caregiver
filial obligation	sandwich generation
five or six generation family	social exchange
generations	social norms
independence and dependence	surrogate family relationships
intergenerational households	surrogate parents
intimacy at a distance	voluntarism
kin-keeping	woman in the middle
latent kin matrix	

Questions for Thought and Reflection

1. Do some genealogical sleuthing and map out the structure of your family tree. Examine such things as the number of siblings in various generations, ages at marriage and at death. What larger social changes in the institution of the family do you see reflected in the history of your own family?

2. Thinking about younger adults of today (in their 20s), what changes in the timing of family events, family norms and individual behaviors are likely to differentiate their cohort experiences of family life from those of individuals in their 70s today?

3. Countries such as China, where family members had a strong tradition of housing and caring for their elders, are seeing threats to those systems as economies modernize and the population urbanizes. Should countries try to enforce traditional patterns through laws and penalties or let go of old ways and adopt more Western styles of meeting the needs of elders for housing, health care, income support, etc.?

4. Matilda White Riley (Riley et al., 1994) describes the family as an age-integrating structure, since it links together individuals of different ages and historical eras. What impact might such age integration have on the various generations involved or the society as a whole?

5. Identify your major partners in social exchange at this point in your life. Consider friends, family, employers, teachers, your college or university, religious or community groups, etc. among the potential partners. Think about what you give and what you get from your ongoing exchanges with these partners. Is exchange theory correct in proposing that you would withdraw from exchanges that are unprofitable (i.e., that cost you more than you get from them)?

TOPICAL ESSAY

Love, Sex, and Longevity

As the old song says, "Love and marriage . . . go together like a horse and carriage." Perhaps, but which comes first? If you are a well-socialized product of American culture, you probably feel strongly that people should get married after they fall in love. However, in other cultures people assume that love will grow within the marriage. Love is not a necessary condition to their decision to marry. Researchers asked college students from eleven different countries whether they would marry someone they did not love. Only about 5 percent of the students in the United States and Australia said that they would marry someone with the right qualities even if they did not love him or her. About 50 percent of the students from India and Pakistan said they would marry without love (Levine, 1993). The cultural practice of arranged marriages still prevails in countries such as India, helping to explain the acceptability of marrying first, then letting love develop later. In India, people still use the term "love marriages" about the small proportion of Indian couples who decide to marry on their own, without parental arrangements, approval, and decision-making.

Though love may not be the basis for the decision to marry in India, it is still highly valued. However, cultural definitions of love vary. In India, love is based on long-term commitment and devotion to the family. On the other hand, the culture of the United States highly prizes romantic love—an idealized view of our partners and of the relationship—based on passion, erotic attraction, and media images of ever growing ardor and tenderness.

Where do these different cultural definitions of love come from? There are a lot of factors that contribute to this ephemeral concept. We suggest here that one of those factors is a quite "unromantic," somewhat prosaic demographic element: the average life expectancy in a society. In "young" countries such as India, where life expectancy is still relatively low, romance may be a luxury. In such societies, people marry younger and begin childbearing earlier, since life is shorter. "Older" societies, like the United States where people live longer, are more likely to value romance and to favor falling in love before marriage.

In Chapter 3 we discussed the emergence of childhood as a differentiated stage of life. Changes in life expectancy were part of the conditions necessary for that new stage of life to develop. People had to live long enough for there to be time in life devoted to education and learning how to become an adult. Similarly, we can argue intuitively that living long enough is a necessary precondition for having the time to search for a desirable partner and to enjoy courtship and engagement prior to marriage. These stages prior to marriage are devoted to romance— the search for the ideal partner; the excitement, passion, and the anticipation of the new relationship; getting to know each other; and making plans for a life together, all of which fuel a romantic view of love and marriage. When we marry in our 20s and live until our 80s, we have the luxury of time to search for the perfect partner and therefore we have to opportunity to sustain the illusion of romantic love. We are also confronted with the prospect of five or six decades with our marriage partners, so our choices in this matter have quite an impact on our lives. The adage, "Marry in haste, repent in leisure," alludes to the care that one should take in this decision and to the potential length of time we spend in marriage.

Longer life expectancy can provide the basis for cultural values about romantic love to develop. These two factors together—longevity and preference for romantic love—are also linked to divorce patterns. "Our culture emphasizes romantic love as a basis for marriage, rendering relationships vulnerable to collapse as sexual passion subsides. There is now widespread support for the notion that one may end a marriage in favor of a new relationship simply to renew excitement and romance" (Macionis, 1997, p. 471). And, since we live long enough, we have time to pursue, develop, and sustain more than one relationship. Serial monogamy—having more than one spouse sequentially but not simultaneously—is a phenomenon unique to societies with long life expectancies. Just as an extended life course provides the opportunities for second careers in the job markets, it also provides for second and third chances at love relationships. Having the time to spend in search of new and improved relationships make it possible to sustain the illusion of an ideal partner, one of the most important elements in romantic love.

Obviously there are factors in addition to longevity that shape a society's values about love and marriage. Other cultural values play important roles. The importance of extended family, the value placed on independence, and the primacy of parental authority are all cultural values that can influence attitudes toward love and marriage. Simmons and associates compared the attitudes of students across cultures toward romantic love1986). They found that Japanese students, who live in a culture that highly values respect toward parental decisions and the importance of the family, placed a significantly lower value on romantic love than did students in the United States or West Germany. The predominance of arranged marriages in India reflects the very strong familial system (Gupta, 1976), while in the United States our emphasis on independence and autonomy would preclude such a practice.

"Older" countries with higher life expectancies thus have the demographic foundation for romanticized views of love and marriage. The life course in these societies is long enough and differentiated enough for time to be spent in the search for at least one "perfect" partner and in the development of those love relationships. But, is

there a time in the life course when people lose interest in this vital endeavor? Do people lose interest in love, romance, and sex as they grow older? According to the stereotypes, they do. According to older people themselves, no, they don't. In some recent research on sexuality and aging, Wiley and Bortz (1996) found that over two-thirds of the middle-aged and older adults in their study were sexually active. While 60 percent reported a decrease in frequency of sexual activity over the past decade, 32 percent reported no change, and 8 percent reported an increase. About half the women and 70 percent of the men in this study stated a desire for increased sexual activity. Availability of a partner is, obviously, one significant factor in sexual activity. One study found that over 80 percent of married people in their 70s were still sexually active (Brecher reported in Barrow 1996). Summarizing findings from a number of studies of sexuality in later life, Barrow (1996) reports additional findings that challenge our own stereotypes about sex, love, and aging. Overall, patterns of sexual activity are established in midlife and remain fairly continuous throughout old age, barring serious illness or disability. But some studies show that nursing home residents often retain their interest in sexuality. Research also reports that three-fourths of older people said their love-making had improved with time; 15 percent of people aged 60 and over reported increased sexual activity over the course of a ten-year longitudinal study. The rate of masturbation increases for women as they get older, partly related to the lack of available partners. Some people have a first homosexual experience in later life. So sexuality does not cease in later life.

We often respond to the idea of love, romance, and sex among older people in an agist, stereotypical way. We may find it hard to believe and even distasteful, or we may find it touching and "cute." Both responses discriminate against older people. Both reactions treat older people as different from the rest of us and presume that age brings with it a fundamental change in our interest in and ability to be sexual beings. From older people we know that, for the most part, interest in sexuality and need for intimacy persists throughout the life course.

Questions for Thought and Reflection

1. Do you know anyone who has had, or expects to have, an arranged marriage? Do you think you could love someone your family or a professional matchmaker found for you? Why or why not?

2. Taking into account what you have read in Chapter Seven and in this essay, what are the benefits of marriage for older people?

3. How do you evaluate the significance of the high percentages of older people who are still sexually active or show interest in sex? Do these figures change your impression of the importance of sex to human beings?

CHAPTER 8

Employment and Retirement

"Aside from issues of war and peace and nuclear holocaust, the most important dramatic social, economic, and political issues and developments facing the societies with aging populations are those associated with the reduction of employment in the life span while the life span itself is extended" (Matras, 1990, p. 75).

Employment as an Organizing Force across the Life Cycle

The interrelated institutions of employment and retirement are one of the cores around which we organize life in complex, modern societies. As societies age, we need to rethink these major institutions and how they fit with the larger social context. One major international trend, the compression of employment into a smaller proportion of our lives, is indeed a fact of life in aging societies worldwide (Guillemard, 1996). As Exhibit 8.1 shows, male labor force participants in the United States today typically enter jobs later, after more extended education, and end employment earlier through early retirement, than was true in the past. Whether or not we agree with Matras that the compression of employment ranks just under the possibility of nuclear holocaust on the list of compelling social issues, it is difficult to argue with the centrality of employment and retirement in the structure of the larger economy and in individuals' lives. In this chapter we use the term employment rather than work, because the latter concept also includes household and other unpaid activities of value (Reskin and Padavic, 1994).

Modern economies organize themselves around employment. We cannot fully understand retirement, for example, without considering its relationship to the structure and meaning of employment; in turn, employment and retirement can only be understood within the context of the socioeconomic structure of the larger society. Highly developed and developing economies differ dramatically in how employment is managed and whether or not retirement exists (Kinsella and Taeuber, 1993). We focus here on issues of employment and retirement from the individual level to the societal level and direct our attention to other aspects of the economies of aging societies in Chapter 9.

One caveat is in order as we begin this examination of employment and retirement. We are in the midst of tremendous economic change throughout the world; these changes are having an impact on jobs and job markets, on the meanings of employment and retirement, and on the questions we pose about these institutions. For example, how will expanded life expectancy and advances in technology alter the capacity of adults to continue employment past

Exhibit 8.1   *Compression of Employment: Male Workers 1950–1990*

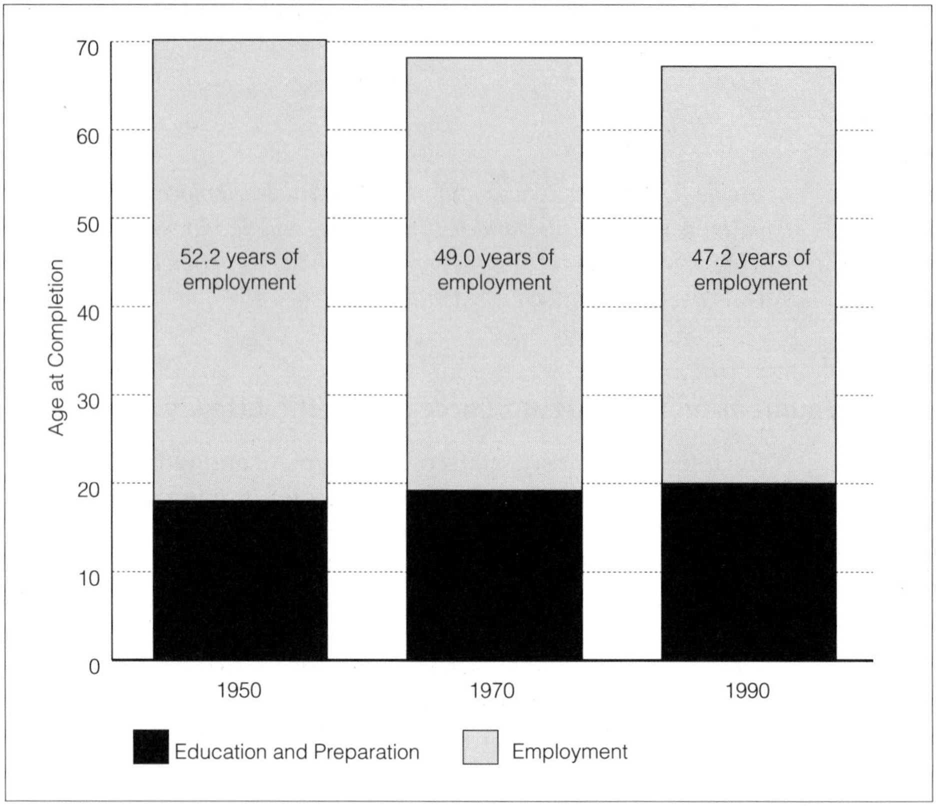

Adapted from: U.S. Bureau of the Census, 1977, 1987.

traditional ages of retirement? Such dramatic changes require that we frame our discussion with an eye to the future. Thus, we describe the critical changes in these institutions and provide some educated speculation about the future of employment and retirement, although predicting the future in such a dynamic system is risky at best.

Dynamics of the Labor Force

Both the **market for labor** (the demand for employees with specific skills) and the **labor force** (the supply of available employees with their particular skills and experience) in a society, a given locality, or a specific company are highly dynamic. Over the past several decades both supply and demand have shifted, changing the opportunities for individuals to find appropriate employment and for employers to meet their needs for skilled labor.

Using a micro-level lens, we tend to see labor as individuals working in particular jobs. But labor can be thought of in a more macro-level way as a com-

Exhibit 8.2   *Changes in Labor Force Participation Rates for Men by Race and Age*

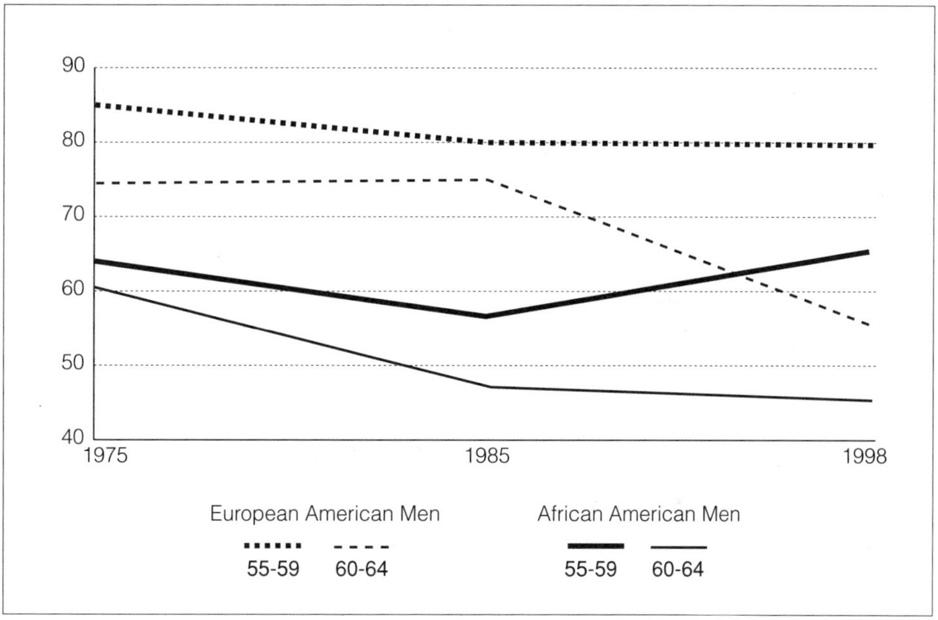

Adapted from: Department of Labor Bureau of Labor Statistice, 1995, 1985, 1975, 2000.

modity in the economic marketplace where supply, demand, and quality change over time. This fits well, except that societies cannot suddenly produce a greater supply of labor, because it takes considerable time to produce and prepare new cohorts to enter the labor market (Cooperman and Keast, 1983). When shortages of labor occur, employers fill the gap with a variety of strategies. They can meet demand for labor by bringing less active groups into the labor force ; for example, luring nonemployed women into the labor force in times of war. Or they can attract immigrants from areas with labor surpluses. Some employers keep current employees on the job longer through wage and benefit incentives or disincentives to retirement. In recent years, for example, there has been a "youth squeeze" in the restaurant, grocery, clothing, and retail sales fields, which typically draw their labor from young adults. When small cohorts enter the labor market, these employers must scramble to meet their labor force needs (Doeringer and Terkla, 1990). When labor is more difficult to find and keep, conditions become more advantageous for workers, and they can bargain for better wages and benefits. When labor is abundant and cheap, however, employers offer lower wages and benefits, because workers are easily replaced (Reskin and Padavic, 1994). One reasons that jobs in the global economy sometimes migrate internationally with major corporations is that abundant labor may be found in other countries, prompting companies to relocate to save costs and meet labor needs.

Exhibit 8.3   *Changes in Labor Force Participation Rates for Women by Race and Age*

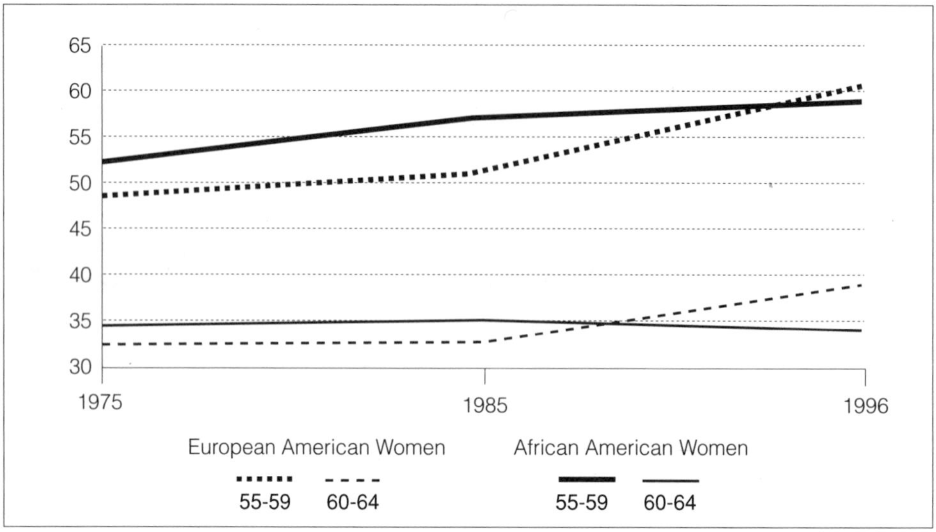

Adapted from: Department of Labor Bureau of Labor Statistics, 1995, 1985, 1975.

Labor force participation rates describe the percentage of the population that is employed (or seeking employment) at a given time and, by extension, indicate how prevalent retirement or other forms of non-employment are among various groups within the population. Exhibit 8.2, showing male labor force participation, identifies two clear trends over time. First, labor force participation has declined among men in the United States over recent decades, especially for those above age 60. Second, there is a clear racial gap in labor force participation for males. In midlife and beyond, African American men and women (see also Exhibit 8.3) more often experience physical disability resulting in labor force exit, a situation that reflects their earlier economic and educational disadvantages (Bound, Scheonbaum, and Waidmann 1996; Hayward, Friedman, and Chen, 1996). While this disability gap means that African American males work fewer years on average, their shorter life expectancy means that they spend a greater percentage of their adult years in the labor force (Hayward et al., 1996).

Trends in labor force participation for mature women show a sharp contrast with those for men. As Exhibit 8.3 shows, during the decades when mature men departed work in large numbers via retirement or disability, more women than ever before remained active in the labor force. This pattern is largely the result of increasing labor force involvement by sequential cohorts of American women. In each cohort since the 1950s, adult women have spent increasing percentages of their adult years in the labor force. These gender differences in employment are rapidly diminishing among younger cohorts. A racial gap is also evident in women's labor force involvement, as European American women catch up to the higher rates of labor force participation long found among African American women.

As more of each female cohort participates in the labor force, more women will face eventual retirement. As a result, retirement may encompass different social concerns and meanings in 2020 than it did in 1950 when nearly all retirees were men. The world has indeed changed since Cumming and Henry (1961) declared, "Retirement is not an important problem for women, because . . . working seems to make little difference to them. Retirement is a man's problem" (p. 144-145).

In general, labor force participation rates of older workers are declining in most developed countries. Exhibit 8.4 shows labor force participation rates in a variety of countries, contrasting males and females in developed and developing nations. For both sexes, rates of participation in the labor force above age 65 are generally lower in developed than in developing countries, probably because more of the developed nations have pensions available (Kinsella and Gist, 1995). The nature of a country's economy (whether it relies mostly on agriculture, manufacturing, modern technology and information, or some combination of these) also shapes the likelihood that the society can make retirement available as an option.

The second major pattern apparent in Exhibit 8.4 is that rates of labor force participation for older women are lower than those for males internationally. We must be cautious, however, because these statistics very likely overlook many economic contributions of women to their families and societies through work in the **underground economy** (jobs such as home-based child care or domestic work, paid in cash with no records kept) or family businesses. Whether this pattern of lower female involvement in the labor force at later ages will persist as cohorts of women with continuous employment histories reach 65 remains to be seen. Women's labor force participation varies considerably among countries, probably reflecting cultural norms regarding the appropriateness of work at older ages for women and men.

Employment and Life Chances

Employment opportunities play a pivotal role in the life chances of individuals. These opportunities result from early life chances (education, social class) and help to shape subsequent life chances through differing incomes, benefits, and levels of social prestige. The varying opportunities that individuals are exposed to, and the resulting differences in the types of occupations they hold, are key to understanding inequality throughout life.

One way to view the effects of differential life chances is to examine occupational segregation by gender and race. The **dissimilarity index** in Exhibit 8.5 compares race/gender groups and shows the proportion of those in one group who would have to change occupations in order to produce a distribution that looks similar to the other group. From the graph we can see that occupational

Exhibit 8.4a   *Labor Force Participation Rates for Men 65 Years and Over in Developed and Developing Countries*

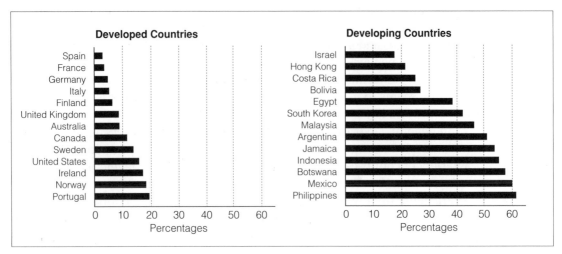

Source: Kinsella and Gist, 1995.

Exhibit 8.4b   *Labor Force Participation Rates for Women 65 Years and Over in Developed and Developing Countries*

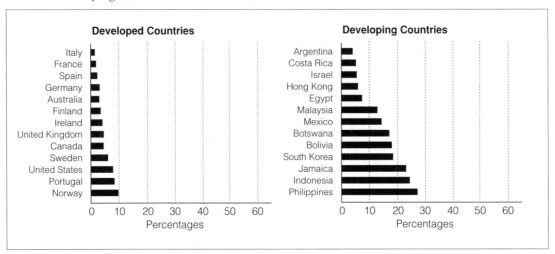

Source: Kinsella and Gist, 1995.

segregation (dissimilarity in jobs) among all of the groups has decreased since 1940. However, the dissimilarity between European American men and women, and between African American men and women, is still over .55 (more than half would need to change occupational categories for the groups to be comparable). In contrast, the differences within gender (between European American and African American women and between European American and African

Exhibit 8.5   *Dissimilarity Indexes of Ocupational Differentiation: 1940–88*

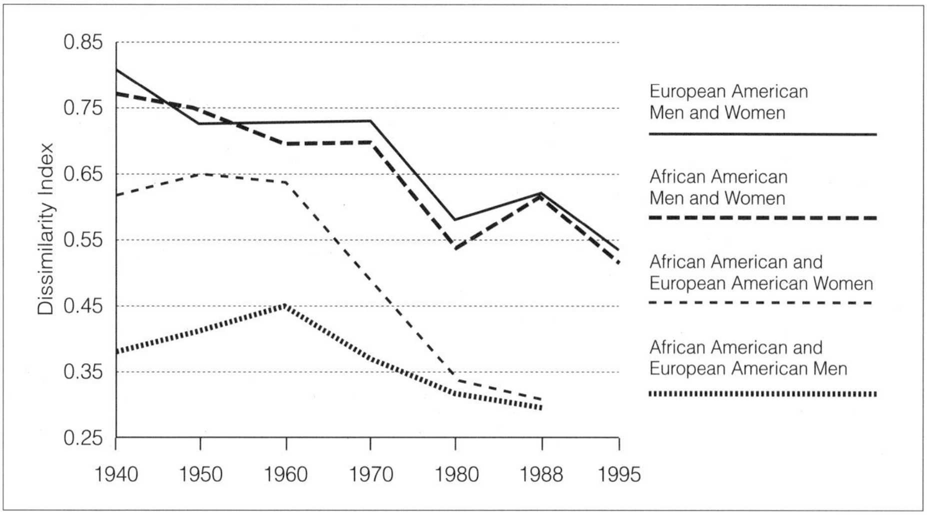

Source: King, 1992, Wooten, 1997.

American men) are relatively small. Although we are progressing toward equal opportunity in the labor force, distinct differences in the occupations held by women and men, and by European American and African American workers, persist. Data from 1995 show that the dissimilarity index by sex remained at .54 (Wootten, 1997).

Why does **sex segregation of occupations** matter? Taking a broad view, Reskin and Padavic argue that "society as a whole pays a price when employers use workers' sex (or other irrelevant characteristics such as age and race) to segregate them into jobs that fail to make the best use of their abilities" (Reskin and Padavic, 1994, p. 46). In addition to these concerns, occupational segregation systematically restricts opportunities (life chances) within the labor market (Baron and Bielby, 1985). Occupational segregation causes inequalities in income and other opportunities. When women are excluded from some jobs, they lose the chance to develop skills, make professional contact and develop meaningful leisure activities. All of these are directly related to life chances in retirement.

Exhibit 8.6 presents further information on sex and race inequality in income. From 1968 to 1998, inequality of income has been reduced somewhat, but notable discrepancies remain. Moreover, the gap in income (measured in constant, inflation-corrected dollars) reflects no income improvement for European American men, but some improvement over the past thirty years for African Americans of both sexes and European American women. Data were not reported on Hispanic Americans as early as 1968, but Hispanic American women and men fare the worst of any group in 1998, with median incomes of only $10,862 and $17,257 respectively (U.S. Bureau of the Census, 1998c).

Exhibit 8.6   *Earnings Inequality by Race and Sex*

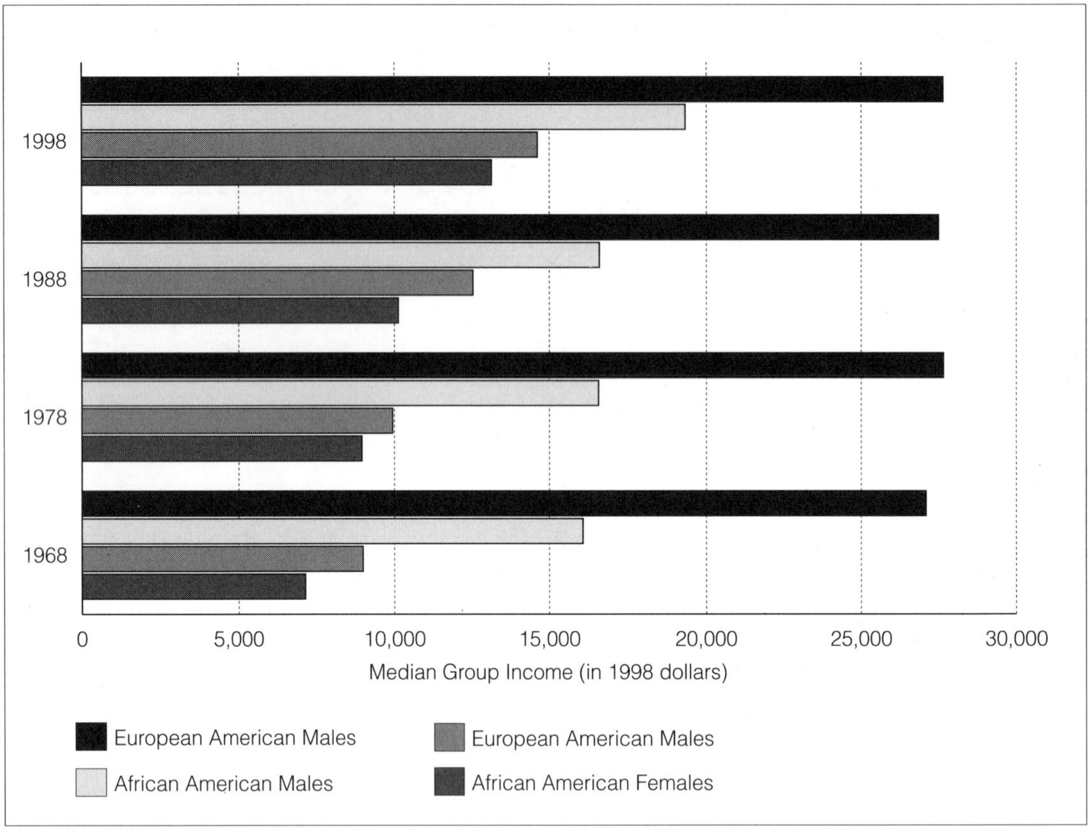

Adapted from: U.S. Bureau of the Census, 1998c.

Income differences during the working years are correlated with later-life economic well-being. Lower earnings, discontinuous employment histories, and occupational segregation combine to significantly diminish the life chances of socially disadvantaged groups as they move through adulthood and into retirement (Hayward, Friedman and Chen, 1998). Women of all races and Hispanic- and African-American men are more likely to suffer these disadvantages. Chapter 9 will show how these occupational opportunities (or their absence) play out in terms of differences in retirement income.

The persistent effects of life chances are seen in the later-life employment and retirement options available to members of racial/ethnic minority groups. Jackson and Gibson (1985) show how limited life chances, because of both lower educational attainment and discrimination, result in employment disadvantage for African Americans throughout adulthood. Current incremental improvements in opportunities will take decades to reach fruition among future older cohorts of African Americans. In recently "retired" cohorts, many African Americans ceased participation in the labor force because of poor health, unemployment, or inability to find jobs (Jackson and Gibson, 1985). Many other African Americans, even those in poor health, had to continue employment to maintain income in later life. In the past, a career as a day laborer or domestic, for example, often did not even carry the guarantee of Social Security and certainly lacked a pension.

Fewer African American retirees receive private pensions, so that more retired African Americans than European Americans are dependent solely on Social Security or welfare programs for retirement income (Jackson and Gibson, 1985). Later-life financial problems, including inadequate incomes, are a legacy of limited life chances during earlier parts of adulthood. Jackson and Gibson argue that a discontinuous employment history might make retirement less meaningful as a concept to African Americans, because intermittent employment often continues into later life to supplement modest Social Security benefits. Lifelong experiences (or life chances) profoundly shape the socioeconomic conditions, either positive or negative, under which African Americans and the rest of us eventually retire (Hayward et al., 1998).

The Occupational Life Cycle: Contemporary Changes

The patterning of employment into the lives of individuals is a taken-for-granted aspect of the life cycle to most of us. But like many age-related phenomena, it is one that is socially constructed and subject to change. Most of us carry in our thinking a socially constructed model of an **occupational life cycle**. As an organizing concept, the occupational life cycle captures the interrelationship of individual lives over time with the social structure of employment and opportunity for advancement, prestige, and rewards. The dominant model in American culture reflects the typical employment pattern of middle-class males.

In this model of the occupational life cycle, a worker, upon completion of education or training, lands an entry-level position with a business or governmental organization. The worker, with the passage of time, advances through the ranks of that occupation, perhaps seeking additional training or changing employers along the way. The worker's earnings increase as he advances through the ranks of skill, experience, and responsibility, reaching a plateau in middle age to late middle age. At that point, advancement may slow or stop in anticipation of retirement with health benefits and a solid pension (Doeringer, 1990). Research has demonstrated some consensus among male workers regarding the ages at which promotions are most likely, with promotions less expected for workers over age 50 (Lashbrook, 1996). A random sample of Chicago-area adults confirmed that most people hold deadlines for completing school, entering full-time employment, settling on a career, and retirement. Fewer women than men had age deadlines for themselves, and people did not agree on the ages by which some events should occur (Settersten and Hagestad, 1996b). For example, retirement for women was suggested at ages from 40 to 75, a considerable range.

This culturally-based, middle-class model is so ingrained into our way of thinking that many of us take it for granted in planning our lives and in doing business. This model creates on a macro level the expectation of how birth cohorts will transform into cohorts of workers for the labor market at particular ages, and then depart via retirement. What would happen, for example, if older workers in large numbers chose not to retire from their senior positions? On a macro-economic level, it could freeze opportunities for advancement by younger workers, violating one of the core elements of the career model— advancement. What if large numbers of young adults were to take time off after training before initiating a career? This violation of expectations of the occupational life cycle model could create a labor shortage for employers, perhaps prompting recruitment of nontraditional workers or improvement of wages, benefits, and working conditions to attract the labor they need.

Although this model of occupational careers represents the experience of many middle-class males, questions have been raised as to whether it has ever characterized the labor force experience of other workers. Further, many wonder whether this model is still viable even for middle-class males in our changing economy. Layoffs from downsizing or corporate mergers, job automation, or worker health problems may interrupt an orderly progression among middle-class males expecting to follow the "traditional" steps of this model (Doeringer, 1990).

There is ample evidence that the idealized occupational life cycle has never fit the experiences of employed women, workers with limited education, or groups who have been discriminated against in employment. First, women continue to carry the bulk of responsibility for household work and child care, even while undertaking employment (Reskin and Padavic, 1994). Employed women often find themselves attempting to reconcile conflicting demands of family and job (Moen, 1994). The years of heaviest career building in the traditional model often coincide with the years of most intensive family responsibility (childbearing and care of small children). Employers have been slow to respond to making employment more "family friendly" in creating alternative models that enable parents to fit employment with parenthood or eldercare (Gonyea, 1997). Second, the jobs occupied primarily by women have shorter career ladders, meaning that female workers have fewer opportunities to advance and attain higher wages, status, and benefits over time (Reskin and Padavic, 1994). Third, the working lives of women have been and continue to be more subject to interruption by family-related needs, such as caring for a child or parent or the pressure to change jobs to follow a husband's career. Such interruptions typically diminish job and wage advancement.

Similarly, the occupational life cycle model of the middle-class male does not fit other types of workers. How would it apply to migrant farmworkers, for instance, who have no career ladder or guarantee of employment, minimal benefits, and no pension? How would the occupational life cycle model fit someone working as an exotic dancer in a nightclub, as a technician repairing office machines, as a waitress in a diner, as a carpenter, or as a telephone sales representative for a mail-order company? Clearly many jobs do not carry the type of career trajectory that we generally associate with the occupational life cycle model, indicating that its usefulness is limited.

The changing nature of the labor market also limits the applicability of the traditional career model. In prior cohorts, career workers were predominantly full-time and had incentives in pay and pension to remain with their firm, so that training and knowledge specific to the company were maintained over time (Henretta, 1994). Recent changes in the labor market, however, include an increase in the number of smaller firms, less manufacturing and more jobs in the service sector of the economy, and the growth of what is called the **contingent labor force**. Contingent employees work as day laborers once did, for the highest bidder for short spans of time (months to years). The difference is that contingent labor runs all the way from manual labor to the executive level. The world of contingent work provides little continuity, career building, or long-term company benefits, such as health insurance or a pension (Rupert, 1991). Estimates in the early 1990s place the contingent labor force at 25 percent of employees, and growing (Rupert, 1991). Eventually there may be so much variability in the patterns of employment that people follow throughout their lives that it may change the age-structured notions of when it is appropriate to have a job and to be retired. These changes could lead to the final demise of the occupational life cycle model (Henretta, 1994). Thus, the lifetime experience of current and future cohorts will likely alter the socially-constructed occupational life cycle into a new and more varied pattern of expectations. It is hoped by some that relaxation of strict age norms with regard to work and career progressions will provide more flexibility in accommodating work, leisure and family responsibilities without the role conflicts often faced by parents today (Loscocco, 2000; Riley and Riley, 1994)

Older Workers and the Dynamics of the Labor Force

Both researchers and policymakers discuss a group referred to as **older workers**. Often this term is not defined or is assigned varying ages of onset, because there is little agreement on a chronological age at which a worker is deemed "older." In fact, career trajectories vary, as do the demands of a job. Workers may be considered "older" at a much earlier chronological age if they are bricklayers than if they are teachers or office managers. Both the demands of the job, physical or mental, and the ages at which workers in the occupation reach their peak in terms of promotion and performance may be keys to defining when "older worker" status begins.

Also essential to understanding the older worker concept are the views of employers. We might argue that workers come to be defined as "older" when their employers start to treat them differently based on ageist assumptions. Perhaps employers stop considering them for promotions, training, or raises. When an employer stops investing in an employee because of age, the employer has implicitly attached a label of "older worker" to the worker. The fate of older workers in the labor force depends both on the demand for labor in the marketplace and on the views held by employers regarding the skills and productivity of older workers.

Chronologically older workers (65 years and older for our purposes) are distributed differently in the labor market than their younger counterparts. Concentrations of older workers are found among the self-employed, in fields where substantial experience is valued, and in declining occupations, such as family-farm agriculture or steel manufacturing in the U.S. (Cooperman and Keast, 1983). In both developed and developing countries, older workers are more concentrated in agriculture and less often found in jobs in the service sector than are younger workers (Kinsella and Taeuber, 1993). Can we explain this pattern by the movement of individuals out of clerical and service jobs and into agriculture as they age? For the most part, the answer is no. Again the key lies in the dynamics of the labor market and the changing distribution of job opportunities presented to various cohorts. Occupational fields that are shrinking, such as agriculture and manufacturing, attract relatively few entrants from younger cohorts, because there are few opportunities. Entering cohorts turn instead to the growth sectors, such as service and clerical occupations. Such shifts in the labor market have marooned older workers in some fields that are in decline, further reducing their employment alternatives.

Skills and Employability of Older Workers

The employment options available to older workers depend in large measure on the overall supply of labor and the mix of skills relative to the demand. Specifically, the number of younger, "prime age" workers (perhaps 25-45) influences whether older workers are in high or low demand. This younger worker/older worker algorithm would be fairly straightforward if the nature of employment and the number and kinds of jobs did not change over time. If jobs were stable, declining numbers of younger workers would simply signal an increasing demand for older workers. But social life is rarely so simple. There remains the question of how many workers overall the economy needs to meet its goals, which depends on the growth (or decline) of the economy and factors such as automation and immigration of workers. Whether the market for labor will grow, remain stable, or shrink in the future is a subject of disagreement among experts, making it difficult to project the demand for older workers (Henretta 2000). Thus, the demand for older workers is related to, but not simply determined by, the number of younger workers available to fill jobs.

Another major influence on the demand for older workers is the perception of older people's competence and desirability as employees. Some of the most common **stereotypes of older workers** are that: older workers miss more time than younger workers because of sickness, are less productive than younger workers, are more likely to suffer injury on the job, are not easily retrained, and are set in their ways. In fact, all of these stereotypes are untrue. Extensive data refute each of these claims against hiring or retaining older workers. Although it is true that a wide range of physical and mental capacities (speed, strength, visual acuity, reaction time) decline somewhat with age, these changes are small until advanced ages and may be compensated for by greater experience (Welford, 1993). In fact, recent research on workers in their sixties shows improvements to health that should enhance coming cohorts' ability to work, improvements that were found for both sexes and all racial/ethnic groups (Crimmins, Reynolds and Saito, 1999). Part of this change is due to cohort compositional shift, with more educated cohorts replacing predecessors with less education and poorer health.

In manufacturing, for example, employee productivity appears to increase with age up to 35-45 years, but this increase may be a result of less efficient employees' dropping out of the pool of workers over time (Welford, 1993). Older workers have fewer work-related accidents, perhaps because of their greater experience. Results of studies on absenteeism are mixed, but managers perceive older workers as less often absent than their younger workers (American Association of Retired Persons, 1995). "A majority of older people continue to function physically and psychologically at a level well above the minimum needed for most adult performance" (Atchley 1994, p. 280).

Less research has focused on the skills of office and managerial workers, because their tasks are more complex and difficult to measure than the speed of workers in manufacturing. A recent study of twelve diverse companies found that managers thought skill and performance was predictably influenced by age only for strenuous tasks. As Exhibit 8.7 shows, managers rated older workers (over age 50) as better in terms of experience, judgment, commitment to quality, low job turnover, and attendance/punctuality while rating them poorer on flexibility, acceptance of new technology, ability to learn new skills, and physical performance in strenuous jobs (AARP, 1995). They rated older and younger workers about the same on another six traits, quite a mixed evaluation (AARP, 1995).

Another study of over 773 employers in 23 countries reports that employers think that productivity peaks at age 43 (on average), but that this performance level is maintained for 14 years before declining (Global Aging Report, 1998). In another questionnaire study, 1,600 middle- and top-level managers were asked to decide about hiring, promotion, discipline, and training one of two applicants, one young and the other older. These managers systematically favored the younger applicant over the older one. All espoused nondiscriminatory views, but older managers (over age 50) were more favorable toward the hypothetical older worker (Rosen and Jerdee, 1985).

In addition, the perceived and real costs of providing benefits are sometimes a barrier to hiring, retaining, or retraining older employees. Senior workers have often achieved substantial salaries, raising questions of whether the same work

Exhibit 8.7   *Manager Assessments of Older Workers by Attribute*

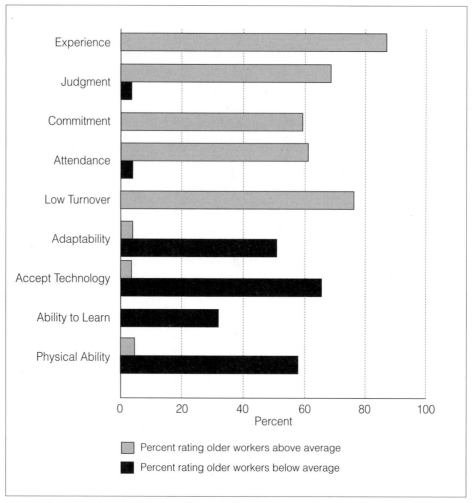

Adapted from: American Association of Retired Persons, 1995.

could be performed at less cost. Employers sometimes weigh these added costs and decide against selecting an older applicant for a job or continuing their older employees.

Special Programs for Older Workers

The literature on employment of older workers and retirees is replete with success stories of companies that have systematically hired older workers or rehired their own retirees. A range of companies have created options in which workers can continue beyond the usual age of retirement, meeting the needs of both the worker and the employer (McNaught, 1994). Typically mentioned are the Days Inn Corporation, which substantially improved productivity and retention after hiring mostly older people as reservation clerks (Miller, 1991). A second example is the Travelers Insurance Company, whose policy of hiring its own retirees to meet short-term personnel needs instead of using temporaries has been in successful operation for many years. Other groups and organizations offer job banks or referral programs for older persons seeking employment (Fuentes, 1991). Many of these programs have been highly successful.

The problem is that only very few employers have considered options for using older workers. In recent decades the greater concern of employers has been how to reduce their labor pool, often through early retirement incentives, rather than how to induce more older workers to come back to or stay in jobs (Rix, 1991). Doubtless the continuing negative attitudes of employers regarding the productivity of older workers has a lot to do with their reluctance to employ these experienced workers. The tantalizing question remains: whether employers will be forced by a shrinking labor pool to reconsider how they can make use of older workers.

Age Discrimination in Employment: Problems and Policies

In 1995 a federal jury awarded three pharmacists more than $2 million in back pay and damages in an age discrimination lawsuit against Kmart. The jury found that the three pharmacists, who were between 62 and 65 years of age when they were fired, had been discriminated against by the company, which wanted to bring younger managers, pharmacists, and staff into its stores (Detroit News, 1995). From cases such as this one, we know that age discrimination in employment still operates.

Age discrimination occurs when an employer makes decisions that disadvantage older workers in the labor force in terms of hiring, promotion, training, wages, or other opportunities. Because age discrimination, stereotypical attitudes, and the "bottom line" of costs for labor certainly influence the demand for older workers, there are policies and laws prohibiting age discrimination in employment practices. The **Age Discrimination in Employment Act (ADEA)**, originally passed in 1967 and amended significantly since then, prohibits the use of age as a criterion in hiring, firing, and personnel policies for workers between ages 40 and 70 (McConnell, 1983). By 1986, the ADEA prohibited mandatory retirement in all but a few occupations. It became illegal to force people to retire when they reached a certain age, and the percentages of workers facing mandatory retirement has declined rapidly. The continued need for lawsuits in the 1990s suggests the need for a closer look at the spirit, effectiveness, and enforcement of ADEA.

Age discrimination is often subtle and difficult to prove legally. If a supervisor selects a younger employee over an older one for a training program, is the choice age discrimination? Not necessarily, because the two employees undoubtedly differ on a variety of other work-related characteristics. Employers often claim legitimate reasons for failing to hire, promote, train, or increase wages to an older employee. The burden of proving age-related reasons for the treatment falls to those bringing suit, a burden that can be lighter if multiple employees shared an experience of discrimination (McConnell, 1983). But if the supervisor systematically selects younger over older workers for various opportunities, even when the qualifications of the older employee are equal or better, it is discrimination. Age discrimination may be conscious or unconscious but is often predicated on negative assumptions by the employer concerning the attitudes and abilities of workers as they age.

Even though mandatory retirement is now prohibited by the ADEA, the law allows for exceptions. Those exceptions are specific occupations in which age is considered a **bona fide occupational qualification (BFOQ)**. Examples include airline pilots, air traffic controllers, and some law enforcement positions. Why is it still legal to force people to leave these jobs at a certain age? Employers have convinced the courts that age has a predictable effect on one's ability to perform these jobs, and the consequences of inability to perform one of these jobs are potentially very serious. On the face of it, there is some logic to the BFOQ exceptions. However, you will recall the case presented at the beginning of this book of airline Captain Al Haynes, credited with saving hundreds of lives during a plane crash. All reports cited his experience as the basis for his ability to handle the crisis. Ironically he was required to retire about six months after the incident because he had reached age 60, the mandatory age of retirement for airline pilots.

This example, and the very existence of BFOQ exceptions, raises two important questions: (1) Does age make a predictable, negative difference for performance in any occupations? (2) Has the ADEA been effective in reducing age discrimination? Although the first question cannot be answered definitively, growing data on how differently individuals are affected by advancing age, and on the importance of experience and effectiveness for many jobs suggest that age may not be a reasonable criterion for removing people from any kind of job. Those who argue in favor of retaining BFOQ exceptions point out that the alternative, testing the performance of each individual after a certain age, is costly and complicated. The fundamental question is which kind of mistake are we more willing to make—forcing potentially productive people out of jobs or retaining people on the job whose abilities may be declining?

Has ADEA been effective in reducing age discrimination? Certainly it has had a legal impact in terms of ending mandatory retirement. Since most workers in jobs with mandatory retirement ages left employment prior to the mandatory age even before the ADEA's passage (Fields and Mitchell, 1984), this change is largely symbolic. Many who have analyzed the policy have concluded that it provides more symbolic than real protection against other forms of discrimination as well. Atchley (1994) notes that the number of complaints of age discrimination reported to the Equal Employment Opportunity Commission have increased, but that the number of ADEA cases prosecuted by the government has dropped.

Age discrimination reflects our society's ambivalent feelings about older workers and retirement. These ambivalent views are reflected in the ideologies and underlying assumptions of two early theories attempting to describe retirement on the individual (micro) level.

■ ■ ■ ■ ■ ■ ■ ■

APPLYING THEORY

Rocking Chairs or Rock Climbing: Disengagement and Activity Theories

Theories mirror the social norms and values of their cultural, social and historical context, reflecting and reinforcing dominant views of what should be the appropriate way to do things. The two theories contrasted here follow this normative pattern. Both disengagement and activity theories socially construct an explanation for not only how individuals' behavior changes with advancing age, but also how it should change (specifying normative patterns of aging).

Disengagement theory was described by Cumming and Henry in 1961. They proposed that people as they reach advanced age undergo a process of an inevitable, beneficial, and universal process of mutual withdrawal of the individual and society from each other . Cumming and Henry thought this **disengagement** was normal and to be expected. This theory argued that it was beneficial for both the aging individual and the society that such a disengagement take place in order to minimize the social disruption caused at the older person's eventual death.

Retirement was a good illustration of this disengagement process, enabling the aging person to be freed of the daily responsibilities of a job and to pursue fewer, more self-selected activities. Through disengagement, Cumming and Henry argued, society anticipated the loss of older people through death and made room to bring new cohorts into full participation within the social world. Although focused primarily on the individual as the unit of analysis, disengagement theory had significant implications for the overall society and its reaction to an aging population. The withdrawal of the older person from various social roles meant that employers would seldom lose a critical employee suddenly, nor would families lose a member with major responsibilities to kin, because disengagement from these responsibilities preceded death.

Reaction to disengagement theory was swift and negative. To many of the activists involved in studying aging at the time, disengagement theory represented a threat to their goal of promoting a more positive and involved lifestyle for older persons (Kastenbaum, 1993). Although the original theory was not stated in these terms, it was quickly interpreted as a normative statement ("Aging people should disengage") rather than as a description of reality ("As they age, people do disengage").

Disengagement theory has had mixed success as a theory. Some argue that it was successful because it stimulated discussion and research (Hochschild, 1975), a major function of any theory. Yet it has been widely criticized as being unfalsifiable, a major failing of any theory (Achenbaum and Bengtson, 1994; Hochschild, 1975). The theory states that disengagement is universal and inevitable, but that its form and timing vary among individuals (Hochschild, 1975). Thus, if a person is not disengaged at age 85, it may be only a matter of time until disengagement occurs, making it impossible to disprove its inevitability or universality. Cumming and Henry also labeled some individuals who continued to be actively involved as "unsuccessful disengagers," suggesting a dysfunctional response to a universal pattern of withdrawal (Cumming and Henry, 1961; Hochschild, 1975). The theory also allows for voluntary reengagement following withdrawal, further muddying the ideas of disengagement as universal and inevitable (Hochschild, 1975).

There are also problems of measurement: How do you determine whether someone is disengaged? What standard is used, the person's own earlier life or peer behavior? Does awareness of approaching death, advancing age, or both factors drive disengagement, if it occurs? None of these questions has been adequately addressed (Hochschild, 1975). So although we may be able to identify the loss of social roles as individuals move into categories of advanced age, this loss does not necessarily signify an inevitable or beneficial process of disengagement.

Activity theory emerged, in part, in response to disengagement theory (Lemon, Bengtson, and Peterson, 1972). Activity theory also represents a normative view of aging: that individuals, in order to age well, must maintain social roles and interaction, rather than disengage from social life. "The essence of this theory is that there is a positive relationship between activity and life satisfaction and that the greater the role loss, the lower the life satisfaction" (Lemon et al., 1972). The activity theory mandate for a retiree was, therefore, to locate some other engaging activity to substitute for employment, maintaining social involvement. Since roles are an essential source of an individual's sense of identity and worth, this activity must substitute for the goals (other than financial) that the job fulfilled for the individual (Atchley, 1976).

This theory has received considerable research attention, but the results are unclear. The research suffers from numerous flaws. Researchers only examined a narrow subset of older adults who were middle-class and married. They used a cross-sectional design, which does not permit the untangling of cause and effect. Critics also thought activity theory suffered from inattention to other factors, especially health and education, that may influence one's level of activity in later life to a very significant degree. It seems that researchers really wanted this theory to be true, since it would confirm mainstream cultural values of remaining active and provide individuals with a means to enhance their well-being in later life.

Both activity and disengagement theories have fallen largely into disuse, but they remain important guideposts regarding normative views on aging and examples of problems to avoid in theory development. Activity theory remains a dominant ideology of successful or productive aging and undergirds the behaviors of individuals and organizations that continue to believe that active aging is successful aging.

Think about these two theories and how they might reflect your expectations about your future aging. Disengagement suggests that you should and will retire from employment, lose friends to death without replacing them, take a less central role in your family, and perhaps withdraw from community activities as you age. You should, in other words, move toward the rocking chair as you move toward your likely date of death. Under the activity theory scenario, in contrast, you should maintain your active involvement in your family and community and replace lost activities or friends with new ones to maintain full involvement as you age. Rock climbing might replace the rocking chair, as long as good health persisted.

What are the implications for the larger society if disengagement is an accurate description of social aging? How will life in our aging society, with 20 percent of the population over age 65, differ if older adults maintain full social involvement? It is clearly an issue with implications for all ages and generations. Both of these approaches take an individual-level view of adaptation/success in later life; they assume that the outcomes experienced by individuals as they age are due to individual choices/decisions. Other perspectives, such as the political economy approach, question why macro-social factors, such as ageism and corporate influence in politics, are overlooked in explaining the well-being of the older population.

■ ■ ■

Retirement

Defining Retirement

Col. K retired from the military after thirty years of service. She receives a military pension and has recently begun a full-time consulting business based on her military expertise.

Basketball superstar Michael Jordan retired from that sport in 1993. He subsequently undertook a career in professional baseball, but later "unretired" and returned to basketball in 1995 at age 32. He "retired" from basketball again–perhaps for good—in 1998.

Mr. L, 70, receives a pension from the accounting firm where he worked for thirty years. For three months of every year, Mr. L works full-time as a tax preparer at a local accounting firm. The remaining nine months, he enjoys an active leisure lifestyle.

Ms. J, age 55, has had a spotty record of employment throughout her adult life, working temporary and part-time jobs when she could find them. Having more trouble than usual in the past few years, she has given up looking for jobs and begun to call herself "retired" when people ask.

Would you categorize any or all of the above persons as "retired"? How do we decide? It is useful to establish some common ground about the boundaries that define retirement in order to develop both policies and research on retirement. As the preceding examples show, the definition is not as simple as it first appears.

Before we can discuss criteria for when retirement occurs or whether an individual is retired, it is necessary to think about what retirement means. Atchley (1976) described several ways in which we use the word **retirement**. It may refer to the event or ceremony marking departure from employment, a phase of the occupational life cycle preparatory to such a departure, a process of separation from employment, or a social role (the "retiree" role). We use the term retirement interchangeably to refer to all of these diverse meanings.

The central focus here is on retirement as a life stage and as a process of separation from employment. Recognizing some ambiguity in how the concept is used, we can now turn to the questions of when retirement begins and when an individual is counted as "retired." We can answer these questions in one of two ways: using self-definitions ("Are you retired?") or using objective indicators. Ekerdt and his colleagues have outlined several indicators used to establish whether or not someone is retired—among them, (1) receipt of a pension, (2) total cessation of employment, (3) departure from the major job of adulthood, or (4) a significant reduction in hours of employment (Ekerdt and DeViney, 1990). As we saw in the cases described at the start of this section, many workers today do not make a clean break from employment by moving from full-time jobs one day to no employment the next (Atchley, 1976). Instead of a clear-cut event, retirement has become somewhat blurrier as a life transition, and we may need several criteria to constitute a working definition of retirement (Mutchler, Burr, Pienta, and Massagli, 1997).

Although there is no agreement about exactly how to measure retirement status, two objective criteria are part of most definitions: receipt of a pension (public or private) and diminished activity in the labor force at some advanced age for reasons other than health (Gendell and Seigel, 1992). Within these general guidelines researchers and policymakers then set more precise limits, depending on their purposes and the data available. Since not everyone uses the same definition, it is important to pay attention to which boundaries of retirement are being used in any given discussion.

The Social Construction of Retirement

Where did retirement come from? If we look at the history of employment and leisure we can easily see that retirement is a social construction. Retirement did not always exist in Western societies and is still not common in many developing nations around the world. Historians date the start of large-scale retirement to the close of the nineteenth century (Quadagno, 1982), arising from a mix of social and economic changes.

Throughout most of history people from all social classes were required to work in order to ensure the survival of themselves and their kin (Quadagno, 1982; Reskin and Padavic, 1994). Labor started early in life, because childhood was not recognized as a separate stage of life to be protected from labor, and continued until death or disability prevented it (Plakans, 1994). Even the nobility of Europe had duties to perform in connection with their station and could not do with their time whatever they wished.

Retirement was not entirely unknown prior to industrialization. Occasionally landowning farmers would have contracts with their inheriting sons to provide care for them (and their widows) once they retired and turned over operation of the farm. Wealthy British men could "retire" to their country estates, undertaking a slower lifestyle. "Retirement in 'modern' society is unique only to the degree that it is associated with massive intergenerational income redistribution through a state bureaucracy. Retirement, itself, is not new" (Quadagno, 1982, p. 199). Historically speaking, however, the option of a large percentage of the population having a block of unstructured time at the end of the life cycle is new.

Four social conditions set the stage for the emergence of retirement as a social institution (Atchley, 1976; Cooperman and Keast, 1983; Plakans, 1994; Quadagno, 1982). First, the society must produce an economic surplus (usually via industrial production) sufficient to support its nonemployed population. Second, there must be some mechanism in place (such as pensions) to divert that surplus to the needs of the nonproducing members of the society. Third, there must be positive attitudes toward not working, legitimating non-employment pursuits as acceptable or desirable. Fourth, people must live long enough to accumulate an acceptable minimum of years of productivity to warrant sup-

Work into the laters years was common in myst societies of the past.

port during retirement (Atchley, 1976). The development of retirement was enabled by the creation of public and private pension schemes, starting in the late 1800s. Retirement incentives, such as pension programs, grew up during periods when labor was in ample supply, as larger youthful cohorts were continually entering the labor force (Cooperman and Keast, 1983). Concurrently, while industrialization created surpluses, it required workers to maintain high-speed movement to keep up with machines, emphasizing speed over skill in productivity (Quadagno, 1982). Given these conditions, it is not surprising that retirement soon emerged.

Attitudes toward retirement were slower to change, but Atchley (1976) contends that sequential cohorts have become more positive in their attitudes toward retirement. Retirement is now generally accepted as an appropriate stage of the adult life cycle and as a legitimate, earned privilege (O'Rand, 1990). The legitimization of leisure has accompanied and reinforced positive attitudes toward retirement, as long as one maintains a high level of activity and involvement (Ekerdt, 1986). Normative support for a leisure lifestyle has reduced the appeal of continued employment, and numerous studies agree that this new phase of life has been accepted by citizens of most Western societies (Atchley, 1994). Even as its meaning continues to change, however, questions are raised regarding whether the concept of retirement has ever been truly meaningful for minority, disadvantaged, and female workers, who often have experienced discontinuous labor force histories and more often continue employment into old age because of financial need (Calasanti, 1996b).

Theoretical Perspectives on Contemporary Retirement

By providing a formal, universal, and manageable exit from the labor force for all people reaching a certain age range, retirement solved a number of problems for industrializing nations with growing populations. Retirement operates at the corporate and societal level as "a mechanism for adjusting the supply of labor to the demand" (Atchley, 1976, p. 123). According to the functionalist perspective, retirement fulfills many functions for society. Retirement controls the flow of labor out of the labor market. Retirement enables employers to more easily remove of older, more highly compensated workers When older workers retire, they make room for younger workers to be hired at lower wages with the promise of future advancement. So retirement smoothes the flow of people into the labor market as well as out of it (Atchley, 1976; Johnson and Williamson, 1987).

From a conflict perspective, however, retirement looks very different. A conflict perspective begins with different assumptions and asks different questions. Who benefits most from the existence of retirement as a social institution? Who controls the process and timing of retirement? Matras (1990) describes the contraction of employment as engendering a "struggle for employment" between workers and employers in which the power is largely in the hands of employers, who control what groups work and receive what wages and benefits.

According to John Myles (1984), politics, not demographics, determine the conditions of life for older people. The exclusion of older workers from employment is not a necessary result of changing demographic realities in an aging society, but instead an act of discrimination. According to the conflict perspective, the social construction of retirement as a time of life without employment builds an army of unemployed but able workers who serve as a mechanism to control the current labor force participants by posing the threat of replacing them (Matras, 1990).

Government policies, such as the age for eligibility of full Social Security benefits, serve the same purpose as corporate decisions about pension eligibility and special early-retirement options. Both operate to manipulate the retirement decisions of individuals to serve the needs of employers. Conflict theorists point out that employers can and do utilize policies to manipulate the labor supply to achieve their own goals. Conflict theorists believe that retirement pits relatively powerless workers against the interests of a powerful organization that may no longer need their services.

Hardy and her colleagues (Hardy and Quadagno, 1995; Hardy, Hazelrigg, and Quadagno, 1996) studied autoworkers who had taken either regular early retirement or "special" **early retirement incentive programs (ERIPs)** created to downsize the work force. Autoworkers are a good case study because their unions have a long history of strong and flexible pensions. Many of the autoworkers in this study were aware that their employers planned to close plants and decrease the labor pool and feared for their jobs. Taking a "voluntary" early retirement (if you were eligible by age and years of service to the company) avoided the risks of layoff and guaranteed a degree of economic security. Their choices, made under threat, appear to be far from truly voluntary. By creating such conditions, employers continue to control the retirement decisions of their employees, even though mandatory retirement is no longer legal and the decisions to retire appear to be purely voluntary.

The Role of Social Security

The creation of the Social Security program in 1935 enabled retirement to become a reality for the majority of American workers (see Chapter 9 for further discussion of the establishment of this program). Social Security has been important in helping to institutionalize and promote retirement in three related ways. First, the existence of Social Security makes retirement socially legitimate as a transition and stage of the life cycle. Second, Social Security benefits enable individuals to retire by providing a reliable source of income to the vast majority of American workers. Currently 92 percent of older adults receive benefits from the program, mostly from its retirement-related aspects (Social Security Administration, 1995b).

Third, Social Security has promoted retirement by creating financial disincentives to continued employment, especially full-time employment

"YOU HAVE TO PREPARE FOR YOUR PENSION YEARS... BEGIN TO TAPER OFF ON FOOD, CLOTHING AND SHELTER."

Lengthy retirements mean that adequate financial resources are key to economic security.

(Burkhauser and Quinn, 1997). One such disincentive is called the **earnings test**. In 1999 Social Security reduced retirement benefits to any individuals aged 65-69 with earnings above $15,500 by $1 for every $3 of additional earnings; thus, the earnings test is essentially a penalty for work after retirement (Social Security Administration, 1999d). Although the earnings test has recently been relaxed (a $30,000 limit will be in effect by 2002), others call for its removal because it has discouraged retirees with Social Security benefits from taking employment.

Although Social Security was created to enable workers to retire, not all of its provisions clearly work in that direction. Policy changes in Social Security now encourages workers to stay in the labor force longer by raising the age of eligibility for full benefits (Burkhauser and Quinn, 1997). Ironically, this change is occurring at the same time that private industry, through pension programs, is often encouraging early retirements! As Exhibit 8.8 shows, Social Security eligibility ages are important. Currently workers can take early (reduced) benefits at age 62 and full benefits at age 65. These are, not coincidentally, the peak ages at which workers start their Social Security benefits, with the trend moving more toward 62 in recent years. By the year 2027, a worker will have to be 67 (rather than 65) in order to retire with full Social Security benefits. This change also increases the financial penalty for early retirement at age 62 because a reduction is built in for every month that retirement is taken early. Benefits will be reduced from the current 80 percent to 70 percent of what they would have been if the worker had waited until the age for full entitlement. Although intended to move the "normal" retirement age upward, analyses done to date suggest that the increased age for full Social Security benefits in itself will have little effect on the timing of retirement (Quinn and Burkhauser, 1990).

The Role of Private Pensions

For workers expecting private pensions, the provisions of those programs and the size of benefits are central to retirement decisions (Wise, 1997). From the perspective of a worker, private pensions can be thought of as compensation deferred from their working years or a reward for past productivity. Although

Exhibit 8.8   *Age at Initial of Receipt of Social Security Retirement Benefits, Males, by Year*

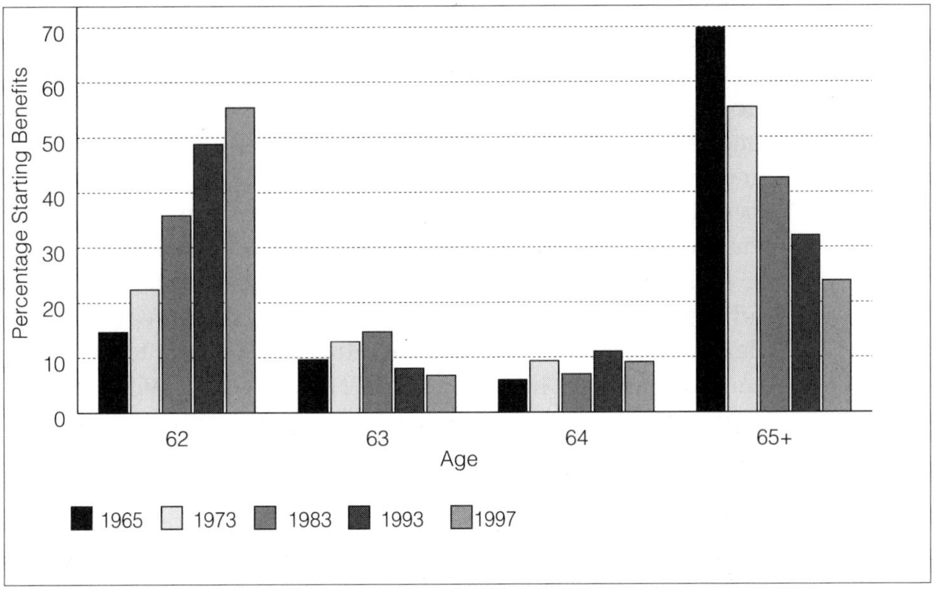

Adapted from: Social Security Administration, 1994b, 1998c

we often think of pensions as an incentive to retire (or to do so early), if policies provide larger benefits if the worker delays retirement another year or more, they can also create a disincentive to retire (Fields and Mitchell, 1984). Pension provisions have a stronger effect on decisions about retirement timing than does Social Security (Hogarth, 1991; Wise, 1997).

From the viewpoint of an employer, pensions look quite different (Burkhauser and Quinn, 1994). Pension programs are designed as policy tools, to be used by the employer to modify their labor pool as needed over time. Many pension programs both enhance employee loyalty during certain earlier spans of the career and later facilitate departures from employment, two goals frequently sought by employers (Hardy et al., 1996). Employers can build provisions into their pensions that create incentives to exit at a certain age by shrinking the value of a pension if it is deferred. In special circumstances (such as a need to reduce a work force suddenly because of economic stress or merger), employers may add incentives, making the pension more attractive and encouraging mature employees to depart early "voluntarily" (Hardy et. al. 1996; Wise, 1997). Employers can add antiwork policies to worker pensions, like financial penalties for transferring to part-time jobs with the same employer, or denying older workers training or opportunities for advancement (Burkhauser and Quinn, 1994).

The use of pension programs as a policy tool is clearly demonstrated in corporate downsizing and layoffs accomplished through early retirement incentive programs (ERIPs). It is no coincidence that these programs flourish during difficult economic times with an oversupply of labor, when it is less costly for an employer to pay pensions than workers' salaries. Early retirement incentive programs are one solution to having too many employees. Incentives in some programs are high, including a dramatic increase in both the monthly and lifetime value of a pension (Hardy et al., 1996). Although the cost is often high and employers cannot choose which employees to retain (such as those with rare or specialized skills), ERIPs are viewed as more humane than layoffs and as creating fewer personnel and legal problems for the company.

Just how the availability and size of a pension influences the decisions of individual workers and the overall trends toward early retirement are complexities beyond the scope of this chapter. Suffice it to say that details of pension programs are highly variable. How pensions will change in the future is unpredictable, but changes will certainly benefit employers at least as much as retirees (Quinn and Burkhauser, 1990). To limit their own costs, many employers are switching to employee-funded and -directed pensions (Quinn and Burkhauser, 1990). In these programs, employees choose from several investment options and contribute, along with their employers, to a pension "nest egg," which is really an investment in stocks and bonds outside the company's control. Advocates suggest that this change fits well with the American ethic of individual responsibility, but it exposes retirement income to risk from a downturn in the stock market or poor management by the pensioner (Quinn and Burkhauser, 1990). In addition, this change means that employers have less leverage over when their employees retire, because they are less able to manipulate provisions of this type of pension program to get people to retire when the company wishes (Quinn and Burkhauser, 1990).

Trends in Retirement

Early Retirement

In recent decades retirement as a stage of life had been expanding at both ends, through increased longevity and earlier retirement. As Quinn and Burkhauser (1990) put it, "If retirement from the labor force marks the passage into old age, then the old among us have grown considerably younger in recent years" (p. 307). In 1950, before Social Security had its early retirement option, the average age for receipt of Social Security retirement benefits was 68.7 for men. By the 1980s, the mean age of receipt of Social Security benefits for both men and women had dropped about five years (Gendell and Siegel, 1992). This pattern holds for both sexes, for both European American and African American workers, and across time (Gendell and Siegel, 1996) (see Exhibit 8.9). Projections in 1992 suggested that retirement ages could decrease a little more by 2005 if current trends continued (Gendell and Siegel, 1992), but not everyone believes that those trends are continuing.

Exhibit 8.9   *Median Age at Retirement by Sex and Race: 1955–90*

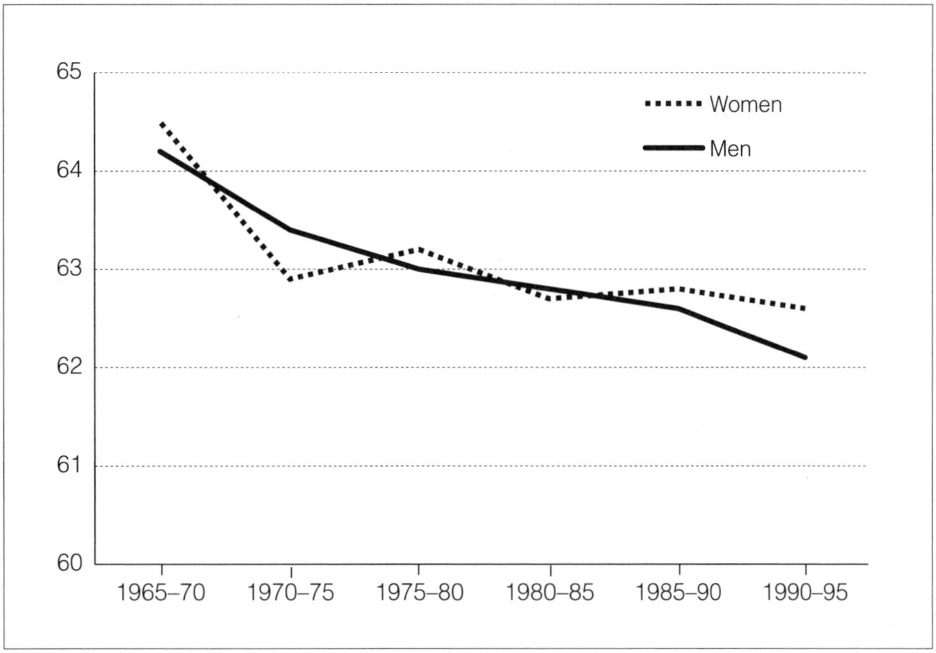

Source: Gendell, 1998.

Early retirement is an international phenomenon and seems illogical given increases in both longevity and health well into the seventh and eighth decades of life (Kohli, 1994; Wise, 1997). Throughout the world, increasing numbers of people are retiring for ever-lengthier periods of time during which they face few demands on their time and have limited opportunities to contribute to societal productivity. Many countries besides the United States have recently passed legislation to raise the age of eligibility for benefits to counteract or minimize the early retirement trend. In the United States we can no longer say that 65 is the appropriate age for retirement, because more workers retire at age 62 than at 65 (Burkhauser and Quinn, 1994).

There is considerable debate about the future of early retirement. If uncertainty in the labor market increases, if fewer workers have pensions, or if Social Security benefits decrease, then average retirement ages may increase to 65 or beyond. In that case, the requirement to work longer will probably weigh most heavily on workers who have had poorer life chances—women, minorities, and the less educated—while early retirement may still prevail for those more advantaged. If, on the other hand, employer priorities, economic cycles and technological change reduce the demand for labor, older workers may continue to be encouraged to take early retirement. In sum, the future of early retirement rests with social and economic forces beyond prediction today. Data from the late 1990s attest to an apparent end to the early retirement trend among men (Henretta, 2000; Quinn, 1997). The direction for future age changes and trends among women and minorities may differ.

Gender and Class Variations in Retirement Trends

As we have seen throughout this chapter, the life chances of persons in different social groups vary in the labor force. It is not surprising that those who are most advantaged during their years in the labor force also have the greatest number of options regarding ending their employment via retirement. Those who freely choose to retire are those who can afford to retire, but who may also have the option of continuing employment. These opportunities are not equally distributed in American society. How do life chances ultimately influence the choices workers face regarding retirement?

It has been projected that women will constitute 47 percent of the labor force by the year 2000; an increasing proportion of women will be labor force participants during most of their adult lives (Guy and Erdner, 1993). Despite this growth, the legacy of women's presumed lack of interest in employment has slowed the study of retirement among women until fairly recently. Historical evidence from the 1800s (Quadagno, 1982) suggests that women often continued employment into old age because of financial need and lack of pensions. In the past, many older women continued in the labor force, even if the jobs available to them were difficult or demeaning. Has the retirement situation improved for women since the early industrial era?

As we saw early in this chapter, women have not followed men into early retirement, at least not the women in the cohorts retiring so far. One reason may be that many of the women in those cohorts entered the labor force at later ages or had interrupted participation, making them less anxious to withdraw from employment and less likely to be eligible for private pensions. As we will see in Chapter 9, there is already a gender gap in pension coverage, even without considering women's lesser time in the labor force, so that women face a different economic landscape if they consider retirement. Early retirement, given fewer economic resources and a longer life expectancy, may seem much less appealing as an option.

Social class is another important source of variation in the conditions facing individuals approaching retirement. Those with sporadic employment histories or who became a part of the underground economy are seldom covered by Social Security. These individuals are often unaware as they approach later life that they have worked for years without contributions being made on their behalf. Too poor to contemplate retirement, many of these individuals continue employment as long as their health permits and opportunities are available, often at menial and physically difficult jobs. Retirement, if it comes at all, arrives with the need to cease employment because of poor health or lack of jobs and the acceptance of SSI or similar welfare-type assistance. It is important for us not to generalize about "the elderly" from the experience of middle-class individuals with pensions and other resources.

Individual Retirement

In addition to its importance to the economy, for corporations, and for the larger society, retirement is also a key life cycle transition for individuals and couples. Since mandatory retirement is illegal (with a few exceptions), one might expect increasing variation in when and how workers withdraw from full-time career employment. For most workers, however, this decision is not freely made. Most people, for instance, cannot decide at age 45 that they wish to retire and be able to do so with economic support from the society. Despite the institutionalization of retirement as part of the occupational life cycle, a surprising number of workers at ages approaching retirement (51-61) have no plans for the transition or its timing (Ekerdt, DeViney, and Kosloski, 1996). A variety of factors shape the decisions about whether and when to retire.

Determinants of the Retirement Decision

Often we think of retirement as determined by age, and in fact an individual's age does play an indirect role by determining eligibility for retirement programs and pensions. The earliest research on retirement behavior in the 1940s focused on mandatory retirement and poor health as causes (Quinn and Burkhauser, 1990). A few decades later, attention turned to the critical role played by retirement income as an enabling factor in retirement. While economists continue to focus on pensions and Social Security benefits, many other factors—health status, job satisfaction, family responsibilities, and the retirement of a spouse—are considered central to retirement decisions today (Quinn and Burkhauser, 1990; Ruhm, 1996).

We assume that every worker reaching ages at which retirements are common among peers periodically considers, based on multiple factors, whether to retire this year, next year, ten years in the future, or never. In fact, the process of reaching this **retirement decision** is probably not as orderly as researchers assume and may involve a variety of individual factors (how much they like their coworkers, the difficulty of their commute, what activities they anticipate during retirement) that remain largely unmeasured (Hardy et al., 1996). Research has focused on more standard items, such as health, availability of pension and other retirement income, marital status, and employment history, which are available for secondary analysis in large national surveys (Quinn and Burkhauser, 1990).

Among the most highly researched topics are financial factors, which are often quite complex (Fields and Mitchell, 1984). The size and rules for private pensions, the value of Social Security benefits, and workers' expectations about the adequacy of these main sources of retirement income over time do influence the decisions individuals make regarding the timing of retirement. A worker might weigh the value of current earnings and future benefits from pensions and Social Security against a year's worth of pension benefits sacrificed if she continues in the current job (Quinn and Burkhauser, 1990). It remains unclear how well typical workers understand such economic intricacies in making their retirement choices.

It was not really until the 1970s that researchers began to investigate retirement among women (Slevin and Wingrove, 1995). Given life-long differences in employment for women, concerns were raised that utilizing a "male model" of retirement would inadequately represent the factors shaping decisions among women. Retirement decisions among women are influenced by a variety of factors that are seemingly less relevant to (and less studied among) men, including family caregiving responsibilities and (for the married) their spouse's health (Weaver, 1994). For example, Ruhm (1996) found that married women with heavy caregiving responsibilities more often withdrew from employment and were much more likely to give family reasons for their decisions. In some studies of women's retirement, financial issues were much less important than health and family factors in determining when retirement occurred (Weaver, 1994). For married couples, a subset of women continue to work after their husbands retire, but some research suggests that wives time their retirements to when their husbands cease employment but that the opposite is not true (Slevin and Wingrove, 1995). Continuing to work after a husband retires may be due to women being younger and thus ineligible for retirement benefits; continuing to work may be a financial necessity. Interruptions in married women's labor force participation, such as delays for child rearing, may also mean they are less ready to retire at the same ages as their husbands (Feuerbach and Erdwins, 1994). Women's attention to couple and family issues, and men's inattention to these issues, suggests that cohorts currently retiring still have not moved very far from past stereotypes of women as primarily rooted in the family and men in their careers.

Decisions on whether to retire and when to retire are also related to the availability of continued employment. There is a resurgent interest in both health and labor-market barriers to continued employment (Quinn and Burkhauser, 1990). Many older workers say they would prefer to work part-time. What they actually mean is that they would like to reduce their hours but remain at the same wages. Employers seldom offer the same wages to part-time workers, so few workers can gradually retire through movement to part-time employment in their same jobs (Quinn and Burkhauser, 1990). Instead, the decision is most often an "either/or" one—either continued full-time employment or complete withdrawal—at least from a primary employer. Such a retirement may not be final, however, because many people become reemployed after retiring from a long-term employment.

Exhibit 8.10 shows the percentage of males by ages that received a pension but were also employed. Some describe this combination as "work after retirement," but it may be more complicated than that. In all three years shown,

Exhibit 8.10 *Percentage of Men by Age with Pensions Who are Employed*

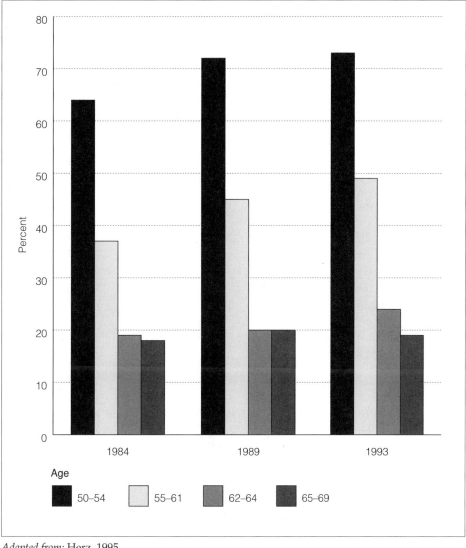

Adapted from: Herz, 1995.

employment with a pension was highest for the youngest group of men (ages 50-54) and dropped substantially for older groups. Employment among the youngest pensioned individuals (under age 62) has been increasing since the mid-1980s, perhaps reflecting the continued employment of men leaving their career jobs through early retirement incentives but not yet ready to withdraw completely from employment. Again, this points out the inadequacy of definitions of retirement.

It may be that our thinking about retirement will eventually evolve into a

Exhibit 8.11   *Alternative Retirement Patterns*

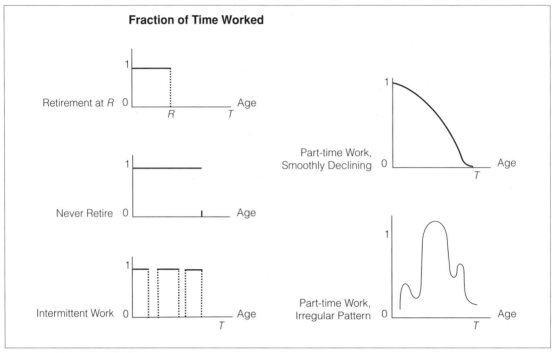

Source: Fields and Mitchell, 1984.

series of decisions on whether to seek a new job once the current job ends (Doeringer, 1990). Fields and Mitchell (1984) have proposed a variety of possible models to substitute for the either/or retirement process, including intermittent work, gradual reduction of work, and varying levels of part-time employment after leaving a primary career (see Exhibit 8.11).

Employment after Retirement—Bridge Jobs

We think about retirement as an abrupt transition, moving from full-time career employment one day to no employment the next. In fact, it is not so simple. A growing percentage of older workers find their career jobs disappearing before they are ready to retire, requiring them to seek what are called bridge jobs. Bridge jobs carry workers over between a career job and full retirement, often with lower pay and fewer benefits (Burkhauser and Quinn, 1994; Doeringer, 1990; Quinn and Kozy, 1996). In a sample of displaced workers in their 50s, average household income loss after reemployment was 24% and health insurance coverage was 14% lower than among current workers, indicating the penalty for job displacement in mid-life (Couch, 1998). Ruhm (1990) reports that half of all workers leave their career jobs and take other employment before fully retiring, with the highest percentages found among minority and female workers.

Employers continue to offer relatively few options for flexible retirement, cling-ing to the occupational life cycle that strictly separates the working phase of life from that of retirement. For example, McDonalds created a McMasters program, intended to attract retirees to employment on a part-time basis for fast-food restaurants at low wages, but this represents substantial downward mobility for a former manager or professional.

Many older workers find new jobs, construct self-employment options, or locate bridge jobs that move them more gradually from full-time employment to complete retirement (Quinn and Burkhauser, 1990). One study found that more than 25 percent of retirees from a career job continued in the labor force, most for at least two years and many in substantially different types of employ-ment (Quinn and Burkhauser, 1990). This pattern helps explain the growing numbers of men with pensions and with jobs seen in Exhibit 8.10. Ruhm (1990) describes the process of leaving a full time career job as similar to the period of labor force entry, when a worker holds several jobs on the way to a career job of longer duration. Mutchler and her colleagues (1997) describe this newly rec-ognized pattern as reflecting "blurred" rather than "crisp" transitions at retire-ment. Departure from employment may involve stepping through a number of jobs as individuals wind down their involvement with the labor force. There are contradictory messages coming from private employers and from the gov-ernment. Private employers incentives and downsizing urge workers to "Retire early" But through increased Social Security eligibility ages, reduced penalties for work in retirement, and removal of mandatory retirement the government says "Retire late." This contradiction in policies may mean that bridge jobs are an increasingly prevalent form of gradual exit from the labor force (Quinn and Kozy, 1996).

Consequences for the Individual and the Couple

Early researchers (in the 1940s and 1950s) studied the consequences of retire-ment with clear expectations. They anticipated, based on their orientations as middle-class males steeped in the "work ethic," that retirees (i.e., male retirees) would experience stress upon separation from employment and lose their core identities as male breadwinners. Since mandatory retirement was much more prevalent at the time, it was feared that workers were being unwillingly "put out to pasture" before they were socially or economically prepared. It was with a great deal of surprise, therefore, that they found that most retired men were not unhappy or maladjusted (Atchley, 1976).

Most early studies of retirement satisfaction showed that retirees were large-ly happy with their situations, not the stressed and "roleless" outcasts that had been expected (Atchley, 1976). A recent longitudinal study of 800 workers found no change in self-esteem and a decline in depression among those who retired, suggesting stability or positive outcomes from retirement (Reitzes, Mutran, and Fernandez, 1996). Not all retirees enjoy retirement equally. Those who retire in good health, who have adequate income, and whose decision to retire was truly voluntary fare better, as do those with strong social networks and activities planned during retirement. The work ethic, as we will see in an upcoming discussion of continuity theory, is transformed into the "busy ethic" of an active leisure in retirement for many of these advantaged individuals.

While clear negative outcomes for male workers have not been demonstrated, the evidence for women is more mixed. Although most of the retirement research has focused on men, an analysis of both men and women showed that women are less satisfied in retirement. Women may be unhappier partly because of other major life events like the illness of self or spouse, relocation, divorce, or widowhood happening near the time of retirement (Szinovacz and Washo, 1992). These mixed findings may also be related to the poorer economic security of retiring women, especially if they are widowed (Guy and Erdner, 1993). Calasanti (1996a) points out that women's satisfaction in retirement is shaped by their experiences in the labor force, which systematically differ from those of men. For women in traditionally female jobs, Calasanti (1996a) found that only health influenced their satisfaction in retirement. Using only the experiences of male workers (often middle-class white male workers at that) gives an unrealistic picture of how the experience of retirement influences workers in other groups (Slevin and Wingrove, 1995).

Volition and choice are important to satisfaction in retirement. Workers who chose to retire and were able to choose the timing of this transition have fared better than those whose health, employment circumstances, family pressures, or other factors forced their retirement at a time not of their choosing. In the study of autoworkers mentioned earlier (Hardy and Quadagno, 1995), those who had anticipated retirement and perceived it as a true choice were more satisfied afterward than those who felt pushed by their employment situation or health problems to leave.

■ ■ ■ ■ ■ ■ ■ ■

APPLYING THEORY
Continuity Theory and the "Busy Ethic"

A central tenet of Western cultures for centuries has been the importance of employment—the **work ethic**.

> The work ethic, like any ethic, is a set of beliefs and values that identifies what is good and affirms ideals of conduct. The work ethic historically has identified work with virtue and has held up for esteem a conflation of such traits and habits as diligence, initiative, temperance, industriousness, competitiveness, self-reliance, and the capacity for deferred gratification. (Ekerdt, 1986, p. 239)

Although sometimes attributed to the Puritans, the contemporary work ethic has a long cultural heritage from a time when labor by all was necessary to survival, and pride in successful employment was central to identity (Plakans,

1994). The work ethic has long been viewed as a pivotal force, driving men (and more recently, women) to seek employment and job-related achievement as a component of self-worth. But how do individuals compensate when retirement removes the status and achievement engendered by employment?

Perhaps a partial answer to this question can be found in **continuity theory**, an individual-level theory spawned (along with activity theory) from the reaction to disengagement theory. Central to continuity theory is the idea that adults adapt to aging by attempting to preserve and maintain existing self-concepts, relationships, and ways of doing things (Atchley, 1989). Activity theory argued for equilibrium. According to this theory, older people replace a lost activity or relationship with an equivalent. "Continuity theory assumes evolution, not homeostasis, and this assumption allows change to be integrated into one's prior history without necessarily causing upheaval and disequilibrium" (Atchley, 1989, p. 183). Faced with change, aging adults select alternatives consistent with who they have been and what they have done in the past. Internal continuity enables individuals to connect current changes with their past, sustaining the sense of self. External continuity is maintained by "being and doing in familiar environments, practicing familiar skills and interacting with familiar people" (Atchley, 1989, p. 185).

Consistent with the tenets of continuity theory, David Ekerdt (1986) posited a moral imperative for involvement during retirement, which he calls the busy ethic.

> Just as there is a work ethic that holds industriousness and self-reliance as virtues, so, too, there is a "busy ethic" for retirement that honors an active life. It represents people's attempts to justify retirement in terms of their long-standing beliefs and values. (p. 239)

He argues that people legitimate retirement and leisure by being highly occupied—keeping busy—much as they did during their years of employment. Rather than unlearning the work ethic, people transform it into the busy ethic, giving content to the "retiree" role once considered devoid of social norms for behavior. The result is a moral continuity between employed and retired statuses that answers many questions about the appropriateness of retirement as a life stage. As a stepchild of the work ethic, Ekerdt argues, the busy ethic lets retirees approach leisure in the same organized and purposeful manner in which they previously approached employment. Retirees don't actually have to pursue constant busyness but should at least talk about their activities and plans to be busy in the future. This busyness represents a high degree of continuity in the lives of individuals, who substitute community work, socializing, and leisure pursuits for a schedule dominated by employment. It structures time in a much more socially acceptable and work-consistent manner than would an ethic of nonconformity and self-indulgence, therefore providing a sense of continuity to individuals and to society. The busy ethic, then, gives middle-class retirees a type of continuity at retirement, minimizing (according to the theory) the risks of disruption and distress.

Those planning activities for future cohorts of the elderly may want to keep the notion of continuity in mind. If continuity is important, then older adults who have retired will probably seek activities in which they can gain both the sense of busyness and the sense of accomplishment formerly provided by employment. These needs may help explain why some older adults eschew participation in today's senior centers, where gossip, arts and crafts, and bingo are often perceived as the core of the day. If such activities do not provide a sense of continuity for individuals who have retired, perhaps rethinking the activities available at senior centers to include meaningful volunteerism and opportunities for part-time employment will make them more relevant to future cohorts of retired Americans. At the same time, given pressures from employers and technologies to work longer hours and more efficiently to the point of stress and burn-out, a more limited but meaningful work-like involvement may be the goal for older adults.

■ ■ ■

Rethinking Employment and Retirement for the Future

It could be argued that the individual, corporate, and societal decisions regarding the future of employment and retirement carry the potential for dramatically reshaping the way we organize the timing and sequencing of events in our lives. How the life course might change and what the place of employment will be within it decades from now are very difficult to predict, given the large flux in both the market for labor and its supply, and the accompanying changes in our notions of employment and retirement. When science fiction writers speculate about possible futures, they often portray societies in which leisure abounds thanks to the labor of robots and other technological advances. One of the great dilemmas facing developed and aging societies, however, is the large amount of unstructured time provided by retirement. Is it useful to society to enable individuals to have this time without social norms for utilizing it toward the social good? The growth of leisure industries, intended to provide enjoyable activities for those able to retire in good financial and physical health, does not confer the social status, social integration, and self-esteem we continue to associate with employment. Nor does it address the pressing social problems of most societies.

Both researchers and policymakers are now considering how to tap the productive potential of an increasing population of healthy and educated individuals past the usual age of retirement. The alternatives include both paid employment and voluntary activities. According to the study by the Commonwealth Fund (1993), 10 percent of the nonemployed population over the age of 55 is willing and able to hold a job but cannot locate suitable employment. Even those who don't desire paid employment may seek interesting vol-

Although our concept of retirement as a time of leisure persists, more older adults may work to advanced ages for economic reasons or if they are self employed and enjoy their jobs.

untary activities using their expertise and experience, providing an untapped resource for dealing with the problems of society.

Productive aging, described in Chapter 6, focuses on the current productivity (both paid and unpaid) of the older population and the potential to tap unused productivity through broadening opportunities for paid, volunteer, and familial work. The productive aging approach also focuses on structural barriers to full use of the productive capacity of the older population, including the retired. Factors such as institutional ageism and age-based rules may structure inactivity for individuals who otherwise could be more productive (Caro, Bass, and Chen, 1993). It is important to point out, however, that older persons already contribute vast numbers of hours in volunteer work for their families and communities, work that currently gains little recognition in society (Commonwealth Fund, 1993).

Changes in Policies and Political Attitudes

The U.S. government has already taken policy steps, including abolishing mandatory retirement and raising the age of full entitlement to Social Security benefits, intended to increase the likelihood of employment into later years of life. The business community has so far not followed suit by modifying pension programs and employment policies to encourage older workers to remain, even in a modified capacity, in the labor force. Business's short-term interests still point to removal, rather than retention, of workers past their early 60s (Rix, 1991). Although the alarm has sounded about the aging of the baby boomers, a variety of political forces and attitudes are involved in shaping the future of employment prospects for older, and therefore for younger, workers.

Policy makers have put forward proposals to raise the age of entitlement to Social Security beyond age 67. One such proposal argues for "equivalent retirement ages," whereby the age of entitlement would be shifted to keep the ratio between years in retirement and working life constant (Chen, 1994). Such a policy would shift the age of entitlement for Social Security benefits upward as life expectancy increases and, presumably, as healthy life expectancy expands. Other proposals simply suggest mandating 70 as the age of eligibility for full entitlements.

Despite policy changes encouraging later retirement (Quinn and Burkhauser, 1990), the pattern of early retirement remains strong in most developed countries (Guillemard, 1996). The synergy between income maintenance programs and the institutionalization of retirement should not be underestimated. Workers lacking financial support do not see retirement as a viable option if it would mean poverty!

Changes in the Economy and the Nature of Work

The productivity of the labor force depends on a number of factors, including the use of advanced technologies such as computers and robotics, as well as the degree of fit between a job's demands and the skills and abilities of a worker filling it. The labor market is changing. Many types of jobs now require high levels of skill and continuous upgrading of education to keep current. Other jobs are becoming deskilled, as machines take over the tasks of workers. In some cases, tasks are accomplished by unskilled workers maintaining machinery. A good example is insurance adjusters, who used to have to use judgement in determining the risks of various people to properly price their insurance policies. Now they plug data into software that calculates risks for them, so that their job requires less skill and they require less training. Their employers can also replace them more easily. **Deskilling jobs** results in lower wages and makes workers more easily replaceable, because their training and knowledge of the business are less important (Auster, 1996). These changes are so fundamental that it remains unclear how they will ultimately shape the needs and the size of the labor force. Given all of the uncertainties, it is difficult to predict the degree to which older workers may be encouraged to continue in current jobs, be retrained into new employment, retire, or move to part-time work.

Employers are changing their policies to move away from lifetime employment of workers. The odds of receiving a pension from a single lifetime employer are mitigated by trends such as contingent employment. By using contingent labor, employers are limiting their current costs, their responsibilities to their employees, and their investment in the labor force over the long term. Employees may pay a price, as retirement once again becomes impractical for many contingent workers lacking pensions (Quinn and Burkhauser, 1990).

These changes also reflect the goals of business and industry as they compete in a global marketplace for goods, labor, and profit. Locking a business into long-term obligations with workers in one country limits its capacity to respond to lower wage rates or abundant labor elsewhere in the world. In addition, employers are starting to think more flexibly about the site of employment, as more information-based jobs can be performed at home, saving the cost of a centralized place of business. The ramifications of these changes for how individuals move through their working lives have not been fully explored.

Robert Kahn (1994) has suggested a rethinking of how we define and organize work. He concurs that the concept of productive aging should be expanded to include activities such as family and household duties and volunteerism. Given the preferences many workers have for part-time jobs, Kahn also suggests that we reengineer time into four-hour work modules that can be flexibly combined into full- or part-time options. This more flexible approach would avoid a false dichotomy between the 35- to 40-hour full-time status and any other type of schedule that now seems to be built into the thinking of employers.

Changes for Individual Workers

For the vast majority of people who survive to age 65, life expectancy is 83; so, an individual who retires at age 65 will live an average of about 20 years in retirement. Since many of those are expected to be healthy, active years, there is a growing concern about what people can, should, and will do after they retire. Attitudes regarding employment and retirement may be critical to deciding how individuals allocate this time.

It seems clear that current changes in the labor market will mean that the occupational careers of individuals will be much less predictable and orderly in the future. We will see the end of the traditional occupational life cycle model as we have known it. Perhaps Riley's suggestion of adulthood as a concurrent and flexible blend of education, leisure, and employment, as discussed in Chapter 6, will become more realistic (See Exhibit 6.6) (Riley and Riley, 1994). One interesting issue will be how individuals coordinate their occupations with roles in the family, especially parenting. The current situation is not optimal, especially for women, as completion of education, heavy demands from early-career employment, and the care of children all overlap substantially in young and middle adulthood. If life scheduling could arrange lower labor force demand during periods of intensive childcare responsibility (and if gender roles encouraged a more equal division of familial/household responsibilities), managing occupational and family roles might become less stressful.

One alternative is **multiple careers**, in which an individual undergoes training and employment two or more times during adulthood, potentially in very different fields. Multiple careers theoretically reduce the risk of boredom for employees, accommodate changing labor market needs, and provide options to deal with skill obsolescence and a longer healthy life expectancy. Training might begin as it does now in late adolescence, followed by a 25-year career in a field. An individual could then experience a period of leisure before retraining for a second career. Multiple careers would require reeducation at midlife, which has not been a typical pattern so far in history. It is also unclear whether there would be sufficient individual choice to make the multiple careers idea work in the manner described. Workers might be discouraged from selecting jobs requiring lengthy training and apprenticeship, such as medicine, under a multiple career system. Downward mobility in earnings and prestige is likely to remain a risk in second careers or bridge jobs (Ruhm, 1990).

The idea of multiple careers also seems to be based on an undersupply of labor, so that workers have choices about jobs and ample salary and benefits to prepare for periods of leisure and training between them. If labor is abundant, however, workers may be competing for scarce jobs while employers pay low wages and benefits and continue to ignore the needs and preferences of older workers. In contrast, if employers need to keep older workers on the job to meet corporate needs when labor is in short supply, options such as part-time or flexible schedules with better pay may become more prevalent than they are today.

With increasing healthy life expectancy, more of us should expect a future with multiple careers, interspersed with periods of training or retraining (Myles and Quadagno, 1995). Rapid-fire changes in technology, jobs, and the economy suggest that flexibility may be a more highly prized quality in workers of the future. In this world of the future, will retirement really be meaningful? That question can only be answered in the decades to come.

Summary

By the year 2006 the U.S. labor force is anticipated to include 147 million individuals (Fullerton, 1995). At the same time, the composition of the labor force will become more diverse, as Hispanic, Asian, and African Americans make up a growing proportion of workers. Women are expected to make up nearly half of the labor force (Fullerton, 1995). The growth in the overall labor force is slower now than it has been in prior decades, forcing society to examine how productivity needs will be met. Will new technologies enable the economy to continue to grow with fewer workers, or will there be increasing pressure to keep older workers in the labor force? Either way, the future will bring changes in how we view work and retirement as part of social life and the individual's life cycle.

Employment helps to organize the sequencing of events in the lives of individuals on a micro level and the flow of cohorts into and out of the labor force at the macro level. Therefore, any changes we devise in how work fits into the life cycle—either extending it, reducing it, or breaking it into different pieces—will have serious social and economic consequences. Although we cannot accurately predict what the demand for labor will be, the life chances that workers of diverse backgrounds have in that labor market will, in turn, shape their options as older workers and potential retirees. Our current concept of the occupational life cycle is moving rapidly toward obsolescence, but new models of employment in the life course are not yet clear.

For the present we continue to face discrimination against older workers, a corporate mentality more interested in creating incentives to retire older workers than in developing them as a resource for the future. As contingent labor grows, will older workers be systematically removed from "career" employment into lower-paying bridge jobs on the periphery? Will work continue to be nomadic, with workers moving regularly between jobs and risking a pensionless future? With the population of older persons growing, it is probable that society will address their needs, both economic and social, to avert some of the worst problems. It remains unclear, however, whether the coming labor market will be an ally or the nemesis of older workers.

We are already seeing the policy underpinnings of a changed conception of retirement, as Social Security raises entitlement ages and reduces penalties for working while receiving benefits. As policy discussions continue regarding the fate of Social Security, societies are actually discussing their concepts of the future of retirement. As the break between employment and retirement becomes less clear, we may one day cease to celebrate this passage in the way we now do—with gold watches and parties—and simply bid farewell to mature workers as they move on to their next employment opportunity. With a dynamic labor market, dynamism in individual lives, and a changing face on the meanings of work and retirement, the best prediction we can make is one of change, either modest or major, in the future of these social institutions.

Web Wise

Retirement Research Foundation

http://fdncenter.org/grantmaker/rrf/new.html

The Retirement Research Foundation is dedicated to supporting programs and projects that better the lives of older Americans. This site outlines areas of funding interests, including improving the quality of long-term care services, and educating/training professionals who serve older adults. This site also provides Foundation related press releases (awards and grant information) as well as lists of facts about older adults.

United States Department of Labor

http://www.dol.gov/

The U.S. Department of Labor (DOL), created by Congress in 1913, is responsible for securing the adequacy of workplaces in America. This comprehensive web site offers information about DOL and its programs, and an opportunity to explore department agencies. The "labor related data" option links the user to access the Bureau of Labor Statistics web site described below. Media releases, the history of minimum wage and the budget for fiscal year 1998 are also topics to explore. A DOL search function is also available.

U.S. Department of Labor
Bureau of Labor Statistics (BLS)

http://stats.bls.gov/

The Bureau of Labor Statistics (BLS) is a national agency within the United States Department of Labor. The BLS gathers, assesses, and disseminates data in the field of labor economics. The agency's web site offers overviews of surveys on employment trends, productivity data, and projections surrounding the labor force, industries, and occupations. The 1997 economy is presented in terms of labor force statistics, productivity, and price indexes; the option to view the data graphically is also available. Opportunities to explore other federal statistical agencies are available as well as publications and research papers, and listings of 1998 and recent archived news releases.

Key Terms

activity theory
age discrimination
Age Discrimination in
    Employment Act (ADEA)
Bona Fide Occupational
    Qualification (BFOQ)
bridge jobs
busy ethic
compression of employment
contingent labor force
continuity theory
deskilling jobs
disengagement
dissimilarity index
Early Retirement Incentive
    Programs (ERIPs)

earnings test
labor force
labor force participation rates
market for labor
multiple careers
occupational life cycle
older workers
private pensions
productive aging
retirement
retirement decision
sex segregation of occupations
stereotypes of older workers
underground economy
work ethic

Questions for Thought and Reflection

1. Given the changes in the occupational life cycle, think about how you might want to plan regarding the careers you may pursue in the future and the timing of other life events relating to the family and education. Will you have one career or more? When amidst work, training and leisure will you fit in time for family roles?

2. Develop some options for how society could better engage the time and skills of retired individuals over the next few decades. Keep in mind that health and education levels are improving. What societal problems might be addressed effectively by paid or unpaid work by older adults?

3. Think about the social policies influencing the timing of retirement. What are the advantages and risks involved in increasing the retirement age for full Social Security benefits to 70? Should the Age Discrimination in Employment Act still permit some jobs to have mandatory retirement (with BFOQs)? Should private pensions still encourage workers to leave early or "on time"?

4. Inequalities by race/ethnicity and gender in employment patterns and opportunities translate to differences faced by individuals facing retirement decisions. Is this a situation where society should intervene? Why or why not? How might change be effectively created through social policy?

TOPICAL ESSAY

E-Elders

The PC revolution and the exponential growth of the Internet are among the most recent in a long line of technological innovations that have touched the lives of current cohorts of older adults. The oldest old have witnessed inventions and innovations ranging from home electrification, airplanes, automobiles, and antibiotics to "smart houses," portable recorded music, cellular phones and microwaves. How are older adults responding to this major transformation of the social and economic worlds? Do older adults embrace or reject the e-revolution? Do reactions of older adults to the emergent cyber-world support or refute stereotypes of resistance among the old to learning new things, including new technologies? Although it may be too soon to have all of the answers to these questions, some early studies of older adults and use of these technologies give us clues.

Exposure and Expansion

Examples of older adults using the web are increasingly visible. One report described an older woman with failing eyesight and mobility limitations who was able to remain in her home. On-line food orders from her grandson some distance away supported her independence (Setton, 2000). Several seniors in a retirement community took a computer training course and commented on how learning to use email affected their lives. One said, "...I have friends all over the country." Another stated that the course "improved my outlook on life. I really can learn something new and it makes me feel more up-to-date." Others expressed concerns about becoming "computer junkies" (White et al. 1999).

Beyond the standing stereotypes about an "old dog learning new tricks," social and economic factors come into play with computers and the Internet. The explosion of the personal computer and the Worldwide Web into the lives of people has not occurred on a level playing field. It often seems as though children and young adults have adapted more quickly to these new ways of connecting to the social world. Programmers first created computer products directed toward youth, like computer games and educational programs, and applications for business and industry. Only recently have programmers and web site developers directed creative attention toward retirement-age adults. While product development for older adults has not begun to match what is targeted to younger markets, there is a significant thrust in designing on-line services and products that are appealing to seniors. Initially, older adults had limited incentives to spend some of their time exploring these new technologies. In many families children became "literate" in applications and hardware first and taught their parents how to use personal computers. Cohorts of cyber-sophisticated youth have now marched into adulthood, but the oldest age cohorts have seen little encouragement until recently to adopt this new technology. Both younger and older adults have shown persistently negative attitudes toward older people taking and succeeding in computer training (Ryan, Szechman and Bodkin, 1992).

Utilization and Benefits

There are varying estimates of the utilization of personal computers and the Internet by adults over age 65 (Post, 1996). One 1995 study suggested that 30% of adults between 55 and 75 owned a computer and about one third of these regularly used an online service, frequently to send e-mail or access the Internet (Adler, 1996). Developers are continuing to create web sites specifically to meet the needs of older adult web-surfers, including "Goldngal: the Cyberspace Granny," "SeniorNet," "Thirdage.com" and a range of others, including some you'll find at the end of chapters in this text (see Furlong, 1997; Setton, 2000). Evidence suggests that older adults use the web for

many of the same purposes as younger users, including gathering information, electronic communication via e-mail or chat groups, and seeking goods and services (Post, 1995).

Advocates for the new technologies cheer the vast potential for practical and innovative uses of computer technology for the older population. Internet access can reduce the social isolation of individuals with mobility limitations that keep them at home much of the time. Older people with health problems can also use the web to reach outside sources of information about their conditions and get health monitoring and medication reminders from healthcare professionals. The web can enhance autonomy among older adults in the community or in long-term care by linking older people to information about services and organizations and by encouraging the maintenance or creation of social networks (Deatrick, 1997; Hunt, 1997; McConatha, McConatha and Dermigny, 1994; Redford and Whitten, 1997; Setton, 2000).

The limited number of studies that have been done with older adults suggest that benefits may accrue to those who are "on line." One study that trained well-educated older adults and monitored their computer usage, found a decrease in loneliness and a sense of mastery in learning something new and innovative (White and McConnell, et. al. 1999).

Limitations

Access to the world opened by the personal computer and the Internet may be hampered for older adults in two significant ways. First, there may be physical or cognitive limitations that make the technology less easy to access. Limited vision or limited finger dexterity due to arthritis or stroke, for example, make use of standard PCs difficult without accessories that may increase costs and require more effort on the part of users

(White and McConnell, 1999). Many older adults had little or no experience with a keyboard in their lives. Fears among older adults about their ability to learn new things (since they may also be victims of the stereotypes about aging) may inhibit some from even trying the new technologies. Research on the willingness and capacity of older adults to learn computer skills is ambiguous (Kelley and Charness, 1995). Although studies do show older adults take more time to learn computers and make more errors than younger adults during training courses (See White and McConnell et. al. 1999); most older adults can and do learn the skills needed. Both spatial and reading ability, for example, correlate well with the performance in computer skills learning (Kelley and Charness, 1995).

Finally, issues referred to as the "digital divide" are likely to influence access to computers among older adults, especially those with limited education or income. Survey data from 1996 showed that 50% of seniors who are college graduates owned computers, compared with only 7% of those with less than a high school education (Adler, 1996). A fundamental part of this divide is economic. Computers can be costly to purchase and update and connection fees may not fit into a fixed income budget that shrinks each year with inflation. Efforts are being made in some quarters to increase access, by placing banks of PCs with internet access in senior centers, senior apartment complexes, and libraries frequented by older adults. It is unclear whether this sort of access will be sufficient to bridge the digital divide. The best way to guarantee meaningful and "on demand" access is for seniors to own computers with internet access in their homes; this model has the best chance of realizing the potential of the internet to enhance the lives of older adults. We are still far from this goal of equity for either old or young in American society today. Equipment and training equity must be addressed if we wish to use the benefits of new technologies to address the needs of the growing numbers of older adults in society.

Questions for Discussion and Review

1. What problems do you think future cohorts of elders will face in being able to utilize technology to improve the quality of their lives?

2. How might technologies, like computers and smart houses, alter the way we provide care and services to older adults in the future?

CHAPTER 9

Economics and the Aging of Society

"The future of old age is uniquely tied to the future history of our welfare state...Politics, not demography, now determines the size of the elderly population and the material conditions of its existence"(Myles, 1984).

The economic structure of a society has a profound influence on the lives of its citizens. The economy affects, and is affected by, politics, social policy, and work and retirement patterns. These interrelationships make it difficult to discuss one social institution without the other. As we explore the economics of aging, it is important to understand how our social policies relating to work, retirement, and income maintenance in later life create, reflect, and sustain the economic dependency of a majority of older people. This link between social policy and the economic situation of older people is not unique to the United States. "Despite enormous national differences in social structure and political ideology, state-administered Social Security schemes are now the major source of income for the majority of elderly in all capitalist democracies" (Myles 1988, p. 322). While an in-depth analysis of the intersections among ideologies, market economies, and the welfare state are beyond the scope of this book, we do need to acknowledge that political processes, power, and agendas play a pivotal role in shaping the economic situation of older people.

Economics, derived from political decisions in any society, influences our lives in other significant ways. How individuals and groups participate in the economy, as producers of goods and services or as consumers, shapes both the vigor of the economy and the direction of its growth. In this chapter we examine both the economic status of the older population, primarily in the U.S., and how older persons as a social group in turn influence the economy. We start by exploring the complex world of policies relevant to providing income support to the older population and their implications for economic well-being.

Policy And The Economic Status Of Older Adults

Income Maintenance Policies

In many countries of the world, older persons are supported by **income maintenance policies** —public or private systems for supporting the poor, ill, and elderly based on entitlement or need. The idea of providing income to maintain older persons at the end of their lives, after they were no longer involved in the labor force, grew from many roots, central among them the British system of

Poor Laws. These laws, which evolved over the seventeenth and eighteenth centuries, defined older persons as among the **deserving poor**—citizens lacking the means to support themselves through no fault of their own. Poor older adults and other paupers who were considered deserving of society's support (those who had worked hard, saved, not drunk or gambled away their money) received either a modest pension or food and lodging in a workhouse or poorhouse run by the community (Quadagno, 1982).

Over time the system kept changing between pensions and poorhouse support. Policy makers were concerned that providing a cash income from public coffers (a pension) to older people in the community would discourage individual virtues like personal saving and the duty of children to provide parental support Erosion of these values would ultimately increase the financial burden to the community. The poorhouse, a truly unattractive alternative, was believed to encourage personal and family responsibility more than pensions (Schulz and Myles, 1990). As you may recognize, this debate about maintaining individual and family responsibility for the care of dependent elders is a continuing legacy today. Many Western societies still struggle with the tension between individualist and collectivist values regarding provision for their dependent populations. Concerns persist today among some groups that "comfortable" levels of government benefits will undermine the responsibility of families and individuals for their own financial support in later life.

The interest of governments in establishing income maintenance policies is not purely altruistic. As Schulz and Myles (1990) point out, countries that develop industrialized economies need ways to deal with those who are unable to participate as workers for reasons of advanced age or poor health. Having some income maintenance system, whether it involves benefits based on need or earned retirement pensions, enables governments to avoid political upheavals from masses of disenfranchised persons. "Very simply, market economies need ways of providing for those who cannot participate in markets; labor markets need welfare states or people will die or revolt (or both!)" (p. 401). Thus, as many countries industrialized and urbanized, it became obvious that issues of income maintenance would have to be addressed.

The British Poor Laws, instituted during an era when industrialization made older workers particularly subject to impoverishment, built the precedent that elders who were no longer able to work deserved at least a modest level of support from society because of their prior contributions through employment and other productive effort. From this beginning has evolved a set of public and private programs in many countries of the world intended to maintain at least a modest flow of income to older persons who have retired or become dependent (Schulz and Myles, 1990).

Although the elderly poor were initially covered by general income maintenance policies, such as the Poor Laws, intended to deal with the indigent of any age, eventually many societies established separate programs of income maintenance for older persons in the form of pensions or similar benefits. Until fairly recently, programs to assist the elderly have benefited from high levels of support from the public and from political leaders (Hudson, 1978). Political support from the older population and their family members (that means most of us) swells the constituency with an interest in seeing that income maintenance is continued (2030 Center, 1999). In recent years, however, income maintenance for older persons has become a controversial issue in many nations of the world, largely because the aging of societies raises the price tag for these programs.

Income Maintenance in the United States

Two distinct premises underlie components of the income maintenance system in the United States. The bulk of income maintenance is predicated on the idea that benefits are earned through prior productivity. Leading examples are Social Security retirement benefits and private pensions, which are based directly on having made a significant contribution in the paid labor force (or being a survivor or dependent of such a contributor). By contributing to productivity and reaching a specified age (or number of years of employment), one becomes eligible for benefits, a system known as **age eligibility**. Additional programs, such as the Supplemental Security Income (SSI) program for poor and disabled older adults, are based on need. When individuals establish that their resources fall below a certain level, they receive benefits based on criteria of **need eligibility**.

Supplemental Security Income, or SSI, a major need eligibility program for income maintenance in the United States, supported about 6.5 million beneficiaries in 1999 with an average monthly benefit (for individuals) of $500 (Social Security Administration, 1999b). Although SSI is administered by the Social Security Administration, it uses need eligibility criteria—in contrast to the age eligibility basis for retirement benefits—to determine who receives support. Because such need entitlement programs carry the stigma of "welfare," they are embraced by neither taxpayers nor their own recipients. In either age or need eligibility, the fundamental ideology behind income maintenance is that older people are economically dependent due to age and (possibly) poor health and are deserving of public support, rather than being left to rely entirely on the family or their own resources.

International Views on Income Maintenance

Although Americans tend to be most familiar with "homegrown" programs, such as Social Security, income maintenance for the elderly is a feature of social policy in most countries of the world (Hoskins, 1992). By 1993 it was estimated that 155 countries, as different in size and economic development as Argentina, Fiji, Romania, the Congo, and Santa Lucia, had some sort of old-age benefit program (Kinsella and Gist, 1995). Most countries' programs began with a minimal benefit, enabling workers to survive when poor health left them unable to earn a living. Some of these programs have grown to be quite elaborate, like

Exhibit 9.1   *Percent of Labor Force Covered by Public Old-Age Pension Program: 1991*

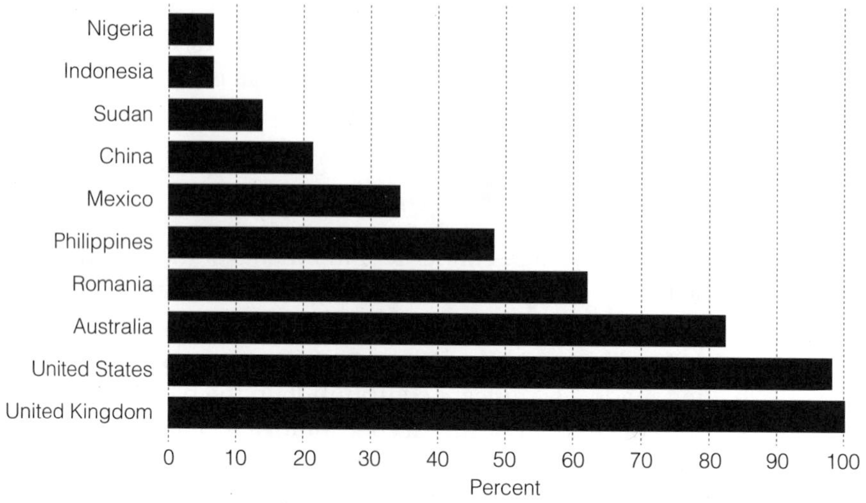

Source: ILO, 1994.

our own, while other systems remain much more rudimentary.

Programs similar to the U.S. Social Security system predominate among the industrialized nations (Schulz and Myles, 1990). Most such retirement programs share the traits of national coverage with compulsory participation, benefit amounts related to earnings or length of employment, contributions from workers and employers, a benefit intended to meet minimum needs, and mechanisms to adapt this benefit to inflation (Schulz and Myles, 1990). Programs in less developed nations may take very different forms, such as mutual benefit societies among occupational groups or compulsory savings programs, called provident funds, to meet a variety of needs including, but not limited to, retirement and old age (Schulz and Myles, 1990). As Exhibit 9.1 shows, the percentage of the labor force covered by public old-age pensions varies widely among countries. Even though 155 countries had such programs in 1993, many of the programs benefited a very small percentage of the country's population compared to the 95 percent or more covered in the United States and the United Kingdom.

The generosity of benefits in these programs also varies considerably, as is apparent in Exhibit 9.2. The bars in this figure compare the disposable incomes of elderly couples and of females (usually unmarried) living alone, adjusted for size and composition of the household, to the median disposable income of that country overall. The numbers reflect the percentage of that adjusted median disposable income available in each type of household in each country. You will note that Australia does a fairly poor job of maintaining incomes for either older

Exhibit 9.2   *Elderly Median Household Income as a Percentage of National Median Household Income, by Type of Household*

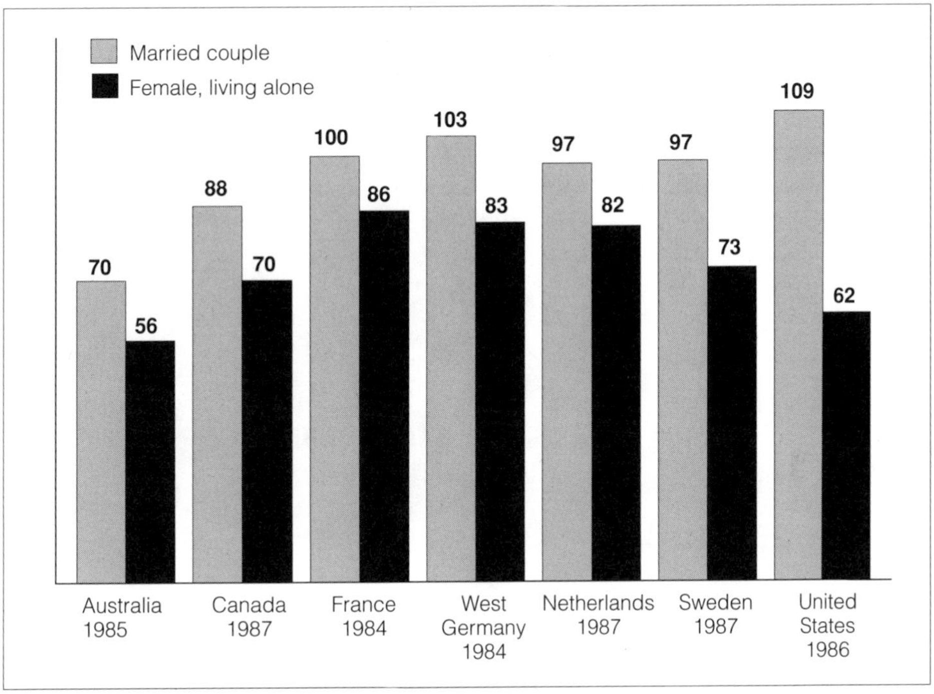

Source: Kinsella and Tauber, 1993.

women or couples, whereas the United States does quite well by married couples but not unmarried women. Other countries provide adequate incomes and show less disparity between married couples and single women than we do in the United States (Holtz-Eakin and Smeeding, 1994).

This comparison and others suggest that the variation in economic well-being among the elderly is greater in the United States than in many countries of Europe (Holtz-Eakin and Smeeding, 1994). Income maintenance in the United States rests on a number of different programs and sources (Social Security, private pensions, SSI, other benefits such as food stamps and housing subsidies) rather than on an integrated system of income maintenance. Thus, some individuals or couples do much better than others here, whereas many European countries have universal social retirement pensions with relatively high minimum benefit levels (Holtz-Eakin and Smeeding, 1994).

Sources of Income

The image used by the Social Security Administration in describing income maintenance for retired Americans is a **three-legged stool**. If any of the three legs is missing, it is impossible for the stool to provide support—it falls over.

Exhibit 9.3   *Percentage of Income from Various Sources, Older Americans: 1996*

Source: Social Security Administration, 1998b.

The three legs (or sources of income) are retirement benefits from Social Security, income from private pensions, and resources from assets and personal savings. The device of the three-legged stool represents the view of its creators that Social Security was not designed to provide an adequate standard of living by itself, but rather to serve as one component of a system of support.

Critics point out that this stool is rather precarious for many older persons, because a majority have stools with only one or two legs (Borzi, 1993; Shaw and Yi, 1997); that is, they lack private pensions, personal savings/assets, or both. In the aggregate these three components, plus earnings, constitute the bulk of the income to households headed by an older person or couple (Social Security Administration, 1998b). As Exhibit 9.3 shows, the income maintenance system actually has four major "legs" (including earnings) when we group all older persons together. This aggregate view of income can be quite misleading, however, because there are striking differences in who gets income from what sources in later life. Before examining these inequalities let us take a closer look at the three basic "legs" of income maintenance for older adults in the U.S.

Social Security: Background and Contemporary Issues

Social Security, initiated in 1935, grew from many historical roots, including the Great Depression and the **Townsend Movement** —a 1930s social movement that advocated granting $200 monthly pensions to older people and requiring

Exhibit 9.4   *Growth in Social Security Payments: 1940–1996*

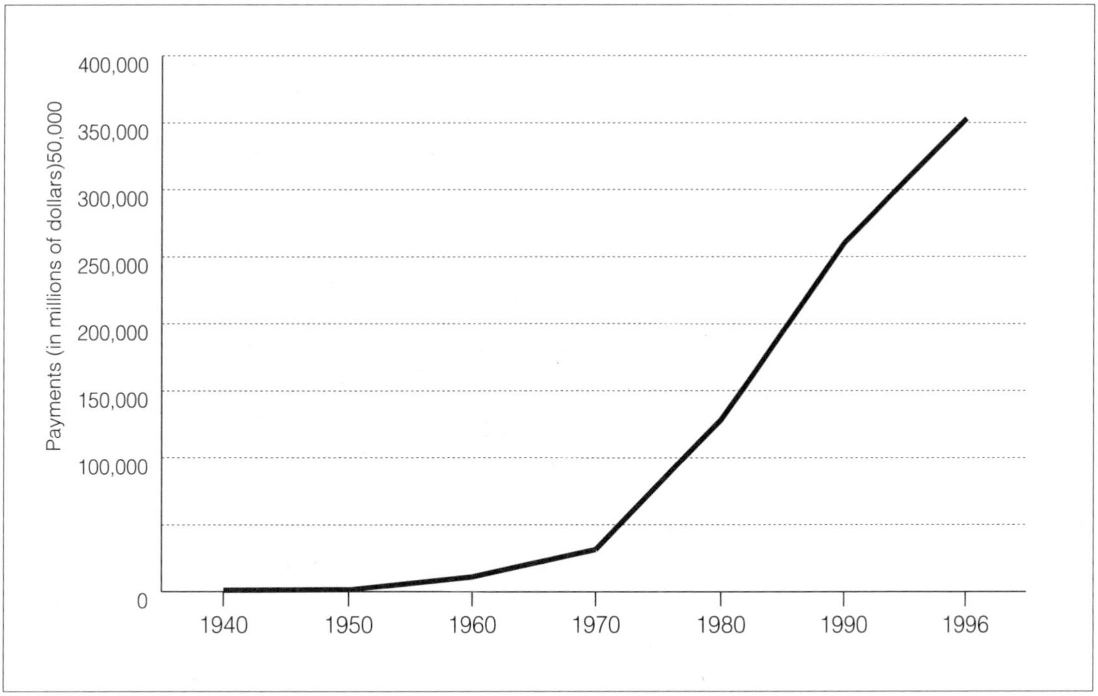

Source: Social Security Administration, 1997.

the funds to be spent within 30 days to stimulate the Depression economy (Quadagno, 1982). Many young people supported both the Townsend movement and Social Security at its outset, since most older adults at that time relied on their kin for financial support. For families, the start of a public pension program reduced their financial burden at a historically critical time, the depths of the Great Depression.

The fundamental premise of the Social Security program is that of a **social insurance program**, in which the population pools resources and collectively shares the risks of growing economically dependent through old age or disability. As with any insurance system, some participants benefit more than others from Social Security, by virtue of higher benefits (based on higher earnings and larger contributions while working) or by living longer (receiving benefits for more months). Some individuals pay into Social Security but recoup few benefits, because they die before or shortly after becoming eligible for benefits; in many such cases their survivors receive benefits.

A second critical aspect of Social Security is that it serves an **income redistribution** function, returning a higher percentage of prior income (known as a higher replacement rate) to poorer individuals and a somewhat lower replacement rate to high-earning retirees (Jones, 1996). This redistribution was built

Exhibit 9.5   *Types of Social Security Beneficiaries*

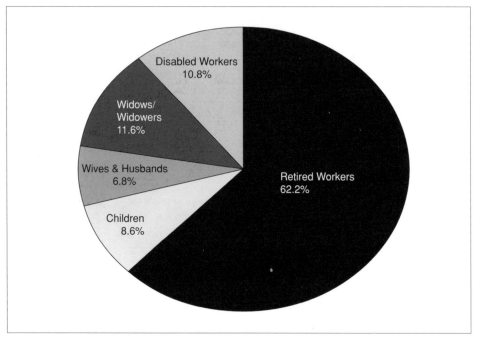

Source: Social Security Administration, 1999a.

into the system and is key to reducing poverty, because fewer individuals with histories of low or inconsistent earnings have private pensions or savings to augment Social Security (Reno, 1993). Although consistent with the social insurance function of Social Security, this redistributive function is politically controversial, because it is somewhat inconsistent with the "contributory" basis of the program, the idea that benefits are directly based on prior contributions to the system.

Social Security is now a massive program, providing benefits in 1999 to 44,366,700 persons, primarily retirees (62.2%) with an average retired worker benefit of $782 (Social Security Administration, 1999a). This program constituted 21.9 percent of the total federal budget in 1995 and expended $178 billion (Social Security Administration, 1995b). The dollar amounts paid by the program have grown dramatically over time, as shown in Exhibit 9.4. More than 90 percent of all workers are in jobs covered by the program (Social Security Administration, 1998b). Any adjustments in the program's provisions or funding have a significant effect not only on retirees and other recipients, but on the overall economy and the federal budget.

As you can see from Exhibit 9.5, retirees are not the only recipients of funds from Social Security. At various points after Congress first approved Social Security for retired workers, it approved extending benefits to others, including

Exhibit 9.6   *Reduction in Poverty Attributable to Social Security: 1992*

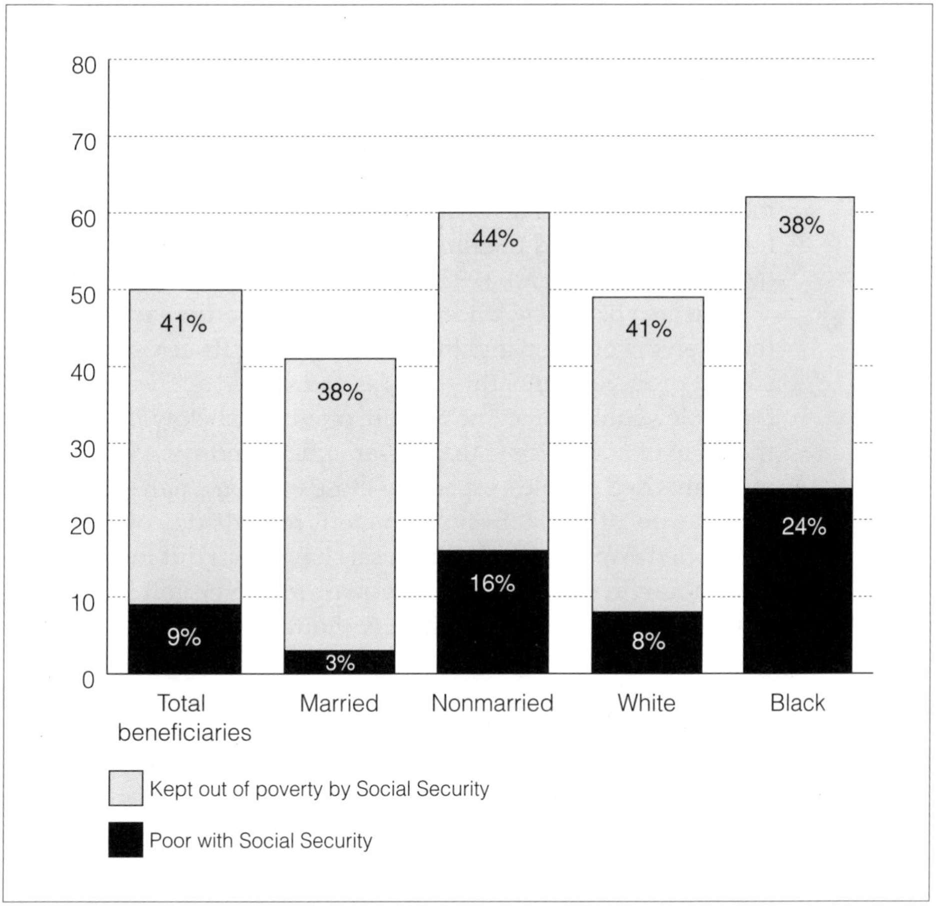

Source: Social Security Administration, 1998b.

dependents of workers (wives, widows, children) and the preretirement-age disabled. Now funds are distributed not only to retirees or the older population, but also to younger persons (Social Security Administration, 1998b). The largest component of dollars paid out by the program and the largest number of recipients, however, are still retired workers.

Many experts agree that Social Security has been highly effective in reducing poverty among the elderly. Without Social Security 50 percent of older beneficiaries would be in poverty instead of 9 percent (Social Security Administration, 1998b). As Exhibit 9.6 shows, both married and unmarried beneficiaries, African Americans and European Americans individuals saw their risks of poverty substantially reduced by the income from Social Security. This success has its limits, however, because there remain many older persons with incomes just above the poverty threshold (Quinn and Smeeding, 1993). In addition, women, concentrated among the unmarried in Exhibit 9.6, continue to face higher risks of poverty than men, and African Americans are at greater risk than are European Americans (Quinn, 1993; Rank and Hirschi, 1999).

What will the effects of societal aging be on the future of Social Security? The contemporary debate regarding Social Security is more fundamental than those in prior years, when modest adjustments, reflecting politically expedient compromises, adapted the program to changing societal needs. Today's debate focuses on fundamental issues: the social insurance premise, using age as a basis for entitlement, and the funding mechanism for the Social Security program (Myles and Quadagno, 1995).

One area of policy concern centers on the **adequacy of benefits** to support those relying on them and the **equity of benefits** across various groups. Under current provisions, monthly benefits to divorced and widowed women are often their sole source of income and are often well below the poverty level, raising the issue of adequacy (Burkhauser and Smeeding, 1994; Weaver, 1997). Currently married couples, especially those with one high-earning worker, fare better in terms of Social Security benefit returns on contributions than do the unmarried (Weaver, 1997). Proposals have been put forward to adjust the benefit amount to married couples downward to permit a more adequate benefit to widowed or divorced women without raising the total costs of Social Security (Burkhauser and Smeeding, 1994; Sandell and Iams, 1997).

Equity concerns are also voiced for married women who have contributed as workers to Social Security, about half of whom receive benefits that are no larger than they would be had they never held jobs and contributed (Quinn, 1993). Under current policies, single-earner couples benefit more than do dual-earner couples or single persons, because of the way benefits are calculated for retirees and their dependents (Harrington Meyer, 1996). These inequities in the returns to beneficiaries compared to what they contributed reflect the outdated notion of the male breadwinner and economically dependent wife as the normative pattern. Although reforms have been discussed for decades, the policies have not been modified substantially to address adequacy and equity of benefits under Social Security.

Debates about the foundations of Social Security have escalated in the face of the "pig in the python" of the baby boom. As these large cohorts move inexorably toward the age of entitlement for Social Security retirement benefits, fears have escalated regarding the ability of smaller cohorts of workers to provide the financial support through their contributions needed to maintain the system. Data from the Social Security Administration's own projections show that the ratio of workers to beneficiaries will decrease from 3.4 in 1990 to 2.0 in 2030 and drop even lower by 2050 (Jones, 1996). This smaller ratio of employees to retirees receiving benefits will require either (1) an increase in payroll deductions from workers and contributions from employers, (2) a reduction in benefits to retirees, (3) revenues from some other sources, (4) policies to raise the retirement age or encourage those in their 60s to keep working, reducing the worker-to-retiree ratio, or (5) some combination of the first four. This list of potential solutions to insure the solvency of Social Security seem relatively straightforward. However, any solution will be the product of complicated policy negotiations, ideological debates, and political battles.

Although the system has primarily been "pay as you go," with funds contributed by today's workers mostly going to support today's retirees, excess funds have always been kept in the **Social Security trust fund**. Changes in 1983, the last major alteration of the Social Security System, built in growth in the trust fund in anticipation of the needs of the baby boom cohorts (Jones, 1996). As contributions are collected from paychecks and employers, extra monies are funneled into this trust fund, which will build up until around 2013. After that time, the retirement of baby boomers will begin to deplete the surplus, and the trust fund, barring additional changes, is projected to run out of money in 2035. Since the alarm has long been raised in Washington, additional changes in the Social Security system will undoubtedly be enacted to forestall depletion of the trust fund. Both Congress and Social Security experts have been actively discussing a range of options to address this shortfall. During the 2000 election while we were writing this book, one item congressional and presidential candidates discussed was how to use projected budget surpluses. Some want to use the hypothetical money to bolster the trust fund for Social Security and Medicare and some to give taxpayers the money back through a tax cut. Others want the federal government to support other programs or initiatives.

The most hotly-debated suggestions focus on changing Social Security to permit some portion of Social Security contributions of individuals to be invested in stocks and bonds, which generally yield higher returns than government bonds. These proposals are referred to as **privatization**. Advocates of privatization prefer the risks of the stock market to the returns of government bonds, especially given the lengthy rise in the stock market in the 1990s. Multiple proposals have been discussed, including those where an independent agency would invest trust fund dollars in stocks and bonds. Another avenue to achieve privatization would be to take a portion of each individual's contributions to Social Security and place them in a personal retirement account, over which the individual would have some choice as to investment options (Goss, 1997). Workers could select one of several government-approved options for investment of their personal retirement funds (Starr, 1988) and these investments would be under some degree of personal control, especially after retirement

Moving toward privatizing Social Security would reduce both the social insurance and the redistributive aspects of the program (Rix and Williamson, 1998) and could have an unknown effect on the stock market. Critics of privatization point out two major concerns with current proposals. First, a privatized universal pension program would provide no protection for individuals who, seeking high returns, invest their money poorly or are swindled by con artists and end up with insufficient funds for even a poverty-level existence in retirement. Social Security and its Supplemental Security Income (SSI) program currently protect people against such impoverishment. Second, the transition to a more privatized system could incur additional costs, as one generation pays twice: once to finance their own retirement and again to pay for the benefits of those older adults already in the existing Social Security system (Starr, 1988).

Alternative scenarios for addressing the funding crisis include adjusting ages for benefits upward, increasing withholding amounts, converting Social Security from an age entitlement to a need entitlement program, recovering benefits from high-income retirees through taxation (Goss, 1997). Unfortunately, most of these proposals have practical or political problems that keep them from being ideal solutions (Myles and Quadagno, 1995). For example, an increase in the retirement age could increase the risk to disadvantaged workers, who both experience higher rates of health problems limiting their employment and rely most heavily on Social Security as part of their later-life income. In fact, Congress has for a long time been moving quietly in these directions by gradually raising the age of entitlement for full Social Security benefits to 67 (currently planned to be phased in by 2027) and raising taxes on higher-income elders to recoup some of their Social Security benefits. Further changes along these lines are contemplated as part of a package of changes intended to address the deficit in the trust fund. Whatever final plan emerges will reflect a lengthy and very political process.

Policy makers are currently debating changes in Social Security intended to guarantee its long-term solvency.

Although many younger people doubt that Social Security retirement benefits will be there for them when they retire (Borden, 1995), the program continues to enjoy considerable social support. Most of us have at least one relative, neighbor, or friend receiving Social Security benefits (Day, 1993b). Social Security is an intergenerational support program in many ways. As Exhibit 9.7 shows, in a study using specific questions, more young people responded in favor of increasing benefits and federal spending than did older people (Day, 1993b). A poll conducted in 1999 suggested that young adults remained strongly behind Social Security, even those who expected reduced or no benefits for themselves (2030 Center, 1999). What would older adults and their families need to do if Social Security suddenly disappeared? Most politicians do not wish to contemplate the answer, and thus they support continuation of some version of the program.

Exhibit 9.7   *Attitudes toward Social Security by Age*

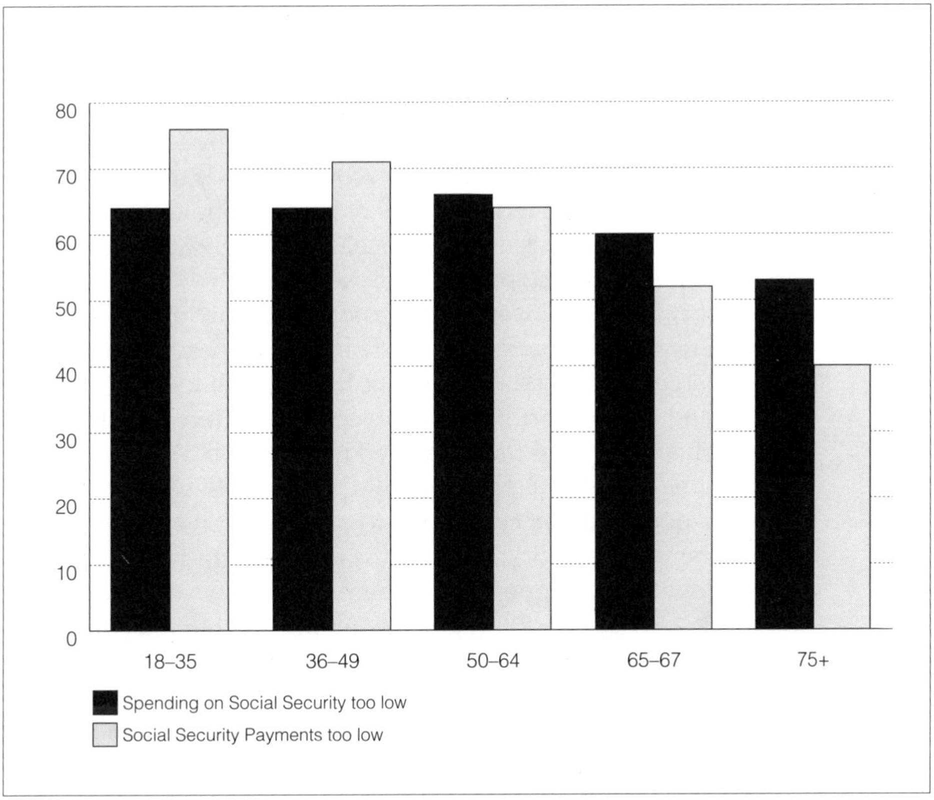

Source: Day, 1993a.

Pensions

Private pensions represent a complex legal, fiscal, and policy area. These retirement income systems are sponsored or organized and often at least partially financed by employers. Their importance in the overall economy is staggering. One estimate claimed that more than $5 trillion is invested in pension and retirement income programs in the United States, making these funds critical capital in financial markets (Salisbury, 1994). Since access to a private pension is often the difference between an economically secure old age and a more marginal existence, both individuals and the larger society must be concerned about how pensions operate and their soundness.

Jobs usually come with or without private pension coverage attached to them, so the type of occupation an individual undertakes and the characteristics of the employer influence the prospects for an eventual pension. Even individuals who are fortunate enough to work for an employer who offers a pension plan must work a minimum period of time for a specific employer to become eligible, or **vested**, for eventual pension benefits. Thus, not everyone employed in a job covered by a pension will eventually receive a pension from that employer. The likelihood of being covered by a pension depends on a variety of factors, including employer, occupation, education, union membership, and gender. Men are more likely than women to be in jobs covered by a pension, but the gap is decreasing, as evidenced by the 25- to 34-year-olds (Reno, 1993). This gender gap in pension coverage is largely due to the lower earnings of female workers and the types of jobs they hold (in the service sector of the economy where pensions are scarce)(Johnson, Sambamoorthi and Crystal, 1999). As we might expect, pension coverage is higher in jobs requiring more education, because employers use pensions to recruit and retain desirable employees. Coverage for pensions is fairly high (79%) for full-time workers in medium and larger private establishments, but is much lower (46%) in smaller companies and among part-time employees (34%) (Bureau of Labor Statistics, 1999).

Private pensions first appeared in the late 1800s, brought about by many of the same forces that created public programs like Social Security. Standard Oil was among the first companies to offer pensions. The public considered pension benefits to workers a reward for merit and a gift from a magnanimous employer (Quadagno, 1988). There was no sense that employers owed their retirees any support. Initially few employers offered private pension options. In the post-World War II era, however, pension coverage grew rapidly in a strong economy, expanding in the 1940s and 1950s to cover a wider range of occupations. This growth is reflected in age differences in pension receipt among those over age 65. While 44 percent of 65-69 year olds have pension income, only 29% of those over age 85 do so (Social Security Administration, 1998a).

The availability of pensions continued to grow until the 1980s; since then it has leveled off or declined in many fields (Quinn and Burkhauser, 1990). This decline is mirrored in the lower pension coverage among younger adults shown in Exhibit 9.8. Pension coverage is becoming more equal by gender, but this convergence is due to a decline in rates of coverage among males not improvement for female workers.

Since employers generally seek to minimize pension costs, sometimes at the expense of the pensioners, the federal government has passed the Employee Retirement Income Security Act of 1974 (**ERISA**) to control how pensions are offered and funded. This law and its subsequent amendments mandate how funds must be collected and credited to employees, how employees become vested, and how pension funds are managed. The legislation was prompted by the failure of a number of pension funds, leaving the retirees without expected resources in retirement (Salisbury, 1993). Now pension funds have some protection through a federal insuring agency, much as the FDIC insures funds in banks.

One cause of economic insecurity among older widows has to do with the rules for private pensions. Because pensions are earned by individual workers, in the past a pension often ended when the worker died. Since most pensioners in past cohorts were male and few wives were eligible for their own pensions, this major source of income would end abruptly for many widows, throwing them into poverty. In 1985 legislation was passed requiring all pensions to offer survivor options and mandating that both spouses approve in writing a choice of either a single life or a survivor option (Miller, 1985). If the survivor option is chosen, the monthly pension amount is decreased but the pension continues to support the survivor after the pensioner dies. In fact, pensions are becoming such an important part of family resources that they are increasingly viewed as jointly earned property, to be allocated like other property in divorce settlements (Women's Initiative, 1993). Both of these changes may reduce the gender gap in later-life poverty for future cohorts.

One major trend in pensions is away from what are called defined benefit systems. In a **defined benefit pension** system the employer controls a worker's pension. The employer invests and controls a common fund under rules defined by ERISA. Benefit amounts are guaranteed on a formula based on the number of years an individual has worked and his or her salary or related factors (Smeeding, Estes and Glass, 1999).

Under such systems workers can know exactly what their pension amount will be. Employers may alter workers' timing of retirement by creating disincentives to working beyond a certain age, but the pension amount is defined and guaranteed. Growing more common are what is known as a defined contribution pension, familiar to some workers as an IRA a 401k plan. A **defined contribution pension** is a system where the worker, the employer or both contribute to a fund held by an independent financial entity so that the money belongs to the worker and is subject to the stock and bond markets to determine benefit amounts. Benefits at retirement are not guaranteed, but may depend on the trends in the stock and bond markets (Smeeding et al., 1999). Payment may come as a lump-sum to be invested or as an annuity, paid over the life of the retiree and/or the spouse. Under this system the worker has control over investment choices (and thus can take risks with it if she or he so chooses), and may either benefit or suffer depending on the stock market and their choices. Employers have less control over the timing of retirement since they don't control the funds or all provisions for their receipt. This change takes the work and control out of the employers' hands, but disadvantages workers, because it divests companies of responsibilities for the adequacy of their workers' pensions. As defined benefit plans have declined, defined contribution plans have grown to more than half of the pension plans offered in recent years (Bureau of Labor Statistics, 1999).

Personal Savings/Assets

Savings and other assets accumulated during years of employment (resources such as home equity, cash in savings or certificates or deposit, stocks, and bonds) are the third support for income maintenance in retirement. **Assets** are all the resources people own that can be converted into money, including home equity, cash savings, stocks, and bonds. Assets "provide housing, serve as a financial reserve for special or emergency needs, contribute directly to income through interest, dividends, or rents, and help to enhance the freedom with which individuals spend their income" (Schulz, 1988, p. 37). Most older persons have savings or assets of some type, although a large percentage of assets, as we will see soon, are tied up in home equity and thus do not generate income, as stocks and bank accounts do.

Like other resources, savings and assets are unequally distributed among the older population, and this inequality has grown in recent years (Quinn, 1993). Accumulation of assets is only made possible by having surplus income to save or invest, limiting the likelihood that lower-income persons will develop independent assets to utilize for their economic security in later life. In a few cases assets are inherited from kin, but most people who develop assets do so through their own productivity in the labor force. Lifetime earnings and benefits (such as stock options) suggest that inequality in asset accumulation is a reflection of income inequality during the working years.

In summary, the three-legged stool of income maintenance for older people is quite a shaky structure today, and it is considerably more wobbly for some groups than for others due to life-long inequalities supplemented by later life events. Social Security is undergoing major reconsideration, private pensions are only available to about 50 percent of the population, and few older people have substantial savings or assets beyond home equity.

Economic Well-Being Of Older Americans

So, how are older Americans doing economically? Armed with your understanding of the three legs of the income maintenance stool for older people in the United States, you are ready to consider questions about the effectiveness and long-term impact of this structure on the economic status of older people. The adequacy of these programs and policies in maintaining some level of economic well-being for older people is an important and complex question. Its import derives in no small part from the fact that future policies are being shaped by today's arguments about its answer.

As we have seen, groups within the older population vary widely in the nature and adequacy of their income sources. This heterogeneity plays an extremely important role in answering the question about the economic status of older people, and we will review major sources of, and explanations for, the variations in a later section. Another basic factor that can influence the picture we are able to draw about the economic status of older Americans is definition and measurement of the concept.

Alternatives for Measuring Economic Well-Being

Two "measurement" issues are involved in answering our question about how well or poorly older people are faring financially. First, we need to clarify the many definitions of economic status. We might look at income, which can include total income, assets, and in-kind income. Poverty level offers another kind of standard of economic well-being. For any measure we might select, the number and nature of financial resources we choose to include in our analysis of economic health will influence our findings. We will review each of these measures, and the sometimes conflicting conclusions they allow us to draw about the economic status of older people. Second, the statistics we use to describe the economic well-being of older adults—such as means, medians, and measures of variability—will similarly have an impact on any conclusions we draw. Those presenting data are sometimes but not always explicit about how the story of economic well-being is constructed through selection of which data to present and how to present it.

Measures of Economic Status

Some economists have suggested that economic well-being encompasses not just income, but also economic responsibilities (including family support and tax liabilities) and economic resources (such as home ownership and medical insurance). Usually, however, it is measured more simply. One obvious way to assess people's financial situation is to find out how much income they receive. Salaries and wages, interest and dividends, and income from public transfer programs (such as Social Security and unemployment compensation) are traditionally included in definitions of **income**. When we compare older people to the younger population on this dimension of economic well-being, we find that older people have lower incomes than younger people, and that people over 75 are more disadvantaged than the 65-74 age group. In 1997, the median income for households headed by someone 65 and older was $20,761; for younger households (headed by people ages 15 through 64), the median income was significantly higher (about $42,000); for people 75 and older, median income was only $17,000 (U.S. Bureau of the Census, 1998a).

Income is only one measure of the financial resources available to people, and our picture of the economic status of older people is more complete, and more complex, when we consider other indicators. Two other measures commonly used in discussing the financial situation of older people are assets and in-kind income.

When assets are included in the calculation, a much more positive picture emerges than if we look only at income, largely because so many older people own their homes. With all appropriate cautions about the variability within the older population, Smeeding (1990) reports an "impressive" level of wealth among the older population (p. 366). The most common asset held by older people is equity in a home, representing about 40 percent of total net worth in the population over age 65 (Holtz-Eakin and Smeeding, 1994). Home ownership by older persons is higher in the United States than in many equally developed European countries (Holtz-Eakin and Smeeding, 1994). Interest-earning assets (savings accounts, savings bonds, and CDs) constitute another 29 percent of total

Exhibit 9.8   *Median Net Worth by Age*

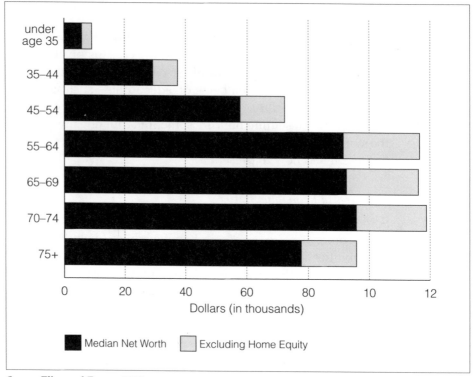

Source: Eller and Fraser, 1995.

wealth, followed by rental property, stocks, bonds, and mutual funds (another 17 percent) (Holtz-Eakin and Smeeding, 1994). As Exhibit 9.8 shows, net worth increases with age, but a substantial percentage of net worth is comprised of home equity value rather than "cash assets." One estimate placed the average asset value for older adults at $9,000 when home equity was excluded. Again, averages can be deceiving, since the top 5% of older adults had assets in excess of $300,000 while those in the bottom 30% had almost nothing (Smith, 1997)

Assets are important not just as a "reserve," but also because some of them provide income through interest and dividends. As you would expect, this financial resource is highly variable among older people. For example, asset income constitutes 28 percent of total income for non-poor aged, but only 4 percent of income for those below the poverty level (United States Congress, 1992). The bottom quintile (20%) of households headed by persons over age 65 had an average net worth around $25,000, all but $3,500 of which was home equity (Holtz-Eakin and Smeeding, 1994). Persons over age 80 have a median net worth (dollar value of home equity and financial assets) that is 80 percent of that for persons 65-69. Widows living alone have net worth less than 70 percent of that for the general population aged 65 to 69, mostly home equity (Radner, 1993). Consistent with lower lifetime incomes and fewer sources of retirement income, about one in four adults over 65 have no equity in a home, but the figure rises to one out of three widows living alone (Radner, 1993). Not surprisingly, those with the highest incomes also had the greatest store of wealth in assets. One analysis of income and assets revealed that about one-fourth of older men and women living alone had no financial assets, and an additional one-third had assets under $15,000 (Schulz, 1988). From this brief sampling of data on income compared to assets, or to assets minus home equity, it should be clear that the question of how older people are doing financially has many answers.

Another way to examine economic well-being is to consider in-kind income. **In-kind income** includes noncash benefits that contribute to economic well-being by reducing necessary expenditures. Publicly funded medical insurance (Medicare) is an example of in-kind income. Subsidized housing and food stamps are other familiar examples of such noncash benefits. The inclusion of in-kind income in calculations of economic well-being can have a major impact on the outcome of those analyses (Shaw and Yi, 1997). In one study, researchers used an "expanded income" measure that measured overall wealth as income plus some other cash and noncash benefits, including health insurance, capital gains, the value of public housing subsidies, and net equity. Using this measure, researchers found that older people as a group were as well-off as the nonelderly (Smeeding, 1990). This is quite a different conclusion from the one we would draw from the data on median personal income or assets exclusive of home equity. One dilemma of such inclusive measures has to do with the role of health benefits. When people are seriously ill, receiving a lot of in-kind income through benefits from Medicare and/or Medicaid, these large amounts are added to their "incomes" to figure their well-being. Even though no money comes to them, such seriously ill people appear wealthy because they receive such high levels of in-kind health care benefits. Such variations in how income is measured reinforce the need for caution in drawing conclusions about income unless you understand the definitions and measures used.

Rates of Poverty

While measures of financial resources answer one kind of question about economic well-being (How well-off are older people?), poverty rates answer another kind of question about economic health: How large or small is the proportion of older people who are in extreme financial jeopardy? Poverty rates tell us the proportion of the population living below a minimum level of income defined as necessary for survival. The U.S. government categorically defines people as "poor" if they earn below a certain income level per year—the **poverty threshold.** If they earn below this threshold, people become eligible for many of our nation's safety net (need eligibility) programs. For example, people whose income is less than 130 percent of the poverty threshold are eligible for food stamps. The poverty rate, the proportion that live below the poverty threshold, is not a measure of how much people have. It is a way for the public to determine how many of people are living in an untenable financial situation.

Researchers and policy makers often use poverty rates and trends to chart how effectively entitlement programs and other social policies have redressed social ills, redistributed resources in ways society desires, and improved the financial situation of various groups. The poverty among elderly Americans was 28.5% in 1966, compared to10.5% in 1997, reflecting substantial improvement. Discussions about the economic status of older people almost always point out the significant decrease in poverty in this population in recent decades. In contrast, poverty rates among children grew from 17.6% in 1966 to 19.9% in 1997, demonstrating slight increase. These statistics feature prominently in current public debate and proposals for changes in income maintenance policies for older adults. Because of the many ways people can use poverty statistics, and because of the many competing agendas that can underlie those uses, it is important to understand the way the US government calculates poverty.

The cost of food was central to the initial calculation of the dollar amount of the poverty threshold. Using food plans that met minimal nutritional requirements, the cost of providing that food was calculated using prevailing prices. The food cost was then multiplied by three (based on data from a 1955 survey which showed that food represented one-third of the average budget for a low-income family) to arrive at the official poverty threshold. Since that time, refinements have adjusted for household size and composition, and the dollar amounts are adjusted upward in tandem with increases in the Consumer Price Index. Households whose incomes fall below that level "qualify" as poor. In 1997, the poverty threshold for a family of four, including two children under the age of 18, was $16,276 (Dalaker and Naifeh, 1998).

The poverty threshold formula is open to serious criticisms. First, the food costs were based on an emergency food plan; no one was expected to survive on these menus for a long time. Second, different food plans were developed for different kinds of households. The plan for a household in which the head of household is under 65 allows for higher food costs than if the head of household is over age 65. The result of this different food plan for older people is a lower poverty threshold, meaning that older people have to have lower incomes than younger people to be considered poor and to quality for need-based entitlement programs. For example, in 1997 the poverty level was $8,350 for a person under age 65, but $7,698 for a person over the age of 65. For two-person households, the threshold was $10,748 if the householder was under 65, but $9,701 if the householder was over 65 (Dalaker and Naifeh, 1998).

A final focus of criticism is the multiplier of three. The idea that food represents about a third of a low-income family's budget, which was apparently the case in 1955, is quite unrealistic today. "Most families require much more than three times their food budget to meet other needs such as housing and transportation costs" (U.S. Bureau of the Census, 1993). Housing takes a much higher proportion of the budget and food a lower proportion than in 1955 (even though food costs are higher today). Moreover, families at different standards of living will have different expenditure patterns; for poor families, necessities such as housing and food will consume a higher proportion of the total budget than in middle-class families of the same size. Wise (1990) estimates that food and housing comprise more than 85 percent of a poor family's budget.

The net impact of the problems in calculating the poverty threshold is to keep that threshold artificially low, meaning that people have to be extremely poor in order to be categorized as living in poverty. Since the poverty level is tied to eligibility for government-funded programs, there is an obvious political stake in keeping those numbers low. Even so, questions about how poverty is and should be calculated are receiving significant attention from researchers, policy analysts, advocates for older people, and the government agencies that produce poverty statistics. Molly Orshansky, who was involved in the original formulation of the poverty threshold, has testified that basing the poverty level on a more realistic food plan would increase poverty rates among older people to almost one-third of the population (Schulz, 1988).

Reflecting these concerns about the adequacy of the poverty level as a standard, poverty statistics are now often reported for those below 100 percent, 125 percent, and up to 200 percent of the poverty threshold. Those falling within 100-150 percent of the poverty threshold are often referred to as "near poor." Dire poverty is sometimes calculated to be 50% of the poverty threshold. In 1997, 10.5 percent of all older people lived below the poverty line ($9,701 for two people, $7,698 for someone living alone); however, almost 40 percent lived below 200 percent (two times) the poverty level (Dalaker and Naifeh, 1998). Thus, hundreds of thousands of older people who are not "categorically" poor according to the official poverty threshold are nonetheless economically vulnerable. Holden and Smeeding (1990) have termed this group the "Tweeners"—older people whose income places them between 100 percent and 200 percent of the official poverty level. He suggests that these people may be most disadvantaged in some ways, because they are not poor enough to qualify for safety net programs but are too poor to be financially secure (p. 372).

A recent study also suggests that we need to be cautious about concluding that poverty is not a serious problem. Rank and Hirschi (1999) examined not just the annual rate of poverty (a cross-sectional, snapshot view), but the likelihood that someone would experience an episode of poverty at some time in later life. In a large, longitudinal study using sophisticated analytic methods, they followed individuals from age 60 and found that 35% experienced poverty by the time they reached 85. Some of the individuals in the study were at greater risk of becoming poor, especially those with less than high school education, those who were unmarried, and those who were African-American. A married white male with more than high school education had a 14% risk of ever experiencing poverty by age 85; risks for a married African-American male who didn't graduate high school reached 60%, and soared to 88% for his female counterpart (Rank and Hirschi, 1999). The life course perspective shows a different picture of the problem of poverty among the elderly than cross-sectional views.

People concerned about how our government defines poverty also question the way income is and should be measured to determine poverty status. Traditionally, income was defined as direct money income, from sources such as wages and salaries, Social Security, public assistance, interest and dividends, and pensions. Current discussion and alternative calculations focus on the inclusion of in-kind income sources and net worth. Analyses based on these alternative definitions can illustrate the impact of in-kind benefits such as government transfer programs on the poverty status of the population. Such analyses can also fuel debate and pave the way for policy changes

Exhibit 9.9 shows what happens to poverty rates among older people using three of the fifteen alternative definitions of income developed by the Bureau of the Census. With data from 1994, using the standard definition of income, about 12 percent of the older population lived in poverty. If we define income as cash from standard sources minus the value of government transfers (in the case of older people, primarily Social Security), the poverty rate rises to 52 percent. In other words, if older people's incomes were reduced by the value of their Social Security benefits and other government transfers, half of them would live in poverty (U.S. Bureau of the Census, 1996a). This figure speaks clearly to the impact of government transfer programs on the economic well-being of older people. If income is defined as money income plus the value of government transfer programs plus tax benefits and net home equity, the poverty rate among older people dropped to 5.7 percent, a rate lower than for any other age group. Again, the political and ideological uses of such information should give us pause.

These kinds of analyses underscore the complexity of answering questions about economic status. Politicians and policy makers draw very different conclusions from one another, but all of them well supported by the same set of facts and figures. Their ideologies, vested interests, and political and social agendas shape these conclusions more than numbers and everyday realities. If an 85-year-old widow subsisting on SSI in her modest house appears to be economically secure because the cost of a temporary nursing home visit is considered "income," we all need to develop a critical eye for the statistics we see on the economic well-being of the elderly.

Summary

The foregoing discussion suggests some of the conceptual ambiguity and social construction inherent in any purely quantitative and completely standardized measure of economic well-being. Whether old people are depicted as rich or poor depends on how income is defined and whether or not in-kind benefits, home equity, and other assets are included.

Exhibit 9.9   *Percent of Older Persons in Poverty, by Definition of Income: U.S. 1994*

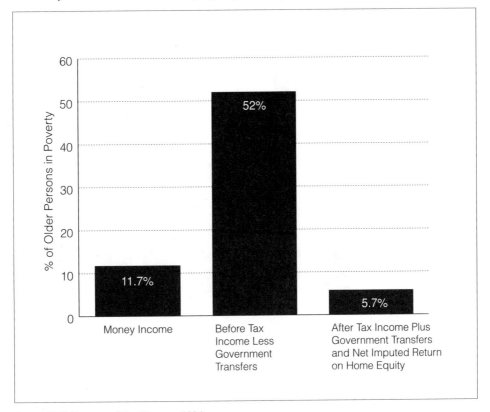

Source: U.S. Bureau of the Census, 1996c.

How are older people doing economically? Obviously, a simple, single answer to this question does not exist. In fact, you can find statistics to support almost any answer, however contradictory. As careful consumers of newspaper reports, published research, and political rhetoric, and as participants in everyday conversations, you need to be aware that people's political or ideological agendas often shape their answers to the economic status question. Those agendas drive the choice of definitions and the statistical summaries presented. Data-based but ideologically motivated statements about the economic status of older people have stereotyped them as "greedy geezers," responsible for the federal deficit, and a drain on the welfare of our children. You are now better prepared to be skeptical about such statements.

Whatever definitions and measures we use, comparing subgroups within the older population will also give us very different answers to the question about economic well-being. Gender, race/ethnicity, and living arrangements are three characteristics on which the economic status of older people is patterned.

Exhibit 9.10   *Diversity of Income Levels in the Older Population: 1996*

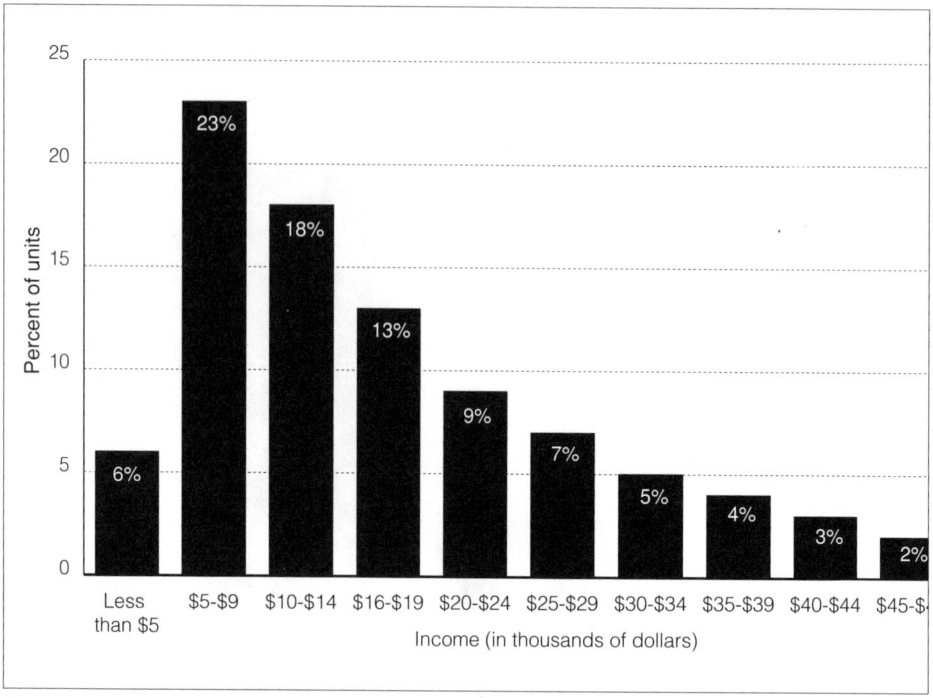

Source: Social Security Administration, 1998b.

Patterns of Economic Well-Being: Social Inequality among Older People

Most researchers agree that there have been striking improvements in the economic well-being of the average older American in the past three decades (Quinn and Smeeding, 1993). For example, married couples over age 65 have experienced a 79 percent increase in median income since 1962 after accounting for inflation (Social Security Administration, 1995). Poverty rates among older people have fallen sharply since the days prior to some of the age-based entitlement programs.

These data documenting a reduction in poverty provide support for political and social agendas seeking to reduce government entitlements to older people. However, despite the historical decline in poverty among older Americans, many still subsist near or below the poverty level, and there remain pockets of severe economic distress in certain social groups (Quinn and Smeeding, 1993). Exhibit 9.10 shows a wide variation in levels of income and a concentration of older adults at the low end of the income distribution.

These wide income variations are reflected in the differing rates of poverty for different groups within the older population. Exhibit 9.11 shows that the

Exhibit 9.11   *Percent of Older Persons in Poverty by Race, Hispanic Origin, Sex, and Living Arrangements: U.S. 1997*

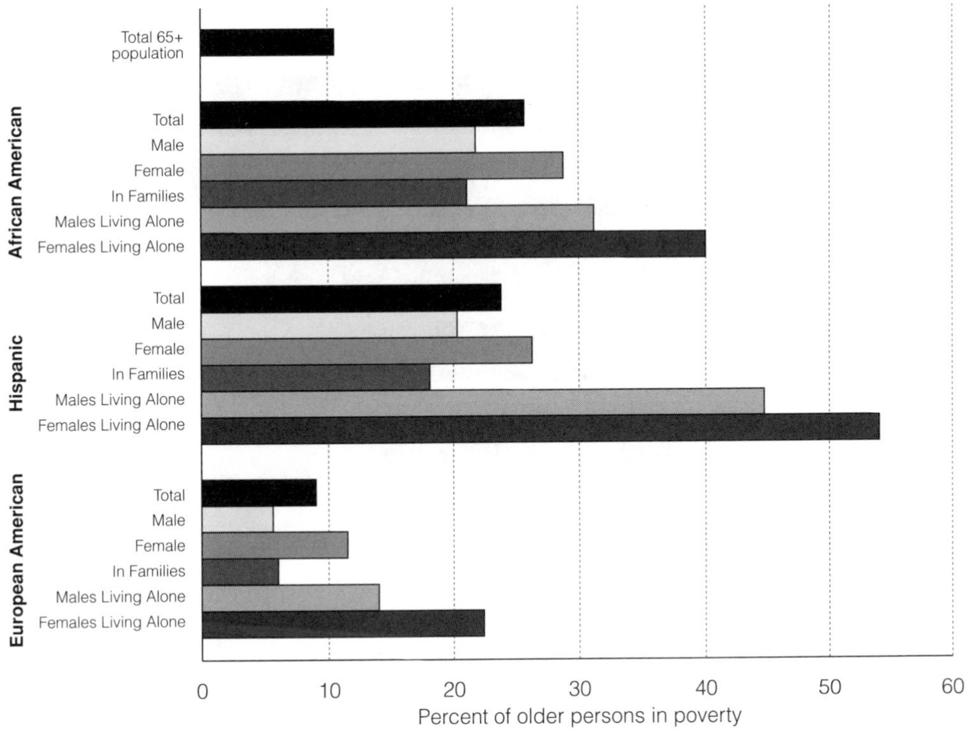

Source: Dalaker and Naifeh, 1998.

overall poverty rate of 10.5 percent masks enormous differences. Being African American, being Hispanic, being female, and living alone are related to serious economic disadvantage. The poverty rates for older African Americans (26%) and Hispanic Americans (23.8%) are much higher compared to 9 percent for older European Americans (Dalaker and Naifeh, 1998). Women of all racial and ethnic backgrounds have poverty rates almost twice as high as their male counterparts. Older African American and Hispanic women who live alone have the highest rates of poverty of any subgroup (See Exhibit 9.11).

In addition, older age itself is associated with economic disadvantage. Although the overall rate of poverty for those over 65 was 10.5 percent in 1997, for those 65 to 74 it was 8.6 percent, and for people 75 and above it was 13 percent (Dalaker and Naifeh, 1998). When examining age differences in economic well-being cross-sectionally, it is important to keep in mind that other factors, associated with age, operate to shape income. Exhibit 9.12 shows median income by age category, along with the percentage of married people and the percent-

Exhibit 9.12   *Income Differences Between Age Groups: 1996*

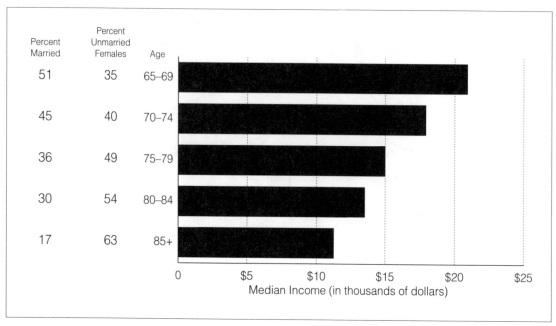

Source: Social Security Administration, 1998b.

age of unmarried females in each age group. As you move from younger to older cohorts, you find not only lower average incomes, but also fewer married couples and more unmarried (mostly widowed) women. As discussed in Chapter 2, cohort composition (the social and demographic characteristics of each cohort) differs with age, explaining a good deal of the apparent age difference in income. Within the "young old" cohort (65-69), 51 percent are married and 35 percent are unmarried women. Among the oldest old (85+), only 17 percent are married and 63 percent are unmarried women, whose incomes are much lower. Are incomes lower for older cohorts because they are older (an aging effect), because pension coverage is better among younger cohorts (a cohort effect), or because the older cohorts include more unmarried females (a composition effect related to aging)? The answer is undoubtedly that all of those factors contribute to the differences we see in income by age when we look cross-sectionally.

As mature cohorts reach age 65 or retirement, each one in recent years has included a higher percentage of people with maximum Social Security benefits and income from pensions and assets. So when we state that the aggregate economic well-being of the older population has improved, it is mostly because poorer members of the oldest cohorts have died and been replaced by more affluent individuals moving into older age groups. It is usually not the case that the economic fortunes of specific persons have improved (Quinn and Smeeding, 1993). Nor is it the case that individuals or couples, as they advance in age, necessarily move to lower levels of income. Some erosion of economic well-being is possible if income sources don't adjust for inflation or if health or family problems require consumption of assets that had been providing income.

■ ■ ■ ■ ■ ■ ■ ■
APPLYING THEORY:
The Stratified Life Course and Economic Diversity

As we have seen, groups within the elderly population differ substantially in rates of poverty and on more "positive" measures of economic status. Married couples fare better than unmarried adults, and European Americans better than Hispanic or African Americans. What brings about these systematic differences, which tend to appear regardless of the measure that you use to evaluate economic well-being? The answer has to do with choices and opportunities throughout the life cycle—prior **life chances**.

These differences must be considered from a life-cycle perspective Differences in life chances including education, health, family, and labor force experiences affect consequent access to various types of resources like income, family support, pensions, and assets. The provision of income maintenance programs is in turn contingent on previous income. (Choudhury and Leonesio, 1997; O'Rand, 1996). Thus life chances, associated with earnings potentials and access to pensions, have long-term consequences for economic well-being in later life. Although later life events may increase the risks of poverty, the people most likely to fall into poverty following these events are those whose economic status was already tenuous as a result of a lifetime's worth of events (Choudhury and Leonesio, 1997; Shaw and Yi, 1997). Sociologists and economists have used the notions of **cumulative advantage** and **cumulative disadvantage. Cumulative advantage** describes how individuals who have early opportunities for success most often build on that success to perpetuate their advantages into later life. **Cumulative disadvantage** describes how those with disadvantages also carry those disadvantages forward through sequential life stages, often resulting in later-life poverty (Crystal and Shea, 1990; O'Rand, 1996). Structural barriers to the full employment of some groups within a society—women, minorities, the less educated—will inevitably result in their greater financial need in old age, unless income maintenance policies correct for those distinctions through income redistribution.

> One interesting implication of a life cycle perspective is that, in the long run, the well-being of the elderly may be more efficiently served by concentrating on programs whose impact occurs long before old age—programs like education, training or health . . . [Such programs] can have great impact on the income, assets, and health status of the elderly-to-be. (Quinn, 1993, p. 21)

As evidence of this, studies continue to confirm that women with children earn lower wages, even after differences of education, experience and job type are taken into account (Waldfogel, 1997). This and similar life course events shape labor force choices, savings and a range of other behaviors over time.

The tendency, then, is for those who have been advantaged in early stages of adulthood to maintain that advantage into later life, with economic disadvantage also following persons as they age. Exceptions to these cumulative patterns of advantage or disadvantage in later life are individuals whose resources are depleted suddenly by major health problems and women whose finances are disrupted following widowhood (Quinn and Smeeding, 1993).

Both race and health influence the accumulation of wealth by affecting life chances: African Americans and those with chronic health conditions generally have lower assets in later life than their more advantaged age peers (Shea, Miles, and Hayward, 1996). African Americans are less likely to own homes or have high equity amounts as they approach later life, giving them fewer resources for the future (Myers and Chung, 1996). Life-course events, such as marriage, divorce, and childbearing, can also influence individuals' long-term economic status. For example, a study of pre-retirement-age women showed that those who had been divorced or widowed had significantly lower incomes and assets than those who remained in first marriages. Even if the divorced or widowed women had subsequently remarried, their economic well-being was lower (Holden and Kuo, 1996).

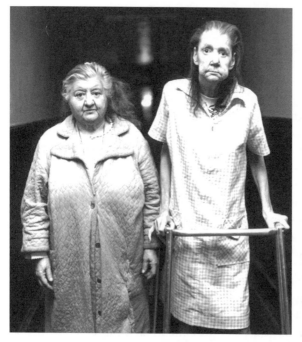 

Older adults in poor health or poverty have often had difficult early lives, resulting in cumulative disadvantage.

Exhibit 9.13 *Sources of Income of Lowest and Highest Income Elderly: U.S. 1996*

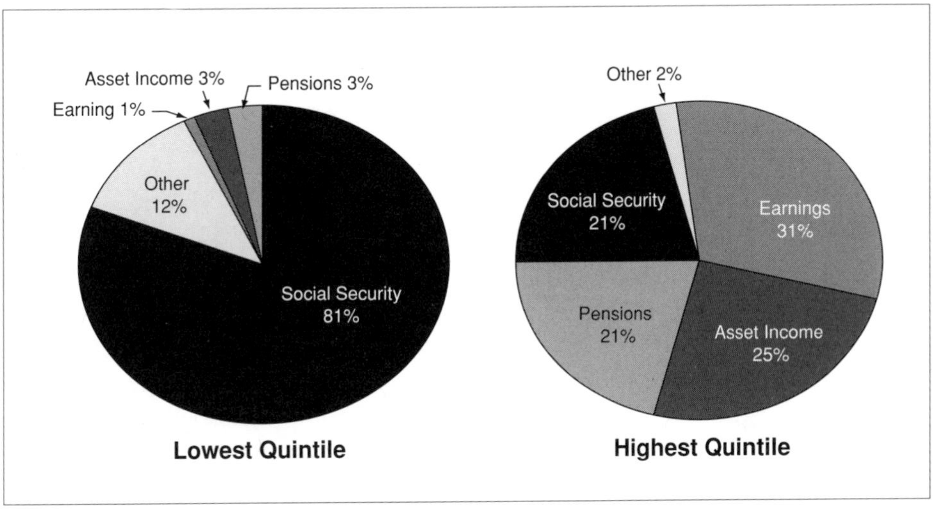

Asset Income 3%   Pensions 3%   Other 2%

Earning 1%

Other 12%   Social Security 81%   Social Security 21%   Earnings 31%

Pensions 21%   Asset Income 25%

Lowest Quintile   **Highest Quintile**

Source: Social Security Administration, 1998b.

Life chances and life experience translate into various groups' being more or less likely to have income from the major sources discussed earlier. Exhibit 9.13 shows that individuals in the highest one-fifth of the income distribution receive substantial income from assets; clearly, those least in need are also most able to save during their working years and develop assets for retirement (Social Security Administration, 1998a). Older persons in the lowest quintile of income receive about four fifths of their income from Social Security, whereas for those in the highest quintile Social Security comprises less than one-fourth of income (Social Security Administration, 1998b). For the poorest 40 percent of the population (annual incomes under $13,000/year) Social Security constitutes 80 percent or more of their total income (Social Security Administration, 1998a). Thus, the mix of income sources of economically secure individuals differ substantially from those who are least economically secure.

Although life chances are associated with membership in particular social groups and categories, the system is not completely deterministic; individuals sometimes do "beat the odds" and do very well, getting excellent jobs, good incomes, and high-paying pensions despite being in a group that fares poorly on average. The notion of life chances simply points out that, to date, individuals in different groups have had different odds of moving successfully through the events of the life course in ways that results in economic security in old age. These different odds, patterned by race, ethnicity, and gender, are the product of our social structure.

Differing life chances for economic security in later life is one kind of diversity among the older population. But diversity can have different meanings and implications. Is diversity a positive, negative, or neutral fact of life in our society? Should we promote diversity or seek to reduce it? Obviously the answer to that question depends on what kind of diversity, and on the ideology of the people discussing it. In the case of economic status, a high degree of diversity may be a negative reflection on our society and may call for policies to reduce differences.

■ ■ ■

Effects Of Population Aging On The Economy

So far we have considered the impact of aging (along with gender, race, and marital status) on the economic well-being of individuals. Another kind of question, using a more macro-level lens, looks at the impact of societal aging on the economy of the nation as a whole. Population aging can have an effect on aggregate economic activity, the size and composition of the labor force, labor force participation rates, productivity, and the structure of demand and consumption (Matras, 1990). Here we will consider some of these effects of societal aging on the economy.

Spending and Saving over the Life Cycle

How will societal aging affect savings behavior in the United States economy and the pool of assets in pension funds and privately owned assets? If future cohorts behave like current ones, the already low level of savings by individual Americans could drop even more. However, we can't necessarily predict the savings behavior of future cohorts from the activities of aging cohorts to date. In the mid-1990s discussions in the media raised alarms about how members of the baby boom cohorts weren't saving enough for their own retirements; more recently, however, these same outlets have attributed the growth in the stock market to these same cohorts investing massive amounts in mutual funds. Either explanation may oversimplify savings dynamics that are driven by many factors, including the rates of employment and the strength of wages and the overall economy, as well as cohorts' experiences and expectations.

Economists propose what they call the **life-cycle hypothesis** of saving and spending. According to this hypothesis, rational economic planners (all of us, presumably) accumulate assets of various types, including personal savings, home equity, and pension wealth, in anticipation of a change in behavior in later life as we become less economically productive at retirement. We defer some of our consumption to support ourselves in later life, spending down these assets as we age (Holtz-Eakin and Smeeding, 1994). A person who adapted perfectly to the life-cycle hypothesis would end up with absolutely no resources at the time of death, having spent all assets that had been saved, but this outcome seldom occurs. Economically secure people often die leaving an estate, whereas the less advantaged often "outlive their money," requiring assistance to pay for basic needs and long-term health care before they die.

Research shows that the oldest age cohorts have fewer accumulated resources than do slightly younger cohorts over age 65. This suggests either that these oldest adults are spending down their accumulated resources as the life cycle hypothesis suggests or that there is a cohort difference. Perhaps the oldest age cohorts started out with fewer resources at age 65 than current cohorts. People do spend down their savings with age, but not as quickly as the life-cycle hypothesis suggests (Holtz-Eakin and Smeeding, 1994). Most people do not add to their accumulated assets in later life, but instead work to hold the resources accumulated in earlier years to meet expected or unexpected needs (a new car, health care expenses). Thus, the aging of the population may not help to increase the low savings rate in this country. In fact, if the life-cycle hypothesis is accurate for most people, the aging of society should reduce private assets, the stock of money in pension funds, and thus the capital available to the economy for investments in new capital or research.

Consumption Patterns

Researchers have analyzed how patterns of saving, spending, and consuming vary by age and other social variables. The amounts and types of spending by older adults may seem of little relevance to the rest of us. However, as the society ages and older consumers become more than one out of five Americans, the degree to which they can afford to consume desired goods and services (discretionary income) will have a major impact on the overall health and size of the economy, indirectly influencing everyone. Choices that this large consumer pool makes will also help to determine the mix of products and services available in the economy.

Early studies on the older population showed a significant percentage of income going for basics—food, health care, utilities, and housing—with discretionary spending on leisure and recreation varying substantially based on income level (Goldstein, 1960). Poorer households could ill afford the travel or recreation consumed by the middle class; as with poor people of any age, nearly all of their incomes went for monthly necessities (food, shelter, transportation). It has been argued that one of the reasons that Social Security passed in 1935 was the hope that consumption by benefit recipients would help spur the economy, which was mired in the Great Depression (Quadagno, 1988).

More recent studies of consumption indicate that the consumption pattern remains largely unchanged for low- to moderate-income households. Fixed costs still constitute a major component of spending by older consumers. A 1992 study by the United States General Accounting Office, for example, estimated that half of older homeowners spend at least 45 percent of their incomes on property taxes, utilities, and home maintenance. Among married couples (with their larger incomes), only about 30 percent of expenditures are for housing-related costs (Nieswiadomy and Rubin, 1995). Other necessary expenditures, such as food and health care, also represent larger percentages of the more modest incomes of unmarried women compared to married couples. In all, Nieswiadomy and Rubin (1995) found that retired couples allocated less than $5, and unmarried women less than $3, of each $100 they spent on entertainment.

One component of consumption that is not entirely predictable is health care. Health care costs, which have varied depending on Medicare's coverage and copayment levels since 1965, were about 12 percent of total expenditures by retirees in the late 1980s (Nieswiadomy and Rubin, 1995). (See Chapter 10 for more detail on health care costs.) Those who can afford to do so seek to control this unpredictable cost by buying insurance that supplements any public or private programs to which they are entitled. Concerns regarding the high cost of health care and the potential for costly catastrophic illnesses may prompt older adults to hold onto savings and suppress current spending, thereby restricting the consumption of the older population in areas other than health care.

Experts disagree on whether consumption patterns will shift substantially in the next decades, as new cohorts enter later life. Johnson and Williamson (1987) claim that the improved health, increased leisure time, and financial status of current and future retirees will result in new products and services targeted to this market. Their side of this debate suggests that specialized products and services, as well as senior-oriented leisure, will be an expanding market as societal aging continues. For example, people over age 60 make up 35 percent of the consumers of vacation cruises (Cruise Lines International Association, 1996). If that percentage remains constant as the population ages, shouldn't enterprising shipbuilders be preparing now for the growing number of customers? There is some evidence that businesses are gearing up to meet expanded demands for consumer goods by a growing cadre of older consumers (Haug, 1995).

On a less optimistic note, as more people survive to ages at which assistance is needed in household tasks and personal care, how much should home health care companies anticipate growing over the next several decades? This question is complicated further if each succeeding cohort has later onset of disability than its predecessors did (Reynolds, Crimmins and Saito, 1998). It remains unclear how quickly or vigorously such markets will shift, in part depending on the level of financial security of the older cohorts of the future.

On the other side of this debate, some researchers voice concerns regarding restricted consumption by the older population. As society ages, they wonder whether the economy will slow if older consumers keep cars and durable goods (such as refrigerators) longer than do younger adults (Kneese and Cooper, 1993). Will the aging of society have a negative effect on consumerism? Again, the answer will turn on whether aging or cohort effects are more potent in these behaviors. Spending and consumption patterns of future aging cohorts may be based more on per capita income and the choices available; we cannot assume that because a society ages, its rate of consumer spending automatically drops (Easterlin, 1996). Future cohorts may be more free-spending or more tight-fisted with their money. Their attitudes will depend on several factors: their lifetime experiences with money and the economy, their anticipations of the future and their levels of disposable income. Social policies in force during their later lives will also shape how they save or spend. For example, will Social Security and Medicare benefits be more limited than today, requiring that more income be devoted to necessities?

One thing that is clear is that business and marketers have discovered the "gray market" for products and services (Minkler, 1991b). This discovery has had the dual effects of recognizing and meeting the needs of this population, but has also resulted in a focus on the affluent among the older population, downplaying the continuing economic marginality of some subgroups within the older population (Minkler, 1991b). Both the senior lobby and private corporations have contributed to the notion of the older population as a vast, untapped resource for marketing goods and services. The fact that we now see "mature" models, even for products not oriented to older adults, is a signal that the older market is no longer marginalized by business (Minkler, 1991b). It remains important, however, for the marketplace to be responsive to the needs of a wide range of older consumers, not just the wealthiest.

Prospects for the Future Economic Status of the Elderly

Predicting the economic well-being of future cohorts of older persons involves many unknowns. Critical among these unknowns are the potential changes in public and private policies for income maintenance and the overall health of the economy. Under a worst-case scenario, the economy would face sustained growth in the elderly population. This would mean a smaller working-age population. Older workers and undereducated youth would dominate the work force. Market forces would then prompt a return to early retirement, increases in the costs of medical care and personal assistance. All together, a graying society could result in stagnant levels of economic growth (Szanton, 1993).

Although we do know that the aging of society will likely proceed, many of the other elements in that worst-case scenario are hotly debated by experts and may deviate dramatically from current trends (Szanton, 1993). For example, the size of the productive work force can vary considerably in a given country depending on immigration policies, and there has been a shift away from the recent pattern of early retirement as incentives to continue working push older employees to continue somewhat longer in the labor force. How close we come to the worst-case scenario is yet to be determined.

Although we have seen improvement in the economic fortunes of recent cohorts, there is no guarantee that this improvement will continue for future cohorts. Recent retirees have been dubbed the **"good times" generation** because of the way in which historical events shaped their lives and their retirement incomes (Moon and Smeeding, 1989). Those born during the 1920s are a privileged cohort. They were in their prime working years during the economic boom following World War II, built careers during the period in which private pension coverage was expanding, and benefited from the windfall of a dramatic

These two women, from different cultures and historical periods, work into their later years due to economic necessity.

increase in the value of real estate during their middle years (Holtz-Eakin and Smeeding, 1994). The coincidence of so many favorable circumstances is unlikely to repeat for future cohorts, who may fare worse than their predecessors.

What also seems likely, however, is that inequality will continue to be problematic among the elderly. In contrast to many other countries, the piecemeal system of income maintenance in the United States leaves some individuals much less secure than others in old age. By attempting to create incentives early in life to work hard and achieve, our income maintenance policies mostly reward high achievers and do less for the unfortunate or unmotivated. As a nation, we will probably be revisiting several pieces of our income maintenance policies in the next few decades, with the outcomes from those political processes shaping the economic well-being of all of us as we age into the future.

Summary

Economic well-being is one area in which it is especially critical to avoid discussions of "the average" older adult. It is clear that economic well-being has improved on the average, but many sizable groups continue to experience high rates of poverty and economic marginality. Lifelong advantages/disadvantages embedded in the labor market and public and private policies of income maintenance result in individuals whose economic histories, for good or ill, follow them into later life to result in security or insecurity. As James Schulz so eloquently put it,

> "The issue is not whether.... we can have better pensions and services for the aged. The issue is whether we want a higher standard of living in our retirement years at the expense of a lower standard in our younger years. Whether we like it or not, the 'economics of aging' begins for most of us quite early in life" (1990, p. 201).

In general, wealthy older people are not suddenly impoverished after retirement, nor are the poorest older persons likely to be in poverty for the first time as a result of retirement.

The choices of a "graying market" regarding saving versus spending, and on what types of goods and services, will have a significant impact on the larger economy in years to come. The economy cannot afford to ignore such a large group of consumers and continue to gear merchandise for the "youth market" only. Whether consumption among older adults will be for necessities only or for leisure and optional goods will depend, to a great extent, on how much disposable income is provided by the public and private systems of income maintenance.

On the societal level, older persons constitute a growing percentage of the population. Income maintenance programs place large and growing demands on both the public and private sectors. We can undoubtedly anticipate some modifications of these policies that will affect future cohorts. The issues facing the United States and most other countries with aging populations are much the same. Can our economies support a growing number of economically dependent adults for increasingly lengthy periods of retirement and still survive in worldwide competition? These issues are likely to challenge political and economic leaders for years to come.

Web Wise

United States Census Bureau

http://www.census.gov/

The United States Census Bureau collects and disseminates data about demographics, the population, and economy of the United States. This site offers information about the Bureau, including its organizational structure and employment opportunities. The current U.S. population and world population data are also available as well as current economic indicators and information on businesses and income, and labor force statistics. To assist the user, a manual and subject search option is provided. A "just for fun" function is also offered, and is more of an interactive approach as the user learns about geography and statistics.

Social Security Administration Home page

http://www.ssa.gov

The Social Security Administration (SSA) provides a great deal of information on various topics including Social Security (SS) benefit information and forms, how to apply for services, direct online services, SS budget and planning, and SS laws and regulations. Quick access to the Office of Research, Evaluation and Statistics (ORES), which offers continuing data and research examinations of the old-age, survivors, and disability insurance (OASDI) and Supplemental

Security Income (SSI) programs, is offered. In addition, current SS information, the most requested top ten SS services, and frequently asked questions are presented. Lastly, separate educational pages for children ages 6-12, teens, teachers, and parents are offered.

Maxwell School: Center for Policy Research, Syracuse University

NIA-Sponsored Research Projects

http://www-cpr.maxwell.syr.edu/

The Center for Policy Research (CPR) is part of the Maxwell School of Citizenship and Public Affairs, Syracuse University. CPR conducts research and related projects in areas including aging and income security policy. This web site offers information about Syracuse University, the Maxwell School, and CPR. It provides links for the user to quickly access the Center for Demography and Economics of Aging and the CPR Aging Studies Program. The user can also explore National Institute on Aging-sponsored research studies as well as other economic and income related projects.

HRS/AHEAD Studies

http://www.umich.edu/~hrswww/

Please see Chapter 2's WEB WISE segment for a summary description.

Key Terms

adequacy of benefits	income maintenance policies
age eligibility	income redistribution
assets	life chances
cumulative advantage	life-cycle hypothesis
cumulative disadvantage	need eligibility
defined benefit pension	poverty threshold
defined contribution pension	private pensions
deserving poor	privatization of Social Security
equity of benefits	social insurance
ERISA	Social Security trust fund
"good times" generation	three-legged stool
in-kind income	Townsend Movement
income	vested

Questions for Thought and Reflection

1. Considering life chances and the pattern of cumulative advantage and disadvantage, what steps are you taking and plans are you making in your current stage of your life that will influence your economic security in later life? In taking the long view, what are the major unknowns about how this will turn out? What choices have you already made and what opportunities granted/withheld from you that will determine this outcome?

2. Social Security has for years battled to reach the goals of adequacy and equity. But they are sometimes inconsistent. Both reflect middle-class American values. Should one of these goals be more important than the other? Should they be weighted equally in policy changes? Explain why you think your choice is best.

3. Imagine yourself at a family gathering where your Uncle Charles asks about your classes this semester. When he hears that you are taking a course in aging, he let you know in no uncertain terms that he thinks older people are selfish and a huge drain on the economy, living comfortably and demanding more than their fair share while giving back nothing. What response would you make to him?

4. Now that you know a little bit more about the social construction of "poverty," do you think that the definition is adequate? Are the assumptions fair? What would be the advantages and disadvantages now to changing the standards for measuring poverty for older and younger people?

CHAPTER 10

Health and Health Care

"We can have a dramatic impact on our own success or failure in aging. What we can do for ourselves, however, depends partly on the opportunities and constraints that are presented to us as we age— the attitudes and expectations of others toward older people, and on policies of the larger society of which we are a part."
(Rowe and Kahn, 1998, p. 18).

"A person's chances for illness and successful recovery are very much the result of specifiable social arrangements... products of deliberate policy choices. In large part, illness, death, health, and well-being are socially produced "(Freund and McGuire, 1999, p.3).

The health status of an older person is the result of many factors, including lifelong health habits (including diet, exercise, and use of health care), heredity, exposure to occupational and environmental hazards, and access to the health care system. These influences on individual health are, in large measure, social forces. As both of the quotes above illustrate, individual health behaviors are affected by societal values and by the practices and habits of the people in our more immediate social world: our families, our peers, and other members of our social groups. For example, your early experiences of eating in your family shaped your current food preferences and eating habits. The current emphasis on the importance of exercise is another example of the way in which societal values can influence individual values and behaviors. Your attitudes about exercise are probably quite different from those of your grandparents.

In addition to the factors that influence our health habits, another social force that has a significant impact on health status is access to health care resources. Race and ethnicity, especially as they influence income and education, significantly affect the nature and extent of a person's access to health care. For example, African American babies are more than twice as likely as European American babies to die before the age of 1 (Weiss and Lonquist, 1997). Low birth weight is the biggest risk factor for infant mortality. Although birth weight is related to individual factors such as the age of the mother and her health habits, the most powerful influence on birth weight is the adequacy of prenatal care, including education about nutrition, smoking, and alcohol consumption. Access to adequate prenatal care is linked to income and the availability of services in the mother's geographic area. Income and availability of services, in turn, are linked to race and ethnicity. In this way, an intensely personal outcome— the life or death of one's infant—is linked to larger social forces such as social inequality. The connections among health outcomes (infant mortality), individual health behaviors (mother's nutrition), and macro-level societal forces (unequal access to prenatal care) operate throughout our lives.

The same social forces that affect infant mortality continue to affect people's heath into later life. In this chapter we explore the health status of older individuals. We consider the factors that influence health in later life, and we examine the patterning of health and illness by gender, race, and social class. In addition, this chapter discusses the way that health care for older people is organized, financed, and delivered in the United States.

The Medical Model: Assumptions and Limitations

Much of our approach to the provision and analysis of health care in the United States is derived from a **medical model** of health and illness. This model of health and health care focuses heavily on the diagnosis and treatment of disease within specific systems of the human body. When we summarize the health status of a group or of the nation, we tend to report the most common conditions or illnesses, the most common causes of death, and the success of various treatments for ill health. These statistics reflect the medical model emphasis. Although a focus on disease is certainly a central dimension of health, some important assumptions and limitations underlie this view of health.

First of all, the medical model implies that **health** is simply the absence of disease: If you are not sick, you are healthy. However, broader definitions of health include positive dimensions such as physical, psychological, and social well-being, and the ability to function in, and perform the tasks associated with, everyday life. So health is not just the absence of something negative (disease), but rather the presence of positive mental and physical conditions.

Second, the medical model is founded on some assumptions that limit the perspective. Freund and McGuire (1999) identify several key aspects of the medical model. **Mind-body dualism** is the assumption that there is a clear separation between physical functioning and psychological, spiritual, behavioral, and emotional dimensions of the person. One outcome of this view is a focus on disease as a physical process, with little attention to the complex interplay between physical and nonphysical states of being. **Reductionism**, which is based on mind-body dualism, is the tendency to reduce any illness to a disorder of the physiological systems of the body of the afflicted individual. With a reductionistic view of health and illness, no attention is given to the social context that affects social, psychological, and emotional states, which in turn have a great impact on physical health. An example is a diagnosis of malnutrition as the absence of essential nutrients and caloric intake. Obviously, to understand why someone is malnourished and what might be done to correct the situation requires a much fuller understanding of the social, economic, and psychological condition of that person. Finally, the medical model rests on the **"doctrine of specific etiology,"** which searches for a specific cause for disease and tends to ignore contextual factors such as nutrition and stress.

The health care system in the U.S., established to focus on acute care, has relatively few physicians trained extensively in geriatrics.

The medical model influences the skills and training of physicians, the expectations of patients and the decisions of insurance providers about how to pay for care. This means most health care is shaped by the three assumptions of the medical model: mind-body dualism, physical reductionism and the doctrine of specific etiology. Health care providers operate with a limited definition of health as the absence of disease, and patients do, too, because of our investment in the medical model.

The implications of a medical model perspective on health and illness are well illustrated by the "discovery" of diseases. Examples of "discovered" diseases from history include drapetomania, which caused slaves to run away from their masters; revolution, an irrational opposition to the "natural rule" of the English monarchy; and onanism (otherwise known as masturbation), which allegedly caused stunted growth, impaired mental capacity, and a variety of other symptoms including headaches, appetite problems, cowardice, and weakness in the back (Freund and McGuire, 1995). The deep-rooted focus of the medical model on physical processes fostered the naming of troubling behaviors as diseases. Our distance from the historical and social contexts that gave rise to the identification of these conditions allows us to see both the profound impact of social forces and, by extension, the limitations of the medical model.

The way in which menopause is commonly defined and treated in American society—as a medical condition—is another manifestation of the medical model perspective. Our current views about menopause have roots in some interesting, startling, and very reductionistic ideas about women's health. The primary assumption underlying our treatment of menopause as a disease is that a woman's reproductive organs define her essence. Giving us an extremely clear example of physical reductionism, a late-19th-century physician stated that the uterus is the "controlling organ in the female body; as if the almighty, in creating the female sex, had taken the uterus and built up a woman around it" (Ehrenreich and English, 1990, p. 277). The uterus and the ovaries were thought to be the source of any abnormality, from irritability to insanity.

This reductionism helped to pave the way for medicalization of menopause. **Medicalization** is "the process of legitimating medical control over an area of life, typically by asserting the primacy of a medical interpretation of that area" (Freund and McGuire, 1995, p. 201). In the case of menopause, medicalization means that we focus on physical symptoms and biochemical processes, focus on these symptoms as unpleasant and uncomfortable, and transform the very natural process of menopause into an estrogen deficiency disease. Defining menopause as a disease has several important implications. First, identifying something as a disease implies a course of treatment. In the case of menopause, the prescribed treatment is estrogen replacement therapy (ERT) which is quite controversial. Artificial hormones help to reduce hot flashes, vaginal dryness, and other symptoms of menopause, but have been implicated in increased incidence of breast cancer. Recent research has found that HRT provides benefits that have nothing to do with menopausal symptoms: lower rates of heart disease and osteoporosis.

While the medical controversy over the advantages and disadvantages of HRT continues, a second concern about the medicalization of menopause persists. Many scholars see "treatment" for menopause as a mechanism of social control, perpetuating the ideology of women as sex objects and as passive participants in managing their own health. "The locus of solution then becomes the doctor-patient interaction in which the physician is active, instrumental, and authoritative and the patient is passive and dependent" (McRea, 1986, p. 298).

Finally, if we focus on menopause as a disease requiring physician intervention, we give less attention to the subjective interpretations and meanings women give to their own experiences. Many women report very positive reactions to this phase of life, including a sense of physical and psychological freedom. Giving greater voice to the subjective social and psychological experiences of women going through menopause would provide a counterbalance to the medical model approach.

Analyzing this approach further, Estes and Binney (1991) suggest that our tendency to medicalize normal physical processes has resulted in the "biomedicalization of aging." They assert that our society has constructed aging as a medical problem, and numerous areas of professional practice (including a huge health care industry, policy efforts, and research agendas) have arisen to deal with this medical challenge. The growth of the aging "industry" means an increasing numbers of professionals involved in dealing with the medical problems of aging. Expanding opportunities for economic gain are accompanied by an increasing social and psychological investment in the medicalization of aging.

In a provocative challenge to the medical model, McKinlay and McKinlay (1990) suggest that traditional "medical care is generally unrelated to the health of populations." They cite data on mortality trends following the introduction of major medical interventions, such as vaccines for polio, smallpox, and flu and treatments for pneumonia and typhoid. They conclude that "at most 3.5% of the total decline in mortality since 1900 could be ascribed to medical measures" introduced for the eight infectious diseases they considered (McKinlay and McKinlay, 1990, p. 21). Social factors such as improved nutrition, rise in real income, and improved sanitation played a more significant role in improving the health of the American population than did the medical measures for treatment or prevention of disease. Although no one would argue against the value of medical measures at the individual level, McKinlay and McKinlay draw our attention to the contextual factors involved in population health and the limitations of the medical model.

One alternative to a purely medical model is the **biopsychosocial model** of health. This approach, offered to clinical practitioners such as physicians, emphasizes a multidisciplinary and holistic view of health care, acknowledging that "complex problems of health and illness are...inherently multidimensional in nature" (Schwartz, 1982, p. 1040), requiring bridges among disciplines, redefinitions of health, and a general paradigm shift within medicine. While focusing somewhat narrowly on clinical processes of diagnosis and treatment, the biopsychosocial model represents an important alternative to unidimensional, mechanistic views of health and illness.

With the assumptions and criticisms of the medical model in mind, we turn to a description of the health status of older people. This description relies heavily on information generated by a medical model approach, because that approach has dominated health care and its analysis in the United States. You can use your awareness of the assumptions of the medical model to place ideas and information in a larger context of alternative views of health, illness, and well-being.

The Health Status of Older People

What happens to health as we grow older? Is there an inevitable increase in illness and poor health that accompanies age? To answer these questions, we can look at the health status of older people overall, compared to that of younger cohorts. However, we also need to look at variations within the older population. Indeed, the degree of heterogeneity and diversity in health suggests that age itself may not be a very strong predictor of health problems. Variations in health status across cultures provide further evidence for the idea that age itself is not the most powerful influence. For example, in Chapter 4 we saw that Americans experience a progressive age-related increase in blood pressure, but in Japan and China resting blood pressure changes very little well into old age.

It is important to keep in mind this question about the primacy of age in predicting health status as we begin to look at statistics from the United States. Because we are focusing on a single culture, it is easy to assume that the age-related patterns we observe are actually due to age. But keep in mind that the patterns we report for the United States do not necessarily hold true for other cultures. Compare, for example, the virtual absence of breast cancer among Japanese women to its exponential increase with age among American women. In the United States in 1991, an average of 32 women per 100,000 died of breast cancer. Among women aged 55 to 59, the death rate was 70 per 100,000; that rate almost triples (to nearly 200 per 100,000) for the 85 and older group. In Japan in 1991, only 9 women per 100,000 died of breast cancer (Cohen and Van Nostrand, 1995; Zarate, 1994). If we just looked at U.S. numbers, we might conclude that something about simply living a certain number of years increases the likeli-

Exhibit 10.1   *Number of Selected Reported Chronic Conditions per 1,000 Older Persons, by Sex and Age: U.S. 1994*

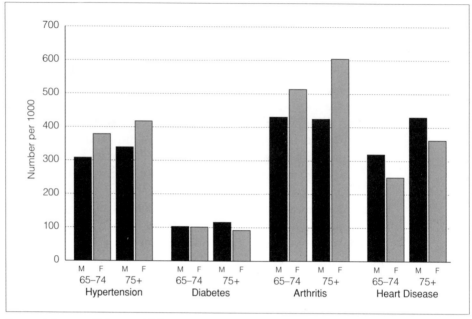

Source: Adams and Marano, 1995.

hood of breast cancer. But the fact that the rate is so much lower in Japan suggests that cultural factors—the context in which one lives out those years—is at least as important as age.

Age can be a marker for increased likelihood of some diseases, but its role as a cause is not at all clear. Chapter 4 makes the point that there is no causal connection between aging and disease, and illustrates that physiological aging is highly variable. Keep these considerations in mind as we review information about the health status of older people. It is useful to have a profile of how healthy older people are, what the most common chronic conditions are, and what the major health care needs are; these kinds of information help us to plan for the provision and financing of health care for our aging society. But the link between age and health is significantly modified by social context, especially by culture, race, gender, and ethnicity.

Measures of Health

As we develop a profile of the health of older people, we need to clarify how health is being defined and measured. Earlier in this chapter we mentioned the idea that health is not merely the absence of disease. Unfortunately, because of the way that the medical model dominates our thinking about and delivery of health care, much of what we know about the health of our population is about diseases and impairments. We have extensive national data on conditions, hospitalizations, and use of ambulatory care. We have virtually no national data on more holistic approaches to health; information on emotional, spiritual, and social well-being is not included in national health surveys. As we consider the health status of older people, the logical extension of the medical model is a focus on the conditions they have and on the major causes. Expanding a bit beyond the medical model, we also provide information on the mental health of the older population, on their self-assessed health status, and on their ability to perform the major tasks of everyday life.

The health status of older adults varies widely among individuals and according to how health is defined.

Prevalence Rates

One of the most common measures of the health of the older population is the prevalence of chronic conditions. **Prevalence rates** indicate what proportion of a given group has a certain condition of interest. These rates, which say something about how common a condition is, are most often reported "per 1000"—how many people per 1000 in the group of interest have the specified condition. For example, in Exhibit 10.1, which shows the prevalence of some common chronic conditions by age and sex, we see a very high rate of arthritis among women 75 and older: 604 out of 1000 (or 60 percent) of these women have arthritis.

Exhibit 10.1 also depicts a number of important patterns. First, prevalence increases with age for three of these conditions—hypertension, arthritis, and heart disease—but diabetes does not vary as consistently with age. Second, there are marked differences between men and women in the prevalence of these four conditions. Men age 65 and over have much higher rates of heart disease, the number one cause of death in the United States among adults, but older women

Exhibit 10.2   *Number of Selected Reported Chronic Conditions per 1,000 Older Persons age 65+, by Race and by Family Income: U.S. 1994*

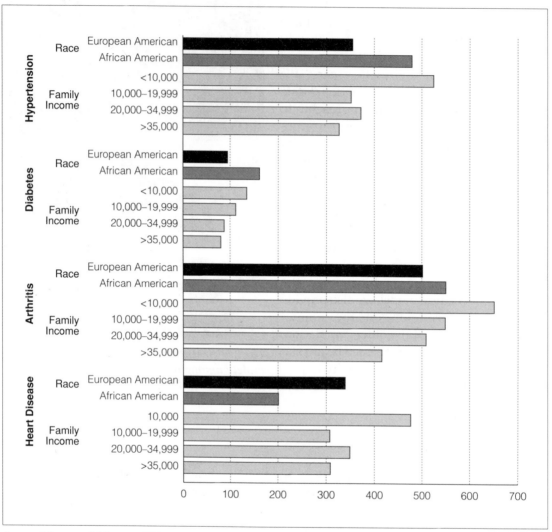

Source: Adams and Marano, 1995.

have higher rates of hypertension and arthritis. This pattern is consistent with the general observation that men have higher rates of the most life-threatening conditions, but women have higher rates of illness and disability overall. This pattern has been summarized (and probably oversimplified) in the statement, "Women get sick; men die." A number of social forces, including gender socialization for risky behavior, attention to bodily symptoms, and seeking help for health problems, contribute to producing this pattern. The gender difference in health is discussed later in this chapter.

Exhibit 10.3 *Percent of Persons Age 70 and Over With and Without Activity Limitations, by Age and Sex: U.S. 1992*

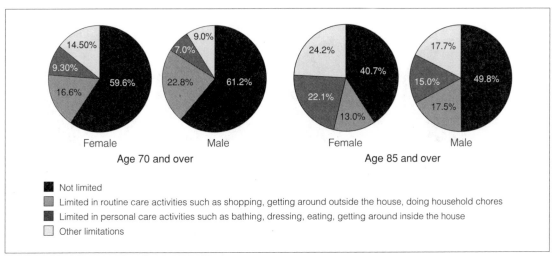

Source: Cohen and Van Nostrand, 1995.

Race and social class are also significantly related to health status. Exhibit 10.2 shows how the same four conditions vary by race and by family income. Hypertension, diabetes, and arthritis are more common among older African Americans, whereas heart disease is more common among older European Americans. All four conditions are much more common among the lowest income groups.

How do we make sense of the race and income findings? Since we know that older African Americans, on average, have lower incomes and higher rates of poverty than older European Americans do, it seems logical to conclude that some of the race difference in health status can be attributed to socioeconomic differences. Income influences lifelong access to health care, which clearly has an impact on health status in later life. We will discuss this explanation, along with other factors that enter into racial and socioeconomic differences in health, later in this chapter. For the present, it is important to note that health in later life is most definitely not a universal, predictable outcome of age alone. Health status in later life varies significantly by race, sex, and socioeconomic status, and these social categories reveal the impact of many social forces, including differential access to health care resources and socialization to different health behaviors.

Functional Ability

Another important indicator of the health status of the older population is the degree of limitation in people's ability to carry out the activities of daily living. Knowing about the conditions older people have is informative, but in order

Exhibit 10.4   *Percent of Persons Age 70 and Over With and Without Activity Limitations, by Age and Race: U.S. 1992*

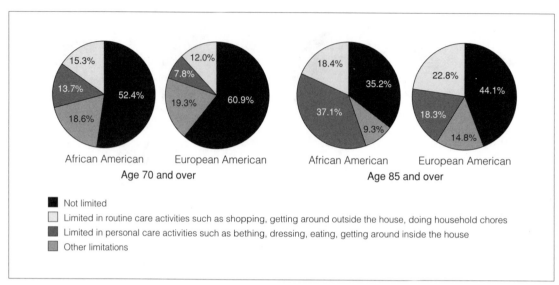

Source: Cohen and Van Nostrand, 1995.

to plan meaningful and effective health services, we need to know how these conditions affect people's lives. Measures of **functional ability** or functional limitation (these terms are used here interchangeably) serve that purpose. These measures evaluate older persons' ability to get through the day by asking about what activities of daily life they are able to do, how difficult a given activity is for them, and whether the help of another person is needed to accomplish a given task. The most common measure of functional ability is the Activities of Daily Living and Instrumental Activities of Daily Living (ADL/IADL) scale, developed by Katz and colleagues (1970) and refined by numerous researchers (Kovar and Lawton, 1994). This measure assesses the extent to which an individual needs help with basic personal tasks such as bathing, eating, and getting dressed, and with household and independent living tasks such as preparing meals, shopping, and transportation. Some version of this measure of functional capacity is used for a wide range of purposes, including determining eligibility for services, evaluating the appropriateness of care plans for people receiving assistance, describing the health status of the older population, and projecting future challenges to our health are system.

From Exhibits 10.3 and 10.4 we can see how limitations in functioning vary by age, race, and sex. It is important to note that these charts use a very specific measure of limitation. Individuals were considered to be limited in an activity if they had difficulty with the activity, if that difficulty was due to chronic health conditions, and if they received the help of another person in performing the activity. The authors of these studies defined people as limited only if they met all three conditions. Because this definition is quite restrictive these are probably conservative estimates of the prevalence of limitations.

Exhibit 10.3 shows that the proportion of men and women with no limitation decreases with age; a smaller proportion of the 85 and older group had no limitations compared to the 70 and older group. Women reported more limitations than men did, especially at the oldest ages. Only 40% of women age 85 and over were free of limitations, while almost 50% of men in this age group functioned without help.

In Exhibit 10.4, we see the same increase with age in the proportion of people who are limited in some way as we did in the preceding chart; the 85+ population is much more likely to have limitations than the 70 and older group. The more striking pattern in this figure, however, is the significant difference between African Americans and European Americans. A much higher proportion of African Americans have limitations than European Americans, in both age groups. Only about a third of the oldest African Americans are free of limitations, compared with 44 percent of the oldest European Americans. More than a third of the oldest African Americans have the most serious level of limitation, in personal care activities such as bathing, dressing, and eating. All of the people at this level of limitation are also presumed to be unable to carry on routine household activities such as shopping and preparing meals. African Americans age 85 and over are twice as likely as European Americans to have this most serious level of limitation. As with the higher prevalence rates for many chronic conditions, the health disadvantage of African Americans is related to many factors, including lifelong access to health care and exposure to occupational hazards.

Data on the prevalence of functional limitations among the older population have implications for planning health care for an aging society, for understanding the dynamics of health status, and for understanding different patterns of aging experiences. Functional limitations have a direct bearing on the issue of long-term care: special services and assistance provided on an ongoing basis (either in nursing homes, in specially designed living units, or in an individual's own home) to people who need help with the activities of everyday life. We will discuss long-term care in more detail later in this chapter. Here it is important to see that functional limitation has significant policy and planning implications.

One of the current questions that will have a bearing on future health needs is whether disability is increasing or decreasing as life expectancy increases. Are we living longer but in poorer shape, or are we moving toward sustained good health and high functioning well into our 80s? This debate about the compression of both morbidity (disease and disability) and mortality into the last years of life is unresolved. Some research suggests that rates of disability are increasing, so that our additional years of life are more likely to be years of poor health and disability. Other, very recent research suggests that chronic disability is

Exhibit 10.5   *Self-assessed Health Status by Race and Age: U.S. 1992*

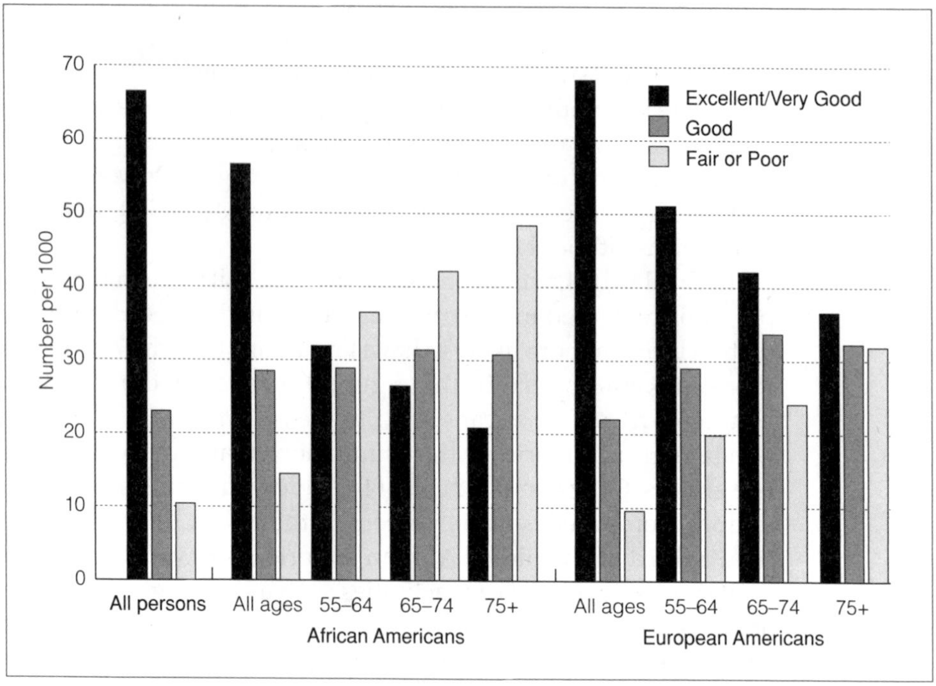

Source: Cohen and Van Nostrand, 1995.

decreasing (Manton, Corder, and Stallard, 1997). Theoretical and empirical investigations of this issue will continue; how it plays out will have significant implications for planning, financing, and delivery of long-term care services for older Americans.

Self-Assessment

Departing a bit from these prevalence-based measures of health status, we can consider a more qualitative, subject measure of the health of the older population: **self-assessed health status**. Asking people to rate their own health as excellent, very good, good, fair, or poor is actually an informative measure of health. It is quite useful to know how people view their own health situation. In addition, self-assessed health "is strongly associated with objective health status such as physical exams and physician ratings" (Cohen and Van Nostrand, 1995, pp. 31-32).

Exhibit 10.5 displays variations in self-assessed health by age and by race. The proportion of people who rate their health as fair or poor goes up significantly with age for both African Americans and European Americans. However, even in the oldest age category, 50 percent of African Americans and 69 percent of European Americans still view their health as good, very good, or excellent.

How does self-assessed health align with the prevalence of chronic conditions? If you look back at Exhibit 10.1, you will see that 60 percent of the oldest women (75 and above) have arthritis, 36 percent have heart disease, and 42 percent have hypertension. Among men in that age category, 42 percent have arthritis, 43 percent have heart disease, and 34 percent have hypertension. The majority of people over age 75 have at least one chronic condition. In the face of the high prevalence of major chronic conditions, how can older people rate their health as good, very good, or excellent?

Some researchers have suggested that older people rate their health highly because expectations about health change and because people tend to compare themselves with age peers (Cockerham, 1998). This explanation implies that people make mental adjustments in the reference point against which they judge their own health. An alternative view suggests that chronic conditions develop gradually so that older people are able to adapt to and compensate for the conditions they have; their health problems have minimal impact on their everyday functioning. "Physical decrements can be accommodated within their customary lifestyle, so that good health is a reality" (Atchley, 1997, p. 86). According to this view, high self-ratings of health are not the result of altered expectations, but are an accurate representation of the ability to perform daily activities.

In addition to the increase with age in proportions who rate their health as fair or poor, and the maintenance of fairly high proportions who rate their health as good or better, Exhibit 10.5 reveals very significant differences between African Americans and European Americans on self-rated health. African Americans are much more likely, at every age, to rate their health as fair or poor, and much less likely to see their health as very good or excellent. These poorer self-assessments are not surprising, given the higher levels of illness and mortality among older African Americans compared to older European Americans.

Mortality

A final measure of health is mortality: who dies, of what, and when. Exhibit 10.6 lists the leading causes of death by sex, race, Hispanic origin, and age. Heart disease and cancer are the two leading causes of death for all sex and race/ethnicity groups ages 45 and over.   You can scan the chart to see differences in leading causes. AIDS is one of the top five causes of death for Hispanic American and African American males between the ages of 45 to 64, but does not appear on the list for other groups. Pneumonia and influenza are leading causes of death for all groups 65 and older. The death rates and rankings have implications for health policy and health promotion efforts, suggesting that such programs be tailored to meet the most pressing health needs of different groups. However, because the largest number people who die are European American

Exhibit 10.6   *Top Five Leading Causes of Death Among People 45 and Older by Race, Hispanic origin, Sex, and Age: U.S. 1992*

	1	2	3	4	5
African American Females age 45–64	cancer	heart disease	CVD	diabetes	COPD
African American Females age 65+	heart disease	cancer	CVD	diabetes	P&I
African American Males age 45–64	heart disease	cancer	CVD	AIDS	A&AE
African American Males age 65+	heart disease	cancer	CVD	COPD	P&I
Hispanic American Females age 45–64	cancer	heart disease	diabetes	CVD	CLD&C
Hispanic American Females age 65+	heart disease	cancer	CVD	diabetes	P&I
Hispanic American Males age 45–64	heart disease	cancer	CLD&C	AIDS	A&AE
Hispanic American Males age 65+	heart disease	cancer	CVD	P&I	diabetes
European American Females age 45–64	cancer	heart disease	COPD	CVD	diabetes
European American Females age 65+	heart disease	cancer	CVD	P&I	COPD
European American Males age 45–64	heart disease	cancer	A&AE	CLD&C	COPD
European American Males age 65+	heart disease	cancer	CVD	COPD	P&I

CVD: cerebrovascular disease   CLD&C: chronic liver disease and cirrhosis
P&I: pneumonia and influenza   COPD: chronic obstructive pulmonary disease
A&AE: accidents and adverse effects

Source: Gardner, Rosenberg, and Wilson, 1996.

males, their experiences have tended to set the agenda for public health efforts, including research, treatment, and prevention.

The ranking of causes of death are based on rates of death due to these diseases. These rates are shown in the table of causes of death. Rates of death tell us how many people per 100,000 in a particular group died of a particular cause in a year. As you would expect, death rates by cause vary significantly. For all groups, death rates go up significantly with age. For example, 510 out of every 100,000 African American males ages 45 to 64 died of heart disease in 1992; for

African American males 65 and older, that rate was more than 2,200 per 100,000 (or 2.2 per 100). There are significant sex variations within race and ethnic categories. For all causes where comparisons can be made, for all age and race/ethnicity groups, men have higher rates of death than do women, except for cerebrovascular disease (stroke) among older European Americans and diabetes among older Hispanics. For most of the causes on which comparisons can be made, African Americans have higher death rates than European Americans do, and European Americans have higher rates of death than persons of Hispanic origin.

Some of the most dramatic differences in mortality patterns, with serious implications for society, are not shown in this table. For African American and Hispanic men between the ages of 25 and 44, the *leading* cause of death is AIDS; for European Americans males of the same age, AIDS is the second leading cause of death, following accidents. The second leading cause of death for African American men between 25 and 44 is homicide and legal intervention, which ranks much lower (sixth) for European Americans males of the same age (Gardner, Rosenberg and Wilson, 1996). These striking variations in leading causes of death and in death rates illustrate that health and illness are complex outcomes of social forces, including social inequality, variations in access to health care resources, lifestyles, and for some groups in our population, immersion in a violent world.

Mental Health and Aging

The foregoing discussion of health status has focused on physical health; the mental health status of the older population is an equally important issue. Just as physical health can be defined and measured in many different ways, the term mental health also has different meanings. It can refer to emotional well-being in our everyday lives. Most often mental health is used to talk about mental illness, just as our discussion of physical health focused primarily on conditions and illnesses that are actually a departure from health. Mental illness includes cognitive, emotional, and behavioral problems, including Alzheimer's disease, depression, and anxiety disorders, as discussed in Chapter 5. A thorough discussion of the comparative prevalence of mental disorders among older people, and of the causes, consequences, and treatment of mental illness, is beyond the scope of this book. However, a description of the overall mental health status of the older population will round out our picture of the health of the older population.

As with physical aspects of health, there is variation in who is more likely to suffer from various conditions. Depression, for example, is more common among people with lower levels of education. A recent study found that the education gap in depression rates increases over the life course (Miech and Shanahan, 2000). Education is linked to social advantage, especially economic advantage. These researchers suggest that a low level of education plays just as decisive a role in mental health as it does in physical health and freedom from disability in later life. Their research contributes to our understanding of the impact of socioeconomic status on mental as well as physical health. In general, rates of such mental health problems are much higher among nursing-home residents than among community-dwelling older people. About 12 percent of older people living in the community have diagnosed mental illnesses, while 65 percent of the nursing-home population is estimated to have some mental disorder. Cognitive disorders such as Alzheimer's disease account for 73 percent of all mental diagnoses in nursing homes (Burns and Taube, 1990). Using the broadest definition, about 15 percent of older people in the community and 25 percent of nursing-home residents suffer from depression (Fogel, Gottlieb and Furino, 1990). Schizophrenia affects less than 1 percent of the older population living in the community, but about one-third of the residents of nursing homes and state hospitals (Fogel et al., 1990). About one in twenty older people in the community have anxiety disorders (Burns and Taube, 1990).

Cognitive impairment refers to the loss of mental capacity for higher-level mental functioning. Some of the symptoms of cognitive impairment, often referred to as **dementia**, are memory loss, confusion, disorientation, and loss of ability to care for oneself. The most common cause of severe cognitive impairment is Alzheimer's disease. Fogel and his colleagues (1990) suggest that about 5 percent of the population 65 and older have severe cognitive impairment. This proportion increases to about 20 percent for the population aged 80 and older. Cognitive impairments like Alzheimer's disease are gradual, progressive deteriorations. In the early stages of the disease, people with Alzheimer's disease are very often cared for at home by family members. "For each demented patient in a nursing home, there are two to three more in the community with equal levels of impairment who are cared for by some combination of family, friends, and paid caretakers" (Fogel et. al. 1990, p. 4). There are many consequences of, and issues related to, family caregiving for Alzheimer's victims. Some of these issues are presented in Chapters 5 and 7.

The burdens of family care for cognitively impaired older people can lead to mental and physical health problems for the caregiver. "Some studies have suggested that more than half of family caretakers of demented patients may suffer from a diagnosable depression at some time during the course of care" (Fogel et al., 1990, p. 4). This latter point—that family caregiving for cognitively impaired older people may cause mental health problems for the caregiver—echoes some of the well-known literature about caregiving in general. Many caregivers enter their own old age with health and financial deficits. This situation is another example of the social production of health and illness. We have a service delivery system that provides few good options for caring for people with Alzheimer's disease. Family caregiving is the foundation of that care system, because it reflects our social values about families' taking care of each other and about the government's not interfering with the primacy of the family unit. This arrangement is the result of policies and programs designed to minimize government responsibility for caregiving. We can fruitfully debate the ideology underlying our current system of caregiving for people with Alzheimer's disease. The point of note here is that our social arrangements surrounding this issue, the policies, social values, and (lack of) programs, contribute to ill health in people affected by the arrangement.

Estimates of the prevalence of other mental health problems vary, depending what data are included. Statisticians may include in their count only diagnosed conditions where individuals have presented themselves to health care professionals. Or they might also include diagnosable conditions, serious enough to reach some threshold for clinical diagnosis if the person presents him/herself. Some estimates also include psychological distress, a disorder not at the clinically diagnosable threshold. In addition, if estimates are developed in order to plan for services, there is sometimes an agenda to keep those rates manageably low so that government financing of treatment is feasible (Burns and Taube, 1990).

There are many interesting questions about the onset, cause, and treatment of these various mental disorders. For our purposes, a general profile of the mental health of the older population is sufficient. In addition, we have given some examples of the ways in which mental health (like physical health) is a product of social factors. Decisions such as how and why a condition gets defined and counted as a mental illness, and how and by whom caregiving for Alzheimer's should be provided, have an impact on assessment of mental health.

Sex and Race Variations in Health

On all of the measures of physical health we have reviewed, we have seen significant differences by race and sex. We have alluded to the various explanations for these differences. For both sex and race patterns of health, these explanations fall into two main categories: biological and social/behavioral. Here we will look more systematically at some of those explanations.

Summing up the dynamics of sex differences in health and mortality, Verbrugge (1990) suggests that risks are "added up over time, and occasionally subtracted. They are derived from a biological foundation . . . and from the overlay of lifetime exposures" (p. 185). Nathanson (1990) further illustrates these two dimensions of the gender gap by pointing out that, while females outlive males in nearly all species, the nature and extent of the difference in human mortality vary across time and across cultures. That the differential persists across contexts provides some support for a biological basis; its variation according to historical and cultural context reinforces its social basis.

In Chapter 3, we discussed some of the biological bases for the female advantage in longevity, including the protective effects of estrogen. We also discussed the different health behaviors of males and females in our society. One of these differences is awareness of, and seeking help for, health problems. Women are more likely to attend to changes in their bodies and to seek the services of health care professionals. This may be because of the emphasis placed on appearance and weight, and because of attention to changes that routinely happen during the menstrual cycle and maternity. One of the results of women's presenting themselves more often to the health care system is that they get diagnosed sooner and more often for many health conditions. Another result is earlier detection and treatment of health problems, which helps to explain women's greater longevity. Although this pattern of women's earlier and more frequent help seeking does not hold for all health problems, it is an important social factor in the gender difference in health and mortality.

Other roles and behaviors to which men and women have been socialized have an impact on risk for illness. For men, these behaviors include smoking, alcohol consumption, hazardous occupations, and driving too fast; for women, competing demands on their time and feeling stressed are two socially produced health risks. Gender differences in health in later life are thus a product of the cumulative effects of biology, lifestyle, and behavior; the latter two effects are strongly influenced by socialization.

Race differences in health are similarly created by a combination of biological and social forces. "Some conditions such as hypertension and sickle cell anemia have a genetic basis, but living conditions associated with poverty influence the onset and course of most physical health problems" (Cockerham, 1998, p. 52). The impact of biology on race differences in health is primarily limited to the genetic component of some diseases and conditions. The social forces that influence racial variation in health patterns are both socioeconomic and cultural. The link between race and poverty means that African Americans have poorer lifelong access to health care than European Americans, greater health risks attributable to occupational hazards, poorer nutrition, and poorer prenatal care (and the impacts of inadequate prenatal care are lifelong). Race and ethnicity can also operate through cultural factors that shape health behaviors related to diet, exercise, and willingness to seek the advice of a health care professional.

Earlier discussion in this chapter suggested the impact of culture and lifestyle on health. An excellent example is the case of the Pima Indians. This group experienced almost no diabetes until, as a result of forced lifestyle changes, they began to eat more processed foods high in simple sugars and fats and to lead more sedentary lives. Today almost half of all adult Pimas aged 35 and older have adult-onset diabetes. The high rate of diabetes among these Native Americans clearly cannot be attributed to a biological predisposition. Another illustration of the cultural (versus biological) explanation of racial and ethnic variation in health: Black Africans do not have rates of stroke or hypertension nearly as high as African Americans do.

Death And Dying

From our discussion of health conditions and mortality rates, it is clear that illness and death are not evenly distributed across the population, either within a society or around the globe. For children in developing countries without sufficient clean food and water and without extensive health care, conditions related to malnutrition and contaminated water and food are major causes of premature death (Bender and Smith, 1997). This unequal distribution of illness and death is another example of the impact of social, economic, and historical context on the lives of human beings.

How, when, and where we die, and how we deal with death are further examples of the social construction of human experience. Looking at the death rituals of any non-Western culture, or at our culture in different historical period, will illustrate how very differently we deal with death in the U.S. today. In India, for example, the body is wrapped in white, laid on a board, carried through the streets while mourners chant and toss flowers, and then taken to be cremated. In earlier times in the U.S. our approach to death was quite different than it is today. Helton (1997) provides an account of how death was handled in rural Kentucky during the early decades of this century. He discusses the central role of family and community in carrying out funeral practices. Women prepared the body, cleaned house, and prepared food; men dug the graves and made the caskets. Body preparation included washing and dressing the body. Women tried to make the body look as good as possible by covering the face of the corpse with a washcloth soaked in baking soda to help preserve the color of the skin. They also had a folk custom of putting coins on the eyes to keep them shut. Helton's description of the traditions and rituals in early twentieth century rural Kentucky, where the body was handled by the family, and the entire community participated in the planning and the experience of the funeral, is in direct contrast with the experience of death in the U.S. today. Our impersonal and business-like approach to death has evolved to the point that we now have drive-through funeral homes.

The majority of deaths in the U.S. occur in hospitals or nursing homes; only about 20% of people die at home (Edmonson, 1997). The place of death tells us something about our attitudes and approaches to death. Death has become highly medicalized and professionalized. Sustaining life and preventing death for as long as possible is a hallmark of the tremendous advances in our medical technology. However, our success at prolonging life has been accompanied by a reluctance to deal with death as a physical reality, or as an ethical and emotional reality. The emergence of "end-of-life" ethical debates about euthanasia, physician-assisted suicide, and Dr. Jack Kevorkian's guilt or innocence reflects the fact that our technological ability to keep people alive has outpaced the development of clear societal values about humane death.

Just as we have come to rely on the medical system to prevent death, we have come to rely on other professionals to deal with death once it occurs. The funeral industry has become firmly established in the American way of death, offering products and services including funeral planning, casket selection, and body preparation. Turning these matters over to practitioners in the funeral industry is consistent with our professionalized and segregated approach to death.

Moller (1996) provides a thorough analysis of the ways in which social and historical context shape the rituals, meanings, and experiences of death. He argues that in the U.S., "the movement away from ritual and community to bureaucratic management and medical treatment of dying patients is consistent with broader patterns of social life" (Moller, 1996, p.25). Moller discusses how individualism, bureaucratization and technological approaches to problem solving characterize our culture's attitude toward death and mourning.

Similarly, our expectations that expressions of grief and mourning will be limited to a specific time and place reflect our societal emphasis on minimizing disruption and getting back to work. Many companies have policies about how long people can stay home from work and even what degree of relationship is required before any time off is allowed. We also have informal norms about appropriate expressions of grief and about how long people "should" be in mourning. When people return to work following the loss of a loved one, they are expected to control their emotions and get on with their lives. Crying and discussing the loss are not acceptable, except with those close to us. While we would be sympathetic if a colleague began to openly grieving during a meeting or a class, it would make most of us very uncomfortable.

These "rules" about how long grieving can legitimately go on, where and how it can happen, and who can legitimately grieve certainly reflect a unique set of cultural values. Doka (1989) offers the idea of "disenfranchised grief" to help us further understand the ways in which experiences surrounding death are socially constructed. He suggests that when "a person who experiences a sense of loss but does not have a socially recognized right, role, or capacity, that grief is disenfranchised" (Doka, 1989). Clearly, the lack of social support and the lack of opportunity to participate in sanctioned, open mourning will make this process much more difficult. The degree to which others acknowledge an individual's sense of loss is crucial. People who are in relationships that are not sanctioned, or in roles that are not clear, or in situations where the death is not recognized are likely to experience "disenfranchised grief." He suggests that when a person experiences a sense of loss but does not have a socially acknowledged role or relationship with the deceased, the "rights" to grief are not recognized and thus that the grief is disenfranchised (Doka, 1989). The legitimation of grief and mourning on the basis of sanctioned and recognized *personal* relationships to the deceased is another example of the individualism that marks our culture; clearly, death is not a collective or community experience in our society.

A sociological analysis of how societies define and deal with death in ways that are consistent with dominant values is not intended to negate the intensely personal and emotional nature of dealing with death. There is extensive literature in both academic journals and the popular press about how people experience and adapt to loss. One of the best known approaches to understanding death and dying is the work of Elizabeth Kübler-Ross who identified five stages that dying patients go through: denial, anger, bargaining, depression, and acceptance (Kübler-Ross, 1969). This model has also been applied to the experience of bereaved persons. Kübler-Ross developed her model out of her conversations

Exhibit 10.7   *A Model of Health Care Access, Behaviors, and Outcomes*

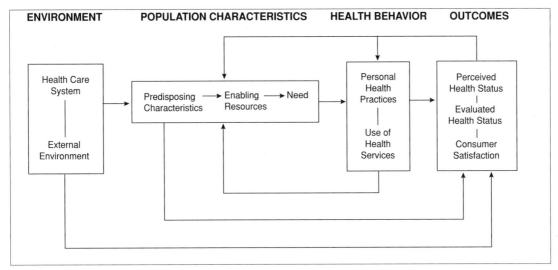

Source: Andersen, 1995. Reprinted with permission.

with dying people. Clearly the model has validity; it summarizes the experiences of many people, and helps both dying people and their loved ones to understand their own experiences. But Moller has critiqued Kübler-Ross' approach for implying that there is a universal trajectory through the phases. He finds the five stages imposing a singular therapeutic approach to this complex phenomenon, and reinforce the medically-based goals of managing the patient by helping them to move to acceptance as quickly as possible (Moller, 1996).

Perhaps in response to the imposition of single "right" ways to experience death and grief, and certainly in response to the over-medicalized, technological, impersonal and individualized way of death in the U.S. today, some countervailing trends are emerging. The growing visibility and popularity of hospice is probably the best example. Hospice emphasizes care-not-cure and uses liberal pain management to keep the person comfortable. The hospice model takes a holistic approach to the dying person and his/her family and loved ones, including everyone in the experience and knowing the dying person as a whole person, not just as a patient. In addition, the ongoing debates about euthanasia ("good death"), quality of life for the dying person, and control over the circumstances of one's own death suggest that we are trying to develop norms and values that will balance our awesome technological capacity to sustain life.

The Health Care System

We have been exploring the health status of older people; variations in health status according to gender, race, and social class; the factors that help to determine health status; and the social construction of illness and death. We have mentioned individual health-related behaviors such as help-seeking, lifestyle, and utilization of health care resources. Societal forces influence individual health-related behaviors. Social structures, processes of socialization, cultural values and preferences, and social institutions all play a role in individual behavior.

One of the most comprehensive and often-cited frameworks for understanding health behavior and outcomes is the Andersen model, which specifies these social influences on individual health behaviors. The most recent version, shown in Exhibit 10.7, is the result of several refinements and revisions by Andersen and his colleagues (see Andersen, 1995, for a discussion of the evolution of this model). Age, sex, and race are examples of predisposing characteristics that influence personal health practices, such as seeking health care and using preventive health care measures. Income and availability of insurance coverage are primary examples of enabling resources—factors that give an individual the economic freedom to seek health care. Our earlier discussion of race, sex, and income differences has verified that these characteristics do indeed have an impact on health status.

It is important to note in the Andersen model the primacy of the health care system. That system has a direct effect on the population characteristics that help shape health behaviors and outcomes. This effect is easiest to see in the case of the enabling resources. Compare a society that provides universal health care access to a country such as the United States, in which access to health care is based on the ability to pay, on having insurance coverage or enough money. Where access is based on ability to pay, some groups in society will not receive the same amount or kind of health care as those with the necessary economic resources. These disadvantaged groups will have lower levels of health care utilization and poorer health outcomes than groups with better access. Van der Maas (1988) discusses the public health implications of the impact of a health care system on population characteristics, health behaviors, and health outcomes. "Under the prevailing government policies, most Western societies tend to produce increasing social inequalities, including access to health care. These developments may lead to a further increase in the health gap between high and low socioeconomic strata, and this may in turn seriously limit our efforts to improve general health levels and longevity" (p. 111).

The way our health care system operates—who has access to health care, under what conditions—has a very powerful influence on the health status of older individuals. The U.S. health care system has been characterized as "high tech, limited access" (Lassey, Lassey, and Jinks, 1997). This means that those who have access have very good, technologically advanced care, while those lacking insurance or financial resources experience serious gaps in health care. These and other features of our health care system are shaped by social forces including politics, ideology about access to care, and the economy. In this section we examine more closely the U.S. health care system for older people. We will review the way in which health care is financed and delivered, including the emergence of managed care, and the special challenges of providing long-term care for an aging population.

An Overview of the U.S. Health Care System

Health care is a fast-growing segment of the U.S. economy. We spend a lot of money on health care. In a comparison of the percentage of gross domestic product (GDP) spent on health care in thirteen countries, the United States ranked first. In 1994, the United States spent 13.6 percent of its GDP for health care, and had the highest rate of per capita health care expenses (Lassey et al., 1997). A number of factors help to explain this rank, including our high-technology system and our aging population. Our cultural preferences are also expensive. We tend to prefer the most technologically advanced care, the "best" care, which is often also the most expensive. Our medical model approach emphasizes solving health problems after they occur, which is more expensive in the long run than preventative care. Our health insurance organizations have relatively high administrative costs for providing insurance and managing health services, and the fee-for-service reimbursement system our insurers use costs more overall.

In **fee-for-service** (FFS) systems of care, doctors, hospitals, and other health care providers are reimbursed for all of the services they provide; the more they do, the more they are reimbursed. Since we tend to value the idea that everything medically possible is being done for us, our expectations as health care consumers help to reinforce the financial incentive for providers to do as much as possible. Our health care costs are spiraling upward on a cycle of fee-for-service reimbursement, technological advances, and demands for the best possible treatment. Such a system encourages innovation, encourages consumer demand for high-tech services, and encourages providers to deliver costly services. The fee-for-service model is gradually being replaced by a prospective payment system, which encourages more limited use of health care resources, especially expensive, high-technology care.

The high-tech, limited-access, medical-model-dominated system of health care in the United States is quite a poor fit to the needs of the older population. The most common conditions that older people have do not lend themselves to high-tech cures or to cures at all, for that matter. The surgical or chemical treatments that are the foundation of our approach to "fixing" health problems simply are not appropriate for ongoing, chronic conditions such as diabetes, arthritis, and heart disease. A system of care that is especially responsive to the health situation of older people would focus on the broader definitions of health, not just the absence of disease. Managing rather than curing a condition, and maintaining or enhancing an individual's ability to function in everyday life, would be the major goals of a health care system matched to the needs of the older population. Instead, we have a system that is oriented toward "curing" illnesses, that is biased toward care provided in institutions such as hospitals and nursing homes, and that is financed in a very fragmented and uneven fashion.

Financing and Delivery of Health Care for Older Americans

In the past several decades there has been a significant change in funding for health care for older Americans. In 1960, the system relied mostly on direct patient out-of-pocket payments. In 1960, just before Medicare legislation was passed, 55 percent of health care costs were paid out-of-pocket, compared to only 23 percent in 1992 (HCFA, 1992). Now the system relies heavily on third-party private and government insurance programs. That transition occurred largely because of two important public policies for the financing of health care: Medicare and Medicaid. In 1992, those two government programs accounted for 35.7 percent of all personal health care expenditures, compared to only 19 percent in 1970 (HCFA, 1992).

Medicare

Medicare is federal health insurance for people 65 and older (and for some younger disabled people). The legislation establishing Medicare passed in 1965, after decades of debate and concerns over whether it was the beginning of the slippery slope toward "socialized medicine." Medicare is virtually universal for the older population, about 97 percent of whom are covered.

Medicare has two sections: Part A and Part B. Part A, sometimes called hospital insurance, covers room, board, and nursing services in the hospital. It also covers up to 100 days of skilled nursing home care in a Medicare-approved facility, provided that certain conditions (such as a three-day prior stay in a hospital) are met. Part A also covers hospice services and, to a very limited extent, some home health care. There are copayments (a certain percentage that the insured must pay) and deductibles (an amount that the insured must pay before

Many older adults with serious health problems continue to live in the community with assistance from some combination of kin, friends, and formal services.

Medicare pays any part of the charges). The yearly deductible for hospitalization is $776 in 2000 (HCFA, 2000).

Part B, sometimes called supplementary medical insurance, covers doctors' fees, outpatient hospital treatment, lab services, and some limited home health care. For doctors' fees and special therapies, there is a deductible ($100 in 2000); Medicare then pays 80 percent of an approved amount. Part B is optional and carries with it a monthly premium. In 2000, the cost to the consumer was $45 a month (HCFA, 2000).

Major successes of the program have included increased access to high-quality medical care, equality of treatment, and high levels of satisfaction reported by beneficiaries (Lave, 1996). The major problem with Medicare is the cost of the program. In 1992, Medicare program payments totaled more than $120 billion (HCFA, 1992). Medicare consumed 13 percent of the federal budget in 1995, and is projected to take up 16 percent of the federal budget in the year 2000 (Lave, 1996). More important, the Medicare trust fund (the fund in which tax dollars accumulate to pay the bill for the Medicare program) currently faces short-term and long-term financial problems.

Other problems with Medicare include its acute-care focus and the lack of coverage for long-term care and for home care. In addition, the copayments, deductibles, and gaps in Medicare coverage mean that many older people need to purchase gap-filler insurance. In 1996, almost 70 percent of older people had some form of private insurance: either gap-filler insurance that they purchased themselves or employer-sponsored insurance (AARP, 1996). While Medicare is a very significant benefit to older people, rising health care costs and gaps in coverage mean that individuals have higher out-of-pocket costs today than before Medicare existed. In addition, the program covers primarily acute care, not long-term care, which is the greatest health care need of the older population in general.

Medicaid

Originally conceived as insurance for the acute health care needs of welfare recipients, Medicaid now plays a crucial role in financing health care for older people. Funded by states and the federal government, and administered by the states, **Medicaid** is the primary health insurance program for low-income individuals and families. Medicaid has always been available for low-income older people, but over the past few decades two important shifts have taken place. First, an increasing proportion of Medicaid expenditures have gone for health care for older people. Second an increasing proportion of those expenditures for older people have gone to long-term care instead of acute care. In 1993, older people represented 12 percent of the Medicaid beneficiary population, but 28 percent of Medicaid expenditures went to services for older people. Medicaid benefits for older people were spent as follows in 1993: 62 percent for nursing home care, 18 percent for acute-care benefits, 12 percent for community-based long-term care (long-term care provided in the community rather than in nursing homes), and 8 percent for Medicare payments (funding the Part B premium for poor Medicare recipients) (Lyons, Rowland, and Hanson, 1996).

How did this shift occur so that Medicaid is now a major payer of institution-based long-term care for older people? From the beginning, Medicaid coverage included nursing facility services. Older people who needed fairly extensive assistance with activities of daily living resorted to Medicaid-financed nursing-home placement because they lacked other options. Most people with long-term care needs do not have the financial resources to stay at home, paying for long-term services out of their own pockets, for very long. Since Medicaid originally covered long-term care only in institutions, older people who came to the end of their own and their families' financial resources often faced the dilemma of not being able to afford home care and not having access to government assistance unless they went to a nursing home.

For decades Medicaid provided almost no financing of community-based services. That situation is changing, with the proliferation of **Medicaid waiver programs**. These programs allow states the option to waive certain restrictions that typically would apply to the delivery of services. Specifically, the waiver programs allow Medicaid dollars to be spent on home and community-based care, rather than institution-based (nursing home) care, for older people who qualify for Medicaid and who are impaired enough to be eligible for nursing-home placement. Since average nursing homes cost about $3,000 per month, and community-based services less than one-fourth of that, the waiver programs are seen as a potential source of cost savings. In addition, most people prefer to receive long-term care services in their own homes, rather than in institutions (Kane, Kane, and Ladd, 1998).

The potential for home and community-based care to save money is of great interest to state and federal agencies. Since states and the federal government jointly fund Medicaid, there is great concern at many levels about the growth of the Medicaid budget. In 1980, Medicaid state and federal spending totaled about $25.5 billion; by 1992, the total was $120.2 billion. Between 1990 and 1992, Medicaid's annual expenditure growth rate jumped to about 28 percent, significantly higher than growth rates for Medicare and private insurance (Tudor, 1995).

In summary, Medicare and Medicaid provide the foundation for the financing of health care for older Americans. Because of the restrictions on what these programs will pay for, they also play an important role in shaping the delivery of health care for older adults. The acute-care and institutional bias in these programs has helped to produce a delivery system that is not particularly responsive to the needs or preferences of the older population. The emergence of Medicaid waiver programs signals a significant attempt to restructure the financing and delivery of some health care services to better fit the demands of our aging population.

Managed Care

No doubt you have heard about and read about **managed care**. This new approach to the provision of health care is being implemented for all age groups, including older adults. Managed care is very different from the traditional fee-for-service (FFS) model for the financing and delivery of health care. Under fee-for-service, physicians make health care decisions; the insurer is billed for the diagnostic procedures, preventive or maintenance services, and treatments the physician has provided to the client. Financing and decisions about the delivery of health care are kept separate in this model. In managed care, financing and delivery are linked. A single organization, which employs physicians and other health care professionals, takes on both financial and clinical decision making and risks. For Medicare recipients who choose to enroll in managed care, the managed care organization, sometimes called a **health maintenance organization** or **HMO** receives a predetermined monthly amount to provide that care (the capitation amount). If the client receives no services that month, or if the client receives extensive services that month, the HMO still gets the same flat fee for that client.

The implications of this approach for quality of care for older (and younger) people are the cause of some concern. There is an obvious incentive to do less, while in a fee-for-service system there is an incentive to do more. Under managed care, the same organization that pays for your care also employs the doctor who decides about your care. While your physician's code of ethics and standards for professional practice still dictates that she do what is best for you, there are new constraints on the decision-making processes.

The challenge for an HMO is to balance quality of care with cost controls. Two major features of managed care are designed to look after that balance: gatekeeping and quality review. **Gatekeeping** is the process whereby a primary care physician coordinates the care a client will receive, providing some of that care and authorizing additional services according to the guidelines of the HMO. The role of the gatekeeper is to provide necessary care at the lowest cost, and to avoid providing unnecessary care. **Quality review** is a process that monitors the adequacy of care provided under an HMO; information from client satisfaction surveys, complaints, and data on the health outcomes for managed care clients form the basis for quality review.

Older Americans are signing up for managed care in increasing numbers. In 1992, only 6.2 percent of Medicare recipients were enrolled in managed care organizations; by 1996, that proportion had increased to 11.5 percent (HCFA, 1992; AARP, 1996). Why would an older person choose to join an HMO, with its built-in incentives to restrict services? The primary advantage of Medicare managed care is that it does away with the need for gap-filler insurance, with very low or no premiums and significantly expanded benefits. For example, prescription drugs are not covered under Medicare, but most managed care organizations do provide such a benefit. The major disadvantages are the loss of choice and control over which physicians and which specialized services a client can seek, and the concern about the incentives to limit the kind and extent of care provided.

How do older people fare under managed care in comparison to traditional fee-for-service Medicare programs? To answer this crucial question effectively, we would need to be able to compare people with the exact same health conditions receiving care under the two different models. Such outcome studies are just beginning to emerge, so the evidence is not complete by any means. So far, there is little evidence of a difference in the health status of HMO versus FFS clients. However, one recent study (Ware, Bayliss, Agers and Kosinski, 1996) found that 68 percent of HMO patients who were both poor and elderly experienced a decline in health over the four-year study period, compared to only 27 percent of similar patients enrolled in FFS.

Whether managed care will be an effective and appropriate means of providing high-quality health care to the older population remains to be seen. The terrain is rapidly shifting at the time of this writing. Even though more older people are signing up for these programs, Medicare managed care organizations continue to pull out of markets because of financial difficulty. Several medicare managed care programs are dropping pharmaceutical coverage, one of the benefits that is most attractive to older consumers.

Long-Term Care for Older Americans

One of the most important issues in thinking about health care for older people is long-term care. **Long-term care** is the system of services provided to people with functional limitations to enable them to function as independently as possible. It is fundamentally different from acute care in its focus. Rather than curing illnesses, long-term care is focused on managing chronic conditions and maximizing functioning. As you have seen at various points in our preceding discussion of the financing and delivery of health care, we do not have a very coherent long-term care system. Where and how care should be delivered (in nursing homes or in the community, by family members or by paid professionals) and how the government should finance it by individuals and their families, or by some combination) are questions on which we have no agreement. These issues have numerous political and ideological overtones. Long-term care is provided in different settings, sometimes by paid formal caregivers, sometimes by unpaid family members and friends. The economic value of the care that is donated by family and friends has been estimated to be between $45 billion and $94 billion. This range of figures certainly challenges us to think about how we think long-term care should be provided and paid for. Clearly "donated" care is an economic, social, and personal foundation for the current system.

Medicare pays for a small amount of long-term care. Medicaid pays for a large portion of institutional care for older people who are poor, or who become poor after they have used up their existing financial resources. Medicaid pays for a small (but growing) portion of home care, for people who are poor enough to qualify. Through Medicare and Medicaid, the federal government is the largest purchaser of long-term care is the federal government. In 1995, these programs paid about 56% of the long-term care bill for older people, amounting to just over $50 billion (Congressional Budget Office, 1999).

Our current system of care does not reflect a carefully crafted vision and plan for the provision of long-term services. Rather, it is a "paradigm by default . . . it arose out of unintended consequences, short-term solutions, and unexamined discrepancies between societal values and common practices" (Applebaum and Kunkel, 1995, p. 28). Medicaid has become a major payer of long-term care in nursing homes, not because that was the original intent of the legislation, but because it could be made to fit the growing need for financing long-term care. Most older people prefer to remain in their own homes, but our current government financing system strongly supports nursing-home care. The emergence of new options for long-term care is a harbinger of change in our long-term care system. There is now government-financed community-based long-term care. A radical departure from the old model is the development of assisted living, specially designed congregate housing units that maximize privacy and independence while efficiently providing needed long-term care services. Currently most assisted living is paid for privately, and thus restricted to those with higher incomes. We have a long way to go, with significant societal values to be clarified and major policy decisions to be ironed out.

Summary

Throughout this chapter we have considered how the health status of older people is a product of lifelong forces, including behaviors, lifestyles, and access to a particular kind of health care system. We have implicitly and explicitly explored the social construction of health, the ways in which health and illness are produced by social arrangements. These social arrangements include gender socialization and socioeconomic variations in access to health care.

The way we think about and describe health and the ways we finance and deliver health care are clear reflections of the medical model. We define, describe, diagnose, and treat conditions. Private and public insurance pay primarily for these efforts to solve the problems of ill health, not for maintaining and enhancing physical, psychological, and social well-being. In the future, our society needs to clarify whether our definition of health is the absence of illness or is a positive state of well-being. Once we have clarified what we mean by health, we can align our financing and delivery of services with that definition.

The medical model has given rise to a system of health care not well suited to the needs of an aging population; it emphasizes acute care when the greatest need among older people is for long-term care for chronic health problems and functional limitations. The financing of health care for older people is fragmented, uneven, and biased toward care provided in an institution, rather than in the community or in people's homes.

Another ideological challenge facing our society in the very near future is coming to terms with the question of whether health care is a right of citizenship (much as education and clean drinking water are) or a privilege (tied primarily to employment). Approximately 40 million Americans currently have no health coverage; apparently we consider health care a privilege rather than a universal right. Concerns about how to design, finance, and provide health care to our older population are part of these larger societal issues.

Even if we can agree that a coherently financed, integrated, and accessible system of health care is our goal, the fundamental problem of how to pay for it remains. The cost of providing health care to an aging population has proved to be an enormous stumbling block in moving toward a better-designed system of care. The large portion of the federal budget currently spent on Medicare is the starting point for projections of an untenable financial burden posed by health care costs of the baby boom generation. However, you should use a critical eye in considering the problems in our health care system and their potential solutions. Certainly the increasing numbers of older people play a part in increasing health care costs to the nation. But the fees charged for health care services have increased also. Blaming older people for rising health care costs is an example of what Robertson (1991) calls **apocalyptic demography,** "the social construction of catastrophe by suggesting that an increasing aging population will place unbearable demands on the health care system" (p. 144). Robertson goes on to suggest that the health care system focuses on the aging population as a growth market and responds by medicalizing many aspects of aging: "creating" diseases, offering treatments for them, and receiving reimbursement for providing those services. The process of providers inducing increased demand for health care services for older people may play a more significant role in increased health care costs than the size of the older population. Certainly the ubiquity of Rogaine commercials, and the instant demand for Viagra when it hit the market, suggests that induced demand is a reality. If that is the case, the solution to the crisis in health care financing may lie in reconsidering what aspects of aging really require medical treatment and limiting the fees charged for health care services.

The crisis in financing is one of the major issues facing our health care system. The resolution of this crisis will depend on our basic values about who has access to health care and who is responsible to provide it. The importance we place on individual responsibility, self-reliance, and independence has stood in the way of major health care reform. Government responsibility is sometimes seen as damaging to private initiative, family responsibility, and independence. However, our current fragmented and underfinanced system of long-term care for older adults is a good example of the need for a system with more integrity. Difficult decisions face us in the very near future, as we prepare for the aging of the baby boomers.

Web Wise

National Center for Health Statistics

http://www.cdc.gov/nchswww/

The National Center for Health Statistics (NCHS) is a part of the Centers for Disease Control and Prevention, United States Department of Health and Human Services. This web site provides background information about NCHS, their products (publications and catalogs), current health-related news releases, and answers to frequently asked health-related questions. Information on NCHS data systems and national health surveys are offered. This site also presents various vital and health statistics, organized in tables from their warehouse. In addition, an opportunity to search chosen topics (older adults) as well as a list of other sites for health-related information and resources are available.

Vital and Health Statistics: Trends in the Health of Older Americans;

Analytic and Epidemiological Studies

http://www.aoa.dhhs.gov/aoa/stats/agetrend/ageguide.html

This site, prepared by R. A. Cohen and J. F. Van Nostrand, includes seventy-one tables presenting data regarding health status patterns as well as determinants of health status of older adults. Specifically, data include hospital and nursing home stays, trends in long-term care, national health expenditures, and the annual rate of selected respondent-reported impairments and chronic conditions by race, age and type of impairment: United States, selected years. The data are provided by the Administration on Aging and is available to the public in two fashions: twelve of the tables are provided in table format for immediate viewing, and all seventy-one are downloadable as *.wk1 spreadsheet files.

Profile of Older Americans: 1999

http://www.aoa.dhhs.gov/aoa/stats/profile/#health

This site, prepared by the Administration on Aging, U.S. Department of Health and Human Services, and the American Association of Retired Persons' Program Resources Department, provides a comprehensive description of older persons. This site offers statistical information on health status and health care trends of older persons. Specifically, data regarding assistance with activities of daily living, most frequently occurring conditions per 100 elderly, and health expenditures for older persons are presented.

Health Care Financing Administration

http://www.hcfa.gov/

The Health Care Financing Administration (HCFA) is the federal agency that governs the Medicare and Medicaid health care programs. Their site provides a description of the agency, information for consumers and professionals on

Medicare and Medicaid, and managed care plans related to both programs. Data on national health care expenditures, individuals covered by Medicare and Medicaid, and health care service utilization are also provided. Easy navigation to each option and other government links is also offered.

Columbia/HCA Health Care Corporation: Mental Illness in the Elderly
http://www.columbia.net/consumer/datafile/menteld.html

This site was prepared by psychiatrist Robert V. Blanche, M.D., and provides information on mental illness in the older population. The site includes a brief discussion of the barriers on assisting older persons with psychiatric illnesses, and offers information on depression, manic depression, dementia, anxiety disorders, and specialized treatment for older adults.

HRS/AHEAD Studies
http://www.umich.edu/~hrswww/

Please see the Chapter Two Web Wise segment for a summary description.

Community Health Status Indicators
http://www.communityhealth.hrsa.gov

This site, funded the federal government's Health Resources and Services Administration, provides data on demographic, health, and economic characteristics of every county in the U.S., and some comparative information with "peer" counties.

Key Terms

apocalyptic demography
biopsychosocial model of health
dementia
doctrine of specific etiology
fee-for-service
functional ability or limitation
gatekeeping
health
health maintenance
    organization (HMO)
long-term care

managed care
Medicaid
Medicaid waiver program
medical model
medicalization
Medicare
mind-body dualism
prevalence rates
quality review
reductionism
self-assessed health

Questions for Thought and Reflection

1. Consider the ways in which individual choice and behaviors affect health, and the ways in which social and cultural conditions play a role. Can you give an example of individual health behaviors that are not influenced by social and cultural factors?

2. Picture two older people whom you know, one who is very healthy and active and one who is in poor health and frail. In what other ways are they different? What social conditions, individual choices, and random events helped to create their health situation?

3. What is your definition of health? Do the policies and practices of our health care system reflect or deviate from your definition?

4. What do you think are the most important health policy issues facing our aging nation? What are the most important issues for older people's lives? What are the most challenging to the health care system?

The Flowering of Gray Power? Political Activism and the Baby Boomers

Nostalgia about the baby boomers often includes a healthy dose of reminiscence about the days of "flower power," free love, Woodstock, use of mind-altering drugs, cultural "be-ins" emphasizing self-expression, and lifestyles including communal living and rejection of consumerism and property. This period also contained a lot of distinctly political activity, including anti-war marches, sit-ins, and efforts to disrupt the military draft, the Vietnam war, and the major parties' political conventions. The events of the 1960s occurred during the formative years of some "boomers" and may have generated attitudes about politics and government that remain significant in shaping their outlooks today, and the ways in which they will act as older citizens and voters. A hallmark of the baby boomer cohorts is the diversity of their members (the oldest now in their mid-50s and the youngest in their 30s) (Williamson 1998).

Separating Myth from Reality

First, nostalgia must be put in its place. Keep in mind that many baby boomers, born over an 18-year span (1946–1964), were much too young to have attended the original Woodstock or to have participated in protests against the Vietnam War. The youngest boomers, still in their 30s in the year 2000, were young children when these events took place. Second, even among those whose ages "fit" these events, only a very small percentage of the baby boomers were actively involved in any of the political or cultural trends described above. Like recent demonstrations by students against the World Trade Organization and World bank and foreign sweatshops producing collegiate sportswear, only a very small subset of these cohorts were political or cultural activists. Most boomers completed school without interruption (from "dropping out, or a stint in jail, Canada, or a commune); married; became parents; and held steady jobs (Williamson 1998). Nonetheless, the efforts of an activist subset of baby boomers made an indelible impression on the historical memory of Americans, since it was the first time that such massive protests against the status quo had been shared widely through television images and news reports. Williamson and others argue that we err in lumping all baby boomers together, since the experiences of the earliest cohorts (1946-1954) are quite different from later boomers (1955-64). The later boomers were too young for the 60s and faced a much less favorable economy as they matured (1998).

A Political Force Waiting to Burst Forth?

Will the experiences of a subset of baby boomers, or our culture's memory of it, prompt unprecedented senior activism once these cohorts are liberated from family responsibilities and the time demands of their employment? Are we about to unleash the most politically active—and some would say liberal and anti-establishment—generation of seniors ever (Alwin 1998)? The threat of a new round of marches on Washington (to support Social Security, protect the environment, expand gender equity or add prescription drug coverage to Medicare) can seem daunting to politicians, who are already cautious about the senior vote. Is it possible that the "activist" character of the baby boomers will carry through to later life, or might they follow the more conventional political behaviors of their predecessors (i.e, voting regularly, keeping informed about issues and candidates)?

Baby boom cohorts have thus far largely followed the path of other cohorts in terms of low voting participation in youth, which grew as these cohorts matured (Alwin, 1998). Fewer of the baby boomers have identified with a major political party than was the case for earlier cohorts, perhaps reflecting some residue of the anti-establishment culture or the Watergate scandal that marked their youth (Alwin, 1998). Beginning in the 1980s, as the overall political climate became more conservative in the U.S., some baby boomers did as well. More registered as Republicans and supported conservative political viewpoints, but the ranks of "Independents" among Boomers still exceed preceding cohorts, and distrust of government institutions has persisted among them (Alwin 1998). Alwin concludes that, while the liberal effect of the baby boom may yet be felt in politics, it may be a mistake to assume that, as they age, these large cohorts will move the political landscape in a dramatically more liberal or unconventional direction.

Brave New Whirl   by Scott-Allen Pierson

Participation in the more "activist" forms of political involvement, such as protest marches, has seemed to decline with age for other cohorts. But recent "adult" marches in Washington (e.g., the "Million Man" and "Million Mom" marches as well as many others) would suggest caution in a conclusion that it will always be so. Other forms of activism, such as learning about candidates and issues, working in campaigns, and writing to elected officials, are very common among older adults today and may be so in the future. Boomers will doubtless use new technologies, such as e-mail and the internet, to make their voices heard and to interact with others sharing common causes and political goals (see Williamson, 1998).

The sheer numbers of baby boomers presage the largest senior vote potential ever, with estimates running from one fourth to over one third of votes cast coming from 65+ voters in 2035 (Binstock, 2000). But it remains unclear whether voting will reflect age-based issues (Alwin, 1997; Binstock, 2000). Thus far, we have not seen older people voting as a monolithic bloc. Lifetime identification with a political party, gender, race, and social class are far better predictors of political opinions than is age.

The large size of the baby boom cohorts does provide a lot of potential for activism, even if only the small percentage of former activists become re-energized in later life to work for political change. The Boomer cohorts will also be different from their predecessors in terms of resources, being more educated and probably healthier, and having longer active life expectancy to do something, including political activism.

A major "wild card" in this formula is retirement. The presumption of baby boomer activism is predicated on having some discretionary time in retirement to accomplish activist goals. If, as the labor market and retirement financial systems evolve, more older adults continue or return to work, the time and energy the baby boomers have for activism would largely be absorbed. A second wild card is the overall political climate and the extent to which political activism ignites people, old and young, to protest, campaign, or vote. While some issues might resonate only with particular age groups, others may see a broad spectrum of ages, working together inside or beyond the borders of the political institutions, to bring about desired results. Whether it is pornography, genetically engineered foods, guns, the death penalty, the environment, the role of the federal government, local school bond referenda, rights for various groups in society, or other emergent issues, the potential for activism and political force among baby boomers will be worth watching!

Questions for discussion and review

1. Do you consider the argument that early life events, such as those experienced by some in the baby boomer cohorts, influence a cohort's later life behaviors realistic? Why or why not?

2. Speculate on how the birth cohorts "coming of age" during political conservative trend led by Ronald Reagan in the 1980s will differ from their baby boomer predecessors in terms of political activities as they age

CHAPTER 11

Politics, Government, and the Welfare State

"Public policy reflects and reinforces the 'life chances' associated with each person's social location within the class, status, and political structures that comprise society. The lives of each succeeding generation are similarly shaped by the extent to which social policy maintains or redistributes those life chances" (Estes, 1991, p. 20).

In the realm of politics, members of the older population are both participants in and the subject of debate. The roles of older persons in politics extend from being voters and advocates for programs such as Medicare and Social Security to holding high electoral office. As a subject of political debate, the aging of the population focuses our attention on the social ties among age cohorts as well as the interests that divide them. We have already begun to discuss the debates surrounding social policies having to do with health care, retirement, and income maintenance. Here we continue and expand those discussions, focusing more directly on politics and the place of the older population in the political system.

Age-Based Government Policies

The Old-Age Welfare State

For the vast stretch of recorded history, older people (in relatively small numbers) were the responsibility of their families or themselves. Governments took no special note of the elderly, often grouping the disadvantaged, frail, or ill among them with disadvantaged individuals of other ages (Quadagno, 1982). Only in the last century have governments assumed any specific responsibility toward their older citizens by developing programs and laws focusing on the older age group. During the same time period, old age has been identified as a unique and distinctive time of life, deserving of special attention and assistance.

Robert Binstock describes American public policy from the 1930s through the 1970s as **compassionate ageism**. By ageism Binstock means "the attribution of the same characteristics, status, and just desserts to a heterogeneous group that has been artificially homogenized, packaged, labeled, and marked as 'the aged' " (1991a, p. 326). Compassionate ageism stereotyped older people as poor, lonely, neglected, in ill health, and inadequately housed. Although founded on stereotypes, Binstock and others argue that the approach was compassionate, intended to help those "deserving and needy" older people who were unable to provide adequately for themselves (Binstock, 1991b; Quadagno, 1982). These stereotypes set the stage for policymakers to clump older persons together and to develop income, housing, and health policies to remedy their collective plight (Jacobs, 1990). Thus, governments in the United States and in many other nations developed a set of programs and policies to address the problems that were believed to afflict most elderly persons in their societies. Political support for these programs was based on two premises: that the problems of the old were not their fault and that they followed years of contribution to society. These societies thus accepted the responsibility to provide help collectively, rather than to rely on individuals or their families to meet all needs (Binstock, 1991a). Exhibit 11.1 outlines the timing of selected social policy developments in the United States, with those during the era of compassionate ageism shaded.

Because they have defined the aged as a distinct and especially deserving population, proponents of compassionate ageism have made public policies that would otherwise have faced potent political opposition. For example, despite vigorous resistance in the United States to any national health insurance program for several decades, in the middle 1960s Congress passed Medicare, a national health insurance targeted to the elderly. Programs and services for the elderly proliferated from the 1930s through the 1960s, and the popularity of helping the elderly rated alongside "Mom and apple pie" or "old-fashioned family values" as campaign issues (Hudson, 1978).

Initiatives to assist older adults saw a peak of activity in the 1960s as part of Lyndon B. Johnson's Great Society (Estes, 1979). The deservedness of the older population, including its high levels of documented poverty, poor health and inadequate housing, was unquestioned, and programs expanded rapidly (Binstock, 1991b). Legislation passed during that era, on both the federal and state levels, led to a wide array of government programs, services, and agencies organized to assist older persons. This system of government programs has been called the **old-age welfare state** (Binstock, 1991a; Myles, 1983). The old-age welfare state of the 1960s had a clear purpose: to ameliorate the serious problems common in the older adult population at that time.

Although we can think about this network of programs as a whole, its development was fragmented, leading to gaps and overlaps. Programs were established on a piecemeal basis, with no single agency, level of government, or group responsible for the well-being of the older population. "Existing social policies for older people include a vast array of fragmented, complicated but important agencies, services and benefits" (Torres-Gil, 1992, p. 37). "The system involves a myriad of administrative autonomies, each with jurisdiction and authority over specific programs and funds. Often, one agency knows nothing of what the others are doing. No single, overarching policy or agency wields responsibility for coordinating services or developing policy direction" (Torres-Gil, 1992, p. 58).

In fact, Torres-Gil (1992) reports that there are programs related to the older population under the auspices of virtually every one of the cabinet agencies

Exhibit 11.1 *Time Line of Selected U.S. Social Policy Developments in Aging*

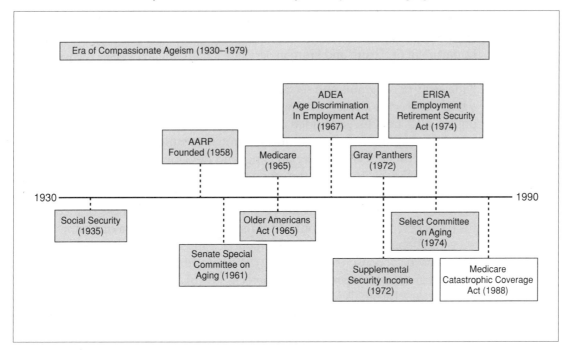

serving the President. The largest concentration of programs is under the Department of Health and Human Services, including Social Security, Medicare, the Administration on Aging, and the National Institutes of Health (Torres-Gil, 1992). The largest program in terms of dollars of assistance each year is Social Security, which provides benefits to the vast majority of people over 65 and many under 65 (Friedland and Summer, 1999). Social Security, Medicare, and Medicaid together account for 40% of all dollars expended in the 1998 federal budget (Friedland and Summer, 1999). Each of these programs is described in more detail in other chapters.

Congress has also expressed its interest in addressing the problems of older people, establishing committees in both the Senate (1961) and the House of Representatives (1974) to hold hearings and develop recommendations to their respective houses of Congress (Congressional Quarterly, 1993). These committees have served as a focal point for discussion of issues that might otherwise get lost in the myriad congressional committees. The House, during its reorganization of committees and in an effort to cut down its operating costs, disbanded the Select Committee on Aging of the House of Representatives in 1993 (Cooper, 1993). It remains unclear whether other committees of the House have taken up the slack and continued attention to issues specifically identified with the older population.

The Older Americans Act

The **Older Americans Act**, intended to serve as the focal point of federal government policy on aging, gave the Administration on Aging, a unit of the Department of Health and Human Services, a mandate to oversee the well-being of older adults (Torres-Gil, 1992). The Older Americans Act (OAA) created a wide array of programs and services intended to enhance the well-being of older adults, defined as anyone over age 60 (Binstock, 1991b). Passed with broad support in 1965, the OAA provided a mandate for the government to deal with the pressing problems of older adults: enhancing employment options, improving long-term care, improving housing, and developing coordinated, comprehensive services to meet the needs of older adults with dependencies (McConnell and Beitler, 1991). The OAA, as an age entitlement, was initially designed to assist all Americans aged 60 and older, regardless of income status (Binstock, 1991a). The context for its passage was the era of compassionate ageism, a booming economy in which public funds seemed plentiful, and a high degree of social consensus regarding the desirability of solving social problems through government programs (Binstock, 1991b).

Although the goals were lofty, the funding has never been sufficient to meet the goals and needs outlined in the OAA (Binstock, 1991b). Through out the existence of OAA, a limited staff and budget have hindered its programs (Estes, 1979; Torres-Gil, 1992). Congress expanded minimal initial funding for OAA in the early years, mostly as additional program responsibilities were added, but the OAA budget has shrunk since 1981 (Binstock, 1991b). Nonetheless, advocates such as Robert Binstock suggest that the Older Americans Act has had some successes.

> "Its accomplishments, at the least, include (1) continuous and dynamic identification of needs of older persons; (2) creation and exemplification of strategies, programs, and services for meeting those needs; (3) provision of tangible and intangible help to innumerable older Americans; (4) development of a nationwide infrastructure for helping older persons, comprising 57 State Units on Aging, 670 Area Agencies on Aging, and about 25,000 associated service-providing agencies; and (5) recruitment and socialization of thousands of career professionals to the field of aging." (Binstock, 1991b, p. 11)

The programs offered under the auspices of the OAA include senior citizen centers, nutrition programs, employment training initiatives, and a network of local and state agencies providing and coordinating services and specific programs that today target the neediest individuals among those over 60. Successive commissioners of the Administration on Aging, faced with inadequate resources to meet the lofty goals of the legislation, have selected priorities for special attention during their administrations (Binstock, 1991b). The legislation and priorities under the OAA have thus shifted over time (Estes, 1979; Quirk, 1991). In the past decade, the OAA has moved significantly toward targeting those in greatest need, low income, frail, and minority elders, rather than ben-efiting all older adults equally. This shift mirrors an important and pervasive debate in today's public policy arena regarding age versus need as a basis for entitlements. We discuss this debate in a later section of this chapter.

In addition, the Older Americans Act has faced considerable uncertainty throughout most of the 1990s. President Clinton elevated the head of the Admin-istration on Aging to the level of Assistant Secretary of the Department of Health and Human Services as part of an overall goal of consolidating programs and services for older adults in this huge governmental agency, enhancing the fed-eral government's visibility (Torres-Gil, 1998). However, providing services at the state and local levels, the model utilized by the Administration on Aging, was viewed as preferable by many conservative politicians (Torres-Gil, 1998). During this tug-of-war between federal and state/local roles, the legislation authorizing Administration on Aging and its services has not been approved by Congress since 1992. Although AoA continues to provide services, the OAA operates in a legislative limbo, without guidelines and with limited funding to meet its extensive original mandate.

The Aging Enterprise

Some have criticized the development of initiatives to assist older persons. Estes (1979) has pointed out that programs and services for older persons can have some unanticipated consequences. The policies and programs established to ameliorate the problems of older adults have generated a system of agencies, service providers, and professionals. Estes calls them the **aging enterprise,** "the congeries of programs, organizations, bureaucracies, interest groups, trade asso-ciations, providers, industries, and professionals that serve the aged in one capacity or another" (p. 2). Estes includes both government and private organ-izations, most of which have grown up since the introduction of major aging legislation in the 1960s, especially Medicare and the Older Americans Act. Over time, Estes argues, the aging enterprise has become a force in itself, with a vest-ed interest in sustaining the dependency of the older population and substan-tial influence on how policies are implemented at the ground level. The aging enterprise has interests of its own and does not always work to the benefit of older people. According to Estes, "the age segregated policies that fuel the aging enterprise are socially divisive 'solutions' that single out, stigmatize, and iso-late the aged from the rest of society" (1979, p. 2). She argues that the programs themselves and by extension the people who implement them reinforce stereo-typic views of older people, create dependency, and sustain a myopic "social problems" approach to dealing with what is now a highly diverse population.

Many experts are now questioning the viability of the old-age welfare state, as political ideologies have shifted and legislative control has moved into the hands of more conservative politicians (Binstock, 1991a; Cole, 1995). The polit-ical process will determine whether these programs and policies will survive with limited funding, be modified in their functions and goals, or be eliminated entirely. Recent battles over the Older Americans Act are symptomatic of this tension, as are general debates over age or need entitlement for governmental benefits.

Age and Need Entitlements

Most programs developed during the era of compassionate ageism share a basis in **age entitlement**. With age entitlement, individuals become eligible for assistance or participation in a program on the basis of chronological age. Usually the legislation includes age limits, such as the 40-70 age range in the Age Discrimination in Employment Act or the age 65 minimum currently in force for Medicare benefits (Quadagno, 1996). Age entitlement provisions are usually set up so that most individuals are eligible for assistance, with only proof of age required. Age entitlement programs are fairly simple to administer, because most people can establish their ages relatively easily.

Since their establishment, age entitlement programs have had two, somewhat contradictory goals: adequacy and equity. "The adequacy goal seeks to protect the most needy by assuring a minimum standard of living and granting special benefits to the disadvantaged. The equity goal seeks to reward individualism and self-reliance by basing government benefits on the amount contributed individually during the working years" (Day, 1990, p. 121). When one goal is met, the other necessarily cannot be fully met, challenging policymakers to weigh the two goals in establishing entitlement for assistance of any type, including assistance based on age. The focus of age entitlement during the period of compassionate ageism was more on adequacy than equity. As we shall see, recent debates have turned attention more toward the equity goal.

Age entitlement contrasts with **need entitlement** a system of providing benefits or services based on need (Quadagno, 1996). Under a need entitlement system, individuals seeking assistance must establish that they have the needs the program was designed to address. For example, they have to prove that they have low income, inadequate shelter, or poor health, and that their income, housing or health is bad enough to meet the program's requirements. Need entitlement results in fewer individuals receiving benefits, which saves the government money. But the need entitlement system also requires more work to establish who is, and who is not, eligible, and that raises administrative costs.

In addition, need entitlement programs in many countries have, in recent years, been subject to reductions when governmental budgets become tight (Hoskins, 1992). Because need-based programs designate recipients as "different from the rest of us," such programs are more politically vulnerable; they lack broad-based, universal, bipartisan support. In fact, an old saying concludes that "programs for the poor become poor programs." The social stigma and negative public opinion regarding welfare benefits for unmarried mothers and their children, for example, indicate the limited support for programs costing tax dollars but providing no direct benefits to those paying the bills (Kingson, 1994).

To reduce expenditures, conservative politicians have suggested changing some current age entitlement programs, such as Social Security and Medicare, to incorporate targeting of benefits based on need (Quadagno, 1996). This push toward need entitlement is evident in the incremental changes that have already occurred in some age entitlement programs. The 1983 Social Security Reform Act started this trend by taxing Social Security benefits for the first time for higher income older persons, in effect reducing benefits dollars going to those with the greatest economic security (Binstock, 1994). Similar changes have been built into the Tax Reform Act of 1986, the Older Americans Act, and the 1993 Omnibus Budget Reconciliation Act (Binstock, 1994). All of these changes have instituted sliding scales for taxes, deductibles, or targeted services based on the level of need of the older person. Thus, as Binstock (1994) reports, "a substantial trend of incremental changes has firmly established the practice of combining age and economic status as policy criteria in old-age benefit programs" (p. 728).

Since the late 1970s, both the stereotypes of the elderly and the political popularity of programs for them have changed dramatically. A growing conservative political tide, increasing government deficits (up until the late 1990s), and shrinking confidence that social programs could successfully resolve social problems all contributed to this transition (Torres-Gil, 1992). Changing views on using age as the basis for entitlements involve two related issues. The first issue is whether age is a good proxy for need. If we were to examine the circumstances of older persons in the early 1960s, we would discover that many of them were poor, inadequately housed, unable to afford medical care, and discriminated against in employment. In other words, by directing social policy interventions at this age group, Congress was fairly certain to hit most of those in need of assistance, and a few who weren't, while keeping administration of the programs simple and inexpensive. So, during the era when many of the programs were established, age was a fairly good proxy for need.

Ironically, the success of programs and policies to alleviate poverty and other old-age problems has left fewer in the older population in dire need of assistance. We have already seen that the economic status of some elderly persons has improved dramatically, and there is evidence of success in other domains as well. This improving situation makes the continuation of policies to assist "the elderly" a more tenuous undertaking (Hudson, 1996). As conditions of older people have become more heterogeneous, age becomes a less adequate proxy for need. The change is reflected in the political rhetoric, which has attempted to shift the stereotype of older Americans from the "deserving elderly" to "greedy geezers" (Binstock, 1995). Efforts toward changing these socially constructed view of the elderly have sometimes been quite explicit and organized, involving advocacy groups and the media (Ekerdt, 1998). The new stereotype is of a mostly affluent elderly population who are also a significant political force, voting in self-interested ways to protect their age entitlement dollars (Binstock, 1991a; Hudson, 1996). (See Chapter 9 for a more detailed discussion of the variations in economic well-being among the elderly.) Although ageism has survived, according to Binstock and others, the compassion has evaporated. The new stereotype of affluent, healthy, and politically savvy elders has undermined the political clout of elderly advocacy groups and engendered resistance from some political interest groups (Torres-Gil, 1992), as well as suggesting a movement away from age entitlements.

The second issue has to do with the American cultural norm of individualism, and whether or not the government should be responsible for helping individuals in need. Whether and how to maintain a "safety net" for older persons who are poor or infirm are questions that reflect the long-term schism in our society over the role of government and the responsibility of individuals for their own well-being. Proponents of he **liberal agenda,** during the ascendance of compassionate ageism, focused on federal programs to address problems of the elderly. Proponents of the **conservative agenda** have challenged the role assumed by government in the middle part of the twentieth century. These conservatives argue that individual responsibility should be the norm and that the role of government in the lives of individuals should be reduced. This battle over old-age entitlements is actually part of a larger conflict over core political ideologies. Our policy dilemmas at this point arise from an absence of consensus on both the meaning and the implications of old age and on the role of government in the welfare of older adults (Torres-Gil, 1992. This is a debate that will not be easily settled.

Aging and Politics

Age Norms and Rules for Political Participation

As many of you know from your high school civics and government classes, the U.S. Constitution includes formal age minimums for holding high federal office. Candidates must be at least 35 years old to run for the presidency, 30 to run for the Senate, and 25 to run for the House of Representatives (Office of the Federal Register, 1995). Presumably these rules were instituted in the belief that sufficient maturity and experience are necessary to fulfill the duties of these offices. Many states also have laws defining the minimum age for office seekers. State laws vary in whether they specify lower limits on age for governors, members of the legislature, or other offices. For example, the most commonly specified minimum age for governor is 30 (in thirty-four states), with three states allowing anyone over 18 to run and six states having no age specified (Council of State Governments, 1994). Lower offices, such as attorney general or lieutenant governor, less often have specific age limits, but almost all states have minimum ages for members of their legislatures. The most common is age 21 (twenty-two states), with fourteen other states specifying 18 and seven more selecting ages 24 or 25 (Council of State Governments, 1994). One interesting point is that none of these laws, state or federal, imposes a *maximum* age for

Exhibit 11.2 *Political Careers of Bill Clinton and Robert Dole*

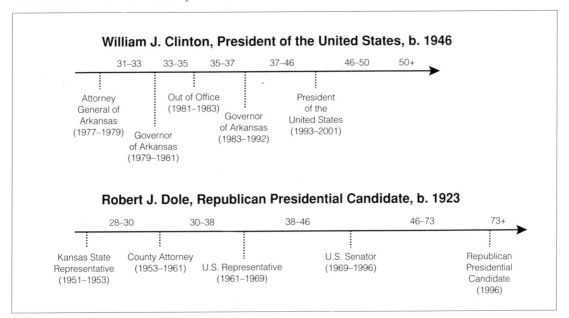

Adapted from: Who's Who in American Politics, 1995–96.

officeholders, a point to which we will return shortly.

Socially constructed age norms guide the timing of events in political careers, just as they do in families and in other occupations. For the ambitious politician, these norms require progress through adulthood from local or regional office to state and possibly national office. Generally the pattern involves expansion of responsibilities with maturation and demonstrated ability, but the timing of political careers can vary widely. As an example, Exhibit 11.2 profiles the political careers, with the ages of holding office, of the two major 1996 presidential candidates. It is especially interesting because of the distinct age difference at the time of that campaign. Both candidates started out in lower-level offices, at the state level, before moving into national-level politics. Clinton's career started early at a fairly high level and at a young age, as attorney general of Arkansas at age 31. He was subsequently governor, entering that office at a precocious age (33). With only a brief interruption in governing Arkansas, Clinton moved directly to the White House in 1992 at age 46, one of the younger presidents. Dole, on the other hand, started as a Kansas state representative, followed by an eight-year term as a county attorney in Kansas. He was then elected to Congress, where he spent eight years in the House followed by twenty-seven years in the Senate, rising to be head of the majority party before resigning to run for the presidency in 1996. Had Clinton lost in 1996, he would have become a 50-year-old former president, a political veteran for whom there are few role models. Dole, on the other hand, had the option to retire gracefully after losing at age 73, consistent with age norms.

Besides the formal rules that set legal age minimums, informal age norms regarding expectations on office holding sometimes become apparent. The media often point up instances in which individuals are violating implicit age norms by seeking public office at inappropriately young or advanced ages. Stories in the media highlight newly elected members entering the House of Representatives at "only age 27" or veterans persisting in the Senate into their 90s. Both Ronald Reagan in 1980 (age 69) and Bob Dole in 1996 (age 73) faced questions regarding age, focusing on the health and vigor necessary for the office. Senator Strom Thurmond (R-SC) was 92 years old when he successfully sought reelection for a 1996-2002 term, also faced questions in the media as to his capacity to fulfill the obligations of the job (Grove, 1996). Whether extremes of age actually hurt a candidate at the voting booth is unclear. The fact that the issue is raised suggests an implicit age norm for being either "too young" or "too old" to become president or hold other high office. If we examine the ages of past presidents of the United States upon entering the office, we find that the youngest to be elected was Teddy Roosevelt, at 42, and the oldest was Ronald Reagan at 69. The median age for presidents upon entering office is 55 years (Kane, 1993). Reactions to extremes of age, in either direction, point out that our socially-constructed norms approve of individuals in the 45-65 age range as most appropriate for high office in the United States.

Aging, Period, and Cohort Effects on Political Behavior

One major topic of debate in the political life of any aging society should be whether the process of aging, period events or the flow of cohorts influences political behaviors such as voting, participating in campaigns, and running for office. An extension of this debate has to do with the issue of political power among the aged. As societies age, is there a potential or likelihood that the older population will take over the political process and control the direction taken by the government? The issue is an important one, because political control determines who fashions the policies of any government. If younger people are politically active in large numbers, politicians in democratic societies will be responsive to their interests and agendas. If, on the other hand, older persons dominate at the voting booth, the voices speaking to elected officials could highlight different issues and the political agenda could take a different path. Do age, period, or cohort really make a difference in how people participate in politics and vote? What are the overall dynamics of these three forces in how individuals and groups interact with and react to the political institutions of society?

Period effects seem likely to be especially potent in the political domain. Social and political events shape the political attitudes of people of all ages, influencing their views of government and of specific policies. It is therefore not surprising that major period events, such as the Watergate scandal in the 1970s, have had negative effects on confidence in government across all age groups

(Kahn and Mason, 1987). But such events may also influence people's orientations toward politics and their attitudes and confidence in the political institutions that govern them, selectively on the basis of age (Peterson and Somit, 1994). Did young adults during Watergate, for example, experience a larger and more enduring reduction in their confidence concerning government than did older cohorts, who had experienced the political solidarity of World War II? Will Clinton's brush with impeachment in the late 1990s influence political attitudes or activities of Generation X or Y? According to Jacobs (1990), such cohort differences do occur. "Distinct political and economic experiences may separate generations and have lasting impact" (p. 350).

Let us revisit the theoretical debate on the relative impacts of aging and cohort. Does aging influence political behaviors and orientations or is cohort experience more influential? Recall Mannheim's hypothesis that, following a formative period in late adolescence and early adulthood, core attitudes and orientations (including political ideas) are set, changing relatively little with advancing age (Alwin and Krosnick, 1991; Mannheim, 1952). If this hypothesis is true, young people's political attitudes are shaped by political socialization within their families and by the political attitudes of the times in which they mature. Thus, if Mannheim is correct, political behaviors and orientations in society would change slowly, as succeeding cohorts with differing attitudes move through the age structure of society (Alwin and Krosnick, 1991). If, however, events can modify political attitudes and behaviors at any age, then Mannheim's view would not be supported and political change could occur at a more rapid pace. If we find evidence that attitudes and political behaviors change dramatically with advancing age, then Mannheim was wrong about the importance of cohorts, and that there may be an aging effect.

Without adequate longitudinal data or a series of repeated cross-sections demonstrating the same pattern associated with aging across historical time, it is difficult to assert an aging effect on political behavior. Fortunately, politics is an area with a fairly long history of data collection enabling us to examine how age groups voted, affiliated themselves with political parties, and participated in other ways in the political system. Using these data resources, we can develop fairly sound answers to our questions about age, period, and cohort.

Voting and Activism: The Potential for Old-Age Political Power

There is a long tradition of political involvement and activism among older adults in the United States.

> Since the Townsend Movement of the 1930s, senior citizens have strongly influenced public policies and political decisions. Their political activism pressured Franklin Roosevelt to pass Social Security, and their alliance with President John Kennedy, labor unions, and the Democratic party helped establish Medicare and Medicaid. (Torres-Gil, 1992, P. 75)

Political activism can take many forms, from voting or participating in campaigns to contributing to political causes, running for office, or simply following political issues in great detail in the media. Research data going back to the 1940s suggest that young adults are less likely to be politically active by writing to their representatives or belonging to political organizations than are members of older age groups (Foner, 1973). Individuals also demonstrate more interest in political campaigns and public affairs debates as they grow older (Torres-Gil, 1992). Torres-Gil argues that both high voting rates and membership in advocacy organizations continue to empower older citizens politically.

One of the most consistent findings in the study of political behavior among the older population is their high rates of participation through voting (Binstock, 2000; Casper and Bass, 1998; Foner, 1973; Jacobs, 1990). This consists of two parts: registering to vote and showing up to cast a ballot on election day. As we saw in Chapter 2, the percentage of eligible voters who cast ballots has been higher among older voters for several decades, suggesting a potential aging effect in this type of political behavior (see Exhibit 2.1). Not only are older people's rates of voting higher, but proportionally more older than younger persons (up to age 85) are registered to vote (Jennings, 1993) (see Exhibit 11.3). At the time of the 1996 presidential election, 66.7% of individuals over 85 were registered, compared to only 43.3% of 18-19 year olds (Casper and Bass, 1998). Although voters over 65 constituted 16.5% of the persons of voting age, they cast 20.3% of the votes in that election (Binstock, 2000). The age gap in voting has increased over time, mostly as a result of declining voting among young adults (Binstock, 2000; Torres-Gil, 1992). Voting among cohorts over 65 might be expected to be lower, because other factors that tend to depress voting (less education, low incomes) are also prevalent among this age category (Peterson and Somit, 1994). In fact, voting does decline slightly for those

Older adults have a long tradition of political activism, including protesting and testifying on issues of concern to them.

Exhibit 11.3   *Voter Registration by Age and Sex*

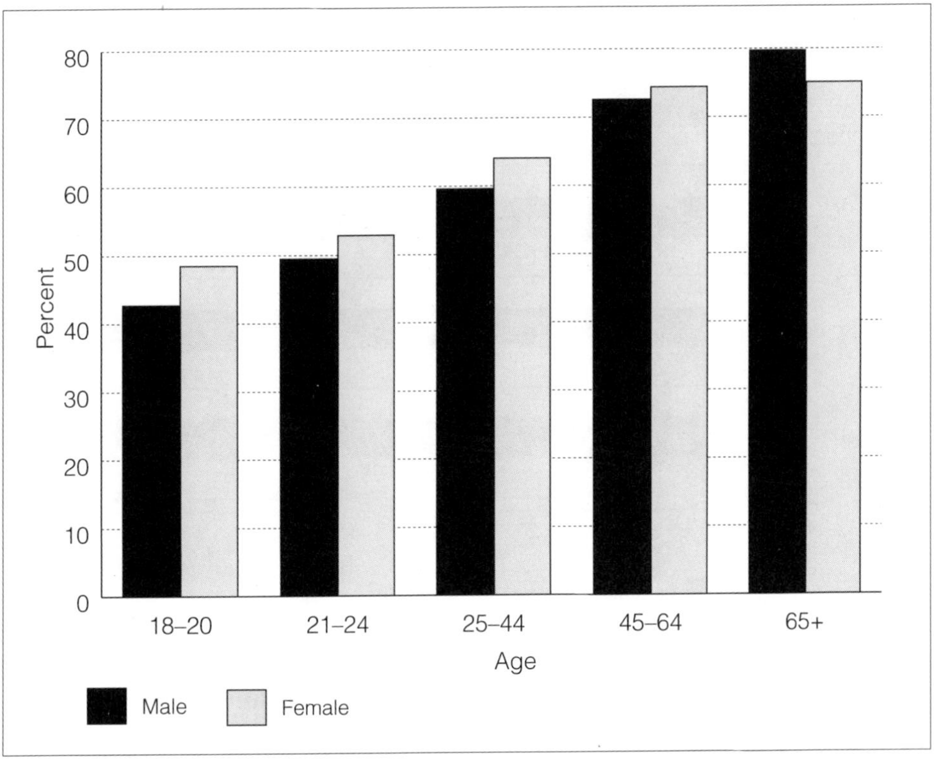

Source: Casper and Bass, 1998.

above age 75, but this pattern is probably due to health limitations (Wallace, Williamson, Lung, and Powell, 1991). Even with such limitations, 50% of adults 85 or older voted in the 1996 presidential election, compared to 30.2% of 18-19 year olds and 33.4% of those 20-24 (Casper and Bass, 1996). As always, it is difficult to sort out the puzzle of age, period, and cohort. These results are based on repeated cross-sectional studies of elections, rather than on longitudinal panel studies following the same individuals over time to determine whether the voting behavior of individuals actually changes in conjunction with aging (Dobson, 1983).

Studying the effects of aging on behaviors such as voting is complicated by factors that are related to both. For example, Exhibit 11.4 shows that among men and women 65 to 74, those with the most education are more likely to vote. Many experts predict that the political activism of the older population will increase further with the rising educational levels of newer cohorts entering later life (Peterson and Somit, 1994; Rosenbaum and Button, 1992), including the cohorts of the baby boom. Among younger cohorts, females outpace males in voter registration (see Exhibit 11.3); this situation is reversed in the cohorts

Exhibit 11.4   *Voting in November 1996 Election by 65–74 Year-Olds by Education and Sex*

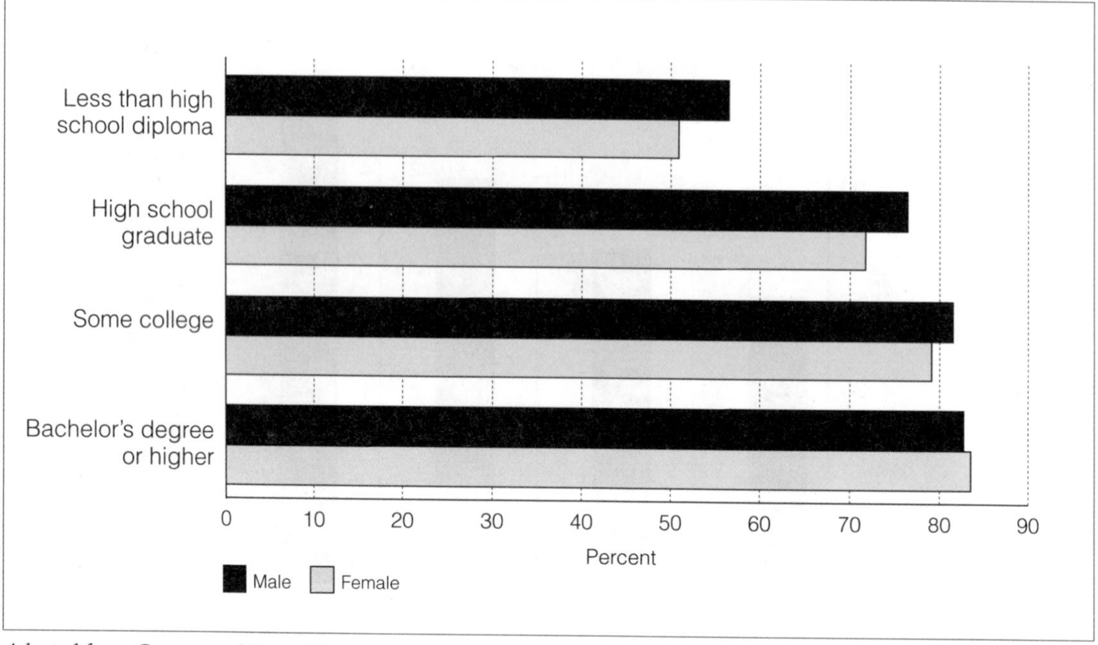

Adapted from: Casper and Bass 1998.

beyond age 65, perhaps as a result of cohort experiences (recall the Nineteenth Amendment women voters from Chapter 2). Thus, voting among older women who are the majority of the older population will likely become even more common as these cohorts move through the life course.

Individuals from higher socioeconomic status (SES) backgrounds tend to vote more regularly than their less advantaged counterparts (Peterson and Somit, 1994; Wallace et al., 1991). They also tend to live longer (Rogot, Sorlie, and Johnson, 1992), meaning that as age increases, the composition of an age cohort shifts more toward higher-SES individuals (Riley, 1987). So, if voting rates increase with age, it may be that part of this increase is due to the "cohort composition effect" discussed in Chapter 2. Selective mortality may leave a higher percentage of individuals who have been engaged in civic matters alive and healthy enough to participate to advanced old age.

Several explanations have been offered for why younger people vote less often. They may have less political experience and feel less attachment to a particular party. Younger people also move more often across boundaries of political jurisdictions, requiring re-registration to make themselves eligible to vote (Foner, 1973). Strate and his associates (Strate, Parish, Elder, and Ford, 1989) suggest that age is related to voting behavior through a variety of forces that increase social integration with advancing age, up to the oldest age groups in which social integration declines. According to the Strate **civic development hypothesis**, young people are neither well socialized into the political process nor do they have the strong connections with family, community, and employment (the social integration) that foster voting among more mature adults (Strate et al., 1989). Strate and his colleagues examined the effects of age on voting in nine presidential elections between 1952 and 1984, attempting to rule out other factors that might account for the age difference in voting. Comparisons of various birth cohorts show that all start with low voting rates and increase over time to a mid-life plateau, after which there is some decline in advanced old age. The authors argue that the differences are not period effects, because they occur for cohorts over a wide range of time during the 32 years studied, and are not cohort effects because the pattern is similar for all cohorts studied.

Through early family socialization and formal education, exposure to the media, ongoing socialization to adult roles, and connection to social institutions, Strate argues, individuals develop a greater sense of obligation to vote as they mature, which is demonstrated in the changing voting activity of each cohort as its members age. Strate argues that it is not age itself, but rather the social changes associated with maturation and changing social roles over the life course that prompt the changes in behavior (Strate et al., 1989). Strate and his colleagues posit that if they could test all of the factors associated with aging that are likely to change voting participation, the consistent association of age and voting would disappear completely.

As you are already well aware, the size (both in absolute terms and as a percentage of the population) of the older population is growing. In addition, through high voter turnout, the population over 65 wields proportionally more influence than their actual percentage of the population. For example, people over 65 represented 22 percent of the total vote in November 1988, a much higher percentage than they represented in the population at that time (*New York Times*, 1989). In eight Florida counties where the 65+ population accounts for 26 percent of the population, they constituted 41 percent of registered voters and 44 to 49 percent of those actually casting ballots in some elections (Button, 1992). With many other jurisdictions likely to approach Florida's current concentrations of older people in the next several decades, this pattern may be a preview of politics in the older populations of the future. In short, if current patterns hold, the older population seems likely to exercise strong political influence through the vote in the future—assuming that they vote on age interests as a political bloc. Candidates already recognize this potential voter power as they seek favor with older voters (Torres-Gil, 1992; Wallace et al., 1991). Candidates often visit senior centers and develop "sound bites" on issues that appeal to older voters, who are more likely to watch the news than are their younger peers. For the 2000 presidential election, both parties identified the senior vote as a key to their strategies, developing positions on Social Security reform, Medicare, and long-term care that were announced early. They develop strategy based on the assumption that older adults will vote based on age-based issues (Binstock, 2000). The question is, will this growing pool of older voters act as a voting bloc?

Do older adults currently vote together on issues or act as a politically cohesive force? For cohorts or age groups to act according to age-based or generational interests requires some degree of **age identification**, labeling themselves as part of an age group or generation. Age identification has been studied for some time, and the results show that many people who are chronologically over 65 do not identify themselves as "older adults," selecting instead the label of middle-aged (Day, 1990). If individuals reject being labeled as part of the older population, it is less likely that they will join age-based organizations or vote (or make other political choices) based on age (Day, 1990). Instead, they may use other sources of identification (gender, religion, region, social class, or party affiliation) that seem to have greater relevance and that they have throughout their lives to make political choices. Although age identification among those over 65 has not coalesced, some predict that it will grow in the future, based in part on greater longevity. Torres-Gil (1992) refers to the baby boomers as the "most age-segregated generation of the century" (p. 129) and hints at the potential for strong age identification among its cohorts. Certainly we might wonder whether the baby boomers, identified throughout their lives as a distinct (albeit highly heterogeneous) "generation," will be more likely to act politically in later life on this basis of experience as an age-identified group (Morgan, 1998).

A related concern in aging societies is the possibility of **gerontocracy,** a society ruled by the elderly. Some nations in recent history could be considered gerontocracies. In the years since its Communist revolution, for example, China has seen the age of its governmental leadership steadily increase as the revolutionary cadres, who have provided political leadership, aged. Now that the last remnants of that revolutionary cohort are dying, however, a new and more youthful leadership is emerging.

When can we say that a gerontocracy exists? One piece of evidence is the domination by older people of positions of power and authority in the political and economic realms. If we look at U.S. history, the median age of presidents at election is 55, hardly old (Kane, 1993). The seniority system in both houses of Congress means that members, as they accumulate years in office, grow in power to head major committees and shape the legislative agenda. However, although members of the 106th Congress ranged in age from late 20s to 90s, the average age was 58.3 for Senators and 52.6 for Representatives—again, not very old (Legislative Research Center, 1999).

A second way to evaluate the possibility of a gerontocracy is to examine whether economic power and wealth are concentrated in the hands of older people. Exhibit 11.5 shows the age distribution of the Fortune 400 wealthiest individuals in 1999. The distribution shows both "self-made" and inherited wealth, so there is no reason to assume that age is necessarily correlated with wealth. The exhibit shows relatively few wealthy individuals under age 30, with the highest concentrations in the age range from 50 to 80. In sum, neither polit-

Exhibit 11.5 *Age Distribution of Forbes Richest 400: 1999*

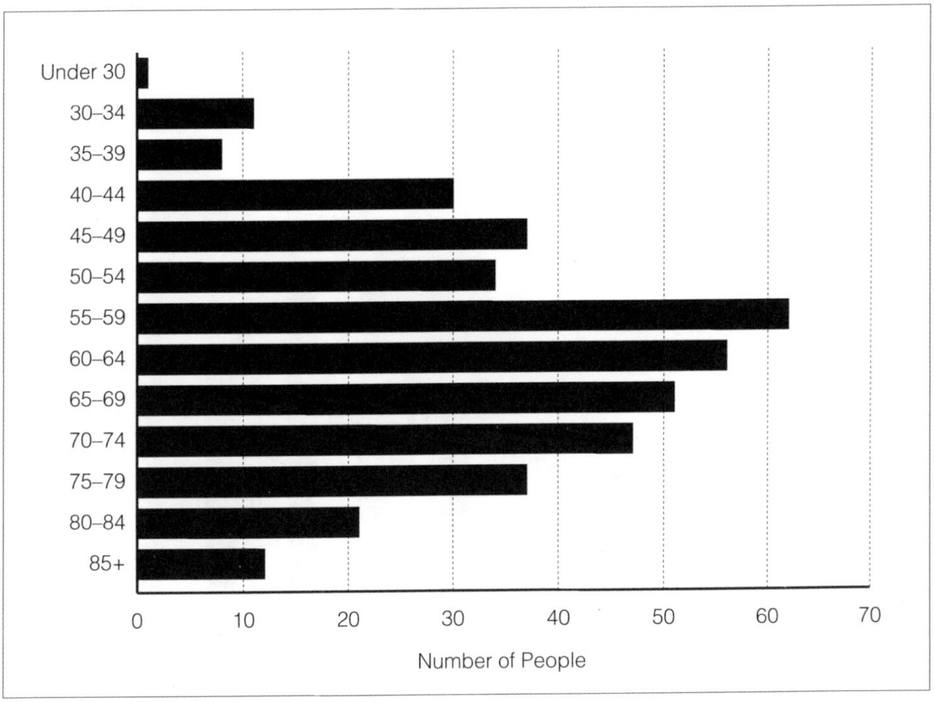

Source: Forbes, 1999.

ical office holding nor the resources of wealth are so concentrated in the hands of those over age 65 or 70 as to warrant concluding that a gerontocracy exists in the United States.

Attitudes and Party Affiliation

Sears (1983) defines two types of political attitudes or orientations. The first, "symbolic" attitudes, are items such as liberal/conservative orientation and party affiliation. Sears contends that such symbolic political attitudes are deeply rooted in the individual's sense of self and less subject to the effects of short-term political events or change with aging. Following the Mannheim hypothesis, he believes that these attitudes are formed in youth and persist across the life course. Sears argues that other, more specific attitudes, such as those toward the budget deficit, gun control, or particular initiatives or candidates, are more subject to the influence of period effects or aging and the passage of time. Let's reserve symbolic attitudes for a moment and examine the nonsymbolic ones first.

Using a life cycle approach, Alwin and Krosnick (1991) have tested the Mannheim hypothesis, described earlier, with regard to changes in political attitudes among various age groups over time. Their study of national samples of

Exhibit 11.6   *Confidence in Major Institutions by Age*

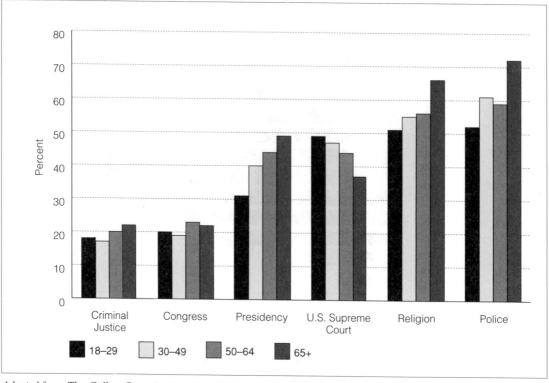

Adapted from: The Gallup Organization, Inc., 1996.

voting-age individuals used two three-wave panel studies, one from the 1950s and one from the 1970s. The analysis showed that the political attitudes of midlife and older adults were only slightly more stable than those of young adults, arguing against the Mannheim hypothesis at least for nonsymbolic political attitudes. Both midlife and older adults demonstrated changes in several political attitudes, albeit slightly less change than the young adults experienced. Detailed analysis of nonsymbolic attitudes, however, failed to show systematic differences by age.

One area of political attitudes that gets wide public attention has to do with confidence in public institutions, including segments of the government. In a May 1996 public opinion poll, the Gallup Organization asked a representative sample of adults whether they had confidence in various social institutions; results of the poll, by age, appear in Exhibit 11.6. It is interesting to note the age differences with regard to some institutions, but not others. People expressed the least confidence in the criminal justice system and in Congress, both hovering around 20 percent across all age groups. Age seemed to make a difference, however, in level of confidence in the presidency, religion, and the police, with those over 65 reporting greater confidence than the younger age groups. Finally, a curious reversal appears for the Supreme Court, where confidence levels shrink with each older age group. What can we conclude from these findings? Perhaps age matters only in some attitudes, and older people do not necessarily have more confidence in social institutions than supposedly disaffected youth.

Turning now to symbolic political attitudes, early studies of the political attitudes of older persons proposed an **aging-conservatism hypothesis**, suggesting that people become more politically conservative as they age—a variation, perhaps, of the "old people are set in their ways" stereotype (Dobson,1983). Research conducted in the late 1960s confirmed that older people espoused more conservative political views than did their younger counterparts. Such cross-sectional results, however, overlooked the complexity of aging, period, and cohort. Most research conducted since the 1960s shows that liberal/conservative orientation, a symbolic attitude, does not change in systematic fashion with aging, supporting the Mannheim hypothesis. Instead, individuals maintain a fairly high level of continuity in their political orientations, with the intervention of period effects likely to have an impact on views across all age groups (Alwin and Krosnick, 1991).

In a similar vein, aging was thought to affect political party affiliation, a related symbolic attitude. Cross-sectional data at that time established that as age increased, affiliation with the Republican party also increased. As an outgrowth of the aging-conservatism hypothesis, maturing individuals were thought to become more attuned to the Republican agenda. Careful analysis of cohorts, however, proved this conclusion to be mistaken. Although comparisons of the elections from 1946 to 1958 seemed to show higher percentages of Republicans among the oldest categories, when cohorts were followed across time Cutler (1969-70) found that party affiliation did not change systematically with age. That finding was reinforced during the 1980s, when older people voted for the candidates of, and were more often affiliated with, the Democratic party in comparison to the young (Jacobs, 1990).

Studies do not show systematic age-related changes in party affiliation. More potent forces shaping party affiliation are family socialization toward political parties and the effects of major period events. Major political victories or scandals do more than age to shape how, when, and whether individuals select a particular party or remain "independent" voters (Jacobs 1990). In the study by Alwin and Krosnick (1991) discussed earlier, stability of party affiliation among various age groups over time was a particular focus. Since they followed various age groups over time—a cohort sequential design—in two separate decades, it became possible to test more directly the aging-versus-cohort issues regarding party affiliation. The results indicate that stability of party affiliation, unlike some other attitudes, increases slowly with age through most of adulthood, with a hint of decrease among those in the oldest groups (Alwin and Krosnick, 1991). The intensity of party identification also increases with age from rather weak to stronger through adulthood, but decreases slightly in the oldest group. People tend to keep their party affiliation as they age, with the

Exhibit 11.7a *Republican Identification by Age Over Time: 1966–1986*

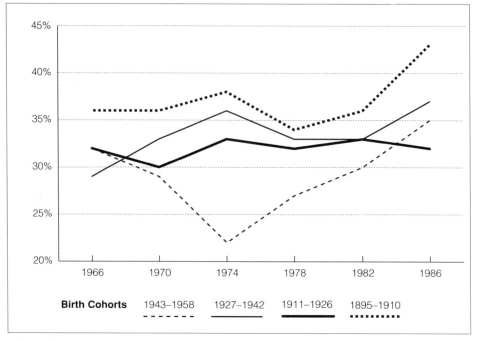

Adapted from: Miller, 1989

Exhibit 11.7b *Democrat Identification by Age Over Time: 1966–1986*

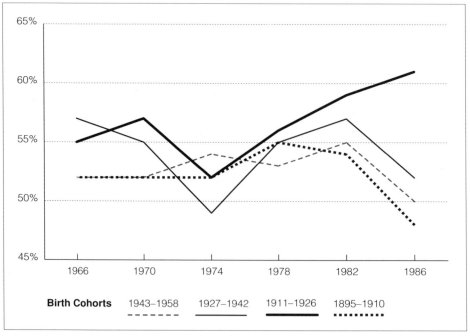

Adapted from: Miller, 1989

intensity of partisanship increasing in the older groups.

The bulk of research fails to demonstrate that political party affiliation changes in systematic ways as individuals age. Exhibit 11.7 suggests that various age cohorts do change their affiliation across the two major parties, but not in any systematic fashion related to age. While some show increasing percentages affiliated with Democratic or Republican parties as they age, other cohorts show essentially no change over time. What is noteworthy is the negative effect on select cohort's affiliation with both parties in 1974, the year Republican president Richard Nixon resigned over the Watergate affair. Among the youngest cohorts shown, affiliation with the Democrats increased and Republican affiliation dropped. Opposite patterns appeared for some (but not all) of the older age cohorts.

Working the Political System: Age-Based Advocacy

An interesting and diverse set of organizations advocates for and provides services to the older population. Most of the advocacy organizations for age-related issues grew up after the advent of the major governmental programs to assist older people (Binstock, 1995), during the period of compassionate ageism. A few earlier movements, such as the Townsend movement that predated Social Security, were critical in the creation of these policies (Torres-Gil, 1992), but most of the major organizations of today have been created since the middle of the twentieth century. Wallace and his colleagues (1991) argue that much of the influence that older adults have exerted has been through organizations and participation in **power elites**, formal or informal groups that build policy and sway public opinion. Numerous age-based organizations, including some that will be described here, have been party to shaping policies on the federal and state levels for many years, regardless of whether or not they represent the full range of older adults. These groups are not organized and run only by older people, but often include and rely upon the work of younger people on behalf of the older population. In this section we describe some of the political battles undertaken by advocacy groups, the government, and the older population.

The Battle over Social Security

Social Security was a political battleground before its passage and has served as the focus of policy and partisan debate many times in its more than sixty-year history. The current debates about reforming Social Security are not new, nor are such discussions occurring only in the United States (Hoskins, 1992). In the early 1990s, most aging societies of the world faced increasing economic pressures that prompted them to examine their Social Security systems and their fiscal capacity to meet their obligations for public pensions to growing populations of older persons. For example, countries in eastern Europe that have recently moved to capitalist economies have experienced both economic recession and dramatic political changes, rendering their former system of old-age income security inappropriate (Hoskins, 1992).

The United States has seen regular political and ideological battles over Social Security, including notable battles surrounding major changes to the program in 1977 and 1983. Prior to his election Ronald Reagan proposed deep cuts to the program, which were formalized as part of a budget proposal in 1981. A tremendous public uproar followed, chastening the new Reagan administration into steadfast support of Social Security (Jacobs, 1990). Like Reagan, other politicians have learned of the dangers of tampering with Social Security. Using the analogy of a subway system, Social Security has been called the "third rail" of American politics. In a subway system, the third rail is the one carrying electrical current. Politicians quickly learn that if you touch the Social Security "third rail," you die! Social Security is a program with a very large and interested constituency, comprising not just those receiving benefits but also those expecting to receive benefits and those whose family members currently receive benefits (Day, 1993a).

Following the abortive Reagan assault on Social Security , many groups have entered the battle over the future of the U.S. Social Security system. These include single-issue advocacy groups, such as Save Our Security and the National Committee to Preserve and Protect Social Security and Medicare, the major political parties, a variety of "think tank" advocates, and the mainstream aging organizations (Day, 1990). As there are additional fights over Social Security, they are likely to be fierce and telling regarding the status of all age entitlement programs.

AARP and Capitol Hill

The American Association of Retired Persons (AARP) boasts 40 million members aged 50 and older, an apparently formidable support group for any candidate or issue (AARP, 1999; Binstock, 1995). The organization, founded in 1958, has grown rapidly in the past few decades as the population has aged (Jacobs 1990). Membership, costing only $8 per year, over-represents European American, middle-class individuals, many of whom would be considered among the middle-aged or "young old" (Day, 1990). It is important to point out that memberships are initiated and maintained primarily for member benefits and discounts (such as travel and insurance discounts, a prescription plan, and a newsletter), rather than for the political agenda that the AARP pursues (Binstock, 1995). By 1994 the AARP received revenue of $469 million and employed a strong professional staff to provide member services and to sustain its reputation for political clout in Washington (Binstock, 1995).

There is question as to whether the AARP can deliver votes for particular candidates and whether its diverse membership supports all of the positions taken by the organization's policy branch during debates in Washington or in individual states (Binstock 1991a). AARP has been accused of using what Binstock calls the "**electoral bluff**." This bluff occurs when organizations of this size implicitly threaten to churn up major support for or against a candidate or proposal, pressuring legislators or policymakers for changes in AARP's chosen direction (Binstock, 1991a). No one knows, in most cases, whether the AARP can deliver on its bluff. Such large membership organizations wield much of their power through high levels of access to elected officials and policymakers. They draw legitimacy from their size when taking positions publicly and work through the media to make their views known (Binstock, 2000). On Capitol Hill, the AARP and its lobbyists actively advocate the organization's positions and make themselves heard on major issues affecting older adults. For example, AARP has recently raised its voice on issues such as improved Social Security benefits for widows and adding drug coverage to Medicare. Current position statements can be viewed on their web site (see the Web Wise section at the end of this chapter).

The Case of Catastrophic Health Care Legislation

One of the most recent efforts to pass significant legislation affecting the older population, and an interesting case history in how the political environment for the elderly has shifted, is the **Medicare Catastrophic Coverage Act** of 1988 (**MCCA**) (Street, 1993). This legislation, intended to provide protection against impoverishment from major, costly illnesses, expanded Medicare benefits for older people for the first time in many years (Torres-Gil, 1992). The MCCA would have placed a cap on out-of-pocket medical expenses for Medicare beneficiaries, expanded coverage for home health care, and protected the income and assets of the spouses of long-term nursing home patients receiving Medicaid (Torres-Gil, 1992). It did not address the situation of most concern to many older adults—the high cost of nursing home care (Wallace et al., 1991).

The legislation passed with strong bipartisan support in the Congress. The AARP was an active advocate in its passage (Jacobs, 1990), strongly supporting the advantages for many of its poorer members. Such politically diverse groups as the Gray Panthers and the Pharmaceutical Manufacturing Association opposed the legislation, but for very different reasons. The Gray Panthers, an activist group emphasizing change, felt that the bill did not go far enough, but would sidetrack momentum for dealing with the key issue of long-term care. The pharmaceutical manufacturers' lobby was concerned that the plan to pay for drugs would lead to government control of medication prices (Holstein and Minkler, 1991). Despite their opposition, MCCA passed.

The bill was repealed one year after its approval; the MCCAs financing scheme was its downfall. Because the elderly were no longer considered "needy" as a group, the program had to be "revenue neutral," adding no costs to taxpayers (Holstein and Minkler, 1991). The financing included a surtax on older adults, based on income, so that the poorest would pay nothing and the wealthiest would pay $800 per person per year (Street, 1993). In contrast to other age entitlements, this one was self-financing, with those more able to afford benefits subsidizing those less able or unable to pay. Once the bill had passed and individuals could identify its specific implications for themselves in terms of added costs and benefits, a small but highly vocal opposition forced repeal of the great majority of the bill's provisions within a year of its passage (Binstock, 1992; Torres-Gil, 1992). Interestingly, research (Day, 1993b) found that neither those who would have to pay the surtax nor those with supplemental insurance coverage (those least likely to benefit from the new coverage) were more likely to oppose the MCCA than other groups of older adults. Nonetheless, the incident characterized older persons as wanting government services but unwilling to pay for them, contributing ammunition to the emergent debate on generational equity, described later in this chapter (Street, 1993).

Crystal (1990) describes the passing and rescinding of the MCCA as a turning point in public policy on aging. The short life of the MCCA demonstrated the power of class politics versus age-based interests. It revealed a schism in the older constituency between the "haves" and the "have nots." In this case, the "haves" were wealthier older persons expected to pay for the services being added, but most likely to have private insurance to meet those needs and the "have-nots" were those in need of services, but not required to pay or able to afford private insurance. The affluent haves had already "opted out" of full dependence on a publicly funded Medicare system via private insurance, and many resented being called upon to finance benefits for others less fortunate (Crystal, 1990). This experience has made some policymakers cautious about proposing new entitlement programs in an era of public resistance to paying for them. This legislation and its repeal also divided the aging advocacy community in a way that had not happened before. According to Crystal (1990), the bill "divided many constituencies who previously have made common cause toward improving services to the elderly" (p. 23). Now advocacy organizations are forced to confront the social class issues that divide the older population and can no longer make clear policy choices that assisted "older people" as a category.

Generational Politics: Conflict and Consensus

The Potential for Generational Conflict

For many years experts in the politics of aging have speculated about generational conflict and the potential for the demands of a large older population to engender resistance among young and midlife adults. Analysts disagree regarding the prospect of **intergenerational conflict** over the distribution of government resources (see Binstock 1991a; Wynne, 1991). Some argue that such conflict will be inevitable if current policies and entitlements remain unchanged; others claim that cross-cutting allegiances pull people into groupings other than age-based ones (Day, 1990). Although conflict between cohorts or generations is often discussed, scant evidence exists for it today or in the past.

This issue of conflict between generations arose in the late 1960s during the era of youthful political activism by the oldest baby boomers, prompting discussions of a "generation gap." The issue has reemerged repeatedly in a variety of contexts. Recent discussions have focused on the possible emergence of "gray power" or gerontocracy political rule by a society's elders, in local politics . Some argue that this power constitutes a "gray peril," with older adults dominating the local political scene to the detriment of other constituencies (Button and Rosenbaum, 1990; Rosenbaum and Button, 1992). The issue boils down to whether the goals and interests of young and old are sufficiently different as to make them adversaries in the political arena. Under a scenario of age-based political conflict, groups would solidify for political action based on age identification. Young people might want more support for public higher education while older adults might want more support for home health care, for example. In times of scarce resources, the argument goes, the old and the young may splinter along age lines, with each group vying for its own distinct political agenda.

The potential for age identification and age-based political action rests on what people's interests are and how narrowly self-centered they are. For example, questions have often been raised about whether older adults vote in support of bond issues for public schools, which affect neither themselves nor their adult children. Environmental advocates wonder whether older voters will care about (and vote to support) pollution-abatement programs to benefit unborn generations of the future, when they will already be dead (Kneese and Cooper, 1993). Although there is some evidence of lower support for school bond issues among older adults (see Button, 1992), the evidence for this sort of generational schism is far from comprehensive. The more persuasive evidence suggests that how old people are does not influence their political positions as much as their social class, education, political party or gender.

In Chapter 7 we discussed reciprocity within the context of the family. It is also useful to consider reciprocity on a societal level between larger groups, including age groups. In this larger context, Social Security can be considered a form of reciprocity—support provided for the elderly in return for their contributions in earlier years to building both the economy and their successor cohorts (Wynne, 1991). Wynne argues for expansion of the concept of reciprocity within the larger society, encouraging civic involvement among young and old for the betterment of society. Under this macro-level version of reciprocity, the age strata of society can be seen to have mutual interests and goals, with exchange among them a natural occurrence (Kingson, Hirshorn, and Cornman, 1986). Generations are pulled together by this reciprocity, not pulled apart.

Day's study (1990) of national public opinion polls shows very little difference by age in how people respond to political issues, including age entitlements. Older adults have priorities similar to those of younger age groups on the great majority of issues. She concludes that "the lines that divide Americans on the issue of government benefits for the elderly are not generational, but economic and partisan" (p. 60). Other research has focused on age-based voting patterns in Florida, a state distinguished by having the largest percentage (about 20 percent) of its population over age 65 as a result of substantial elderly in-migration (Button and Rosenbaum, 1990). Florida is as ripe for political conflict based on age as any location in the United States. Evidence from the work of Button and Rosenbaum suggests that the "gray peril" is an overstatement of the possible effect of high proportions of older voters (Button and Rosenbaum, 1990). Nonetheless, rapid growth of the older population in Florida jurisdictions is associated with perceptions by local government officials of a potential for age-based conflicts in their communities (Rosenbaum and Button, 1992). These public officials consider their older citizens activists, although few can point to specific instances in which elder activism has brought about changes in policies or laws (Rosenbaum and Button, 1992). The government officials perceive the older population to be resistant to increasing taxes or development of the local economy, changes that would not be in their self-interest (Rosenbaum and Button, 1992). Finally, local age-related strife has arisen over issues that might not immediately be perceived as age-based. One such issue is the location of congregate housing, nursing homes or retirement communities for the elderly. A second issue is driving speed, with young and old mutually critical of each other's speed on local roads (Rosenbaum and Button, 1992). Despite all of these potential rifts, government officials did not see the older populations in their localities acting as a coherent bloc in terms of voting or supporting issues, because many traits also divided them. In other words, age-based politics were more expected than real.

A second aspect of age-based conflict is the potential for a **backlash against the older population** by young and midlife individuals (Rosenbaum and Button, 1992). Many analysts and politicians argue that the perception of the elderly as greedy and willing to fight politically to maintain entitlements raises the specter of the elderly fighting over resources with young families or disadvantaged groups, such as the poor or the physically or mentally disabled (Rosenbaum and Button, 1992). Day (1990) argues that backlash is fueled by the failure of aging advocacy groups to lobby effectively for the needs of the most disadvantaged groups in the older population, a critique raised by such diverse groups as the Gray Panthers and the conservative Americans for Generational Equity. This potential for backlash remains in the realm of speculation, however, with little evidence to support the idea of the young or middle-aged forming a voting force to ratchet down age-based entitlement spending.

Political conflict between generations can occur only if issues emerge that elicit voting or other forms of political activism based on age identification. Although people have suggested for many years that such an old-age voting bloc could develop (a version of Binstock's "electoral bluff"), it has yet to materialize (Binstock, 1997; Dobson, 1983). A galvanizing event or issue, such as a threat to the continuation of Social Security, might pull together the older population into a coherent interest group that might act together in voting and advocacy for their cause (Dobson, 1983). Evidence from exit polls during the 1996 presidential election suggests that Medicare, used as an issue by both sides in the campaign, was not effective in eliciting such a response (Binstock, 1997). Wallace and his associates (1991) claim that when older adults have been mobilized to act on an issue, it has been more on the basis of economic issues than of age, as we saw in the case of the Medicare Catastrophic Care Act.

Other characteristics, such as gender and social class, appear to make *more* difference in candidate choice than does age in most cases (Binstock,1991a). Older voters vary in how they stand on the issues, just as younger voters do (Jacobs, 1990). And, however much the older population increases, it will remain smaller than the 20- to 65-year-old voting population (Wynne, 1991). The general absence of collective age identity and political cohesiveness among the older population undoubtedly reflects the close linkages between older and younger persons in the economic, religious, and family institutions of society (Dobson, 1983). We can take the absence of an elderly voting bloc as an indicator that more connects us politically than separates us by age.

We saw examples of this connectedness of generations earlier in the widespread support for programs such as Social Security across all age groups, despite the fact that primarily the older population benefits from them (2030 Center, 1999). Research by Day (1993a) has found that among older adults, political ideology and party affiliation dominate views toward old-age benefits, whereas among those under age 65 socioeconomic status is the strongest influence. Some analysts see older voters basing their choices more on economic self-interest than on their identities as older adults, with a potential schism based on social class looming even larger in future cohorts (Wallace et al., 1991). Similarly, Day (1990) describes older people as "deeply divided on aging policy issues, particularly along economic and partisan lines" (p. 36). Her research shows relatively little evidence that the older population acts cohesively and in an age-identified fashion.

Aside from age, individuals and groups of persons have a variety of social identifications and allegiances. They remain members of families, social classes, communities, regions, political parties, religions, and a variety of more specialized groups that both indicate and shape their interests in social policies and the political process (Day, 1990). These identifications as "an avid-reader, female, Baptist, Democrat" or a "Southern, middle-class, attorney, ecologist, fiscal conservative" do not simply evaporate as people age. Instead, people may add to their repertoire of allegiances a potential new allegiance—that of being an older person in society. Not everyone adopts this identity. Some actively avoid it, whereas others embrace it and make it a focus of their self-concept :they develop age identification. Peterson and Somit (1994) conclude from their research that "it is important to consider the elderly not as a single bloc (although there are some commonalities that bind them together), but as a complex mosaic made up of many different groups, with distinct and often competing interests" (p. 3).

The fact that the older population will be growing more racially and ethnically diverse as current cohorts age may further dilute the likelihood of an elderly voting bloc emerging (Torres-Gil, 1992). Torres-Gil projects that activism and organizations may become more focused and specialized, addressing the needs, for example, of disadvantaged older women rather than the economic issues of the elderly as a whole. Age, he argues, may be less compelling as an organizing force than as a common interest when the older population is so diverse. Keep this focus on diversity and heterogeneity in the older population in the forefront of your mind when we revisit age stratification theory later in this chapter.

The Generational Equity Debate

Politicians and the media have paid attention to one specific aspect of generational conflict in recent years, the generational equity debate. The United States, like a variety of other nations throughout the world, transfers resources between individuals who are economically productive (i.e., workers) and those who are not (dependent children, disabled adults, and older persons). We often take these transfers for granted; we tax local property owners to finance public schools and tax wages to pay for Social Security and Medicare, among other examples.

The growth of the older population has prompted politicians, economists, and sociologists to examine the fundamental assumptions behind such transfers (Cornman and Kingson, 1996). Medicare, Medicaid and Social Security are the three most costly components of these transfers to older adults. In contrast, families are responsible for much of the support to dependent children with the major exception of public education, while the public systems of the old age welfare state provide more of the support provided to older people (Achenbaum, 1992). This system has emerged through a lengthy process of social construction (here via legislation) based on our unique cultural values and our history and reflecting the political and social processes peculiar to our society. Some European countries provide much more public support for children's needs than the Unit-

Generational equity groups suggest that society must make choices that penalize one age group in society, but not everyone agrees.

Exhibit 11.8   *Percentage of Federal Spending Devoted to Entitlements*

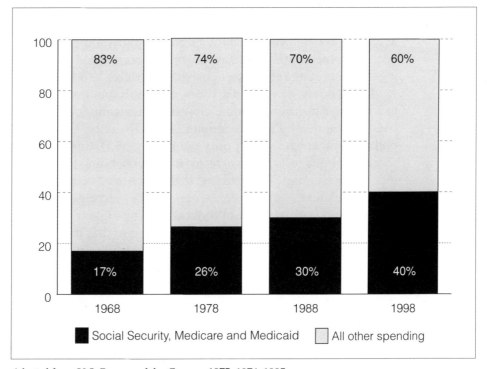

Adapted from: U.S. Bureau of the Census, 1975, 1976, 1995c.

ed States does, reflecting differences in values and beliefs (Quadagno, 1989). Our federal government spends more money on programs for the older population than on programs for children, raising questions about priorities.

Demographers had long predicted the growth of the older population in the United States and many other countries. Nevertheless, it was not until the late 1970s that politicians and advocates for the elderly recognized the growing costs of transfers for older citizens. Hudson (1978) called this process the **graying of the federal budget** (see also Binstock, 1991a). This "graying" refers to the growing percentage of the federal budget each year allocated to entitlements (transfer programs mandated by law) for the older population, including the dollars spent on Medicare, Medicaid and Social Security. Exhibit 11.8 shows the increase between 1968 and 1998 in the percentage of the federal budget allocated to these entitlements.

Alarms have sounded in some circles as the baby boom cohorts move toward old age and as life expectancy continues to increase. These factors, combined with the ongoing commitment to pay for these entitlements in future generations, have congealed into a narrowly focused debate on whether the economy can afford old-age entitlements (Cornman and Kingson, 1996), a debate with many assumptions that are seldom examined in detail. A major part of this debate has to do with the future financing of Social Security and Medicare and some of the alternatives proposed for their funding. We describe these debates in greater detail in earlier chapters. Surprisingly, some countries with populations older than the United States have not encountered public resistance to paying the costs of age entitlement programs (Myles 1996).

An advocacy group in the 1980s, responding to the entitlement alarm and to a broader political agenda, created **Americans for Generational Equity** (AGE). Founded by former Senator David Durenberger (R, Minn.) with both political and corporate support (Minkler, 1991a), this group argued that we should look at age as a critical factor in understanding the linkage between politics and economics. AGE pointed to the improved economic well-being of the older population — the lower rate of poverty— and high rates of poverty among children and posited a causal connection. The organization asserted that society was throwing resources at older people and that these resources would be better spent to alleviate poverty and educate future cohorts (Quadagno, 1991). AGE argued that older adults have fared much better politically than have children or unborn cohorts, because the elderly are effective in advocating for their own agenda, including funding for age entitlement programs.

AGE and its successors, including the Concord Coalition, advocate movement away from age entitlements to entitlement programs based on need. This change, they said, should happen in steps, by eliminating cost-of-living increases and raising the retirement age for Social Security and by using tax policies to encourage private old-age insurance (Quadagno 1991)—all of which are now under discussion in Washington. With these changes, AGE argued, we would no longer need to pay Social Security benefits to millionaires (who would be ineligible under need entitlement) and could reallocate resources to pay down the federal debt and to benefit children and future cohorts. Rather than viewing programs like Social Security as part of society's solutions to its problems, AGE considered old-age entitlements to be part of the problem, in effect faulting older persons for societal problems and the federal budget deficit (Minkler, 1991a). Holstein (1995) points out that reducing entitlements for older people in no way guarantees that those resources would be redistributed to children. A very public debate between Congress and the President in 1999 focused on just these issues. In spite of such critiques, AGE was successful in altering the nature of the debate about age entitlements from its prior focus on adequacy of benefits to issues of equity—specifically, intergenerational equity (Quadagno, 1989).

Is the fundamental generational inequity argument of AGE accurate? At first glance, Exhibit 11.8 seems to provide support for this contention. The largest increase in entitlement spending occurred after the enactment of Medicare in 1965 and has slowed substantially in recent years (Friedland and Summer, 1999; Quadagno, 1996). The percentage growth has also been fueled by cuts in discretionary spending, such as government-funded research and small business programs, making both interest on the deficit and entitlement costs larger percentages of the overall budget (Quadagno, 1996). Using some standard economic measures for the costs of programs, neither Social Security nor overall entitlements to the elderly have grown in real terms much since the early 1970s. Instead, as recent conservative Congresses have cut spending in other areas and the Reagan administration reduced taxes on individuals and corporations in the 1980s, old-age entitlements have become a larger percentage of significantly reduced overall spending, creating a false impression of dramatic growth in the dollars being spent (Quadagno, 1996). In other words, the size of the federal budget pie in recent years is, in real financial terms, smaller than a few decades ago. Quadagno concludes that the entitlements "crisis" has been socially constructed through careful rhetoric to advance a political agenda of reducing government programs, rather than emerging as a consensual social problem to be resolved.

Achenbaum (1992) has pointed out that equity, a key term in this debate, can have several meanings, from fairness in how an individual is treated over the life course to a group's standing relative to its peers. While equity sounds good, he argues, it is a loose term that could be tuned to varied meanings for policy. Theodore Marmour and his colleagues argue that Social Security has become "a scapegoat for anxieties engendered by a distressingly volatile economic environment" (1990, p. 127). Quadagno (1991) concludes that AGE recommendations simply shift economic support functions back to families and would most hurt those individuals who rely primarily on Social Security for income—those lacking private pensions from their employers. This group is disproportionately composed of women and minorities. As a consequence, she argues, many of these most disadvantaged individuals would need to continue working in low-wage jobs into advanced old age, having inadequate finances to retire on reduced Social Security benefits (Quadagno, 1991).

Quadagno's strongest complaint with the AGE agenda is its contention that childhood poverty is somehow caused by greater entitlements to the older population. During the time that old-age entitlements have increased, other significant social changes have contributed to poverty among children. One of these important changes is an increase in the number of families headed by single women who are unable, in a gender-segregated economy, to earn sufficient income to adequately support their children (Quadagno, 1991). AGE implies that because the decline in old-age poverty and the increase in childhood poverty occurred at the same time, one caused the other, ignoring other, concurrent changes.

It is apparent that AGE and its supporters have been quite effective in getting their political message out. Many popular magazines and other media now use the rhetoric of "greedy geezers" and sound the alarm regarding financing of entitlements in the future (Ekerdt, 1998). In contrast, Achenbaum (1992) argues that it is necessary to make manifest the transgenerational benefits of programs like Social Security to ensure their political survival for the future.

Cornman and Kingson (1996) point out that we invest resources in children in anticipation of their future contributions to society and assist the elderly in reciprocity for their prior contributions, evening out the balance sheet over the life course. It is only if we freeze the picture and define entitlements as a zero-sum game that the old and the young seem like drains on society.

Debate continues regarding when and whether the economy will experience a crisis based on the growth of the older population. One major wild card in any projection is the performance of the economy in the future; many economic projections are flawed because the assumptions they use are not found to be valid (Quadagno, 1996). In sum, it is difficult to project whether a crisis will emerge and, if so, its seriousness. Politicians and policymakers, however, are acting as if the crisis is sure and imminent and are formulating policy based on the rhetoric that organizations like AGE have been quite effective at promulgating.

By some measures, the programs of the old-age welfare state have been successful in dealing with the problems they were created to address. As Chapter 9 discussed, overall poverty has been greatly reduced by the presence of Social Security benefits. The housing and health of the older population have improved, albeit only partly through the efforts of federal government programs (Quirk, 1991). Some aging advocates argue that these programs are victims of their own success. Because the condition of the average older person has improved significantly in recent decades, there is less momentum to maintain the programs that have helped to bring about (and to maintain) that success. In addition, there remain a substantial number of older persons, primarily minority individuals and widowed women, who are poor and receive little help from this "safety net." It is a major failing of the old-age welfare system that it leaves behind some severe pockets of disadvantage (Binstock, 1991a).

■ ■ ■ ■ ■ ■ ■ ■
APPLYING THEORY
Age Stratification Theory

Age stratification theory posits that we divide the population into strata (or layers), that are ranked hierarchically. As in other stratification theories focusing on social class, race, or gender rather than age, the population is divided into groups; age stratification substitutes age as the criterion upon which individuals are divided. In age stratification, age is used to cluster groups of people together (into age strata or, in the term we have used most often, cohorts) and to differentiate among people on the basis of the age stratum to which they belong (Dowd, 1980). We can ask, for example, whether someone belongs to an age stratum in the teenage years or in "old old" age and, on that basis, make some educated guesses about the person. These guesses are based on the assumption that people in the same stratum have significant social characteristics in common and that members of different strata are different in critical ways. To visualize the idea of age strata you need look no farther than the population pyramids presented in Chapter 3. Age stratification systems are straight-forward in a sense, because chronological age allows us to readily order individuals into groups and rank them hierarchically as having more or fewer accumulated years of life. In contrast, class stratification systems require considerable effort to define the boundaries and characteristics of strata and the placement of individuals within specific social classes. In age stratification, it is clear that someone who is 35 is older, and therefore in a different stratum, from someone who is 15. The question remains, however, whether the distinction between those two chronological ages is socially meaningful. And since age strata usually include several chronological ages (e.g., ages 25-34), the boundaries dividing strata may be arbitrary and certainly debatable, as in the debate about when someone qualifies as an older person.

What about age stratification based on stages of the life course? Once we attempt to develop stratification based on life-course stages, the strata become even less clear and distinct (O'Rand, 1990). What criteria must one meet, for example, to be considered an "adult"? Using life-course events, people might be considered adults when they married, got a full-time job, left their parents' home, had children, or some combination of these events (Hogan and Astone, 1986). It is much simpler, although not necessarily conceptually meaningful, to use chronological age; for voting purposes, for example, you are an adult when you become 18 years of age.

Age stratification theory goes beyond the recognition that societies divide their populations by age or into cohorts, and examines how societies offer different rewards and opportunities to members of different age strata. According to Dowd (1981), "both age strata and social classes may be defined by their differential possession of valued resources and differential access to the means of acquiring these resources" (p. 158). People in the 35-40 age stratum as a rule hold more socially valued resources and are given more opportunities to augment those resources than someone who is 15 or 85. Age, like many other bases for stratification, serves as a basis of structured social inequality (Foner, 1973). Riley and her colleagues (1973) point out that we give opportunities to (or place requirements on) individuals to be enrolled in educational institutions at certain ages and limit access to other activities (such as marrying, voting, or holding office) until a certain age has been achieved. Informal norms and sanctions that go with them also encourage people to "act their age," performing in ways that are consistent with the expectations associated with their location in the stratification system (Riley, Johnson, and Foner, 1973). The hierarchy of age stratification is not as straightforward as the system of social class stratification, however, because those "higher" in the stratification system (the aged) do not necessarily benefit from greater resources than those in the middle. Therefore, the concept of age stratification is less clear-cut from the perspective of social inequality (Cain, 1987).

Another element of age stratification that differentiates it from stratification by social class has to do with social mobility. **Social mobility** refers to the move-

Despite dire predictions of intergenerational conflict, many interests and goals are shared across diverse age cohorts.

ment of an individual between levels of the stratification system. In stratification systems based on gender or race, such mobility is extremely limited; most of us are stuck with our race and gender. In the case of social class, mobility between strata is quite possible. For example, when a young person from a poor background seeks an advanced education and achieves a high-level professional career, he moves to a higher social class. In age stratification, mobility through the age stratification system is automatic and unavoidable. You can't avoid growing older (Riley et al., 1973). In fact, according to Riley, aging is mobility. Simply by virtue of surviving, individuals and cohorts are "upwardly mobile" in the age stratification system; but upward age mobility, unlike social class mobility, does not necessarily mean an improvement in one's social and economic situation. In social class stratification, higher is better; in age stratification, older may or may not be better.

Although we are introducing age stratification theory in an official manner here, we have already used elements of age stratification theory throughout this book, especially in discussions of cohorts and their movement through the society. Dowd's explanation of exchange theory, described in Chapter 7, also includes elements of age stratification; he argues that older persons have, by virtue of their location in the stratification system, less power and fewer resources, which disadvantages them in exchange relationships. Age stratification also has roots in modernization theory, described in Chapter 3. Modernization theory examines the relative status of older age groups (compared with younger adults) in more and less developed societies, positing that as societies modernize, older individuals lose the foundations that gave them power and prestige in less developed economies (O'Rand, 1990). Although modernization theory has been heavily criticized, it nonetheless directs attention to age stratification systems.

Age stratification theory is flexible, enabling us to look at movement of individuals through age-related roles and expectations on a micro level or focus attention on the flow of cohorts through social institutions on the macro level, adding the important element of inequality between strata (O'Rand, 1990). Age stratification theory focuses our attention on the issues that age cohorts have in common—how society structures both opportunities and expectations based on the age of the individual, ignoring potentially important differences that exist among 20- or 70-year-olds. O'Rand (1990) points out that in the twentieth century the state has imposed more standardization on the lives of the youngest and oldest in society—for example, creating regulations requiring school attendance and institutionalizing retirement. In this way governments define the civil rights and responsibilities of individuals in these age strata. You have doubtless felt the restrictions of age boundaries already in your life—being "too young" or "too old" to participate in certain activities—and may have celebrated passing a milestone birthday as you experience mobility through the age stratification system.

To focus on age stratification in no way invalidates other systems of stratification. It is often informative to use multiple systems of stratification—for example, examining age strata and then, within age strata, looking at variations by gender, social class, or race to see how these interlocking systems augment or diminish opportunities and disadvantages for the individuals within their ranks. Stratification theory—using age, class, gender, or other criteria for establishing strata—encourages using the sociological imagination and taking a macro-social view of inequality of opportunity.

The fundamental question today for age stratification is its usefulness, given the fuzziness of boundaries and definitions of age strata, the expectations for increasing diversity in the older population of the future (Torres-Gil, 1992), and the importance of other dimensions of stratification intersecting with age. Will age really matter more than social class, educational background, gender, or race and ethnicity in understanding the social placement and life chances available to individuals in various groups? The answer may be no, but as long as age-based restrictions on opportunities in society continue, there is some utility in using an age stratification framework to examine social and political issues.

■ ■ ■

Summary

As we have seen in earlier chapters, there is every reason to expect that the political experience of future cohorts will differ from those of contemporary cohorts of older Americans. For example, the concept of later life and the inclusiveness of an elderly constituency might change. Those past 65 who are employed, in good health, and with thirty or more years of future life expectancy might not consider themselves part of the interest group of older adults (Torres-Gil, 1992), and might behave accordingly.

Will old age continue its relevance as a focal category for social policy, or will crosscutting issues such as social class, disability, or race/ethnicity prove more politically powerful as the foci for societal intervention (Binstock ,1992)? Analysts disagree about the future of both advocacy and policy relative to old age. Torres-Gil (1992) expects a future of old-age politics that differs from what we have experienced in recent decades. He argues that social class and need will become the basis for government programs and that the strong advocacy network for old-age issues will self-destruct. Not everyone agrees, arguing that the baby boomers, by their sheer numbers and education, will be a political force to be reckoned with for many years (Cornman and Kingson, 1996). What seems apparent is that the pressure of the baby boomers has brought many of these policy discussions into sharp focus, even though the cohorts that immediately follow them will be much smaller in size. As policy is formulated, we need to ask whether the decisions make sense not only for the baby boomers, but also for the cohorts who will follow them into later life.

While some researchers have spent considerable time forecasting conflict between the generations over entitlements and policies, others have begun to speculate about the possibility of **intragenerational conflict** (Day, 1993a). Intragenerational conflict—conflict among members of the same generation or age group—might be predicated on socioeconomic status, with many analysts predicting increasing distance between the advantaged and disadvantaged elderly of the future (Torres-Gil, 1992). AARP and the Gray Panthers, for example, are two aging organizations that differ significantly in terms of member demographics and interests. Many other organizations that focus on issues related to age have more specific agendas, often with opposing goals. It is already overly simplistic to discuss advocacy on behalf of "the elderly," because that population includes so many constituencies and interests. Such diversity may promote more intragenerational conflict in the future.

Torres-Gil (1992) predicts the growth of vertical alliances across cohorts or age strata, based on social class, race and ethnicity, or common interests, that would strongly divide age groups and minimize the potential for age-based alliances in support of policies. Some experts predict that transgenerational alliances (for example, an alliance between older people in frail health and younger disabled people) focused on specific issues such as health care, housing, or income may make the politics of age obsolete (Day, 1990). For example, in 1996 the House of Representatives passed legislation that would enhance criminal penalties for crimes of violence against both the elderly and children. Previous legislative approaches might have singled out one group or the other. Here, policy attention is given to both groups together, based on the presumption of their shared vulnerability to crime.

Should age become less salient as a criterion for policy, it could be politically difficult to maintain current programs of age entitlements, and disadvantaged elders would find themselves vying with younger poor persons for the limited resources that society provides those in need. The current debate may signal the doom of age as a significant political and policy force as we have known it in recent decades in most developed societies.

The role of government in ensuring the well-being of older people is a subject of continuing debate. Although concerns regarding "demographic as destiny" have driven these debates on age-based policies and entitlements in many aging societies, the issues are much more complex than just the dependency ratio (Friedland and Summers, 1999). Political commitments and public attitudes, which have largely favored societal attention to the needs of older adults, are potent forces in shaping how collective resources are allocated. With regard to intergenerational politics and issues, Moody (1992) suggests, the "political argument comes down to a matter of confidence and legitimization: a feeling that institutions of intergenerational transfer—whether Social Security or the public schools—can be counted on to do their job and remain reliable for successive cohorts" (p. 239).

Web Wise

Administration on Aging/Older Americans Act

http://www.aoa.dhhs.gov/aoa/pages/aoafact.html

One of the major pieces of legislation establishing the "aging network" was the Older Americans Act (OAA). This site, provided by the Administration on Aging, the governmental agency charged with fulfilling the mandate of the OAA, describes the legislation and how it has been implemented. The OAA provides a wide range of services based on a combination of age and need at the federal, state, and local levels.

Senior Law

http://www.seniorlaw.com/index.htm

This site, which is maintained by attorneys Goldfarb & Abrandt specializing in Senior Law, provides information on legal/legislative updates in Medicare and Medicaid, a reference to articles on elder law topics, and other senior law information. If you are seriously interested in the law, you may wish to check out their "way cool sites," which includes topics reaching well beyond senior law.

American Association for Retired Persons—Where We Stand

http://www.aarp.org/where.html

As the largest membership group in the country, the American Association for Retired Persons is active in developing positions, advocating on behalf of causes related to older adults, and encouraging/educating older adults to be vocal on their own behalf. This site contains issue papers describing AARP's stand on a variety of topics from advance directives and elder abuse to older drivers and federal entitlement programs. There is also information about hot policy topics, including managed care and Social Security, and informational "how to" segments for those interested in lobbying or expressing their views to policy makers.

National Council of Senior Citizens (NCSC)

http://www.ncscinc.org

The National Council of Senior Citizens is an activist organization for older adults, working on a range of issues from housing and the Older Americans Act to improvements in health care coverage. Their issues and some analysis of current developments relating to them in Washington (and elsewhere) can be found on this easily navigated site.

National Aging Information Center (NAIC)

http://www.aoa.dhhs.gov/naic/

The National Aging Information Center (NAIC), operated by the U.S. Administration on Aging (AoA), is a central source for a wide variety of program- and policy-related materials and demographic and other statistical data on the health, economic, and social status of older Americans. Established under the Older Americans Act (OAA), NAIC opened its doors to the public in September 1995. It is a useful gateway to other sites and statistical information through its alphabetical site index.

Key Terms

age entitlement
age identification
age stratification
aging-conservatism hypothesis
aging enterprise
Americans for Generational
   Equity (AGE)
backlash against the older population
civic development hypothesis
compassionate ageism
conservative agenda
electoral bluff

gerontocracy
graying of the federal budget
intergenerational conflict
intragenerational conflict
liberal agenda
Medicare Catastrophic Coverage
   Act (MCCA)
need entitlement
old-age welfare state
Older Americans Act
power elites
social mobility

Questions for Thought and Reflection

1. Period effects are thought to influence peoples' political party affiliation and their confidence in institutions, such as the government. Thinking through your life and through history, what are some of the events that you might expect would have a significant effect on these political views?

2. Think about or discuss with others the reasons people choose to vote or not to vote (including reasons not to register). What are the major themes that appear to be central for young adults compared to people of other ages? Can you identify any strategies that might accomplish what political parties have tried in recent decades—to get out the "youth vote?" What are the implications if few young people continue to vote in upcoming elections?

3. Generational equity proposes moving toward need-based entitlement for government benefits. What major programs would this influence? How would changes to need entitlement influence your neighbors, family and friends?

4. Does it make sense to have minimum ages mandated for running for political offices? Would you suggest that we have maximum ages for holding high office? If so, what age would you suggest and why would it be the relevant one to choose?

The Future

The chapters that have been presented thus far have described the processes of aging and the social contexts that structure and give meaning to aging in various cultures. But what will aging be like in the future? Will science fiction predictions of extended life span or of immortality become real? Advances in technology, efforts in health promotion, changes in our attitudes about aging, and changes in our age structures will all contribute to a new experience of aging.

In recent years a woman in her sixties gave birth to her first child with the assistance of a fertility clinic. Senator John Glenn of Ohio, the first American to orbit the globe as an astronaut in the early 1960s, has returned to space in his late 70s. Senator Glenn's mission in part studied the effects of weightlessness on an aging body.

Clearly we need to start to stretch our ideas about what aging means. Some scholars suggest that we will probably rethink many of our assumptions about aging and life stages as more of us survive to ages close to the century mark. In the next (and final) chapter, we examine some of what we know about the future now and some of the speculations about the issues that we face in aging societies and an aging world.

CHAPTER 12

Conclusion:
The Dynamics of Aging in Our Future

At the end of the 20th century, later life remains a season in search of its purposes. It is clear that the moral status of older people cannot rest simply on their entitlements, or their roles as abstract bearers of rights, or their image as dependent, passive recipients of treatment. But what do older people owe society? their families? themselves? (Cole, 1995, p. 342).

Most of us easily conceptualize aging on an individual level as the physical and social changes that come as we move through various ages and stages of the life course. It is somewhat more difficult to understand how the aging of the larger society and the accompanying high rates of social change affect this personal experience. Aging is an individual journey through time, `shaped by individual choices (regarding employment, family, financial planning) and behaviors (building a history of good nutrition and exercise and a strong network of social support). But aging is also a collective, shared experience constructed by the political and economic forces in society, by public values and debates, and by changing social institutions. It has been one of our goals here to make the larger social context and the implications of an aging society more visible.

We age in a social context that dramatically influences us in both positive and negative ways. This socially-constructed and culturally-specific context not only defines the opportunities available to us based on age, but also the way we think of ourselves and others as young, middle-aged, or older persons. Our collective attitudes toward later life in the U.S. continue to be fairly negative, despite the positive reports we get from older people regarding their well-being and satisfaction with life. Myths and stereotypes about aging are perpetuated, giving way incrementally to a more realistic view of the diverse situations we probably will face as we move into later life.

On the positive side, frailty, loss, and disadvantage do not necessarily characterize later life. Certainly there are older persons who experience these problems, but most older people live autonomously in the community, are financially independent of their families, and despite some health conditions, fend for themselves. Recent evidence strongly suggests that many dimensions of the quality of life, from age of onset of disease and disability to economics well-being and social engagement, should improve in coming cohorts, in part through positive lifestyle choices of individuals (Rowe and Kahn, 1998). We are, in many cases, agents in shaping our futures. Aging is not a spectator sport; choices we each make every day will bear fruit over the long term in terms of

Exhibit 12.1   *Serious Problems by Age Group*

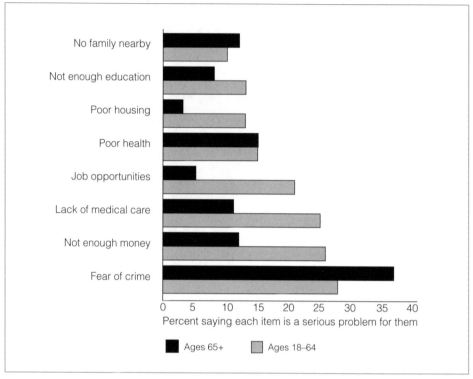

Source: Speas and Obenshain, 1995.

health, housing, economic status, and social networks.

It is also encouraging that older people today do not see a picture nearly as negative as the stereotypes portray. In fact, later life may have advantages. Exhibit 12.1 shows the responses to a large national survey of adults (age 18 and over) regarding their experience with eight common problem areas. In only two of these areas (fear of crime and having no family nearby) were respondents over 65 more likely than younger adults to report problems as being "serious" for themselves. Contrary to the negative images many of us carry of later life, more younger than older people reported serious problems with money, lack of health care, poor housing, or inadequate education (Speas and Obenshain, 1995). Many older adults, according to this study, do not find later life a stage of endless problems and decline.

Clearly the luckiest of us will approach later life with good health, strong family and friendship networks, a secure financial future, and opportunities to contribute to society in ways we find meaningful. Despite the positive changes we can anticipate in future cohorts of aging individuals, including ourselves as we grow older, individuals and subgroups within the older population will benefit unequally from those changes. Some individuals will experience poor health, inadequate housing or income, or other disadvantages as a result of the cumulative effects of a lifetime of poverty, disability, or educational disadvantage. Alternatively, negative consequences may result from disruptive life events, such as unexpected job loss, disability, or divorce. Although we as individuals have a certain amount of control over our future selves as older persons, some factors remain beyond our control and planning. Some changes are random; some are patterned and socially produced.

Each society with an aging population is now making decisions regarding what types of assistance it is collectively willing and able to provide for aging individuals in need. These decisions reflect our ideologies about whether disadvantaged elders are responsible for their own fates. Each culture has different ideas about the appropriate roles of families and communities in assisting elders in need. If someone is poor in later life, society may be much more sympathetic if the problem occurs because of a disabling workplace injury than if the person was a lifelong spendthrift. Policies being formulated today reflect our societal viewpoint on the elderly. The media push since the 1980s in the U.S. to identify the elderly as uniformly well-to-do "greedy geezers" has implications for social policies that affect not just the wealthy elders but also those at the other end of the income spectrum. If we reduce Social Security benefits based on an incorrect stereotype of all elders as wealthy, we undoubtedly harm some individuals who differ from that stereotype.

In this chapter we summarize some key points about understanding aging in this dynamic social context and describe trends for the future of aging as a process in society. We also address some of the challenges that remain relevant to understanding aging in the new millennium.

Aging in a Changing Social World

Rethinking Old Age and the Life Course

Life stages did not always exist as we currently understand them. Not all cultures have distinguished childhood from adulthood, or adulthood from later life, in the ways that we do today (Aries, 1962; Cole, 1992). There is nothing natural or fixed about the set of life-course stages that we have today and no reason why we could not reorganize life into more, fewer, or different stages than we now have. We already find that researchers and practitioners are dissatisfied with "old age" as a stage, often differentiating it into two or three stages, such as "young old" and the "oldest old." Such categorizations point out the socially constructed nature of our current life-course stages. We determine the boundaries of these stages and the fact that we utilizing some criteria, perhaps a combination of chronological age, physical characteristics, and social role obligations. Once we socially construct them and imbue them with meaning, they become a taken-for-granted part of our culture and way of looking at the world—they become reality for us.

It is important to recall that old age as we now think of it is a social construct that has been generated by and given meaning in various cultures (Cornman and Kingson, 1996). Whether older adults are revered or discarded depends on the cultural/historical context. Such ideas are, therefore, changeable. One potential trend to watch is whether our definitions of old age and how we divide the life course into socially meaningful stages change as societal aging progresses. Americans apparently continue to share notions of age-appropriate timing of life events (Settersten and Hagestad, 1996a, b; Zepelin, Sills, and Heath, 1986-87), but some experts argue that chronological age is becoming less relevant as a marker of human life and the social roles of adulthood (Neugarten, 1979).

In a sense we can already see signs that some redefinition is underway, because chronological age often does not help us make valid distinctions between individuals and groups. It is difficult to see meaningful physical, social, or psychological commonalities between those who have just reached age 65 and those approaching a century of life, but both groups are currently called "old." In the future we may, for example, raise the lower boundary of "old age" to age 75 or 80, modify existing life stages, or add new ones. Policies are already in place to gradually increase the age for full Social Security benefits to 67 from 65, and politicians are discussing moving beyond that age in the future. If people continue most adult roles and maintain good health until age 75, is there any reason to continue to use 65 as the benchmark for when later life begins? The signs point to the need for individuals, social institutions, and entire societies to rethink our stereotypes, definitions of what aging means, and the relevance of "old age" as a social category.

Do our existing life-course stages still fit the way that the life course is evolving? Will these stages remain meaningful in light of increasing life expectancy? In several ways the life course fits the current realities poorly. The addition of years at the end of life means an increasingly long period of socially undifferentiated "adulthood," followed by an undifferentiated period of "old age." As people spend, on average, more time in these phases of the life course, we find ourselves pulled toward making finer distinctions. When most people died in what we today call "middle age," it was less important to consider differences between 60-year-olds and centenarians. In most countries of sub-Saharan Africa, for example, where life expectancies are lower and where AIDS is devastating the population, there is little discussion of aging compared to countries with growing populations of older adults.

A second important question about the life course refers to a consistent theme throughout this book—the extent to which aging is constituted differently for various gender, race, class or ethnic groups. Is there uniformity across diverse social groups in how they move through the life course and in the timing of major events? We have some clues, but further research is required for definitive answers. The preponderance of research studies on European American, middle-class adults, especially males, makes our understanding of other social classes, ethnic and racial groups, and of all women more tenuous. Differences in life expectancies and functional health across racial groups, for example, may result in different boundaries for being "middle-aged" or "old." Higher rates of physical disability result in more early retirements among African Americans. If being retired places one in the category of "old age," then disadvantaged African Americans may reach that benchmark chronologically sooner (Jackson and Gibson, 1985). In another example, working-class individuals may engage in the social roles such as grandparenthood at earlier chronological ages than those in the middle class may. Working-class careers plateau earlier and at a lower level than do those of middle-class workers. People in this category often start families earlier so their children are grown sooner. From these few examples, it is clear that not all groups move through life-course stages in chronological lockstep. To the extent that these differences persist, life-course stages may be less useful as a social concept for researchers in a more diverse society.

A third question about the life course can shed some light on future change. Do biological and psychological maturation correspond meaningfully to the socially constructed stages of life? Perhaps not; certainly physical development sometimes outpaces and other times lags behind the social stages that we have developed. Puberty occurs long before ages at which many societies encourage marriage or reproduction, and retirement is socially timed for ages when a majority of individuals are quite capable of continued productivity on the job. In addition, there are individuals whose health is impaired early in life through disease or accident, raising the question of whether they share social characteristics with the "old old" despite chronological age differences. Therefore, using physical traits or functional capacity to evaluate life stage or "old age" continues to be problematic.

Fourth, how might we reorganize the stages of life to modify our existing patterns? Who does the reorganizing, and how does it happen? The answers to these questions are more obscure. Consider the area of employment. Currently we have roles temporally structured in the life course in such a way that young adults face the pressures of attempting to succeed in jobs at the same time that they are bearing and parenting small children (Loscocco, 2000). Yet it is difficult to defer childbearing beyond the currently accepted years of career building, especially for women. Knowledge is now becoming obsolete more quickly, suggesting that scheduling education to be completed before employment begins will be less useful over a 30- to 40-year career. Multiple careers, with individuals taking a mid-life sabbatical for updating their knowledge in a field or changing careers entirely, or simultaneous employment and education, could become more common and should become more expected and accepted (Dannefer, 2000). In fact, although full-time students are more often of "traditional ages," data on enrollments show that 47.1% of undergraduate and 63.4% of graduate students attending part-time are over age 30, suggesting that lifelong education is already here (Chronicle, 1999). Each of these changes will have implications for social policy and other social institutions, such as the family, education and the economy.

Finally, as later life lengthens and we see greater diversity among the population in what we now call "old age," we may both move that baseline age back (say to 75 or 80) and construct new stages within this lengthening period. For example, we may differentiate an early, healthy stage during post-retirement years, in which activity and community service become normative expectations, and a later stage, in which health limitations and some degree of dependence are expected (Laslett, 1991).

Implications of a Global Economy

The world's human population is, as we saw in Chapter 3, aging. But different countries' populations are aging at various speeds. Nations' population profiles are related to their levels of economic development, as well as a range of other social and cultural factors. A global economy, communications technology that connects all parts of the world, and changing worldwide employment patterns underscore the relevance of aging in all parts of the world. The rapid aging of the Chinese population will have implications far beyond the borders of that country, as the Chinese government moves to control the population through the one-child policy. Production and consumption in China may change as the population ages and shrinks in size; Chinese experts may seek internationally for alternatives to traditional family care as their older population skyrockets. As the world gets smaller, it is important to keep the larger world economy, and those of its many aging societies, in mind.

As some countries age more quickly, they face problems and opportunities in this wider economy. Aging nations might become more open to immigration to bolster the shrinking size of their labor forces. Such migration will raise questions about support of elderly kin left behind in the migrants' home countries and the impact immigration has on the culture of the receiving country.

In the global economy, it is probably safe to bet that neither employment patterns nor retirement as we know it will survive without dramatic alterations. Jobs will become more technological. Workers will need advanced education to be competitive in the marketplace. As health status and longevity improve, will older workers be prevented from retiring when they desire? Either governments or employers could alter their pension policies if the supplies of youthful workers entering the job market are insufficient to meet demand.

The distinctions between the economic "haves" and the "have-nots" are growing, not shrinking, in many nations of the world. Analyses of pension coverage of U.S. workers show declining rates of pensions, with the steepest declines for Hispanic and African American workers (Chen and Leavitt, 1997). Because disadvantages in early-life stages with regard to education, jobs, health, and pensions have ramifications throughout the life course, it is too simplistic to presume that problems of a nation's underclass will disappear in the future or that most elders will be financially secure. For example, more women throughout the world are working full-time for pay throughout most of their adult lives. But the types of employment women hold internationally, often in family businesses, continue to be less likely to offer pensions; perhaps women's work will not have the same long-term "payoff" as a lifetime of work for men. If pension coverage continues to decline, especially as contingent employment becomes more common, the financial security of more older people may be a question mark rather than a given. Even in countries where private pensions are widely available today, policymakers may need to revise provisions (both public and private) for their aging populations in the future. Recall that many countries have no pension system or only rudimentary pension coverage, as they deal with problems of economic modernization, hunger, disease, population growth and, all too often, political strife or war. As the populations in these economically challenged nations age, it is unclear that resources will be available to avoid many of the problems addressed in more developed countries. The future elderly will, if current trends continue, include some very advantaged and some very disadvantaged groups. Coping with that reality will continue to challenge societies in which those holding the advantages tend to make the policies.

Societies must also address issues of productivity as their populations age. Population projections clearly identify a growing population in many societies of "young old" individuals under age 75 or 80. Some consider the "young old" an "untapped resource" for productivity (Commonwealth Fund, 1993). If employment policies do not change to dramatically increase their involvement in jobs, societies must ask themselves how they can both integrate those individuals into the society and harness some of their skills, experience, and energy to improve their communities and nations. Could or should societies strengthen norms of volunteerism so that healthy and willing retirees give a significant portion of their time to fighting poverty, illiteracy, teen pregnancy, environmental problems, or other social issues? Such norms, and the social policies supporting them, would have implications for income maintenance policies —would such work be paid or unpaid? If healthy retirees volunteer in large numbers, would the marketplace for leisure activities like golf and cruise vacations suffer? How would volunteers affect family life and other areas of social life —would there be less support available from older to younger generations?

Developing additional options for "young old" individuals not engaged in paid employment remains an unmet challenge in many aging societies. Nonetheless, research shows that adults over 55 already make tremendous contributions to their families, their communities, and the nation through voluntary activity as well as paid employment (Bass, 1995). Many are interested in contributing more, in either paid or unpaid work settings (Commonwealth Fund, 1993).

Changing Family Structure

Dramatic changes within families over the past several decades will play themselves out in future cohorts of elders. More women are employed full-time, making them less available as family caregivers (Bianchi and Spain, 1996). In addition, lower fertility means that future cohorts will have fewer adult children as potential caregivers. Who will undertake caregiving for the childless or those with children whose children are geographically or emotionally distant? One answer is for the economy to respond with market alternatives such as home health care services or assistive housing to meet the needs of those unable to be fully independent. Yet such solutions require either public or private financing to ensure access for all elders needing such help. When neither family nor society provides needed care, is society willing to accept negative fallout such as insufficient care or increased deaths?

This photo of an 83 year-old with her great-great granddaughter was a rare family experience in the past, but is becoming more common as life expectancy increases.

We have yet to encounter the full ramifications of "serial monogamy" (sequential divorce and remarriage) on family relationships in later life. Its impact both on filial obligation toward non-custodial and step-parents, as well as on step- and half-sibling relationships, is far from clear. Will having eight or more full and step-grandparents be advantageous to a child, compared with having only four? On the one hand, we might be pessimistic that the family will relinquish its role of providing primary support to frail elders; on the other hand, the relationships that persist may be stronger ones than those engendered through only a sense of duty.

For individuals, some family relationships will be longer-lasting than today. A newspaper story chronicling the birthday of a 115-year-old woman in Maryland will soon not warrant coverage as "special" as the number of centenarians grows. In the story, the mentally intact and physically healthy 115-year-old was visited daily by her 92-year-old daughter and less often by a 70-year-old grandson. Three generations of one family were receiving Social Security! All six generations of this family, including a 2-month-old great-great-great-granddaughter, were present for the woman's birthday celebration (Vitez, 1995). Although most of us will probably not achieve the century mark, having the potential for a century of fairly healthy life warrants a serious rethinking of how, and when in life, we do certain things.

Future Cohorts of Older People

What We Can Accurately Predict

Predicting the future is a notoriously difficult (and risky) process, especially for those with some allegiance to the rules of scientific method. Given the large number of unknown factors, what can we really say about the future and what the older population will be like in the year 2020 or 2050? It is perhaps easier than it seems, because the people who will be part of the over-65 population in those years are already born. We can examine these cohorts and identify ways in which they are similar to and different from current cohorts above the age of 60 or 70. Based on these differences from their predecessors, we can speculate about how they may age differently. Let us first examine a few of the differences we can quantify, and later speculate about other social changes and cohort experiences likely to make these cohorts very distinct from their predecessors as they age.

The federal government routinely makes projections of future socio-demographic characteristics for the purpose of planning. According to Easterlin (1996), "Projections of population in developed countries over the next half century consistently assume that the rate of childbearing will remain low, total population size will stabilize or decline, and the proportion of the older population will rise markedly" (p. 73). Some projections assume that there will not be a significant rise in the fertility rate, nor will there be major breakthroughs that will significantly extend average life expectancy. Should major changes occur, the projections would be off, either underestimating or overestimating the size or characteristics of future elderly. With that caveat in mind, let us examine what we are expecting to see in the next several decades.

Growth and Diversity

We have talked throughout this book about the impact of the growing older population on society and on the lives of individuals. Just how significant is that growth? Exhibit 12.2 shows population trends through 1990 and projections starting in 2000 for those over 65. Several things are readily apparent. First, the growth in the population over age 65 will continue to be a major social phenomenon, with the U.S. population over age 65 more than doubling between 2000 and 2050. Second, the growth will be fastest among those above age 85, who will have grown from near invisibility as recently as the 1940s to nearly one-fourth of the over 65 population by 2050 if current assumptions hold true. In contrast, the size of the "young old" population (ages 65-74) is expected to grow quite slowly during this time period.

The growth of the population over 65 will not be matched by growth among the population aged 64 and under, according to population projections. Therefore, the median age of the society will increase. Exhibit 12.3 shows the projections for median age of the U.S. population to 2050, demonstrating an increase to nearly 40 years before a slight downturn. Keep in mind that the median age

Exhibit 12.2   *Population Trends and Projections by Age: 1900–2050*

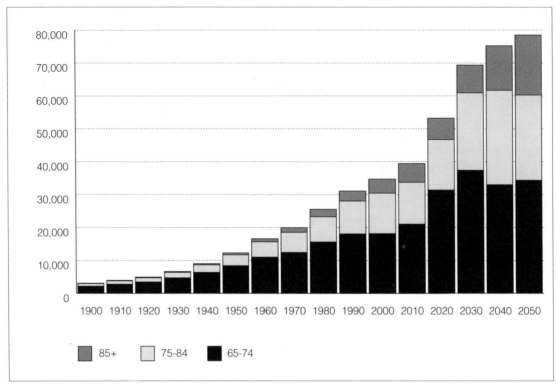

Source: Hobbs and Damon, 1996.

Exhibit 12.3   *Projected Median Age: 1940–2050*

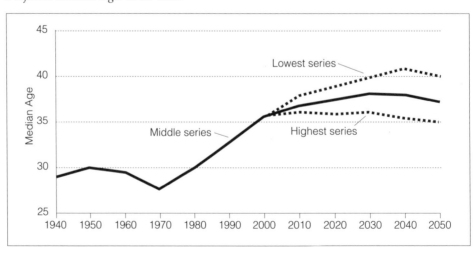

Source: U.S. Bureau of the Census, 1996a.

Growing racial and ethnic diversity means that the face of later life is changing.

is shaped by mortality, fertility and sometimes by migration. The dotted lines indicate projections with either higher or lower fertility assumptions, which might result in either an "older" society or a "younger" society, as indicated by the median age (U.S. Bureau of the Census, 1996a).

Another way to look at these projections is in terms of the dependency ratio, as discussed in Chapter 3. Exhibit 12.4 divides the dependent population into its two chronological components, those under age 18 and those 65 and over. Clearly there have been dramatic historical changes in the dependency ratio during the twentieth century, and we can expect continuing drama in the first fifty years of the twenty-first century. The level of dependency is expected to increase until about 2030, and then essentially level off. This growth is largely accounted for by the growth in the population 65 and over, with relatively little change expected in the number of dependents under 18. Even with the growth of the older population, however, total dependency is not expected to exceed the levels of the peak years of childhood dependency of the baby boom cohorts (see Exhibit 12.4). Barring unforeseen changes (such as a dramatic upturn in fertility rates, or a breakthrough reducing old age mortality), we can anticipate that the older population will become an increasingly large component of the population of the United States and many other aging societies. This aging of society is somewhat moderated by the "baby boom echo," the large number of births at the end of the 20th century to the very large number of mothers in the baby boom itself (Morgan, 1998). The number of births in the 18-year span from 1980-1998 (72.3 million) approaches the size of the original "boom" (75.9 million), providing some counter-weight to the base of the population pyramid as baby boomers age

Exhibit 12.4   *Number of Dependents per 100 Persons Age 18 to 64 Years: 1900–2050*

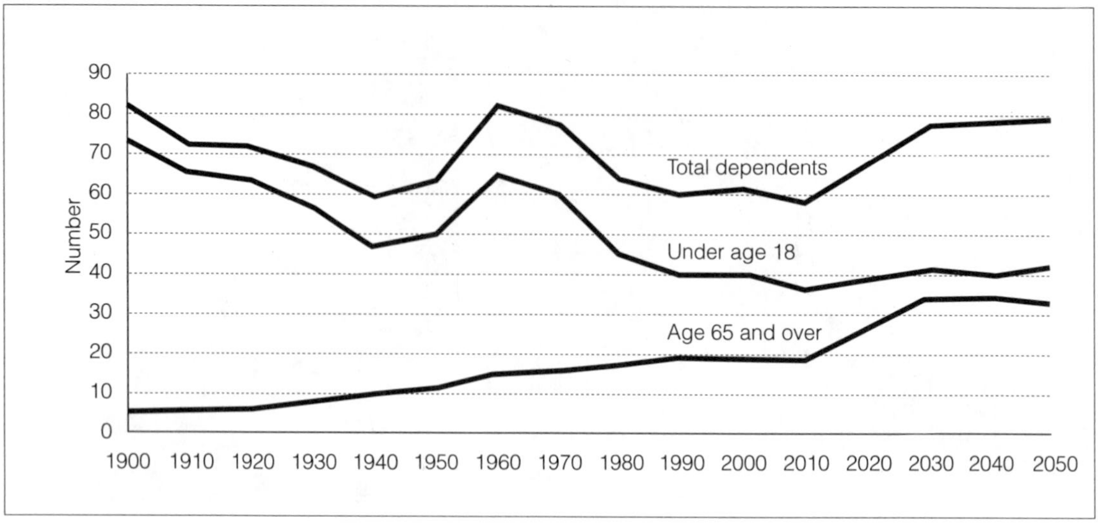

Source: U.S. Bureau of the Census, 1996a.

(Friedland and Summer, 1999).

One final population projection also suggests growing racial/ethnic diversity within the older population in the United States. Exhibit 12.5 compares the percentage of the population 65 and over by race/ethnicity from 1990 to 2050 (U.S. Bureau of the Census, 1996a). The trend over the next fifty years is clearly toward a decreasing percentage of non-Hispanic European Americans and only modest increases among African and Native American groups. The strongest growth will be among Asian/Pacific Islander and Hispanic populations, deriving from recent levels of migration of these groups into the United States and higher-than-average fertility in some of their subgroups.

Education

Education is an area of some complexity, requiring consideration of cohort differences and changing age norms to understand recent changes and future trends. Two related areas are worthy of examination. The first is that of the trends in educational attainment through high school and college among various birth cohorts. The second area is the growing trend toward education beyond "traditional" ages, currently referred to as adult or continuing education, already mentioned earlier in this chapter.

First, the education of successive cohorts has increased, as was indicated earlier in Exhibit 2.1. As we contrast younger cohorts and older cohorts, it is clear that more and more people are completing high school, attending some college, or completing college. Between 1960 and 1994 the proportion of high school

Exhibit 12.5   *Percent Distribution of Population Age 65 and Over by Race and Hispanic Origin: 1990–2050*

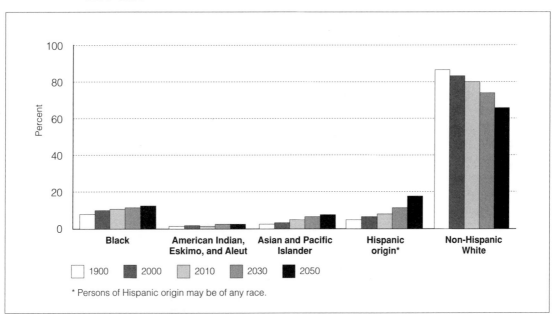

* Persons of Hispanic origin may be of any race.

Source: U.S. Bureau of the Census, 1996a

graduates who were enrolled in college during the October following gradua-tion increased from 45.1 percent to 61.9 percent (U.S. Bureau of the Census, 1996b). As a consequence of these long-term trends, the educational profile of the adult population is shifting; members of older, less educated cohorts die and younger and better educated cohorts move into adulthood and eventually later life. Exhibit 12.6 compares the educational attainment of the population over 65 in 1990 with projections for 2030 (Hobbs and Damon, 1996). Clearly the trend toward more education is apparent for both men and women, with increased percentages expected to complete high school and college. Despite ongoing con-cerns about high dropout rates and the "cumulative disadvantage" potential of undereducated individuals in a technologically-savvy job market, the older population overall will continue to grow more educated over the next several decades. Since more-educated individuals often fare better in later life, all else being equal (which it never is), this trend is an encouraging one.

The second issue, education among individuals of non-normative ages, is one of growing interest to educators. Data on education have often reflected the out-of-date expectation that most people over age 25 seek little addition-al education. Educational institutions have been age-segregated in the past, enrolling children and young adults. Increasingly since the 1970s, enrollments have grown dramatically for more "mature" students, including those return-

Exhibit 12.6   *Educational Attainment of the Elderly by Sex: 1990 and 2030*

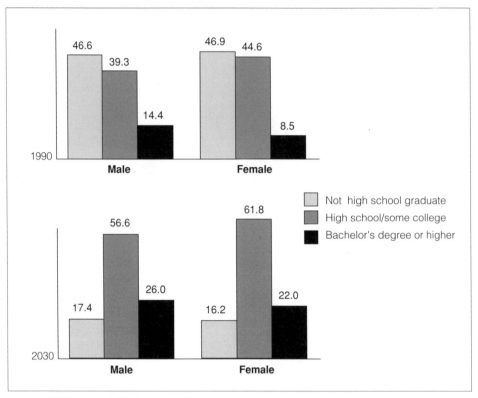

Source: U.S. Bureau of the Census, 1990.

ing to school after many years of involvement in work, family, or both. Also included in this trend, however, are those who are extending their education to the graduate or professional levels, where the extra years of training push completion to age 30 or beyond. From 1970 to 1994 the numbers of individuals enrolled in some type of schooling (mostly college) between ages 25 and 29 more than doubled, and the numbers for adults ages 30 through 34 grew threefold (U.S. Bureau of the Census, 1996b). This trend portends a gradual transition of education to an age-integrated, rather than age-segregated, social institution (Riley and Riley 1994). Between 1980 and 1998 school enrollments among those over age 35 more than doubled, but this trend started from a very low number, with the result that only 2.5 percent of adults over 35 were enrolled in school in 1998 (Martinez and Curry, 1998; U.S. Bureau of the Census, 1996b). Of course, these cross-sectional "snapshots" of enrollment in specific years may hide the fact that more adults are enrolled in school at one time or another throughout adulthood than indicated by the percentages. If education continues to become more integrated throughout adulthood, we

Exhibit 12.7   *Trends and Projections of Marital Status for Women Aged 65+: 1980–2050*

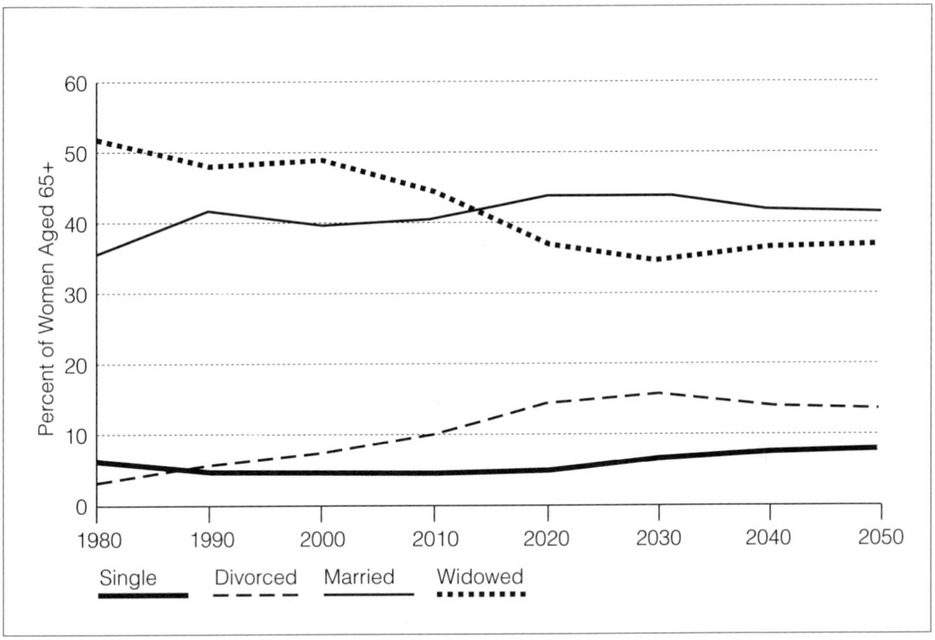

Adapted from: U.S. Bureau of the Census, 1975, 1976, 1995c.

may find it less relevant to distinguish among students of traditional ages and those augmenting their education in other stages of life. Being a student may become an "ageless" role.

Sharing Lives and Households

Marital status, non-marital relationships, and living arrangements in later life are the product of a lifetime of opportunities and decisions, some not under the control of the individual. Will the prevalence and outcome of these major life events differ markedly for future cohorts? Significant social changes have continued to sweep through the institution of the family, mirrored in sometimes dramatic changes in the lives of individuals of different cohorts. An example is marriage. In 1970 about 36 percent of women ages 20-24 and 11 percent of those 25-29 had never married. By 1994 the comparable figures for women were 66 percent and 35 percent, indicating both the possibility of delayed marriage (with ramifications for the timing of other family events) and the increased likelihood of never marrying at all (Saluter, 1996). Men also experienced dramatic changes; 9 percent of men 30-34 had not married in 1970, compared with 30 percent in the mid-1990s, with these trends apparently continuing (Lugaila, 1998). Exhibit 12.7 shows projections of the marital status of the female population over 65 through 2050, assuming that current trends hold (Hobbs and Damon, 1996). Among women, who constitute the majority of the older population and whose marital fates differ substantially from those of men, we can expect a substantial increase in the percentage divorced, a slight increase in the percentage who remain single, and corresponding declines in the widowed population. The percentage of the female population over age 65 who are expected to be married remains remarkably stable across this time period (Hobbs and Damon 1996). Dramatic increases in divorce mean that fewer women will reach later life with a sufficiently lengthy marriage to quality for spouse benefits from Social Security (Smeeding, 1999).

These projections represent the current marital status of women 65 and over, not their marital histories. Given the continuing high levels of divorce, more individuals will approach later life having lived independently, perhaps having experienced one or more marriages or long-term relationships along the way. The smaller percentage of adults who will approach old age having experienced a lengthy, continuous marriage, with its expectations of substantial mutual support and economic security, may have significant implications for issues such as caregiving. One neglected area is the potential for companionship and social support provided by non-marital couple relationships with either same- or opposite-sex partners (Kimmel, 1993). Researchers have generally paid attention to whether or not someone is married, but not to other, non-marital forms of partnering that may be meaningful and may be more openly practiced by future cohorts. The baby boomers, who spearheaded the cohabitation trend of the 1970s, may also be pioneers of alternative lifestyles in their later years.

In terms of living arrangements, households headed by someone over age 75 already constituted 8.4 percent of all U.S. households and will increase substantially in number by 2010, even before the baby boomers reach 75, starting in 2020 (U.S. Bureau of the Census, 1996b). One of the major trends regarding households is the increasing number and percentage of older adults living alone (Szinovacz and Ekerdt, 1996). Future developments in alternative forms of housing, however, may change where older people choose to live as they age. Alternatives such as continuing care retirement communities, where independent elders have their own apartments but may move to more supportive environments as needed, are becoming more commonly available to those who can afford them (Newcomer and Preston, 1994).

Political Participation

The area of politics and political participation is one in which we might strongly suspect that cohort effects will create differences in the behaviors and attitudes of cohorts. Once it was thought that aging led to political conservatism; today some might speculate that aging leads to liberalism, because more older adults than in the past have voted for Democratic candidates. Major events, such as the Vietnam and Persian Gulf wars, various political scandals from Watergate to Whitewater, and the swings that occur from domination by the Republicans or the Democrats are likely to influence these cohorts. But only sketchy information is available to try to predict how these events will influence older voters of the future.

Data available on the party affiliation of older and younger cohorts and on the strength of their political attitudes suggest that, if cohorts continue to maintain their party affiliations throughout life, the older population will eventually swing back toward a more Republican concentration than is the case today. This swing will reflect the eventual aging of the Reagan Republicans of the 1980s (U.S. Bureau of the Census, 1996b). A related issue has to do with the impact of the aging population on the profile of voters. Exhibit 12.8

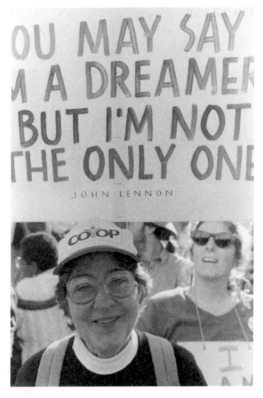

Some experts expect greater activism among coming cohorts of older adults.

shows the 1992 age structure of the voting population and projections for 2020. You can see in the chart the shift toward older age groups dominating the voting population as the large baby boomer cohorts swell the ranks of the population over 65. If older adults ever coalesce into a coherent voting bloc, their potential impact in the years between 2030 and 2050 could be considerable.

Speculations about Coming Cohorts

It is difficult to anticipate the nature and extent of changes in a number of areas, including health, disability, life expectancy, and the labor force. Many experts believe in a biological limit to human life span of around 120 years but others debate this figure. Aging experts are also divided on the prospect that a major breakthrough in understanding the biological mechanisms of aging might enable an extension of average life expectancy. Such changes raise important ethical questions regarding access to costly life-extending technologies that have, until only recently, been the subject of science fiction. Most biologists are not optimistic that a major breakthrough will be forthcoming in the near term; if it is, its social implications are potentially staggering. Completion of mapping the

Exhibit 12.8   *Percent Distribution of Voters by Age: November 1992–2020*

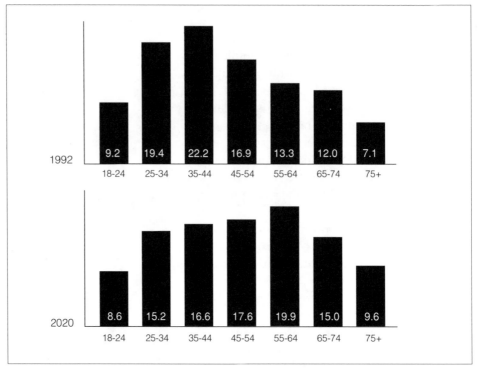

Source: U.S. Bureau of the Census, 1992b and Day, 1998 .

human genome raises the prospect of genetic interventions in diseases and the fundamental aging process (Rowe and Gatz, 2000). This prospect raises questions about the policies and institutions that might alter dramatically in the face of dramatically extended human life.

Nor can we predict what small changes in health practices and preventive care will mean for health or longevity. For example, dietary changes from 1970 to 1994 included average per-person declines in consumption of 15 percent for red meat and 20 percent for distilled liquor and increases of 25 percent for fruits and 33 percent for the healthiest vegetables (U.S. Bureau of the Census, 1996b). Widespread fluoridation of water, which began in the middle of the twentieth century, might mean that more elders retain their teeth and therefore get more satisfactory nutrition into their later years. Will larger portions in restaurant food, more meals eaten away from home and the average weight gain of Americans portend health problems? Will the recent fashions of drinking more water or smoking cigars have long-term effects? How have childhood immunizations for measles and flu shots for adults changed the outcomes for health and life expectancy? How will the movement toward management of AIDS shape mortality from that single cause of death? How will the countervailing trends toward more exercise and more sedentary jobs and leisure activities (like television watching or web surfing) influence long-term health prospects? The changes are so numerous that it is difficult to isolate the single effects of any one. Nonetheless, the cumulative effect of these changes will influence life expectancy and the types and ages of onset of illnesses/disabilities.

In a recent book entitled *Successful Aging*, authors Rowe and Kahn outline what they refer to as many aspects of "usual aging," including high blood pressure, weight gain and inactivity, which are easily modified by changing behaviors (1998). Usual aging is a complex of changes that are typical, but not caused by aging, per se. These authors argue that changes in behavior, such as quitting smoking or starting exercise, even later in life, will have a dramatic effect on the health of older adults in the future. Individuals, while certainly not in control of all aspects of aging, do have a role to play as agents in mapping their physical, social and emotional futures as they age. The extent to which coming cohorts engage in these positive behaviors, versus the negative ones of eating fatty foods, being "couch potatoes," and smoking, may alter the profile of functional health among the elderly in a striking positive direction.

The Risks of Prediction

Despite the predictions outlined here, there remains the potential for dramatic and as yet unanticipated changes that will reshape current and future cohorts as we age. It is difficult to speculate, for example, about how some changes we can see today will play out. Among adults between 25 and 44 almost 13 percent have accessed the Internet, compared with only 1 percent of adults over 65 (U.S. Bureau of the Census, 1996b). If utilizing such technologies is a cohort-based phenomenon, we might expect a gradual increase in the likelihood that older adults will be "surfing the net," and we can contemplate ways to make use of that technology in providing services and even conducting research. If restrictions in pensions and Social Security reduce the disposable incomes of older adults, however, fewer may be able to keep up with cutting-edge technology or afford access to the Internet.

While many changes are already upon us, we cannot anticipate what the "next big thing" will be that will reshape social life. Will some dramatic reorganization of family life or employment or politics make our understood ways of doing things, including growing older, no longer relevant? Will social attitudes about age and life stages change dramatically? Will a worldwide economic crisis mean that older people who are fit must continue to work and contribute to society? These possibilities are only a few of the endless alternatives. We cannot predict these kinds of changes-either positive or negative-nor can we always identify them as being the "next big thing" when they first appear. What is likely, however, given the pace of social and technological change in a global economy, is that major and currently unanticipated historical changes, generating period and cohort effects, will come.

Challenges and Opportunities for the Field

Throughout this book we have outlined what we know about aging and, just as important, what we don't know about aging today. The field is obviously still a "young" one, with growing pains evident over recent decades. In this section we discuss some of the issues facing the study of aging and some key opportunities for enhancing our understanding of this dynamic social process.

In order to organize the material in various chapters, we have drawn distinctions based on disciplines used to study aging, the level of analysis along the micro/macro continuum, and the subject matter under consideration. In preparing to conclude this book, one critical message to remember is that *it is all connected*. Although we have divided material into categories for purposes of clarity in presentation, in the real world of aging societies and in the lives of aging individuals *everything is connected* in complex and interactive ways that blur many of the distinctions we have drawn.

Disciplinary Frameworks

In much of this book we have taken a disciplinary approach to the study of aging. Much of the material presented has taken its frame of reference from social sciences, using the concepts and the research methods most often applied by researchers trained in sociology, political science, economics, and history. Each of the many disciplines used to study aging has information and perspectives to offer if we seek to understand the process of aging in all of its complexity. In fact, we doubt that anyone trained in the study of aging would argue for the usefulness of one discipline to the exclusion of all others in addressing the puzzle that is human aging in social context.

Applied aging research often occurs in a truly interdisciplinary fashion, with researchers from numerous disciplines, including history, epidemiology, economics, biochemistry, and physiology, coming together to address a question or policy issue. A project might, for example, utilize theories from sociology, economics, and psychology and borrow research techniques applied in these or other disciplines to seek answers to the research question. This interdisciplinary approach strengthens, rather than weakens, the research process, because the physical, psychological, and social aspects of aging are all simultaneously interactive on the micro and macro levels. In fact, biologists, sociologists, psychologists, and those in other disciplines have a lot to teach each other about the process of aging for individuals, groups, organizations, and nations.

Micro/Macro Distinctions: Implications for Policy and Practice

Just as the distinctions among disciplines are instructive but sometimes fuzzy, micro/macro frames of reference actually represent a continuum. In this book we have identified issues that can have serious implications for policy or practice on both the individual and the societal levels. The example of longevity is a handy one. Any significant extension of human life expectancy would raise important dilemmas for aging individuals. How would the extended years of life be used? Would longer-lived humans demand more of a role for themselves in the later years than they do today? On a mid-level of this continuum, we could think of how increased life expectancy would influence family relationships, the world of employment, and other social groups and institutions. On a macro level, using the widest-angle lens possible, we would confront the issues of societies already aging, which might need to restrict births in order to avoid overpopulation and need to address changes in economic dependency in later years created by the current system of retirement.

When we point to questions on these various levels, it is important to emphasize that there are generally related questions for practice and policy. As the processes of social aging evolve, we examine whether policies based on chronological age have appropriate age limits. For example, is the age range of 40 to 70 appropriate for laws on age discrimination in employment, or should these cutoffs be altered? We also consider whether age criteria remain relevant to the issues the policies seek to address. For example, many programs (Older Americans Act services and even Social Security) have moved from eligibility based solely on age to a combination of age and need as the older population has grown more socioeconomically diverse.

As we examine social issues along the micro/macro continuum, it is important to consider all of the levels. Will the increasing rates of divorce in future cohorts of older adults mean less informal support from kin, resulting in the need for more assistance from public programs? Will the preventive health behaviors of individuals in these same cohorts mean that the onset of disability will be delayed to later ages, reducing the burden on families and on the overall society? Will changes in Social Security policy, increasing the retirement age, result in impoverishment of older adults forced by ill health to retire before they can receive full benefits? The changes on one level reverberate in the others. We encourage you to consider how changes at both the individual level and the societal level of the micro/macro continuum are intricately connected.

The Interrelatedness of Social Domains

Our discussions about aging in various social institutions have also drawn some distinctions with a limited basis in the real world. Many issues within the social domains discussed in the previous five chapters, families, work, economics, health, and politics are highly interrelated. Although each was discussed separately, it is necessary to move across these boundaries in thinking about either an intervention to assist an older person or a social policy intended to affect the entire society. The complexity of these connections is overlooked only at our peril!

On the micro level of the individual, connections between these domains are fairly easy to see. As individuals move through the life course, the family shapes their initial socioeconomic status, thereby influencing their life chances and opportunities for education and occupation. The family teaches early health care and habits that will have long-range repercussions on health and disability into advanced old age. The attitudes people learn in their families are likely to shape their political orientation and party selection. Throughout adulthood, work, economic status, and health are likely to have mutual influences; persons in poor health cannot be as competitive in work, and those who are poorer or work in less advantaged jobs are less likely to have health care coverage. For women especially, work may influence their involvement in family life, and their family responsibilities shape their likelihood of working full-time.

As the life-course perspective reminds us, the behaviors undertaken and choices made in early and mid-life have clear effects on the later-life well-being of individuals. Today's working poor, for example, are less likely to have pensions, good health, or complete choice about when to retire, resulting in their continued vulnerability into later life (Meyer and Greenwood, 1997). Seldom do those who are economically marginal find themselves in a financially comfortable old age. Generally those in excellent health or poor health find those statuses the starting ground for whatever changes they experience in self-sufficiency and health with advancing age. Those intervening among physically frail or poor elders would do well to look beyond the initial problems (such as poor health, or poverty) to examine other issues, such as the availability of family support or adequacy of housing, in developing their strategies to provide assistance. Physicians, for example, sending an older person home after a health crisis may presume the availability of either family caregivers or money to hire surrogates to provide that care. Absence of such support could mean a dangerous situation for the individual and a costly return to the hospital, if not worse.

On a macro or societal level we must also keep in mind the interrelatedness of these social domains. Improvements or declines in the economy shape the political process and the likelihood that Congress will fund programs to assist older adults. Political trends, such as the decline in public confidence in government in recent decades, also signal changes in the government's ability or willingness to get public cooperation in collecting taxes. Inability to raise taxes, in turn, constrains the amount of health care provided to older adults, putting more responsibility onto families. Health care policies determine who will receive what care when, and ultimately help to shape the wellness of both younger and older citizens.

Employers shift their retirement policies in response to both government mandates and the economic pressures of the global economy. Currently, the government encourages people to work longer before retiring and is looking ahead to raising the age of entitlement to full Social Security benefits, while the private sector may offer incentives for early retirement. Families may constrain their childbearing in response to their need for two incomes to meet expenses. Societies cannot develop new (and perhaps badly needed) programs to assist the elderly or any other group unless both economics and political opinion are on their side.

Firming Our Theoretical Foundations

Among the ongoing problems encountered by the study of aging is that most research is not clearly directed by theory (Bengtson, Burgess, and Parrott, 1997). Theoretical development in the study of aging has, according to many experts, lagged behind theoretical development in traditional disciplines, such as economics and sociology (Passuth and Bengtson, 1988). In fact, Linda George (1995) goes so far as to call the research in aging "theoretically sterile or unsatisfying" (p. S1). Her argument suggests that the field has generated a lot of testable hypotheses and specific conceptual models (what she calls theory with a small t), rather than examining "broad views of fundamental processes underlying social structure and social life," or theory with a capital T (p. S1). Theoretical development in the study of aging has sometimes been quite narrow, generating specialized, small-scale theories relating to specific points or data of limited scope. In a study of published research in eight leading social-gerontological journals from 1990 to 1994, Bengtson and his colleagues (1997) concluded that 80 percent of the articles lacked a theoretical framework for their research findings.

Researchers studying the social aspects of aging would do well to look to their disciplinary traditions in history, psychology, or social work for theoretical frames of reference applicable to the needs of the field. Such theoretical frameworks assist in compiling the pieces of the research puzzle into a larger whole. Passuth and Bengtson (1988), for example, advocate examining the dynamic contexts of everyday life in which social aging occurs. Such a contextual view would examine historical, political, and economic aspects of aging as well as the ongoing construction of everyday life among aging individuals and groups (Passuth and Bengtson, 1988). We might draw from politics, economics, sociology and anthropology, among others, to look at the context in which older adults move from what are defined as "productive" roles in families and in the workforce to "non-productive" leisure or volunteer pursuits. We might ask how that definition takes shape both in public policies, the corporate and business world, and the lived experience of older adults. Each discipline contributes perspectives that enrich the others in disentangling the complicated web of political, attitudinal, economic and cultural forces shaping the way we socially construct life at older ages.

Perhaps some of the reluctance to theorize on the grand scale derives from the early experience with disengagement theory. Highly controversial when it was introduced, disengagement theory was immediately attacked, including some rather hostile reactions (Achenbaum and Bengtson, 1994). Attacks were based both on scientific criteria and on implicit value positions of researchers oriented toward activity as the successful mode of adaptation to later-life changes. This first major attempt to examine the impact of aging on the relationship of the individual to the social world may have dissuaded theoretically minded individuals from putting forward a brash or potentially flawed theoretical orientation that might experience a similar fate (Achenbaum and Bengtson, 1994).

Yet another barrier to the development of theory has been the applied origins of the field. Both the "social problems" background of the study of aging and the funding available for research, which tends to focus on policy-relevant problems and outcomes, have sometimes diverted attention from theoretical considerations. Some consider theorizing to be less productive than pragmatic problem solving. Thus, by virtue of its roots and research funding, the field has been turned away from attention to theoretical concerns.

What is lost when we lack theoretical models to organize our knowledge of the changes that we see with aging? In the absence of theory, research provides a set of unrelated bits of knowledge that fail to build a larger picture, undergird effective interventions, or predict how future cohorts will age differently. Results of research not driven by theory become an array of "factoids"—what Seltzer (1993) calls "itty-bitty" gerontology—which fail to contribute to our understanding of the underlying process of aging. Theories assist us in creating a meaningful, albeit tentative, framework for understanding the complexities of the social world in which we operate. Both research and practice need theories to connect results and make them more coherent and effectively applicable. As Bengtson and his colleagues note, "A policymaker would have difficulty supporting a program that does not have clearly stated goals and a plan for how they will be achieved. And it is intellectually irresponsible for a program of research to proceed without a similar set of statements—in short, a theory" (Bengtson et al., 1997, p. S73). They conclude that there is nothing so practical as a good theory!

Refining Methodologies for Applied Research

The study of aging is still far from having the research tools needed to answer all of the fascinating questions that have been posed. One major lack in prior decades was a methodology to bridge different levels of analysis (Campbell and O'Rand, 1985). Since individual behaviors/choices and large-scale social trends are connected, emerging approaches to understand these connections will help us understand the role of social context on aging and its outcomes for individuals (Campbell and Alwin 1996). How the effects of a government policy change with regard to retirement influence both corporations' pension and retirement policies and individuals' decisions about the timing of retirement remains a question difficult to answer. Because social trends are actually aggregations of individual decisions and happenings, shaped by larger institutional forces, the interplay between individual aging and social change can only be addressed when these linkages are articulated.

Aging has successfully borrowed research techniques from a wide range of disciplines. A good example is the event history approaches described in Chapter 2, which are now often applied to longitudinal data to examine changes in the life course. Certainly scales and measures to tap a variety of concepts of concern to aging researchers have been refined and tested by researchers. Nonetheless, relatively few new approaches to studying the "moving target" of aging cohorts within an ever-changing social structure have emerged to satisfy a wide range of basic and applied research needs.

The study of aging grew from an interest in resolving social problems. As we move into a new millennium, the issues have become even more complex. It is more difficult to formulate effective and politically feasible policies based on age because the older population and younger cohorts have become much more diverse (Torres-Gil, 1992). Serious problems persist for some groups within the older population—notably, older women, racial and ethnic minorities, and the oldest old—all of whom may be experiencing the fruits of cumulative disadvantage throughout their lives paired with the perils of later life. Thus, research needs to focus as much on diversity within age groups as differences between them.

Policy decisions will be made with or without good-quality information from researchers. Growing sophistication in the methods we use to study of aging individuals, groups, and populations will provide a more textured and detailed picture of the "universals" or aging as well as the varied paths followed to later life. Undoubtedly better policy and practice could come from an informed study of these complexities with methodological techniques yet to be developed.

Addressing Diversity in Policy and Practice

It is clear that the older population is becoming more diverse; in sociological terms, the older population is more differentiated by structural factors, such as age, race, ethnicity, social class, and cohort (Calasanti, 1996b). Even though it has always been problematic to discuss "the elderly," it will become increasingly critical to focus on which components of the older population are under consideration. Formulating policy for older adults as a single category may be a thing of the past (Torres-Gil, 1992). The life experiences, and hence the later-life trajectories, of various social groups differ in ways that are obvious but also in more subtle ways. Matters from dietary preferences and filial obligation to willingness (and financial resources) to use community services or housing alternatives are all likely to vary broadly in this diverse population of older adults.

Can we expect, for example, that an African American woman, aged 85, with a large network of family but little income will have much in common with a newly retired European American professional man who has remained single and childless? Not only do their objective circumstances of aging differ, but also perhaps more important, they may interpret their situations and even the meaning of later life very differently. For example, retirement for the man just described may mean free time, with opportunities to pursue new hobbies, travel, and participate in community service. For the woman, retirement may mean moving from two jobs one in the home and one for pay, to one job, and with that a dramatic reduction in income (Calasanti, 1996a) Clearly retirement for these two examples does not have the same meaning at all.

Programs and activities for the older population increasingly serve a diverse population.

We have already emphasized the changing racial/ethnic profile of the older population. Those planning future social policy or preparing interventions overlook the growth in diversity among older adults, especially among Hispanic and Asian/Pacific Island groups, at their own peril. Even a local nutrition program will need to recognize the diverse palates of the people it is serving and be responsive to the dietary and cultural needs of these groups. Even more than today, it will be inappropriate to discuss "the elderly" as a social category.

Not only must we think about diversity in terms of race, class, ethnicity, gender, education, and similar social structural variables but also in terms of age cohorts (R. Gibson, 1996). At any given point in time, 60- and 90-year-old cohorts have experienced different slices of history and been differentially shaped by historical events. Baby boomers and their parents and children are good examples. Many parents of baby boomers were part of the "good times generation," coming of age in the strong economy following World War II and experiencing job security and growing pension coverage. Many baby boomers, however, entered a stagnant economy, where job security and pensions were evaporating at the same time as Watergate reduced their confidence in the political system. Their children, as part of the large baby boom echo, are moving toward maturity in the age of computers, as a global economy alters employment toward contingent labor and Social Security trust funds are described as endangered. As these three groups age, their outlooks, expectations, and well-being can be expected to differ substantially.

In the face of this growing diversity, we need to reconsider the standard traditionally used as the reference group for older adults: married, middle-class, European American males. Because men face shorter life expectancies, divorce is increasing, and ethnic diversity is growing, it will be increasingly unrealistic to use males of the dominant culture as our benchmark for how various groups are doing as they age (R. Gibson, 1996). This tendency to use male experience as the norm casts other groups into the role of "the other," being compared with a standard. Instead, perhaps female experience should be promoted as the norm, because they represent a growing majority with increasing age (R. Gibson, 1996), or no group should be considered the standard against which other groups are evaluated.

Transforming Knowledge to Inform Policy and Practice

Research on aging grew from a tradition of identifying and ameliorating the problems of aging individuals within societies. Now we recognize that not only individuals but also entire societies face challenges as their populations grow older. As both societies and individuals work to face these challenges, high-quality information is essential. More than ever before, those formulating policy need to have access to accurate information, not only on current cohorts in later life but also on the differences to be expected in future cohorts.

The policy process often focuses on immediate problems, without much consideration of the long-term view as new and different cohorts move through the age structure of society. As the 1990s came to a close, for example, members of Congress are struggling with ways to modify both Social Security and Medicare to secure their trust funds into the future. Making decisions regarding the best way to reform these and other policies should, in the best of all possible worlds, consider the likely needs of individuals just born, not just individuals already receiving benefits or the cohorts of the baby boom on the horizon of eligibility. Talk of the baby boom was not accompanied by talk of their children, the baby boom echo, of nearly the same size (Friedland and Summer, 1999). Right now, it appears that the policy process is responding mostly to the immediate threat of the large cohorts entering retirement in the next 30 to 40 years. If policymakers do not consider this longer-term view of the population, will the policies enacted now also be suitable for the next sets of cohorts to move into later life? Unfortunately, the policymaking process seldom encourages consideration of these longer-range views.

Researchers, too, have a critical role to play in making research results accessible to the public and to those making policy. As the research process has become more sophisticated and technical, it often becomes more difficult to translate the results of research into language easily comprehensible by nonscientists. Many researchers studying aging are hesitant, given the complexities of the connections among aging, period effects, and cohort differences, to make definitive statements about trends and recommendations to intervene in the most effective fashion. It is incumbent on both groups, scientists and policymakers alike, to work toward better understanding of the complexities of the others' work and make their own work more accessible.

Summary

The process of aging is not just an individual journey, but also a societal transformation, developing within a political/historical/economic context that both shapes individuals and their cohorts and, in turn, is shaped and altered by the passage of those age cohorts through the society (Riley, 1987; 1994). The study of aging is the attempt to capture an ever-changing process that affects us all as we move through our individual lives, through the domains of family, work, and the political world.

Your aging will not be like that of your parents or your grandparents. The dynamic interplay between social change and the aging of cohorts, including your cohort, guarantees that the only thing we can count on is that aging in the future will be different socially, economically, and (to some degree) physically. Predicting the form that those differences will take, however, is a much riskier task.

Even if age is a socially constructed phenomenon, and thought by some people therefore to be "unreal," we must recall W. I. Thomas's wisdom that such phenomena, if perceived as real, are real in their consequences. We have constructed as part of our social world a complex understanding of aging and what it means that extends far beyond the physical parameters and changes experienced by individuals. We organize much of our social lives based on age, with access to opportunities and relationships among individuals constrained by the formal and informal rules of age stratification systems. This reality, which we share as part of our culture, comes to be a system by which society organizes itself and through which individuals plan their lives. Just because it is socially constructed does not mean it isn't a powerful force. The next time someone encourages an individual to "act their age"—regardless of whether that age is 6 or 66—remember that you are seeing the power of age as a social construction in operation.

It is not simply for individuals, however, that age is significant. Social life would be chaotic if we lacked some rules and orderliness of events and relationships imposed by the social construct of age. We all rely on the rules of the system and build it into our social planning in complex ways. There seems to be little likelihood that a completely "age irrelevant" society is on the horizon. Nonetheless, many of the distinctions we make today, between someone who is 16 and 18 or between 63 and 66, for example, are subject to serious question.

We must recognize the power of aging as a concept. Individual and larger-scale planning, as we face an aging society, must include flexibility. Social scientists do not have a very good track record of predicting trends far into the future, and the aging of society is one of the most potent trends we face today. One goal of any planning is certain: If you plan, you must plan for change. The future of aging is uncertain; only the fact that we are all aging is firmly guaranteed.

Web Wise

Association for Gerontology in Higher Education Student Page

http://www.aghe.org/studepg.htm

The Association for Gerontology in Higher Education has a page of resources for students. It includes information on a database (with tailored searches available for a $10 fee for students) to identify specific types of educational programs in gerontology/geriatrics nationwide, information on scholarships and fellowships for advanced study in aging/gerontology, and information on careers in aging for the potential professional.

Elderhostel

http://www.elderhostel.org/

Elderhostel has been a source of social activity, travel, and education for older adults for many years. A visit to their web site demonstrates the richness and diversity of education/travel programs they offer and provides a notion of what some adults do in their retirement years. Although courses do carry costs and primarily cater to a middle-class clientele, some scholarships are available. Check out activities located at a wide range of locations throughout the U.S. and Canada ("Programs in the U.S. and Canada") and view some of the courses available in your state or elsewhere through the online catalogs.

Senior Net

http://www.seniornet.com/

Senior Net is a non-profit organization of 30,000 or more computer-using adults ages 50 or above. The goal of the site is to enhance the lives of those in this stage of life and to share knowledge that is useful. This lively site has a lot of information and linkages to other useful sites related to active, engaged maturity.

Senior Women Web

http://www.seniorwomen.com/

Started by a mature journalist, Senior Women Web is a site focusing on issues of concern specifically to women. It includes news stores, sections on art, politics, fitness, and media and provides linkages to other woman-oriented web sites.

Baby Boomers Envision their Retirement

http://research.aarp.org/econ/boomer_seg_toc.html

This page, provided by AARP, outlines results of a study done of the baby boom cohorts as they look toward later life. The results demonstrate considerable diversity among baby boomers and differences between these cohorts' expectations and the current older population. The methodology of their study and the findings are outlined on this site.

Questions for Thought and Reflection

1. If you were working for a service provider planning for the future needs of the elderly, what steps would you recommend right away based on what we know about changes in the older population? What specific changes are going to be most important to those planning for service needs?

2. Do we have too many life cycle stages, too few, or just the right number? Since these are socially constructed, it is possible to change them. As the average life expectancy grows, does that mean we should have more stages or should we move toward making age irrelevant to more aspects of society?

3. Now that you are more educated about the complexities of aging, what steps can you take right now to maximize a "good old age" for yourself, including the avoidance of "usual aging?" Answering this question requires you to consider what makes for successful aging according to your value system.

4. Speculate on the likely changes to later life that may be brought by the large cohorts of the baby boom. What have their cohort experiences suggested about this large age group that may transform later life?

AARP Public Policy Institute. 1996. *Reforming the Health Care System: State Profiles 1996.* Washington, DC: AARP.

Achenbaum, W. A. 1992. With justice for all? Social Security, symbolic politics, and generational equity. *In Depth, 2* (3), 13-36.

Achenbaum, W. A. and V. L. Bengtson. 1994. Re-engaging the Disengagement Theory of Aging: On the history and assessment of theory development in gerontology. *The Gerontologist, 34* (6), 756 -763.

Adelman, R. C. 1977. Definition of biological aging. Pp. 9-13 in *Second Conference on the Epidemiology of Aging*, S. G. Haynes and M. Feinleib, (Eds.). Washington: U.S. Department of Health and Human Services.

———. 1995. The Alzheimerization of aging. *The Gerontologist, 35* (4), 526-532.

Adler, R. P. 1996. Older adults and computers: Report of a national survey. Available: http://www.seniornet.org/intute/survey2.html.

Akiyama, H., T. C. Antonucci, and R. Campbell. 1990. Rules of support exchange among two generations of Japanese and American women. Pp. 127-138 in *The Cultural Context of Aging*, J. Sokolovsky, (Ed.). New York: Bergin & Garvey.

Alessio, H. M. and E. Blasi. 1997. Physical activity as a natural antioxidant booster. *Research Quarterly for Exercise and Health, 68,* 292-302.

Alessio, H. M., R. G. Cutler, and A. H. Goldfarb. 1988. Malonaldeyde content increases in fast and slow twitch skeletal muscle with intensity of exercise in a rat. *American Journal of Physiology, 255,* C874-C877.

Alessio, H. M. and A. H. Goldfarb. 1988. Lipid peroxidation and scavenger enzymes during exercise. *Journal of Applied Physiology, 64,* 1333-1336.

Allaire, J. C. and M. Marsiske. 1999. Everyday cognition: Age and intellectual ability correlates. *Psychology and Aging. 14,* 627-644.

Allen, S. M., F. Goldscheider, and D. A. Ciambrone. 1999. Gender roles, marital intimacy, and nomination of spouse as primary caregiver. *The Gerontologist, 39* (2), 150-158.

Alwin, D. F. 1998. The political impact of the baby boom: Are there persistent generational differences in political beliefs and behavior? *Generations, 22* (1), 46-54.

Alwin, D. F. and J. A. Krosnick. 1991. Aging, cohorts, and the stability of sociopolitical orientations over the life span. *American Journal of Sociology, 97,* (1), 169-195.

Amato, P. R., S. J. Rezac, and A. Booth. 1995. Helping between parents and young adult offspring: The role of parental marital quality, divorce, and remarriage. *Journal of Marriage and the Family, 57,* (2), 363-374.

American Association of Retired Persons (AARP). 1995. *Valuing Older Workers: A Study of Costs and Productivity.* Washington, DC.

———. 1999. *Annual Report for 1998.* Accessed 11/1/99 from http://www.aarp.org/ar98.

American Psychiatric Association. 1994. *Diagnostic and Statistical Manual of Mental Disorders* (4th ed.). Washington, DC: American Psychiatric Assn.

Andersen, R. M. 1995. Revisiting the behavioral model and access to medical care: Does it matter? *Journal of Health and Social Behavior. 36* (1), 1-10.

Aniansson, A., Grimby, G., and Hedberg, M. 1992. Compensatory muscle fiber hypertrophy in elderly men. *Journal of Aplied Physiology, 73,* 812-816.

Anschutz, L., C. J. Camp, R. P. Markley, and J. J. Kramer. 1987. A three-year follow-up on the effects of mnemonics training in elderly adults. *Experimental Aging Research 13,* 141-143.

Antonucci, T. C. 1990. Social supports and social relationships. Pp. 205-226 in *Handbook of Aging and the Social Sciences* (3rd Ed.) R. H. Binstock and L. K. George, (Eds.). San Diego: Academic Press.

Antonucci, T. C. and H. Akiyama. 1987. Social networks in adult life and a preliminary examination of the convoy model .*Journals of Gerontology, 42,* 519-527.

———. 1995. Convoys of Social Relations: Family and Friendships Within a Life Span Context. Pp. 355-371 in *Handbook of Aging and the Family,* R. Blieszner and V. H. Bedford, (Eds.). New York: Greenwood Press.

Applebaum, R. A. and C. Austin. 1990. *Long-Term Care Case Management.* New York: Springer.

Applebaum, R. and S. Kunkel. 1995. Long-term care for the Boomers: A public policy challenge for the 21st Century. *Southwest Journal on Aging. 11* (1), 25-34.

Applegate, W. B. 1996. Elevated systolic blood pressure, increased cardiovascular risk and rationale for treatment. *American Journal of Medicine, 101,* 35-95.

Aries, P. 1962. *Centuries of Childhood: A Social History of Family Life.* New York: Vintage.

Atchley, R. C. 1976. *The Sociology of Retirement.* New York: Schenkman.

———. 1989. A continuity theory of normal aging. *The Gerontologist 29,* (2), 183-190.

———. 1997. *Social Forces and Aging* (8th ed.) Belmont, CA: Wadsworth.

Auster, C.. 1996. *The Sociology of Work: Concepts and Cases.* Thousand Oaks, CA: Pine Forge Press.

Bachu, Amara. 1997. Fertility of American women: June 1995 (Update). *Current Population Reports.* P20, No. 499. Accessed 10/6/99 at http://www.census.gov.

Baltes, B. and M. M. Baltes. 1990. Psychological perspectives on successful aging: The model of selective optimization with compensation. Pp. 1-34 in *Successful Aging: Perspectives From the Behavioral Sciences,* P. B. Baltes and M. M Baltes, (Eds.). New York: Cambridge University Press.

Baltes, B. and R. Kliegl. 1992. Further testing of limits of cognitive plasticity: Negative age differences in a mnemonic skill are robust. *Developmental Psychology, 28,* 121-125.

Baltes, B. and U. Lindenberger. 1988. On the range of cognitive plasticity in old age as a function of experience: Fifteen years of intervention research. *Behavior Therapy, 19,* 283-300.

Baltes, B., D. Sowarka, and R. Kliegl. 1989. Cognitive training research on fluid intelligence in old age: What can older adults achieve by themselves? *Psychology and Aging, 4,* 217-221.

Baltes, B. and U. M. Staudinger. 1993. The search for a psychology of wisdom. *Current Directions in Psychological Science, 2,* 75-80.

———. 1996. *Interactive Minds: Life-Span Perspectives on the Social Foundation of Cognition.* New York: Cambridge University Press.

Baltes, M. M. 1995. Dependency in old age: Gains and losses. *Current Directions in Psychological Science, 4,* 14-19.

———. 1996. *The Many Faces of Dependency in Old Age.* Cambridge, England: Cambridge University Press.

Baltes, M. M. and L. L. Cartensen. 1996. The process of successful aging. *Aging and Society 16,* 397-422.

Baltes, M. M., K. P. Kühl, and D. Sowarka 1992. Testing for limits of cognitive reserve capacity: A promising strategy for early diagnosis of dementia? *Journals of Gerontology, 47,* 165-167.

Baltes, P. B. 1987. Theoretical propositions of life-span developmental psychology: On the dynamics between growth and decline. *Developmental Psychology, 23,* 611-626.

———. 1993. The aging mind: potentials and limits. *The Gerontologist, 33,* 580-594.

Baron, J. N. and W. T. Bielby. 1985. Organizational barriers to gender equality. Pp. 233-251 in *Gender and the Life Course,* A. Rossi, (Ed.). New York: Aldine.

Barrow, G. M. 1992. *Aging, the Individual, and Society* (5th ed.) St. Paul, MN: West Publishing Company.

Bass, S. A. (Ed.) 1995. *Aging and Active: How Americans Over 55 Contribute to Society.* New Haven: Yale University Press.

Becker, G. 1993. Continuity after a stroke: implications of life-course disruption in old age. *The Gerontologist, 33* (2), 148-158.

Bedford, V. H. 1989. Understanding the value of siblings in old age: A proposed model. *American Behavioral Scientist, 33,* 33-44.

———. 1995. Sibling relationships in middle and old age. Pp. 201-222 in *Handbook of Aging and the Family,* R. Bleiszner and V. H. Bedford, (Eds.). Westport, CT: Greenwood Press.

Bender, W, and Smith, M. 1997. Population, food, and nutrition. *Population Bulletin, 51 (4)*. Population Reference Bureau Inc.

Bengtson, V. L., E. O. Burgess, and T. M. Parrott. 1997. Theory, explanation, and a third generation of theoretical development in social gerontology. *Journal of Gerontology: Social Sciences, 52* (B), S72-S88.

Bengtson, V. L., and J. A. Kuypers. 1971. Generational differences and the 'developmental stake.' *International Journal of Aging and Human Development, 2,* 249-260.

Bengtson, V. L., N. E. Cutler, D. J. Mangen, and V. W. Marshall. 1985. Generations, cohorts, and relations between age groups. Pp. 304-338 in *Handbook of Aging and the Social Sciences,* R. H. Binstock and E. Shanas, (Eds.). New York: Van Nostrand Reinhold.

Bengtson, V. L., C. Rosenthal, and L. Burton. 1990. Families and aging: Diversity and heterogeneity. Pp. 263-287 in *Handbook of Aging and the Social Sciences* (3rd ed.) R. H. Binstock and L. K. George, (Eds.). San Diego: Academic Press.

Bengtson, V. L. and M. Silverstein. 1993. Families, aging, and social change: Seven agendas for 21st-Century researchers. Pp. 15-38 in *Annual Review of Gerontology and Geriatrics: Focus on Kinship, Aging, and Social Change, Vol. 13,* G. L. Maddox and M. P. Lawton, (Eds.). New York: Springer.

Berg, W. P., H. M. Alessio, E. M. Mills, and C. Tong. 1997. Correlates of recurrent falling in independent community dwelling older adults. *Journal of Motor Behavior, 29,* 5-16.

Berkman, L. F. and S. L. Syme. 1979. Social networks, host resistance, and mortality: A nine-year follow-up study of Alameda County residents. *American Journal of Epidemiology, 109,* 186-204.

Berkman, L. 1988. The changing and heterogeneous nature of aging and longevity: A social and biomedical perspective. In *Annual Review of Gerontology and Geriatrics, Vol. 8,* G. Maddox and M. P. Lawton, (Eds.) New York: Springer.

Bernard, J.. 1972. *The Future of Marriage.* New York: World.

Bianchi, S. M. and D. Spain. 1996. Women, work, and family in America. *Population Bulletin 51* (3), 2-48.

Binstock, R. H. 1991a. Aging, politics, and public policy. Pp. 325-340 in *Growing Old in America* (4th ed.) B. B. Hess and E. W. Markson, (Eds.) New Brunswick, NJ: Transaction.

———. 1991b. From the Great Society to the Aging Society-25 Years of the Older Americans Act. *Generations 15* (3), 11-18.

———. 1992. Aging, disability, and long-term care: The politics of common ground. *Generations 16* (1): 83-88.

———. 1994. Changing criteria in old-age programs: The introduction of economic status and need for services. *The Gerontologist 34* (6): 726-730.

———. 1995. A new era in the politics of aging: How will the old-age interest groups respond? *Generations 19* (3): 68-74.

———. 1997. The 1996 election: Older voters and implications for policies on aging. *The Gerontologist 37* (1): 15-19.

———. 2000. Older people and voting participation: Past and future. *The Gerontologist 40* (1):18-31.

Blackburn, J. A., D. Papalia-Finlay, B. F. Foye, and R. C. Serlin. 1988. Modifiability of figural relations performance among elderly adults. *Journal of Gerontology: Psychological Sciences 43,* 87-89.

Blackmar, F. W. 1908. *The Elements of Sociology.* New York: MacMillan.

Blair, S. N., H. W. Kohl, R. S. Paffenbarger, D. G. Clark, K. H. Cooper, and L. W. Gibbons. 1989. Physical fitness and all cause mortality. *Journal of the American Medical Association, 262,* 2395-2401.

Bodnar, A. G., M. Ouellete, M. Frolkis, S. E. Holt, C. P. Chiu, G. B. Harley, J. W. Shay, S. Lichteiner, and W. E. Wright. 1998. Extension of life span by introduction of telomerase into normal human cells. *Science, 279,* 349-352.

Bonnefoy, M., T. Kostka, M. C. Patricot, S. E. Berthouze, and J. R. LaCour. 1998. *Age and Ageing, 27,* 745-751.

Bortz, W. M. IV and W. M. Bortz II. 1996. How fast do we age? Exercise performance over time as a biomarker. *Journal of Gerontology, 51A,* M223-M225.

Borzi, P. C. 1993. A Congressional response to pensions reform. Pp. 111-112 in *Pensions in a Changing Economy,* R. V. Burkhauser and D. L. Salisbury, (Eds.). Washington, DC: Employee Benefit Research Institute.

Bosman, E. A. 1993. Age-related differences in the motoric aspects of transcription typing skill. *Psychology and Aging, 8,* 87-102.

Botwinick, J. 1978. *Aging and Behavior.* New York: Springer.

Bound, J., M. Scheonbaum, and T. Waidmann. 1996. Race differences in labor force attachment and disability status. *The Gerontologist, 36,* (3): 311-321.

Brandtstädter, J., D. Wentura, and W. Greve. 1993. Adaptive resources of the aging self: Outlines of an emergent perspective. *International Journal of Behavioral Development, 16,* 323-349.

Brecher, E. 1984. *Love, Sex, and Aging: A Consumers' Union Report* . Boston: Little, Brown.

Brody, E. M. 1981. Women in the middle. *The Gerontologist, 21,* 471-480.

———. 1985. Parent care as normative family stress. *The Gerontologist, 25,* 19-29.

Brubaker, T. H. 1990a. *Family Relationships in Later Life.* Newbury Park, CA: Sage.

———. 1990b. Families in Later Life: A Burgeoning Research Area. *Journal of Marriage and the Family 52,* (4), 959-981.

Bryson, K., and L. M. Casper. 1999. Coresident grandparents and grandchildren. *Current Population Reports.* P23, No. 198. Accessed 10/8/99 from http://www.census.gov.

Bureau of the Census Press Release CB93-117 (June 28, 1993).

Bureau of Justice Statistics (BJS) 1994. *Elderly Crime Victims.* Washington, DC: U.S. Department of Justice (Publication # NCJ-147186).

Bureau of Labor Statistics 1999. Employee Benefits in Medium and Large Private Establishments, 1997. *Bureau of Labor Statistics News.* Accessed 11/11/99 from http://stats.bls.gov/special.requests/ocwc/och/ebs/ebnr0005.pdf.

Burkhauser, R. V. and J. F. Quinn. 1994. Changing policy signals. Pp. 237-262 in *Aging and Structural Lag,* M. W. Riley, R. L. Kahn, and A. Foner, (Eds.). New York: Wiley-Interscience.

———. 1997. Pro-work proposals for older Americans in the 21st Century. *Policy Brief,* No. 9/1997, Syracuse, NY: Syracuse University Center for Policy Research.

Burkhauser, R. V. and T. M. Smeeding. 1994. Social Security reform: A budget neutral approach to reducing older women's disproportionate risks of poverty. *Policy Brief,* No. 2/1994, Syracuse, NY: Syracuse University Center on Policy Research.

Burns, B. J. and C. Taube. 1990. Mental health services in general medical care and in nursing homes. Chapter 4 in Fogel, Furino, and Gottleib (Eds.), *Mental Health Policy for Older Americans: Protecting Minds at Risk.* Washington, DC: American Psychiatric Press, Inc.

Burton, L.M. 1996. Age norms, the timing of family role transitions, and intergenerational caregiving among aging African American women. *The Gerontologist, 36 (2),* 199 – 208.

Burton, L. and C. DeVries. 1995. Challenges and rewards: African-American grandparents as surrogate parents. Pp. 101-108 in *Families and Aging,* L. Burton, (Ed.). Amityville, NY: Baywood.

Bush, T. L. 1990. The epidemiology of cardiovascular disease in post-menopausal women. *Annals of the New York Academy of Science, 592,* 263-266.

Butler, R. N. 1989. Dispelling ageism: The cross-cutting intervention. *Annals of the American Academy of Political and Social Sciences, 503,* 138-147.

Button, J. W. 1992. A sign of generational conflict: The impact of Florida's aging voters on local school and tax referenda. *Social Science Quarterly 73* (4): 786-797.

Button, J. and W. Rosenbaum. 1990. Gray power, gray peril, or gray myth?: The political impact of the aging in local Sunbelt politics. *Social Science Quarterly 71* (1): 25-38.

Byrd, M. and T. Bruess. 1992. Perceptions of sociological and psychological age norms by young, middle-aged, and elderly New Zealanders. *International Journal of Aging and Human Development, 34* (2): 145 -163.

Cain, L. D. 1987. Alternative perspectives on the phenomena of human aging: Age stratification and age status. *The Journal of Applied Behavioral Science, 23* (2): 277-294.

Calasanti, T. M. 1996a. Gender and life satisfaction in retirement: An assessment of the male model. *Journal of Gerontology: Social Sciences 51B* (1): S18-S29.

———. 1996b. Incorporating diversity: Meaning, levels of research, and implications for theory. *The Gerontologist 36* (2): 147-156.

Campbell, D. T. and J. C. Stanley. 1963. *Experimental and Quasi-Experimental Designs for Research.* Chicago: Rand McNalley & Co.

Campbell, R. T. 1988. Integrating conceptualization, design, and analysis in panel studies of the life course. Pp. 43-69 in *Methodological Issues in Aging Research,* K. W. Schaie, R. T. Campbell, W. Meredit, and S. C. Rawlings, (Eds.). New York: Springer Publishing.

Campbell, R. T. and D. F. Alwin. 1996. Quantitative approaches: Toward and integrated science of aging and human development. Pp. 31-31 in *Handbook of Aging and the Social Sciences.* New York: Academic Press.

Campbell, R. T. and A. M. O'Rand 1985. Settings and sequences: The heuristics of aging research. Pp. 58-79 in *Handbook of Aging and the Social Sciences,* J. E. Birren and V. L. Bengtson, (Eds.) New York: Springer.

Cantor, M. H. 1983. Strain among caregivers: A study of experience in the United States. *The Gerontologist, 23,* 597- 604.

———. 1995. Families and caregiving in an aging society. Pp. 135-144 in *Families and Aging,* L. Burton, ed. Amityville, NY: Baywood.

Canter, G. J., R. Torre, and M. Mier. 1961. A method for evaluating disability in patients with Parkinson's disease. *Journal of Nervous and Mental Disorders, 133,* 143-147.

Carey, J. R., P. Liedo, D. Orozco, and J. W. Vaupel. 1992. Slowing of mortality rates at older ages in large medfly cohorts. *Science, 258,* 457-461.

Caro, F. G., S. A. Bass, and Y.-P. Chen. 1993. Introduction: Achieving a productive aging society. Pp. 3-25 in *Achieving a Productive Aging Society,* S. A. Bass, F. G. Caro, and Y.-P. Chen, (Eds.). Westport, CT: Auburn House.

Carstensen, L. L. 1992. Social and emotional patterns in adulthood: Support for socioemotional selectivity theory. *Psychology and Aging, 7,* 331-338.

———. 1993. Motivation for social contact across the life span: A theory of soicioemotional selectivity. Pp. 205-254 in *Nebraska Symposium on Motivation,* Vol. 40, J. Jacobs, (Ed.). Lincoln, NB: University of Nebraska Press.

Casper, L. M., and L. E. Bass, U.S. Bureau of the Census. 1998. Voting and registration in the election of November 1996. *Current Population Reports.* P20, No. 504. Accessed 10/17/99 from http://www.census.gov.

Cassata, D. 1994. Freshman class boasts resumes to back up 'outsider' image. *Congressional Quarterly, 52* (44), 9-12.

Cavalieri, T. A., A. Chopra, P. N. Bryman. 1992. When outside the norm is normal: Interpreting lab data in the aged. *Geriatrics, 47,* 66-70.

Center for Human Resource Research. 1995. *NLS Handbook, 1995.* Columbus, OH: Ohio State University.

Cerami, A. 1985. Glucose as a mediator of aging. *Journal of American Geriatrics Society, 33,* 626-634.

Chappell, N. L. 1990. Aging and social care. Pp. 438-454 in *Handbook of Aging and the Social Sciences* (3rd ed.) R. H. Binstock and L. K. George, (Eds.). San Diego: Academic Press.

Chen, Y.-P. 1994. 'Equivalent retirement ages' and their implications for Social Security and Medicare financing. *The Gerontologist 34* (6): 731-735.

Chen, Y.-P. and T. D. Leavitt. 1997. The widening gap between white and minority pension coverage. *The Public Policy and Aging Report 8* (1): 10-11.

Cherlin, A. J. 1992. *Marriage, Divorce, Remarriage* (2nd ed.). Cambridge, MA: Harvard University Press.

Cherlin, A. and F. Furstenberg. 1986. *The New American Grandparent.* New York: Basic Books.

Choudhury, S., and M. V. Leonesio. 1997. Life cycle aspects of poverty among older women. *Social Security Bulletin. 60* (2), 17-36.

Chronicle of Higher Education, 1999. *The Chronicle of Higher Education Almanac: 1999.* Cited 8/23/99 at http://chronicle.com/weekly/almanic/1999.

Cicirelli, V. G. 1991. Sibling relationships in adulthood. *Marriage and Family Review 16* (3/4): 291-310.

Clarke, E. J., M. Preston, J. Raksin, and V. L. Bengtson. 1999. Types of conflicts and tensions between older parents and adult children. *The Gerontologist. 39* (3):261-270.

Coale, A. 1964. How a population ages or grows younger. In *Population: The Vital Revolution*, R. Freedman (Ed.). Garden City, NY: Anchor Books.

Cockerham, W. C. 1998. *Medical Sociology*. Seventh edition. Upper Saddle River, NJ: Prentice-Hall.

Cohen, G. D. 1990. Psychopathology and mental health in the mature and elderly adult. Pp. 359-371 in *Handbook of the Psychology of Aging* (3rd ed.) J. E. Birren and K. W. Schaie, (Eds.) San Diego, CA: Academic Press.

Cohen, L. E. and K. C. Land. 1987. Age structure and crime: Symmetry versus assymetry and the projection of crime rates through the 1990s. *American Sociological Review 52* (2), 170 -183.

Cohen, R. A. and J. Van Nostrand. 1995. *Trends in the Health of Older Americans: United States. 1994.* National Center for Health Statistics. *Vital and health Statistics 3*, (30).

Cohen, S. and T. A. Willis. 1985. Stress, social support, and the buffering hypothesis. *Psychological Bulletin, 98*, 310-357.

Cohn, L., A. G. Feller, M. W. Draper, I. W. Rudman, and D. Rudman. 1993. Carpal tunnel syndrome and gynecomastia during growth hormone treatment of elderly men with low circulating IGF-1 concentrations. *Clinical Endocrinology, 39*, 417-429.

Cohler, B. 1983. Autonomy and interdependence in the family of adulthood: A psychological perspective. *The Gerontologist, 23*, 33-39.

Cohler, B. J. and K. Altergott. 1995. The family of the second half of life: Connecting theories and findings. Pp. 59-94 in *Handbook of Aging and the Family*, R. Blieszner and V. H. Bedford, (Eds.). Westport, CT: Greenwood Press.

Cole, Thomas R. 1983. The 'enlightened' view of aging: Victorian morality in a new key. *Hastings Center Report, 13*, 34-40.

———. 1992. *The Journey of Life: A Cultural History of Aging in America*. New York: Cambridge University Press.

———. 1995. What have we 'made' of aging? *Journal of Gerontology: Social Sciences, 50*, (6): S341-S343.

Commonwealth Fund. 1993. *The Untapped Resource: Final Report of the Americans Over 55 at Work Program*. New York: The Commonwealth Fund.

Condie, S. J. 1989. Older married couples. Pp. 143-158 in *Aging and the Family*, S. J. Bahr and E. T. Peterson, (Eds.). Lexington, MA: Lexington Books.

Congressional Quarterly. 1993. *Congress and the Nation: Volume VIII 1989-1992*. Washington, DC: Congressional Quarterly, Inc.

Conley, J. J. 1985. Longitudinal stability of personality traits: A multitrait- multimethod-multioccasion analysis. *Journal of Personality and Social Psychology, 49*, 1266-1282.

Connidis, I. A. and L. Davies. 1992. Life transitions and the adult sibling tie: A qualitative study. *Journal of Marriage and the Family, 54*, 972-982.

Cook, N. R., M. S. Albert, L. F. Berkman, D. Blazer, J. Taylor, and C. H. Hennekens. 1995. Interrelationships of peak expiratory flow rate with physical and cognitive function in the elderly: MacArthur Foundation Studies of Aging. *Journal of Gerontology: Medical Sciences, 50A*, M317-M323.

Cooney, T. and P. Uhlenberg. 1990. The role of divorce in men's relations with their adult children after mid-life. *Journal of Marriage and the Family, 52*, 677-688.

Cooper, K. J. 1993. Four House Select Committees expire as symbols of reform. *Washington Post*, April 1.

Cooperman, L. F. and F. D. Keast. 1983. *Adjusting to an Older Work Force*. New York: Van Nostrand Reinhold.

Cornelius, S. W. and A. Caspi. 1987. Everyday problem solving in adulthood and old age. *Psychology and Aging, 2*, 144-153.

Cornman, J. M. and E. R. Kingson. 1996. Trends, issues, perspectives, and values for the aging of the baby boom cohorts. *The Gerontologist 36*, (1), 15-26.

Costa, P. T. and R. R. McCrae. 1988. Personality in adulthood: A six-year longitudinal study of self-reports and spouse ratings on the NEO Personality Inventory. *Journal of Personality and Social Psychology, 54*, 853-863.

Couch, K. A. 1998. Late life job displacement. *The Gerontologist. 38* (1), 7-17.

Council of State Governments. 1994. *The Book of the States* (1994-95 ed.) Vol. 30. Lexington, KY: The Council of State Governments.

Cowgill, D. 1972. A theory of aging in cross-cultural perspective. In *Aging and Modernization,* D. Cowgill and L. Holmes, (Eds.). New York: Appleton-Century-Crofts.

Craik, F. I. M. 1977. Age differences in human memory. Pp. 384-420 in *Handbook of the Psychology of Aging.* J. E. Birren, and K. W. Schaie (Eds.). New York: Van Nostrand Reinhold.

Craik, F. I. M. and T. A. Salthouse. (Eds.) 1992. *The Handbook of Aging and Cognition.* Hillsdale, NJ: L. Erlbaum Associates.

Cress, M. E., D. M. Buchner, K. A. Questad, P. C. Esselman, B. J. deLateur, and R. S. Schwartz. 1999. Exercise: Effects on physical functional performance in independent older adults. *Journal of Gerontology, 54A,* M242-M248.

Crimmins, E. M., S. L. Reynolds, and Y. Saito. 1999. Trends in health and ability to work among the older working-age population. *Journal of Gerontology: Social Sciences. 54B* (1), S31-40.

Cross, S. and H. Markus. 1991. Possible selves across the life span. *Human Development, 34,* 230-255.

Crown, W. H., P. H. Mutschler, J. H. Schulz, and R. Loew. 1993. *The Economic Status of Divorced Older Women.* Waltham, MA: Policy Center on Aging, Brandeis University.

Cruise Lines International Association. 1996. *The Cruise Industry: An Overview.* New York: CLIA.

Crystal, S. 1990. Health economics, old-age politics, and the catastrophic Medicare debate. *Journal of Gerontological Social Work 15* (3-4), 21-31.

Crystal, S. and D. Shea. 1990. Cumulative advantage, cumulative disadvantage, and inequality among elderly people. *The Gerontologist 30* (4), 437-443.

Culligan, R. C., D. Osborne, W .M. Swenson, and K. P. Offord. 1983. *The MMPI: A Contemporary Narrative Study.* New York: Praeger.

Cumming, E. and W. H. Henry. 1961. *Growing Old: The Process of Disengagement.* New York: Basic Books.

Curtis, H. J. 1964. Cellular processes involved in aging. *Federated proceedings, 23,* 662.

Cutler, N. E. 1969-70. Generation, maturation, and party affiliation: A cohort analysis. *Public Opinion Quarterly, 33,* 583-588.

Cutler, R. G. 1982. Longevity is determined by specific genes: Testing the hypothesis. In R. C. Adelman and G. S. Roth (Eds.). *Testing the Theories of Aging.* Boca Raton, FL: CRC Press, 25-114.

Cutler, S. J. 1995. The methodology of social scientific research in gerontology: Progress and issues. *Journals of Gerontology: Social Sciences 50B,* (2) S63-64.

Dalaker, J., and M. Naifeh. 1998. Poverty in the United States: 1997. *Current Population Reports,* Series P60, No. 201, Washington, DC: U.S. Government Printing Office.

Dannefer, D. 1988a. Differential gerontology and the stratified life course: Conceptual and methodological issues. Pp. 3-36 in *Varieties of Aging, Annual Review of Gerontology and Geriatrics,* Vol. 8, Maddox and Lawton, (Eds.).

———. 1988b. What's in a name? An account of the neglect of variability in the study of aging. Pp. 356-384 in *Emergent Theories of Aging,* J. E. Birren and V. L. Bengtson, (Eds.). New York: Springer.

Dannefer, D. 2000. Paradox of opportunity: Education, work and age integration in the United States and Germany. *The Gerontologist, 40* (3), 282-286.

Davitz, J. R. and L. L. Davitz. 1996. *Evaluating Research Proposals: A Guide for the Behavioral Sciences.* Upper Saddle River, NJ: Prentice Hall.

Day, C. L. 1990. *What Older Americans Think.* Princeton, NJ: Princeton University Press

———. 1993a. Public opinion toward costs and benefits of Social Security and Medicare. *Research on Aging, 15* (3), 279-298.

———. 1993b. Older Americans' attitudes toward the Medicare Catastrophic Coverage Act of 1988. *Journal of Politics 55,* 167-177.

Day, J. C., and A. E. Curry. 1998. Educational attainment in the United States: March 1998 (Update). *Current Population Reports,* P20, No. 513. Cited 9/9/99 at http://www.census.gov/prod/3/98pubs/p20-513pdf.

Deatrick, D. 1997. Senior-Med: Creating a network to help manage medications. *Generations, 21* (3), 59-60.

Demming, J. A. and S. L. Pressey. 1957. Tests 'indigenous' to the adult and older years. *Journal of Counseling Psychology, 4,* 144-148.

Denney, N. W. 1984. A model of cognitive development across the life span. *Developmental Review, 4,* 171-191.

Denney, N. W. and K. A. Pearce. 1989. A developmental study of practical problem solving in adults. *Psychology and Aging, 4,* 438-442.

Department of Health and Human Services. 2000. Medicare Basics. (www.medicare.gov/Basics/Amounts2000.asp)

Detroit News. 1995. Kmart pharmacists win $2.17 million in age-discrimination case. August 5.

Diehl, M., S. L. Willis, and K. W. Schaie. 1995. Everyday problem solving in older adults: Observational assessment and cognitive correlates. *Psychology and Aging, 10,* 478-491.

Dixon, R. A. and O. N. Gould. 1996. Adults telling and retelling stories collaboratively. Pp. 221-241 in *Interactive Minds: Life-Span Pespectives on the Social Foundation of Cognition,* P. B. Baltes and U. M. Staudinger, (Eds.). Cambridge: Cambridge University Press.

Dobson, D. 1983. The elderly as a political force. Pp. 123-144 in *Aging and Public Policy: The Politics of Growing Old in America,* W. P. Browne and L. K. Olson, (Eds.). Westport, CT: Greenwood Press.

Doeringer, P. B. 1990. Economic security, labor market flexibility and bridges to retirement. Pp. 3-19 in *Bridges to Retirement: Older Workers in a Changing Labor Market,* P. B. Doeringer, (Ed.). Ithaca, NY: Cornell University.

Doeringer, P. B. and D. G. Terkla. 1990. Business necessity, bridge jobs, and the nonbureaucratic firm. Pp. 146-171 in *Bridges to Retirement: Older Workers in a Changing Labor Market,* P. B. Doeringer, (Ed.). Ithaca, NY: Cornell University/ILR Press.

Doka, K.J. 1989. *Disenfranchised Grief: Recognizing Hidden Sorrow.* New York: Lexington Books.

Dowd, J. J. 1975. Aging as exchange: A preface to theory. *Journal of Gerontology, 30,* 585-594.

———. 1980. *Stratification Among the Aged.* Monterey, CA: Brooks/Cole.

———. 1981. Age and inequality: A critique of the age stratification model. *Human Development, 24,* 157-171.

Dura, R., E. D. London, and S. I. Rapoport. 1985. Changes in structure and energy metabolism of the aging brain. Pp. 595-620 in C. E. Finch and E. L. Schneider (Eds.). *Handbook of the Biology of Aging,* New York: Van Nostrand Reinhold.

Duvall, E. M. and B. C. Miller. 1985. *Marriage and Family Development* (6th ed.) New York: Harper & Row.

Dwyer, J. W. 1995. The effects of illness on the family. Pp. 401-421 in *Handbook on Aging and the Family,* R. Blieszner and V. H. Bedford, (Eds.). New York: Greenwood Press.

East, P. L. 1998. Racial and ethnic differences in girls' sexual, marital, and birth expectations. *Journal of Marriage and the Family, 60* (1),150-162.

Easterlin, R. A. 1987. *Birth and Fortune: The Impact of Numbers on Personal Welfare* (2nd ed.) Chicago: University of Chicago Press.

———. 1996. Economic and social implications of demographic patterns. Pp. 73-83 in *Handbook of Aging and the Social Sciences,* R. H. Binstock and L. K. George, (Eds.). New York: Academic Press.

Edmonson, B. 1997. The facts of death. *American Demographics,* April, 46 – 53.

Ehrenreich, B. and English, D. 1990. The sexual politics of sickness. Pp. 270 – 284 in P. Conrad and R. Kerns (Eds.) *The Sociology of Health and Illness: Critical Perspectives.* New York: St. Martin's Press.

Ekerdt, D. J. 1986. The busy ethic: Moral continuity between work and retirement. *The Gerontologist, 26* (3), 239-244.

Ekerdt, D. 1998. Entitlements, generational equity, and public-opinion manipulation in Kansas City. *The Gerontologist, 38* (5), 525-536.

Ekerdt, D. and S. DeViney. 1990. On defining persons as retired. *Journal of Aging Studies, 4* (3), 211-229.

Ekerdt, D. J., S. DeViney, and K. Kosloski. 1996. Profiling plans for retirement. *Journal of Gerontology: Social Sciences, 51B* (3), S140-S149.

Eller, T. J. and W. Fraser. 1995. *Asset Ownership of Households: 1993.* U.S. Bureau of the Census, Current Population Reports, P-70, No. 47. Washington, DC: U.S. Government Printing Office.

Erikson, E., J. M. Erikson, and H. Kivnick. 1986. *Vital Involvement in Old Age: The Experience of Old Age in Our Time.* London, England: Norton.

Epstein, J. S. 1994. *Adolescents and Their Music: If It's Too Loud, You're Too Old.* New York: Garland.

Ershler, W. B. 1993. The influence of aging and immune system on cancer incidence and progression. *Journal of Gerontology, 48,* B3-B7.

Estes, C. L. 1979. *The Aging Enterprise.* San Francisco: Jossey-Bass.

———. 1991. The new political economy of aging: Introduction and critique. Pp. 19-36 in *Critical Perspectives on Aging: The Political and Moral Economy of Growing Old,* M. Minkler and C. L. Estes, (Eds.). Amityville, NY: Baywood.

Estes, C. and E. Binney. 1991. The biomedicalization of aging: Dangers and dilemmas. Pp. 117-134 in M. Minkler and C. Estes (Eds.), *Critical Perspectives on Aging: The Political and Moral Economy of Growing Old.* Amityville, NY: Baywood Publishing.

Estes, C., J. Swan, and L. Gerard. 1989. Dominant and competing paradigms in gerontology: Toward a political economy of aging. Pp. 25-36 in *Readings in the Political Economy of Aging,* Minkler and Estes, (Eds.). Farmingdale, N.Y: Baywood.

Estes, C. L., J. H. Swan and Associates. 1993. *The Long Term Care Crisis: Elders Trapped in the No-Care Zone.* Newbury Park, CA: Sage.

Evans, D. A. 1996. Descriptive epidemiology of Alzheimer's disease. In Z. S. Katchaturian and T. Radebaugh (Eds.). *Alzheimer's Disease: Causes, Diagnosis, Treatment, and Care.* Boca Raton, FL: CRC Press, 51-60.

Evans, W. J. 1995. What is sarcopenia? *Journal of Gerontology, 50A,* 5-8.

Everitt, A. V., B. D. Porter, and M. Steel. 1981. Dietary, caging, and temperature factors in the ageing of collagen fibers in rat tendon. *Gerontology, 27,* 37-41.

Ewing, O. R. 1951. Our aging population. In *Man and His Years.* Health Publications Institute, Inc., Raleigh, North Carolina.

Fahy, T. W. 1995. *NLS Annotated Bibliography: 1968-1995 Edition.* Columbus, OH: Ohio State University.

Fanestil, D. D. and C. H. Barrows, Jr. 1965. Aging in the rotifier. *Journal of Gerontology, 20,* 462-469.

Ferraro, K. F. and R. L. LaGrange. 1992. Are older people most afraid of crime? Reconsidering age differences in fear of victimization. *Journal of Gerontology: Social Sciences, 47* (5), S233-244.

Ferraro, K. F. 1997. The gerontological imagination. Pp. 3-18 in *Gerontology: Perspectives and Issues,* K. Ferraro, (Ed.). New York: Springer.

Festinger, L. 1954. A theory of social comparison process. *Human Relations, 7,* 117-140.

Feuerbach, E. J., and C. J. Erdwins. 1994. Women's retirement: The influence of work history. *Journal of Women and Aging, 6* (3), 69-85.

Fiataronne, M. A., E. C. Marks, N. D. Ryan, C. N. Meredith, L. A. Lipsitz, and W. J. Evans. 1990. High intensity strength training in nonagenerians. *Journal of the American Medical Association, 263,* 3029-3034.

Fiatronne, M. A., E. F. O'Neill, N. Doyle, K. M. Clements, S. B. Roberts, J. J. Kehayias, L. A. Lipsitz, and W. J. Evans. 1993. The Boston FICSIT study: The effects of resistance training and nutritional supplementation on physical frailty in the oldest old. *Journal of the American Geriatric Society, 41,* 333-337.

Fields, Gary S. and O. S. Mitchell. 1984. *Retirement, Pensions, and Social Security.* Cambridge, MA: The MIT Press.

Finch, C. E., C. Pike, and M. Witten. 1990. Slow mortality rate accelerations during aging in some animals approximate that of humans. *Science, 249,* 902-905.

Fine, J. T., G. A. Colditz, and E. H. Coakley. 1999. A prospective study of weight change and health-related quality of life in women. *Journal of the American Medical Association, 282,* 2136-2142.

Finley, N. J., M. D. Roberts, and B. F. Banahan. 1988. Motivators and inhibitors of attitudes toward aging parents. *The Gerontologist, 28* (1), 73-78.

Finn, S. E. 1986. Stability of personality self-ratings over 30 years: Evidence for an age/cohort interaction. *Journal of Personality and Social Psychology, 50,* 813-818.

Firebaugh, G. and K. Chen. 1995. Vote turnout of Nineteenth Amendment women: The enduring effect of disenfranchisement. *American Journal of Sociology, 100* (4), 972-96.

Fogel, B. S., G. Gottlieb, and A. Furino. 1990. Minds at risk. Chapter 1 in Fogel, Furino, and Gottlieb (Eds.), *Mental Health Policy for Older Americans: Protecting Minds at Risk.* Washington, DC: American Psychiatric Press, Inc.

Foner, A. 1973. The polity. Pp. 115-159 in *Aging and Society. Vol 3: A Sociology of Age Stratification,* M. W. Riley, M. Johnson, and A. Foner, (Eds.). New York: Russell Sage Foundation.

———. 1996. Age norms and the structure of consciousness: Some final comments. *The Gerontologist, 36* (2), 221-223.

Forbes Magazine. 1999. Forbes 400 richest people in America. Cited 12/1/99 at http://www. forbes.com/toolbox/rich400/asp/rich.asp.

Fossel, M. 1998. Implications of recent work in telomeres and cell senescence. *Journal of Anti-Aging Medicine, 1,* 39-43.

Fowler, F. J., Jr. 1988. *Survey Research Methods.* Newbury Park, CA: Sage.

Fozard, J. L., M. Vercruyssen, S. L. Reynolds, P. A. Hancock, and R. E. Quilter. 1994. Age differences and changes in reaction time: The Baltimore Longitudinal Study of Aging. *Journal of Gerontology, 49,* P179-P189.

Freund, A. M., and P. B. Baltes. 1998. Selection, optimization, and compensation as strategies of life-management: Correlations with subjective indicators of successful aging. *Psychology and Aging, 13,* 531-543.

Freund, P. E. and M. B. McGuire. 1995. *Health, Illness, and the Social Body.* Englewood Cliffs, New Jersey: Prentice-Hall.

___. 1999. *Health, Illness, and the Social Body.* 3rd edition. New Jersey: Prentice-Hall, Inc.

Friedland, R. B., and L. Summer. 1999. *Demography Is Not Destiny.* Washington, DC: National Academy on Aging, Gerontological Society of America.

Fries, J. F. 1980. Aging, natural death and the compression of morbidity. *New England Journal of Medicine, 303,* 130-135.

Fuentes, B. 1991. Bank of American-An advocate for older workers. Pp. 73-75 in *Resourceful Aging: Vol IV Work/Second Careers.* Washington, DC: American Association of Retired Persons.

Fullerton, H. N. 1995. The 2005 labor force: Growing, but slowly. *Monthly Labor Review, 118* (11), 29-44.

Furlong, M. 1997. Creating online community for older adults. *Generations, 21 (3),* 33-35.

Ganong, L., M. Coleman, A. K. McDaniel, and T. Killian. 1998. Attitudes regarding obligations to assist an older parent or stepparent following later-life remarriage. *Journal of Marriage and the Family, 60* (3), 595-610.

Gardner, E. F. and R. H. Monge. 1977. Adult age differences in cognitive abilities and educational background. *Experimental Aging Research. 3,* 337-383.

Gardner, P., Rosenberg, H, and Wilson, R. 1996. Leading Causes of Death by Age, Sex, Race, and Hispanic Origins: United States, 1992. *National Center for Health Statistic, Vital and Health Statistics,* 20 (29).

Garibaldi, R. R. and B. A. Nurse. 1986. Infections in the elderly. *American Journal of Medicine, 81,* 53.

Gates, G. and J. Cooper. 1991. Incidence of hearing decline in the elderly. *Acta Otogolaryn, 111,* 240-248.

Gates, G., J. L. Cobb, R. B. D'Agostino, and P. A. Wolf. 1993. The relation of hearing in the elderly to the presence of cardiovascular disease and cardiovascular risk factors. *Archives of Otolaryngology Head and Neck Surgery, 199,* 156-161.

Gatz, M., J. E. Kasl-Godley, and M. J. Karel. 1996. Aging and mental disorders. Pp. 365-382 in *Handbook of the Psychology af Aging* (4th ed.) J. E. Birren and K.W. Schaie. (Eds.). New York: Academic Press, Inc.

Gatz, M., V. L. Bengtson, and M. J. Blum. 1990. Caregiving families. Pp. 404-426 in *Handbook of the Psychology of Aging,* J. E. Birren and K. W. Schaie, (Eds.). San Diego, CA: Academic Press.

Gendell, M. 1998. Trends in retirement age in four countries. *Monthly Labor Review, 121,* (August):20-30.

Gendell, M. and J. S. Siegel. 1992 Trends in retirement age by sex, 1950-2005. *Monthly Labor Review, 115* (7), 22-29.

———. 1996. Trends in retirement age in the United States, 1955-1993, by sex and race. *Journal of Gerontology: Social Sciences, 51B* (3), S132-S139.

George, L. K. 1995. The last half-century of aging research-and thoughts for the future. *The Journal of Gerontology: Social Sciences, 50B* (1), S1-S3.

Gergen, K. J. 1977. The social construction of self-knowledge. Pp. 139-169 in *The Self: Psychological and Philosophical Issues*, T. Mischel, (Ed.). Totowa, NJ: Rowman and Littlefield.

Gerike, A. E. 1996. On gray hair and oppressed brains. Pp. 155-163 in *Aging for the Twenty-First Century*. S. Scribner (Ed.). New York: St. Martin's Press.

Gibson, D. 1996. Broken down by age and gender: 'The problem of old women' redefined. *Gender & Society, 10* (4), 433-448.

Gibson, R. 1996. The black American retirement experience. Pp. 309-326 in *Aging For The Twenty-First Century*, Quadagno and Street, (Eds.). St. Martin's Press: New York.

Glazer, N. Y. 1993. *Women's Paid and Unpaid Labor*. Philadelphia: Temple University Press.

Glenn, N. D. 1998. The course of marital success and failure in five American 10-year marriage cohorts. *Journal of Marriage and the Family, 60* (3), 569-576.

Glick, P. C. 1977. Updating the life cycle of the family. *Journal of Marriage and the Family, 39* (1), 1977.

Global Aging Report. 1998. A global view of age and productivity: Performance peaks early say executives worldwide. *Global Aging Report, 3* (3), 3.

Goffman, 1969. *The Presentation of Self in Everyday Life*. London: Allen Lane.

Goldstein, C. and C. M. Beall. 1983. Modernization and aging in the third and fourth world: Views from the rural Hinterland in Nepal. *Human Organization, 1*, 48-49.

Goldstein, S. 1960. *Consumption Patterns of the Aged*. Philadelphia: University of Pennsylvania Press

Gonyea, J. G. 1997. The real meaning of balancing work and family. *The Public Policy and Aging Report, 8* (3), 1, 6-8.

Goss, S. C. 1997. *Comparison of financial effects of Advisory Council plans to modify the OASDI Program*. Retrieved 8/22/99 from http://www.ssa.gov/search97cgi/.

Gould, O., D. Kurzman, and R. A. Dixon. 1994. Communication during prose recall conversations by young and old dyads. *Discourse Processes, 17*, 149-165.

Goyal, R. S. 1989. Some aspects of aging in India. In *Aged in India: Sociodemographic Dimensions*, R. N. Pati and B. Jena, eds. New Delhi: Ashish Publishing House.

Goycoolea, M., H. Goycoolea, L. Rodriguez, C. Farfan, G. Martinez, and R. Vidal. 1986. Effect of life in industrialized societies on hearing in natives on Easter Island. *Larngoscope, 96*, 1391-1396.

Grady, D., S. M. Rubin, D. B. Petitti, C. S. Fox, D. Black, V. Ernster, and S. R. Cummings. 1992. Hormone therapy to prevent disease and prolong life in post menopausal women. *Annals of Internal Medicine, 117*, 1016-1037.

Grasl-Kraupp, B., W. Bursch, B. Ruttkay-Nedecky, A. Wagner, B. Lauer, and R. Schulte-Hermann. 1994. Food restriction eliminates preneoplastic cells through apoptosis and antagonizes carcinogenesis in rat liver. *Proceedings of the National Academy of Sciences, 91*, 9995-9999.

Green, D. R., and J. C. Read. 1998. Mitochondria and apoptosis. *Science, 281*, 1309-1312.

Green, E. J., W. T. Greenough, and B. F. Schlumpf. 1983. Effects of complex or isolated environments on cortical dendrites in middle-aged rats. *Brain, 264*, 233-240.

Grimby, G., Aniansson, H. Hedberg, G. B. Henning, U. Grangard, and H. Kvist. 1992. Training can improve muscle strength and endurance in 78-84 year old men. *Journal of Applied Physiology, 73*, 2517-2523.

Grimby, G. 1995. Muscle performance and structure in the elderly as studied cross-sectionally and longitudinally. *Journal of Gerontology, 50A*, 17-22.

Gross, C. P., G. F. Anderson, N. R. Powe. 1999. The relation between funding by the National Institutes of Health and the burden of disease. *New England Journal of Medicine, 340*, 1881-1886.

Grove, L. 1996. The 100-year-old senator? Some fans, foes say quit. Strom Thurmond says no. *The Washington Post*, April 8.

Guillemard, A.-M. 1996. The trend toward early labor force withdrawal and the reorganization of the life course: A cross-national analysis. Pp. 167-176 in *Aging for the Twenty-First Century*, J. Quadagno and D. Street, (Eds.). New York: St. Martin's Press.

Guy, R. F. and R. A. Erdner. 1993. Retirement: An emerging challenge for women. Pp. 405-409 in *Encyclopedia of Adult Development*, R. Kastenbaum, (Ed.). Phoenix: Oryx Press.

Hagburg, B. 1995. The individual's life history as a formative experience to aging. Pp. 61-76 in *The Art and Science of Reminiscing*, B. K. Haight and J. D. Webster (Eds.). Washington, DC: Taylor & Francis.

Hagestad, G. and B. L. Neugarten. 1985. Age and the life course. In *Handbook of Aging and the Social Sciences* (2nd ed.) Binstock and Shanas, (Eds.). New York: Van Nostrand Reinhold.

Hampton, J. K. *The Biology of Human Aging*. Dubuque, IA: William C. Brown, Pp. 91-93.

Hann, N., R. Millsap, and E. Hartka, E. 1986. As time goes by: Change and stability in personality over fifty years. *Psychology and Aging, 1*, 220-232.

Hardy, M. A. and J. Quadagno. 1995. Satisfaction with early retirement: Making choices in the auto industry. *Journal of Gerontology: Social Sciences, 50* (4): S217-228.

Hardy, M. A., L. E. Hazelrigg, and J. Quadagno. 1996. *Ending a Career in the Auto Industry: Thirty and Out*. New York: Plenum.

Hardy, M.A., and Waite, L. 1997. Doing time: Reconciling biography with history in the study of social change. Pp. 1- 21 in M.A. Hardy (Ed.) *Studying Aging and Social Change*. Thousand Oaks: SAGE Publications.

Hareven, T. K. 1993. Family and generational relations in the later years: A historical perspective. Pp. 7-22 in *Families and Aging*, L. Burton (Ed.). Amityville, NY: Baywood.

———. 1994. Family change and historical change: An uneasy relationship. Pp. 130-150 in *Aging and Structural Lag*. M. W. Riley, R. L. Kane, and A. Foner (Eds.). New York: Wiley-Interscience.

———. 1995. Historical perspectives on the family and aging. Pp. 13-31 in *Handbook of Aging and the Family*. R. Blieszner and V. H. Bedford (Eds.) Westport, CT: Greenwood Press.

Harrington Meyer, M. 1996. Making claims as workers or wives: The distribution of Social Security Benefits. American *Sociological Review, 61*, 449-465.

Harris, S. B. 1995. Spouse abuse in the elderly: Is it spouse abuse grown old? Doctoral Dissertation, Cornell University, Ithaca, NY: Dissertation Abstracts International.

Haug, M. R. 1995. Elderly power in the 21st Century. *Journal of Women & Aging, 7* (4): 3-10.

Hayflick, L. and P. S. Moorehead. 1961. The limited in vitro lifetime of human diploid cell strains. *Experimental Cell Research, 25*, 585-621.

Hayward, M. D., S. Friedman, and H. Chen. 1996. Race inequalities in men's retirement. *Journal of Gerontology: Social Sciences, 51B* (1): S1-S10.

———. 1998. Career trajectories and older men's retirement. *Journal of Gerontology: Social Sciences, 53B*, S91-103.

Hazelrigg, L. 1997. On the importance of age. Pp. 93 – 128 in M.A. Hardy (Ed.). *Studying Aging and Social Change*. Thousand Oaks: SAGE Publications.

HCFA (Health Care Financing Administration). 1992. *Health Caqre Financing Review: Medicare and Medicaid Statistical Supplement*. Baltimore: U.S. Department of Health and Human Services.

Heckhausen, J. and R. Schulz. 1995. A life-span theory of control. *Psychological Bulletin, 102*, 284-304.

Heidrich, S. M. and N. W. Denney. 1994. Does social problem solving differ from other types of problem solving during the adult years? *Experimental Aging Research, 20*, 105-126.

Heidrich, S. M. and C. D. Ryff. 1991. The role of social comparisons processes in the psychological adaptation of elderly adults. *Journals of Gerontology, 48*, 127-136.

Helton, D.R. 1997. A look at how Kentuckians in Knox County once treated the dead. *Kentucky Explorer, April*, 34 –39.

Hendricks, J. 1992. Generations and the generation of theory in social gerontology. *International Journal of Aging and Human Development, 35 (1)*, 31 –47.

Henretta, J. C. 1988. Conflict and cooperation among age strata. Pp. 385-404 in *Emergent Theories of Aging*, J. E. Birren and V. L. Bengtson (Eds.). New York: Springer.

———. 1992. Uniformity and diversity: Life course institutionalization and late-life work exit. *Sociological Quarterly, 33* (2), 265-275.

———. 1994. Social structure and age-based careers. Pp. 57-79 in *Age and Structural Lag*, M. W. Riley, R. L. Kahn, and A. Foner (Eds.) New York: Wiley-Interscience.

———. 2000. The future of age integration in employment. *The Gerontologist, 40* (3), 282-286.

Herskind, A. M., M. McGue, N. V. Holm, T. I. Sroensen, B. Harvald, and J. W. Vaupel. 1996. The heritability of human longevity: A population-based study of 2872 Danish twin pairs born 1870-1900. *Human Genetics, 97,* 319-323.

Herz, D. E. 1995. Work after early retirement: An increasing trend among men. *Monthly Labor Review, 118* (4), 13-20.

Herzog, A. R., and H. R. Markus. 1999. The self concept in life span and aging research. Pp. 227-252 in *Handbook of Theories of Aging*. V. L. Bengtson and K. W. Schaie (Eds.). New York: Springer.

Hess, B. B. and J. H. Waring. 1978. Changing patterns of aging and family bonds in later life. *Family Coordinator, 27,* 303-314.

Hill, R. 1965. Decision making and the family life cycle. Pp. 114-126 in *Social Structure and the Family: Generational Relations*, E. Shanas and G. F. Streib (Eds.). Englewood Cliffs, NJ: Prentice-Hall.

———. 1970. *Family Development in Three Generations*. Cambridge, MA: Schenkman.

Hirsch, C. H., L. P. Fried, T. Harris, A. Fitzpatrick, P. Enright, and R. Schulz. 1997. Correlates of performance-based measures of muscle function in the elderly: The cardiovascular health study. 1997, *Journal of Gerontology, 52A,* M192-M200.

Ho, D. H., P. A. Hansen, M. M. Chen, and J. O. Holloszy. DHEA treatment reduces fat accumulation and protects against insulin resistance in male rats. *Journal of Gerontology, 53A,* B19-B24.

Hobbs, F. B. and B. L. Damon. 1996. 65+ in the United States. *Current Population Reports,* P-23, No. 190. Washington, DC: U.S. Government Printing Office.

Hochschild, A. R. 1975. Disengagement theory: A critique and proposal" *American Sociological Review, 14* (5, 553-569.

Hogan, D. P. and N. M. Astone. 1986. The transition to adulthood. *Annual Review of Sociology, 12,* 109-130.

Hogan, D. P., D. J. Eggebeen, and C. C. Clogg. 1993. The structure of intergenerational exchanges in American families. *American Journal of Sociology, 98* (6), 1428-58.

Hogarth, J. M. 1991. Involving older persons in the labor force: An agenda for the future. Pp. 101-108 in *Resourceful Aging: Volume IV Work/Second Careers*. Washington, DC: American Association of Retired Persons.

Holden, K. C. and T. M. Smeeding. 1990. The poor, the rich, and the insecure elderly caught in between. *The Milbank Quarterly, 68* (2).

Holden, K. C. and H.-H. D. Kuo. 1996. Complex marital histories and economic well-being: The continuing legacy of divorce and widowhood as the HRS cohort approaches retirement. *The Gerontologist, 36* (3), 383-390.

Holstein, M.. 1993. Women's lives and women's work: Productivity, gender, and aging. Pp. 235-248 in Caro, F. G., S. Bass, and Y. Chen. "Introduction: Achieving a Productive Aging Society." In *Achieving a Productive Aging Society*, Bass, Caro, and Chen, (Eds.). Westport, Connecticut: Auburn House.

———. 1995. The normative case: Chronological age and public policy. *Generations, XIX* (3), 11-14.

Holstein, M. and M. Minkler. 1991. The short life and painful death of the Medicare Catastrophic Coverage Act. Pp. 189-204 in *Critical Perspectives on Aging: The Political and Moral Economy of Growing Old*, M. Minkler and C. L. Estes (Eds.). Amityville, NY: Baywood.

Holtz-Eakin, D. and T. M. Smeeding. 1994. Income, wealth, and intergenerational economic relations of the aged. Pp. 102-145 in *Demography of Aging*, L. G. Martin and S. H. Preston (Eds.). Washington, DC: National Academy Press.

Hooker, K. and C. R. Kaus. 1992. Possible selves and health behaviors in later life. *Journal of Aging and Health, 4,* 390-411.

Horgas, A. L., H. Wahl, and M. M. Baltes. 1996. Dependency in late life. Pp. 54-75 in *The Practical Handbook of Clinical Gerontology*, L. L.Carstensen, B. A. Edelstein, and L. Dornbrand (Eds.). Thousand Oaks: Sage.

Horn, J. L. and R. B. Cattell. 1966. Age differences in primary mental ability factors. *Journal of Gerontology, 21,* 210-220.

Horn, J. L. and S. M. Hofer. 1992. Major abilities and development in the adult period. Pp. 44-49 in *Intellectual Development,* R. J. Sternberg and C. A. Berg (Eds.). New York: Cambridge University Press.

Horowitz, A. 1985a. Family caregiving to the frail elderly. *Annual Review of Gerontology and Geriatrics, 6,* 194-246.

———. 1985b. Sons and daughters as caregivers to older parents: Differences in role performance and consequences. *The Gerontologist, 25* (6), 612-617.

Hoskins, D. D. 1992. Developments and trends in Social Security, 1990-1992: Overview of principal trends. *Social Security Bulletin, 55,* (4), 36-42.

Hu, Y. and N. Goldman. 1990. Mortality differentials by marital status: An international comparison. *Demography, 27* (2): 233-250.

Hudson, R. 1978. The 'graying' of the Federal budget and its consequences for old-age policy. *The Gerontologist, 18,* 428-440.

———. 1996. The changing face of aging politics. *The Gerontologist, 36* (1), 33-35.

Hultsch, D. F., and R. A. Dixon. 1990. Learning and memory in aging. Pp. 258-274 in *Handbook of the Psychology of Aging.* Third Edition. J. E. Birren and K. W. Schaie (Eds.). New York: Academic Press.

Hunt, G. G. 1997. Cleveland Free-Net Alzheimer's Forum. *Generations, 21,* (3), 37.

Huyck, M. H. 1995. Marriage and close relationships of the marital kind. Pp. 181-200 in *Handbook of Aging and the Family,* R. Blieszner and V. H. Bedford (Eds.). Westport, CT: Greenwood Press

Ikels, C. 1993. Chinese kinship and the state: Shaping of policy for the elderly. Pp. 123-146 in *Annual Review of Gerontology and Geriatrics: Focus on Kinship, Aging, and Social Change,* Vol. 13, G. L. Maddox and M. P. Lawton (Eds.). New York: Springer.

Inter-University Consortium for Political and Social Research. 1985. *Data Collections National Archive of Computerized Data on Aging.* Ann Arbor, MI: University of Michigan.

Ismail, A. I., D. L. Corrigan, D. F. MacLeod, V. L. Anderson, R. N. Kastgen, and P. W. Eliot. 1973. Biophysiological and audiological variables in adults. *Archives Otolaryn, 97,* 447-451.

Jackson, J. S. and R. C. Gibson. 1985. Work and retirement among the black elderly. Pp. 193-222 in *Work, Retirement, and Social Policy,* Z. S. Blau (Ed.). Greenwich, CT: JAI Press.

Jacobs, B. 1990. Aging and politics. Pp. 349-361 in *Handbook of Aging and the Social Sciences* (3rd ed.) R. H. Binstock and L. K. George (Eds.). San Diego: Academic Press.

Jarrett, W. H. 1985. Caregiving within kinship systems: Is affection really necessary? *The Gerontologist, 25* (1), 5-20

Jennings, J. T. 1993. Voting and registration in the election of November 1992. *Current Population Reports.* P-20, No. 466. Washington, DC: U.S. Government Printing Office.

Ji, L. L. 1995. Exercise and oxidative stress: Role cellular antioxidant systems. *Exercise and Sport Sciences Review, 23,* 135-166.

Johnson, C. L. 1995a. Divorce and reconstituted families: effects on the older generation. Pp. 33-41 in *Families and Aging,* L. Burton (Ed.). Amityville, NY: Baywood.

———. 1995b. Cultural diversity in the late-life family. Pp. 307-331 in *Handbook of Aging and the Family,* R. Blieszner and V. H. Bedford (Eds.). Westport, CT: Greenwood Press.

Johnson, E. S. and J. B. Williamson. 1987. Retirement in the United States. Pp. 9-41 in *Retirement in Industrialized Societies,* K. S. Markides and C. L. Cooper (Eds.). New York: John Wiley and Sons.

Johnson, F. B., D. Sinclair, and L. Guarente. 1999. Molecular biology of aging. *Cell, 96,* 291-302.

Johnson, R. W., U. Sambamoorthi, and S. Crystal. 1999. Gender differences in pension wealth: Estimates using provider data. *The Gerontologist, 39* (3), 320-333.

Jones, T. W. 1996. Strengthening the current Social Security System. *The Public Policy and Aging Report, 7* (3), 1, 3-6.

Jung, C. G. 1960. The stages of life. In *Collected Works,* Vol. 8, Princeton, NJ: Princeton University Press.

Juster, F. T. and R. Suzman. 1995. An overview of the health and retirement survey. *The Journal of Human Resources, 30,* S7-S56.

Kahn, J. R. and W. M. Mason. 1987. Political alienation, cohort size, and the Easterlin Hypothesis. *American Sociological Review, 52,* (2), 155-169.

Kahn, R. L. and T. C. Antonucci, 1980. Convoys over the life course. Attachment, roles and social support. Pp. 254-283 in *Life-Span Development and Behavior.* P. B. Baltes and O. G. Brim (Eds.). New York: Academic Press.

Kahn, R. L. 1994. Opportunities, aspirations, and goodness of fit. Pp. 37-53 in *Aging and Structural Lag,* M. W. Riley, R. L. Kahn, and A. Foner (Eds.) New York: Wiley-Interscience.

Kalton, G. and D. W. Anderson. 1989 Sampling rare populations. Pp. 7-30 in *Special Research Methods for Gerontology,* M. P. Lawton and A. R. Herzog (Eds.) Amityville, NY: Baywood.

Kane, R.A., Kane, R.L., and Ladd, R.C. 1998. *The Heart of Long-Term Care.* New York: Oxford University Press.

Kane, J. N. 1993. *Facts About the Presidents.* New York: H. W. Wilson.

Kannel, W. B., W. P. Castelli, and T. Gordon. 1979. Cholesterol in the prediction of atherosclerotic disease: New perspectives based on the Framingham Study. *Annals of Internal Medicine, 90,* 85-91.

Kasl, S. V. 1995. Strategies in research on health and aging: Looking beyond secondary data analysis. *Journal of Gerontology: Social Sciences, 50* (4), S191-S193.

Kastenbaum, R. 1993. Disengagement theory. Pp. 126-130 in *Encyclopedia of Adult Development,* R. Kastenbaum (Ed.). Phoenix: Oryx Press.

Katz, S., T. Downs, H. Cash, and R. Grotz. 1970. Progress in the development of the Index of ADL. *The Gerontologist 10* (1), 20-30.

Kavanagh, T., D. J. Mertens, V. Matosevic, R. J. Shephard, and B. Evans. 1989. Health and aging of masters athletes. *Clinical Sports Medicine, 1,* 72-88.

Kelley, C. L., and N. Charness. 1995. Issues in training older adults to use computers. *Behaviour & Information Technology, 14* (2), 107-120.

Kennedy, G. E. 1990. College students' expectations of grandparent and grandchild role behaviors. *The Gerontologist, 30* (1), 43-48.

Keyfitz, N. and W. Flieger. 1990. *World Population Growth and Aging: Demographic Trends in the Late Twentieth Century.* Chicago: University of Chicago Press.

Kimmel, D. C. 1993. The families of older gay men and lesbians. Pp. 75-79 in *Families and Aging,* L. Burton (Ed.). Amityville, NY: Baywood Publishing Co.

King, M. C. 1992. Occupation segregation by race and sex, 1940-1988. *Monthly Labor Review, 115* (2), 30-36.

Kingson, E. R., B. A. Hirshorn, and J. M. Cornman. 1986. *Ties That Bind: The Interdependence of Generations.* Washington, DC: Seven Locks Press.

Kingson, E. R. 1994. Testing the boundaries of universality: What's mean? What's not? *The Gerontologist, 34* (6), 736-742.

Kinsella, K. and Y. J. Gist. 1995. *Older Workers, Retirement, and Pensions.* Washington, D.C.: U.S. Bureau of the Census.

Kinsella, K. and C. M. Taeuber. 1993. *An Aging World II.* Washington, DC: U.S. Bureau of the Census.

Kirby, J. B., and P. Uhlenberg. 1998. The well-being of adolescents: Do coresident grandparents make a difference? Paper Presented at the Annual Meeting of the Population Association of America.

Kliegl, R., J. Smith, and P. B. Baltes. 1990. On the locus and process of magnification of age differences during mnemonic training. *Developmental Psychology, 26,* 894-904.

Kneese, A. and C. L. Cooper. 1993. Demography, resources, and the environment: Further considerations. Pp. 61-68 in *Aging of the U.S. Population: Economic and Environmental Implications.* Washington, DC: American Association of Retired Persons.

Koenig, H. G. and D. G. Blazer. 1992. Mood disorders and suicide. Pp. 379-407 in *Handbook of Mental Health and Aging* (2nd ed.) J. E. Birren, R. B. Sloane, and G. D. Cohen (Eds.). San Diego, CA: Academic Press, Inc.

Kohli, M. 1994. Work and retirement: A comparative perspective. Pp. 80-106 in *Aging and Structural Lag.* M. W. Riley, R. L. Kahn, and A. Foner (Eds.) New York: Wiley-Interscience.

Kominski, R. and A. Adams. 1994. Educational attainment in the United States: March 1993. *Current Population Reports,* P-20, 476. Washington, DC: U.S. Government Printing Office.

Kovar, M. G., and M. P. Lawton. 1994. Functional disability: Activities and instrumental activities of daily living. Pp. 57-75 in *Annual Review of Gerontology and Geriatrics: Focus on Assessment Techniques, Vol. 14.* New York: Springer.

Kranczer, S. 1994. Outlook for U.S. population growth. *Statistical Bulletin, 75* (4), 19-26.

Krause, N. 1995. Assessing stress-buffering effects: A cautionary note. *Psychology and Aging, 10,* 518-526.

Kubler-Ross, E. 1969. *On Death and Dying.* New York: Macmillan.

Kunkel, S. and R. A. Applebaum. 1992. Estimating the prevalence of long-term disability for an aging society. *Journal of Gerontology: Social Sciences, 47* (5), S253-S260.

Kunkel, S. and R. C. Atchley. 1996. Why gender matters: Being female is not the same as not being male. *American Journal of Preventive Medicine, 12* (5), 294-295.

Kunkel, S. and J. Subedi. 1996. Aging in South Asia: How "imperative" is the demographic imperative? Pp. 459-466 in *Sociology of Aging,* Minichiello, Chappell, Kendig, and Walker (Eds.). Melbourne: International Sociological Association, Toth Publishing.

Lachman, M. E., M. A. Ziff, and A. Spiro. 1994. Maintaining a sense of control in later life. Pp. 216-232 in *Aging and the Quality of Life.* R. P. Abeles, H. C. Gift, and M. G. Ory (Eds.). New York: Springer.

Lang, F. R. and L. L. Carstensen 1994. Close emotional relationships in late life: Further support for proactive aging in the social domain. *Psychology & Aging, 9* (2), 315-324.

Lashbrook, J. 1996. Promotional timetables: An exploratory investigation of age norms for promotional expectations and their associations with job well-being. *The Gerontologist, 36* (2), 189-198.

Laslett, P. 1991. *A Fresh Map of Life: The Emergence of the Third Age.* Cambridge: Harvard University Press.

———. 1995. Necessary knowledge: Age and aging in the societies of the past. Pp. 3-80 in *Aging in the Past: Demography, Society and Old Age,* D. I. Kertzer and P. Laslett (Eds.). Berkeley: University of California Press.

Lassey, M., W. Lassey, and M. Jinks. 1997. *Health Care Systems Around the World.* Upper Saddle River. NJ: Prentice Hall.

Laub, J. H., D. S. Nagin, and R. J. Sampson. 1998. Trajectories of change in criminal offending: Good marriages and the desistance process. *American Sociological Review, 63* (April), 225-238.

Lave, J. 1996. Rethinking Medicare. *Generations XX,* (2), 19-23.

LaViest, T. A. 1995. Data sources for aging research on racial and ethnic groups. *The Gerontologist, 35* (3), 328-339.

Lawrence, B. S. 1996. Organizational age norms: Why is it so hard to know one when you see one? *The Gerontologist, 36* (2), 209-220.

Lawton, M. P. and A. R. Herzog. 1989. Introduction. Pp. v-viii in *Special Research Methods for Gerontology,* M. P. Lawton and A. R. Herzog (Eds.). Amityville, NY: Baywood.

Lee, G. R. 1988. Marital satisfaction in later life: The effects of nonmarital roles. *Journal of Marriage and the Family, 50* (3), 775-783.

Lee, G. R., C. W. Peek, and R. T. Coward. 1998. Race differences in filial responsibility expectations among older parents. *Journal of Marriage and the Family, 60* (2), 404-412.

Lee, I. M. and R. S. Paffenbarger. 2000. Association of light, moderate, and vigorous intensity physical activity with longevity: The Harvard Alumni Health Study. *American Journal of Epidemiology, 151,* 293-299.

Legislative Research Center. 1999. Demographic information provided via e-mail 11/1/99 on demographics of the Congress from LRCGeneralPublicRequests@mail.house.gov.

Lemon, B. W., V. L. Bengtson, and J. A. Peterson. 1972. An exploration of the activity theory of aging: Activity types and life expectation among in-movers to a retirement community. *Journal of Gerontology, 27,* 511-523.

Leung. J. C. B. 1997. Family support for the elderly in China: Issues and challenges. *Journal of Aging and Social Policy, 9* (3), 87-101.

Lexell, J., C. Taylor, and M. Sjostrom. 1988. What is the cause of the aging atrophy? *Journal of Neurological Science, 84,* 275-294.

Liang, J. and R. H. Lawrence. 1989. Secondary analysis of sample surveys in gerontological research. Pp. 31-61 in *Special Research Methods for Gerontology,* M. P. Lawton and A. R. Herzog (Eds.). Amityville, NY: Baywood.

Lichtenberg, P. A. 1999. *Handbook of Assessment in Clinical Gerontology.* New York: John Wiley & Sons.

Lindenberger, M., and R. Kliegl. 1993. Speed and intelligence in old age. *Psychology and Aging, 8,* 207-220.

Linton, R. 1942. Age and sex categories. *American Sociological Review, 7,* 589-603.

Litwak, E. 1960. Geographic mobility and extended family cohesion. *American Sociological Review, 25,* 385-394.

———. 1965. Extended kin relations in an industrial society. Pp. 290-323 in *Social Structure and the Family: Generational Relations,* E. Shanas and G. Streib (Eds.). Englewood Cliffs, NJ: Prentice-Hall.

Longino, C., D. Jackson, and R. Zimmerman. 1991. The second move: Health and geographic mobility. *Journals of Gerontology 46,* S218-224.

Lopata, H. Z. 1979. *Women as Widows: Support Systems.* New York: Elsevier.

Loscocco, K. A. 2000. Age integration as a solution to work-family conflict. *The Gerontologist. 40* (3), 292-301.

Luescher, K. and K. Pillemer. 1998. Intergenerational ambivalence: A new approach to the study of parent-child relations in later life. *Journal of Marriage and the Family. 60* (2), 413-425.

Lugaila, T. A. 1998. Marital status and living arrangements: March 1998 (Update). *Current Population Reports.* P-20, No. 514. Accessed 10/8/99 from http://www.census.gov.

Lund, D. A., M. S. Caserta, M. F. Dimond, and S. K. Shaffer. 1989. Competencies, tasks of daily living, and adjustments to spousal bereavement in later life. Pp. 135-152 in *Older Bereaved Spouses,* D. A. Lund (Ed.). New York: Hemisphere.

Lutz, W. 1994, June. The future of world population. *Population Bulletin 49* (1). Population Reference Bureau, Inc.

Lyons, B., D. Rowland, and K. Hansom. 1996. Another look at Medicaid. *Generations XX,* (2), 24-30.

Machemer, R. 1992. The news in the biology of aging: The good, the bad, and the confusing. Paper presented at annual meeting of the Association for Gerontology in Higher Education. Baltimore, Maryland.

Mader, S. 1984. Hearing impairment in elderly persons. *Journal of the American Geriatric Society, 32,* 458-553.

Maddox, G. L. 1968. Retirement as a social event in the United States. Pp. 357-365 in *Middle Age and Aging,* B. L. Neugarten (Ed.). Chicago: University of Chicago Press.

Maddox, G. L. and M. P. Lawton. 1993. *Annual Review of Gerontology and Geriatrics: Focus on Kinship, Aging, and Social Change.* New York: Springer.

Mannheim, K. 1952. *Ideology and Utopia.* New York: Harcourt, Brace & World.

———. 1952. (edited by P. Kecskemeti) *Essays on the Sociology of Knowledge.* New York: Oxford University Press.

Manson, J., H. M. Alessio, M. Cristell, and K. M. Hutchinson. 1994. Can cardiovascular health mediate hearing ability? *Medicine and Science in Sports and Exercise 26,* 866-871.

Manton, K., L. Corder, and E. Stallard. 1997. Chronic disability trends in elderly United States populations: 1982-1994. *Proceeding of the National Academy of Sciences USA: Medical Sciences, 24,* 2593-2598.

Manton, K. G. and K. Liu. 1984. The future growth of the long-term care population: Projections based on the 1977 National Nursing Home Survey and the 1982 Long-Term Care Survey. Paper presented at Third National Leadership Conference on Long-Term Care Issues, Washington, D.C.

Manton, K., E. Stallard, and K. Liu. 1993. Forecasts of active life expectancy. *Journal of Gerontology 48*, 11-26.

Markides, K. S., J. Liang, and James S. Jackson. 1990. Race, ethnicity, and aging: Conceptual and methodological issues. Pp. 112-129 in *Handbook of Aging and the Social Sciences* (3rd ed.) R. H. Binstock and L. K. George (Eds.). San Diego: Academic Press.

Markus, H. 1977. Self-schemas and processing information about the self. *Journal of Personality and Social Psychology 35*, 63-78.

Markus, H. R. and A. R. Herzog. 1991. The role of the self-concept in aging. *Annual Review of Gerontology and Geriatrics 11*, 111-143.

Markus, H. and P. Nurius. 1986. Possible selves. *American Psychologist 41*, 954-969.

Markus, H. and E. Wurf. 1987. The dynamic self-concept: A social psychological perspective. *Annual Review of Psychology 38*, 299-337.

Marmour, T. R., J. L. Mashaw, and P. L. Harvey. 1990. *America's Misunderstood Welfare State: Persistent Myths, Enduring Realities.* New York: Basic Books.

Marsiske, M., F. R. Lang, P. B. Baltes, and M. M. Baltes. 1996. Selective optimization with compensation: Life-span perspectives on successful human development. Pp. 35-79 in *Compensating for Psychological Deficits and Declines*, R. A. Dixon and L. Backman (Eds.). Mahwah, NJ: Lawrence Erlbaum Associates.

Marsiske, M. and S. L. Willis. 1995. Dimensionality of everyday problem solving in older adults. *Psychology and Aging 10*, 269-283.

Martin, L. and K. Kinsella. 1994. Research in the demography of aging in developing countries. In *Demography of Aging*, L. Martin and S. Preston (Eds.). Washington D.C.: National Academic Press.

Martin, P. J. 1995. *Sounds and Society: Themes in the Sociology of Music.* Manchester: Manchester University Press.

Martinez, G. M. and A. E. Curry. 1998. School Enrollment - Social and Economic Characteristics of Students (Update). Accessed 1/11/00 from http://www.census.gov:80/population/www/socdemo/school.html.

Matras, J.. 1990. *Dependency, Obligations, and Entitlements: A New Sociology of Aging, the Life Course, and the Elderly.* Englewood Cliffs, NJ: Prentice Hall.

Matthews, A. M. and C. J. Rosenthal. 1993. Balancing work and family in an aging society: The Canadian experience. Pp. 96-119 in *Annual Review of Gerontology and Geriatrics: Focus on Kinship, Aging, and Social Change*, Vol. 13, G. L. Maddox and M. P. Lawton (Eds.). New York: Springer.

Maxwell, S., A. Cruickshank, G. Thorpe. 1994. Red wine and antioxidant activity in serum. *Lancet, 344*, 193-194.

McAuley, J. 1987. *Applied Research in Gerontology.* New York: Van Nostrand-Reinhold.

McConatha, D., J. T. McConatha, and R. Dermigny. 1994. The use of interactive computer services to enhance the quality of life for long-term care residents. *The Gerontologist. 34* (4) 553-556.

McConnell, S. R. 1983. Age discrimination in employment. Pp. 159-196 in *Policy Issues in Work and Retirement*, H. S. Parnes (Ed.). Kalamazoo, MI: W.E. Upjohn Institute.

McConnell, S. and D. Beitler. 1991. The Older Americans Act after 25 years: An overview. *Generations 15* (3), 5-10.

McFalls, J.A. 1998. Population: A lively introduction. *Population Bulletin, 53 (3).* Population Reference Bureau Inc.

McGrew, K. 1989. Personal Communication with Kunkel.

McKinlay, J., and S. McKinlay. 1990. Medical measures and the decline of mortality. Pp. 10-23 in Conrad and Kerns (Eds.). *The Sociology of Health and Illness: Critical Perspectives.* New York: St. Martin's Press.

McNaught, W. 1994. Realizing the potential: Some examples. Pp. 219-236 in *Aging and Structural Lag*, M. W. Riley, R. L. Kahn, and A. Foner (Eds.). New York: Wiley-Interscience.

McCrae, R.R. and Costa, P.T. Jr. 1982. Aging, the life course, and models of personality. Pp. 602 – 613 in T. M. Field et al. (Eds.) *Review of Human Development.* New York: Wiley.

Mead, G.H. 1934. *Mind, Self, and Society.* Chicago: University of Chicago Press.

Metropolitan Life Insurance Company, 1991. Longevity gains continue. *Statistical Bulletin, 72,* 19-26.

Meyer, J. A. and Daphne Greenwood. 1997. Back to the future: Poverty among the elderly in the Twenty-First Century. *The Public Policy and Aging Report 8* (1), 1, 17-20.

Miech, R. A. and M. J. Shanahan. 2000. Socioeconomic status and depression over the life course. *Journal of Health and Social Behavior, 41* (2), 137-161.

Miller, B., S. McFall, and R. T. Campbell. 1994. Changes in sources of community long-term care among African-American and white frail older persons. *Journal of Gerontology: Social Sciences 49* (1) S14-24.

Miller, D. 1985. The Economic Equity Act of 1985. *Washington Social Legislation Bulletin 29,* 61-64.

Miller, R. A. 1999. Are there genes for aging? *Journal of Gerontology, 54,* B297-B307.

Miller, S. 1991. Days Inns recruits older workers. Pp. 65-67 in *Resourceful Aging, Vol IV Work/Second Careers.* Washington, DC: American Association of Retired Persons.

Miller, W. E. 1989. *American National Election Studies Data Sourcebook, 1952-1986.* Cambridge, MA: Harvard University Press.

Mills, C. W. 1959. *The Sociological Imagination.* New York: Oxford University Press.

Minkler, M. 1991a. "Generational equity" and the new victim blaming. Pp. 67-80 in *Critical Perspectives on Aging: The Political and Moral Economy of Growing Old,* M. Minkler and C. L. Estes (Eds.). Amityville, NY: Baywood.

———. 1991b. Gold in gray: Reflections on business discovery of the elderly market. Pp. 81-93 in *Critical Perspectives on Aging: The Political and Moral Economy of Growing Old,* M. Minkler and C. L. Estes (Eds.). Amityville, NY: Baywood.

Mitchell, J. and J. C. Register. 1984. An exploration of family interaction with the elderly by race, socioeconomic status, and residence. *The Gerontologist 24* (1), 48-54.

Moen, P. 1994. Women, work and family: A sociological perspective on changing roles. Pp. 151-170 in *Aging and Stuctural Lag,* M. W. Riley, R. L. Kahn, and A. Foner (Eds.). New York: Wiley-Interscience.

Moen, P., D. Dempster-McClain, and R. M. Williams, Jr. 1989. Social integration and longevity: An event history analysis of women's roles and resilience. *American Sociological Review 54,* 635-647.

Moller, D.W. 1996. *Confronting Death.* New York: Oxford University Press.

Moody, H. R. 1992. *Ethics in an Aging Society.* Baltimore: Johns Hopkins University Press.

———. Overview: What is critical gerontology and why is it important? In *Voices and Visions of Aging: Toward a Critical Gerontology,* T. R. Cole, et al. (Eds.). New York: Springer.

Moon, M. and T. M. Smeeding. 1989. Can the elderly really afford long term care? Pp. 137-160 in *The Care of Tomorrow's Elderly: Encouraging Initiatives and Reshaping Public Programs,* S. Sullivan and M. E. Lewin (Eds.) Washington, DC: University Press of America.

Moore, P. 1985. *Disguised.* Waco, TX: Word Books.

Morgan, D. L. 1998. Facts and figures about the baby boom. *Generations. (Spring),* 10-15.

Morgan, L. A. 1984. Changes in family interaction following widowhood. *Journal of Marriage and the Family 46* (2), 323-332.

———. 1991. Economic security of older women: Issues and trends for the future. Pp. 275-292 in *Growing Old in America* (4th ed.) B. B. Hess and E. W. Markson (Eds.). New Brunswick: Transaction.

Morrell, R. W., D. C. Park, and L. W. Poon. 1990. Effects of labeling techniques on memory and comprehension of prescription information in young and older adults. *Journals of Gerontology 45,* 166-172.

Morris, J. N., A. Kagan, D. C. Pattison, M. J. Gardner, and P. A. B. Raffle. 1966. Incidence and prediction of ischemic heart disease in London busmen. *Lancet, 2,*553-559.

Morrison and Hoff. 1997. Life and death of neurons in the aging brain. *Science, 278,* 412-419.

Must, A., J. M. Spadano, E. H. Coakley. 1999. The disease burden associated with overweight and obesity. *Journal of the American Medical Association, 282,* 1523-1529.

Mutchler, J. E., J. A. Burr, A. M. Pienta, and M. P. Massagli. 1997. Pathways to labor force exit: Work transitions and work instability. *Journal of Gerontology: Social Sciences 52B* (1) S4-S12.

Mutran, E. 1985. Intergenerational family support among blacks and whites: Response to culture or to socioeconomic differences. *Journal of Gerontology 40* (3), 382-389.

Myers, S. L. and C. Chung. 1996. Racial differences in home ownership and home equity among preretirement-aged households. *The Gerontologist 36* (3), 350-360.

Myles, J. F. 1983. Conflict, crisis, and the future of old age security. *Millbank Memorial Fund Quarterly/Health and Society 61,* 462-472.

——. 1984. *Old Age in the Welfare State: The Political Economy of Public Pensions.* Boston: Little, Brown and Co.

——. 1996. Social Security and support of the elderly: The western experience. Pp. 381-397 in *Aging for the Twenty-First Century,* J. Quadagno and D. Street, (Eds.) New York: St. Martin's Press.

Myles, J. and J. Quadagno. 1995. Generational equity and Social Security reform. *Aging Research & Policy Report 3* (5), 12-16.

Nathanson, C. A. 1990. The gender-mortality differential in developed countries: Demographic and sociocultural dimensions. Pp. 3-24 in M. Ory and H. Warner (Eds.). *Gender, Health and Longevity: Multidisciplinary Perspectives.* New York: Springer.

National Alliance for Caregiving. 1997. *Family Caregiving in the U.S.: Findings from a National Survey.* Bethesda, MD: NAC and AARP.

National Center for Health Statistics. 1989. Advance report on final mortality statistics, 1987. *Monthly Vital Statistics 38,* (5), 1-48.

——. 1994. *Vital Statistics of the U.S., 1990 Life Tables.*

Nelson, J. F. 1995. The potential role of selected endocrine systems in aging processes. In E. J. Masoro (Ed.), Pp. 377-394 in *Handbook of Physiology: Section 11: Aging.* New York: Oxford University Press.

——. 1994. *Vital Statistics of the U.S., 1990 Life Tables.*

Nesselroade, J. R. 1988. Sampling and generalizability: Adult development and aging research issues examined within the general methodological framework of selection. Pp. 13-42 in *Methodological Issues in Aging Research,* K. W. Schaie, R. T. Campbell, W. Meredith, and S. C. Rawlings (Eds.). New York: Springer Publishing.

Neugarten, B. and N. Datan. 1973. Sociological perspectives on the life cycle. Pp. 53-71 in *Life-Span Developmental Psychology,* P. B. Baltes and K. W. Schaie (Eds.). Academic Press.

Neugarten, B., J. Moore, and J. Lowe. 1965. Age norms, age constraints, and adult socialization. *American Journal of Sociology 70,* 710-717.

——. 1968. Age norms, age constraints, and adult socialization. Pp. 22-28 in *Middle Age and Aging,* B. L. Neugarten (Ed.). Chicago: University of Chicago Press.

Neugarten, B. L. 1979. Time, age, and the life cycle. *American Journal of Psychiatry 136* (7), 887-894.

Newcomer, R. and S. Preston. 1994. Relationship between acute care and nursing unit use in two continuing care retirement communities. *Research on Aging, 16* (3), 280-300.

New York Times. 1989. The political power of the aging: Part I. July 23.

Nieswiadomy, M. and R. M. Rubin. 1995. Change in expenditure patterns of retirees: 1972-1973 and 1986-1987. *Journal of Gerontology: Social Sciences 50* (5), S275-S290.

Nordin, A. A. and T. Makinodan. 1974. Humoral immunity in aging. *Federated Proceedings, 33,* 2033.

O'Brien, R. M., J. Stockard, and L. Issacson. 1999. The enduring effects of cohort characteristics on age-specific homicide rates, 1960-1995. *American Journal of Sociology. 104* (4), 1061-1095.

O'Rand, A. M. 1990. Stratification and the life course. Pp. 130-148 in *Handbook of Aging and the Social Sciences* (3rd ed.) R. H. Binstock and L. K. George (Eds.). San Diego, CA: Academic Press.

——.1996. The Precious and the precocious: Understanding cumulative disadvantage and cumulative advantage over the life course. *The Gerontologist 36* (2), 230-238.

Office of the Federal Register. 1995. *The United States Government Manual 1995/1996.* Washington, DC: U.S. Government Printing Office.

Orr, W. C. and R. C. Sohal. 1994. Extension of life span by overexpression of superoxide dismutase and catalase in Drosophila melanogaster. *Science, 263,* 1128-1130.

Paffenbarger, R. S., A. L. Wing, and R. T. Hyde. 1978. Physical activity as an index of heart attack risk in college alumni. *American Journal of Epidemiology, 108,* 161-175.

Paffenbarger, R. S., M. E. Laughlin, A. S. Gima, R. A. Black. 1970. Work activity of longshoremen as related to death from coronary heart disease and stroke. *New England Journal of Medicine, 282,* 1109-1114.

Pak, C. Y. C. 1983. Post menopausal osteoporosis. In H. J. Buchsbaum (Ed.). *The Menopause.* New York: Springer-Verlag.

Palmore, E. 1975. *The Honorable Elders: A Cross-National Analysis of Aging in Japan.* Durham, NC: Duke University Press.

———. 1988. *The Facts on Aging Quiz.* New York, NY: Springer Publishing Company, Inc.

———. 1989. Medical records as sampling frames and data sources. Pp. 127-135 in *Special Research Methods for Gerontology,* M. P. Lawton and A. R. Herzog (Eds.). Amityville, NY: Baywood.

Parker, R. G. 1995. Reminiscence: A continuity theory framework. *The Gerontologist 35* (4), 515-525.

Parsons, T. and R. F. Bales. 1955. *Family Socialization and Process.* New York: Free Press.

Parsons, T. 1959. The social structure of the family. Pp. 241-274 in *The Family: Its Function and Destiny* (2nd ed.) R. Anshen, (Ed.). New York: Harper and Row.

Passuth, P. M. and V. L. Bengtson. 1988. Sociological Theories of aging: Current perspectives and future directions. Pp. 333-355 in *Emergent Theories of Aging,* J. E. Birren and V. L. Bengtson (Eds.). New York: Springer.

Pavalko, E. K. and G. H. Elder, Jr. 1990. World War II and divorce: A life-course perspective. *American Journal of Sociology 95* (5), 1213-1234.

Pendergrast, D. R., N. M. Fisher, and E. Calkins. 1993. Cardiovascular, neuromuscular, and metabolic alterations with age leading to frailty. *Journal of Gerontology, 48,* 61-67.

Peterson, L. R., M. Courtois, L. F. Peterson, M. R. Peterson, V. G. Davila-Roman, P. J. Spina, and B. Barzilai. 2000 Estrogen increases hyperemic microvascular blood flow velocity in post menopausal women. *Journal of Gerontology, 55A,* M174-M179.

Peterson, S. A. and A. Somit. 1994. *The Political Behavior of Older Americans.* New York: Garland Publishing.

Pineo, P. C. 1961. Disenchantment in the later years of marriage. *Marriage and Family Living 23,* 3-11.

Plakans, A. 1994. The democratization of unstructured time in western societies: A historical overview. Pp. 107-129 in *Aging and Structural Lag,* M. W. Riley, R. L. Kahn, and A. Foner (Eds.). New York: Wiley-Interscience.

Poon, L. W., P. Martin, G. M. Clayton, S. Messner, C. A. Nobel, and M. A. Johnson. 1992. The influences of cognitive resources on adaptation and old age. *International Journal of Aging and Human Development, 34,* 31-46.

Post, J. A. 1996. Internet resources on aging: Seniors on the net. *The Gerontologist.* 36 (5), 565-569.

Preston, S., I. Elo, and I. Rosenwaike. 1996. African-American mortality at older ages: Results of a matching study. *Demography 33,* 193-209.

Pruchno, R. 1999. Raising grandchildren: The Experiences of black and white grandmothers. *The Gerontologist.* 39 (2), 209-221.

Quadagno, J. 1982. *Aging in Early Industrial Society.* New York: Academic Press.

———. 1988. *The Transformation of Old Age Security: Class and Politics in the American Welfare State.* Chicago: University of Chicago Press.

———. 1989. Generational equity and the politics of the welfare state. *Politics and Society 17,* 353-376.

———. 1991. Generational equity and the politics of the welfare state. Pp. 341-351 in *Growing Old in America* (4th ed.) B. B. Hess and E. W. Markson (Eds.). New Brunswick, NJ: Transaction.

———. 1996. Social Security and the myth of the entitlement "crisis." *The Gerontologist 36* (3), 391-399.

Queen, S., G. Pappas, W. Harden, and G. Fisher. 1994. The widening gap between socioeconomic status and mortality. *Statistical Bulletin 75* (2), 31-35.

Quinn, J. F. 1987. The economic status of the elderly: Beware the mean. *Review of Income and Wealth 33*, 63-82.

———. 1993. *Poverty and Income Security Among Older Persons: Overview of Proceedings.* Syracuse: National Academy on Aging.

———. 1997. Retirement trends and patterns in the 1990s: The end of an era? *The Public Policy and Aging Report. 8* (3),10-14.

Quinn, J. F. and R. V. Burkhauser. 1990. Work and retirement, Pp. 307-327 in *Handbook of Aging and the Social Sciences* (3rd ed.) R. H. Binstock and L. K. George (Eds.). San Diego: Academic Press.

———. 1994. Retirement and labor force behavior of the elderly. Pp. 50-101 in *Demography of Aging,* L. G. Martin and S. H. Preston (Eds.). Washington, DC: National Academy Press.

Quinn, J. F. and T. M. Smeeding. 1993. The present and future economic well-being of the aged. Pp. 5-18 in *Pensions in a Changing Economy,* R. V. Burkhauser and D. L. Salisbury (Eds.). Washington, DC: Employee Benefit Research Institute.

Quinn, J. F. and M. Kozy 1996. The role of bridge jobs in the retirement transition: Gender, race, and ethnicity. *The Gerontologist 36* (3), 363-372.

Quirk, D. 1991. An agenda for the nineties and beyond. *Generations 15* (3), 23-26.

Radner, D. B. 1993. Economic well-being of the old: Family unit income and household wealth. *Social Security Bulletin 56* (1), 3-19.

Rakowski, W. and V. Mor. 1992. The association of physical activity with mortality among older adults in the longitudinal study of aging (1984-1988). *Journal of Gerontology 47,* M122-M129.

Rank, M. R., and T. A. Hirschi. 1999. Estimating the proportion of Americans ever experiencing poverty during their elderly years. *Journal of Gerontology: Social Sciences. 54B* (4), S184-S193.

Raskind, M. A. and E. R. Peskind. 1992. Alzheimer's Disease and other dementing disorders. Pp. 477-513 in *Handbook of Mental Health and Aging* (2nd ed.) J. E. Birren, R. B. Sloane, and G. D. Cohen (Eds.). San Diego, CA: Academic Press, Inc.

Raskind, M. A., S. C. Risse, and T. H. Lampe. 1987. Dementia and antipsychotic drugs. *Journal of Clinical Psychiatry, 48,* 16-18.

Recker, R. R., K. M. Davies, S. M. Hinders, R. P. Heaney, M. R. Stegman, and D. B. Kimmel. 1992. Bone gain in young adult women. *Journal of the American Medical Association 268,* 2403-2408.

Redford, L. J., and P. Whitten. 1997. Ensuring access to care in rural areas: The role of communication technology. *Generations. 21* (3), 19-23.

Regelson, W. and M. Kalimi, 1994. Dehydroepiandrosterone (DHEA) the multifunctional steroid: Effects on the ENS, cell proliferation, metabolic, vascular, clinical and other effects. *Annals of the New York Academy of Science 719,* 564-575.

Reitzes, D. C., E. J. Mutran, and M. E. Fernandez. 1996. Does retirement hurt well-being? Factors influencing self-esteem and depression among retirees and workers. *The Gerontologist 36 (5),* 649-656.

Rendell, P. G., and D. M. Thomson. 1999. Aging and prospective memory: Differences between naturalistic and laboratory tasks. *Journal of Gerontology: Psychological Sciences. 54B (4),* P246-255.

Reno, V. P. 1993. The role of pensions in retirement income. Pp. 19-32 in *Pensions in a Changing Economy,* R. V. Burkhauser and D. L. Salisbury (Eds.). Washington, DC: Employee Benefit Research Institute.

Reskin, B. and I. Padavic. 1994. *Women and Men at Work.* Thousand Oaks, CA: Pine Forge Press.

Reynolds, S. L., E. M. Crimmins, and Y. Saito. 1998. Cohort differences in disability and disease presence. *The Gerontologist. 38* (5), 578-590.

Riley, M. W. 1983. The family in an aging society: A matrix of latent relationships. *Journal of Family Issues. 4,* 439-454.

———. 1987. On the significance of age in sociology. *American Sociological Review 52,* 1-14.

———. 1994. Aging and society: Past, present, and future. *The Gerontologist 34* (4), 436-446.

———. 1996. Discussion: What does it all mean? *The Gerontologist 36* (2), 256-258.

Riley, M. W., M. Johnson, and A. Foner. 1973. *Aging and Society: Vol 3: A Sociology of Age Stratification.* New York: Russell Sage Foundation.

Riley, M. W. and J. Riley. 1994. Age integration and the lives of older people. *The Gerontologist 34,* 110-115.

Riley, M. W., R. L. Kahn, and A. Foner (Eds). 1994. *Aging and Structural Lag.* New York: Wiley-Interscience.

Rix, S. E. 1991. Making resourceful aging a reality. Pp. 85-91 in *Resourceful Aging: Vol IV Work/ Second Careers.* Washington, DC: American Association of Retired Persons.

Rix, S. E., and J. B. Williamson. 1998. *Social Security Reform: How Might Women Fare?* Washington, DC: AARP Public Policy Institute.

Roberto, K. A. 1990. Grandparent and grandchild relationships. Pp. 100-112 in *Family Relationships in Later Life* (2nd ed.) T. H. Brubaker (Ed.). Newbury Park, CA: Sage.

Robertson, A. 1991. The politics of Alzheimer's disease: A case study in apocalyptic demography. Pp. 135-152 in M. Minkler, and C. Estes (Eds.). *Critical Perspectives on Aging: The Political and Moral Economy of Growing Old.* Amityville, NY: Baywood.

Rogers, R.. 1992. Living and dying in the U.S.A.: Sociodemographic determinants of death among blacks and whites. *Demography, 29* (2,) 287-304.

———. 1995. Marriage, sex and mortality. *Journal of Marriage and the Family 57* (2), 515-526.

Rogot, E., P. D. Sorlie, and N. J. Johnson. 1992. Life expectancy by employment status, income, and education in the National Longitudinal Mortality Study. *Public Health Report 107,* 457-461.

Rook, K.S. 1984. The negative side of social interaction. *Journal of Personality and Social Psychology 46,* 1097-1108.

———. 1990. Stressful aspects of older adults' social relationships: Current theory and research. Pp. 173-192 in *Stress and Coping in Later-Life Families,* M. A. P. Stephens, J. H. Crowther, S. E. Hobfoll, and D. L. Tennenbaum (Eds.). New York: Hemisphere.

Rosen, B. and T. H. Jerdee. 1985. *Older Employees: New Roles for Valued Resources.* Homewood, IL: Dow Jones-Irwin.

Rosenbaum, W. A. and J. W. Button. 1992. Perceptions of intergenerational conflict: The politics of young vs. old in Florida. *Journal of Aging Studies 6* (4), 385-396.

Rosenhall, U. 1979. Degenerative changes in the human vestibular sensory epithelia. *Acta Oto-Laryngologica 1975, 79,* 67-80.

Rosenmayr, L. and E. Kockeis. 1963. Propositions for a sociological theory of action and the family. *International Social Science Journal 15,* 410-426.

Rosenmayr, L. 1989. Wandlungen der gesellschaftlichen sicht und bewertung des alters [Changes in society's perspective toward and evaluation of aging]. Pp. 96-101 in *Erfolgreiches Altern: Bedingungen und Variationen [Successful Aging: Conditions and Variations],* M. M. Baltes, M. Kohli, and K. Sames (Eds.). Bern: Huber.

Rosenthal, C. J., S. H. Matthews, and V. W. Marshall. 1991. Is parent care normative? The experiences of a sample of middle-aged women. Pp. 427-440 in *Growing Old in America,* B. B. Hess and E. Markson (Eds.). New Brunswick: Transaction.

Rosow, I. 1985. Status and role change through the life cycle. In *Handbook of Aging and the Social Sciences,* (2nd ed.) R. H. Binstock and E. Shanas (Eds.). New York: Van Nostrand Reinhold.

Rowe, J. W. and M. Gatz. 2000. Implications of genetic knowledge for public policy. *Generations.* 24 (1), 79-83.

Rowe, J. W. and R. L. Kahn. 1987. Human aging: usual and successful. *Science 237,* 143-149.

———. 1998. *Successful Aging.* New York: Pantheon Books.

Rubenstein, L. Z., K. R. Josephson, P. R. Trueblood, S. Loy, J. O. Harker, F. M. Pietruszka, and A. S. Robbins. 2000. Effects of a group exercise program on strength, mobility, and falls among fall-prone elderly men. *Journal of Gerontology, 55A,* M317-M321.

Rudman, D. A., G. Feller, H. S. Nagraj, G. A. Gergans, P. Y. Lalitha, A. F. Goldberg, R. A. Sclenker, L. W. Rudman, and D. E. Mattson. 1990. Effects of human growth hormone in men over 60 years old. *New England Journal of Medicine, 323,* 1-6.

Ruhm, C. J. 1990. Career jobs, bridge employment, and retirement. Pp. 92-107 in *Bridges to Retirement: Older Workers in a Changing Labor Market,* P. B. Doeringer. Ithaca, NY: Cornell University/ ILR Press.

———. 1996. Gender differences in employment behavior during late middle age. *Journal of Gerontology: Social Sciences 51B* (1), S11-S17.

Rupert, P. 1991. Contingent work options: Promise or peril for older workers. Pp. 51-53 in *Resourceful Aging: Vol IV Work/Second Careers.* Washington, DC: American Association of Retired Persons.

Russell, A. and N. McWhirter. 1987. *1988 Guinness Book of World Records.* New York: Bantam Books.

Ryan, E. B., B. Szectman, and J. Bodkin. 1992. Attitudes toward younger and older adults learning to use computers. *Journal of Gerontology: Psychological Sciences. 47* (2), 96-101.

Ryder, N. B. 1965. The cohort as a concept in the study of social change. *American Sociological Review 30,* 843-861.

Ryff, C. D. 1991. Possible selves in adulthood and old age: A tale of shifting horizons. *Psychology and Aging. 6* (2), 286-295.

Salisbury, D. L. 1993. Policy implications of changes in employer pension protection. Pp. 41-58 in *Pensions in a Changing Economy,* R. V. Burkhauser and D. L. Salisbury (Eds.). Washington, DC: Employee Benefit Research Institute.

———. 1994. Preface. Pp. xi-xii in *Pension Funding and Taxation: Implications for Tomorrow,* D. L. Salisbury and N. S. Jones, (Eds.). Washington, DC: Employee Benefit Research Institute.

Salk, D., K. An, H. Hoehn, and G. Martin. 1981. Cytogenics of Werner's syndrome cultured in fibroblasts: Variegated translocation mosaicism. *Cytogenic Cell Genetics, 30,* 92-107.

Salthouse, T. A. 1991. *Theoretical Perspectives on Cognitive Aging.* Hillsdale, NY: Erlbaum.

Saluter, A. F. 1996. Marital status and living arrangements: March 1994. *U.S. Bureau of the Census, Current Population Reports,* Series P-20, No. 484. Washington, DC: U.S. Government Printing Office.

Sandell, S. H., and H. M. Iams. 1997. Reducing women's poverty by shifting Social Security benefits from retired couples to widows. *Journal of Policy Analysis and Management, 16* (2), 279-297.

Sankar, A. and J. Gubrium. 1994. Introduction. Pp. vii-xvii in *Qualitative Methods in Aging Research,* J. Gubrium and A. Sankar (Eds.). Thousand Oaks, CA: Sage.

Sarma, S. T. Sahi, M. Koskenvuo, and J. Kaprio. 1993. Increased life expectancy of world class athletes. *Medicine and Science in Sports and Exercise, 25,* 237-244.

Schacter, F., Fauere-Delanef, F. Geunot, H. Rouger, P. Froguel, L. Lesbier-Ginot, and D. Cohen. 1994. Genetic associations with human longevity at the APOE and ACE loci. *Nature Genetics, 6,* 29-34.

Schaie, K. W. and I. A. Parham. 1976. Stability of adult personality traits: Fact or fable? *Journal of Personality and Social Psychology 34,* 146-158.

Schaie, K. Warner and C. Hertzog. 1982. Longitudinal methods. Pp. 91-115 in *Handbook of Developmental Psychology,* B. B. Woman (Ed.). Englewood Cliffs, NJ: Prentice-Hall.

Schaie, K. W. and S. L Willis. 1986. Can intellectual decline in the elderly be reversed? *Developmental Psychology 22,* 223-232.

Schaie, K. W. 1994. The course of adult intellectual development. *American Psychologist 49,* 304-313.

———. 1996. *Intellectual Development in Adulthood: the Seattle Longitudinal Study.* Cambridge, New York: Cambridge University Press.

Schmittroth, L. 1991. *Statistical Record of Women Worldwide.* Detroit: Gale Research, Inc.

Schnohr, P., J. Nyboe, P. Lange, and G. Jensen. 1998. Longevity and gray hair, baldness, facial wrinkles, and arcus senilis in 13,000 men and women: The Copenhagen City heart Study. *Journal of Gerontology, 53A,* M 347-M350.

Schone, B. S., and R. M. Weinick. 1998. Health-related behaviors and the benefits of marriage for elderly persons. *The Gerontologist 38* (5), 618-627.

Schulz, J. H. 1980. *The Economics of Aging.* Belmont, CA: Wadsworth.

Schulz, J. H. and J. Myles. 1990. Old age pensions: A comparative perspective. Pp. 398-414 in *Handbook of Aging and the Social Sciences,* R. H. Binstock and L. K. George (Eds.). San Diego: Academic Press.

Schulz, R. and J. Heckhausen. 1996. A life span model of successful aging. *American Psychologist 26,* 702-714.

Schulz, R., P. Visintainer, and G. M. Williamson. 1990. Psychiatric and physical morbidity effects of caregiving. *Journals of Gerontology 45,* 181-191.

Schutt, R. K. 1996. *Investigating the Social World: The Process and Practice of Research.* Thousand Oaks, CA: Pine Forge Press.

Schuman, H. and J. Scott. 1989. Generations and collective memories. *American Sociological Review 54* (3), 359-381.

Schwartz, G.E. 1982. Testing the biopsychosocial model: The ultimate challenge facing behavioral medicine? *Journal of Consulting and Clinical Psychology, 50 (6),* 1040 – 1053.

Scogin, F. and J. L Bienias. 1988. A three-year follow-up of older adult participants in a memory-skills training program. *Psychology and Aging 3,* 334-337.

Scott, J. P. 1990. Sibling interaction in later life. Pp. 86-99 in *Family Relationships in Later Life* (2nd ed.) T. H. Brubaker (Ed.). Newbury Park, CA: Sage.

Scrutton, S. 1996. Ageism: The foundation of age discrimination. Pp. 141-154 in *Aging for the Twenty-First Century,* Quadagno and Street (Eds.). St. Martin's Press: New York.

Sears, D. O. 1983. The persistence of early political predispositions: The roles of attitude object and life stage. Pp. 79-116 in *Review of Personality and Social Psychology,* Vol. 4, L. Wheeler (Ed.). Thousand Oaks, CA: Sage.

Seeman, T. E., M. L. Bruce, and G. J. McAvay. 1996. Baseline social network characteristics and onset of ADL disability: MacArthur studies of successful aging. *Journal of Gerontology: Social Sciences 51B,* S191-S200.

Seligman, M. E. P. and G. H. Elder. 1986. Learned helplessness and lifespan development. Pp. 377-428 in *Human Development and the Life Course: Multidisciplinary Perspectives.* A. B. Sorensen, F. E. Weinert, and L. R. Sherrod (Eds.). Hillsdale, NJ: Erlbaum.

Seltzer, M. M. 1993. Personal communication to Kunkel.

Sen, C. 1995. Oxidants and antioxidants in exercise. *Journal of Applied Physiology, 79,* 675-686.

Settersten, R. A. and G. O. Hagestad. 1996a. What's the latest? Cultural age deadlines for family transitions. *The Gerontologist 36* (2), 178-188.

———. 1996b. What's the latest? II: Cultural age deadlines for educational and work transitions. *The Gerontologist 36* (5), 602-613.

Setton, D. 2000. Cyber granny. *Forbes. 165* (12), 40-41.

Shanas, E. 1967. Family help patterns and social class in three countries. *Journal of Marriage and the Family 29* (2), 257-266.

———. 1979a. Social myth as hypothesis: The case of family relations of old people. *The Gerontologist 19,* 3-9.

———. 1979b. The family as a social support system in old age. *The Gerontologist 19,* 169-174.

Sharma, R. Theories of aging. 1994. In P. S. Timiras (Ed.) *Physiological Basis for Aging and Geriatrics.* New York, CRC Press, Pp. 37-46.

Shaw, L. B. 1983. *Unplanned Careers: The Working Lives of Middle-Aged Women.* Lexington, MA: Lexington Books.

Shaw, L. B., and H.-y. Yi. 1997. How elderly women become poor: Findings from the new beneficiary data system. *Social Security Bulletin. 60* (4), 46-50.

Shea, D. G., T. Miles, and M. Hayward. 1996. The health-wealth connection: Racial differences. *The Gerontologist 36* (3), 342-349.

Shock, N. W. 1983. Aging of physiological systems. *Journal of Chronic Diseases, 38,* 137-142.

Siegler, I. C., L. K. George, and M. A. Okun. 1979. Cross-sequential analysis of adult personality. *Developmental Psychology 15,* 350-351.

Silverman, H. G., and Mazzeo. 1996. Hormonal responses to maximal and submaximal exercise in trained and untrained men of various ages. *Journal of Gerontology, 51A,* B30-B37.

Silverstein, M., V. L. Bengtson. 1997. Intergenerational solidarity and the structure of adult child-parent relationships in American families. *American Journal of Sociology. 103,* (2), 429-460.

Silverstein, M., X. Chen, and K. Heller. 1996. Too much of a good thing? Intergenerational social support and the psychological well-being of older parents. *Journal of Marriage and the Family 58,* 970-982.

Silverstein, M., J. D. Long. 1998. Trajectories of grandparents' perceived solidarity with adult grandchildren: A growth curve analysis over 23 years. *Journal of Marriage and the Family 60,* (4), 912-923.

Silverstein, M., T. M. Parrott, and V. L. Bengtson. 1995. Factors that predispose middle-aged sons and daughters to provide social support to older parents. *Journal of Marriage and the Family 57,* (2), 465-475.

Simmons, C.H., Vom Kolke, A., and Hideko, S. 1986. Attitudes toward romantic love among American, German, and Japanese students. *The Journal of Social Psychology,* 126, 327 - 336.

Singleton, R. A., Jr., B. C. Straits, and M. Miller Straits. 1993. *Approaches to Social Research.* (2nd ed.) New York: Oxford University Press.

Slevin, K. F., and C. R. Wingrove. 1995. Women in retirement: A review and critique of empirical research since 1976. *Sociological Inquiry 65,* (1), 1-21.

Smeeding, T. M. 1999. Improving benefit adequacy and economic security for women. *Policy Brief #16.* Syracuse: Maxwell School, Syracuse University.

Smeeding, T. M., C. L. Estes, and L. Glasse. 1999. Social Security in the 21st Century: More than deficits: Strengthening security for women. *Gerontology News (August-special insert),* 1-8.

Smith, A. D. 1996. Memory. Pp. 236-250 in *Handbook of the Psychology of Aging.* Fourth Edition. J. E. Birren and K. W. Schaie (Eds.). New York: Academic Press.

Smith, J. 1997. The changing economic circumstances of the elderly: Income, wealth and Social Security. *Policy Brief #8.* Syracuse: Maxwell School, Syracuse University.

Smith, J. and M. Marsiske. 1994. Abilities and competencies in adulthood: Life-span perspectives on workplace skills. *OECD/NCAL Technical Report.* Philadelphia, PA: National Center on Adult Literacy and Organization for Economic Cooperation and Development.

Snowden, D. A. 1997. Aging and Alzheimer's disease: lessons from the nun study. *The Gerontologist, 37,* 150-156.

Snowden, D. A., S. J. Kemper, J. A. Mortimer, L. H. Greiner, D. R. Wekstein, and W. R. Markesbery. 1996. Linguistic ability in early life and cognitive function and Alzheimer's disease in late life. Findings from the nun study. *Journal of the American Medical Association, 275,* 528-532.

Social Security Administration. 1994a. *Income of the Aged Chartbook, 1992.* SSA Publication #13-11727. Washington, DC: U.S. Department of Health and Human Statistics.

———. 1994b. *Social Security Bulletin: Annual Statistical Supplement: 1994.* Washington, DC: U.S. Government Printing Office.

———. 1995a. *A Brief History of Social Security.* SSA Publication #21-059. Washington, DC: U.S. Government Printing Office.

———. 1995b. *Fast Facts and Figures about Social Security.* SSA Publication #13-11785. Washington, DC: Department of Health and Human Services.

———. 1998a. *Income of the Population 55 or Older, 1996.* SSA Publication No. 13-11871. Washington, DC: U. S. Government Printing Office.

———. 1998b. *Income of the Aged Chartbook, 1996.* SSA Publication No. 13-11727. Washington, DC: U. S. Government Printing Office.

———. 1998c. *Social Security Bulletin: Annual Statistical Supplement. Table 6B1.* Washington, DC: U. S. Government Printing Office.

———. 1999a. Highlights of Social Security, June 1999. Accessed on July 27, 1999 at http://www.ssa.gov/statistics/highssd.html.

———. 1999b. *Social Security Update, 1999*. SSA Publication 05-10003. Accessed 9/7/99 at http://www.ssa.gov/pubs/10003.html.

———. 1999d. *How Work Affects Your Benefits*. Publication 05-10069. Washington, DC: U.S. Government Printing Office.

Social Security Bulletin. 1997 Annual Statistical Supplement: 1997. Washington, DC: U. S. Government Printing Office.

Sontag, W. E., C. D. Lynch, W. T. Cefalu, R. L. Ingram, S. A. Bennett, P. L. Thornton, and A. S. Khan. 1999. Pleitropic effects of GH and IGF-1 on biological aging: Influences from moderate caloric restricted animals. *Journal of Gerontology, 54A*, B521-538.

Speas, K. and B. Obenshain. 1995. *AARP Images of Aging in America: Final Report*. American Association of Retired Persons: Washington, DC.

Spencer, G. 1993. What are the demographic implications of an aging U.S. population structure during the 1990 to 2030 period? Pp. 7-16 in *Aging of the U.S. Population: Economic and Environmental Implications*. Washington, DC: American Association of Retired Persons.

Spencer, J. T. Self help for healthy hearing, the cardiovascular factor. *Speech Health and Hearing Journal*. 1993, May/June: 29-30.

Spirduso, W. W. 1995. Physical dimensions of aging. 1995. Champaign, Illinois: *Human Kinetics*, Pp. 390-417.

Spitze, G. and J. Logan. 1990. Sons, daughters, and intergenerational social support. *Journal of Marriage and the Family, 52*, 420-430.

Sprott, R. 1999. Biomarkers of aging. *Journal of Gerontology, 54A*,B464-B465.

Starr, P. 1988. Social Security and the American public household. Pp. 119-148 in *Social Security: Beyond the Rhetoric of Crisis*, T. R. Marmour and J. L. Mashaw (Eds.). Princeton, NJ: Princeton University Press.

Staudinger, U. M. and P. B. Baltes. 1996. Interactive minds: A facilitative setting for wisdom-related performance? *Journal of Personality and Social Psychology, 71*, 746-762.

Staudinger, U. M., M. Marsiske, and P. B. Baltes. 1995. Resilience and reserve capacity in later adulthood: Potentials and limits of development across the life span. Pp. 801-847 in *Developmental Psychopathology*, Vol. 2, D. Cicchetti and D. J. Cohen (Eds.) New York: Wiley.

Steffensmeier, D., C. Streifel, and M. D. Harer. 1987. Relative cohort size and youth crime in the United States, 1953-1984. *American Sociological Review 52* (5), 702-710.

Steffensmeier, D. J., E. A. Allan, M. D. Harer, and C. Streifel. 1989. Age and the distribution of crime. *American Journal of Sociology 94* (4), 803-831.

Stein, C. H., V. A. Wemmerus, M. Ward, M. E. Gaines, A. L. Freeberg, and T. C. Jewell. 1998. "Because they're my parents." An intergenerational study of felt obligation and parental caregiving. *Journal of Marriage and the Family. 60* (3), 611-622.

Steinmetz, S. K. 1988. *Duty Bound: Elder Abuse and Family Care*. Newbury Park, CA: Sage.

Stephens, M. A. P. and M. M. Franks. 1995. Spillover between daughters' roles as caregiver and wife: Interference or enhancement? *Journal of Gerontology: Psychological Sciences, 50B*, 9-17.

Stephens, Mary A. P., M. M. Franks, and A. L. Townsend. 1994. Stress and rewards in women's multiple roles: The case of women in the middle. *Psychology and Aging, 9*, 45-52.

Stephens, M. A. P., J. M. Kinney, V .K. Norris, and S. W. Ritchie. 1987. Social networks as assets and liabilities in recovery from stroke by geriatric patients. *Psychology and Aging, 2*, 125-129.

Stephens, M. A. P. and A. L. Townsend. 1997. The stress of parent care: Positive and negative effects of women's other roles. *Psychology and Aging, 12*, 376-386.

Stoller, E. P. and K. L. Pugliesi. 1989. Informal networks of community-based elderly: Changes in composition over time. *Research on Aging, 10*, 499-516.

Stone, R., G. L. Cafferata, and J. Sangl. 1987. Caregivers of the frail elderly: A national profile. *The Gerontologist 27* (5), 616-626.

Stone, R. I. and P. Kemper. 1989. Spouses and children of disabled elders: How large a constituency of long-term care reform? *The Millbank Quarterly, 67*, 485-506.

Strate, J. M., C. J. Parrish, C. D. Elder, and C. Ford III. 1989. Life span civic development and voting participation. *American Political Science Review, 83* (2), 443-464.

Street, D. 1993. Maintaining the status quo: The impact of old-age interest groups on the Medicare Catastrophic Care Act of 1988. *Social Problems, 40,* 431-444.

Strehler, B. L. 1962. Further studies on the thermally induced aging of Drosophilla melanogaster. *Journal of Gerontology, 17,*347-___.

Stryker, S. S. 1986. Identity theory: Development and extensions. In *Self Identity.* K. Yardley and T. Honess (Eds.). New York: Wiley.

Suitor, J. J., and K. Pillemer. 1993. Support and interpersonal stress in the social networks of married daughters caring for parents with dementia. *Journal of Gerontology: Social Sciences, 48,* S1-8.

Suitor, J. J., K. Pillemer, S. Keeton, and J. Robison. 1994. Aged parents and aging children: Determinants of relationship quality. Pp. 223-242 in *Handbook of Aging and the Family,* R. Blieszner and V. H. Bedford (Eds.). Westport, CT: Greenwood Press.

Summary of the Second Report of the National Cholesterol Education Program Expert Panel on Detection, Evaluation, and Treatment of High Blood Cholesterol in Adults (1993). (Adult Treatment Panel II). *Journal of the American Medical Association, 269,* 3013-3023.

Sussman, M. B. 1985. The family life of old people. Pp. 415-449 in *Handbook of Aging and the Social Sciences* (2nd ed.) R. H. Binstock and E. Shanas (Eds.). New York: Van Nostrand Reinhold.

Sussman, M. B. and L. Burchinal. 1968. Kin family network: Unheralded structure in current conceptualizations of family functioning. Pp. 247-257 in *Middle Age and Aging,* B. L. Neugarten (Ed.). Chicago: University of Chicago Press.

Swenson, M. W., J. S. Pearson, and D. Osborne. 1973. *An MMPI Source Book.* Minneapolis: University of Minnesota Press.

Szanton, P. 1993. Implications of an aging population: predictions, doubts, and questions. Pp. 69-76 in *Aging of the U.S. Population: Economic and Environmental Implications.* Washington, DC: American Association of Retired Persons.

Szilard, L. 1959. On the nature of the aging process. *Proceedings of the National Academy of Sciences, 45,* 30-45.

Szinovacz, M. E. 1998. Grandparents today: A demographic profile. *The Gerontologist, 38* (1), 37-52.

Szinovacz, M. and C. Washo. 1992. Gender differences in exposure to life events and adaptation to retirement. *Journal of Gerontology: Social Sciences, 47* (4), S191-196.

Szinovacz, M. and D. J. Ekerdt. 1996. Families and retirement. Pp. 375-400 in *Aging and the Family: Theory and Research,* R. Blieszner and V. H. Bedford (Eds.). Westport, CT: Praeger.

Taylor, S. E. and M. Lobel. 1989. Social comparison activity under threat: Downward evaluation and upward contacts. *Psychological Bulletin, 96,* 569-575.

Theodorson, G.A., and Theodorson, A.G. 1969. *A Modern Dictionary of Sociology.* New York: Thomas Y. Crowell Company.

Thompson, H. 1967. *Hell's Angels.* New York: Ballantine Books.

Thompson, J. N, R. C. Woodruff, and H. Huai. 1998. Mutation rate: A simple concept has become complex. *Environmental and Molecular Mutagenesis, 32,* 292-300.

Thompson, L. and A. Walker. 1987. Mothers as mediators of intimacy between grandmothers and their young adult granddaughters. *Family Relation, 36,* 72-77.

Thompson, W. S. and P. K. Whelpton. 1933. *Population Trends in the United States.* New York: McGraw-Hill.

Timiras, P. S. 1994. *Physiological Basis of Aging and Geriatrics,* 2nd edition. New York: CRC Press.

Torres-Gil, F. M. 1992. *The New Aging: Politics and Change in America.* Westport, CT: Auburn House.

———. 1998. Policy, politics, aging: Crossroads in the 1990s. Pp. 75-88 in *New Directions in Old-Age Policies.* J. S. Steckenrider and T. M. Parrott (Eds.). Albany: State University of New York Press.

Tout, K. 1989. *Aging in Developing Countries.* New York: Oxford University Press.

Townsend, P. 1968. The emergence of the four-generation family in industrial society. Pp. 255-257 in *Middle Age and Aging*, B. L. Neugarten (Ed.). Chicago: University of Chicago Press.

Treas, J. 1995. Older Americans in the 1990 and beyond. *Population Bulletin, 50* (2), 2-46.

Tudor, C. G. 1995. Medicaid expenditures and state responses. *Health Care Financing Review, 16,* (3), 1-10.

2030 Center. 1999. Young Americans and Social Security: A public opinion study conducted for the 2030 Center by P. D. Hart Research Associates. http://www.2030/org.fr990719.html.

Uhlenberg, P. 1993. Demographic change and kin relationships in later life. Pp. 219-238 in *Annual Review of Gerontology and Geriatrics: Focus on Kinship, Aging, and Social Change*, Vol. 13, G. L. Maddox and M. P. Lawton (Eds.). New York: Springer.

——. 1996. Mutual attraction: Demography and life-course analysis. *The Gerontologist, 36* (2), 226-229.

Uhlenberg, P., T. Cooney, and R. Boyd. 1990. Divorce for women after midlife. *Journal of Gerontology: Social Sciences, 45* (1), S3-11.

U.N. Department of Economics and Social Information and Policy Analysis. *World Population 1994.*

U.S. Bureau of the Census. 1975. *Statistical Abstract of the United States: 1975.* Washington, DC: U.S. Government Printing Office.

——. 1976. *Historical Statistics of the United States, Colonial Times to 1970.* Bicentennial Edition. Washington, DC: U.S. Government Printing Office.

——. 1977. *Statistical Abstract of the United States.* Washington, DC: U.S. Government Printing Office.

——. 1985. *Statistical Abstract of the United States.* Washington, DC: U.S. Government Printing Office.

——. 1987. *Statistical Abstract of the United States: 1987.* Washington, DC: U.S. Government Printing Office.

——. 1991a. Marital status and living arrangements: March, 1990. *Current Population Reports,* Series, P-20, No. 450. Washington, DC: U.S. Government Printing Office.

——. 1991b. *Global Aging: Comparative Indicators and Future Trends.* Washington DC: U.S. Department of Commerce.

——. 1992. Marital status and living arrangements: 1991. *Current Population Reports,* Series, P-20, No. 461. Washington, DC: U.S. Government Printing Office.

——. 1993. *Statistical Abstract of the United States: 1993.* Washington, DC: U.S. Government Printing Office.

——. 1994. *Statistical Abstract of the United States: 1994.* Washington, DC: U.S. Government Printing Office.

——. 1995a. Income, poverty, and valuation of noncash benefits: 1993. *Current Population Reports,* Series, P-60, No. 188. Washington, DC: U.S. Government Printing Office.

——. 1995b. Income, poverty, and valuation of noncash benefits: 1994. *Current Population Reports,* Series P-60, No. 189. Washington, DC: U.S. Government Printing Office.

——. 1995c. *Statistical Abstract of the United States.* Washington, DC: U.S. Government Printing Office.

——. 1996a. Population projections of the United States by age, sex, race, and Hispanic origin: 1995 to 2050. *Current Population Reports,* Series P-25, No. 1130. Washington, DC: U.S. Government Printing Office.

——. 1996b. *Statistical Abstract of the United States: 1996.* (116th ed.) Washington, DC: U.S. Government Printing Office.

——. 1998a. Money income in the United States: 1997. *Current Population Reports,* P-60, No. 200. Washington, DC: U. S. Government Printing Office.

——. 1998b. *Statistical Abstract of the United States: 1998.* Washington, DC: U. S. Government Printing Office.

——. 1998c. Money Income in the United States: 1998. *Current Population Reports,* P-60, No. 206. Washington, DC: U. S. Government Printing Office.

——. 1999a. Poverty in the United States: 1998. *Current Population Reports,* P-60, No. 207. Washington, DC: U. S. Government Printing Office.

U.S. Congress, Congressional Budget Office. 1995. *The Economic and Budget Outlook: Fiscal Years 1996-2000.* Washington, DC: U.S. Government Printing Office.

U.S. Department of Health and Human Services and U.S. Department of Agriculture. 1986. *Nutrition Monitoring in the United States: A Progress Report from the Joint Nutrition Monitoring Evaluation Committee.* DHHS Pub. No (PHS) 86-1255. Washington, DC: U.S. Government Printing Office.

U.S. Department of Health and Human Services. 1996. *Physical Activity and Health: A Report of the Surgeon General Centers for Disease Control and Prevention.* National Center for Chronic Disease Prevention. Atlanta, GA: U.S. Government Printing Office.

U.S. Department of Labor, Bureau of Labor Statistics. 1975. *Employment and Earnings 22,* (3), 21.

———. 1985. *Employment and Earnings 32,* (11), 10-11.

———. 1995. *Employment and Earnings 42,* (11), 21-22.

U. S. Department of Labor, Bureau of Labor Statistics. 2000. *Employment and Earnings: January 2000.* Accessed 10/23/99 at http://stats.bls.gov/cpsaatab.htm#empstat.

U.S. General Accounting Office. 1992. *Elderly Americans: Health, Housing and Nutrition Gaps Between the Poor and Nonpoor.* Washington, DC: U.S. Government Printing Office.

U.S. Senate Special Committee on Aging. 1991. *Aging America: Trends and Projections.* Washington, DC: U.S. Department of Health and Human Services.

Van der Mass, P. J. 1988. Aging and public health. Pp. 95-115 in Schroots, J., J. Birren, and A. Svanborg (Eds.). *Health and Aging: Perspectives and Prospects.* The Netherlands: Swets and Zeitlinger.

Velkoff, V. (2000). Centenarians in the United States, 1990 and Beyond. *Statistical Bulletin, 81 (1),* 2 – 9.

Verbrugge, L. M. 1990. The twain meet: Empirical explanations of sex differences in health and mortality. Pp. 159-200 in M. Ory and H. Warner (Eds.). *Gender, Health and Lingevity: Multidisciplinary Perspectives.* New York: Springer.

Verdery, R. B., D. K. Ingram, G. S. Roth, and M. A. Lane. 1997. Caloric restriction HDL2 levels in rhesus monkeys. *American Journal of Physiology, 273,* E714-E719.

Verhaeghen, P., A. Marcoen, and L. Goosens. 1992. Improving memory performance in the aged through mnemonic training: A meta-analytic study. *Psychology and Aging, 7,* 242-251.

Vinick, B. H. and D. J. Ekerdt. 1992. Couples view retirement activities: Expectations versus experience. Pp. 129-144 in *Families and Retirement,* M. Szinovacz, D. J. Ekerdt, and B. H. Vinick (Eds.). Newbury Park, CA: Sage.

Vinton, L. 1991. Abused older women: Battered women or abused elders? *Journal of Women and Aging, 3* (3): 5-19.

Vitez, M. 1995. Ripeness is all, in centenarians as in cheeses. *The Sun.* November 29.

Vuori, I. 1995. Exercise and physical health, musculoskeletal health and functional capabilities. *Research Quarterly for Exercise and Sport, 66,* 276-285.

Waldfogel, J. 1997. The effects of children on women's wages. *American Sociological Review, 62* (April), 209-217.

Waldron, I. 1993. Recent trends in sex mortality ratios for adults in developed countries. *Social Science and Medicine, 36* (4), 451-462.

Walford, R. L., S. B. Harris, and M. W. Gunion. 1992. The calorically restricted low-fat nutrient-dense diet in Biosphere 2 significantly lowers blood glucose, total leukocyte count, cholesterol, and blood pressure in humans. *Proceedings of the National Academy of Sciences, 89,* 11533-11537.

Walford, R. L. and S. R. Spindler. 1997. The response to calorie restriction in mammals shows features also common to hibernation: A cross adaptation hypothesis. *Journal of Gerontology, 52A,* B179-B183.

Walker, A. J., S. K. Martin, and L. L. Jones. 1992. The benefits and costs of caregiving and care receiving for daughters and mothers. *Journal of Gerontology: Social Sciences, 47,* S130-139.

Wallace, H. 1996. *Family Violence: Legal, Medical and Social Perspectives.* Needham Heights, MA: Allyn and Bacon.

Wallace, S. P., J. B. Williamson, R. G. Lung, and L. A. Powell. 1991. A lamb in wolf's clothing? The reality of senior power and social policy. Pp. 95-114 in *Critical Perspectives on Aging: The Political and Moral Economy of Growing Old.* M. Minkler and C. L. Estes (Eds.). Amityville, NY: Baywood.

Wang, S. M., C. Nishigori, T. Yagi, and H. Takebe. 1991. Reduced DNA repair in progeria cells and effects of gamma-ray irradiation on UV-induced unscheduled DNA synthesis in normal and progeria cells. *Mutation Research, 256,* 59-66.

Ward, R., J. Logan, and G. Spitze. 1992. The influence of parent and child needs on coresidence in middle and later life. *Journal of Marriage and the Family, 54* (1), 209-221.

Ware, J., M. Bayliss, W. Rogers, and M. Kosinski. 1996. Differences in four-year health outcomes for elderly and poor, chronically ill patients treated in HOM and Fee-for-Service systems. *JAMA 276,* (13), 1039-1047.

Weaver, D. A. 1994. The work and retirement decisions of older women: A literature review. *Social Security Bulletin, 57* (1), 3-24.

———. 1997. The economic well-being of Social Security beneficiaries, with an emphasis on divorced beneficiaries. *Social Security Bulletin, 60* (4), 3-17.

Weeks, J. R. 1994. *Population: An Introduction to Concepts and Issues.* Belmont, CA: Wadsworth Publishing Company.

Weindruch, R. 1997 The retardation of aging by caloric restriction. *Toxicology Pathology, 24,* 742-745.

Weindruch, R. R., R. L. Walford, S. Fligiel, and D. Guthrie. 1986. The retardation of aging in mice by dietary restriction: Longevity, cancer, immunity, and lifetime energy intake. *Journal of Nutrition, 116,* 641-654.

Weishaus, S. and D. Feld. 1988. A half century of marriage: Continuity or change? *Journal of Marriage and the Family, 50* (3), 763-774.

Weismann, A. 1891. Life and death (a paper presented in 1883). Pp. 111-157 in E. B. Poulton, S. Schonland, and A. E. Shipley (Eds.), *Essays Upon Heredity and Kindred Biological Problems.* Oxford: Clarendon Press.

Weiss, G. L. and L. E. Lonnquist. 1997. *The Sociology of Health, Healing, and Illness.* New Jersey: Prentice-Hall, Inc.

Welford, A. T. 1993. Work capacity across the adult years. Pp. 541-552 in *Encyclopedia of Adult Development,* R. Kastenbaum (Ed.). Phoenix: Oryx Press.

Wellman, B. and S. Wortley. 1989. Brothers' keepers: Situating kinship relations in broader networks of social support. *Sociological Perspectives, 32,* 273-306.

Whipple, R., L. Wolfson, C. Derby, D. Singh, and J. Tobin. 1993. Altered sensory function and balance in older persons. *Journal of Gerontology, 48,* 71-76.

Whitbourne, S. K. 1985. The psychological construction of the life span. Pp. 594-618 in *Handbook of the Psychology of Aging* (2nd ed.) J. E. Birren and K. W. Schaie (Eds.). New York: Von Nostrand Reinhold.

White, H., E. McConnell, E. Clipp, L. Bynum, C. Teague, L. Navas, S. Craven, and H. Halbrecht. 1999. Surfing the net in later life: A review of the literature and pilot study of computer use and quality of life. *Journal of Applied Gerontology, 18* (3), 358-378.

White, L. and J. N. Edwards. 1990. Emptying the nest and parental well-being: An analysis of national panel data. *American Sociological Review, 55* (2), 235-242.

White, L. K. and A. Reidmann. 1992. When the Brady Bunch grows up: Step/half- and full sibling relationships in adulthood. *Journal of Marriage and the Family, 54,* 197-208.

White, L. and D. Peterson. 1995. The retreat from marriage: Its effect on unmarried children's exchange with parents. *Journal of Marriage and the Family, 57* (2), 428-434.

Who's Who in American Politics 1995-96. 1995. New Providence, NJ: R.R. Bowker.

Williams, J. K., M. R. Adams, H. S. Klopfenstein. 1990. Estrogen modulates responses of atherosclerotic coronary arteries. *Circulation, 81,* 1680-1687.

Williamson, J. B. 1998. Political activism and the aging of the baby boom. *Generations, 22* (1), 55-59.

Willis, S. L., R. Blieszner, and P. B. Baltes. 1981. Intellectual training research in aging: Modification of performance on the fluid ability of figural relations. *Journal of Educational Psychology, 73,* 41-50.

Willis, S. L. 1987. Cognitive training and everyday competence. *Annual Review of Gerontology and Geriatrics, 7*, 159-188.

———. 1991. Cognition and everyday competence. *Annual Review of Gerontology and Geriatrics, 11*, 80-109.

———. 1996. Everyday problem solving. Pp. 287-307 in *Handbook of the Psychology of Aging* (4th ed.) J. E. Birren and K. W. Schaie (Eds.). New York: Academic Press, Inc.

Willis, S. L., G. M. Jay, M. Diehl, and M. Marsiske. 1992. Longitudinal change and the prediction of everyday task competence in the elderly. *Research on Aging, 14*, 68-91.

Willis, S. L. and C. S. Nesselroade. 1990. Long-term effects of fluid ability training in old-old age. *Developmental Psychology, 26*, 905-910.

Willis, S. L. and K. W. Schaie. 1986. Training the elderly on the ability factors of spatial orientation and inductive reasoning. *Psychology and Aging, 1*, 7-12.

———. 1994. Cognitive training in the normal elderly. In *Plasticite Cerebrale et Stimulation Cognitive,* F. Forette, Y. Christen, and F. Boller (Eds.). Paris: Foundation Nationale de Gerontologie.

Wise, D. A. 1997. Retirement against the demographic trend: More older people living longer, working less, and saving less. *Demography, 34* (1), 83-95.

Wolf, D. R. 1991. *The Rebels: A Brotherhood of Outlaw Bikers.* Toronto: University of Toronto Press.

Wolf, N. 1991. *The Beauty Myth.* New York: Doubleday & Co., Inc.

Wolf, O., E. Naumann, D. H. Hellhammer, and C. Kirschbaum. 1998. Effects of DHEA replacement in elderly men on event-related potentials, memory, and well-being. *Journal of Gerontology, 53A*, M385-M390.

Wolfson, L., J. Judge, R. Whipple, and M. King, 1995. Strength is a major factor in balance, gait and the occurrence of falls. *Journal of Gerontology, 50A*, 64-67.

Women's Initiative. 1993. *Women, Pensions and Divorce: Small Reforms That Could Make a Big difference.* Washington, DC: American Association of Retired Persons.

Wood, J. V. 1989. Theory and research concerning social comparisons of personal attributes. *Psychological Bulletin, 106*, 231-248.

Woodruff, R. C. and A. G. Nikitin. 1995. PDNA element movement in somatic cells recues life span in Drosophilla melanogaster: Evidence in support of the Somatic Mutation Theory of aging. *Mutation Research, 338*, 35-42.

Woolacott, M. H. 1993. Age-related changes in posture and movement. *Journal of Gerontology, 48*, 56-60.

Woods, J. A., J. K. Evans, B. W. Wolters, M. A. Ceddia, and E. McAuley. 1998. Effects of maximal exercise on natural killer cell cytotoxicity and responsiveness to Interferon-alpha in the young and old. *Journal of Gerontology, 53A*, B430-B437.

Wootton, B. H. 1997. Gender differences in occupational employment. *Monthly Labor Review,* April, 15-24.

Wynne, E. A. 1991. Will the young support the old? Pp. 507-523 in *Growing Old in America* (4th ed.) B. B. Hess and E. W. Markson (Eds.). New Brunswick, NJ: Transaction Books.

Yaukey, D. 1985. *Demography: The Study of Human Population.* Prospect Heights, IL: Waveland Press.

Yu, B. P., E. J. Masoro, and C. A. McMahan. 1995. Nutritional influences on aging of Fischer 344 rats. I. Physiological, metabolic, and longevity characteristics. *Journal of Gerontology, 40*, 657-670.

Zarate, A. O. 1994. *International Mortality Chartbook: Levels and Trends 1955-1991.* Hyattsville, Maryland: Public Health Service.

Zepelin, H., R. A. Sills, and M. W. Heath. 1986-87. Is age becoming irrelevant? An exploratory study of perceived age norms. *International Journal of Aging and Human Development, 24* (4), 241-256.

Zeyuan, D., T. Bingying, L. Xialin, H. Jimming, C. Yifeng. 1998. Effect of green tea and black tea on the metabolism of mineral elements in old rats. *Biological Trace Element Research, 65*, 75-86.

Zuev, S. M., A. I. Yashin, K. G. Manton, E. Dowd, L. B. Pogojev, and R. N. Usmanov. 2000. Vitality index in survival modeling: How physiological aging influences mortality. *Journal of Gerontology, 55A*, B10-B19.

A

Abridged Life Expectancy Test, 89

Achenbaum, W. Andrew, 409

activism is when researchers take a stand on critical social issues of importance and provide applied research findings oriented toward solving these problems. 39

Activities of Daily Living (ADLs), 12, 20, 36, 354

Activities of Daily Living and Instrumental Activities of Daily Living (ADL/IADL), 354

activity theory is a normative aging theory suggesting that individuals, in order to age well, must maintain social roles and interaction, rather than disengage from social life. 275-277

acute care is health care aimed at treating a short-term condition, often with a sudden onset. Usually acute care refers to hospital-based care, either emergency room, inpatient or outpatient treatment. 372

acute conditions are health problems with sudden onset, and lasting for a relatively short time. 350

adaptive functioning, 145

adequacy of benefits is an issue within income maintenance policies, such as Social Security, when benefit levels to some groups or entire populations are low. 316

Administration on Aging/Older Americans Act web site, 415

advanced glycosylated end products (ages) result from cross-linking of protein and glucose molecules, associated with disease. 122

African Americans

activity limitations of, 354-355

dissimilarity indexes for, 264

family reciprocity of, 218

grandparent relationships among, 235-236

intergenerational exchanges among, 241

labor force participation rates for, 264-265

median age of retirement for, 429

percent of older persons in poverty, 331

prevalence rates of health of, 352

research on families of, 214

sibling relationships among, 232

top five leading causes of death among, 358

See also race

age-based advocacy, 399-402

age-condensed is a structure of generations within the family where parent and child ages are closer than dictated by societal norms. 248

Age Data web site, 102

age deadlines, 198

age discrimination in employment occurs when an employer makes decisions that disadvantage older workers in the labor force in terms of hiring, promotion, training, wages, or other opportunities. Decisions by others that unfairly advantage or disadvantage particular age groups, especially on the basis of stereotypes, also constitute age discrimination. 273-275

Age Discrimination in Employment Act (ADEA) is federal legislation, originally passed in 1967, prohibiting the use of age in hiring, firing, and personnel policies for those 40-70 years of age. 273-275, 384

age eligibility is a system or policy where one becomes eligible for benefits by reaching a particular age (or number of years of employment). 309

See also age entitlement

age entitlement is a system or policy under which individuals become eligible for assistance or participation in the program on the basis of chronological age. 384-386, 400-413

age-gapped is a system of generations of the family where parent and child ages are clearly farther apart than dictated by societal norms. 249

age group

criminal behavior by, 44, 54

income differences between, 332

labor force participation by, 261

living arrangements by, 217

marital status by, 224

mean and median, 82

median net worth by, 324

nursing home populations by, 94

opinions on Social Security by, 319

percentage voting by, 41

political reciprocity of, 403

self-assessed health status by, 356

serious problems by, 426

social network and, 166-169

U.S. resident population by, 101

voter distribution by, 442

voter registration by, 390

Americans for Generational Equity (AGE) is an advocacy group promoting the generational equity debate, which has argued that we should look at age as a critical factor in understanding the linkage between politics and economics. 404, 408

American Psychological Assn. Division 20: Adult Development and Aging web site, 181

American Sociological Association-Section on Aging and the Life Course web site, 207

Andersen model, 365-366

antioxidants are substances that act to remove free radicals and other active oxygen species before they attack cells and tissues. 134

Antonucci, T. C., 168, 218, 230, 241

apocalyptic demography the social construction of catastrophe suggests an increasing aging population will place unbearable demands on the health care system. 374

apoptosis is a form of cell death that comes from an active, programmed process. 135

applied research is any research which uses scientific methods to provide answers to important questions of policy and practice. 33-34

See also research

Asset and Health Dynamics among the Oldest Old Study (AHEAD), 68, 342

assets refer to the resources people own which can be converted into money, such as home equity, cash savings, stocks and bonds. 321-322

Association for Gerontology in Higher Education Student Page web site, 453

Atchley, Robert, 189, 201, 271, 278, 291

atherosclerosis is a progressive accumulation of fat on the inside of arteries carrying blood throughout the body. 118, 135

B

baby boomers
concerns over Social Security and, 296, 316, 407
dependency ratios of, 77, 82-84
expected predictions on, 9, 16
as most age-segregated generation, 394
musical preferences of, 28-29
as "pig-in-the-python," 78
population pyramid of, 77
societal aging of, 9
topical essay on, 379-382

backlash against the older population is an expected negative reaction by young and middle-aged individuals deriving from the political conflict over age entitlements. 404

Baltes, M., 143, 145, 173

Baltes, P., 147, 148, 150, 151

Barrow, G. M., 256

beanpole family is a new shape for the family tree, where from a narrow base of one couple, fewer children and grandchildren will eventually emerge. 246

the Beatles, 28

Becker, G., 37

Beginners Central, 25

Bengtson, V.L., 276, 447, 448

bereavement, 176

Berlin Aging Study, 150

Bernard, J., 224, 226

"Big Five" personality dimensions, 160

Binney, E., 348

Binstock, R., 379, 383, 386, 389, 390, 404, 408

biomarkers of aging are more precise changes in the body and its organs and systems used by physiologists to reflect aging changes. 115

biomedicalization of aging refers to the tendency to medicalize normal conditions and processes of aging; this tendency has been criticized as helping to create and maintain a medical industry to deal with the socially constructed medical problems of aging. 348

biopsychosocial model of health emphasizes a multidisciplinary and holistic view of health care, requiring bridges among disciplines, redefinitions of health, and a general paradigm shift within medicine. 349

Biosphere 2 experiment, 131

birth cohorts are groups of individuals born at approximately the same time in history and sharing a collection of historical life experiences. 42

See also cohorts

Birth and Fortune (Easterlin), 54

Blazer, D. G., 175, 177

blood cholesterol levels, 110

bona fide occupational qualification (BFOQ) exceptions allowed by the law for those occupations where mandatory retirement is allowed. Examples include airline pilots, air traffic controllers, and some law enforcement positions. 274

bone density, 108-110

Bortz, W. M., IV, 256

Brandtstädter, J. 164

breast cancer, 348, 349

T

tannins are substances commonly found in red wines and many teas that act as antioxidants. 134

target cells allow select hormones to activate their receptors and initiate a subsequent series of reactions inside the cell. 126

Tax Reform Act of 1986, 385

Taylor, S. E., 165

telomerase is an enzyme that repairs and replaces part of the telomere lost during replication. 123-124

Telomere Theory of Aging is a recent aging theory that explains how, over time, a shortened telomere eventually results in a loss of genes that are critical to reproducing exact copies of chromosomes. With unique characteristics of parent cells lost, new cells do not function appropriately and die. 123-124

theories
    activity, 276
    age stratification, 410-413
    aging and social, 185-88
    continuity, 292-294
    demographic transition, 73-76
    disengagement, 187, 275-277
    Easterlin hypothesis, 54-55
    error, 119-129
    exchange, 186
    family life cycle, 221-222
    modernization theory, 92-93, 416
    nuclear family, 212
    on physiological aging, 118-123
    on population aging, 72-74
    political economy, 187
    programmed, 119
    scientific method and, 37
    social exchange, 185, 237-238
    stratification, 202
    synergy between research method and, 37
    telomere, 123-124

Thomas, W. I., 449

Thompson, W., 14, 15

three-legged stool of income consists of retirement benefits from Social Security, payments from private pensions, and income from assets and personal savings. 311-312, 322

Thurmond, Strom, 388

Torres-Gil, F.M., 380, 390, 394, 406, 414

Tout, K., 90

Townsend Movement was a 1930s social movement advocating $200 monthly pensions for older people, requiring the funds to be spent within 30 days to stimulate the Depression economy; a precursor to passage of Social Security. 312-313, 89, 399

Travelers Insurance Company, 270

typing mechanics, 148

U

Uhlenberg, P., 197, 231, 237

underground economy involves jobs such as home child care or domestic work where pay may be in cash and no records are kept; many workers may be ineligible for Social Security or pensions. 263

United Arab Emirates population pyramid, 78

United States Census Bureau web site, 341

United States Department of Labor web site, 300

United States population pyramid, 77

unit of analysis describes the scope of the elements under study (blood cells, families, health care delivery systems, nations) in research and relates to the micro/macro continuum. 38-39

upward social comparison is the idea that in order to motivate ourselves to do better, we will look for those who are better off, and set them as the standard by which we evaluate ourselves. 165

V

Van Nostrand, J. F., 364

variability with aging, 51

Verbrugge, L., 361

vested describes when a worker has been employed sufficiently long with a given employer to be eligible for eventual pension benefits. 319-320

Vital and Health Statistics: Trends in the Health of Older Americans web site, 375

voluntarism in family relationships is the extent to which individuals have choices regarding whether and when to meet individual vs. collective [family] needs. 218-220

"voodoo demographics," 79

voter participation, 439

voter registration, 391

W

Wallace, H., 399, 405

"The Waltons" TV show, 233-234